BLACKAMOORES:
*Africans in Tudor England,
Their Presence, Status and Origins*

BLACKAMOORES:
Africans in Tudor England, Their Presence, Status and Origins

Sometimes people hold a core belief that is very strong. When they are presented with evidence that works against that belief, the new evidence cannot be accepted. It would create a feeling that is extremely uncomfortable, called cognitive dissonance. And because it is so important to protect the core belief, they will rationalize, ignore and even deny anything that doesn't fit in with the core belief.

Frantz Fanon, *Black Skin, White Masks* (Paris: Editions du Seuil, 1952).

Revised Edition Copyright © 2013/2014 by Narrative Eye and The Circle with a Dot.
First Edition Copyright © 2013 by Narrative Eye and The Circle with a Dot.
Published 2013 by Narrative Eye and The Circle with a Dot.

All rights reserved. No part of this book may be reproduced or transmitted in any form by any means, electronic, mechanical, photocopying, recording, or otherwise, without the consent, of the publisher, for information on obtaining permission for reprints or excerpts, contact the author or distributor.

ISBN 978-0-9533182-1-6

Printed in London

Front cover: Hans Memling. *Triptych of Jan Floreins*, central panel with *Adoration of the Magi*, 1425/40-1494. Bruges, Memling Museum. © 2013. Photo Scala, Florence.

Rear inside cover: Andres Sanchez Galque. *Los Tres Mulatos de Esmeraldas*, (Detail), (Portrait of Don Francisco de a Robe and sons Don Pzzas and Don Domingo), Madrid, 1599, oil on canvas. Museo Nacional del Prado, Madrid, ref. P04778. Reproduced by kind permission of Photographic Archive. © Madrid, Museo Nacional del Prado.

Rear cover: Andres Sanchez Galque. *Los Tres Mulatos de Esmeraldas*, (Portrait of Don Francisco de a Robe and sons Don Pzzas and Don Domingo), Madrid, 1599, oil on canvas. Museo Nacional del Prado, Madrid, ref. P04778. Reproduced by kind permission of Photographic Archive. © Madrid, Museo Nacional del Prado.

Layout by Daniel Palmer
Production by Narrative Eye.
Front inside cover photograph: *'Contemplation'* by George West.
Website: www.narrative-eye.org.uk
Email: info@narrative-eye.org.uk

Contents

Preface	vii
Introduction	xii
Parish records and the subsidy rolls	xix
Other primary evidence	xxiv

CHAPTER 1
The Status of Africans in Tudor England — 1

The First Letter	4
The Second Letter	9
The Proclamation of 1601	12
Conclusion	28

CHAPTER 2
How Africans were described in Tudor England — 41

The words used to describe Africans in Tudor England	42
Africans in Tudor England and their otherness	46
The 'curse of Ham'	49
Others	54
How Africans were not the epitome of otherness in Tudor England	56
How stories of 'noble' Africans affected otherness	66
Conclusion	70

CHAPTER 3
Africans from continental Europe in Tudor England — 107

Africans in Tudor England who came from continental Europe	108
Africans who came from Spain and Portugal	112
Iberian Africans living in Jewish households	126
Iberian Africans in England in the later part of the sixteenth century	129
Conclusion	135

CHAPTER 4
West Africans in Tudor England   152
West Africans present in Tudor England   153
How West Africans were seen in Tudor England   163
Africans in Tudor England and their relationship to African kingdoms   170
Trade and the presence of West Africans in late Tudor England   174
Conclusion   180

Africans in Tudor England:
Their Presence, Status and Origins   211
The Conclusion   211
Can he speak for himself?!   221
Lucy Negro and her sisters   226

Afterword   239

Bibliography   242
List of Images   341

Index   343

Preface

If we cannot see England clearly, do we imagine her as a book with white pages and no black letters in? Then we need to be reminded, as the archivist and historian Arthur Schomburg said in 1921 that African history represents 'the missing pages of history.' This statement inspired the young Professor John Henrik Clarke to go and research African history, and in particular African-American history.[1] But what is true for African history in general is even more so for the history of Africans in England. In the United States of America there is an acknowledgement that Africans were present on American soil at all the key moments during the life of that nation.[2] That same acknowledgement does not exist here in England, even though my twenty-seven years of research suggests it is true.

So in 1986, I began to search for evidence of Africans in England from antiquity to the sixteenth century. By 1992 this had blossomed into a desire to write a book revealing such a presence, but within a discreet period of English history. Five years into my research I discovered that the Tudor period had the largest amount of primary evidence, so I began to focus my study on that period. When I did, I developed acute concerns about how English history was being presented in books such as those by the historian Geoffrey Rudolph Elton.[3] His book *Life Under the Tudors,* and others listed in the Bibliography did not mention that Africans were present in Tudor England – although some might argue that because Elton's book does not focus on issues of 'race' that such an omission is not surprising.[4] But I found it so, because I knew Africans were present here during this time, and since his and other writers' silence and/or indifference on this subject was a feature of their books whether they were written recently or twenty or thirty years ago. I also looked at biographies of notable Tudor personalities such as Raleigh Trevelyan's *Walter Raleigh*, hoping to learn about Raleigh's relationship with Africans present in Tudor England. But I found that although the author concentrated on the swashbuckling aspects of Raleigh's life, he did not mention that there were Africans living in Tudor England who had been part of his entourage or accompanied him on his adventures.[5] The same applies to the books of Alison Weir and Antonia Fraser such as *The Six Wives of Henry VIII.*[6]

What also encouraged me to research and write on this subject was the mistaken idea presented in newspapers and television programmes that in the past when England was 'great' it had an all white population.[7] This false idea worryingly appears to influence public policy on immigration and the content of school curriculums, and paints a distorted picture of England's history. I thought and still think, that this distorted image was not being sufficiently contested by those who most had responsibility to do so, in other words, because it is historically inaccurate it is historians who should take up this challenge.[8]

Similar issues were, and are, faced by writers attempting to reclaim the voice of women in Tudor England.[9] But as the historian Laura Gowing points out, using the work of Patricia Crawford as an example, there is 'overwhelming evidence that the experiences of women can be retrieved from sources with predominately male perspectives, and their voices are capable of offering alternative views [on themselves and Tudor society.]'[10] This idea is even more a' droit when applied to the subject of Africans in Tudor England, whose existence can be 'retrieved' from contemporary sources which they did not write, and where they may not be the primary subject of discussion – but are nevertheless mentioned in. Moreover, in a similar way as writers about women in the Tudor period developed their own methodologies to discover these voices, so those seeking to find an African voice are forced to do the same.[11] This book is part of that growing body of research which refuses to allow the history of Africans in Tudor England to be submerged, and ultimately lost, in a wider discussion on early modern society.[12]

However, having an idea to write a book on Africans in Tudor England is quite different from actually doing it. This is not just because any research will place demands on the writer, but also because this subject relates to issues of race and identity which can create psychological problems for anyone wishing to tackle them. But in my case my past experiences helped to prepare me for some of these issues. This experience included the period of time I spent from 1997 applying to universities to do a doctorate on this subject, where I received over fifty-two rejections – most of which were justified on the basis that there was no one within their department who had the knowledge to supervise my thesis. During those years I had to overcome feelings of failure and resignation – which I did, and later when these emotions resurfaced during the course of the doctorate, because of what I had gone through I was able to manage these new emotions effectively.

Nevertheless, my coping mechanisms did not involve seeking access to specialist support teams, and this was fortunate as the changes that were taking place at my University meant that the history department that I had enrolled into no longer existed. Shortly thereafter my director of supervision Hakim Adi also ceased to be employed at the University. It was fortunate that both he and Erica Fudge both agreed to continue supervising me at a time when I most needed their input. Later, when I encountered more serious problems which questioned my research methods and the entire basis of my work, my resolve was tested again. I was forced to resolve these issues too, and with the help from colleagues (and you know who you are) I did.

This book is a direct result of my research. What has nourished my desire is a belief that this work is important. I believe that understanding England's past is fundamental to help us see the society we now live in. In many ways this feeling has grown, rather than be diminished by the various obstacles that have been put in my way. I have always been mindful that these impediments originate from an English academic community which too often is riddled with people who are indifferent, ignorant and sometimes unwittingly prejudiced.

My research goes on.
Onyeka
London, England, 2013.

Note

In this book the words 'Black' and 'Alien' begin with a capital letter when they refer to people who are called such, but the latter is in lower case when it refers to documents called alien registers. This is unless such words are being quoted directly from a text that does not capitalise. I use hyphens to join two or more words together when they describe somebody or something else such as with: 'sixteenth-century moriscoworke with gilt edge;' but not here 'in the sixteenth century moriscos worked.' This can lead to the same words relating to dates, descriptions of people etc. being hyphenated and not hyphenated in the same paragraph. Furthermore, words such as West Africans, Iberian Moors, Iberian Africans are not hyphenated unless they describe West-African society or people etc. However, the term African-American is hyphenated (unless it comes from a quotation or the title of a book that does not.) In addition, I have not modernised the spelling used by writers in the past and these are written as quotations. On footnotes, in this book there may be a long list of entries, because for example it supports a theory stated in the text that 'many historians' have made this argument, or the idea being justified may be considered as controversial. These entries are either arranged sequentially as they appear in the text, chronologically by date of publication, alphabetically by author, or more often thematically with the most important or significant first. Where 'ibid.' is used in footnotes it refers to all the items above and this may be more than one text. And in the footnotes films and television programmes are underlined to differentiate them from books and articles. Finally commas and full stops are included within quotation marks, not outside of them if the quotation is part of the main body of the paragraph.

Notes

[1] Michael Warren Williams, *The African American Encyclopedia*, Volume 2 (New York/London: Marshall Cavendish Corp, 1993), p. 334. (On Schomburg and Clarke).

[2] Kwame Anthony Appiah, Henry Louis Gates, *Africana: The Encyclopedia of the African and African American Experience* (Oxford: Oxford University Press, 2005), preface and introduction.

[3] The Bibliography contains a list of the books I consulted and includes Geoffrey Rudolph Elton, *England Under The Tudors* (1974, revised edition, London: Methuen, 1995); Robert Tittler, *Townspeople and Nation: English Urban Experiences, 1540–1640* (Stanford: Stanford University Press, 2001); and Robert Tittler and Norman Jones (eds.), *A Companion to Tudor Britain, Blackwell Companions to British History* (Oxford: Wiley Blackwell, 2004), all throughout.

[4] The idea of 'race' is complex and seen by some as controversial. The word is used in this book in a similar way as Jonathan Schorsch does in, *Swimming the Christian Atlantic: Judeoconversos, Afroiberians, and Amerindians in the Seventeenth Century* (Leiden/Boston/Biggleswade: Brill Extenza Turpin, 2004), p. 5 (6), 'Without wishing to enter into an enormous and dangerous topic, race/ethnicity is real, i.e., 'natural' insofar as different population groups often manifest different biological conditions [genotype]: immunities to particular diseases or lack thereof, manifest specific patterns of disease (lactose intolerance, sickle cell anaemia, Jays-Sachs diseases, etc.). Different population groups may also manifest statistically–notable somatic uniqueness [phenotype]: eye shape, particularly light skin, height, etc ...'

[5] Raleigh Trevelyan, *Sir Walter Raleigh* (London: Allen Lane, 2002); and Michael Dobson, Nicola Watson, Susan Doran and David Starkey (eds.), 'Elizabeth's Legacy,' *Elizabeth: The Exhibition at the National Maritime Museum* (London: Chatto and Windus, 2003).

[6] Antonia Fraser, *The Six Wives of Henry VIII* (1977, revised edition, London and Arizona: Phoenix, 2002); and Alison Weir, *The Six Wives of Henry VIII* (New York: Grove Press, 1991). But I acknowledge that Weir briefly refers to an African in Elizabeth's entourage in Alison Weir, *Elizabeth the Queen* (London: Jonathan Cape, 1998), p. 253.

[7] This idea is implied by television programmes and films such as Simon Schama, et. al., *A History of Britain*, 2 Entertain Video, 2000–2002; Michael Hirst, et. al., *The Tudors*, Showtime/Reveille/Working Title, 2007; Shekhar Kapur, et. al., *Elizabeth*, Polygram, 1998; Shekhar Kapur, et. al., *Elizabeth the Golden Age*, Universal Studios, 2007; Charles Jarrott, et. al., *Anne of the Thousand Days*, Universal Pictures, 1969; Fred Zinnemann, et. al., *The Man for all Seasons*, Columbia Pictures, 1966; but see, Gareth Roberts (writer), Charles Palmer (director), *The Shakespeare Code, Dr Who Series*, British Broadcasting Corporation, 7 April 2007.

[8] The question of immigration and race in post-war Britain is a widely discussed theme of writers such as Kathleen Paul, in *Whitewashing Britain: Race and Citizenship in the Postwar*

PREFACE

Era (New York/London: Cornell University Press, 1997), passim; and Colin Holmes, *John Bull's Island: Immigration and British Society, 1871–1971* (Basingstoke: Macmillan, 1988), passim. A similar view on English school curriculums is expressed by Marika Sherwood, in 'In this curriculum, I don't exist,' The Institute of Historical Research, University of London School of Advanced Study, http://www.history.ac.uk/resources/history-in-british-education/first-conference/sherwood-paper, accessed 27/ 7/11.

[9] Susan Broomhall and Stephanie Tarbin (eds.), *Women, Identities and Communities in Early Modern Europe* (Aldershot: Ashgate, 2008), passim; Patricia Crawford, 'Public Duty, Conscience and Women in Early Modern England,' in, John Morrill and Paul Slack (eds.), et. al., *Public Duty, and Private Conscience in Seventeenth-Century England: Essays Presented to G. E. Aylmer* (Oxford: Clarendon Press, 1993), pp. 201–234; Crawford, *Exploring Women's Past; Essays in Social History* (Carlton: Sisters Publishing, 1983), passim; other writers include: Laura Gowing, Philippa Maddern, Jodi Mikalachki, some of whose work is discussed throughout this book or listed in the Bibliography.

[10] Laura Gowing in Broomhall, Tarbin (eds.), *Women, Identities*, p. 2.

[11] This is discussed extensively by a range of historians who include Patricia Clarkson, Laura Gowing, and Philippa Maddern. Also see Selene Scarsi, in *Translating Women in Early Modern England: Gender in the Elizabethan Versions of Boirado, Ariosto and Tasso* (Farnham: Ashgate, 2001), pp. 1–13, 73–123 (on translating, interpreting and identifying the 'hidden' or women subject).

[12] I give a similar argument in Onyeka, 'The Missing Tudors, Black People in Sixteenth-Century England,' *BBC History Magazine*, 13, No. 7, July 2012, pp. 32–33.

Introduction

There were Africans present in Tudor England and this book examines their status and origins. These Africans were present in cities such as London, Plymouth and Bristol, but also towns and villages such as Blean in Kent, Hatherleigh in Devon, Holt in Worcestershire and Salisbury in Wiltshire. This population included men, women and children, such as Catalina de Cardones an Iberian Moor part of Katherine of Aragon's entourage, and John Blanke the 'black trumpeter' who was living in London in 1507. There was 'Christopher Cappervert a blackemoore,' who was buried in St Botolph without Aldgate, London on 22 October 1586; and there are the baptismal records of 'Mary Fillis, a black more, being about xx years old and dwelling with Millicent Porter, a seamester,' on 3 June 1597. We know that Symon Valencia 'a Blackamoore' lived in St Botolph without Aldgate, London at the same time; and 'Fortunatus [was] a blackmoor seruant to Sr Robert Cicill,' who was buried on 21 January 1602 in Westminster. In Plymouth, records exist for 'Bastien, a Blackmoore of Mr Willm Hawkins,' buried on 10 December 1583, and 'Anthony, John, a Neyger' on 18 March 1587; whilst in the same parish there are baptism records for 'Helene, daughter of Cristian the negro svant to Richard Sheere, the supposed father binge Cuthbert Holman, illeg.,' dated 2 May 1593.[1]

In this book I argue that some of these Africans brought skills with them to Tudor England from where they came from, and that these skills meant they did not automatically have the status of slaves. Instead, most Africans in Tudor England seem to have occupied positions ranging from household servants to visiting dignitaries. However, not all of the Africans mentioned above or others discussed in this book were immigrants or temporary visitors. Some Africans were born here, whilst others were domiciled, although the status of native and foreign-born Africans appears to have been dependent on the personal relationships they developed in Tudor society and not the colour of their skin. Furthermore, some of these Africans appear to have been considered as liege subjects and loyal members of their English parishes. I argue this despite the existence of two Letters written in 1596, and a Proclamation drafted in 1601, which talk about Africans in Tudor England being foreign and strangers and which attempted to classify or treat groups of 'those kindes of people' as slaves. As I discuss in the next chapter these documents failed and this reveals much about the status of Africans in England at this time.²

Some of the Africans who were present in Tudor England were born in Africa and others were of Black African descent. I use the word African to describe both sets of people, but I acknowledge that in Tudor records these people are described by terms such as 'Blackamoore,' 'Moor' and 'Negar.'³ Some of these terms originate from the way Ancient Greek and Roman writers referred to Africans; and the meaning of words such as Moor may also have been influenced by the way that Africans were described in continental Europe and parts of West Africa. In some cases this shows that some of the Africans present in Tudor England came from those places.⁴ This was confirmed through my research in Tudor parish records and other documents. And in a number of cases, this evidence has enabled me to locate and map the place in Africa or elsewhere that an African present in Tudor England came from. But I acknowledge that this may not prove in all cases that because an African came from a place that they originate from there.

This issue illustrates the difficulty of researching in this area, and may explain why there have only been a few modern historians who have examined this subject. It also explains why as a researcher I was forced to rely on primary evidence, often with very little additional information from elsewhere.⁵ I acknowledge that my approach in interpreting this evidence may pose problems for some modern readers who are unfamiliar with Black British history or Black history in general.⁶ Especially, as a general knowledge of the Tudor period, may not provide a reader with the skills to fully understand what is contained in this book. As most researchers of the Tudor period are within an academic culture which states or implies Africans were not present. Evidence which proves this presence, whether it originates from primary sources or not, is often reinterpreted as merely being about blackness as an abstract metaphor; or the evidence of Africans in parish records disappears into a discussion about Tudor writing styles, or some other subject that a modern historian may feel more confident discussing.⁷ This means that those historians trained only with traditional research methods will tend to be more limited and restricted in what they are willing to claim about Africans in Tudor England; whereas those with a wider knowledge of African history will tend to be more interpretive and 'innovative.'⁸

This tension exists and to some extent is inevitable until Black history and in particular the study of Africans in the Diaspora is taken more seriously.⁹ That is why in this book I have tended to include a range of different sources to support my arguments and where appropriate other historians' counter arguments. But I suggest that to really understand the history of Africans in Tudor England it would be useful to get an understanding not only of this period but also of African history as a field of study. These themes and ideas I return to throughout this book.

Some of these issues help to explain why I started my research not with books about Tudor England written by modern historians, but by finding Africans in parish records. My research initially focused on cities and towns such as London, Plymouth, Bristol and Barnstable (the reason why I started with these places is explained later). This process took three years, and then I spent a further two months in Spain exploring the connection between Africans there and those here. However in 2008, Imtiaz Habib's *Black Lives in the English Archives* was published. Habib provides evidence much of it in the form of chronological lists, with information arranged by date, which reveals the presence of hundreds of Africans in towns, cities and villages throughout Tudor England.[10] Habib's book means that I no longer have to prove that Africans were present in England because his work does this. I was thus able to make a shift in the emphasis and direction of my research, and focus on the status and origins of Africans in Tudor England which are subjects that I had always found more interesting and important.

Habib's book was not the only important text about Africans in Tudor England which was published in 2008. Another was Gustav Ungerer's *The Mediterranean Apprenticeship of British Slavery*. In this book and other work by the same author, he talks about the presence and status of Africans in Tudor society. Ungerer claims that this presence was entirely the result of slavery conducted by English pirates and other Europeans who stole Africans from West Africa and brought them to Tudor England. He suggests that these West Africans were regarded as naked-pagan savages who were slaves in English society, and that these two factors eventually led to the systematic enslavement of African people during the eighteenth and nineteenth centuries in the Americas and the Caribbean. Habib also suggests something similar, and these are the kinds of views that I will be challenging.[11]

Habib and Ungerer are not the first historians, however, to suggest that all or most of the Africans present in Tudor England were slaves. Other historians whose focus is on Africans in the eighteenth, nineteenth and early-twentieth centuries also do this. This includes: Faiza Ghazala, Folarin Shyllon, Paul Edwards, James Walvin, Madge Dresser and David Dabydeen.[12] But I will show that because these historians focus on issues which relate to a later African presence some of their theories are doubtful. This applies not only to what they say about the status and origins of Africans in Tudor England, but also to the numbers of Africans who they claim were present in that society. For example in *The Oxford Companion to Black British History,* Dabydeen claims that in '1601, in London alone the Black [African] population of England was 15,000–20,000.'[13] If *The Oxford Companion*'s figures are accurate, when compared with a total English population of 3–4 million, it would mean that Africans in 1601 represented a similar proportion of that population as they do now.[14] In other words, Africans would be a visible and substantial presence in late Tudor England. However, the figure of '15–20,000' is likely to be a misquotation. Dabydeen confirmed in an email to me that these figures were obtained from the historian Miranda Kaufmann.[15] However, Kaufmann states the figures are from *Daily Life in Eighteenth-Century England* by Kirstin Olsen, where they refer to the African population in England in the late eighteenth century. So the figure of 20,000 is generally regarded as a 'reasonable estimate' for the African population in Georgian not Tudor England.[16]

Dabydeen's misquotation probably occurs because of a lack of research on the African presence in Tudor England. To avoid that problem I have sought to concentrate on finding evidence from the Tudor period. I have been aided in this process by the work of a few historians such as Marika Sherwood and Mike Sampson. Since 2000, these historians have been collecting evidence on an African presence in Tudor England. Sherwood published an important article that lists the names, baptisms and burials of Africans present in England in the sixteenth century,[17] whilst Sampson has been doing this same sort of evidence gathering in conjunction with a group of historians called the Friends of Devon Archives. Other researchers who have also looked at this area include those at the Guildhall of London who have compiled evidence of an African presence in England from 1485 until the early-twentieth century. Their evidence has been a useful tool which I use to cross-reference with information that I have already found on this subject.[18]

Another two historians who have examined the presence and status of Africans in Tudor England include Peter Fraser and Miranda Kaufmann. Fraser in his article 'Slaves or Free People,' suggests that Africans were not automatically slaves in Tudor England – whilst Kaufmann, who completed her doctorate at Oxford University in 2012, wrote her thesis on 'Africans in Britain 1485–1640.' She published an important article suggesting that the Letters of 1596, and the Proclamation of 1601, were not effective because they were not supported by public officials with the power to implement them. She has also done field research discovering 350 Africans in early modern records.[19]

It is only recently, however, that Habib, Ungerer and Sampson have produced enough evidence which demonstrates that Africans were present in

Tudor England. But I suggest that most historians' reticence or indifference about an African presence in Tudor England remains; moreover, this kind of thinking still influences the work of those who do write about 'those kindes of people.' This may explain why most historians before Sampson and Sherwood were tentative in their claims about the presence of Africans in Tudor England, but still offer in some cases misleading statements about their status and origins. One of these historians is Peter Fryer in *Staying Power,* who in a similar way to Habib and Ungerer claims that Africans were either slaves or a few 'strolling players,' isolated, strange and transient.[20] But, as I shall reveal Fryer's ideas about Africans in Tudor England are not supported by the evidence I have found, although other information in his book about Africans in the eighteenth and nineteenth centuries is detailed and comprehensive. This latter evidence has enabled me to compare the status of Africans in Georgian and Victorian Britain with that of 'those kindes of people' in Tudor England.[21]

Other earlier historians who have also postulated about an African presence in Tudor England include Kenneth Little in *Negroes in Britain* written in 1947. But in a similar way to Fryer, Little says he doubts 'if the Blackman whether of African or East Indian origin was a familiar figure [in England] until well on in the [sixteenth] century, except as a chance visitor or when imported from Portuguese and colonial territories [in Africa and the Caribbean].' The word 'imported' in Little's quote suggests that he thinks the few Africans present in Tudor society were slaves, who had arrived in England as the property of their owners. More recently, some historians such as Kim Hall seem to repeat similar ideas in their work. For example Hall suggests that Africans in Tudor England were very few in numbers, and that they were 'too accidental and solitary to be given a historical statistic,' implying that their presence was not significant enough to warrant any serious academic analysis.[22]

Throughout this book I will be challenging these sorts of views on the presence, status and origins of Africans in Tudor England. I also examine important legal issues such as whether it was legal to enslave Africans in Tudor England simply because of the colour of their skin, or ethnic origins, as it was later to be in Britain's colonies in the eighteenth and nineteenth centuries. In the latter, Africans were treated as property and systematically stigmatised, so that ideas about their inherent inferiority became commonplace. These ideas were developed into a coherent system supported by science and religion which classified Africans as slaves at birth and attempted to ensure they would remain so perpetually. This system was not only morally justified but was also maintained on the basis of economic necessity.[23]

INTRODUCTION

In this book I will show that this does not appear to be what happened in Tudor England.

There are a few other historians who share the views I have just outlined. But their research is about the status and origins of Africans in sixteenth-century continental Europe. These historians who are African-American and African-Caribbean often have their research ignored by the English historians who I have mentioned earlier. This may be because these historians from the African Diaspora are perceived as lacking evidence for their theories, or they are accused of falsifying history. However, I find many of these historians' conclusions are supported by evidence, and I suggest that sometimes their work is being treated with indifference for other reasons. These reasons may be based on non-academic issues such as the writers' ethnicity or that their work is produced by small-independent publishing companies.

I therefore include the work of African-American writers such as Edward Scobie, Joel Augustus Rogers and the African-Guyanese historian Ivan Van Sertima.[24] These historians have written about an African presence in sixteenth-century Europe and this work helped me understand more about Africans in Tudor England. Their work also shows that Africans in Europe were not all slaves and that 'those kindes of people' occupied various positions in sixteenth-century European society. Scobie has written five articles for the *Journal of African Civilisation* and three of his articles in particular are of note: 'The Black in Western Europe', 'African Women in Early Europe' and 'The Moors and Portugal's Global Expansion'.[25] He also wrote *Black Britannia: A History of Blacks in Britain*, and his further work in *The African Presence in Early Europe* incorporates his previous articles on the subject with some new references and footnotes.[26]

It is not just African-American historians who write on the African Diaspora who have their work ignored. The English historian Basil Davidson, and the African British author Robin Walker in *When We Ruled*, provide more evidence about Africans having power and influence in the fifteenth and sixteenth centuries, and their work is treated with indifference, probably because it offers this positive perspective.[27]

My research also refers to evidence from writers such as Nabil Matar and Daniel Vitkus that focuses on the presence of Muslims in Tudor and Stuart England. The evidence they reveal is important because it shows there were African Muslims in England in the sixteenth and seventeenth centuries, and that some came from the Ottoman Empire and North-African kingdoms such as Morocco. Readers wishing to understand more about this particular African presence may examine their research.[28] However, the evidence in this book suggests that not all Africans in Tudor England were Muslims and this therefore is the limitation of their research, since the comments that they make about non-Muslims do not seem to be supported by evidence. For example, Matar states that 'the likelihood [in Tudor or Stuart Britain] of an Englishman or Scotsman meeting a Muslim [were] higher than that of meeting ... a Sub-Saharan African.'[29] In this book I suggest that this matter is more complex than Matar's statement implies.

Interestingly, a group of much earlier historians attempted to address some of these issues and this includes the nineteenth- and early-twentieth-century historians David MacRitchie and Gerald Massey. Their work contains a considerable amount of information[30] some of which has been useful in my research, for example, by examining MacRitchie's books it helped me find information on African performers in sixteenth-century Scotland and how similar performers were present in Tudor England.[31] But despite this, historians such as Stephen Howe have dismissed the work of MacRitchie and others such as Godfrey Higgins as being merely a regurgitation of myths and legends – when in fact they are attempting to find the facts behind those mythical stories.[32] More recently, a few historians such as Ahmed Ali and Ibrahim Ali have confirmed in their books that some of the kinds of ideas that MacRitchie writes about can be supported by evidence, and they support his claim that there was an African presence in England long before the Tudor period.[33]

Nevertheless, writers such as MacRitchie do not appear to have found the evidence that I draw upon in this book. But this also applies to recent historians as well. In addition, even those historians such as Habib and Ungerer who have found some of the evidence I have, often seem to come to starkly different conclusions. This means that their arguments often provide contrary views to those offered here – but their ideas are included nevertheless as they may enable the reader to gain a greater understanding of the issues in this book.

Some of the differences between what Habib and Ungerer propose, and what I claim are because we draw different conclusions from the same evidence. These differences occur as the historians Stephanie Tarbin and Susan Broomhall suggest because of our 'innovative' interpretations of the evidence. This method of examining records should be seen as a way of interpretation, rather than speculation, and is a tool writers about women in Tudor England have been using for decades.[34] For Tarbin and Broomhall these methods of interpretation are necessary, as they uncover evidence of women in Tudor documents much of which has been neglected, lost or concealed. For similar reasons I adopt an analogous approach with evidence about the presence, status and origins of Africans in Tudor England.[35]

INTRODUCTION

Parish records and the subsidy rolls

My investigations have led me to evidence contained in Tudor parish records. These documents include parish registers, some of which are written on single sheets of paper, others are bound together as books. The latter also include memorandum daybooks an important source of information which often contain notes written by a parish priest or clerk about the people who they baptised, married or buried.

However, these parish documents can be very difficult to understand as the information in them is sometimes indecipherable through age, or the way they are written. Moreover, even after finding a reference to an African in one parish register, it may have taken me another year before I found something else to corroborate this person's existence or status. In some cases this meant revisiting evidence which I had earlier disregarded. Notwithstanding these difficulties, I have found descriptions of Africans in Tudor parish records, and details about their baptisms, marriages and burials. These records also occasionally provide indications about an African's status and origins. The reasons why some parish records provide this information are linked to these documents' historical development. Up to the Dissolution of the monasteries 1538–1541, monks had been the principal record keepers. But because of a feeling that they were the 'harbingers' of 'popery' and 'idolatry,' this responsibility was passed to the parish priests and clerks.[36] On 29 September 1538, Thomas Cromwell issued the following order: 'a priest, parson or vicar ... [should] kepe one boke or reistre wherin ye shall write the day and yere of every weddyng christenyng and buryeng made wtin yor pishe.' In other words, that there should be one authentic record for everyone in the parish. This is important because if this order was followed we would find all the Africans in Tudor England who were baptised, married or buried by the Church simply by examining these records. The order goes on to say that each and 'every time' there is a 'weddyng, christenyng and buryeng' the person should be recorded and this should be done in front of 'said wardens.' According to the order the priest has no discretion as to whether to record – it must be done. The order then says the parish records are to be locked up for 'sauff keeping,' with rather elaborate means for the retention of keys and punishments for failure to comply.[37]

In 1563 and 1598 two further orders were made, the first stating that a copy of the parish records had to be sent to a Bishop. The second in 1598, reiterating this and stating all records from 'the beginning of her Majesty's [Elizabeth I's] reign ... are to be added.'[38] This is important because most of the parish records that are available are from these second set of records. But the problem with them is that they may not be as comprehensive as those made under the first order in 1538.[39] Many priests and clerks started their records from 1558 and failed to copy those falling outside of Elizabeth I's reign. So with the exception of those parish records from Perlethorpe and Carburton in Nottinghamshire, we have few records for the first fifty years of the Tudor period.[40] It is not known if these earlier parish records contain information about an African presence, but it does mean that the evidence in this book is weighted towards the end of the sixteenth century, suggesting there were more Africans present in England at the end of that century than at the beginning.[41]

In this book I use 232 entries from parish records that describe Africans using terms such as 'Moor,' 'Blackamoore' and 'Negar.' A further 73 entries contain these same terms, but it is not clear whether they describe Africans. A selection from both types of records are discussed in this book and included in the bibliography. Of the 232 entries, they were found throughout Tudor England in areas such as Hatherleigh, Northampton, Preston, Lancaster and Salisbury. However, I concentrated on forty-two parishes from four major cities and towns: London, Plymouth, Bristol and Barnstable. I was able to identify these areas because of information in contemporary records such as letters and books, which showed that Africans were living in those places. My research revealed that London has the largest number of parish records referring to Africans: 77 entries and this appears to reflect that there were more Africans living there than in other cities. It may also show that Africans were drawn to this city because it was a port and a centre for commerce and trade.[42] The same is also true for Plymouth which was the place with the second largest number of entries. Interestingly, the evidence suggests that Africans were living in the centre of these two cities and this may show that 'those kindes of people' were part of the cultural heart of those places. For example the parishes with the most number of entries referring to Africans are St Botolph without Aldgate, where Africans appear at a ratio of 1:15, and St Olave Hart Street in London, with the St Andrew's ward in Plymouth being the third largest. In the St Olave and St Andrew's parishes, Africans appear at a ratio of 1:20. This creates the possibility that Africans constituted 6%, 5% and 5% respectively of the populations of these areas between the years of 1538 (when records began) and 1603.[43]

I am not in a position, however, to state how many Africans were living in Tudor England. This is because despite the clear words in the various orders, there does not appear to have been an effective administrative infrastructure capable of recording all the Africans present. Africans may be hidden or missing in some Tudor records as 'parish clerks [and priests] were careful to conceal' the existence of 'controversies.'[44] In other words, recording a person with an epithet or moniker which describes their ethnicity may have been considered a 'controversy' or more likely, unnecessary, because as I shall show Tudor writers did not see race as we do now. What this means is that some parishes appear to have more evidence of an African presence than others: for example, St Olave Hart Street has more records where 'those kindes of people' are described than Whitechapel in London. This may mean that there were more Africans living in Hart Street in Tudor times than Whitechapel,[45] and/or, it might suggest that the parish priest or clerk in Hart Street was more comfortable at using terms that we now know refers to Africans than his counterpart.

Therefore there are likely to be Africans who are living in Tudor England who are not revealed by the records. This idea is supported by the notion that some documents which describe Africans may have been lost, especially if they were contained in non-conformist churches where this information was never collated, or perhaps was destroyed during the Reformation.[46] But whilst there is insufficient evidence to say conclusively how many Africans were present in Tudor England, there is sufficient information to claim that the numbers of African men, women and children were not negligible as Fryer claims. And there is enough evidence to raise issues, propose theories and explanations for these people's demographic presence.

Some of these demographic issues relate to the disproportionate recording in Tudor parish records of African women compared to men: 55 to 141. This is explained by the historians Hall and Benjamin Braude who claim that African women are obscured in Tudor records because they were hidden inside English households. Lowe takes this point further and infers that Tudor writers either did not know how, or were afraid to record African women.[47] Jose Piedra suggests something similar. However, Hall, Braude, Lowe and Piedra seem to base their conclusions on the fact that in some early modern plays such as *Othello* and *Titus Andronicus* African men are present and African women are either absent, or only referred to in a sub-plot.[48] Some of the issues that are raised by these facts are discussed throughout this book, others that relate more to the development of early modern literature are not. However the important point that I shall return to later is that Tudor parish records do suggest there were fewer African women living in Tudor England.

Parish records list the baptisms, marriages and burials of African men, women and children, but they do not record births.[49] Nevertheless, sometimes in the record for the baptism of an African child there is a comment about them being illegitimate. For example, there is a record of a baptism on

23 June 1603 at St Andrew's Plymouth, for 'Richard, son of Marye a Neger, base, ye reputed father Rog Hoggett.'[50] Records such as these indicate information not only about the status of the mother and child but also highlight another issue. This is that there are only a few references to 'Blackamoore children' and even fewer to Africans marrying other Africans. Amongst the records discovered so far, the most common types of sexual relationships are those unions between white men and African women. Of the thirty-two mixed-parentage children only twelve of them appear to be the product of a relationship between an African father and a white mother. Marriages where both parties are African do not appear frequently in Tudor parish records. This may be because African men and women in Tudor society were having non-Christian marriages. But we have little evidence to support this. So with the information I have discovered so far, it is more likely that the evidence does accurately show there were only a small number of Africans marrying other Africans in Tudor England.[51]

So some parish records contain information about the relationships Africans had or their status and origins. It is possible as the historian Andrew Spicer suggests that if some Africans were thought of as Aliens then priests or clerks would record information about their ethnicity in case they were foreign spies or agents. War may have increased this fear, as England had internal civil and religious struggles or conflicts with France and Spain.[52] Certain parish records may then have become an additional record of Aliens that could be used in similar ways to the subsidy rolls.[53] This may be one reason which explains a record such as 'Katherin the negar,' who was buried on 24 August in 1594 at St Stephen Coleman Street, London and who is noted as 'dwelling with the prince of Portugal.'[54] Katherin may have been described in this way because she was 'dwelling' with a high profile Portuguese dignitary. It may also imply that she too has foreign origins. However, most parish records contain few statements or comments on the origins of the Africans being baptised, or buried, in order for us to determine whether they were newly arrived immigrants, or domiciled. Of course, it is possible that some of these people may be English-born as in the example of 'Iferdynando,' who was buried on 19 January 1597 at Dartford, Kent and is simply described as 'a blackamore svannte [servant] to Alexander Neuby.'[55]

If Africans living in Tudor England, however, were Aliens or immigrants then they may have appeared on another set of records known as the alien, lay or local registers: referred to here as the subsidy rolls. The subsidy rolls required every adult over sixteen who was not born in England but was 'under the King's Obeisance' to be registered.[56] If the Alien's income fell below a tax threshold (that was one established as a minimum for 'native-born') then they had to be taxed at a standard rate 'that is 8d.' The assessors or clerks were asked to list the name, nationality and status if known of the Alien. These rolls had existed since medieval times, but in 1523 Henry VIII attempted to standardise how they ran – now 'every person' had to pay a charge but Aliens paid more, usually double the rate. Aliens were identified on these records because they had to pay extra, but the rates were not standardised, nor was the extra they had to pay.[57] During Henry VIII's war with France, the subsidy rolls were used as a way of making money to pay for this conflict. He did this by taxing immigrants such as Italians, Normans, Dutch and Flemish Huguenots, many thousands of whom had settled in London and on the south-coast of England in towns such as Southampton, Poole and Bournemouth, or Norwich in Norfolk.[58] But the rolls were not created to specifically identify the race of the people who they taxed but to show if they were foreign or not. In other words, they are likely to have missed a number of Africans present in Tudor England because they were domiciled or had the status of being liege.[59]

This may explain why the subsidy rolls contain only fifteen entries that have a clear reference to an African person. For example in the Langborne ward of London in 1582, there is a record for 'the house of John Baptista Sambitores: [where] Fardinando a blackamore [lives].' But other records in the subsidy rolls contain words that require investigation to find out if terms such as 'Blackamoore' and 'Moor' are merely the names of people described in those records, or whether they are describing their ethnicity. For example as with 'Fraunces Negro' who was living in the Aldersgate ward of London in 1583, and was paid 'for fee and wages x li…xxxs' and 'Dyego Negro servaunt' who in 1541 lived at St Mary's Woolnoth, London and was assessed at '4d.'[60] In this way these records resemble some parish records that raise similar issues such as that of 'Philip Blackamore,' who was christened on 18 January 1599 in Cardington, Bedfordshire.[61] In some cases I suggest that these types of records do describe African people, but in most situations I endeavour to find other evidence before claiming this.

Nevertheless, Tudor parish records seem to contain more evidence about Africans than the subsidy rolls. This may be because parish records are more comprehensive perhaps, because they had more effective punishments for failure to complete them. They therefore appear to have been checked more often and by more people than the subsidy rolls. The rolls on the other hand, seem to have relied on clerks or priests having a personal interest in keeping them up to date.[62] Because of this it has not been possible to track many Africans who appear on both records. Perhaps, this is because these records were not designed to be, nor are, complementary.[63] In other words there are Africans recorded as being foreign-born in parish records, but they are missing from the subsidy rolls.[64] This may be because another person paid for the African's tax burden and then expunged them from the rolls. It may also mean that in Tudor England only a small number of Africans were being officially recorded as having the status of Aliens or immigrants. Africans may also have been exempt from the subsidy rolls because these records did not apply to some people employed as servants or soldiers. For example, a foreign-born African called Diego Negro who was a friend of Francis Drake and lived in England for four years from 1573 is absent from the rolls.[65] Other Africans in Tudor England who were transitory or here for short-term visits also appear to be missing from the rolls and the parish records: this includes the Moroccan Ambassador and his entourage who visited Elizabeth I in 1600. This is despite him being painted in England and his entourage being referred to in a number of other English documents.[66]

Other primary evidence

The parish records and the subsidy rolls are not the only contemporary, official public documents that mention Africans. There is also a Letter written on 11 July, and a second on 18 July in 1596 that are both signed by Elizabeth I. In addition there is a Proclamation drafted in 1601 that purports to have been written in the hand of Elizabeth I but lacks her or any other signature on it. These documents are significant because they show that some officials in Tudor England recognised and were willing to publicly acknowledge an African presence. This is so despite Africans in Tudor England occupying positions predominately in the private sphere of that society.[67] In that private sphere some of these Africans may have been obscured or hidden. But these documents show that Africans were sufficiently visible and significantly numerous that they could be labelled as a social, political and economic problem in late Tudor society.[68]

However, most documents that talk about Africans in Tudor England are not legal ones. Africans are also only rarely mentioned in the work of official Tudor historians such as Raphael Holinshed, John Stow and William Harrison. The lives of most Africans in Tudor society appear to have been obscured or are part of the 'missing pages of history.' In this way the lives of Africans resemble that of the poor and women.[69] However, with Africans this reticence is more pronounced, there are no books written by Tudor writers which talk exclusively about Africans in England at that time. Holinshed, Stow and Harrison's work concentrates on subjects such as constitutional reform, trade, religion and the succession to the throne of England as these were the subjects their patrons were no doubt interested in. These writers often seem to present English history so that it pleases those who sponsored their work.[70] They thus give prominence to groups 'capable of concerted' political action such as the King, Queen or aristocratic lords inside the royal court.[71] I have found no evidence of a resident African group that was powerful enough to commission or sponsor an alternative vision of Tudor England that consistently included them as fully-functioning agents. This means that some late Tudor or early Stuart historians saw their own history with a revisionist perspective, and it might mean that Africans were obscured or ignored, perhaps deliberately. However, this is not always the case and in one important example in Chapter 3 of this book, a historian writing at the beginning of the Stuart period uses primary records written during the Tudor era to edit an African in. This may suggest that noting the presence of some Africans may not have been as problematic as first thought. Or that for this particular African his legacy was so significant that it was not socially acceptable to ignore him.

So, only occasionally do we find clear references to Africans living in Tudor England in contemporary books. More often evidence about these Africans comes from personal letters sent between individuals or other correspondence not written for publication. This includes a letter written in 1501, by the Tudor politician Thomas More to his friend John Holt and others by George Best that talk about Africans being present in Tudor England.[72] Other writers who also make such references as an aside or in a matter-of-fact way include Richard Hakluyt and Samuel Purchas.[73] There are also other books by English travellers such as Andrew Boorde's *Introduction to the Book of Knowledge,* published in 1550 and the work of the sixteenth-century Moorish scholar Leo Africanus, translated by John Pory in 1600 that describe the customs and culture of Africans. The latter is important because it includes the views of Africans about other Africans.[74] Africans also appear in *A Notable Historie of the Saracens,* written by the sixteenth-century Italian writer Augustinus Curio and Edward Blount's translation in 1600 of *The Historie of the Uniting of Portugal.* In addition, *The Spanish Dictionary* of John Minsheu created in 1599 is significant as it provides important sixteenth-century definitions of words used to describe Africans.[75]

I also suggest that the work of writers such as Boorde, Best and Africanus may have been one of the factors that influenced Tudor playwrights such as Shakespeare, Ben Jonson and Christopher Marlowe to include Africans and references to Africans in their plays[76] – although the presence of Africans in Tudor London, and the stories they brought with them may have been a more significant factor, especially since Blackamoores were living close to where Shakespeare and others were writing and performing their plays.[77] This offers the possibility that some of the words spoken by characters such as Othello and Aaron are the echo of the voices of an otherwise silent population. But I acknowledge the fact as Habib, Matar and many other historians suggest that these playwrights provide few, if any, direct references to a resident Tudor African population.[78] Despite this, I suggest that some of these plays can indicate popular perceptions and ideas about Africans present in Tudor society. The historians Harry Lee Faggett and Sujata Iyengar come to similar conclusions.[79]

Apart from written documents such as books and plays there are also a few images and paintings that show Africans present in Tudor England. There is the painting of the Moroccan Ambassador (Fig. 1), and we have images of a John Blanke the 'blacke trumpeter' in 1511 on the *Westminster Tournament Roll* (Fig. 2).[80] In addition, there are a few other images of Africans in Thomas Earle and Kate Lowe's *Black Africans in Renaissance Europe* which include an African woman or man on the Hawkins' family crest. However, it is significant that we have more images of Africans present in continental Europe than Tudor England and the reasons for this are numerous and daedalian.[81] Nevertheless, in the next chapter we shall see that though there is a dearth in contemporary visual images of Africans in Tudor England, their presence was recognised in some official public documents such as the Letters and the Proclamation. These documents are important because they raise issues that are pertinent to the status of Africans throughout the entire Tudor period, despite the fact that they were written at the end of the sixteenth and beginning of the seventeenth centuries. And that is why I discuss them in Chapter 1.[82]

In the Letters and the Proclamation, Africans are described by a variety of names and terms. This raises a number of issues which are not addressed in Chapter 1 because they are convoluted. Nevertheless I feel that they cannot be ignored as they reflect on our understanding of the identity, ethnicity and therefore the origins of Africans present in Tudor England. That is why in Chapter 2 I analyse what these different terms mean, and that people in English society did not categorise Africans as some modern anthropologists do now. The way that Africans are described in Tudor parish records and letters suggests that ideas about their racial identity and perhaps status were based on shifting criteria, such as the personal views of the contemporary writer, or were reflective of how individual Africans saw themselves. This can be seen in records in Plymouth and London such as that for Domingo who was buried in the St Botolph area of London in 1586, and was described as a 'negar,' 'Ginnye,' and 'a black' in various parish records.[83]

In addition, I propose that some of the terms used to describe Africans which are discussed in Chapter 2 of this book, had their origins or were influenced by words that may have come from the Iberian Peninsula or from classical writings. I also suggest in Chapter 4 that some of the terms used to define Africans in Tudor England may have had their source in the stories that Africans told about themselves. Some of these stories are fantastic and give a negative and/or prurient image of the African. In Chapters 2 and 4, I consider whether these stories led to 'those kindes of people' being seen as 'less than,' or as examples of 'otherness' in Tudor England. The term otherness in this book refers to 'difference,' 'distinctness' or 'strangeness.' It also relates to whether the 'blackness' associated with Africans made them outsiders in Tudor society.[84] I suggest in Chapter 2 that Africans were not considered as strange as other peoples such as Native-Americans, and that this may have been because 'those kindes of people' had been present in England since medieval times, and Englishmen had ideas about them from the stories that were told.

In Chapters 3 and 4 some of these Africans' lives are traced from their time here, all the way back to the country or countries they came from. I believe this helps us see not only their origins more clearly but also their status as well. As a result, I intend to show particular Africans in Tudor England as real people, not just as a statistic or an anomaly. In the next chapter this is revealed as I discuss the status of Africans in Tudor England.

Notes

[1] The references for the records that contain these Africans are to be found throughout this book and in the Bibliography.

[2] Author unknown, Letter to Lord Mayors, signed by Queen Elizabeth, National Archives, Kew, London, PC 2/21, p. 304, 11 July 1596; Author unknown, Letter signed by Queen Elizabeth, National Archives, Kew, London, PC 2/21, f. 306, 18 July 1596; and Author unknown, Proclamation ca January 1601, National Archives, Kew, London, *Tudor Royal Proclamations,* 1601/ 804.5-805. The phrase 'those kindes of people' originates from this Proclamation and the second Letter where it is used to describe Africans present in Tudor England.

[3] *Oxford Dictionary of English* (Oxford: Oxford University Press, 2nd edition 2003), p. 28; Including those records in Guildhall Library, London (and thereafter referred to as G. L.), GL Ms 28867, GL Ms 9243–9245, GL Ms 4310, GL Ms 9222 and Plymouth and West Devon Record Office, Plymouth, St Andrews/MF1–4.

⁴ The meaning and origins of these words is discussed in Richard Percyvall, *A Dictionarie in Spanish and English, First Published by R Percivale Now Enlarged by J Minsheu. Hereunto is Annexed in Ample English Dictionarie with the Spanish Words Adjoined* (London: E Bollifaunt, 1599), p. 172; and revealed in John Pory, (translator (tr.)), Leo Africanus, *A Geographical Historie of Africa, Written in Arabicke and Italian ... by Iohn Leo a More ...* (London: John Pory, 1600), pp. 6, 42.

⁵ The idea of what is a primary source is open to some interpretation, a workable definition used in this book is material created at or close to the Tudor period. In analysing what is primary and what is not I have found the work of E. Sreedharan useful in, *A Textbook of Historiography, 500 B.C. to A.D. 2000*, (New Delhi: Orient Longman, 2003), pp. 79–89, 301–303; Martha C. Howell and Walter Prevenier, *From Reliable Sources: An Introduction to Historical Method* (Itacha: Cornell University Press, 2001), pp. 21–22; and Jennifer Bowers and Peggy Keeran, *Literary Research and the British Renaissance and Early Modern Period: Strategies and Sources* (Plymouth: Scarecrow Press, 2010), pp. introduction.

⁶ The term 'Black' used here includes the study of African, Asian and other minority-ethnic people see David Dabydeen and James Gilmore (eds.), *The Oxford Companion to Black British History* (Oxford: Oxford University Press, 2007), pp. introduction; and Josna Pankhania, *Liberating the National History Curriculum* (London: Falmer Press, 1994), pp. 1–7. On Black studies in general see, Molefi Asante and Ama Mazama (eds.), *The Encyclopedia of Black Studies* (2004, new edition, London: SAGE publications, 2005), passim.

⁷ These views are shared by many others including Pankhania, *Liberating the National History Curriculum*, passim; and Marika Sherwood, in 'In this curriculum, I don't exist,' The Institute of Historical Research, University of London School of Advanced Study http://www.history.ac.uk/resources/history-in-british-education/first-conference/sherwood-paper, accessed 27/ 7/11.

⁸ A similar 'tension' exists when writing about women, in Susan Broomhall and Stephanie Tarbin (eds.), *Women, Identities and Communities in Early Modern Europe* (Aldershot: Ashgate, 2008), p. 7 (definition of 'innovative' interpretations).

⁹ Onyeka, 'The Missing Tudors, Black People in Sixteenth-Century England,' *BBC History Magazine*, 13, no. 7, July 2012, pp. 32–33.

¹⁰ Imtiaz Habib, *Black Lives in the English Archives, 1500–1677: Imprints of the Invisible* (London: Ashgate, 2008), pp. 1–18, 274–334.

¹¹ Gustav Ungerer, *The Mediterranean Apprenticeship of British Slavery* (Madrid: Verbum Editorial, 2008), p. 76; Gustav Ungerer, 'Recovering a black African's voice in an English Lawsuit,' *Medieval and Renaissance Drama in England* (Madison: Fairleigh Dickinson University Press, 2004), pp. 255–271; and Gustav Ungerer, 'The Presence of Africans in Elizabethan England and the performance of *Titus Andronicus*, at Burley-on-the-Hill, 1595–96,' *Medieval Renaissance Drama in England Annual*, Volume 21, 2008, pp. 19–56.

¹² Faiza Ghazala, Greater London Council Ethnic Minorities Unit, *A History of the Black Presence in London* (London: Greater London Council, 1986), pp. 7–8; Folarin Shyllon, *Black People in Britain* (Oxford: Oxford University Press, 1977), pp. preface, 1–10; Paul Edwards, James Walvin, 'Africans in Britain, 1500–1800,' in *The African Diaspora: Interpretive Essays* (Cambridge: Harvard University Press, 1976), pp. 173–204; James Walvin, *Black and White: The Negro in English Society, 1555–1945*, pp. 1–31; *Black Ivory: A History of British Slavery* (1992, 2ⁿᵈ edition, London: Harper Collins, 2001), preface; and Madge Dresser, *Slavery Obscured: The Social History of the Slave Trade in an English Provincial Port* (2001, new edition, Bristol: Redcliff Press, 2007), p. 11. Other books expressing similar views by James Walvin, Madge Dresser, Peter Fleming and others are included in the Bibliography.

INTRODUCTION

¹³ Dabydeen and Gilmore (eds.), *The Oxford Companion to Black British History*, p. 146; Peter Fryer, *Staying Power: The History of Black People in Britain Since 1504* (1984, reprint, London: Pluto Press, 1989), pp. 33–66, 67–89; Charles Malcolm Macinnes, *England and Slavery* (London: Arrowsmith, 1934), pp. 107–139; and Nigel File, Chris Power, *Black Settlers in Britain 1555–1958* (London: Heinemann Educational Books, 1981), pp. 1–32.

¹⁴ Office for National Statistics, *Ethnicity and National Identity in England and Wales 2011*, http://www.ons.gov.uk/ons/dcp171776_290558.pdf accessed 02/03/13 and Office for National Statistics, Population estimates for the UK, http://www.statistics.gov.uk/cci/nugget.asp?ID=6, accessed 02/03/13.

¹⁵ Dabydeen and Gilmore (eds.), *The Oxford Companion to Black British History*, p. 146; David Dabydeen, personal email sent 11/11/08, accessed 11/11/08; and Miranda Kaufmann, personal email sent 11/11/08, accessed 11/11/08.

¹⁶ Kirstin Olsen, *Daily Life in 18th-Century England* (Oxford: Greenwood Publishing Group, 1999), pp. 29, 310. These books and articles quote similar figures for the numbers of Africans in eighteenth-century England: Gretchen Holbrook Gerzina, *Black London: Life Before Emancipation* (New Jersey: Rutgers University, 1997), p. 5; Kathy (Kathleen) Chater, *Untold Histories: Black People in England and Wales During the Period of the British Slave Trade, c. 1660–1807* (Manchester: Manchester University Press, 2008), pp. 23–30; and Joel Augustus Rogers, *Nature Knows no Colour Line* (St Petersburg: Helga Rogers, 1952), p. 156 quotes, 'Anglicanus,' *Gentleman's Magazine* XXXIV, October, 1764, pp. 493, 495.

¹⁷ Mike Sampson, 'Black burials and deaths 16th century' (Email), from Devon Record Office, Devon, 16 April 2006; Mike Sampson, 'Friends of Devon Archives, the Black connection,' *Friends of Devon Newsletter*, Issue 25, May 2000, pp. 12–15 quoted in Lucy MacKeith, *Local Black History: A Beginning in Devon* (London: Archives and Museum of Black Heritage, 2003), p. 35; and Marika Sherwood, 'Blacks in Elizabethan England,' *History Today*, 53: 10, 2003, pp. 40–42.

¹⁸ Sherwood, 'Blacks in Elizabethan England,' pp. 40–42; and G. L. 'Black and Asian people discovered in records held by the Manuscripts Section,' *Manuscripts Section*, Aldermanbury, London.

¹⁹ Peter Fraser in Randolph Vigne and Charles Littleton (eds.), 'Slaves or Free people, the status of Africans in England 1550–1750,' *From Strangers to Citizens: The Integration of Immigrant Communities in Britain, Ireland, and Colonial America, 1550–1750* (Eastbourne: Sussex Academic Press, 2001), pp. 254–261; and Miranda Kaufmann, 'Caspar Van Senden, Sir Thomas Sherley and the 'Blackamoor' project,' *Historical Research*, 81: 212, May 2008, pp. 366–371.

²⁰ Fryer, *Staying Power*, pp. 1–14, 113–133, 146, 191–236; The quotation is from Samuel Parsons Scott, *History of the Moorish Empire in Europe* (New York: Lippincott, 1904), p. 355.

²¹ On the importance of Fryer's work see the following: James Walvin in Peter Fryer, *Rhythms of Resistance: African Musical Heritage in Brazil* (London: Pluto Press, 2000), p. 2; Marika Sherwood, 'Britain, Slavery and the Trade in Enslaved Africans,' *History in Focus*, Issue 12, http://www.history.ac.uk/ihr/Focus/Slavery/articles/sherwood.html posted spring 2007, accessed 03/12/08; Gemma Romain, *Black British History*, Birkbeck University, Faculty of Continuing Education, London, England, 2007–2008 http://www.bbk.ac.uk/ce/history/documents/FFHI232UACB_003.pdf 05/11/08; and suggested by the Qualifications and Curriculum Authority (QCA) Website, 'Innovating with History,' http://www.qca.org.uk/history/innovating/history_matters/worked_for_me/ks3/cameo9.htm, accessed 18/07/08.

²² Kenneth Little, *Negroes in Britain* (London: Routledge, Kegan Paul, 1947), pp. 6, 166 (quotation), 187–216; Habib, *Black Lives*, p. 1, quotes Kim Hall in *Things of Darkness: Economies of Race and Gender in Early Modern England* (1995, 2nd edition, New York: Cornell

University Press, 1996), p. 13; Fryer, *Staying Power*, pp. 4, 5, 8. Other historians with similar views include: Walvin, *Black and White*, pp. 1–16, 16–31; Shyllon, *Black People in Britain 1553–1833*, pp. 1–10; and Edwards and Walvin, 'Africans in Britain, 1500–1800,' pp. 173–204.

²³ Fraser in Vigne and Littleton (eds.), 'Slaves or Free people,' pp. 254–261; Ottobah Cugoano, *Thoughts and Sentiments on the Evil and Wicked Traffic of the Slavery and Commerce of the Human Species ...* (London: T. Beckett, 1787), p. 142; Chancellor Williams, *The Destruction of Black Civilisation: Great Issues of a Race from 4500 BC to 2000 AD* (Chicago: Third World Press, 3rd edition 1987), pp. 176–195, 243–272 (how slavery was enforced and maintained); Naim Akbar, *Chains and Images of Psychological Slavery* (Jersey City: New Mind Productions, 1984), pp. 1–8; and Naim Akbar, *Breaking the Chains of Psychological Slavery* (Jersey City: Mind Productions and Associates, 1996), pp. 1–8, 27.

²⁴ Stephen Howe is one of those writers who claims most of the African-American and Caribbean historians noted below are polemic fantasists in *Afrocentrism: Mythical Pasts and Imagined Homes* (1998, 2ⁿᵈ edition, London: Verso, 1999), pp. 1–16, 215–229. These historians include: Edward Scobie, *Black Britannia: A History of Blacks in Britain* (Chicago: Johnson Publishing Company, 1972), pp. 190–203; Joel Augustus Rogers, *World's Great Men of Colour*, Volume I and II (1931, new edition, New York: Touchstone Books, 1995), pp. 1–7; *Sex and Race*, Volumes I–IV (Petersburg: Helga Rogers, 1941/2), Volume I, pp. 151–160, 196–220; and Sertima,' The African Presence in Early Europe,' pp. 190–223.

²⁵ Scobie in, Ivan Van Sertima (ed.), *Journal of African Civilizations*, New Brunswick, New Jersey, Rutgers University, 1985, Issue 3, n. p. These are edited and included in *African Presence in Early Europe*, pp. 190–223.

²⁶ Scobie, *Black Britannia*, pp. 190–203; Sertima (ed.), *African Presence in Early Europe*, pp. 190–203, 203–223; Edward Scobie, 'The Moors and Portugal's Global Expansion,' *Department of Black Studies Pamphlet* (New York: City College, City University of New York, 1996), p. 37. Also quoted by Wayne Chandler, in Sertima (ed.), *African Presence in Early Europe*, pp. 144–176.

²⁷ Basil Davidson, *African Civilization Revisited: From Antiquity to Modern Times* (Trenton: Africa World Press, 1991), passim; Basil Davidson, *Black Mother: A Study of the Precolonial Connection Between Africa and Europe* (London: Longman, 1970), passim; and Robin Walker, *When We Ruled* (London: Every Generation Media, 2005), passim.

²⁸ Nabil Matar, *Islam in Britain, 1558–1685* (New York: Cambridge University Press, 1998) and *Turks Moors and Englishmen in the Age of Discovery* (New York: Columbia University Press, 2000), passim; Daniel Vitkus, *Turning Turk: English Theatre and the Multicultural Mediterranean, 1570–1630* (New York: Palgrave Macmillan, 2003), pp. 21–50; Imtiaz Habib, *Shakespeare and Race: Postcolonial Praxis in the Early Modern Period* (Lanham: University Press of America, 1999), pp. 157–205; and Virginia Mason Vaughan, *Performing Blackness on English Stages, 1500–1800* (Cambridge: Cambridge University Press, 2005), pp. 57–60.

²⁹ Matar, *Islam in Britain*, p. 2.

³⁰ David MacRitchie, *Ancient and Modern Britons: A Retrospect*, 2 Volumes (1884, 3ʳᵈ edition 1985, reprint, Los Angeles: Preston, 1986), Volume I, p. 67, Volume II, pp. 125, 186; Gerald Massey, *Ancient Egypt the Light of the World, Containing an Attempt to Recover and Reconstitute the Lost Origines of the Myths and Mysteries ... with Egypt for the Mouthpiece and Africa as the Birthplace*. Volume I, *Egyptian Origines in the British Isles* (1881, republished, London: Secaucus University Books, 1974); Godfrey Higgins, *Anacalypsis, An Attempt to Draw Aside the Veil of the Saitic Isis: or, an Inquiry into the Origin of Languages, Nations, and Religions* (1883, 1878, new edition, London: TGS Publishing, 1927); Albert Churchward, *The Signs and Symbols of Primordial Man ... The Evolution of Religious Doctrines from the Eschatology of the Ancient Egyptians ...* (London: EP Dutton and Co, 1910), n. p. passim; and

INTRODUCTION

Edward Williams Byron Nicholson, *Keltic Researches: Studies in the History and Distribution of the Ancient Goidelic Language and Peoples* (Oxford: Oxford University Press, 1904), pp. 1–8.

[31] MacRitchie, *Ancient and Modern Britons,* Volume I, pp. 212–213, 253, 347.

[32] Howe, *Afrocentrism: Mythical Pasts and Imagined Homes,* pp. 66–70 claims that MacRitchie et. al. are romantic fantasists.

[33] Ahmed Ali, Ibrahim Ali, *The Black Celts: An Ancient African Civilisation in Ireland and Britain* (Cardiff: Punite Publications, 1992), pp. 14–47; Paul Dunbavin, *Picts and Ancient Britons: An Exploration of Pictish Origins* (London: Third Millennium Publishing, 1998), pp. preface, 1–8.

[34] Susan Broomhall and Stephanie Tarbin (eds.), *Women, Identities and Communities in Early Modern Europe* (Aldershot: Ashgate, 2008), p. 7.

[35] For a longer discussion on this see, Onyeka, 'The Missing Tudors,' pp. 32–33.

[36] The quotations are from Thomas Cromwell, 'Order for keeping parish registers,' on 29 September 1538, 'Parish Records: 1538, 1563 and 1598,' National Archives, *Parish Records* http://www.nationalarchives.gov.uk/familyhistory/guide/people/parish.htm, accessed 12/08/08; http://freepages.genealogy.rootsweb.ancestry.com/~framland/acts/pre1812.htm, accessed 25/12/06; and Thomas Cromwell, 'Supplication against the Ordinaries,' a petition passed by the House of Commons in 1532 in Geoffrey Rudolph Elton, *Studies in Tudor and Stuart Politics and Government: Papers and Reviews* (1973, new edition, Cambridge: Cambridge University Press, 2003), pp. 63–68. On how records were collected see Raphael Holinshed, *The Late Volume of Chronicles England, Scotland and Ireland with their Descriptions* (London: J. Harrison, 1587), p. 1524; David Cressy, *Literacy and the Social Order: Reading and Writing in Tudor and Stuart England* (Cambridge: Cambridge University Press, 2006), pp. 118–142; and John Vivian Kitto, 'St Martins in the fields the accounts of the church wardens, 1525–1603,' *British History Online,* 1901, pp. 457–475, http://www.british-history.ac.uk/report.aspx?compid=81909 accessed 25/10/08 (on the role of priests and parish clerks).

[37] Cromwell, 'Order for keeping parish registers,' on 29 September, 1538, National Archives, *Parish Records,* 'And for the sauff keping of the same boke the pishe shalbe boude [bound] to puide [provide] of there comen charges one sure coffer with twoo lockes and keys wherof the one to remain wt [with] you …'

[38] Author unknown, 'Order of 1563,' National Archives, *Parish Records*; Author unknown, 'A provincial constitution of Canterbury,' 25 October 1597 but approved in 1598, National Archives, *Parish Records.*

[39] Anton Gill, Nick Barratt, *Who Do You Think You Are?: Trace Your Family History Back to the Tudors* (London: Harper Collins, 2006), n. p. introduction; Including those in London: GL Ms 28867, GL Ms 9243–9245, GL Ms 4310, GL Ms 9222 and Plymouth and West Devon Record Office, Plymouth, St Andrews/MF1–4.

[40] William Brewer Stephens, *Sources for English Local History* (Cambridge: Cambridge University Press, 1981), p. 56; and Guy Etchells, 'Timeline of events concerning the keeping of records pre 1812,' *Genealogy RootsWeb,* 'The records of Perlethope and Carburton include about forty registers and they begin in 1528, containing one or two entries per year up to 1538' http://freepages.genealogy.rootsweb.ancestry.com/~framland/acts/pre1812.htm, accessed 12/12/05.

[41] Evidence on this latter point can be seen in Habib, *Black Lives,* pp. 274–334.

[42] Evidence and clues came from Holinshed, *The Chronicles* (1587), p. 1524; John Stow, *A Summary of the Chronicles of England, Abridged and Continued unto 1598 …* (1565, new edition, London: R. Bardocke, 1598), pp. 768–769; John Stow, Edmund Howes, *The Annales, or Generall Chronicle of England …* (London: Thomas Dawson for Thomas Adams, 1615),

p. 790; George *Best, A True Discourse ...* (London: H Bynyman, 1578), pp. 28-32; Sherwood, 'Blacks in Elizabethan England,' pp. 40-42; Sampson, 'Black burials and deaths 16th century;' and Rory Lalwan (ed.), *Sources for Black and Asian History at the City of Westminster Archives ...* (London: Westminster City Archives, 2005), pp. 9, 10.

[43] London: GL Ms 28867, GL Ms 9243-9245, GL Ms 4310, GL Ms 9222; and Plymouth and West Devon Record Office, Plymouth, St Andrews/MF1-4.

[44] The quotations are in Habib, *Black Lives in the English Archives*, pp. 7, 19-63, 96, 119; and Paul Griffiths, 'Secrecy and Authority in sixteenth and seventeenth century London,' *Historical Journal*, 40-4, 1997, pp. 925-51. A similar view on how parish clerks wrote their records is expressed by Stephens, *Sources for English Local History*, pp. 52-56.

[45] GL Ms 28867, GL Ms 9243-9245; and Habib, *Black Lives*, pp. 274-334.

[46] Christopher Haigh, *English Reformations: Religion, Politics, and Society under the Tudors* (Oxford: Oxford University Press, 1993), pp. 3-17; and Geoffrey Rudolph Elton, *The Reformation 1520-1559* (Cambridge: Cambridge University Press, 1990), pp. 262-288.

[47] Benjamin Braude, 'Collective Degradation: Slavery and the Construction of Race, Ham and Noah: Sexuality, Servitudinism, and Ethnicity:' from proceedings of the *Fifth Annual Gilder Lehrman Center International Conference* (New Haven Connecticut: Yale University, November 8, 2003), n. p. passim; Hall, *Things of Darkness*, pp. 13, 211; Thomas Earle and Kate Lowe (eds.), *Black Africans in Renaissance Europe* (Cambridge: Cambridge University Press, 2005), pp. 102-103. Similar views are expressed by Margo Hendricks, 'Surveying race in Shakespeare,' *Shakespeare and Race* (Cambridge: Cambridge University Press, 2000), pp. 1-23; and George Kirkpatrick Hunter, 'Othello and Colour Prejudice,' *Proceedings of the British Academy* 53, 1967, p. 153.

[48] Jose Piedra, 'In search of the Black stud,' in Louise Fradenburg and Carla Freccero (eds.), *Premodern Sexualities* (New York: Routlegde, 1996), pp. 22-44; and Braude, 'Collective Degradation,' n. p. passim.

[49] National Archives, *Parish Records*.

[50] Plymouth and West Devon Record Office, St Andrews/ June 23/1603 MF 1-4, 'Register of St Andrews,' p. 110; and Habib, *Black Lives*, p. 333.

[51] Evidence in London: GL Ms 28867, GL Ms 9243-9245, GL Ms 4310, GL Ms 9222; Plymouth and West Devon Record Office, St Andrews/MF1-4; and Habib, *Black Lives*, pp. 115, 116, 136.

[52] Andrew Spicer, in Nigel Goose and Lieun Luu (eds.), *Immigrants in Tudor and Early Stuart England* (Eastbourne: Sussex Academic Press, 2005), p. 94; John Knox Laughton, *State Papers Relating to the Defeat of the Spanish Armada, Anno 1588* (Aldershot: Publications of the Navy Records Society, 1987), n. p. preface, introduction; and Holinshed, *The Chronicles* (1587), pp. 1427-1567, 'Cornish Rebellion 1497,' 'The Spanish Armadas 1588, 1596, 1597' and 'The Anglo Spanish War 1585-1604,' etc.

[53] Roger Schofield, *Taxation Under the Early Tudors 1485-1547* (London: Blackwell, 2004), 73-74, 81, 94, 101, 104, 108, 115, 124.

[54] GL Ms 4448.

[55] Medway Archives and Local Studies Centre, Rochester, Kent, 19/January/1596/7/Dartford/ MF1/P110.

[56] William George Hoskins, *Local History in England* (1959, 3rd edition, Harlow: Longman, 1984), pp. 140-2; and Richard Kirk and Ernest Kirk (eds.), *Returns of Aliens Dwelling in the City and Suburbs of London from the Reign of Henry VIII. To that of James I.* Volume IV, Quarto Series 10 (London: Huguenot Society of London, 1900-8), pp. 241, 248.

[57] Quotations from Cyril Coffin, 'Aliens in Dorset 1525,' *the Dorset page*, http://www.thedorsetpage.com/history/Aliens/Aliens.htm posted 2000, accessed 02/01/07. On how the

INTRODUCTION

rolls worked see, Author Unknown, *Lay Subsidy Records, Returns for the City of London in 1292–1392* ... National Archives, Kew, London, PRO E179/144/2 and E179/144/3; Hoskins, *Local History in England*, pp. 140–2; and Lara Hunt Yungblut, *Strangers Settled Here Amongst Us: Policies, Perceptions, and the Presence of Aliens in Elizabethan England* (1996, new edition, London: Routledge, 2003), p. 55.

[58] Cyril Coffin, 'Aliens in Dorset 1525;' Goose and Luu (eds.), *Immigrants in Tudor and Early Stuart England*, pp. 41–57; and Sally Mckee (ed.), *Crossing Boundaries: Issues of Cultural and Individual Identity in the Middle Ages and the Renaissance* (Turnout: Brepols, 1999), pp. 268–272.

[59] Suggested by David Cressy, *Society and Culture in Early Modern England* (London: Ashgate, 2003), pp. 40, 107; and Sherwood, 'Blacks in Elizabethan England,' pp. 40–42.

[60] Richard Lang (ed.), *Two Tudor Subsidy Assessment Rolls* (London: The London Record Society Publications, 1993), pp. 87–95, '1582 Langborne Ward;' Sherwood, 'Blacks in Elizabethan England,' pp. 40–42; and Kirk and Kirk (eds.), *Returns of Aliens Dwelling in ... London*, Volume I, p. 46, Volume II (1902), p. 339, Volume IV (1908), pp. 241, 248.

[61] Jesus Christ Church of Latter day Saints, *International Genealogical Index*, G Batch N. P003891, File 0845460, Call number 6905932, http://www.familysearch.org/eng/default.asp, accessed 15/08/08.

[62] Stephens, *Sources for English Local History*, pp. 77–80; Coffin, 'Aliens in Dorset 1525.'

[63] Hoskins, *Local History in England*, pp. 140–2.

[64] Evidence in GL Ms 28867, GL Ms 9243–9245, GL Ms 4310, GL Ms 9222; Plymouth and West Devon Record Office, Plymouth, St Andrews/MF1–4; But not in Kirk and Kirk (eds.), *Returns of Aliens Dwelling in the City and Suburbs of London*, Volume IV, pp. 241, 248.

[65] Kirk and Kirk (eds.), *Returns of Aliens*, Volume IV, pp. 241, 248. (As far as I can tell Diego Negro is no relation to Dyego Negro mentioned earlier.)

[66] Artist unknown, *Abd el-Ouahed Ben Messaoud Ben Mohammed Anoun, Moorish Ambassador to Queen Elizabeth I*, Oil on Oak Panel, 1145 x 790mm, about 1600, Tate Britain, London, from the University of Birmingham, The Barber Institute of Fine Arts, Birmingham, Ref: A0427; see figure 1; Matar, *Turks Moors and Englishmen*, p. 43; Stow, *The Chronicles* (1615), p. 790; and Thomas Purfoot, *The Historical Discourse of Muley Hamet's Refining the Three Kingdoms, of Moruecos Fes and Sus. The Religion and Policies of the More or Barbarian* ... (London: Clement Knight, 1609), pp. A3, B2, 5.

[67] The idea that societal life can be divided between private and public spheres is discussed widely by social historians and others. The private sphere is generally regarded as being unfettered by public policy see Jurgen Habermas and Martin Heidegger in Thomas Burger, Frederick Lawrence (eds. trs.) *The Structural Transformation of the Public Sphere: An Inquiry into a Category of Bourgeois Society* (Cambridge: MIT Press, 1989), introduction. For a discussion on the private sphere in Tudor society see Lena Cowen Orlin, *Locating Privacy in Tudor London* (Oxford: Oxford University Press, 2007), passim; Conal Condren, 'Public, Private, and the Idea of the 'Public Sphere' in Early-Modern England,' *Intellectual History Review*, 19, 1, 2009, pp. 15–28; Paula Backscheider (ed.), *The Intersections of the Public and Private Spheres in Early Modern England* (London: Frank Cass, 1996), passim.

[68] Author unknown, Letter to Lord Mayors, signed 11 July 1596; Author unknown, Letter to the Lord Mayors, signed 18 July 1596; and Author unknown, Proclamation ca January 1601.

[69] Africans not in, Stephen Alford, 'Politics and Political History in the Tudor Century,' *Historical Journal* 42 (Cambridge: Cambridge University Press, 1999), pp. 535–548. The term 'missing pages' in relation to African history was coined by the African-American historian Arthur Schomburg in, Benjamin P. Bowser, Louis Kushnick, Paul Grant (eds.), *Against*

the Odds: Scholars who Challenged Racism in the Twentieth Century (Amherst: University of Massachusetts Press, 2002), p. 9

⁷⁰ On writers pleasing their patrons see Cressy, *Society and Culture in Early Modern England*, p. 1; Francis Bacon, *The Two Bookes of Francis Bacon of the Proficience and Advancement of Leaning, Divine Humane* (London: Henrie Tomes, 1605), p. 1; and Antonia Gransden, *Historical Writing in England, c. 550–1307* (1970, new edition, London: Routledge, 1996), n. p. introduction.

⁷¹ Similar views are expressed in Peter Holbrook, *Literature and Degree in Renaissance England: Nashe, Bourgeois Tragedy, Shakespeare* (Newark: University of Delaware Press, 1994), pp. 169–170; and Louise Schleiner, *Tudor and Stuart Women Writers* (Bloomington: Indiana University Press, 1994), pp. introduction, 1–30.

⁷² Elizabeth Francis Rogers (ed.), Thomas More, *The Correspondence of Sir Thomas More* (Princeton: Princeton University Press, 1947), p. 4; and George Best, *A True Discourse of the Late Voyages of Discovery, for the Finding of a Passage to Cathya, by the Northwest, under the Conduct of Martin Frobisher ...* (London: H Bynyman, 1578), pp. 28–32.

⁷³ Rayner Unwin, *The Defeat of John Hawkins* (London: Allen Unwin, 1961), p. 205; John Hawkins, *Letter to Queen Elizabeth*, 16 September 1567, National Archives, Kew, London, SP 12/44, f. 16 16/9/1567; Richard, Hakluyt (ed.), *The Principal Navigations ...* Volume VI (London: Hakluyt's Collection, 1598), p. 137; Samuel Purchas, *Purchas his Pilgrimage; or Relations of the World and the Religions Observed in all Ages and Places Discovered from the Creation unto the Present ...* (London: William Stansby for Henrie Fetherstone, 1613), pp. 540–541; Thomas Wyndham, in John Hamilton Moore (ed.), *A New and Complete Collection of Voyages and Travels ... Including ... Voyages and Travels ... With the Relations of Maghellan, Drake, Candish, Anson, Dampier, and all the Circumnavigators, Including ... the ... Voyages and Discoveries ...* (London: John Hamilton, 1785), pp. 86–87; and Margo Hendricks, Patricia Parker, *Women, 'Race' and Writing in the Early Modern Period* (New York: Routledge, 1994), p. 336 (has a different view).

⁷⁴ Andrew Boorde, *The First Boke of the Introduction of Knowledge. The Whych Doth Teach a Man to Speake and Parte of All Maner of Languages and to Know the Vsage and Fashion of all Maner of Countries ... with Woodcuts* [images] (London: William Copeland, 1550); and John Pory (tr.), Leo, Africanus, *A Geographical Historie of Africa, Written in Arabicke and Italian ... by Iohn Leo a More ...* (London: John Pory, 1600).

⁷⁵ Caelius Augustinus Curio, *A Notable History of the Saracens ...* (London: William How and Abraham Veale, 1575), pp. 25–26, 139; Edward Blount (tr.), Ieronimo Conestaggio, *The Historie of the Uniting of the Kingdom of Portugal to the Crowne of Castill ...* (London: A. Hatfield for E. Blount, 1600), n. p. passim; Minsheu, *A Dictionarie in Spanish and English*, pp. 172, 175.

⁷⁶ Habib, *Shakespeare and Race*, pp. 35, 49, 74; Christopher Marlowe, *The Famous Tragedy of the Jew of Malta ...* (London: Nicholas Vavasour, 1633), Act 2, no scene, n. p. ; *Tamburlaine the Great* (London: Marlowe, 1592), No Act, or Scene, pp. A3, D4, E4, F2, F3, F4, G1–2; and *The Tragedy of Dido Queen of Carthage* (London: Thomas Nash, 1594), n. p. passim; William Shakespeare, *Othello* in Richard Proudfoot, Ann Thompson and David Scott Kastan (eds.), *The Arden Shakespeare Complete Works* (Walton on Thames: Thomas Nelson and Sons, 1998), pp. 939–978; *Titus Andronicus*, pp. 1123–1150; *Romeo and Juliet*, Act I, Scene V, Line 46, p. 1013, 'As a rich jewel in an Ethiop's ear;' *The Merchant of Venice*, Act II, Scene I, Line 1–46, pp. 835–836, Act II, Scene VII, Line 1–79, p. 840; *Macbeth*, Act V, Scene III, Line 11–12, p. 794, 'The devil damn thee black/ thou cream-faced loon.'

⁷⁷ Harry Lee Faggett, *Black and Other Minorities in Shakespeare's England* (Prairie View: Prairie View Press, 1971), pp. 34, 35, 43, 46, 48; Including evidence in: GL Ms 28867, GL Ms

INTRODUCTION

9243–9245, GL Ms 4310, GL Ms 9222, GL Ms 4515/1; and Lalwan (ed.), *Sources for Black and Asian History … Westminster Archives*, pp. 9, 10.

[78] Habib, *Black Lives*, p. 7; Habib, *Shakespeare and Race*, pp. 35, 49, 74; Matar, *Islam in Britain*, pp. 50–70; Leslie A. Fiedler, *The Stranger in Shakespeare* (New York: Stein and Day, 1972), pp. 139–199; Hall, *Things of Darkness*, p. 211; Hendricks, 'Surveying race in Shakespeare,' pp. 1–23; Hunter, 'Othello and Colour Prejudice,' p. 153; Jose Piedra, 'In search of the Black stud,' pp. 23–44; Braude, 'Collective Degradation,' passim; Joyce Green Macdonald, 'Black Ram, White Ewe: Shakespeare, Race and women,' *A Feminist Companion to Shakespeare* (Oxford: Wiley Blackwell, 2001), pp. 188–207. Other authors including Jonathan Burton, Ania Loomba and Patricia Parker are listed in the Bibliography.

[79] Faggett, *Black and Other Minorities in Shakespeare's England*, pp. 30, 37–39; Sujata Iyengar, *Shades of Difference: Mythologies of Skin Colour in Early Modern England* (Philadelphia: University of Pennsylvania Press, 2008), p. 92, 99; and suggested by Ungerer, 'The Presence of Africans in Elizabethan England and the performance of *Titus Andronicus*,' pp. 19–56; Benjamin Braude, 'The Sons of Noah and the Construction of Ethnic and Geographical Identities in the Medieval and Early Modern Periods,' *William and Mary Quarterly LIV*, January 1997, pp. 103–142.

[80] Artist unknown, Author unknown, *Westminster Tournament Roll 1511*, The College of Arms, London, E 36/214 f.109, see figures 2, and 20.

[81] This issue is discussed, and some images of these Africans are present in Earle, Lowe (eds.), *Black Africans in Renaissance Europe*, pp. 17–26, 27, 28–42, 42–48, 70–94, 113–125. The references for more images of Africans from continental Europe are listed in the Bibliography.

[82] Author unknown, Letter to Lord Mayors, signed Queen Elizabeth, National Archives, Kew, London; Letter Author unknown, signed Queen Elizabeth, National Archives, Kew, London; and Author unknown, Proclamation ca January 1601, National Archives, Kew, London.

[83] Plymouth and West Devon Record Office, Plymouth, original records on microfiche, St Andrews/MF1–4; Author unknown, *St Botolph without Aldgate Memorandum Daybook*, Volume I (London: Parish of St Botolph without Aldgate, 1586–1588), p. 127; G. L. Ref P69/BOT2/ A/ 01/MS 9234/1; GL Ms 9234; and Hendricks, 'Surveying race in Shakespeare,' p. 15 (has a similar view).

[84] *Oxford Dictionary of English*, p. 1247 (quotations on otherness). On strangeness and otherness see Ania Loomba, Jonathan Burton, *Race in Early Modern England: A Documentary Companion* (Basingstoke, Palgrave Macmillan, 2007), n. p. preface, introduction; and Tony Bennett, Lawrence Grossberg, Meaghan Morris (ed.), *New Keywords: A Revised Vocabulary of Culture and Society* (Oxford: Blackwell, 2005), pp. 249–250.

CHAPTER 1

The Status of Africans in Tudor England

This chapter is about the status of Africans in Tudor England. But this is not a straightforward subject as the position of 'those kindes of people' in sixteenth-century English society was not often written about by contemporary writers. So, without clear statements by Tudor writers, recent historians such as Gustav Ungerer and Imtiaz Habib have suggested that Africans in sixteenth-century English society were slaves, and that ideas present in international law were used to justify slavery against them. These historians refer to documents such as *Dum Diversas,* a papal bull issued on 18 June 1452 by Pope Nicholas V which authorised the Portuguese to 'reduce any non-Christians to the status of slaves.' This same Pope in 1455, issued a further papal bull *Romanus Pontifex* that said there must be a 'war against [infidels],' and that the 'enslavement of non Christian people' was permitted because they had 'primitive living practices' which were 'a violation of natural law.' Later in 1493, Spain and Portugal were blessed by another Pope Alexander VI to carry out slave trading in the 'new world.' In 1494, the Treaty of Tordesillas divided the 'newly discovered world' between Spain and Portugal and legally gave authority to these nations to conduct slavery within their empires. Even as late as 1595, Philip II of Spain under the Portuguese merchant Pedro Gomes Reinal had legal authority over all the slave trade in West Africa.[1] However in Tudor England, most of these documents and enactments are likely to have been seen by Englishmen as attempts by Spain, Portugal, and the Pope to gain and then hold on to international power. As we shall see in this chapter it is extremely unlikely that these international laws could be, or were used to enslave Africans in Tudor England. In fact when England became a Protestant nation, it is probable that the English government would have resisted laws originating from the Popes, especially those that imposed the status of 'slave' on people who were members of Tudor parishes.

In Tudor records, however, we do occasionally find references to Englishmen treating Africans as slaves abroad, and occasionally this treatment leads to those 'same kindes of people' having a low status in England.

One incident which appears to demonstrate this relates to a group of Africans, Portuguese and Spaniards who were apparently brought to Bristol on board a captured foreign ship in 1590 by a Captain Jonas Bradburie an English privateer.[2] I say apparently, because their presence cannot be verified by local records such as the *Mayor's Audit Books* because these are missing for the years 1588–1594, whilst other local records and correspondence be it fiscal or administrative are strangely muted on the matter.[3] But the visitors are referred to in letters written by the Mayor of Bristol William Hopkins to William Cecil, one of them co-authored by the Chamberlain of Bristol. These letters and another by an Englishman called William Bland (which is a supporting statement) are written on 14, 18 and 20 October when the visitors had already been sent back to Portugal.[4] Hopkins' letters written to Cecil are essentially inventories listing expenses incurred as a result of the visitors stay in the 'Cittie' (the Portuguese and Spaniards) and the 'barne' (the Africans); the upkeep of the vessels used in the capture of the foreign ship and its outrigging for the return trip back to Portugal, and other miscellaneous costs for English 'labourers' 'who work[ed] by night' in connection to this project.[5] Some aspects of these lists are detailed, including that the visitors ate 'Biskitts,' 'oranges,' and that the Africans were also given 'cows bollocks.' There also seems to be several entries for the Africans to have 'strawe' in their 'barne' for them to rest on, and an entry for a 'man [servant] to keepe them … and give them their victualls …'[6]

However, the Hopkins' documents are not what they appear to be. Hopkins and his colleagues were privateers looking to fund future privateering adventures abroad and these letters should be seen in that light. They are retrospective requests for costs which even contemporary commentators such as Cecil or his officials could not verify, as by the time the letters were written the ship was on its way back to Portugal. It is likely that Hopkins and his colleagues are deliberately inflating the numbers of Africans to claim more money from Cecil. But what is interesting is that this idea does not appear to have been coherently worked through as Hopkins' claims for 'vituails' for the Africans resembles the same amounts requested for the 32 Europeans. This may suggest the number of Africans was closer to 32 than 135. But most significantly of all, in the original documents written by Hopkins the actual number of Africans has been scribbled over several times, almost as if he was not sure how many Africans were actually in this 'barne.'[7]

In addition, the letters are missing any detail about who these Africans are. They are referred to merely as 'negroes,' we do not know how many were men, women, or children.[8] Apart from the three letters mentioned earlier, there seems to be little information on these Africans in other Bristonian correspondence despite them spending a week in the city. This is especially important because this kind of detail would usually be available if the Africans really were slaves, as it would help determine their value.[9] So the Africans are not referred to as slaves in any documents, but the inference is that by them being speedily transported out of England as if they were, they are going to be treated as such elsewhere. In England these Africans' status is uncertain, but it seems to resemble that of the Spaniards and the Portuguese who they are with, despite them being lodged in separate locations.[10] But significantly, no attempt seems to have been made by Jonas, Hopkins, or anyone else to sell the Africans or the other visitors to a third party. The reasons for this will become evident through further discussions of other evidence in this chapter.

In sixteenth-century England no laws existed which used race, religion, colour or an African's origins to justify making them into slaves. However, there are two Letters written in 1596 and signed by Queen Elizabeth I, and a Proclamation created in 1601 which when they are first read seem to suggest otherwise.[11] The Letters and the Proclamation attempt to politically and socially justify giving some or all Africans in Tudor England an inferior status by claiming that they are foreign, strange or 'infidels.' But contrary to what these documents claim evidence in this book shows that Africans in Tudor England could be native or liege, that is 'a person born in a specified place or associated with a place by birth,' or a 'natural citizen.' Other Africans were domiciled, treating 'the country ... as their permanent home, or [having a] substantial connection with [it];' while some were 'denizen,' meaning an 'inhabitant of or an alien admitted into the country that now has rights.'[12]

The meaning and effectiveness of these documents thus raises important issues about the presence and status of Africans in Tudor England and that is why they are being analysed in this first chapter.[13] Here, the issues that are specific to each document are examined and then the legal, religious and practical reasons that prevented them being enforced are discussed. This approach shows us these three documents were poorly drafted and it is doubtful whether the measures included in them could be implemented. This view is shared by others such as Habib, Sherwood and Kaufmann, but not by John Gabriel who suggests that these documents did lead to racial pogroms and the mass deportation of Africans.[14]

Furthermore, these documents attempt to link or blame Africans for the poverty and hardships that ordinary people in England were suffering, and use this as a means to circumscribe the status of 'those kindes of' persons in Tudor England. The drafter of these documents may have felt that this would have made the measures they suggest more popular. Certainly in England from the 1590s until after 1603, there were genuine concerns about the country's economic situation, as shown by the proclamations issued on the shortage of wheat in England's cities and the lack of gold coin in England's treasury.[15] As part of this economic depression, flour prices in London trebled from 1593 to 1597 as the harvests of 1595 and 1597 failed. A Poor Law was introduced in 1601 to alleviate some of this distress amongst the very poor, and a group of people known as 'strangers' (a movable term describing people who were perceived as not being 'native' citizens) were blamed for the economic problems.[16] Many of these 'strangers' were white European Protestant immigrants, and they were attacked violently by 'unruly youths' during the 'outrages' of 1592 and 1595. This is important because although the Letters and the Proclamation contain rhetoric directed against Africans, I have not discovered any evidence which shows that the 'mobs' targeted Africans in these outrages, or blamed them for the poverty that they suffered.[17] Evidence indicates that most Africans were so integrated into Tudor society[18] that they may have even been part of the mobs of unruly youths, and this idea is explored as we examine each document in detail.

The First Letter

This Letter was signed by Elizabeth I on 11 July 1596, and it is addressed to the Aldermen and Mayors of London and other cities. It reads:

> An open letter to the Lord Maiour of London and the alermen his brethren, And to all other Maiours, Sheryfes, &c. Her Majestie understanding that there are of late divers Blackmoores brought into the Realme, of which kinde of persons there are all ready here to manie, consideringe howe God hath blessed this land w(i)th great increase of people of our owne Nation as anie Countrie in the world, wherof manie for want of service and meanes to sett them on worck fall to Idlenesse and to great extremytie; Her Ma(jesty)s pleasure therefore ys, that those kinde of people should be sent forth of the lande. And for that purpose there ys direction given to this bearer Edwarde Banes to take of those Blackmoores that in this last voyage under Sir Thomas Baskerville were brought into this Realme to the number of Tenn, to be transported by him out of the Realme. Wherin wee Req(uire) you to be aydinge & assisting unto him as he shall have occacion and thereof not to faile.[19]

The Letter is signed by Elizabeth I, but it seems more likely that it was written by a member of her Privy Council or Edward Banes who is mentioned in it. Edward Banes was an English adventurer and merchant who appears to have been involved in activities related to this Letter up until 1597. But after that date his name does not appear in any of the correspondence relating to this or the second Letter, and this may mean that he ceased being involved in this 'project.'[20]

Habib, Kaufmann and Sherwood suggest that the writer of this Letter is attempting to give Banes authority over all the Africans in Tudor England. Nevertheless, I suggest the writer is only genuinely interested in the presence and status of Africans who have come with Thomas Baskerville. Then as the writer of the Letter talks about these Africans he confirms the existence of a larger African presence in England in 1596. Furthermore, it describes these Africans in such a way that they fall into three groups. The first group are the ones who have come 'of late.' The second are of the same 'kind' as the first but 'are all ready here too manie.' In other words, these Africans were present in England before 1596. The third group are singled out as a specific number of ten Africans brought into England by Thomas Baskerville. I propose that it is only these Africans that the writer believes have a status which will enable them to be sent 'forth [out] of the land.'[21] Each of these groups of Africans are discussed in more detail below.

The first group of Africans mentioned in this Letter are those who have come to Tudor England 'of late' or recently. The Letter describes these Africans as 'divers.' This word could mean that they are numerous and/or of a diverse origin and 'kind.' I suggest that it means both and implies that this group of Africans includes more than the ten who came to England with Baskerville in 1596. However, the Letter does not say how many more, when they arrived in England, or where they came from. This may be because in Tudor England there was no effective border control or immigration service and so nobody really knew.[22]

The Letter implies that there is a second group of Africans who 'are already here to manie.' In other words, that these Africans are substantial in number and can be distinguished from the new arrivals mentioned earlier, but whether the Letter is implying they have a different status is not clear. The phrase 'already here' may also refer to Africans who were born here, some of whom may have been in England for more than one generation. The evidence in parish records confirms that Africans had been present in England long before 1596.[23] In the next chapter I suggest that Africans have been present in England for hundreds of years before this Letter was written, although this Letter is probably not referring to that historical reality, but is attempting to offer simple answers to explain the presence of 'blackamores' in late Tudor society.

The third group of Africans the Letter mentions are perhaps part of the 'divers' lately arrived 'blackmores,' but are specifically set aside as the 'ten' who came with Baskerville. The Letter is the only major official document that specifically mentions these ten Africans but even here their names are not recorded.[24] This may suggest the writer intends that these Africans should be perceived as objects, and that consequently in Tudor England they were regarded as having an inferior status. Moreover, that their status was so low that their individual persona was not relevant to anyone in that society.[25] It is therefore difficult for us to find out more about these Africans.

Nevertheless, there is a possibility that the writer and some of his Tudor audience knows more about these Africans than at first it appears. This is because these particular Africans arrived in England at a specific time in 1596, and their arrival was associated with memorable events. The events in question are a series of debacles that took place in Panama and Puerto Rico that Francis Drake in 1596 and John Hawkins in 1595 died in.[26] Consequently, that the names of some of these Africans are known to officials present in Tudor England. In other words, it may not be because these Africans are strange that their names are absent from the Letter, but it is likely to be because of expediency, or to fulfil the requirement of brevity in 'official' public correspondence.[27] The ten Africans in the Letter are not a random group, but a particular set of people whose status was in question because they were attached to the activities of English pirates Drake and Hawkins. The Letter attempts to transfer 'authority' over these Africans to Banes, from Drake and Hawkins who would have been the 'natural employers'.[28] So by tracing Drake's and Hawkins' activities we may find out more about the status of these Africans.

These Englishmen's expedition was written about by a Spanish Captain called Don Bernaldino Delgadillo De Avellaneda. In England, his writings are referred to as *A Libell of Spanish Lies*. In it, Avellaneda speaks about the expedition led by Drake, Hawkins and Baskerville as they tried to take control of a port and trading station in Puerto Rico. They failed to obtain either, and Drake and Hawkins two of England's most able commanders died.[29] The whole campaign also ended in financial loss which would have been passed on to those who financed it. These financers may have initially included Elizabeth I and some members of her Privy Council, since they were known to secretly fund these types of ventures.[30]

To make a profit from these activities English merchants and pirates sometimes exchanged or sold Spanish and English prisoners. Occasionally, Africans were also involved in these exchanges.[31] Whether these enterprises did 'turn a profit' was often determined by the prices obtained for the people who were being smuggled.[32] As explained in the accounts of Hawkins (1569), Hakluyt (1598) and others, these people exchanges invariably took place outside of England, where they could be economically justified as a collateral part of acquiring 'booty,' 'much gold,' silver or other precious metals that England's treasury was in 'dire need of.'[33] This, as we shall see later, may have been because of how English law regarded these types of transactions.

If these 'blackamores' who came to Tudor England with Baskerville were from Puerto Rico, they are likely to have been under Spanish or Portuguese authority, and have been held in some kind of servitude or even been slaves. As Hawkins himself suggests, Spain and Portugal were more 'advanced' than most European nations in developing slave plantations in the Caribbean and South America and reducing the Africans and native peoples there to slavery or servitude. By the middle of the sixteenth century the Spanish had become 'quite efficient' at creating plantations, at a time when England was only 'dabbling.'[34] Within this context these Africans could have 'believed themselves to be slaves' on arrival in England, although, how long they had been so we cannot at present determine, and whether they continued to believe this is also uncertain.[35]

This uncertainty in their status would remain even if contrary to what has been said these Africans were free and had defected to Drake and Hawkins by choice. This may have happened because of 'perceived bad treatment' by the Spanish, Portuguese and/or other Africans, as with those whom Hawkins came across during his voyages to Guyana.[36] Nevertheless, no matter where they were from or what their initial status was, to have Africans treated as slaves in Tudor England because of the colour of their skin would be problematic. This is perhaps why the Letter attempts to provide a reason for this treatment based on these Africans taking resources or benefits from 'liege' or 'natural' citizens.[37] Implicit in this argument is an idea that Africans in Tudor England are not liege or natural subjects. But, as stated at the beginning of this chapter and discussed later, this part of the writer's argument appears unfounded.

There seems to be a discrepancy between the status that the writer of the Letter says Africans have, and what other contemporary evidence shows. This becomes apparent through examining the statement that they 'for want of service and meanes to sett them on worck fall to Idlenesse and to great extremytie.' If this statement relates to the plight of 'native' Englishmen it can be seen as highlighting the problem of poverty present in late Tudor society. But if more interestingly, the 'manie' in the Letter is including or referring to the 'manie' Africans that it talks about earlier, it could be saying Africans fall into 'idlenesse and great extremytie,' and that they have 'want of service.' This may have initiated an idea about the employment and status of 'those kindes of people' which is later developed in the 1601 Proclamation. This is that Africans were 'brought into the Realme' to be useful, but they are now 'idle' and in poverty. What this 'idlenesse' means is not clarified, but if they are 'idle' as the Letter suggests, then they may also have taken up lawless activities. However, none of the proclamations passed during this time state Africans were part of the gangs of 'masterless men' or 'unruly youths.' But there are proclamations that describe some of these miscreants as ex-domestic servants. So it is possible that because Africans were employed as servants in some households some may have become 'masterless,' and settled in areas of Southwark (London) or other areas, where they felt they could live without punishment.[38]

In addition, amongst the masterless men were vagrants and the 'homeless,' and in Tudor England there is evidence of Africans who have that status and are in that predicament. One of them was 'a young man negroe,' whose 'name was not known,' who 'dyed in the street' in the parish of St Botolph without Aldgate in London and was buried on 6 October in 1587. There is also another African from St Olave Hart Street, London, who was buried on 29 June in 1588 and was simply described as 'a man blacamore [who] laye in the street.'[39] Other evidence of apparently 'homeless' Africans are to be found in Plymouth records, which suggests that there were African vagrants in other Tudor cities.[40]

Nevertheless in the sixteenth century, even in cities such as London and Plymouth, it is unlikely that Africans constituted the majority of those classified as vagrants. The writer of this Letter may therefore be trying to mislead his audience about the status of Africans in Tudor England. This may be to get those that read or heard this Letter to think that if Africans were deported this would resolve the problem of vagrancy. But for the writer to conceptualise that this kind of idea would be plausible, the African presence amongst that population must have been visible enough to be portrayed as significant.

Viewed in this way, the Letter could be seen as part of a number of documents created as a reaction to the problem of vagrancy between the years of 1590 to 1597. This was a problem which had been developing throughout the Tudor period and was not just fiscal and logistical but also moral.[41] Perhaps the writer hoped that by linking the presence of Africans to the problem of vagrancy in sixteenth-century England, this would create a moral justification for deporting 'those kindes of people.'[42] Indeed, this appears to be what happened with some Africans present in eighteenth-century London, who were expelled 'for their own' and 'society's good.'[43] But there is no evidence that this took place in Tudor England, and even in the Bristol case, the Africans return to Portugal seems to have been based on administrative and fiscal considerations not moral ones.

Furthermore in Tudor England, if Africans were part of what had become '12,000' 'sturdy beggars' it would have taken an army to extricate them. In the later part of Elizabeth's reign, the English Government did not have such an army or the administrative capacity. Justices of the Peace were barely able to keep order.[44] But more importantly, if some Africans were numbered amongst the 'masterless,' 'idle' and 'poor,' they are not likely to have had the status of perpetual slaves, as Little, Fryer, Hall and others say they had.[45] This is because a slave can never be idle, and can legally be brought back to his owner and compelled to work, a slave is the personal property of his employer and can be 'disposed of at will.' Slaves 'have no rights whatsoever.'[46] Therefore, if some Africans were poor and idle in Tudor England as this Letter suggests, this may mean that the authorities did not have the power to force them to work as a slave. Of course this Letter may have been an attempt to impose some sort of slave status on 'idle' Africans who were part of this class. In this way it would resemble similar legislation created for 'sturdy beggars,' but other evidence cited below, and the fact that a second Letter was created seven days later, shows that the first Letter failed to create such a power.

The Second Letter

18 July an open warrant to the L(ord) Maiour of London and to all other vyceadmyralles, Maiours and other publicke officers whatsoever to whom yt may apprertain. Wheras Casper van Senden a merchant of Lubeck did by his labor and travel procure 89 of her ma(jest's) subiectes that were detained prisoners in Spaine and Portugall to be released, and brought them hither into this Realme at his owne cost and charges, for the w(hi)ch his expenses and declaration of his honest minde towards those prisoners, he only desireth to have lycense to take up so many Blackamoores here in this Realme and to transport them into Spaine and Portugall. Her Ma(jes)ty in regard of the charitable affection the suppliant hathe shewed being a stranger to work the dlivery of our contrymen that were there in great misery and thralldom and to bring them home to their native contry, and that the same could not w(i)thout great expence and also considering the reasonableness of his requests to transport so many Blackamoores from hence doth thincke yt a very good exchange and that those kinde of people may well be spared in this Realme being so populous and numbers of hable persons the subjects of the land and xpian [Christian] people that perishe for want of service, wherby through their labor they might be mayntained. They are therefore in their L(ordships) name req(ui)red to aide and assist him to take up suche Blackamores as he shall finde

within this Realme with consent of their masters, who we doubt not considering her Ma(jesty) good pleasure to have those kindes of people sent out of the lande and the good deserving of the stranger towards her Ma(jesty's) subiectes, and that they shall doe charitable and like Christians rather to be served by their own contrymen then with those kynde of people, will yilde those in their possession to him.[47]

This Letter was written on 18 July in 1596 and was signed by Elizabeth I. But it is possible that it may have been drafted by a member of her Privy Council such as Robert or William Cecil, who appear to have been initially involved in this matter.[48] The Letter could then have been developed by others such as Senden, Thomas Sherley or his son of the same name (albeit with the latter offering only minor input). However, the Sherleys unlike Banes and Senden are not named directly in these documents, but are probably included under the term 'assignee' in the Proclamation.[49]

One reason which may explain the exclusion of the Sherleys' names from the Letter is suggested by Kaufmann. She states that they were both English gentlemen at Elizabeth's court who sought to gain a financial monopoly using royal patronage and excluded their names as part of a strategy. What supports this argument is the emphasis the writer of the Letter places on what Senden wants, with words such as 'his honest minde,' and 'his requests,' suggesting the views expressed in these epistles are not the Queen's. Moreover, the writer of this Letter uses similar language and proposes solutions that resemble those offered in the first Letter.

Both Letters refer to a general African presence but only seem genuinely interested in the presence and status of the few Africans who have 'come of late' and those who employers have 'possession' of. This second Letter may simply be another attempt to gain possession of the ten Africans brought to England by Thomas Baskerville in 1596. The difference is that this Letter proposes that these Africans should be given to Senden so he can be compensated for his release of eighty-nine English prisoners. Four years later in a petition to Robert Cecil, Thomas Sherley (elder) claims that Senden has released two hundred prisoners from Lisbon in addition to the eighty-nine stated here. In both documents Sherley states that Senden has already 'procure[d]' these prisoners, but it is not clear how many Englishmen he has actually brought back to England, or whether he needs the Africans to complete these exchanges. This latter query is all the more pertinent because in the Proclamation the actual numbers of prisoners Senden 'procure[d]' is not stated.[50]

Senden may have been chosen for this task because in 1596 there was an absence of men living in England who had 'skill [s]' to carry out slave trading. Hawkins died in November 1595 and Drake in January 1596. Also in 1595, the exiled Portuguese Prince Don Antonio who was involved in slave trading passed away suddenly[51] and the merchants William Towerson, William Winter and Martin Frobisher died in 1584, 1589 and 1594 respectively.[52] By 1596, John and Martin Lok were in semi-retirement, and although Sir Walter Raleigh the notorious merchant adventurer was back in the Queen's favour, he was occupied in military campaigns in Europe.[53] This lack of 'qualified' Englishmen may have meant that despite any sixteenth-century preference for employing 'natives' to carry out these sorts of tasks, Senden may have seemed one of the few viable choices. This would probably have been influenced by his experience as a known slave trader from Lubeck in Germany.[54] His devout Protestant faith may also have made him attractive to some English officials. In *Power, Knowledge and Expertise*, Eric Ash outlines how some English officials used religion to determine the suitability of foreigners who were going to be employed in assignments or ventures connected to public enterprises.[55]

Senden's slave trading experience is not mentioned in the Letter, however. Rather, he is portrayed as a man of virtue who because of his own 'honest minde' wants to help Englishmen escape 'thralldom' in Spain and Portugal. Senden's past and intent are concealed behind what many people in England would have regarded as a popular task of freeing Englishmen from foreign prisons. This task is also likely to have been popular with the English Privy Council, since they had sometimes sponsored the activities these Englishmen were being held prisoner for.[56] But releasing Englishmen from Spanish and Portuguese prisons was a difficult task because Spanish authorities were understandably unwilling to give them up. This Letter attempts to link this difficult but popular task with the presence of Africans in Tudor England. Perhaps, the writer hopes that by doing this he will provide a moral compulsion for employers to give up the Africans they have 'possession of.'[57] This also seems to suggest that the writer thinks that in Tudor England Africans have such an inferior status that some of their employers can 'dispose' of them at will. This is unlikely, but even if it were true, employers are unlikely to give up their employees purely on the grounds of altruism.

Most employers would probably be aware that these sorts of activities were about making money, even though the writer of these documents has placed a patriotic or charitable facade on them.[58] This strategy of seeking to appeal to public morality and patriotism, and ignoring more complicated issues regarding the status of Africans in Tudor England is even more evident in the third document the Proclamation. By exploring this

Proclamation we will also discover more about how this strategy failed with all three documents.

The Proclamation of 1601

> Wheras the Queen's majesty, tendering the good and welfare of her own natural subjects, greatly distressed in these hard times of dearth, is highly discontented to understand the great Numbers of Negroes and blackamoors which (as she is informed) are carried into this realm since the troubles between her highness and the King of Spain; who are fostered and powered here to the great annoyance of her own liege people that which co(vet) the relief which these people consume, as also for that the most of them are infidels having no understanding of Christ or his gospels; hath given a special commandment that the said kind of people shall be with all speed avoided and discharged out of this her Majesty's realms; and to that end and purpose hath appointed Casper Van Senden, merchant of Lubeck for their speedy transportation, a man that hath somewhat deserved of this realm in respect that by his own labor and charge he hath relieved and brought from Spain divers of our English nation who otherwise would have perished there. These shall therefore be to will and require you and every of you to aid and assist the said Casper Van Senden or his assignees to taking such Negroes and blackamoors to be transported as aforesaid he shall find within the realm of England; and if there shall be any person or persons which be possessed of any such blackamoors that refuse to deliver them in sort aforesaid, then we require you to call them before you and to advise and persuade them by all good means to satisfy her majesty's pleasure therein; which if they shall eftsoons willfully and obstinately refuse, we pray you to certify their names to us, to the end her majesty may take such further course therein as it shall seem best in her princely wisdom.[59]

The existence of the 1601 Proclamation is important for all the reasons already stated, but not because as a statement of royal or prerogative intent it was ever supported by national laws, enforced in the courts or by administrators as some proclamations were.[60] Moreover, it does not appear amongst the proclamations that were published in Elizabeth I's reign, and it may be a document that was drafted but never implemented.[61] This Proclamation in a similar way to the Letters makes sweeping accusations and generalisations about an African presence and their status in Tudor England, and then it raises questions about their origins. However, the writer only seems genuinely interested in the presence and status of a specific group of them. These appear to be the 'said' and 'such blackamoors' who have been 'fostered in

England' 'since the troubles between her highness [Elizabeth I] and the King of Spain.' In other words, since the beginning of the Anglo-Spanish war that began in 1585.[62] This would probably include the ten Africans mentioned in the first Letter and it may refer to an indeterminate number of 'late' arrivals mentioned in the second Letter.

The Proclamation seems to have been written in a hasty manner, in this way it is similar to the Letters and may indicate it was created by the same person or people. Perhaps, the writer believed that if his arguments were incorporated into a Proclamation, with the threat (written at the end of it) of some sort of future but undisclosed punishment for failure to comply, it would mean his ideas would be implemented.

This theory is all the more likely since the Proclamation follows Sherley's (elder) request to Robert Cecil on 29 December in 1600 to create a legal instrument with 'a stronger purpose.' Sherley says:

> I most humbly thank you for your willingness touching the suit of Van Zenden for the transport of the Moores, at my request ... I did not perceive by my son that you thought it not meet to have these kind taken from their masters compulsorily ... I beseech that the letter which Van Zenden formerly had may be renewed to some stronger purpose than before ...[63]

Altogether four petitions were written to Robert Cecil to enforce the Letters or create new powers so Thomas Sherley could gain possession of the Africans. These petitions some of which are attributed to Senden, but all are likely to have been written by Sherley, use similar specious arguments as those contained in the Letters and the Proclamation. The first signed on a day unspecified but in November 1600 says,

> In reward for his procuring the release in 1596 of 89 of the Queen's subjects who were prisoners in Spain and Portugal, and transporting them to England, the Queen granted him [Senden] licence to take up such blackamoores as he could find in the realm and transport them into those countries. The masters of the blackamoores, however seeing by his warrant that he could not take them without the master's good will, would not suffer him to have any of them ... In consideration ... and seeing that all the blackamoores in England are regarded but only for the strangeness of their nation, and not for service to the Queen, and ... may be very well spared out of this country, prays again for a licence to take up and carry away into Spain and Portugall all the blackamoors he shall find, without interruption of their masters or others.[64]

In a third petition from Sherley also in November 1600, he asks for 'aid in his suit concerning the blackmoors,' because of Senden's 'services to [the] distressed English in Spain and Portugal.'⁶⁵ Lastly on 29 November, 1600 Sherley writes:

> Of the suit concerning the blackemoores, wherof he once moved Cecil for Jasper Van Zenden, whose petition he encloses [probably the third petition above]. When he first moved Cecil therin, Cecil seemed not to like that a commission of that nature, to take what pleased him ... Prays Cecil, for his (Sherley's good), to assent to the matter, with such limitations to the commission as he best likes.⁶⁶

These petitions show that the Letters were unsuccessful and illustrate that the unsigned Proclamation was created to bring into effect what the Sherleys requested obtaining 'possession' 'of the 'ten blackmoores' mentioned in the first Letter, the 'lately arrived' Blackamoores in the second, and perhaps those who were 'already here to manie.' But by 1600, Sherley (elder) now seems desperate to gain 'possession' of any Africans he 'can find.' In other words any African no matter how long they have been here or how they arrived. This issue we will return to later in this chapter.⁶⁷

As stated earlier Sherley (elder) who wrote these petitions and influenced the development of the Letters and the Proclamation is not specifically named in any of the latter. One reason which may explain why is because the Sherley family was well-known to the Privy Council as men who 'embezzled' goods and did not pay rent even when according to the English gentleman Thomas Fanshaw they owed it to the Queen. Furthermore, on 13 April 1600, the merchant Fernando Garges describes Sherley (elder) in a petition to Robert Cecil as a 'poor gentleman ... in a ... miserable estate, afflicted with extremity of sickness, destitute of honest and trusty servants, and matched with an unruly rout of mariners ...'⁶⁸

Interestingly, Senden is also described in a similar way in a petition written in 1598 as being in debt from creditors and seeking 'consideration' and 'protection' from them because he had 'procured the release of 200 prisoners in Lisbon, and has sent them home to England.'⁶⁹ In a second petition by an English gentleman William Andrews in 1600, Senden is accused of using his 'warrant from Cecil,' which may well be the one granted to him from the Letters as a means to 'protect him' from arrest. But Andrews says that Senden should not avoid 'arrest' or 'imprison[ment]' and 'asks that Cecil will not' allow 'the merchant stranger' to act 'in contempt' of the law.⁷⁰

Neither Senden nor the Sherleys seem to have had good reputations within the English court. But Sherley's (elder) notoriety preceded him, he was known in the 'vulgar press' and by contemporary commentators as 'gentleman on the make' and as 'a very strange man to deal withal, promising much' but performing 'nothing'.[71] Sherley was part of a notorious family who were involved in economic extravagance, 'chicanery, larceny, adultery ... treachery' and also more importantly were regarded as being incompetent, because their business ventures were publicly known to fail.[72] The Sherleys seems to have been involved in this task opportunistically, because of their own impecuniosity, and we shall see how their involvement may have contributed to the Proclamation's failure, because they did not have the wherewithal to understand how to implement the measures this document suggests.

The Sherleys' ineptitude, however, is not the only reason why this Proclamation was ineffective. A major problem with this document is the generalisations that are included in it. Not only are these generalisations about the status of Africans in Tudor England, they are also about the presence of 'those kindes of people.' It says that there are 'great Numbers of Negroes and blackamoors' 'carried in' to Tudor England. But the first Letter written five years earlier stated Africans 'are already here too manie.' Both documents seem to be contradicting each other. I suggest that there is insufficient evidence, even if one believes the numbers quoted in the Bristol case, to support the idea that the African presence of 1601 is the result of a sudden mass influx of Africans into Tudor England.

There is also insufficient evidence to prove that the term 'too manie' in the Proclamation is an accurate description of how Africans were concentrated, even though evidence in parish records illustrates that some Africans were gathered in parishes located near the centre of cities such as Plymouth and London. In other words, despite what the Proclamation may imply the concentration of Africans does not appear to have been large enough to pose the problem the Proclamation suggests.[73] Even in the last quarter of the sixteenth century, when the numbers of Africans may have been greater, white immigrants in the same areas appear to have outnumbered them, with the latter making up a small majority in St Botolph and Hart Street in the 1590s: the parish records of these areas confirms this.[74]

Nevertheless, if the writer's claim of 'too manie' in the Proclamation and 'divers' in the Letters is not based on any facts, then he could have picked any racial group to label in that way. This includes Native-Americans and Inuits who were living in London and Plymouth. William Harrison refers to them and their customs in his *History of England* and Stow does the same in *The Chronicles*.[75] But perhaps no Tudor writer does this because it would be difficult even for the most xenophobic to create an argument where thirty or so Native-Americans are 'too manie.' Africans therefore, are likely to have been more significant in numbers than Native-Americans, and constituted more than a 'few strolling players.' Africans appear to have offered in numbers and visibility the potential of being portrayed as a threat, even though they are unlikely to have been one.[76]

The writer of the Letters, Proclamation and the petitions, however, appears to be speaking about Africans with a xenophobic misanthropy. The evidence suggests that Tudor society was not free of xenophobia, but it is unlikely that the status of Africans would have been decided purely on the basis of their ethnic origins or the colour of their skin. One indication of this is a book called *The Gaping Gulf*, written by John Stubbs in 1579. This book is a tirade against all things foreign especially Frenchmen and Catholicism. Stubbs, apart from saying that marriage with a 'foreigner is against God's law,' he also states that 'a foreigner is barred from the highest positions' in the country, and cannot 'inherit land or become a steward.'[77] Some of Stubbs' views are echoed in the obiter dicta of *Calvin's Case* decided in 1608. This case suggests that an Alien could become a citizen, but that they had different rights and obligations to 'natural citizens.'[78] All this seems to indicate that between 1579 and 1608, some English lawyers may have been suspicious of Aliens obtaining certain positions of power.[79] However, it is doubtful whether English officials ever publicly supported Stubbs' rampant nationalism, exemplified by his suggestion that 'it is lawful to seize the property of aliens.' After all, many of the 'unruly youths' who tried to do the latter were put to death by English authorities, whilst Stubbs had his hand cut off for his writings, and a proclamation was enforced to prevent the dissemination of his work.[80]

Furthermore, the judges in *Calvin* make no mention of race as a factor in determining who a citizen is; and even Stubbs had ambiguous ideas about Africans and their status.[81] It is doubtful even if one followed his xenophobic furore that we can find a justification for the views expressed in the Letters and the Proclamation. For example when Stubbs talks about Africans his attitude seems at odds with the animosity that is present within the Proclamation. He praises the 'Moor' 'for holding more faith with strangers than these French doe' and says if Elizabeth I is to marry a 'foreigner,' then she should marry with 'these Moores beyonde Spain,' rather than with a French man. In other words, Elizabeth's marriage to a French monarch offers a danger that such a union with an African would not. This may imply that the status of Africans is not automatically below that of some continental Europeans, and the former may possess a number of qualities which make them superior to the latter.[82]

Nevertheless, the writer of this Proclamation wants his audience to see Africans in Tudor England as having an inferior status, and to recognise that they are a social problem. The writer claims that Africans 'are carried into this realm since the troubles between her highness [Elizabeth I] and the King of Spain' and 'are fostered and powered here to the great annoyance of her own liege people.' This suggests that Africans in Tudor England have come recently from Spain or Spanish colonies, and/or it could imply that they arrived as result of destabilisation caused by the Anglo-Spanish War. The evidence in Chapter 3 suggests that both theories are true for some but not all Africans in England at this time. In addition, perhaps the writer is trying to claim that the lately-arrived Africans were more foreign or strange than others who had come here before and therefore that their status is different.[83] In this way, the Proclamation seems to repeat ideas stated in the Letters: that is in describing the 'lately' arrived Africans as not being liege. We know what Sherley's (elder) true intentions were, but perhaps it is only these Africans that the Proclamation is crudely attempting to bar from citizenship with a perfunctory time qualification. Even though this measure would seem particularly inequitable as it would then deny naturalisation to people who may have been living in England for sixteen years. It is unlikely that other citizens would have to spend so long in England before they could become 'liege.'[84]

I suggest, in a similar way to Peter Fraser, that the true status of Africans in Tudor England resembled other people present in that society, and they could become native, naturalised or liege by being born in England, baptised in an English church and/or by being married to, or having sexual relationships with an English person. Indeed these relationships may have made some foreign-born Africans of a low status feel that they had rights or were equal to English-born whites. In Tudor fiction this process seems to be what happened with Aaron in *Titus Andronicus,* and to be echoed in the relationships of some real African men living in Tudor London.[85]

For foreign-born African women, if they had relationships with white Englishmen these unions may have granted them rights to remain in England. This is likely to be for practical reasons as in some cases they either carried or were about to carry the 'reputed' child of an Englishman. For example, as in an entry for 'Richard, son of Marye a Neger, base, ye reputed father Rog Hoggett.' Richard was baptised in the St Andrew's ward in Plymouth on 23 June 1603. His reputed father Rog Hoggett was a white Englishman who lived in Plymouth. Even if Mary was foreign-born to deny her or her son Richard the right to stay here in England would probably have required special 'Race Laws' which as stated above do not appear to have existed.[86]

Marriage or a relationship with a white English person, were not the only ways that Africans could become integrated members of their parishes.

Some Africans who were born abroad are likely to have become naturalised by becoming 'ordinarily resident' in England. In Tudor England, there does not seem to have been racial restrictions on Africans altering their status to become naturalised as there was in some British colonies in the eighteenth and nineteenth centuries.[87] This may be why the Proclamation attempts to concoct religious and moral reasons.

For example the Proclamation claims that 'most of them [Africans] are infidels having no understanding of Christ.' This seems to have been stated to emphasise Africans' otherness and perhaps that they are dangerous and should have an inferior status. It implies that this is the reason why some or most cannot be natural citizens. But the majority of Africans found in Tudor records are baptised or buried as Christians. This includes 'Pedro Katheren' who was baptised on 4 October in 1596, at 'St Andrew's Plymouth,' 'daughter of don Pedro a basterd Neger.'[88]

Perhaps the writer of the Proclamation has heard about these Africans, and knows his arguments are tenuous, and this may be why he uses an additional idea that 'those kindes of people' consume 'the charity' meant for the Queen's 'liege subjects' and that is why they have to be 'discharged' from the land. However, this claim in a similar way to the first is doubtful. This is because as already stated, even though there may be some Africans in Tudor England apparently living in poverty, the evidence discovered so far does not support the idea that there are so many of them that they prevented 'other subjects' from receiving charitable relief. Furthermore, if the Proclamation is suggesting policies to deny charitable relief to Africans simply because they are Africans it is unlikely that parishes in Tudor England could consider such a policy apposite, valid or enforceable. The question of race or someone's skin colour being a disqualification for poor relief is absent from the laws or practices which governed this area. This includes: the Vagabonds Acts 1530, 1547 and 1597, the Poor Acts 1551 and 1575, the Act for the Relief of the Poor 1597, and the Poor Laws of 1598 and 1601.[89]

Such a disqualification is also absent from the documents entitled *An Ease for Overseers of the Poore,* and a *Plea for the Poore* written in 1601 and 1616 respectively. The first was created to provide poor law administrators and overseers with guidance from all the existing laws in how charitable relief should be administered. The *Plea for the Poore* was written by John Downame who by the end of the sixteenth century had served in the parishes of St Olave and Jewry, and St Margaret Lothbury in London. It is interesting that Downame during the Tudor period served in parishes in which we know Africans were present, so it is very significant that he does not mention race, or skin colour as a disqualification for charitable relief.[90] I suggest that if Africans were born in the local area, had been living there for a long time, and/or had conceived a child with a local person, that in practical terms these Africans would probably have been considered as having a status akin to the white people who lived in the same parishes. Therefore, the statements made in the Proclamation make it difficult to know whether the arguments in these documents could form the basis of a serious legal instrument, which could be enforced, or if it is simply a 'wish-list' coupled with a hyperbolic rant. This last issue is discussed throughout the remainder of this chapter, as is the question of whether the two Letters would have had legal validity.

Legal reasons for the failure of the Letters and the Proclamation

The legal issues which explain the failure of the Letters and the Proclamation are closely related to questions about the status of Africans in Tudor England. Legal ambiguities about people-smuggling or slavery were intensified when transactions took place in England. And this may be why in the Bristol case the Africans and others were speedily removed from English soil. Smuggling people against their will would probably have meant using force or violence to enforce slavery upon them. The courts of law in Tudor England appear to have been reluctant or unwilling to allow people to use force to impose 'a slave status.'

This reluctance was grounded in legal, moral and practical reasons. In 1569, in a case called *In the Matter of Cartwright*, a Russian slave present in England was severely beaten by his master.[91] The English Court decided that it was 'morally' 'unfair' for any human being to be subject to such violence. It has been reported in eighteenth-century cases such as *Somersett* or *Shanley and Harvey*, which did relate to the status of enslaved Africans,[92] that *Cartwright* stated that 'England was too pure an air for slaves to breathe.'[93] However, whether this was the rule in *Cartwright*, or whether this was an idea inserted by later cases similar to *Somersett* is still unclear.[94]

The Tudor courts' position on this matter may be clarified by a London case decided in 1579 involving an unnamed African present in England. This African 'utterly refused to serve' his employer who was called Hector Noviemies. The English Court decided that the African could not be compelled to work for Noviemies, and they were unwilling or unable to force the African into the status of being a slave.[95] Taking Noviemies' and Cartwright's cases together it appears that the courts of law in Tudor England were not willing to see people beaten, tortured or sold, and then have the employer justify it by calling the person a 'slave.' The term 'slave' may not have been a functional definition of any person's status in Tudor England.[96]

Moreover, for all the reasons stated throughout this book, recent attempts by historians such as Noami Tadmor to retrospectively claim that slavery was a functional status by using the position of Africans in English society are unsupported.[97] As I suggest throughout, the longer Africans such as the ones who came with Baskerville stayed in England, the more difficult it would be to treat them as slaves. This may explain why the writer of the Letter and the Proclamation is trying to get groups of these Africans out of the country quickly – so that they can be treated as slaves elsewhere.[98] But, it would be difficult to remove Africans from English society even if they had only come to England since the Anglo-Spanish war, because even by then they are likely to have been 'securely lodged,' or integrated in their parishes.[99]

The status of Africans in Tudor England also appears to have been determined by their ability to speak for themselves. Some Africans arriving in England from Spanish or other colonies may have thought themselves slaves on arrival, and if they remained dumb subalterns it may have been possible to exploit them.[100] However, once any African opposed that status by refusing to be sold or treated as a slave, Tudor law seems unable or unwilling to impose slavery on them. The same would happen if anyone connected to an African spoke on their behalf, as happened in the case of Maria Moriana an African woman living in England in 1470. Moriana spoke little English and appears to have been 'innocent' of her employer's intention to sell her as a slave until those around her objected.[101] She then voiced her disapproval. Once she did, she appears to have assumed the status of a free citizen and the courts of law had no power or were unwilling to take that status away.[102]

In Tudor England, the courts of law do not seem to have labelled Africans as perpetual slaves simply because of the colour of their skin, or their ethnic origins, although, what some of these people's status is appears uncertain. In his article 'Slaves or Free people,' Fraser concurs noting that imposing the status of slave on anyone in Tudor England was rare, and that maintaining that status was even more difficult.[103] This dilemma seems to be echoed by what William Harrison says in 1577, when he writes 'as in theft therefore, so in adultery and whoredom, I would wish the parties trespassing to be made bond or slaves unto those that received the injury.' But he then states, 'as for slaves and Bond men ... we [in England] have none.'[104] Harrison seems to be saying in the first statement that slavery could exist, but then he says there are no slaves here.

Modern historians such as Norma Pilbeam and Ian Nelson echo what Harrison has said, as they discuss how slavery may have existed as a potential punishment for those accused of vagrancy. Pilbeam says that those found guilty of vagrancy could be branded with a 'V' on their skin.[105] In an

Ease for Overseers of the Poor, this same idea is repeated, when the author looking back at earlier Tudor legislation on the poor says, that in the time of King Edward VI, 'idle wanderers ... [were] marked with a letter V. [so] ... the presenters might take them for slaves ... and feed them bread ... and water.' But this comment should be seen in context, for the author is suggesting that slavery in the past was used as a punishment for the crime of being 'idle and sturdy'.[106] But in Tudor times, these laws on vagrancy were not being used to impose a perpetual status on their recipients, although the 'V.' sign on the skin does suggest that those punished would be recognised elsewhere for their crime. Rather this legislation because of its draconian nature was trying to deter people who were 'sturdy' from becoming vagrants.[107] Therefore to claim that the intention behind this sixteenth-century legislation was the same, or even similar to that later imposed on Africans in the Caribbean, the Americas, and elsewhere would probably be a grave error. Since, the intention of the later legislation was to arbitrarily make as many slaves as possible on the grounds that they were racially inferior.[108] In Tudor England this simply does not seem to have happened.

Furthermore, it is actually questionable how often vagrants were actually branded and treated as the author in *Ease* suggests. Even in *Ease* the author states that the poor should be 'provided for,' and that overseers of the poor should not be there to punish, but 'provide a special title of inspiration,' exercising their duties without prejudice or 'malice' but with 'conscience and discretion.'[109] Similar views are also included in the medieval text *D. Pauper* or *Dives and Pauper* which was read in Tudor England by administrators and priests.[110] Pilbeam and the historian A. L. Beier add to this idea when they suggest that in Tudor England, the more harsher types of punishments for vagrancy such as branding, fell into disuse because they were not 'practical' or enforceable. Moreover, that they sometimes made the public sympathetic to the one being punished, or stirred up animosity against the authorities.[111]

In Tudor England, therefore, even when the term 'slave' was used to describe some people's status, it seems to have been a temporary or transitory term. It certainly did not describe a permanent status determined by a person's race. Those Africans discussed in this book, some of whom are called slaves in Tudor documents, also seem to have this status on a temporary basis, perhaps reflecting a past punishment, or more likely, an echo of their status abroad – rather than a statement of their functional status in English society.[112]

The systematic labelling and treatment of Africans as plantation or personal slaves was not a feature of Tudor England, but of the British Empire in the eighteenth century. It was then that there were legal enactments and legislation that supported that status.[113] At that time the British Empire enslaved more Africans than any nation in the world, and genuine horrors and cruelty were committed against them, however, the status of an African actually living in Georgian Britain was not certain. In many ways, the law did not discriminate against these Africans in the same way, 'the son of a black born in England shall be admitted if he be a Protestant to all municipal rights [,] whilst they shall be unmercifully denied to a white because he is a Catholic.' Sometimes, Africans in Georgian Britain gained their freedom and acquired independent wealth or property. Some became equal or socially superior members of the families they once served.[114] The implication of this is that in Tudor times, when it was not legal to enslave Africans, their status is even more likely to have been based on the personal relationships they established.[115]

This is all the more pertinent since jurists in Tudor England tended to only interfere in the personal relationships between an employer and employee when there were situations of 'manifest injustice' or 'cruelty.' In other words the courts would be extremely reluctant to arbitrarily enforce an inferior status on someone else's servant.

These ideas are bound up in legal principles about 'restraint of trade,' since the Letters, Proclamations and petitions sought to grant warrants and authority to Banes, Senden and the Sherleys over certain groups of Africans, employed by others. Edward Coke, who was the Attorney General in the last quarter of the sixteenth and at the beginning of the seventeenth centuries, was a legal champion for the rights of the merchant class against 'royal patronage.' In 1592, Coke stated that the monarch needed 'a positive legal instrument' before she could grant a monopoly that might result in individual financial gain, or might restrict the trading or activities of another. This also applied to those acting in the name of the monarch. Similar views, but for different reasons were expressed on this subject by other leading lawyers, such as James Dyer and Edmund Anderson, Chief Justices of the Court of Common Pleas.[116]

Nevertheless, in the petitions of 1600, Sherley (elder) states that he believes that a document of 'stronger purpose' can be drafted. He says this is needed because the 'masters' of the Africans would not allow them to be taken. Of course this presupposes that all the Africans no matter how long they have been in England, or how they came have masters. But Sherley's statement 'find' repeated several times seems to allude to at least some Africans not having masters, almost as if he can just pick them up. Sherley seems to be offering ideas which conceptually contradict themselves because either the

Africans have 'masters' or they do not; either they 'are fostered and powered here,' or they are 'idle,' 'covet relief' and offer no 'service to the Queen.' What we know is that Sherley admits he cannot get 'possession' of any Africans; and this is likely to be for reasons other than what he is admitting. In other words for Sherley to succeed he would have to do more than compel the 'masters' of Blackamoores to comply. Sherley wants the Proclamation to be the document with that 'stronger purpose' which can make Africans into slaves.[117]

Sherley acknowledges, however, that Cecil does not 'like a commission of that nature,' which allows Sherley 'to take what pleased him,' or one where the Africans could be taken 'from their masters compulsorily.' So what Sherley wants is unlikely to happen, not just because he appears to have misunderstood what the status of Africans in Tudor England is, but also because any attempts by Banes, the Sherleys or Senden to use a royal warrant to force employers to release Africans to them would probably fail for another legal principle which is the prohibition against decrees which granted absolute powers.[118] This would especially be the case since no compensation was being offered. In *The Necessarie Verse and Fruit of the Pleadings,* Coke states how the law should defend the merchant class against a monarch's absolute power and decrees that resulted in despotism.[119] In the case of Darcy and Allen in 1603, Coke stated that the 'Monarch did not have the [legal] authority' to make a grant of a monopoly to another arbitrarily, even where she attempted to do so on the 'grounds of public good.' The case sought to disqualify 'unscrupulous courtiers' who tried to use royal patronage for their own financial benefit. Senden and the Sherleys were precisely the sort of 'purveyors' gaining 'authoritie' through 'commission' that Coke attempted to keep out of the financial affairs of well-respected Englishmen. Coke's views represented the dominant legal position in late Elizabethan and early Stuart jurisprudence. The legal tide had turned against either the monarch or another in the name of the monarch behaving as these men intended to do.[120]

The Proclamation seems to acknowledge that it has no legal force when it states that those employers who 'refuse to deliver' Africans to the authorities shall first be 'call[ed] ... before you [the relevant authority, but does not say who this is] and ... advise[d] and persuade[d] ... by all good means [of] ... her majesty's pleasure therein.' If this does not force compliance, and for all the reasons stated so far this is likely, their 'names' are to be given to the authorities and 'her majesty may take such further course therein as it shall seem best in her princely wisdom.' This last threat seems vague, and this is probably because there was no appropriate legal punishment for employers who refused to comply.

Some of the reasons for this are that late Tudor jurists such as Coke empowered the merchant class. Some of the men who employed Africans were powerful merchants in the process of expanding England's colonies. The status of the Africans who worked in their households was linked to that of their employers. The English government tried to work with this class rather than antagonise them by attempting to give their African employees to a foreigner or a notorious interloper. England relied on the favour of English merchants especially during times of economic hardships. Robert Cecil appears to have understood this, and this may be why (by 1600) he only initially expressed 'willingness touching [Senden's and Sherley's]… suit.'[121] Perhaps Cecil understood that if there were any legal disputes, and the cases went to trial, the judicial trend against 'purveyors' would mean that the judges would decide in favour of the Africans or their employers.

Without the law enforcing 'some stronger purpose,' however, Banes, Senden or the Sherleys are unable to gain 'possession' of any Africans,[122] and this may explain why Banes is granted a further warrant on 10 May 1597, for the payment of '35l. 8s.4d' 'for his expenses, victuals … for 22 Spanish prisoners.'[123] It may also indicate that as early as 1597, Banes had moved on to another venture because he had failed to acquire the ten Africans who came with Baskerville. Of course it is also possible that the twenty-two Spanish prisoners included these Africans – but because of Sherley (elder) and Senden's admissions that they had failed to 'get any' it is unlikely that Banes had been more successful.

The difficulty of slave trading in England is also underlined by another of Sherley's petitions in April 1600. In it he admits to having a 'West Indies man,' probably a Native-American from the Caribbean islands, and he expresses doubts about whether he will be able to hold onto him. He says:

> It hath please God to send me the prizes, the one a West Indies man, the other a ship of Hamburg laden with Portingales goods … Since our strangers in London are very apt to give men impediment where they have any hope to benefit themselves, I am bold to beseech you that I may have my right, with as much favour as may be.[124]

In this petition Sherley is requesting that Cecil grants him 'possession' of the 'West Indies man': a ship, and another from Hamburg, because it is 'his right.' But his statement that 'our strangers in London are very apt to give men impediment where they have any hope to benefit themselves,' may well be an acknowledgement that holding possession and making profit from these 'goods' may have inherent difficulties. So this is an acknowledgement that it was difficult to hold on to goods. Holding onto 'ten or manie' Blackamoores as property would be even more problematic.

Slavery and people-smuggling were hazardous activities, filled with danger. The Englishmen who participated in it and obtained a profit such as Drake, Hawkins and Raleigh seemed to understand how to. Other Englishmen including Hopkins and Jonas in the Bristol case, appear to have made a loss, so to 'return ... a profit' from your activities often required ruthlessness. By Hawkins' own admission, the voyage of 1567 was 'troublesome', and he gained 'captives' by 'gun and the sword' only 'with great hurte and damage.'[125] But the Sherleys were certainly different to Hawkins who could kill for profit or country, although, they did portray themselves as such.[126]

Furthermore, Englishmen such as Drake, Hawkins and Raleigh appear to have understood they operated outside of the black-letter of English law; and kept the Africans who they intended to retain as slaves outside of England and therefore away from the jurisdiction of English jurists. As discussed in Chapter 4, it is likely that these Englishmen were aware of the issues about trying to impose a 'slave' status on Africans present in Tudor England. Indeed, as we shall see later these Englishmen seem to have regarded those Africans who lived 'amongst' them in England, as having a different status to those who they captured and sold abroad.

Robert Cecil may not have possessed the practical knowledge or experience of slave trading that Drake, Hawkins and Raleigh had, and so Sherley (elder) may be asking the wrong person when he asks Cecil for help.[127] Moreover, though Senden had experience as a slave trader abroad, his apparent reliance on Sherley to plead his case seems to show that the Dutch man did not understand English law and customs. They then both appear to make a mistake that is similar to a group of Italian witnesses in an English court case of 1547. This case at the High Court of the Admiralty features an African called Jacques Francis who was a diver working in England on the sunken remains of the *Mary Rose*.[128] The Italian witnesses in this case presumed that English law could be used to bar Jacques Francis' testimony because they said he had the status of 'a slave'. The English courts however, were unwilling to endorse that view. It seems that these Italian witnesses, in a similar way to the Sherleys, Senden, Noviemies and Maria Moriana's employers, are mistaken about what English law can or is willing to do. The law in Tudor England seems unwilling to impose slavery on an African simply because the testimony of another may have asked for this.[129] However, this legal principle is not the only reason why these documents failed. Another is related to religious and superstitious fears connected to imposing a slave status on human beings.

Late Tudor England was a deeply religious and superstitious country. In 1596, the English Admiral Charles Howard stated that England had defeated Spain in 1588 because of the latter's 'sins and wickedness.' John Stow in 1598 repeated this idea in *The Chronicles*.[130] Another Tudor writer Walter Thomas Rogers, whose book the *Second Coming of Christ* is recommended in *The Chronicles*, claimed that the 'false, corrupt and detestable' sins of Spain that included slavery and the Spanish Inquisition were the activities of the servants of the Antichrist.[131] Just before Hawkins died he wrote in his will dated 6 June 1595, that the 'wrath of the Allmightie' had fallen on his 'head' because he was a 'grievous sinner.' The historian Harry Kelsey suggests that the 'sin' Hawkins is referring to includes those associated with slave trading.[132] He may not have been alone in that fear as the Portuguese Prince Don Antonio, who died in 1595, expressed similar regrets of a life that included participation in slave trading. In his personal confessions written in the form of psalms and published in 1596, he describes himself as a 'wicked man,' who lived by 'the most wicked ways.' His confessions seem to go beyond an 'ordinary' attempt to atone for his sins.[133] Some English officials may have felt that the death of these men within a year of each other was also a sign, not only that imposing the status of slave on any human being was morally and religiously wrong, but any trade linked to this was as well.[134]

These men's deaths may also have alarmed members of the English establishment, but what certainly did was the worsening economic situation, riots and failed harvests and the lack of a male successor to Elizabeth I. Together all of these occurrences in late Tudor England, seem to have confirmed Rogers' assertion that 'the second coming of Christ' was 'nigh at hand,' and that England's calamities were 'signs' that the 'end of the world' was also 'nigh.'[135] This may be why officially and publicly, Elizabeth I expressed in 1600, she had no desire or 'pleasure therin' to be involved in schemes related to domestic slavery, despite her and her Privy Council's private sponsorship of these very activities abroad.[136]

The Africans who had 'lately arrived' in England, through Drake and Hawkins' expedition, may thus have been a reminder of England's 'sinful activities' abroad. If there was retribution to come from God, these Africans may bring it with them and that is why some officials or others may have felt that they ought to be 'discharged' from English soil. This would explain some of the language of fear expressed in these documents and the urgency to have 'those kindes of people' 'avoided.' In other words, the language in these documents may not reflect an intrinsic fear of the African, but rather a superstitious concern surrounding the activities that had brought them here. However to remove these Africans, especially by force, would probably mean participating in more 'sinful acts.' Perhaps the reason why men such as Banes, Senden and the Sherleys had been employed was that by 1596, they were the only ones willing to 'risk their souls' in such activities.[137] Ironically by the end of 1600, faced with these legal issues about status, conflicting superstitions and religious matters, English officials such as Robert Cecil seem to have eventually decided that doing nothing was the most 'moral' and practical approach.

Practical reasons for the failure of the Letters and the Proclamation

Cecil's approach was probably influenced by all the factors discussed in this chapter, with the addition that most Africans in Tudor England were too useful inside their English communities to have the status of being mere commodities which could be deported at will in groups or en masse. These Africans were also too useful to be exchanged with foreign merchants. The Letters and the Proclamation may be acknowledging this when they say that Africans are 'fostered' and 'powered' here. Some of these Africans may have come to Tudor England voluntarily. This is especially likely as English gentlemen encouraged artisans and immigrants of all colours and complexions from different parts of the world. Some of these Africans were coming from societies that were intellectually and economically more advanced than Tudor society. In 1578, George Best argued that 'Englishmen should wake' and catch up with the rest of Europe.[138] If Africans could help England 'wake,' or if they offered skills that other men in England did not have, they would be respected and useful within their communities. This is more likely in towns such as London, Plymouth, Bristol and Southampton that were developing an economic autonomy based on trade.[139] Moreover, as we shall see in Chapters 4 and 5, the merchants and traders of these towns were more interested in activities that would make them money, and would oppose or ignore royal edicts and proclamations that did not help them do this.[140] The Letters and the Proclamation would almost certainly fall into the latter category.

However, Africans were not just useful in Tudor towns but were also personally so to Elizabeth I and members of her Privy Council. This contradicts Sherley (elder) and Senden's claim that 'all the blackamoors in England are regarded but only for the strangeness of their nation and not for service to the Queen.'[141] In fact, there were Africans living in Tudor England who were either directly in royal service, or being paid through royal patronage, and this includes Jacques Francis and John Blanke the 'blacke trumpeter.'[142] In addition, in 1572, Elizabeth I had a 'favourite lytle Blackamore' who she had a special suit made for that was a 'Garcon coat of white taffeta cut and lined and stripped with Gold and silver, [and] painted with prints and ribbons.'[143] The question is, were any of 'those kindes of' Africans who were performing royal duties included within the scope of these documents. As I shall show these Africans certainly do not have an inferior status to their white counterparts, nor do they 'have want of service,' or 'fall into extremity.' Other Africans though not in royal service still appear to have been members of their communities. These include: an African woman such as Mary Fillis the servant of Millicent Porter, Bastien the servant of William Hawkins, and Cabrew Lazia the Negro merchant.[144] The rhetoric contained in the Letters, and the Proclamation presents an image of Tudor England that leads us to assume these people did not exist. But we know they did.

Furthermore, an African called Fortunatus appears to have been personally employed and useful to the most important member of Elizabeth I's Privy Council, Robert Cecil.[145] In 1601 Cecil was a powerful man because of his position as the Spymaster General. He was in charge of England's secret service and was constantly watching for dangers real or perceived to the peace, moral health, and the wealth of the nation.[146] With that background, it is significant that he had an African servant called Fortunatus working for him in 1601. Fortunatus was buried in St Clement Danes, London, on 21 January 1602.[147] It is not likely that Cecil included Fortunatus amongst the Africans who are classified in the Letters and the Proclamation as having an inferior status and being strange, dangerous and foreign. But if Cecil agreed with these documents' rhetoric, perhaps he should not have had any African servants at all. The presence of an African within Cecil's personal household suggests that despite Cecil's initial involvement, in a similar way to most other Englishmen he was too pragmatic to enforce what was an opportunistic wish-list infused with demagoguery.

Conclusion

The Letters and the Proclamation are important documents concerning the presence and status of Africans in Tudor England. These documents reveal that there was an African presence and suggests that this was significantly large in the centre of some of England's major cities such as London and Plymouth. However, these poorly drafted documents do not appear to have resulted in a decline in that population's numbers. This is because the Letters and the Proclamation appear to have been weak legal instruments that ignore fundamental legal issues present in sixteenth-century English jurisprudence. These issues are that if Africans had the status of slaves, then no special Letters or Proclamation would be needed to have them sold or exchanged. In other words since these documents exist, Africans were not automatically slaves, and if they were free people it would probably be illegal simply on the basis of their race and ethnic origins to have them treated as chattels or bond men. The fact that these documents became defeasant illustrates that these questions were not resolved. The evidence infers that even those Africans who were servants had a position akin to that of indentured workers: that is they had a low status and there were few laws to protect them, but they were not regarded as 'property' in the same way as a slave is.[148]

These issues above are why the Letters and the Proclamation could not be enforced for legal, religious, but above all practical reasons. The status of Africans who were 'fostered' and 'powered' in Tudor England appears to have been determined by their own skills, abilities and usefulness. Furthermore, the men entrusted to carry out the measures suggested in these documents were either: incompetent, corrupt or ignorant as to how to. Their desire to have new documents created with a 'stronger purpose' confirms their own impotence. Therefore, these Letters and the Proclamation are not as Kaufmann suggests, merely a matter of Sherley and Senden's business transactions going 'wrong,' although, the evidence indicates that they do show that too. Rather, the hyperbolic statements that these documents contain are likely to have been seen by the Tudor audience that read or heard them as a ruse to make money, or an attempt at royal interference in their households.

Nevertheless, the Africans spoken about in these documents were not just objects for making money. They were real people who lived. But these epistles just as those in the Bristol case refer to them from a distance. Consequently, it is difficult to get a full understanding of who these Africans were simply by examining these documents. For example we do not know what the ten Africans who came with Baskerville would have thought about the measures discussed in this chapter. In order to find out more about the status of Africans in Tudor England, it is necessary to look beyond documents such as these. In the next chapter, I will look at a range of other evidence that reveals much about the meaning of words used to describe the Africans who are talked about in the Letters, Proclamation and petitions. Some of this evidence supports what we have already learnt about the status and origins of Africans in Tudor England, other evidence resolves new questions.

Notes

[1] Quotations from James Walvin, *Slaves and Slavery: The British Colonial Experience* (Manchester: Manchester University Press, 1992), pp. 17–19; and William Philips, *Slavery from Roman Times to the Early Transatlantic Trade* (Manchester: Manchester University Press, 1985), pp. 142–144. On the power and 'crueltie' of Spain and Portugal see Samuel Purchas, *Purchas his Pilgrimage; or Relations of the World ...* (London: William Stansby for Henrie Fetherstone, 1613), pp. 746–752.

[2] William Hopkins, *Letter to Lord Burghley*, October 1590, in *Lansdowne Manuscripts*, no. 115, item 83, pp. 236–239; A privateer is someone attacking foreign ships with the authority of letters from the government, for more on this see: Kenneth R. Andrews, *Elizabethan Privateering: English Privateering during the Spanish War, 1585–1603* (Cambridge: University Press, 1964); William Jessop, *Privateering in Elizabethan Bristol: A Case Study on John Hopkins*, (Unpublished, 2004); Peter Leeson and Alex Nowrasteh, 'Was Privateering Plunder Efficient?' *Journal of Economic Behavior and Organization*, 79, issue 3, August 2011, pp. 303–317. A more detailed version is available at http://www.peterleeson.com/Efficient_Plunder.pdf.

[3] These letters are not in: Authors various, *Mayors Audit Books*, for the city of Bristol (Bristol: Bristol City Council, 1501–1558, 1594 onwards); *Ordinances of Common Council*, 1506–1598 ref. 04272, Bristol Record Office, Bristol; Maureen Stanford (ed.), *The Ordinances of Bristol* (Bristol: Bristol Record Society, 1990); Author Various: *Little Red Book*; *Great Red Book*; *Great White Book*; Robert Ricart, *Ricart's Kalendar*, 1479–1895 ref. 04720/1/A all at Bristol Record Office; Jean Vanes (ed.), *Documents Illustrating the Overseas Trade of Bristol in the Sixteenth Century* (Bristol: Bristol Record Society, 1979); D. M. Livock (ed.), *City Chamberlain's Accounts in the Sixteenth and Seventeenth Centuries* (Bristol: Bristol Record Society, 1966).

[4] Hopkins, *Letter to Lord Burghley*, pp. 236–239; William Bland, *Letter to Lord Burghley*, October 1590, in *Lansdowne Manuscripts*, no. 115, item 84, p. 241.

[5] Quotations from Hopkins, *Letter to Lord Burghley*, p. 236.

[6] Ibid., (on the servant), p. 238.

[7] Hopkins, *Letter to Lord Burghley*, p. 239 (victuals; and the number of Africans is scribbled over).

[8] See previous note (3).

[9] For how African slaves were categorised, measured, listed and sold in transactions from the sixteenth to the twentieth century see, United Nations Educational Scientific and Cultural Organization, 'The Slave Route Project,' *Culture*, http://www.unesco.org/new/en/culture/themes/dialogue/the-slave-route/, accessed on 12/10/11.

[10] Ibid., p. 238.

[11] Author unknown, Letter to Lord Mayors, signed by Queen Elizabeth, London, National Archives, Kew, London, PC 2/21, p. 304, 11 July 1596; Author unknown, Letter signed by Queen Elizabeth, National Archives, Kew, London, PC 2/21, f.306, 18 July 1596; and Author unknown, Proclamation ca January 1601, National Archives, Kew, London, *Tudor Royal Proclamations*, 1601/ 804.5-805.

[12] *Oxford Dictionary of English*, pp. 515, 1171(definitions of 'native' etc.); on who is 'native' and 'liege' see Lien Luu, *Immigrants and the Industries of London, 1500–1700* (Aldershot: Ashgate, 2005), pp. 142–144; and Harry Lee Faggett, *Black and Other Minorities in Shakespeare's England* (Prairie View: Prairie View Press, 1971), pp. 1–6.

[13] The word 'writer' is used here and throughout with an acknowledgement that there may have been more than one writer of these documents, see Faiza Ghazala, Greater London Council Ethnic Minorities Unit, *A History of the Black Presence in London* (London: Greater

London Council, 1986), pp. 8–12; and Miranda Kaufmann, 'Caspar Van Senden, Sir Thomas Sherley and the 'Blackamoor' project,' *Historical Research*, 81, 212, May 2008, pp. 366–371.

[14] Imtiaz Habib, *Shakespeare and Race* ... (Lanham: University Press of America, 1999), pp. 1–5; Marika Sherwood, 'Blacks in Elizabethan England' *History Today*, 53: 10, 2003, pp. 40–42; Peter Fryer, *Staying Power* ... (1984, reprint, London: Pluto Press, 1989), pp. 10–12; Folarin Shyllon, *Black People in Britain 1553-1833* (Oxford: Oxford University Press, 1977), p. 3; Emily Carroll Bartels, 'Too many Blackamoors: Deportation, discrimination and Elizabeth 1,' *Studies in English Literature* ... 46: 2, Spring 2006, pp. 305–322; and John Gabriel, *Whitewash: Racialized Politics and the Media* (London: Routledge, 1998), pp. 44 , 99.

[15] Humfrey Dyson (collator), *A Book Containing all such Proclamations as were Published by the Reigne of the Late Queen Elizabeth 1559-1602* (London: Bonham Norton and John Bull, 1618), pp. 1–6, 88, 146, 267, 284, 338, 371.

[16] John Stow, *A Summary of the Chronicles of England, Abridged and Continued unto 1598* (1565, new edition, London: R. Bardocke, 1598), pp. 768–769; Jessica Browner, 'The wrong side of the river: London's disreputable Southbank in the sixteenth and seventeenth century,' *Essays in History*, 36, 1994, http://etext.virginia.edu/journals/EH/EH36/EH36.html accessed 12/06/2007; Susan Styles, *The Poor Law* (London: Macmillan Education, 1985), n. p. preface. For explanations of who is a 'stranger' see *Oxford Dictionary of English*, p. 1746; Faggett, *Black and Other Minorities*, pp. 1–6, 25; and Ian Smith, *Race and Rhetoric in the Renaissance: Barbarian Errors* (Basingstoke: Palgrave Macmillan, 2009), pp. 23–43, 46–62, 121.

[17] Stow, *A Summary of the Chronicles of England*, pp. 768–769; Andrew Spicer, in Goose and Luu (eds.) *Immigrants in Tudor and Early Stuart England*, p. 92; Faggett, *Black and Other Minorities*, p. 6; and Smith, *Race and Rhetoric*, pp. 10–12.

[18] A similar view is offered by Peter Fraser, Randolph Vigne and Charles Littleton (eds.), 'Slaves or Free people, the status of Africans in England 1550-1750' ... (Eastbourne: Sussex Academic Press, 2001), pp. 254–261.

[19] Author unknown, Letter to Lord Mayors, signed 11 July 1596.

[20] Also suggested by Miranda Kaufmann but for different reasons in, 'Caspar Van Senden, Sir Thomas Sherley and the 'Blackamoor' project,' pp. 366–371; and Kris Lane, *Pillaging the Empire: Piracy in the Americas* ... (New York: ME Sharpe, 1998), pp. 56–57.

[21] Author unknown, Letter to Lord Mayors, signed 11 July 1596; and Emily C. Bartels, 'Too many Blackamoors, Deportation, discrimination and Elizabeth 1,' pp. 305–322 (has a different view).

[22] On the last point a similar view is expressed by Spicer, in Goose and Luu (eds.), *Immigrants in Tudor and Early Stuart England*, pp. 1–7.

[23] Author unknown, Letter to the Lord Mayors, signed 11 July 1596; Including evidence in: Guildhall Library, London, GL Ms 28867, GL Ms 9243–9245, GL Ms 4310, GL Ms 9222; Plymouth and West Devon Record Office, Plymouth, St Andrews/MF1-4; Imtiaz Habib, *Black Lives in the English Archives* ... (London: Ashgate, 2008), pp. 274–334; Sherwood, 'Blacks in Elizabethan England,' pp. 40–42; and Sampson, 'Black burials and deaths 16th century,' (Email).

[24] Thomas Baskerville, *An Approbation of this Discourse, by Sir Thomas Baskeruile* (London: John Windet, 1596), n. p. passim; and Casper Van Senden and Thomas Sherley, 'Cecil Papers Petition, Merchant of Lubeck to the Queen,' 29 November 1600, *Calendar of the Manuscripts of the Most Honourable the Marquess of Salisbury*, Volume 10 (London: Historical Manuscripts Commission, 1883–1976), p. 399.

[25] Habib, *Black Lives*, pp. 1–18 raises similar points.

[26] Bernaldino Delgadillo De Avellaneda, *A Libell of Spanish Lies: Found at the Sacke of Cales, Discoursing the Fight in the West Indies, Twixt the English Nauie being Fourteene Ships*

and Pinasses, and a Fleete of Twentie Saile of the King of Spaines, and of the Death of Sir Francis Drake. With an Answere Briefely Confuting the Spanish Lies ... (London: John Windet, 1596), n. p. passim.

[27] On the writing style of officials inside the Tudor court see Robert Beale, Clerk to the Privy Council's 'A Treatise of the office of a Councellor and Principall Secretaire to her Majesty,' written in 1592, in Conyers Read, *Mr. Secretary Walsingham and the Policy of Queen Elizabeth*, Volume I (Oxford: Clarendon Press, 1925), pp. 423–443.

[28] Edward Coke, *Les Reports de Edward Coke ... de Diuers Resolutions & Judgemens Donnes ... per les ... Judges, & Sages de la ley ... Durant les Tresheureux Regiment de ... Roigne Elizabeth...* (1600, new edition, London: Tomas Wight, 1607), n. p. preface; and Kaufmann, 'Caspar Van Senden, Sir Thomas Sherley and the 'Blackamoor' project,' pp. 366–371.

[29] Lane, *Pillaging the Empire*, pp. 56–57; De Avellaneda, *A Libell of Spanish Lies*, pp. preface, 20; and Harry Kelsey, *Sir John Hawkins: Queen Elizabeth's Slave Trader* (London: Yale University Press, 2003), p. 258.

[30] Kelsey, *Sir John Hawkins: Queen Elizabeth's Slave Trader*, pp. 262–263 (Hawkins' Will); and Fryer, *Staying Power*, pp. 8, 410–411 (speech of John Archer on this subject in 1918).

[31] Richard Hakluyt, *Voyages of Hawkins, Frobisher and Drake: Select Narratives from the 'Principal Navigations' of Hakluyt/ edited by Edward John Payne; with additional notes, maps, etc, by C. Raymond Beazley* (Oxford: Clarendon Press, 1844–1905), pp. 1–69; Richard Hakluyt, *The Principal Navigations* (London: Hakluyt's Collection, 1598), p. 359; and Nabil Matar, *Turks Moors and Englishmen ...* (1998, new edition, New York: Columbia University Press, 1999), pp. 43, 181–185.

[32] John Hawkins, *Declaration of the Troublesome Voyage, of John Hawkins to the Parties of Guynea and the West Indies in the Yeares of Our Lord, 1567–1568* (London: Thomas Purfoot, 1569), p. 8; Hakluyt, *The Principal Navigations* (1598), p. 359; and Richard Eden, *Decades of the Newe World West India* (London: William Powell, 1555), p. 176.

[33] Quotations from Hawkins, *Declaration of the Troublesome Voyage*, p. 8; Lane, *Pillaging the Empire*, pp. 45–57; Kelsey, *Sir John Hawkins*, pp. 46–51; and David Williams Davies, *Elizabethans Errant. The Strange Fortunes of Sir Thomas Sherley and his Three Sons* (Ithaca: Cornell University Press, 1967), pp. 7, 188.

[34] Hawkins, *A True Declaration of the Troublesome Voyage*, pp. 8–18; Fryer, *Staying Power*, p. 8 (last quotation). This view is also strongly supported with primary evidence by, Toby Green, *The Rise of the Trans-Atlantic Slave Trade in Western Africa, 1300–1589* (New York: Cambridge University Press, 2012), passim; and by Basil Davidson, *African Civilization Revisited: From Antiquity to Modern Times* (Trenton: Africa World Press 1991), pp. 3–45, 127–131, 203–226.

[35] David Dabydeen and James Gilmore (eds.), *The Oxford Companion to Black British History* (Oxford: Oxford University Press, 2007), p. 402 (quotation); and Fraser, Vigne and Littleton (eds.), 'Slaves or Free people, the status of Africans in England 1550–1750,' pp. 254–261.

[36] Hawkins, *A True Declaration of the Troublesome Voyage*, pp. 3–5; and Kelsey, *Sir John Hawkins*, pp. 23–26.

[37] Fraser, Vigne and Littleton (eds.), 'Slaves or Free people,' pp. 254–261; Author unknown, Letter to the Lord Mayors, signed 11 July 1596; and Bartels, 'Too many Blackamoors, Deportation, discrimination and Elizabeth 1,' pp. 305–322 (suggests Africans are 'scapegoats').

[38] Humfrey Dyson (collator), *A Book Containing all such Proclamations as were Published by the Reigne of the Late Queen Elizabeth, 1559-1602*, pp. 1–6, 300, 324, 356; Browner, 'The wrong side of the river,' p. 42; and Stow, *The Chronicles* (1615), pp. 325, 327, 328, 671, 769 (on masterless men).

[39] Author unknown, *St Botolph without Aldgate Memorandum Daybook,* Volume I (London: Parish of St Botolph without Aldgate, 1586–1588), pp. 30, 149; G L, Ref P69/BOT2/A/ 01/MS 9234/1, GL Ms 9234; and St Olave Hart Street, Parish Register, GL Ms 28867, p. 121.

[40] Including evidence in: London, GL Ms 28867, GL Ms 9243–9245, GL Ms 4310, GL Ms 9222; Plymouth and West Devon Record Office, Plymouth, St Andrews/MF1–4; G. L. 'Black and Asian people discovered in records,' *Manuscripts Section*; Mike Sampson, 'Friends of Devon Archives, the Black connection,' *Friends of Devon Newsletter,* Issue 25, May 2000, pp. 12–15; and Habib, *Black Lives in the English Archives,* pp. 274–326.

[41] Dyson (collator), *A Book Containing all such Proclamations,* pp. 1–6, 167, 324, 356; and William C. Carroll, *Fat King, Lean Beggar: Representations of Poverty in the Age of Shakespeare* (Ithaca/ London: Cornell University Press, 1996), pp. 1–36.

[42] On the general problem of vagrancy in Tudor England see, A. L. Beier, *The Problem of the Poor in Tudor and Early Stuart England* (London: Methuen, 1983), pp. 4–13, 13–19, 29–36; Steve Hindle, *On the Parish?: The Micro-Politics of Poor Relief in Rural England, c. 1550–1750* (Oxford: Clarendon, 2004), pp. 1–36; and Marjorie Keniston McIntosh, *Poor Relief in England, 1350–1600* (New York: Cambridge University Press, 2011), pp. 139–173 (begging and fraud) , 186–214 (almshouses, hospitals, and fiscal problems) and 225–252 (determining parish poor).

[43] Quotations from, Fryer, *Staying Power,* pp. 191–207, 538–541; Stephen J Braidwood, 'Initiatives and Organisation of the Black Poor 1786–1787,' Paper presented at International Conference on the History of Blacks in Britain, London, 28–30 September 1981; Ottobah Cugoano, *Thoughts and Sentiments on the Evil and Wicked Traffic of the Slavery and Commerce of the Human Species ...* (London: T. Beckett, 1787), p. 142; Norma Myers, *Reconstructing the Black Past: Blacks in Britain, 1780–1830* (Liverpool: University of Liverpool, 1990), pp. 10, 23–26, 51–53, 89–97, 127–139.

[44] Dyson (collator), *A Book Containing all such Proclamations,* pp. 1–6, 84, 276, 300, 324, 356 ('sturdy beggars'); Queen Elizabeth I, *Proclamation Against Idlers and Vagrants in London. 15 Feb 1601* (London: Barker, 1601), passim; Stow, *The Chronicles* (1615), pp. 325, 327, 328, 671, 769; A. L. Beier, *Masterless Men: The Vagrancy Problem in England 1560–1640* (London: Methuen, 1985), pp. 29–51, 69–86, 123–146; and Browner, 'The wrong side of the river,' p. 42 ('12,000').

[45] Kenneth Little, *Negroes in Britain* (London: Routledge, Kegan Paul, 1947), p. 187; Fryer, *Staying Power* (1984), pp. 1, 5, 8 , 9; Kim Hall, *Things of Darkness: Economies of Race and Gender in Early Modern England* (1995, 2nd edition, New York: Cornell University Press, 1996), p. 211; Gustav Ungerer, 'The Presence of Africans in Elizabethan England and the performance of *Titus Andronicus,* at Burley-on-the-Hill, 1595–96,' *Medieval Renaissance Drama in England Annual,* Volume 21, 2008, pp. 19–56; and Gustav Ungerer, *The Mediterranean Apprenticeship of British Slavery* (Madrid: Verbum Editorial, 2008), p. 76.

[46] Fraser, Vigne and Littleton (eds.), 'Slaves or Free people,' pp. 257, 254–261; and Author unknown, *A Forensic Dispute on the Legality of Enslaving Africans held at the Commencement in Cambridge New England, July 21, 1773* (Boston: John Boyle, 1773), p. 5 (quotations).

[47] Author unknown, Letter to the Lord Mayors, signed 18 July 1596.

[48] Suggested by Casper Van Senden and Thomas Sherley, 'Cecil Papers Petition, Merchant of Lubeck to the Queen,' *Calendar of the Manuscripts of the Most Honourable the Marquess of Salisbury* (London: Historical Manuscripts Commission, 1883–1976), Volume 10, p. 341 and Volume 14, p. 143; and Sherwood, 'Blacks in Elizabethan England,' pp. 40–42.

[49] Author unknown, Letter to Lord Mayors, signed 11 July 1596; Author unknown, Letter to the Lord Mayors signed 18 July 1596; and Author unknown, Proclamation ca 1601.

50 Senden, Sherley, 'Cecil Papers Petition, Merchant of Lubeck to the Queen,' Volume 14, p. 143; and Author unknown, Proclamation ca 1601.

51 Thomas Purfoot, *The Historical Discourse of Muley Hamet's ...* (London: Thomas Purfoot, 1609), pp. 71–73 (how to trade in Guinea); and Don Antonio, Federike Morell (tr.), *Psalmes of Confession, Found in the Cabinet of the Most Excellent King of Portingal, Don Antonio ... Written with his Owne Hand ...* (London: G. Bishop, R. Nuberie, R. Barker, 1596), n. p. passim.

52 Evidence in, Ungerer, *The Mediterranean Apprenticeship of British Slavery*, pp. 81, 84, 90; and Eric Ash, *Power, Knowledge, and Expertise in Elizabethan England* (Baltimore: John Hopkins University Press, 2004), pp. 124–130.

53 Stow, *The Chronicles* (1615), pp. 783, 795.

54 Author unknown, Letter to the Lord Mayors signed 18 July 1596; Author unknown, Proclamation ca 1601; and Sherwood, 'Blacks in Elizabethan England,' pp. 40–42.

55 Ash, *Power, Knowledge, and Expertise*, pp. 19, 20–21.

56 Robert Greene, *The Estate of English Fugitives under the King of Spain and his Ministers* (London: John Drawater, 1595), pp. 1–2; and Purfoot, *The Historical Discourse of Muley Hamet's Rising*, n. p. chapter xv.

57 Greene, *The Estate of English Fugitives under the King of Spain and his Ministers*, pp. 3, G1, G2, L2; and Author unknown, Letter to the Lord Mayors, signed 18 July 1596.

58 This same issue is discussed by Davies, *Elizabethans Errant. The Strange Fortunes of Sir Thomas Sherley*, pp. 7, 17, 188; and Greene, *The Estate of English Fugitives*, p. 3.

59 Author unknown, Proclamation ca 1601.

60 On the enforcement and status of proclamations see Rudolph W. Heinze, *The Proclamations of the Tudor Kings* (Cambridge: Cambridge University Press, 1976), pp. 250–293; and Frederick A. Youngs, *The Proclamations of the Tudor Queens* (Cambridge: Cambridge University Press, 1976), passim.

61 Dyson (collator), *A Book Containing all such Proclamations as were Published by the Reigine of the Late Queen Elizabeth 1559–1602*, pp. 1–6; and Kaufmann, 'Caspar Van Senden, Sir Thomas Sherley,' pp. 366–371.

62 Bartels has a similar view in 'Too many Blackamoors,' pp. 305–322.

63 Senden, Sherley, 'Cecil Papers Petition, Merchant of Lubeck to the Queen,' Volume 10, p. 431. Full text quoted in the bibliography.

64 Senden, Sherley, 'Cecil Papers Petition, Merchant of Lubeck to the Queen,' Volume 14, p. 143.

65 Ibid., p. 144.

66 Senden, Sherley, 'Cecil Papers Petition, Merchant of Lubeck to the Queen,' Volume 10, p. 399.

67 Quotations from the 1596 Letters; 1601 Proclamation; and Senden, Sherley, 'Cecil Papers Petition, Merchant of Lubeck to the Queen,' Volume 10, pp. 399, 431, Volume 14, p. 143.

68 Senden, Sherley, 'Petitions to Robert Cecil,' Volume 10, p. 108 (Garges), Volume 14, pp. 128–129 (embezzling), pp. 272 (Fanshaw), 277 (debts).

69 Senden, Sherley, 'Petitions to Robert Cecil,' Volume 14, p. 89.

70 Senden, Sherley, 'Petitions to Robert Cecil,' Volume 14, p. 154.

71 The quotations are from Davies, *Elizabethans Errant. The Strange Fortunes of Sir Thomas Sherley*, pp. 1, 188; and Kaufmann, 'Caspar Van Senden, Sir Thomas Sherley,' pp. 366–371.

72 Davies, *Elizabethans Errant. The Strange Fortunes of Sir Thomas Sherley*, pp. 1, 4, 188.

73 Evidence in, London: GL Ms 9243–9245, GL Ms 4310, GL Ms 9222; Author unknown, *St Martin in the Fields Parish Register*, Volume I (London: No publisher, 27 September 1571), p. 116; Plymouth and West Devon Record Office, Plymouth, St Andrews/MF1-4;

Devon Record Office, East Allington/20/08/1577 PR; and Northampton Records Office, Northampton, Microfiche 120, pp. 1–3.

[74] In St Botolph the white immigrants are about 53 %, and in Hart Street 51% of the total population, see, Richard Kirk and Ernest Kirk (eds.), *Returns of Aliens Dwelling in the City and Suburbs of London,* Volume I (Aberdeen, Huguenot Society, The Publications of the Society, 1900), pp. preface, xii; GL Ms 28867, GL Ms 9220, GL Ms 92221, GL Ms 9234; St Olave Hart Street GL Ms 28867; Author unknown, *St Botolph without Aldgate Memorandum Daybooks,* Volume I–VI (London: Parish of St Botolph without Aldgate, 1586–1603 etc), G. L. Ref P69/BOT2/ A/ 01/MS 9234/1–6. For a commentary on this see Luu, *Immigrants and the Industries of London, 1500–1700,* pp. 126–127.

[75] William Harrison, 'Description of England,' *Modern History Sourcebook,* http://www.fordham.edu/halsall/mod/1577harrison-england.html, accessed 10/09/2007; and Stow, *The Chronicles* (1615), p. 485.

[76] The last quote is from, Samuel Parsons Scott, *History of the Moorish Empire in Europe* (New York: Lippincott, 1904), p. 355.

[77] John Stubbs, *The Discoverie of a Gaping Gulf Whereinto England is Like to be Swallowed by an other French Marriage, if the Lord Forbid not the Banes, by Letting her Maiestie see the Sin and Punishment Thereof* (London: H. Singleton, 1579), pp. 30, 31.

[78] Edward Coke, *The Famous Case of Robert Calvin a Scots-man; as Contain'd in the Reports of Sir E. Coke ... as it was Argued in Westminster-Hall...* (Edinburgh: James Watson, 1705), n. p. passim.

[79] See Author unknown, *A Declaration of Great Troubles Pretended Against the Realme a Number of Seminaries, Priests and Jesuits, Sent and very Secretly Dispersed in the Same, that Work Great Treasons under a False Pretence of Religion ...* (London: Christopher Barker, 1600), p. 96.

[80] Stow, *A Summary of the Chronicles of England* (1598), pp. 768–769 (on Stubbs); Stubbs, *The Discoverie of a Gaping Gulf,* n. p. hand written note, inside leaf, dated 1581; John Stubbs, *The Gaping Gulf with Letter and other Relevant Documents* (1968, new edition, Charlottesville: The University Press of Virginia, 1978), p. 114; Elizabeth I, *A Proclamation Against Stubs, 'Gaping Gulf' 27 Sept. 1579* (London: Christopher Barker, 1579), n. p. passim. A longer discussion on nationalism in Tudor England is contained in the Conclusion.

[81] Coke, *The Famous Case of Robert Calvin,* n. p. passim.

[82] Stubbs, *The Discoverie of a Gaping Gulf,* pp. 4, 32, 35, 42, (Nevertheless, Stubbs makes the qualification that England should not make the mistake of Spain, where the 'Turke and his Saracens [a term that may include Africans] ... [made] war within the Nation.')

[83] Although Senden and Sherley's petitions written in 1600 suggests any Africans they can find are 'strange,' see Senden, Sherley, 'Cecil Papers Petition, no 151, Merchant of Lubeck to the Queen,' Volume 10, pp. 399, 431 and Volume 14, p. 143.

[84] Spicer, Goose and Luu (eds.), *Immigrants in Tudor and Early Stuart England,* pp. 57–72.

[85] Fraser, Vigne and Littleton (eds.), 'Slaves or Free people,' pp. 254–261; William Shakespeare, *Titus Andronicus* in Richard Proudfoot, Ann Thompson and David Scott Kastan (eds.), The Arden Shakespeare Complete Works (Walton on Thames: Thomas Nelson and Sons, 1998), Act II, Scene I, Line 517–525, p. 1130 (although I acknowledge the play is set in Ancient Rome, and a persuasive interpretation is that Aaron had overreached his status). On African men and white English women in Tudor England see Richard Hakluyt, *The Principal Navigations,* p. 359; Richard Eden, *Decades of the Newe World ...* (London: Richard Jug, 1555), p. 176; and Best, A True Discourse, pp. 28–32.

[86] Marye's record is at the Plymouth and West Devon Record Office, St Andrews/ June 23/1603 MF 1-4, 'Register of St Andrews,' p. 110; and Habib, *Black Lives,* pp. 115, 116, 136,

333; Other evidence is at GL Ms 28867, GL Ms 9243-9245, GL Ms 4310, GL Ms 9222; Plymouth and West Devon Record Office, Plymouth, St Andrews/MF1-4; Kim Hall, 'Object into Object, Some thoughts on the Presence of Black Women in Early Modern Culture,' pp. 346-380, in Peter Erickson and Clarke Hulse (eds.), *Early Modern Visual Culture: Representation, Race, Empire in Renaissance England* (Philadelphia: University Press, 2000); George Monger, *Marriage Customs of the World: From Henna to Honeymoons* (Santa Barbara: ABC CLIO, 2004), p. 173; George Bourne, *Slavery Illustrated in its Effects on Women and Domestic Society* (Boston: Issac Knapp, 1837), pp. 7, 33-45, 64, 101, 111, 124, 127; and Race is not listed as a bar in Tudor marriage ceremonies: Vivien Brodsky-Elliott, 'Single women in the London Marriage market: Age status and mobility, 1598 -1619,' *Studies in the Social Mobility of Marriage* (London: RB Outhwaite,1981), pp. 81-100.

[87] Leon Higginbotham, *In the Matter of Colour* ... (1978, new edition, New York: Oxford University Press, 1980), pp. 320-329; Author unknown, *A Forensic Dispute on the Legality of Enslaving Africans held ... in Cambridge New England July 21, 1773*, pp. 1-16; and William Blackstone, John Frederick Archbold, John Taylor Coleridge, et. al. *Commentaries on the Laws of England* (1765, new edition, London: GW Childs, 1867), pp. 332-335.

[88] Author unknown, Proclamation ca 1601; Including those in London: GL Ms 28867, GL Ms 9243-9245, GL Ms 4310, GL Ms 9222; Plymouth and West Devon Record Office, Plymouth, St Andrews/MF1-4, Original record: St Andrews/October 4/1596/MF1-4; and James Walvin, *Black and White: The Negro and English Society* (London: Allen Lane and the Penguin Press, 1973), p. 9 (believes Africans were not all 'infidels' but for different reasons).

[89] The following contain a summary and comments on the legislation, Beier, *The Problem of the Poor*, pp. 1, 39-42, appendix; Styles, *The Poor Law*, preface; Paul Slack, *The English Poor Law, 1531-1732* (Basingstoke: Macmillan Education, 1990), pp. 9-21, 41-48, 51-57.

[90] Author unknown, *An Ease for Overseers of the Poore, Abstracted from the Statutes* (Cambridge: Publisher unknown, 1601), passim; John Downame, *A Plea of the Poore, or a Treatise of Beneficence and Almes-Deeds: Teaching How These Christian Duties Are Rightly to be Performed* (London: E. Griffin for R. Tubbe, 1616), passim. On Tudor poor relief see, Marjorie Keniston McIntosh, *Poor Relief in England, 1350-1600* (New York: Cambridge University Press, 2011), passim; and Steve Hindle, *On the Parish?: The Micro-Politics of Poor Relief in Rural England, c. 1550-1750* (Oxford: Clarendon, 2004), pp. 1-92, 103-104, 259 (on John Downame).

[91] Case: *In the Matter of Cartwright*, 11 Elizabeth, 2 Rushworth's College (1569), p. 468.

[92] Case: *Somersett's Case, R. v. Knowles, ex parte Somersett*, 20 State Tr (1772), p. 1; Case: *Shanley v Harvey*, 2 Eden (1763), pp. 126, 127; also discussed in Onyeka, 'Diversity in Early Modern Britain Podcasts,' *The Historical Association*, http://www.history.org.uk/resources/secondary_resource_4714.html, accessed 05/06/12.

[93] Quoted in, Higginbotham, *In the Matter of Colour*, pp. 320-329; and Dabydeen and Gilmore (eds.), *The Oxford Companion to Black British History*, pp. 401, 402.

[94] David Brion Davis, has a similar view in, *The Problem of Slavery in the Age of Revolution, 1770-1823* (1975, new edition, New York: Oxford University Press, 1999), pp. 472-473.

[95] National Archives, Kew, London, *The Court of Chancery Legal Records*, Req2 /164/17; Roslyn L Knutson, 'A Caliban in St.Mildred Poultry,' *Shakespeare and Cultural Traditions* (Delaware: University Press, 1994), pp. 114-116; and Habib, *Black Lives*, pp. 313-314.

[96] This view raises complex issues but is shared by Alison Sim, *Masters and Servants in Tudor England* (Stroud: Sutton, 2006), passim; Norma Pilbeam and Ian Nelson (eds.), *The Poor Law Records of Mid Sussex, 1601-1835* (Lewes: Sussex Record Services, 2001), pp. 4, 5; Fraser, Vigne and Littleton (eds.), 'Slaves or Free people,' pp. 254-261; John Baker, '*Personal Liberty under the Common Law of England, 1200-1600*,' *The Origins of Modern Freedom in the West* (Stanford: Stanford University Press, 1995), pp. 178-202. But I acknowledge that a

kind of 'slavery' was imposed on some vagrants as a punishment and this is discussed later in this chapter.

[97] Naomi Tadmor, *The Social Universe of the English Bible: Scripture, Society and Culture in Early Modern England* (Cambridge: Cambridge University Press, 2010), pp. 82–106, 113–114, 169.

[98] This is suggested by Senden in, Senden and Sherley, 'Cecil Papers Petition, Merchant of Lubeck to the Queen,' Volume 10, pp. 399, 431, Volume 14, p. 143; Dabydeen and Gilmore (eds.), *The Oxford Companion to Black British History*, p. 146; and B. J. Sokol, *Shakespeare and Tolerance* (Cambridge: Cambridge University Press, 2008), pp. 120–121, 142–174.

[99] The phrase 'securely lodged,' is from Walvin, *Black and White*, p. 8.

[100] The idea of the 'dumb subaltern' is a widely discussed issue in Gayatri Chakravorty Spivak, 'Can the subaltern speak?' in Cary Nelson and Lawrence Grossberg (eds.), *Marxism and the Interpretation of Culture* (Urbana: University of Illinois Press, 1988), pp. 271–313.

[101] The phrase 'innocent' is used several times to describe Moriana's knowledge of her employer's intentions, in National Archives, Kew, London, *Early Chancery Proceedings* (ECP), C1/148/67; and Alwyn Ruddock, *Italian Merchants and Shipping in Southampton 1270–1600* (Southampton: University College, 1951), pp. 126–127, 138.

[102] Ibid.; Fraser, Vigne and Littleton (eds.), 'Slaves or Free people,' pp. 254–261.

[103] Ibid. pp. 257, 254–261.

[104] William Harrison, 'Description of Elizabethan England,' Chapter 1, *Modern History Sourcebook*.

[105] Norma Pilbeam and Ian Nelson (eds.), *The Poor Law Records of Mid Sussex, 1601–1835* (Lewes: Sussex Record Services, 2001), pp. 4, 5.

[106] Author unknown, *An Ease for Overseers of the Poore*, pp. 23–25 (definitions of 'impotent' and 'sturdy'), 38 (both quotations).

[107] Pilbeam and Nelson (eds.), *The Poor Law Records*, pp. 4, 5; and A. L. Beier, 'Poverty and Progress in Early Modern England,' in, A. L. Beier and David Cannadine and James R. Rosenheim (eds.), *The First Modern Society: Essays in English History in Honour of Lawrence Stone* (Cambridge: Cambridge University Press, 1989), pp. 201–241.

[108] Similar views are expressed by Fraser, in, Vigne and Littleton (eds.), 'Slaves or Free people, the status of Africans in England 1550–1750,' pp. 257–258. On the legislation about African slavery see, Blackstone, Archbold, Coleridge, et. al. *Commentaries on the Laws of England*, pp. 92, 334–335, 455; and Peter Davis (ed.), *William Looney, Victorian Naval Surgeon*, http://www.pdavis.nl/Legislation.htm accessed 03/03/09.

[109] Author unknown, *An Ease for Overseers of the Poore*, pp. A3 (how to administer relief), 10–11(conscience and discretion), 13 (without 'malice').

[110] Parker, Henry (ed.), *D. Pauper. End. Here Endeth a Compendyouse Treatyse Dyalogue of D. and Pauper. That is to Saye, the Riche the Poore ...* (London: Wyken de Worde, 1496. New edition, London: Thomas Bertheleti, 1536), p. 1 says the rich and poor are both made in the 'image' and 'likeness of God' and neither should be punished for their economic status, pp. 1–11 but criminal vagrants should be punished.

[111] Pilbeam and Nelson (eds.), *The Poor Law Records of Mid Sussex*, pp. 4, 5; Beier, 'Poverty and Progress in Early Modern England,' pp. 201–241; and Browner, 'The wrong side of the river,' passim.

[112] Fraser, Vigne and Littleton (eds.), 'Slaves or Free people,' pp. 257–258; and suggested in Boorde, *The First Boke of the Introduction of Knowledge*, pp. 88–89.

[113] Blackstone, Archbold, Coleridge, et. al. *Commentaries on the Laws of England*, pp. 92, 334–335, 455; and Peter Davis (ed.), *William Looney, Victorian Naval Surgeon*, http://www.pdavis.nl/Legislation.htm accessed 03/03/09 (legislation on slavery).

[114] The quotation is from Henrie Gregoire, *On the Slave Trade and on the Slavery of the Blacks and of the Whites, by a Friend of Men of All Colours* ... (London: Josiah Conder, 1815), p. 60; and Fryer, *Staying Power*, pp. 67-113; and for more on this see Onyeka, *The Black Equestrians: The African Gentlemen of Georgian England* (London: Narrative Eye, 2014), passim.

[115] These matters are explored by Onyeka, in, 'Diversity in Early Modern Britain Podcasts,' *The Historical Association;* and Onyeka, *The Black Equestrians,* passim.

[116] Quotations from Edward Coke, *The Lord Coke his Speech and Charge. With a Discouerie of the Abuses and Corruption of Officers* ... (London: Nathaniell Butter, 1607), pp. 52-55. On Coke, Anderson, and Dyer see Allen Boyer, *Sir Edward Coke and the Elizabethan Age* (London: Stanford University Press, 2003), pp. 99-300; and John Baker, 'Human Rights and the Rule of Law in Renaissance England,' *Northwestern Journal of International Human Rights,* Volume 2, Spring, 2004, www.law.northwestern.edu/journals/jihr/v2/3/ accessed 10/01/13.

[117] Quotations from the 1596 Letters; 1601 Proclamation; and Senden, Sherley, 'Cecil Papers Petition, Merchant of Lubeck to the Queen,' Volume 10, pp. 399, 431, Volume 14, p. 143.

[118] On the abhorrence and 'fear' of arbitrary power in the late Tudor period see Malcolm Smuts, *Culture and Power in Tudor England, 1585-1685* (Basingstoke: Macmillan, 1999), pp. 76-78.

[119] Senden, Sherley, 'Cecil Papers Petition, Merchant of Lubeck to the Queen,' 29 November 1600, Volume 10, p. 399; and Edward Coke, *Le Necessarie vse & Fruit de les Pleadings, Conteine en le lieur de le Tresreuerend Edward Coke, Lattorney General la Roigne...* (London: Thomas Wight, 1601), passim.

[120] Boyer, *Sir Edward Coke and the Elizabethan Age,* pp. 99-300; Coke, *The Lord Coke his Speech and Charge,* pp. 52-55 (quotations); and Coke, *Le Necessarie verse & Fruit de les Pleadings,* passim.

[121] Quotations from Senden, Sherley, 'Cecil Papers Petition, Merchant of Lubeck to the Queen,' Volume 10, pp. 399, 431 and Volume 14, p. 143.

[122] Quotations from Senden, Sherley, 'Cecil Papers Petition, no 151, Merchant of Lubeck to the Queen,' Volume 14, p. 143.

[123] Robert Lemon, *Calendar of State Papers, Domestic Series, of the Reigns of ... Elizabeth ...* Volume 4 (London: Record Office, 1856-72), p. 410.

[124] Senden, Sherley, 'Cecil Papers Petition, Merchant of Lubeck to the Queen,' Volume 10, pp. 102-103.

[125] Hawkins, *Declaration of the Troublesome Voyage,* pp. 1, 2 (quotations); and Author unknown, *A Declaration of the Demeanour, and Carriage of Walter Raleigh Knight as well ...* (London: Bonham Norton and John Bull, 1618), pp. 2, 19.

[126] Davies, *Elizabethans Errant,* pp. 44, 62, 119, 118.

[127] Evidence in: Senden, Sherley, 'Cecil Papers Petition,' Volume 10, pp. 399, 431 and Volume 14, p. 143. This view is shared by Davies, *Elizabethans Errant,* p. 3.

[128] National Archives, Kew, London, *High Courts of Admiralty (HCA) Reports,* 1547, Ref. 24/39/49-51.

[129] Ibid.; Senden, Sherley, 'Cecil Papers Petition,' Volume 10, pp. 399, 431 and Volume 14, p. 143.

[130] Charles Howard, *A Declaration of the Causes Moving the Queen Majesty ... to ... Send a Navy to the Seas for the Defence of her Realms ...* (London: Christopher Barker, 1596), pp. 1-6; Stow, *The Chronicles* (1615), pp. 747-748; and Walter Thomas Rogers (ed.), Scheltco Geveren, *Of the End of this World, and Second Coming of Christ ...* (London: Henrie Middleton, 1583), pp. 13, 57.

[131] Stow, *The Chronicles*, (1615), p. 748; Rogers (ed.), Scheltco Geveren, *Of the End of this World, and Second Coming of Christ*, pp. 21, 32, 43–44, 53, 57; and Author unknown, *A Packe of Spanish Lies Sent Abroad in the World: First Printed in Spain, in the Spanish Tongue, and Translated out of the Original. Now Ripped Up, Unfolded, and by Just Examination Condemned, as Containing False, Corrupt and Detestable Wares, Worthy to be Damned and Burned* (London: Christopher Barker, 1588), preface.

[132] John Hawkins, Will 6 June 1595, PRO Prob11/94 fols 100–105, quoted in Kelsey, *Sir John Hawkins*, p. 258.

[133] Don Antonio, Federike Morell (tr.), *Psalmes of Confession, Found in the Cabinet of the Most Excellent King of Portingal*, pp. A3, B4, B10, B11.

[134] Suggested by Kelsey in, *Sir John Hawkins*, p. 263.

[135] Rogers (ed.), Geveren, *Of the End of this World, and Second Coming of Christ*, pp. 1–8, 18, 22, 24.

[136] Quotation from Senden, Sherley, 'Cecil Papers Petition,' Volume 10, p. 431. Dabydeen suggests she had 'moral squeamishness,' Dabydeen and Gilmore (eds.), *The Oxford Companion to Black British History*, pp. 144–145.

[137] Suggested in Kelsey, *Sir John Hawkins*, p. 4.

[138] Best, *A True Discourse*, pp. 16, 28–32, 'Fithe Chapter.'

[139] Catherine F. Patterson, 'Town and City Government,' in, Robert Tittler and Norman Jones (eds.), *Companion to Tudor Britain* (Oxford: Wiley, Blackwell), pp. 116–133; and William George Hoskins, 'English Provincial Towns in the Sixteenth-Century,' *Transactions of the Royal Historical Association*, 5th Series, 6, 1956, pp. 1–19. Stephen Alford suggests this quest for independence began much earlier with some servants with skills escaping their servile obligations in towns, 'Urban Safe Houses for the Unfree in Medieval England: A reconsideration,' *Slavery and Abolition*, 32, Issue 3, September 2011, pp. 363–375.

[140] Richard Britnell, 'The Economy of British Towns 1300–1540,' in, D. M. Palliser, *The Cambridge Urban History of Britain: c. 600–c.1540*, Volume I (Cambridge: Cambridge University Press, 2000), pp. 313–333; and Britnell, 'Town Life,'in Rosemary Horrox (ed.), *A Social History of England 1200–1500* (Cambridge: Cambridge University Press, 2006), pp. 134–178: 152–163 (Commercialism and urban culture).

[141] Senden, Sherley, 'Cecil Papers Petition, no 151, Merchant of Lubeck to the Queen,' Volume 14, p. 143.

[142] Evidence in, Habib, *Black Lives*, pp. 274–326; Dabydeen and Gilmore (eds.), *The Oxford Companion to Black British History*, pp. 145–146; Gustav Ungerer, 'Recovering a black African's voice in an English lawsuit: Jacques Francis and the salvage operations of the *Mary Rose* and the *Sancta Maria* and *Sanctus Edwardus*, 1545–ca 1550,' *Medieval and Renaissance Drama in England, Annual 2005*, http://findarticles.com/p/articles/mi_6723/is_17/ai_n28529708 accessed 12/03/06 and Author unknown, 'Black Settlers in Tudor Times,' *National Archives*, http://www.nationalarchives.gov.uk/pathways/blackhistory/early_times/settlers.htm accessed 11/03/06.

[143] Janet Arnold, *Queen Elizabeth's Wardrobe Unlocked ...* (Leeds: Maney, 1988), p. 106.

[144] GL Ms 9234/6 (Mary Fillis); Susan Cerasano, *Medieval and Renaissance Drama in England*, Volume 20 (New York: Fairleigh Dickinson University Press, 2003), p. 81; Plymouth and West Devon Record Office, St Andrews/December 10/1583/MF1–4 (Bastien); and Plymouth and West Devon Record Office, St Andrews/March 11/1591/ MF 1–4 (Cabrew).

[145] Fortunatus' reference is below. Phyllis Margaret Handover, *The Second Cecil: The Rise to Power 1563–1604 of Sir Robert Cecil Later First Earl of Salisbury* (London: Eyre & Spottiswoode, 1959), n. p. preface; and Earl of Leicester, *Copies of Letters to the Right Honourable Earl of Leicester* (London: Christopher Barker, 1586), pp. 1–9.

[146] Elizabeth I, *The History of the Life and Reign of ... Queen Elizabeth I ...* (London: Publisher unknown, 1739), p. 287; and Robert Cecil, *An Answer to Certaine Scandalous Papers ...* (London: Thomas Basson, 1606), n. p. preface.

[147] City of Westminster Archives Centre, London, 1601/2 January/21/St Clements Dane/Volume 1 Burials/MF 1.

[148] Similar views are expressed by Higginbotham, *In the Matter of Colour*, pp. 21, 320–329; and William Blackstone, John Frederick Archbold, John Taylor Coleridge, et. al. *Commentaries on the Laws of England* (1765, new edition, London: G. W. Childs, 1867), pp. 332–335. Other historians offer a different view in Davis, *The Problem of Slavery in the Age of Revolution, 1770–1823*, pp. 472–473; Don Jordan, Michael Walsh, *White Cargo, The Forgotten History of Britain's White Slaves in America* (New York: New York University Press, 2008), n. p. preface.

CHAPTER 2

How Africans were described in Tudor England

This chapter discusses a number of complex and convoluted issues such as the meaning of the words used to describe the race and ethnic origins of Africans in Tudor England. As stated throughout this book, I use the word 'African' to refer to people who are not just born in Africa, but also those who have a direct African ancestry.[1] However, I am aware that using the word African in this way raises important issues that have not yet been addressed. The most important of which concerns why the same 'kindes of people' in Tudor documents such as parish records are referred to as 'Blackamoores,' 'Blacks,' 'Moors,' 'Negroes' ('Negars,' 'Negras,' 'Negyers,' 'Neygers,'[2] 'Nigers,' 'Nigros') and 'Ethiopians' ('Aethopians').[3] Another issue is that Africans are an ethnically diverse set of people, and many historians such as the eminent Cheikh Anta Diop, and others such as Mary Lefkwich claim that the people referred to as 'Moors' in Tudor documents are not 'dark skinned' or 'black Africans'[4] and in this chapter I challenge this idea.

The information in this chapter also seeks to resolve some of the issues caused by modern interpretations of words such as 'Moor' and 'Negro' in current versions of *The Oxford English Dictionary* and the *Oxford Dictionary of English*.[5] By resolving some of these issues it is intended that this will later help the reader to follow my arguments about the origins of Africans in Tudor England. In other words by knowing who these Africans are enables us to see more clearly where they may have come from.

Another important issue that has emerged is that in Tudor England, the words Blackamoore, Moor, Negro and Ethiopian did not automatically describe people who were considered as the prime example of otherness. I propose that key evidence contained in Tudor parish records, letters, and books written at the time shows that Africans were more familiar to people in Tudor England than historians such as Peter Fryer and Emily Carroll Bartels suggest.[6] In this view I stand against not only Fryer and Bartels, but a significant number of other historians who have written about Africans in early modern England. These writers propose that in Tudor society the blackness of Africans was automatically regarded as negative, and this meant they were thought of as strange in that society.[7] Furthermore, Fryer and Bartels suggest that because words such as Moor and Ethiopian are associated with classical and medieval stories, some of which describe Africans as strange or fantastic, this proves that in Tudor England 'those kindes of people' were regarded in the same way. But I will show that there are also positive stories about Africans that Tudor writers could and did refer to, and that these are likely to have neutralised any negative fantasies.[8]

The words used to describe Africans in Tudor England

Some Tudor writers use the word 'Blackamoore': a conjunction of the words 'Black' and 'Moor' to describe Africans.[9] This is confirmed by the books of Andrew Boorde, and John Pory's translations of Leo Africanus. Moreover, these words written as 'Black a Moor' or 'Blackamoore' were commonly used by Tudor writers such as George Best to describe Africans living in Tudor England.[10] These words can be found in the parish record of 'Cornelius Blacke a More,' who was buried on 2 March 1593/4 at St Margaret's Lee, Deptford, London.[11] The conjoined word Blackamoore is also used in a significant number of other parish records such as in Susan's baptism, on 1 July 1596 at St Andrew's Plymouth, where she is described as a 'daughter of a Blackmoore' and the same derivatives of this word are also used in the Letters and the Proclamation.[12]

In Europe during the medieval and early modern period, however, the word 'Moor' could be used to describe Africans without the adjective 'Black.'[13] This is because the word Moor by itself means Black. As a result in books such as Minsheu's *Spanish Dictionarie*, the word 'Moor' is connected to the words: 'Mauros' from the Greek meaning Black, 'Maur' from the Latin meaning the same and another word 'Mudarra' which is used to describe Africans from Spain.[14] So the use of these words by sixteenth-century writers is not just a reflection of their inability to follow modern rules of grammar.[15] Rather, I suggest these words when used in parish records or other documents reflect the word Moor's linguistic and rich cultural heritage, and this is why it and its variants were used to describe Africans:[16] including dark-skinned or 'Black Africans' in Tudor England.[17]

However, Elliot Percival Skinner, Nabil Matar and Joseph Greenberg suggest that the word Moor was not used in this way,[18] and their views seem to be supported by anthropological statements by UNESCO.[19] But Tudor writers such as John Pory and Edward Blount define the word 'Moor' quite differently; they use it interchangeably with 'Blackamoore.' This same approach is followed in Minsheu's *Dictionary,* where he uses the colour 'Black' to define and describe who Moors are: 'Moro – a blacke Moore of Barberie or a Neager ... Moronez – a blackish swartie colour.'[20] I suggest that this seems to have been a standard approach for using these terms even up to the eighteenth century, and can be seen in the revised edition of Samuel Johnson's *Dictionary*, where he writes, '(... Maupos [(Greek)], Niger, More ...) A Negro a blackamoor.'[21] In these examples, these words all describe Africans and emphasise the 'blackness' of their complexion. This same approach is adopted by a significant number of other books and documents written in Tudor England.[22]

In Tudor England being Black in complexion appears to be the prime qualification for being described as a Moor. However, some of the references in *The Oxford English Dictionary* and arguments from writers such as Bartels, suggests that in Tudor England people who were called Moors were also automatically Muslims.[23] Evidence in some Tudor documents appears to support this notion. For example the 1601 Proclamation states that the Blackamoores in England have 'no understanding of Christ and his gospels' and this may mean that they follow any religion other than Christianity. In addition, Boorde claims that Moors are 'infydels and unchritened' and that they 'do kepemuche of Maconites lawe as the Turkes do,'[24] whilst Minsheu's *Dictionary* defines Africans as: 'Moro – a blacke Moore ... that followeth the Turkish religion [Islam] ...'[25]

Boorde and Minsheu do not state, however, that Moors have to be Muslims, but merely that they may be.[26] This is supported by evidence in Tudor parish records, where Africans who are Christians are also described as Moors and Blackamoores. For example as with Julyane aged 22 who was christened on the 29 March 1601 at St Mary Bothaw London, and who is referred to as a 'blackamore servant.'[27] And this is an idea which seems to have been generally agreed upon in the early-seventeenth century, and can be seen in the marriage record of James Curres. He is identified as 'beinge a Moore Christian,' when he married 'Margaret Person a maid,' on 24 December 1617 in the church at the parish of Holy Trinity in London.[28] These records indicate that in the sixteenth- and early-seventeenth centuries the words Moor and Blackamoore could be used to describe Africans no matter what religion they are. The Moorish writer Leo Africanus corroborates this, when he states that there are Moors of the Muslim, Christian, Jewish and the Animist persuasions.[29] In this respect the words Moor and Blackamoore are both similar to another word 'Negro,' which is also used to describe Africans in Tudor parish records and the subsidy rolls.[30]

Some of these subsidy roll records where Africans are described as 'Negroes' appear in Kirk and Kirk's *Return of Aliens*. These records reveal

Africans living in Tudor England and include those for 'Clar' who is described as 'a Negra at Widdows Stokes.' Another woman called 'Maria' is also referred to as 'a Negra at Olyver Skynners,' whilst another person called 'Lewse' is called 'a Negro at Mitons.' Finally, a fourth known as 'Marea or Mary' is noted as 'a Negra at Mr Woodes.' All of these Africans were taxed as Aliens and were present in the parish of Tower Ward, London, on 1 October 1598. One year later, Clar and Marea were still there recorded in a similar way and still taxed as Aliens. Nevertheless, Maria and Lewse do not appear in these latter records and this may be because they ceased being registered as Aliens, had left the parish or died – although at present I cannot confirm this.[31]

The word 'Negro' as used in the records above seems to have a different meaning to that offered in some modern publications such as *The Oxford Dictionary of English,* where it says that the words 'Negro' and 'Niger' (below), only defines those Africans who come from West Africa.[32] However, in Tudor England, the word Negro was interchangeable with others such as Blackamoore, Moor and Ethiopian and could describe Africans from all over Africa and in the Diaspora.[33] For example, the explorer John Lok certainly uses the word 'Negro' to describe the West Africans who he brought to England in 1555. But he also uses the word 'Blackamoore' as well.[34] This same pattern is followed in the work of writers such as Best, Boorde, Caelius Augustinus Curio and Minsheu and is also acknowledged by the early-twentieth-century scholar J.A. Rogers, and the modern historian William Wright.[35] Nevertheless, though the words Blackamoore, Moor and Ethiopian were interchangeable with Negro, by the end of the sixteenth century and into the seventeenth the term Negro was used more frequently. This can be seen in parish records already mentioned in this book, and also includes one for Grace who was buried on 13 July 1590 at St Olave Hart Street, London. In her record she is described as 'a negro out of Doctor Hector's.'[36] The reasons for the increase in the use of the word Negro are complicated but may relate to the origin of this word.

The word Negro originates from the Latin word Niger meaning Black. The term Niger was used before the term Negro to describe Africans in England and this may be one reason why the word Negro only later became popular.[37] As Richard Eden the Tudor writer and traveller and Ben Jonson (1575) the dramatist say, the words 'Niger' and 'Nigrite' describe Africans who are now 'called ... Negroes and are the blackest in the world.' Similar phrases are found in translated versions of *A Notable Historie of the Saracens* by the sixteenth-century Italian Curio.[38] So in Tudor times, the word Negro was a 'new' word that only gained popularity in England as the older word Niger became unfashionable. Perhaps this was because of increased Spanish and Portuguese influence on English culture as revealed by the popularity of Minsheu's *Spanish Dictionaire*.[39]

Another word that is often associated with Negro and Moor in Tudor documents is Barbary. However, when the word Barbary and its derivatives such as Barbarian are used it is not always clear whether it refers to where a person is from, or something else about their ethnicity. For example, in the baptismal record for 'Lambert Waterson' dated between 20 March and 30 July 1568 at St Giles in the Fields London, he is described as a 'barbaryen.'[40] But in Lambert's record it also says he 'goeth to his parish church,' so in a similar way to James Curres (above), Lambert is probably an active Christian. This may indicate that the word 'barbaryen' used in his record is probably not a reference to his religion but indicates something else about his ethnicity. Boorde supports this idea when he uses the word 'Barbary' to describe where 'a blake More' is 'borne.' He says in 'Barbary ... the inhabytors ther be called Mores.'[41] These comments imply that the word 'Barbary' could describe where an African is from and 'barbaryen' could describe an African. This is supported by historians such as Ivan Van Sertima who quotes from the classical works of Pliny and Herodotus.[42] However, this issue is more complex as Curio states that the word Barbary only describes specific areas within North Africa.[43] Nevertheless, other contemporary evidence from writers such as Best and Pory's translation of Leo Africanus suggests that by the middle of the sixteenth century the word Barbary could refer to various parts of West Africa and elsewhere. A similar view on this issue is expressed by other historians including Habib and Sherwood.[44]

As well as the word Barbary, the word Ethiopian is sometimes used in conjunction with the word Moor to describe Africans in Tudor documents.[45] However, in those documents, the word 'Ethiopian' is used quite differently to how it is in some modern texts such as *The Oxford English Dictionary* and *Oxford Dictionary of English*. These texts sometimes quote misleading ideas about this word that originate from information published by UNESCO in 1972. This is that there are different types of Africans, such as 'Hamites ... Forest Negroes, [and] Bantu speaking Negroes' and the term Ethiopian is now only applied to 'Hamites.'[46] But in medieval and Tudor England, the term Ethiopian could be used to describe all Africans, and this probably comes from its classical Greek origins where it referred to all of 'those kindes of people,' not just natives 'or national[s] of Ethiopia or ... person[s] of [direct] Ethiopian descent.' It is used in this way in the record of Bartholomew who is described as an 'Ethiopian' twice in the *Patent Rolls* of 1259.[47] The reason why the word 'Ethiopian' has been included in Bartholomew's record is to emphasise his blackness. As we have seen in the sixteenth century a similar approach is adopted when the words Black and Moor are used together in the word Blackamoore. However, in Bartholomew's record he is also described as a 'Saracen,' and it appears that in medieval England the word 'Saracen' was also capable of describing Africans as it does in the *Flores Historiarum*,[48] where it describes an African also known as the 'Ipswich Man' who was buried in Grey Friar's monastery in the thirteenth century, (more about the scientific evidence that confirms this man's ethnicity can be seen in the research of Professor Sue Black).[49]

Therefore there were a number of terms medieval writers used to describe Africans; some of these terms such as Saracen were not often used by Tudor writers to refer to 'those kindes of people.' But in Tudor England the word Ethiopian retained its popular use, for example in 1501 when the Tudor politician and writer Thomas More describes the Africans who came to England with Katherine of Aragon, he says they were 'barefoot pygmy ... Ethiopians,' and in 1578 George Best uses the word 'Ethiopian' to describe Africans living in Tudor parishes.[50] The term is also used in the parish record of an African woman called Maria Mandula who was buried in Colne in Wiltshire on 10 December 1585 and is referred to as an 'Aethiopo.'[51] And the Tudor writer Barnabe Rich, translating from the Greek historian Herodotus in 1584 uses the same word to describe Africans. Moreover, in Minsheu's *Dictionary* it says, '[a] Negrillo – [is] a little black More somewhat blacke, [a] Negro ... [is] also a blacke Moore of Ethiopia ... Negror,' and Pory does the same.[52] A similar idea is also present in Jonson's *Masque of Blackness,* where the river 'Niger' is 'presented in human form' and described as 'a forme and color of an Aethiope his hare and rare beard curled.'[53]

These sorts of descriptions of Africans as Ethiopians, Moors, Blackamoores, Negroes and Nigers are to be found in a significant number of English documents dating from the sixteenth to the early-seventeenth centuries. I suggest that the evidence on this matter is overwhelming,[54] but this does not resolve all the issues about the words that are used to describe Africans in Tudor England. One of these issues is expressed by Kim Hall and it is that Africans in Tudor England were considered as the epitome of otherness because of how they are described.[55] I examine this idea in the rest of this chapter.

Africans in Tudor England and their otherness

The issue of otherness in Tudor society is a widely discussed matter in books by historians, linguists, anthropologists and other academics. Nevertheless, as a word, 'otherness' does not appear in Tudor documents, rather it is something that may be inferred when Tudor writers use terms such as 'strangeness,' 'foreign,' 'enemy alien' or propose that a person is inherently inferior.[56] In many ways this chapter continues the discussion begun in Chapter 1. In that chapter, I quoted comments made by Thomas Sherley (elder) and the slave trader Casper Van Senden in 1600, which suggest that Africans were the epitome of otherness when they say that 'all the blackamoors in England are regarded but only for the strangeness of their nation and not for service to the Queen.'[57] This comment and others in the Letters and the Proclamation imply that some people in Tudor England believed Africans should be treated as if they were inherently inferior. But as I stated in Chapter 1 the Letters and the Proclamation failed, and this is likely to illustrate that the words 'blackamore,' 'neger' and 'black' despite being used in these documents to suggest otherness did not automatically prove Africans were seen in that way.[58]

The writer of the Proclamation and the Letters, however, is not the first to attach ideas of otherness to his descriptions of Africans present in England. A medieval English monk called Richard Devizes makes comments about Africans which resemble those made in the Letters and the Proclamation. In his *Chronicle ... Concerning Richard the First, King of England* written between 1192 and 1198 he says:

> When you reach England if you come to London pass through it quickly, for I do not at all like that city. All sorts [kinds] of men crowd together there from every country under the heavens. Each race brings its own vices and its own customs to the city [*omne hominium genus in ilam conflict ex omni nations que sub celo est*] ... You will meet with ... braggarts ... the number of parasites is infinite. Actors, jesters, smooth skinned lads, Moors [*Garamantes*], flatterers, pretty boys, effeminates, pederasts, singing and dancing girls, quacks, belly dancers [*crissarie*], sorceresses [*phitonisee*], [*vultuariae magi*] ['black magicians'] ... all this tribe fill all the houses.[59]

Devizes' image of medieval London, with Africans in it, echoes that offered of Tudor London by the writers of the Letters and the Proclamation. Devizes' words also reveal a startling and important idea as we have a twelfth-century writer suggesting that Africans are present in London as a social problem, and are a significant, visible, recognisable part of its under-class – since in Devizes' text the only ethnic or racial group that is specifically mentioned is 'Garamantes' or Africans. This may suggest that they are significant enough in numbers to be specifically identified as part of that social decay. However, Africans may also be included in the phrases 'all kinds of men,' and 'from every country under the heavens.'[60] The last phrase implies that the people he is talking about are not native-born. But Devizes does not state which nations these Africans have come from or whether they are 'lately come.' Perhaps Devizes' lack of clarification on the origins of these Africans may mean that he does not want to confuse or mislead his audience unlike the drafters of the 1601 Proclamation.[61]

Furthermore, Devizes' description of twelfth-century London is so similar to that offered in the Letters and the Proclamation of Tudor London, that it might illustrate an underlying idea in English thought about how Africans should be seen. This is illustrated by the language that Devizes uses such as 'crowd together,' or 'come together,' 'braggarts, parasites,' 'quacks ... sorceresses ... magicians,' and suggests that there are groups of people of which Africans are a part, who are moral degenerates, religious heretics or pagans and that they are not only visually different but are also culturally so. In the Letters and the Proclamation similar language is used to describe Africans when they are accused of 'all ready [being] here to manie,' that there are 'great Numbers of Negroes and blackamoors,' and that 'most of them are infidels having no understanding of Christ or his gospels,' or as Sherley remarks Africans in Tudor England are known for their 'strangeness.'[62] The difference is that in these Tudor documents groups of Africans are being portrayed as the source of the problem, whereas in Devizes' description Africans are merely part of a greater social decay.[63]

There are other texts which are even more likely to have influenced how Tudor writers describe Africans who were 'living amongst' them. These writers do not talk about Africans in England as Devizes does, but they do talk about 'blacknesse' and describe the continent of Africa. One of them is an early- seventeenth-century translation by the Englishman Philemon Holland of the Roman writer Pliny's work. Pliny's books, whether in Latin or English were popular in Tudor times and in his work some Africans are described as 'strange' and 'fantastic,'[64] because they have 'no heads,' are 'satyrs' or 'limber-legged,' and are accused of 'moving their members [genitals]' as a greeting. Furthermore, Pliny describes an African king with 'an eye in the middle of his forehead' and says in Africa, fairies often appear in the 'shape of men and women but vanish soone away like fantasticall illusions,' and that there is 'a river that can turn black men white [and vice-versa].'[65] These sorts of ideas are likely to have inspired similar ones in Pory's translation of Leo Africanus, and those in Richard Eden's *The Decades of the New World* published in 1555. Eden's book is one of the first to be widely distributed in Tudor England which has detailed descriptions of Africa. The question I will be considering is whether because these sorts of books were read in Tudor England this means that ideas about the otherness of Africans were widely believed.[66]

The 'curse of Ham'

Best and a priest called Meredith Hanmer are two Tudor Englishmen who appear to have been influenced by some of these ideas. Let us examine Best first. His notions about Africans show a mixture of religious myths and classical fables and in a similar way to Africanus and Pliny he claims 'all these Moores which are in Africa' are descended from a 'black ... Chus:' who was a son of Ham. But Best takes this idea further by saying that Chus was 'cursed' and born 'black and loathsome' through a 'blot of infection of blood,' that 'can not [now] be cured.' According to Best, this blackness is a sign of Chus' 'disobedience to God.' But Pliny and Africanus do not state that all Africans are 'cursed,'[67] so Best seems to be conflating, and mixing contradictory ideas about the blackness of Africans to make sense of how 'those kindes of people' keep their complexion in England's 'clime.' This makes his comments confusing, but also very important because he is talking about Africans living in Tudor England.

Best's ideas about the blackness of Africans being caused by a 'curse' would seem to classify them as perpetually inferior and the epitome of otherness. But I will suggest that his comments reveal that Tudor writers did not have a systematically negative racial policy regarding Africans. Best says that the original Man as he 'manifestly and plainely appeareth by Holy Scripture ... [was] white, and their wives also, by course of nature should have begotten and brought forth white children.' As a Christian following this theory of religious monogenesis, Best believes that all human beings were descended from one couple or family. Therefore, the racial origin and appearance of that family would not only show what the prophets looked like, but also be representative of the appearance of God, since in the Bible the original Man is made in the image of God.[68] So on one hand Best's ideas suggest that the colour of African people makes them the epitome of otherness, but in a contradictory way he is also saying 'those kindes of people' do come from the original family.

In one version of the story of the 'curse of Ham,' the curse is bestowed on Ham by his father Noah, because the former had carnal knowledge of his wife when God had forbidden it.[69] Hanmer expresses similar ideas and does use them to explain the blackness of Africans in Africa and elsewhere, but not to explain the complexion of 'those kindes of people' present in Tudor England. Hanmer obtained his doctorate of divinity from Oxford University and by April 1567 was Chaplin of Corpus Christi College. In 1581 he became vicar of St Leonards Church Shoreditch, and it is whilst there that he wrote and delivered his sermon on 2 October 1586.[70] It was published the same year and in it Hanmer refers to this 'curse'. Hanmer's sermon was given at the baptism of a man called Chinano who was aged 'about 40 years old' 'a Turke' born at Euboea in Negroponte.[71] This Chinano had been 'rescued' from Spanish slavery by Francis Drake, brought to England by him, and by 1586 the 'Turke' appears to have showed his willingness in Spanish, because he did not speak English to become a Christian.

In Hanmer's sermon he expresses how important Chinano's conversion to Christianity is, but then digresses to talk about Africans using terms such as 'Moor', 'Nigritae', 'Negro', 'Barbarian', and 'Saracen' to describe them. Hanmer says these Africans, as well as Arabians, Asians and 'Turkes' are all 'cursed' because they have received the 'cursed doctrine of Mahomet'. But he adds that the blackness of Africans shows that they 'are the progenie of Cham [who] ... Noe [Noah] cursed.'[72] So Hanmer's theory of Africans being twice 'cursed' comes from a misreading or misquoting of ideas present in the Bible – since it does not explicitly state there that Africans are the children of Ham. The idea that they are, probably originates from the way some Muslims interpreted the Quran in the Ottoman Empire.[73] And since these are all borrowed ideas and myths it is interesting that Hanmer a doctor of divinity is talking about them as if he believes them.

According to David Whitford, Hanmer and Best's ideas are symptomatic of the same kind of theories that in the eighteenth and nineteenth centuries were used to classify Africans as perpetually-inferior slaves, who were doomed to be 'hewers of wood' and 'drawers of water.'[74] However, I shall show that this analysis is not accurate and that in sixteenth-century England there was no such coherent system. For example, in the popular sixteenth-century *Thomas Matthew's Bible* Africans do not appear as the 'cursed children of Ham,' although it does depict Adam and Eve in the Garden of Eden and all the people in the Old Testament as white.[75] This is important and may show that in a different way to Best and Hanmer, the compilers of this Bible did not think that Africans were 'cursed,' although it may also indicate that they felt Africans were not part of the original family of mankind either. Perhaps, the compilers of the *Matthew's Bible* did not know where or how to include Africans and this may show that the writers considered Africans were other than original, but not necessarily the epitome of otherness.

The absence of images or words in the *Matthew's Bible* which corroborate Best and Hanmer's ideas may show that their notions were not shared by others in Tudor England. In fact I have not found evidence of other sixteenth-century English writers using the 'curse of Ham' myth to claim that Africans in England should be treated as inferior. Moreover, even Best does not propose as some eighteenth-century writers do that racial integration in England should stop, or that Africans should be removed from English soil.[76] This is also true of Hanmer who lived in London and is likely to have seen Africans who lived nearby in the parish of St Olave Hart Street, such as 'Isabell a blackamore' who was buried there on 6 June 1588.[77] But Hanmer does not aim his comments at Africans present in England, nor in fact does he even mention them at all.[78] Rather Hanmer is primarily talking about those Africans abroad who are in league with 'the Great Turke.' The motivation behind Hanmer's sermon seems in part to come from a desire to champion the cause of protestant Christianity, something which he was zealous in the pursuit of.[79] To emphasise that Hanmer's real focus is on religion and not race, we can see the way in the same sermon that he gives qualified praise for a nation of Africans who are under the authority of 'Prester John the great King of Aethiopia ... professeth the[ir] faith in Christ.' I say qualified praise because he later says these Africans do not practice Christianity as 'purely as it is to be wished.'[80] But Hanmer is not above praising non-Christian Africans as well, when he says:

> Nigros in the kingdom of Senega, [despite] being of the faith of Mahomet ... are not malicious neither stubbornly bent against the Christians: they are delighted with the behaviour of the Christians and [regard] ... our faith and religion to be holer and the better ... [81]

These comments by Hanmer raise a number of questions. The most important of which is whether he believes the Africans under the authority of Prester John are 'cursed' despite being Christians, and whether those in 'Senega' are also. The way he describes both sets of Africans seems to suggest that he does not. Moreover, the way he talks about the blackness of all these Africans seems to imply that he does not believe that it marks them as perpetual slaves, but rather as 'wandering sheep,' who need to become part of 'one sheepfolde' under Jesus Christ. This is an idea echoed in Samuel Purchas' work and that of other Tudor writers.[82] But there are also other possible reasons behind Hanmer's sermon, and these have got more to do with making money rather than evangelicalism. Hanmer admits in the same sermon that Englishmen are 'gredily bent to gete the earthly commodities of Affrike and Asia.'[83] The knowledge of what possible wealth could be secured from foreign expeditions was known to Hanmer as illustrated by his support for Drake.[84] Indeed, this sermon may be an attempt to provide religious propaganda to justify adventures in Africa and Asia.

This idea is supported by more evidence that we have about Hanmer's character and a bogus marriage that may directly relate to Chinano's baptism. The sixteenth- early- seventeenth-century historian Weever tells us Hanmer 'converted the brass of several ancient monuments into coin for his own use' and 'plucked up many plates fixed in the grave-stones, and left no memory of such as had been buried under them.'⁸⁵ Furthermore, in a legal case of 1584 regarding the Earl of Shrewsbury, Hanmer was called to give evidence and may have perjured himself for money. At the court case the recorder William Fleetwood says that Hanmer 'regardeth not an oath, surely he is a very bad man.'⁸⁶ And, there is evidence that 'Dr Hanmer vicar of Shoreditch married Richard Turke of Dartford, and Gertrude, the wife of John Wynd, without barns and licesse.'⁸⁷ The Richard Turke named in this marriage may be the baptised name for Chinano. But without more evidence it would be difficult to say. What is certain is that Hanmer was capable of committing fraud and telling lies to make money. The nineteenth- early-twentieth-century historian Henry Ellis goes further, and says that 'There is a great tradition among the inhabitants of Shoreditch that the doctor [Hanmer] committed suicide [because of his sins].'⁸⁸

So Hanmer's statements do not provide evidence of a coherent racial ideology that condemns Africans to slavery, rather his sermon should be seen in a similar way to Sherley's' petitions, and shows a man opportunistically seeking future pecuniary advancement. But, one can see how later English writers may have taken some of the ideas expressed by Best and Hanmer to justify discriminating against Africans.⁸⁹

However, in Tudor England there is little evidence of systematic racial discrimination against Africans. But that does not mean there are not negative ideas about blackness present in some Tudor books and plays. For example, in Minsheu's *Dictionary*, the words Negro and Niger are linked to the terms 'Negreguedo:' which means 'Blacked made blacke, Negr – disgraced unfortunate,' and another word 'Negromantio [meaning] – a worker of negromacy, Negror – blackness.' These terms imply that in Tudor England, the words Negro and Niger are also linked to death and 'black magic.'⁹⁰ A few of these ideas seem to have filtered into some popular fiction. African characters such as Othello, Aaron and Eleazar are mocked for using black magic.⁹¹ In the case of Othello his adversaries claim this is how he won Desdemona's love, although he proves that the only 'magic' he has used is his eloquence.⁹² But characters such as Aaron in *Titus Andronicus*, or Eleazar in *Lust's Dominion* do have a 'dangerous' sexuality and commit villainous acts under the auspices of some sort of 'black code' or magic: which may make their 'soul[s] black like [their] … face[s].' These sorts of ideas may show that for a Tudor audience an Africans' otherness was more than skin deep.⁹³

No matter how popular these plays were in Tudor England, however, the negative aspects of these portrayals do not seem to have led to Africans being treated as if they were 'cursed' simply because of the colour of their skin. For example, despite strong elements of xenophobia in the Letters, the Proclamation, and Stubbs' *Gaping Gulf* these documents do not mention this idea.[94] On the contrary, evidence discussed throughout this book suggests that ideas about Africans being foreign or strange would alter as people had contact with 'those kindes of people' in sixteenth-century England. This seems even more likely as there was no coherent system which categorised Africans as the epitome of otherness or automatically as enemies of the state.[95]

In other words, contact with Africans present in Tudor England may have encouraged some people including contemporary writers to never form, or reject the idea that Africans were the prime example of otherness. This kind of thinking may explain the comments of the well-known Tudor politician and writer Thomas More in *The First Boke,* written in 1528. More says 'it would be against reason' and 'nature' to state that it is not 'the heate [that] maketh his country blacke, and of lyke reason of other countries must make the[ir] people white.' In other words, 'what maketh Black men' was the Sun and not 'astronomy [magic or the stars].'[96] More is using the idea of heliotropism to make sense of the blackness of Africans. This theory is found in the classical works of writers such as Pliny, and in the seventeenth-century by English writers such as Francis Bacon and Thomas Browne and it is a concept that the blackness of Africans is caused by either extreme heat or sunlight.[97] But More seems to be rejecting the more fantastic aspects of heliotropism as told by the ancient Roman writer Ovid, that it was mystical or cataclysmic acts caused by the Sun god Phoebus' son Phaethon,[98] or 'manifold strange and wonderful forms' and 'curses,'[99] which caused Africans to acquire their complexion.

It is significant that Bacon and Browne follow the same pattern as More in rejecting the idea that magic causes the complexion of Africans.[100] Bacon says in 'the coloration of black and tawny Moors,' in *Novum Organum* (1620), that an African's skin tone is the result of 'heat' and 'moisture;'[101] whilst Browne says,

> ... men affirm the colour [of Africans] was a curse, I cannot make out the property of that name, it neither seeming so to them, nor reasonably unto us, for they take so much constent ... that they esteeme deformity by other colours, describing the Devil, and terrible objects white ...[102]

Browne is doing more than just say that the blackness of Africans does not make them 'cursed.' He is also saying that Africans have their own value system in which their blackness is not denigrated, but whiteness is. This is very significant not least because it shows a desire for a seventeenth-century Englishman to evaluate blackness through the eyes of Africans, but also because Browne believes that their views provide the definitive rebuttal of the 'curse of Ham' theory. Moreover, in a similar way to Higden and More, Browne never went to Africa,[103] and yet he is talking about Africans who he appears to know, in other words those present in seventeenth-century Europe.

In sixteenth-century England, More seems to share some of the ideas stated by Browne when he says that if an 'Inde ... never came out of hys country nor never had seen any white man or women in his life ... and [having seen only] innumerable black people [,] he might [think] that it were against nature of men to be white.'[104] More uses the term 'Inde' with the word 'black.' The former term arises from a belief that the people being described are 'infidels' and 'strange' – not that they owe their origin to India. In this way, the word 'Inde' can be used to convey a strong sense of otherness.[105] However, More's comments seem to suggest that he is attempting to make sense of blackness, without describing 'black people' as the epitome of otherness. Moreover, he seems to be speculating on how 'those kindes of people' see their own complexion. This way of looking at 'black people' may have been influenced by his contact with Africans, as twenty-seven years earlier in 1501, he saw Africans who came to England with Katherine of Aragon;[106] and he is also likely to have seen more Africans who were working and living in Tudor London.[107]

Others

The way More uses the terms 'Inde' and 'black,' raises more questions about otherness, as it is unclear whether these words distinguish between Africans and other non-white people. This way of referring to non-white people in a generic way is different to what other Tudor writers do. This can be seen with John Stow in his *Annales of England,* who describes the Native-Americans he saw in Bristol in 1502 quite differently from Africans.[108]

Other Tudor writers such as Best also seem to distinguish between Native-Americans and Africans,[109] as do recorders and clerks in Tudor parish records. But not only do these writers distinguish between Native-Americans and Africans, they also seem to describe the former as being more of an example of otherness than the latter, and this may be because Africans were more familiar to most Tudor writers than Native-Americans.[110] Moreover, although a few Native-Americans were integrated into Tudor society, many others seem to have lived apart from whites.[111] This includes those who the sixteenth-century European traveller Lupold von Wedel describes, came to England with Walter Raleigh in 1584. Their names were Wanchese and Manteo and although they were very useful to Walter Raleigh in his activities, they were described by Wedel and other contemporary writers as the epitome of otherness, and 'most childish and silly figure[s],' but also 'fierce and cruel.'[112]

The few Inuits present in Tudor England seemed to have been treated in a similar way. Some of these Inuit people who were also from North America were present in England in 1576/7. Two came with the English traveller Martin Frobisher when he returned from Baffin Island and their pictures were drawn by another Englishman John White (Figures 6 and 7). In those pictures and in the accounts written about them they were described as the epitome of otherness.[113]

It is not only by looking at Inuits and Native-Americans that we can understand how people in Tudor England regarded otherness. The way 'Egyptians' were treated and described also helps reveal how Tudor society looked at otherness. But there are complex issues related to this, as the word 'Gypsy' is a shortened version of the word Egyptian. Historians such as Paul Clarke use the word Gypsy to describe 'vagrants' or a people's 'way of life.' And both words Egyptian and Gypsy may refer to any set of people who have no fixed abode.[114] Notwithstanding this, the term 'Egyptian' was used in Tudor documents to identify people regarded as a social problem. Egyptians more than any other set of people had specific Acts of Parliament created to control them, the first being in 1511-12 in which they were described as a particular class of 'disorderly persons.' Specific legislation aimed at controlling or expelling Egyptians continued throughout the reign of Henry VIII and into that of Elizabeth I. In some later Vagrancy Acts they were incorporated into the general 'cozening' class, or fell under the Poor Law Acts passed during Elizabeth I's reign.[115]

Egyptians were legislated against in Tudor England in a way in which Africans were not, even though the language used in some of these laws resembles that in the Letters and the Proclamation. However, we saw how attempts in the Letters and Proclamation to classify Africans as a social problem did not succeed. But the measures against Egyptians did lead to their persecution, imprisonment, expulsion and execution, suggesting they were thought of as dangerous in a way that Africans were not.[116] This may have been underlined by an idea that many Egyptians viewed themselves, and wanted to be seen as part of independent nations that only happened to be within the geographical boundaries of England, Scotland, Wales and

Ireland. In this way Egyptians offered a very different and extremely dangerous kind of otherness,[117] an idea alluded to by writers such as David Mayall in *Gypsy Identities*.[118] Africans in Tudor England did not offer this type of dissident otherness, evidence in parish records shows that most appear to have been integrated members of their local parishes – not part of communities claiming to be independent nations.[119]

How Africans were not the epitome of otherness in Tudor England

The idea above underlines that Africans were not the epitome of otherness in Tudor society. Moreover, Africans were seen and spoken about more often in sixteenth-century England than other non-white people, and this may mean that 'those kindes of people' were familiar to people living in Tudor society. For example we find in recent research by William Ingram and Alan Nelson in the parish of St Saviour in Southwark, London an African named 'Reson' and described as 'a Blackmore.' The parish of St Saviour included parts of the Bishop of Winchester's diocese called the 'liberty of the clink.' This is where bear baiting, theatrical productions and prostitution were known to take place. In this area known for moral permissiveness, it is not surprising bearing in mind what we discussed in Chapter 1, that in 1579 we find an African such as Reson living on the west side of the parish and recorded as the head of a household. We do not know what sex this person is, but we do know that this record was found in the *Token* books which were collected at Easter each year. Parishioners were invited to buy tokens and show they were members of their parishes. The heads of the households were recorded in the books. So it is significant that an African is recorded as head of a household in the area.[120]

However, this inclusion of Africans in some written Tudor records is not reflected in there being numerous images of Africans in English documents and books. For example, there are no pictures of Africans in any of the fifteenth- and sixteenth-century books I have mentioned in this chapter, including Boorde's *Introduction to the Book of Knowledge*,[121] and this is despite Boorde having images of other peoples such as Ottomans. The one contemporary book that does give positive representations of dark-skinned Africans is the *Degli Habiti*, by the Italian painter Cesare Vecellio (see Fig. 8).[122]

There are also images of Africans that show Tudor society did not inherit from its medieval past, an idea that 'those kindes of people' were automatically inferior. Some of these images show that Africans were familiar to people in medieval England and other representations imply that they had useful roles in that society. One of these representations is of an African man in the *Abbreviatio Domesday Book* (1241), and it is important because in a similar way to some Tudor images, the African is not portrayed as fantastic or strange. He appears in the section concerning the county of Derbyshire and he is dressed as a medieval artisan or tradesman and is looking upwards at the letter 'I.'[123]

In addition, there is an image of an African man in Westminster Abbey in St Faith's Chapel. This image dates from circa 1250 when Nicholas Pevsner suggests the South Transcript of Westminster Abbey was constructed and is an image of a 'blackman's head.'[124] The African's head is one of a number of 'corbel' stone heads created to show a cross-section of medieval society. The stone heads consist of this African, a monk, a woman in a linen headdress and what appears to be a lord or merchant. Laura Kinsey, a researcher and press officer at Westminster Abbey, suggests that all four corbel heads were created from the likeness of 'people the master masons may have known or seen.'[125] If this is so, then this African may represent others who were part of an integrated population living in medieval London. Kinsey says that 'St Faith's chapel is part of Henry III's thirteenth-century church' and this would fit with other similar images of Africans created during the medieval period.[126]

These medieval images of Africans resemble those found in Tudor England such as John Blanke's on the *Westminster Tournament Roll*, which show Africans as members and not 'others' in English society. The ways in which some of these Africans interacted with the rest of Tudor society is also recorded in documents and books that I have been discussing throughout. However, sometimes it is difficult to know whether a writer such as Boorde is talking about Africans he has met in Tudor England, or he is referring to those from elsewhere.[127] But with the comments that some Tudor writers make it is clearer that they are talking about Africans present in Tudor society. For example this appears to be the case with some of the remarks in Richard Eden's *Decades of the New World,* which are the paraphrased statements of John Lok the English explorer made in 1555, and describe some African men who were 'brought' to England as being 'taule and strong men and could well agree with our meats and drinkes. [Even though] The cold and moist air dooth somewhat offend them.'[128] These comments suggest a familiarity with the Africans whom they describe: they are not fantastic – but are people who Lok knows are living in Tudor England. In Chapter 4 I discuss who these Africans could be. But what is important to discuss here is that Lok's comments are a contrast from the fantastic illusions stated earlier. Similar matters become apparent when we revisit Best's comments, and as I return to what he and another writer Hidgen says, we will discover more about the presence and status of Africans in Tudor England.

Best's comments on Africans in Tudor England are an attempt to make sense of 'those kindes of people' present in that society. He uses observation but also stories from the past to rationalise how Africans can keep their complexion in England's 'clime'. Best may well have read the medieval English writer Ranulphus Higden who does something similar in *Polychronicon*. This is especially as Caxton's 1480 publication of his work was widely available during the Tudor period as a source on history, science and geography.[129] Higden says, because 'the beame of the sun' consumes the 'humores' of the 'blacke men of Affrike [Africa]' they are Black and 'feynte in heart.' Higden's comments seem to suggest that if Africans went to 'the Northe partes' they would lose their complexion. Initially, this may suggest that Higden is implying Africans are foreign and an example of otherness because they only live in Africa where there is heat. But Higden never went to Africa, and yet he tells us he knows about the colour and temperament of Africans. This may mean he is describing Africans who live in Europe. My theory is supported by other comments that Higden makes on the complexion of Africans.[130]

Best in a similar way to Higden discusses a number of ideas about Africans which seem to suggest they are the epitome of otherness, but then he acknowledges that 'those kindes of people' are familiar enough for him to know them, and believes his audience will know them to. Of course, no matter how negative the comments of Best are, they tell us there is an African presence in sixteenth-century England. But Best takes this idea much further and very significantly admits that despite Africans being as 'black as cole' they can be 'native' to England.[131] Best is confirming what was said in the last chapter, which is that in Tudor England no laws existed which prevented Africans from being 'liege' or 'citizens.'

Best believes that racial integration and interracial relationships have created Africans who are 'native.' However, Best still explains the blackness of these Africans in negative ways. He says a 'faire [white] English woman' in a relationship with an African man 'begat[s] a sonne in all respects as blacke as the father was,' with the African 'expunging' the 'good white blood' of their spouse.[132] Evidence in parish records confirms that interracial marriages took place in Tudor England. This is evident in a burial record from St George's Parish, Bristol in 1603. It contains an entry for 'Joane Pontying the wife of Thomas Pontying being a Blackamoore, now buried on the xiii(?) day of the plague (September).' The word 'Blackamoore' may relate to Joane as she is the one being buried, but it is more likely to refer to Thomas as these terms were usually juxtaposed next to the name of the person.[133] This record describes the relationship between an African man and a white woman. It may reveal what Best has already told us that marriages between African men and white English women happened in Tudor England – although why we have found little evidence of this is difficult to ascertain. Perhaps, as I have suggested earlier, for some Tudor recorders noting the ethnicity of their subject may not have seemed important. This is especially likely for marriages, where the focus of Tudor priests was to record that a legal and religious contract had been agreed, and ensure that future children were legitimised.[134]

It is interesting, however, that Best offers no comments on African women having interracial relationships with white men although, as stated earlier, the unions between them and white Englishmen appear to have been more common. Furthermore, those Tudor priests and clerks who do record these unions, make no pejorative comments about the blackness of the children or the mother – although they do often note the child's illegitimacy. These priests and clerks also sometimes emphasise the children's Black complexion by referring to them as 'a black,' 'a negyer,' or 'a Blackamoor.' Other comments in these records about the mother's ethnicity imply that the children resemble their African mother more than the 'supposed' white father, or that the recorder is unsure who the 'real' father actually is. This latter point seems to be evident in an entry for Fortunatus. His baptism took place on 24 December 1594 at St Andrew's Plymouth. He is described as the 'son of a Negro of Thomas Kegwins, the supposed father being a Portugall.'[135] This is also true for Cristien who was baptised on 17 November 1594, at St Andrew's Plymouth, and who was a 'daughter of Mary, a negro of John Whites and the supposed daughter of John Kinge, a Dutchman, illeg.'[136]

Nevertheless, in the fictional and symbolic portrayal of interracial unions by Jonson in *The Masques of Blacknesse* and *Beautie* (1605), these relationships are described as providing opportunities for Africans to 'improve their colour' by 'washing' themselves white. Jonson in the *Masque* suggests that the 'daughters of Niger,' who are African women, can do this by engaging in unions with white men under the gaze of the King of England.[137] These sorts of ideas may explain why one Tudor priest noted on the baptism record of a child called 'Elizabeth,' that she was 'born white,' despite her mother being 'a negro.' The girl was baptised on 25 September 1586 at the parish of St Botolph Bishopsgate, London.[138] These notes written as part of Elizabeth's record describe what the recorder could see, her colour.[139] Perhaps Tudor writers were used to children being 'born black' from Blackamoore mothers, and that is why the writer in Elizabeth's record appears to have found it strange that this child was 'born white,' and it may be an interesting example of a recorder noting whiteness as being 'abnormal.' But, whether this 'abnormality' meant that this child was considered as inferior or superior to an African 'child born Black,' is unclear. Having said that, there are examples of stories told, written, and translated in Tudor England where whiteness is seen as strange. One of them is by Thomas Underdowne, called *An Æthiopian Historie*. Underdowne's work was written in 1569 and is a translation from the Ancient Greek writer Heliodorus. In this story the principal white character attempts to prove despite her whiteness that she is part of an Ethiopian royal family. As the historian Sujata Iyengar states, in this legend 'the aristocracy is black, and it is the white body which shows up as aberrant … cast out and ultimately subjected through battery and enslavement to control.'[140]

In other ancient and medieval stories, however, which were retold in Tudor England interracial relationships are described in a positive way.[141] The historian Benjamin Kedar suggests that in medieval Europe, some people believed that the interracial/intercultural marriages between white English men and 'Saracen' women offered an opportunity for all of 'God's children' to become 'one people,' and this idea is dramatically portrayed in *The Man of Law's Tale* and the Becket legend.[142] The Becket legend concerns Thomas Becket's mother being a Saracen/African woman.[143] Thomas Becket was Lord Chancellor of England and Archbishop of Canterbury until he was executed in the twelfth century. Upon his death he became a venerated martyr and saint as shown in Chaucer's *The Canterbury Tales* and other works written throughout the medieval and Tudor period. Therefore the twelfth-century story of Becket's mother – irrespective of whether it is true – shows that Englishmen in medieval times were willing to include Africans in their stories as wives and lovers.[144] These sorts of stories may also show why people in Tudor England never created legal or religious restrictions on interracial unions, and why such relationships occur in early modern fiction such as: *Othello, Lust's Dominion, Titus Andronicus* and *The Masque of Blackness*.

The medieval and Tudor stories in which Africans have interracial unions are important, because many of them were believed in Tudor times.[145] To illustrate this point, it is worth returning to the Becket legend, and evidence contained in the armorial crest of the Worshipful Company of Brewers. They received their royal charter from Henry VI in 1437. Evidence in Bromley's work suggests that because of the Brewers' 'loyalty to [the] St Thomas' story they carried the image of an African woman as their crest into the sixteenth century. In other words, the story of Becket's mother was the inspiration for their crest.[146] We shall see in the next chapter that this was not the only image of an African from medieval times which was used in Tudor England to represent a guild or livery company. The images of Africans decorating these livery companies would have created a striking impression on the streets of Tudor London.

On these same streets, these depictions would show to all of those who saw them, including resident or visiting Africans, that Africans had been present in England for a long time and that their blackness could be seen as positive. This kind of iconography becomes even more significant, because as stated earlier there was a dearth of visual images of 'those kindes of people.' This means that the crest of the Worshipful Company of Brewers may have been one of the more common and popular depictions of Africans that ordinary people in London saw.

The image of the African on the crest of the Worshipful Company of Brewers is an example of how 'those kindes of people' were more familiar than writers such as Barthelemy claim. I suggest that this familiarity meant that in records written in the sixteenth and early-seventeenth centuries it became less important to emphasise the 'blacknesse' or ethnicity of Africans living in a local parish, and that words such as Negro, Moor and 'barbary' were included as an after-thought. Let us return to the parish record of 'Lambert Waterson,' as it illustrates this point. He is described as a '(denizen) barbaryen, tenaunte of Gabriell Levesy, grocer, [who] goeth to his parish church, St Giles in the Fyldes.'[147] In Lambert's record there is a strong sense of otherness and familiarity recorded side by side. This is because earlier I said the word 'barbaryen' could describe an African, but it also has other meanings. It owes its origins to the Latin word: 'Barbarus' or 'Barbari' and has its roots in the Greek 'Barbaros.' Classical writers such as Pliny used these words to label anyone who was 'other than Greek or Roman.'[148] In Tudor society, the word 'barbaryen' was used to describe those people who Englishmen may have regarded as Aliens, foreigners or strangers. It is used in this way in *Othello,* when he is mocked by Iago and called a 'Barbary horse.'[149] However, in Lambert's case his apparent otherness is qualified by the fact that the word 'barbaryen' is juxtaposed with that of 'denizen' in parenthesis, and the latter means he is a settled Alien seeking citizenship.[150] Lambert is also the 'tenaunte of' a 'grocer' whom other parishioners may know, and 'he goeth to his parish church.' So Lambert is an integrated member of his parish, and is therefore less strange than the word 'barbaryen' at first implies.

Thus other Tudor priests because they lived with or near, met, saw or heard about Africans in their parishes were likely to have been affected by this contact as the priest in Lambert's case seems to have been. After all, some of these Africans gave birth to children of long-standing members of their community, and in that context it is doubtful whether they could be seen as the epitome of otherness as writers such as Barthelemy and Bartels suggest. As the historian Philippa Maddern states the idea of 'community' and 'belonging' in Tudor England was a broad concept which was used by:

> contemporaries when they discussed social relations ... from rural peasants to urban guilds to gentry-governed 'country communities' to towns and cities, people organised, or simply belonged to, collectives based upon something they held in common.[151]

Using this broad definition of community many of the Africans discussed throughout this book could be said to 'belong' to the 'communities' they were recorded in.[152]

Furthermore, this integration of Africans within Tudor society is likely to have meant that the terms and monikers used to describe these people's ethnicity may have lost their significance, been subject to summarisation and eventual deletion. For example in the record for 'Christian Ethiopia,' who was baptised on 18 March 1602 at St Dunstans and All Saints, Stepney, London, Christian is described 'as a daughter of a Blackmore.'[153] For the sake of brevity, Christian's ancestors could be expected to drop the descriptive phrase about being the descendant of 'a Blackmore.' Indeed, for her immediate descendants, their complexion and the word 'Ethiopia' would have been enough to highlight their African roots. But later on the meaning of why they were called 'Ethiopia' would probably be forgotten, especially if through integration with local white people they lost their colour.

In another set of English records in the first quarter of the seventeenth century we see evidence of this process. The records include one for Elizabeth, who is the daughter of an African called 'George.' He was married to Marie Smith at All Saints Church, Staplehurst, Kent, on 16 October 1616. In that record he is recorded as 'George a blackmore.' Six years later his daughter Elizabeth is baptised in the same parish church on 19 May 1622. This record says, 'Elizabeth blackamore D [daughter] of George 'the Blackamore.''[154] In this record the word 'Blackamore' that was once being used to describe George as an African is now being used as a last name by his daughter Elizabeth. This dropping of the 'a' in Elizabeth's record is unlikely to be the result of an intention to conceal her African heritage; as the inclusion of references to her father's race tells any reader where her name comes from and what it means.

Nevertheless, Elizabeth's records illustrate how the meaning of terms used to describe Africans in parish documents, over time could lose their meaning or be obscured. But I suggest this process did not begin in the seventeenth century but originated earlier in the sixteenth century when priests and clerks tried to standardise the way parish records were written.[155] Other records from different parts of the country illustrate this very point, and they include those for 'Henrie Anthony Jetto' and his family from the village of Holt in Worcestershire. His baptism records describe him as 'A Blackemore being 26 or year aboute ... baptised the 21 day of Marche ...' 1596.[156] In Henrie's record the word 'Jetto' is a moniker which refers to his blackness and the words 'A Blackemore,' refer to his race.[157] But later in the seventeenth century, in the Holt records which refer to Henrie and his family, the word 'Blackemore' has been dropped as a description of him, but 'Jetto' retained as a last name.[158] In Salisbury in Wiltshire a further record illustrates this process, where Elizabeth is described at her burial on 26 January 1653 as 'Elizabeth the Blackmore that lives[d] at white Hart;' but in the Bishops' transcripts written later in the seventeenth century this has been changed to 'Elizabeth blackmore [that] lives[d] at white hart.'[159]

It is possible that this practice of simplifying terms which describe the ethnicity of Africans may have been used in earlier Tudor records, such as the marriage record for 'Mr Blackmor and Sarah ffyson,' made on 9 June 1573 at St Mary Magdalene, Bermondsey, London. Or in the burial record of 'Wm. Blackmore' on 19 September 1573, at St Mary Magdalene, Bermondsey, London.[160] And that is why I have included a selection of these types of records in the bibliography; with the caveat that I know there may be other explanations for the use of these words in these particular records.

Nevertheless, the simplifying of descriptive terms relating to Africans may also explain some records where the people are described/named as a Moor who arrived from another country. For example such as 'Georgis de More of Ouldenor[?],' 'who is of no churche and came into this realme about V years ago to serve the said Giles Hoffingele.'[161] Giles Hoffingele was from Antwerp in Belgium but originated from Spain. From the evidence available so far it is not certain that Georgis was an African, but it is possible because a literal translation of his entry in the alien registers is 'Georgis the More of Ouldenor.' It is unlikely that 'More' is a reference to where he was from: Oudenaarde in Flanders; and the way that he is described is reminiscent of how Africans were, such as the character 'Othello the Moor of Venice.'[162] Georgis was employed as 'one of the servants to oversee and learne other men to winde and thirste the silk,' and the Moors were famous throughout Europe for being silk weavers.[163] On 10 November 1571, he was living in the Candlewick Street Ward of London and was noted in the subsidy rolls as an Alien. It is possible in a similar way to Elizabeth that twelve years later he may have shortened and anglicised his name to 'George More,' and be the 'silk weaver' living at St Olaves, Southwark London.[164] This may be for all the reasons stated above.

In the records for other people the words Niger and Negro can also describe that they are Africans. In some cases, these words seem to have gone through a similar process of transition from being used as descriptions to now being names. This makes it difficult to prove that all the people who J. A. Rogers lists with names such as 'Niger' and 'Negro' in *The World's Great Men of Colour,* or *Sex and Race* are Africans.[165] The same applies when similar names occur in Tudor records such as with 'John Baptist de Monte Nigro' who was present in London from 1538. This record is interesting because John is noted as a 'merchant stranger,' and the inclusion of the words 'de Monte' that are Spanish or Italian and mean 'mountain,' 'moat' or 'in the area of' may support an idea that he is from Spain or Portugal. But his name may also mean that he is from the Black Mountain or even Montenegro near Serbia.[166] This may imply that he is not an African, although, there appears to have been an African presence in Montenegro in the sixteenth century.[167]

In other examples, however, it seems clearer that the word Niger is being used to describe an African, although even here the descriptive term/epithet seems to have been included as an after-thought. This may be seen in the record for 'Thomas Bull niger,' who was a servant connected to the Old Eydon or Annesley Halls in Northamptonshire. He was buried on 16 December 1545.[168] The way the word 'Bull' and 'niger' are used in Thomas' record suggests that they are not just names but are also descriptions of his physical and racial appearance. In other words he is a 'Bull niger,' or a strong African – an idea supported by historians at the Northamptonshire Record Office.[169]

It is possible of course that names, monikers and descriptions used to describe Africans such as 'Thomas Bull niger' or 'Symon Valencia' 'a black A moore' may have been influenced by how Thomas or Symon wanted to be recorded; since, before a recorder listed the ethnicity of an African for a baptism or a marriage, they may have asked them about their identity and even how they wanted this to be described. Moreover, even some burial records echo how Africans defined themselves in their lives. As I discuss in the next two chapters, some Tudor parish records may reflect Africans' perception of themselves. This is because a significant number of 'those kindes of people' may have been born in England, and others came from countries where the people spoke languages which Tudor writers could have understood.

If some Africans in Tudor England were choosing the terms that were used to describe them, this would illustrate they had a sense of their own identity, and were not dumb subalterns – but also that they were not perpetually-inferior slaves, branded with racial epithets by their owners.[170] What is also likely is that some terms used in Tudor England were a mixture of those used by an African in their lifetime and others suggested by a recorder or employer after their death. This is a complicated issue because in most cases we do not have the written voice of Africans who lived in Tudor England to tell us how they saw themselves. So it is through what is written about them, that we must now infer how Africans may have seen their own identity. Furthermore, as Habib suggests the same descriptive term could be imposed on one subject and yet be chosen by another.[171] For example, the unnamed African who apparently nobody 'knew,' and who was buried in St Olave Hart Street, London on 29 June 1588, was simply called 'a man blacamore' who 'laye in the street.' This African, because we know that nobody 'knew' him, probably had the word 'blacamore' applied to his record posthumously, without reference to how he defined himself.[172]

However, other Africans coming to Tudor England from abroad may have carried their identity with them. For many of them, Blackamoore is used as a description of their ethnicity. This can be seen in the record of Symon Valencia who was '20 years old' when he was buried on 20 August 1593 at St Botolph without Aldgate, London. Symon was described as 'a black moore servaunt to Stephen Drifyeld a nedellmaker.'[173] In Symon's record although the term 'black moore' is used to describe him in his burial records, it is likely to echo how he saw himself while he lived, reflecting his own Spanish-Moorish origins. In other words, he was calling himself a 'moore' long before he reached Tudor England. This may also be true of 'Cassangoe,' buried on 8 October in 1593 in St Botolph without Aldgate, London, and who is described as 'a blacke A moore tenant to Mrs Barbor.'[174] This theory is explained in more detail in the next chapter, when I discuss other Africans present in Tudor England who come from continental Europe.

Furthermore, it is worth discussing another African whose Tudor record seems to reflect her identity before she came to England. This is the African woman Mary Fillis who was baptised on 3 June 1597 at St Botolph without Aldgate, London. She and her father 'Fillis' are both described in that entry as being 'of Morisco' and being 'black mores.' Mary has a detailed note in the *Memorandum Daybook for St Botolph without Aldgate*.[175] It is significant that in Spain and Portugal where the word Morisco originates, it was applied to all Africans who were baptised and incorporated into the Spanish state at the end of the sixteenth century.[176] But in Tudor England the term Morisco was only occasionally used to describe Africans. It is highly likely that Mary and her father had the description of 'Morisco' applied to them in Spain before they arrived in England, and that the inclusion of this word in church records, reflects ideas they already had about their identity, rather being a epithet imposed on them by an English recorder.

The different ways Africans such as Mary are described in parish records illustrates that they were more familiar to people in Tudor society than writers such as Fryer suggest. What also suggests this is the presence of Africans in some early modern plays and books. This is especially since Shakespeare, Marlowe and Jonson resided in places where Africans also lived.[177] I suggest that contact with Africans in England may have influenced why these writers sometimes include in their work positive comments about 'those kinds of people,' and in the remainder of this chapter, I will concentrate on other positive ideas and stories about Africans.

How stories of 'noble' Africans affected otherness

Stories that contain positive ideas about blackness, not as just a metaphor, but related to the skin complexion of Africans are found in biblical, Ancient Greek, Roman and medieval texts. They were then translated and retold in Tudor England. These stories portray Africans as virtuous and noble. The ideas of the 'blameless,' 'long lived' and 'mighty Ethiopians' are as much a part of Herodotus' work as their 'limberlegged' and 'fantastic' counterparts are a part of Pliny's.[178] In Herodotus' stories, Africans are sometimes shown as kings, queens, scientists and warriors within a classical world that includes Egypt and Ethiopia. These stories include the biblical legend quoted by the Tudor writer Samuel Purchas that Moses' wife was a 'Black Kushite' African, and that the kings of Ethiopia are descended from King Solomon and the Queen of Sheba.[179]

The same positive notions are present in the ancient idea believed in fifteenth- and sixteenth-century Europe, that one of the three kings who visited the infant Jesus was a youthful African Magi called Balthazar, who through his youth represents a new kind of Christianity. This idea is strongly represented in depictions of the *Adoration of the Magi* and can be seen in images in churches and paintings across Europe and in Tudor England.[180]

Other legends present in Tudor England contain ideas about a Black Virgin/Madonna. These legends appear to have had an effect on the way Africans were seen and described in Tudor England, even though some of these stories originated from Catholic European countries, where iconography played a more important role.[181] However, despite England's split from the Church of Rome in 1534, myths and legends about the Black Madonna are still found here.[182] This is present in Walter Thomas Rogers' book, *Second Coming of Christ,* written in 1583. Rogers was an Englishman whose book was a popular and well-known treatise on religion which was recommended by Stow in *The Chronicles,* and Rogers writes:

> The chaste daughter of Sion and beloved spouse of Jesus Christ ... thou art blacke and browne, by reason of the extreme heate of the Sunne ... For thy blacknesse by his holy spirite he hath turned into beautifulnesse and ... [your] unseeming spottes of sinne by his precious blood are now white ...[183]

The 'blacknesse' mentioned in this passage is symbolic, but it also relates to an actual African woman. This is the 'daughter of Sion' the 'beloved spouse of Jesus' who is 'blacke' because of the Sun. The idea proposed by Rogers offers an alternative view of beauty and divinity being white and is present in a number of early modern writers' work some of whom are discussed here; others are examined at length by the historian Iyengar. Iyengar outlines that this tradition may have been supported by passages in the Bible especially those contained in the psalms known as the *Song of Songs*.[184] But I suggest it also echoes medieval English and other European traditions of the Black Madonna. In some of those traditions the Black Madonna and the Moors who accompany her are defenders of virtue, chastity and divinity.[185]

Some of these traditions also include the Black Knight and Black Lady Days practised in sixteenth-century Scotland. In these events the King of Scotland symbolically dressed as a 'Black Knight,' and Africans such as Peter the Moryan or Morien were employed in planning these pageants and the activities associated with them,[186] whilst African women such as 'Elen More' and 'Black Margret' were engaged to play the 'Black Lady.' Although how the 'Black Lady' as a character became involved in the legends of the Black knights is still uncertain; writers such as Habib suggest that these characters were incorporated into pageants by James IV of Scotland, Henry VII, Henry VIII and James I as a result of European fashions.[187] However, I suggest that the ideas of Black knights were also strongly inspired by ancient legends of Saint Maurice the African Roman soldier who refused to kill Christians because of his faith;[188] and the medieval English legends which place Africans in Ancient Britannia and medieval society as representative members of England's equestrian-chivalric class.[189] These stories offer a stark contrast to any ideas of Africans automatically being part of an underclass or a social problem. These legends also offer an additional explanation as to why it was thought appropriate for some Africans such as John Blanke to have prominent positions in sixteenth-century English pageantry.[190]

Stories of Black knights also appear in several legends about King Arthur which were popular in Tudor times. This includes Thomas Malory's *La*

Morte d'Arthur, first published in 1469, and then republished in the reigns of Henry VII and Mary I in 1529 and 1557 respectively.[191] In another Arthurian legend called the *Romance of Morien* the title character is an African. In this story Morien represents the highest ideals of English medieval society and he is not the epitome of otherness, but virtue, dignity, honour and courage.[192] For a Tudor audience the stories of Africans such as Morien written in the thirteenth, fourteenth and fifteenth centuries would have shown that Africans were not outside of God's grace, and were capable of being divine representations of mankind. This idea forms a stark contrast to the notions that blackness was a 'curse,' and illustrates that in Tudor society there were ideas about Africans, which portrayed them as iconic symbols of grace and military prowess.[193] Perhaps Peter Morien who we mentioned earlier, who organised some of these pageants in sixteenth-century Scotland was known as 'Morien' or 'Moryan' as a moniker because it linked him to the *Romance of Morien*.[194] This may also be true for another person known as 'Mathias the Morian,' who was buried on 22 February 1602 at Salisbury Cathedral.[195]

There may be other Black knights present in Tudor England, who continued the equestrian and chivalric traditions of Morien. One of them according to Habib and Sherwood was a man called Sir Peter/Pedro Negro or 'Mogo.' Peter Negro was a knight, soldier, pirate, mercenary and landowner living in England in the sixteenth century.[196] He was employed by the English Privy Council from 1545 until his death in 1552.[197] However, Ungerer strongly states that Peter was not an African, whilst Kaufmann provides a more ambivalent perspective on this matter. Their arguments can be examined in more detail in their work.[198]

The underlying notion is that people in Tudor England may have inherited from Arthurian legends the belief that 'those kindes of people' could be noble knights and this may have helped them accept such people in their society. This premise relies on Englishmen in the sixteenth-century looking into their past, whether it was imagined, or real and believing the legends to be true. Having said that I acknowledge some medieval Englishmen such as Caxton and Chaucer were questioning whether all the Arthurian legends were true,[199] nevertheless, in Tudor England stories such as *Sir Gawain and the Green Knight, La Morte d' Arthur* and *The Romance of Morien* were part of the cultural heritage that inspired people in England. This is also true for Tudor monarchs and can be seen in the care that Henry VIII displayed with those manuscripts containing Arthurian legends that were given to Sir George Cotton in 1544.[200] Moreover, all social classes in Tudor England had access to, and were influenced by, Arthurian stories whether this was from manuscripts or stories that were told orally in ballads and songs. So this means that at the time these positive notions about Africans were widely known.[201]

Legends of Black knights and Rogers' comments also echo an idea discussed earlier, that the blackness of Africans could be more natural, 'pure,' 'unspotted' and divine than whiteness; and is to be preferred over the seemingly 'artificial' beauty of the 'white' 'whore of Babylon.'[202] Rogers' ideas show that not only in the classics read in Tudor England, but in treatises which were believed, some English people saw Africans as heroes. Moreover, I am willing to go further and suggest that the image of the 'daughter of Sion,' her blackness, and adult conversion to Christianity, provides a key to unlock the idea of the universality of the English Church. This is because the redeemed African woman present in Rogers' work is a gentile, whose conversion offers for all gentiles no matter what their colour, the example of redemption. In this way this African woman and others in the psalms are metaphors for the newly formed Anglican Church, which in a similar way is 'natural' and 'true.'[203] This explanation helps us to see why Rogers would begin his treatise on the *Second Coming of Christ* with an African woman, as she is a representation not only of her sex and race but of the English Church itself. Of course the idea that such a positive notion about Africans and their blackness could be present in Tudor England is challenged by modern historians such as Ean Begg and Regina Buccola. They suggest that the 'kind of blackness' stated in the *Second Coming of Christ* is only symbolic and has nothing to do with Africans.[204] But I suggest Rogers' use of iconic terms to describe his 'virgin' does not make her less of an African woman.[205]

Other writers in the Tudor period also appear to have used positive ideas about blackness drawn from notions present in the culture of that society, and then used this to inform their understanding of Africans they met, saw or heard about. Shakespeare seems to do this in his *Sonnet* 127 as George Bagshawe Harrison in *Shakespeare at Work* confirms. Harrison suggests that Shakespeare in all or some of the 'dark lady sonnets' from 127–154 is talking about blackness that is related to the complexion of Africans, and Ivan Sertima in at least three of his books agrees.[206] Their ideas are based on stories of a Lucy Negro who was otherwise known as Luce Morgan, Banthym or Baynam. These stories may also be related to that of 'the negress' of Clerkenwell who was a prostitute. The latter is referred to by the Tudor gentleman Dennis Edwards in his letter of 28 May 1599 to Thomas Lankford, where he says she works at an inn called the Swan in London. But other accounts by Harrison suggest she was employed at the Gray's Inn Tavern.[207] However, the consistent element in all these accounts is that Lucy Negro was an African woman living in Tudor London who had a sexual relationship with Shakespeare and other writers at the time. The story says that she later spurned Shakespeare's advances for a younger man, but not before giving him a sexual disease. These apologues are analysed in more detail by a number of other writers including Hugh Calvert.[208]

The important point is that Shakespeare's writings suggest that he had contact with Africans, and his *Sonnets* 127, 131 and 137 imply that blackness does not always have to be negative. Shakespeare writes, 'in the old age black was not counted fair.' But later in *Sonnet* 131 he states that blackness can be the 'fairest in my judgements place' and in *Sonnet* 137 that 'beauty herself is black.' Shakespeare is suggesting that although 'his' beauty has 'breasts dun [black or dark]' and her hair is 'black wires, [that] grow on her head,' she represents an alternative image of 'comeliness.'[209]

The idea that the blackness of Africans could be *superior* to whiteness is also evident in two poems written in the early modern period by Edward Lord Herbert of Cherbury. They are a *Sonnet of Black Beauty* and *Another Sonnet to Black Itself*. In them Herbert states that the 'hue' of 'Black people' contains the 'hidden power' of the cosmos, whilst in a third poem *To Her Face*, Herbert says, 'Sure Adam sinn'd not in this spotless Face.' Herbert is implying that whilst the original man was not Black, blackness may be purer than whiteness and free from 'original sin.'[210]

Conclusion

In Tudor England there are many terms used to describe Africans. The most common is Black used with Moor as two words, or as one to create Blackamoore. But other words include Moor by itself, Negro (Niger, Negyer, Negra) and Ethiopian (Aethiopian). Most of these words appear to originate from an interpretation of classical works, mixed with observational descriptions of African peoples' complexions. Some modern definitions of the words Blackamoor, Moor, Negro and Ethiopian include confusing and in some cases misleading connotations. One of these is the qualification that Moors or Blackamoores must be Muslims, when Tudor documents such as the 1601 Proclamation use the word 'Moor' to refer to all Africans irrespective of religion. The same principle applies to the modern qualifications that Moors must be from North Africa or that they are Arabs.[211] The word Arab was not used to describe Moors in Tudor England but the words Blackamoore, Black, Negro and Ethiopian were.[212]

Nevertheless, some of the terms associated with Africans in Tudor England are linked to geographical areas and these include the words Barbary and Morisco. These words could be used to explain where a particular African living in Tudor England was from. However, Gustav Ungerer suggests that terms such as Barbary and Blackamoore are deliberately being used in Tudor documents to obscure the origins of Africans present in England. He claims that an accurate record of an African's existence or origins may have highlighted the illegal activities of English merchants who brought them to the country. Habib and Paul Griffiths propose something similar.[213] Ungerer's theory may explain why some Africans are occasionally described without name, sex or place of birth, such as in the record for an African on 15 December 1567, at St Olaves Coleman Street, London. Here the individual is not named but is simply noted as 'Niger 1,' and this word marks that African's presence but nothing else.[214] A similar way of referring to Africans occurs in the Hopkins' letters mentioned earlier, and that of the *Bottomry* case, where the Africans described are simply noted in official court transcripts as a 'cargo of negroes.' This case was heard before the High Courts of Admiralty of England in 1600, and relates to how goods should be compensated in the result of financial loss.[215]

This does not mean however, that all the terms used to describe Africans in Tudor England were negative, pejorative or denied them personhood. Rather, some of the terms being used in parishes to describe Africans may reflect these people's own ideas of their identity. So in the absence of documents written by Africans in Tudor England which shows us how they saw their own identity and ethnicity, our reading of Tudor parish records may reveal that some of the words they contain may be self-generated, reflecting 'those kindes' of people's perceptions of themselves. This underlines that in Tudor England except for rare examples the terms being used to describe Africans do not label them as property.

Furthermore, the evidence suggests that Africans in Tudor society were the most visible and numerous non-white people in sixteenth-century England. And that Africans were more familiar to people in Tudor society than other non-white people such as Native-Americans or Inuits.[216] Moreover all of these non-white people may have been considered as less dangerous than white European Catholics after England became a Protestant nation. A writer such as John Stubbs helps us to understand this.[217] Pursuant to this the records that we have found so far suggest that most Africans were integrated into their local communities in a way that many white European immigrants were not. This seems to be reflected in how some of the terms, labels, names and epithets used in Tudor England to describe Africans could have changed over time or eventually disappeared. Those terms which are used to describe Africans in Tudor England tended not to be based on ideas that Africans were scientifically or linguistically inferior to white people.[218] Furthermore, even where mythical, religious or quasi-scientific theories such as the 'curse of Ham' are quoted by Best or Hanmer, this does not give rise to a systematic way of discriminating against Africans, but rather are used to answer questions arising from what some Englishmen have seen.[219]

This is probably because there were also positive ideas about Africans present in Tudor England. Some of these positive ideas originate from similar notions about the symbolic nature of blackness or come from stories and images of Africans from medieval England. They appear to have offered a more believable alternative to the fantastic and strange ideas also present in sixteenth-century England. It is probable that the presence of Africans in Tudor parishes would have further rationalised ordinary English people's perception of 'those kindes of people;' this view is supported by the fact that some of these Africans were born here, and they were not all immigrants, even though the 1601 Proclamation may suggest the contrary.[220] Some parish records overtly state the African is born in England, whilst others imply it such as with Frauncis the African servant to Peter Miller, that according to a certain reading of his parish record dated 3 March 1595 was 'dwelling at the signes of the hartes [and was] borne in the Libertie of East Smithfield.' However, Habib and the Guildhall Manuscripts team in London interpret the word 'borne' as 'horne' and relate it to the word that precedes it, in other words suggesting Peter was not born in England.[221]

There are also other Tudor baptismal records in which it can be inferred that those identified as Africans or the children of Africans were born in England. This includes that of Elizabeth mentioned earlier, where the description of her colour at birth infers that the recorder or someone close to the recorder has witnessed this in England. Or in an entry for William Harris who is noted as 'a blackamoor' at his christening, and is recorded as being 'baseborn' on 7 August in 1595 at St Margaret's Westminster, London.[222] This note about his status implies that the birth was recent and took place in England. The same could be said where baptismal entries say 'supposed' or 'reputed father,' for example as with the record of 'Richard son of Marye a Neger, base, ye reputed father Rog Hoggett.' Richard was baptised on 23 June in 1603, at St Andrew's Plymouth.[223] This example and other evidence similar to it suggests that the African population in Tudor England included a significant number of 'native' born, and this refutes the claim in the 1601 Proclamation that these 'kindes of people' are 'lately come.'[224] This is a theory that I examine in the next chapter.

Notes

[1] For a wider discussion on these matters beyond what is included here, please see Onyeka in, 'What's in a Name?,' *History Today*, 62: 10, 2012, pp. 34–39.

[2] In addition, other 'contemptuous' derivatives of the word Niger such as 'Nigger' were apparently not in use in Tudor England to describe Africans. The word 'Nigger' 'remains one of the most racially offensive [and derogatory] words in the [English] language,' *Oxford Dictionary of English*, p. 1189. In Tudor records it is absent even as an insult. This suggests it probably emerged much later through a bastardised use of 'Neyger' or 'Neger,' see Richard B. Moore, *The Name Negro its Origin and Evil Use* (Baltimore: Black Classic Press, 1960), pp. 16–18.

[3] George Best, *A True Discourse of the Late Voyages of Discovery ...* (London: H. Bynyman, 1578), pp. 28–32; and including evidence in: Guildhall Library, London, GL Ms 9243–9245, GL Ms 4310, GL Ms 9222. Similar issues are discussed in Mary Floyd Wilson, *English Ethnicity and Race in Early Modern Drama* (Cambridge: Cambridge University Press, 2003), pp. 1–13; and B. J. Sokol, *Shakespeare and Tolerance* (Cambridge: Cambridge University Press, 2008), pp. 113–115.

[4] Cheikh Anta Diop, in Ivan Van Sertima (ed.), *Golden Age of the Moor* (Piscataway: Transaction Publishers, 1992), p. 185; Mary Lefkowitz, *Black Athena Revisited* (Chapel Hill: University of North Carolina Press, 1996), pp. 113–120; John Gunther, *Inside Africa* (London: Hamish Hamilton, 1955), pp. 21–25; Elliott Percival Skinner, *Peoples and Cultures of Africa: An Anthropological Reader* (Washington: Natural History Press, 1972), pp. 61–63; Joseph Greenberg, *The Languages of Africa* (1963, 3rd edition, Bloomington: Hague by Mouton & Co., 1970), pp. 24, 42, 45; and Emily Bartels, *Speaking of the Moor: From Alcazar to Othello* (Philadelphia: University of Pennsylvania Press, 2008), pp. 1–7.

[5] *The Oxford English Dictionary* (London: Oxford University Press, 1998), pp. 49, 401, 1058; *Oxford Dictionary of English* (Oxford: Oxford University Press, 2nd edition 2003), pp. 1139, 1178; and *Chambers Dictionary of Etymology* (New York: Harrap Publishers, 1988), pp. 676, 699. But that does not mean that these same dictionaries have not provided important and significant links to primary sources that are used in this book.

[6] Evidence in, London: GL Ms 9243–9245, GL Ms 4310, GL Ms 9222; Author unknown, *St Martin in the Fields Parish Register,* Volume I (London: No publisher, 27 September 1571), p. 116; Plymouth and West Devon Record Office, Plymouth, St Andrews/MF1-4; Devon Record Office, East Allington/20/08/1577 PR; and Northampton Records Office, Northampton, Microfiche 120, pp. 1–3.

[7] Peter Fryer, *Staying Power: The History of Black People in Britain* (London: Pluto Press, 1984), pp. 135–146; Anthony Gerard Barthelemy, *Black Face, Maligned Race: The Representation of Blacks in English Drama from Shakespeare to Southerne* (London: Louisiana State University Press, 1987), pp. 77, 96, 98, 99, 111, 115, 116, 121, 124, 133, 166, 167; Emily Carroll Bartels, *Spectacles of Strangeness: Imperialism, Alienation, and Marlowe* (Philadelphia: University of Pennsylvania Press, 1993), n. p. introduction; Kim Hall, *Things of Darkness ...* (New York: Cornell University Press, 1996), pp. 13, 211; and Kenneth Little, *Negroes in Britain* (London: Routledge, Kegan Paul, 1947), p. 166.

[8] George Kirkpatrick Hunter, *Dramatic Identities and Cultural Tradition ...* (Liverpool: Liverpool University Press, 1978), p. 32 (has a different view).

[9] See, *The Oxford English Dictionary*, p. 1058.

[10] Andrew Boorde, *The First Boke of the Introduction of Knowledge The Whych Doth Teach a Man to Speake and Parte of All Maner of Languages and to Know the Vsage and Fashion of all Maner of Countries ... with Woodcuts* [images] (London: William Copeland,

1550), pp. 88–89; John Pory (tr.), Leo Africanus, *A Geographical Historie of Africa, Written in Arabicke and Italian ... by Iohn Leo a More* ... (London: John Pory, 1600), p. 6; George Best, *A True Discourse*, p. 28; and John Minsheu, *A Dictionarie in Spanish and English, First Published by R Percivale Now Enlarged by J Minsheu ... Hereunto is Annexed in Ample English Dictionarie with the Spanish Words Adjoined* (London: E Bollifaunt, 1599), p. 172.

11 Local History and Archives Centre, Lewisham, London, A78/18M/A1/1; Lewis Leland Duncan and Oswald Barron (eds.), *The Registers of all the Marriages, Christenings and Burials in the Church of St Margaret's Lee in the County of Kent, From 1579-1754* (Lee: C. North for Lewisham Antiquarian Society, 1888), p. 40.

12 Plymouth and West Devon Record Office, St Andrews/May 2/1593/MF1-4; Author unknown, Letter to Lord Mayors, signed Queen Elizabeth, National Archives, Kew, London, PC 2/21 p. 304, 11 July 1596; Author unknown, Letter signed Queen Elizabeth, National Archives, Kew, London, PC 2/21, f. 306, 18 July 1596; and Author unknown, Proclamation ca January 1601, National Archives, Kew, London, *Tudor Royal Proclamations*, 1601/804.5-805.

13 *The Oxford English Dictionary*, p. 1058; Minsheu, *A Dictionarie in Spanish and English*, pp. 172, 175; Pory (tr.), Africanus, *A Geographical Historie of Africa*, p. 6; and Rogers, *Nature Knows no Colour Line* (St Petersburg: Helga Rogers, 1952), pp. 78–82.

14 Minsheu, *A Dictionarie in Spanish and English*, p. 172; Boorde, *Introduction to the Book of Knowledge*, pp. 88–89; Pory (tr.), Africanus, *A Geographical Historie of Africa*, p. 6; and Edward Blount (tr.), Ieronimo Conestaggio, *The Historie of the Uniting of the Kingdom of Portugal to the Crowne of Castill ... The Description of Portugal, their Principal Townes, etc.* (London: A. Hatfield for E. Blount, 1600), pp. 1, 5, 7, 39.

15 On early modern English grammar see, David Cressy, *Literacy and the Social Order: Reading and Writing in Tudor and Stuart England* (Cambridge: Cambridge University Press, 2006), pp. 20–25, 56; Lynda Mugglestone (ed.), *The Oxford History of English* (Oxford: Oxford University Press, 2006), pp. 1–6, 121, 133, 139, 221; and Joan Simon, *Education and Society in Tudor England* (Cambridge: Cambridge University Press, 1979), pp. 76–77.

16 *The Oxford English Dictionary*, p. 1058; Minsheu, *A Dictionarie in Spanish and English*, pp. 172, 175; Pory (tr.), Africanus, *A Geographical Historie of Africa*, p. 6; and Rogers, *Nature Knows No Colour Line*, pp. 78–82.

17 Evidence in: London, GL Ms 9243-9245, GL Ms 4310, GL Ms 9222; Author unknown, *St Martin in the Fields Parish Register*, Volume I, p. 116; Plymouth and West Devon Record Office, Plymouth, St Andrews/MF1-4; Devon Record Office, East Allington/20/08/1577 PR; Northampton Records Office, Northampton, Microfiche 120, pp. 1–3; and Imtiaz Habib, *Black Lives in the English Archives* ... (London: Ashgate, 2008), pp. 274–334. For definitions of 'dark-skinned' see Molefi Asante and Ama Mazama (eds.), *The Encyclopedia of Black Studies* (2004, new edition, London: SAGE publications, 2005), p. 370.

18 Nabil Matar, *Islam in Britain, 1558–1685* (Cambridge: Cambridge University Press, 1998), p. 2; Skinner, *Peoples and Cultures of Africa*, pp. 61–63; and Greenberg, *The Languages of Africa*, pp. 24, 42, 45.

19 Though written forty years ago the following documents still express modern anthropologists views on race, Ashley Montagu (ed.), *UNESCO Statement on Race, An Annotated Elaboration and Exposition of the Four Statements on Race Issued by the United Nations Educational, Scientific, and Cultural Organization* (1st edition not known, 3rd edition, New York: Oxford University Press, 1972), p. 78.

20 Minsheu, *A Dictionarie in Spanish and English* (1599), p. 172; Pory (tr.), Africanus, *A Geographical Historie of Africa* (1600), p. 6; and Blount (tr.), Conestaggio, *The Historie of the Uniting of the Kingdom of Portugal* (1600), pp. 1, 5, 7, 39.

21 Samuel Johnson, *A Dictionary of the English Language* (1755, new edition, London: Longman Rees, 1827), p. 511.

22 Blount (tr.), Conestaggio, *The Historie of the Uniting of the Kingdom of Portugal*, pp. 10, 27, 39; Pory (tr.), Africanus, *A Geographical Historie of Africa*, p. 6. Similar views are offered in: Mythili Kaul, *Othello: New Essays by Black Writers* (Washington: Howard University Press, 1997), pp. 95-96; Ivan Van Sertima (ed.), *African Presence in Early Europe* (New Jersey: Transaction Publishers, 1985), pp. 12-15; Wilson, *English Ethnicity and Race in Early Modern Drama*, pp. 1-13; and *The Oxford English Dictionary*, p. 1058.

23 *The Oxford English Dictionary*, p. 134; and Bartels, *Speaking of the Moor*, pp. 1-15.

24 Author unknown, Proclamation ca January 1601; and Boorde, *Introduction to the Book of Knowledge*, p. 89.

25 Minsheu, *A Dictionarie in Spanish and English*, p. 172.

26 Ibid. and Boorde, *Introduction to ...*, pp. 88-89.

27 G. L. Registers of St Mary Bothaw, GL Ms 4310.

28 G. L. Registers of Holy Trinity the Less, GL Ms 9155.

29 Pory (tr.), Africanus, *A Geographical Historie of Africa*, pp. 6, 42; Shari Berke, Rick Gold, 'The Jews of Timbuktu,' *Washington Jewish Week*, 30 December, 1999. http://kulanu.org/timbuktu/JewsofTimbuktu.php, accessed 21/02/07; and implied by Roger Prior, in, 'Jewish Musicians at the Tudor Court,' *The Musical Quarterly*, 69: 2, Spring 1983, pp. 253-265.

30 Including records in: GL Ms 9243-9245, GL Ms 4310, GL Ms 9222; Author unknown, *St Martin in the Fields Parish Register*, Volume I (London: No publisher, 27 September 1571), p. 116; Plymouth and West Devon Record Office, Plymouth, St Andrews/MF1-4; Devon Record Office, East Allington/20/08/1577 PR; Northampton Records Office, Northampton, Microfiche 120, pp. 1-3; and Habib, *Black Lives*, pp. 274-334.

31 Kirk and Kirk (eds.), *Returns of Aliens Dwelling in the City and Suburbs of London*, Volume III, (1907), pp. 28, 54; Habib, *Black Lives*, p. 326.

32 *The Oxford English Dictionary*, pp. 49, 401; *Oxford Dictionary of English*, pp. 1178, 1189; and Chambers, *Dictionary of Etymology*, p. 699.

33 See, Norman Verrle MacCullough, *The Negro in English Literature* (Ilfracombe: A. Stockwell, 1962), pp. 23-47, 143-144; Richard B. Moore, *The Name Negro its Origin and Evil Use* (Baltimore: Black Classic Press, 1960), pp. 16-18; and Mike Sampson, 'Black burials and deaths 16th century' (Email), from Devon Record Office.

34 Richard Hakluyt, *The Principal Navigations, Voyages, Traffiques & Discoveries of the English Nation: made by Sea or Overland to the Remote and Farthest Distant Quarters of the Earth at any time within the Compass of these 1600 years* (1598, new edition, London: JM Dent and Sons, 1927), p. 131; and Peter Fraser, 'Slaves or Free people, the Africans in England 1550-1750,' in Randolph Vigne and Charles Littleton (eds.), *From Strangers to Citizens: The Integration of Immigrant Communities in Britain, Ireland, and Colonial America*, 1550-1750 (Eastbourne: Sussex Academic Press, 2001), pp. 254, 255.

35 George Best, *A True Discourse*, pp. 28-32; Andrew Boorde, *Introduction to the Book of Knowledge*, pp. 88-89; Caelius Augustinus Curio, *A Notable History of the Saracens ...* (London: William How and Abraham Veale, 1575), pp. 25-26; Minsheu, *A Dictionarie in Spanish and English*, pp. 172, 175; Ben Jonson, *The Character of Two Royall Masques, the One of Blacknesse. The Other of Beautie Personated By the Most Magnificent of Queenes Anne Queene of Great Britain, with her Honourable Ladys 1605 and 1608 at White hall* (London: Thomas Thorp, 1605), pp. 3-5; Joel Augustus Rogers, *World's Great Men of Colour*, Volume I and II (1931, new edition, New York: Touchstone Books, 1995), p. 94;

Joel Augustus Rogers, *Sex and Race, Negro Caucasian Mixing in all Ages and all Lands*, Volume I (Petersburg: Helga Rogers, 1942), pp. 86–88; and William Wright, *Black History and Black Identity: A Call for a New Historiography* (Westport: Greenwood Publishing Group, 2002), pp. 99–101.

[36] G. L. Registers of St Olave Hart Street, GL Ms 28867.

[37] *Oxford Dictionary of English*, p. 1178; and MacCullough, *The Negro in English Literature*, pp. 23–47, 143–144; Moore, *The Name Negro*, pp. 16–18.

[38] Richard Eden, *The Decades of the New World* ... (London: Richard Jug, 1555), p. 356; Jonson, *The Character of Two Royall Masques*, pp. 3–5; Caelius Augustinus Curio, *A Notable History of the Saracens* ... (London: William How and Abraham Veale, 1575), pp. 24–26; and Omoh Ojior, *Africa and Africans in the Diaspora: An Evaluation of the Impact they have on each other* (Hampton: UB and US Communications Systems, 1996), pp. 158–161.

[39] MacCullough, *The Negro in English Literature*, pp. 23–47, 143–144; Moore, *The Name Negro*, pp. 16–18; Minsheu, *A Dictionarie in Spanish and English* (1599), n. p. introduction. On Minsheu's popularity and importance see Catherine Alexander and Stanley Wells (eds.), *Shakespeare and Race* (New York: Cambridge University Press, 2000), pp. 16–21; Christopher Baker (ed.), *Absolutism and the Scientific Revolution, 1600–1720: A Biographical Dictionary* (Westport/London: Greenwood Press, 2002), p. 266; Although a different view is offered by Jurgen Schafer, 'John Minsheu Scholar or Charlatan?,' *Renaissance Quarterly*, 26: 1, 1973, pp. 23–35.

[40] Kirk and Kirk (eds.), *Returns of Aliens Dwelling in* ... *London, Volume III* (1907), p. 407; Habib, *Black Lives*, p. 304. On the word 'Barbary' see Bolton (ed.), *Alien Communities of London in the Fifteenth Centuries*, pp. 1–15, 42.

[41] Boorde, *Introduction to the Book of Knowledge*, p. 88.

[42] Sertima (ed.), *Golden Age of the Moor*, p. 141.

[43] Curio, *A Notable History of the Saracens*, pp. 25–26, 139; suggested by: *The Oxford English Dictionary*, pp. 945, 946, 1058 (those areas bordering the Barbary coast including modern day Algeria, Morocco, Libya and Tunisia); *The Concise Oxford English Dictionary* (New York: Oxford University Press, 11th edition 2008), p. 927; and Montagu (ed.) *UNESCO Statement on Race*, p. 78.

[44] Best, *A True Discourse*, pp. 28–32; Pory (tr.), Africanus, *A Geographical Historie of Africa*, p. 6; Ian Smith, *Race and Rhetoric in the Renaissance: Barbarian Errors* (Basingstoke: Palgrave Macmillan, 2009), pp. 23–43; *The World Book Encyclopedia* (Chicago: World Book inc, 2002), pp. 105–106; Habib, *Black Lives*, n. p. preface, introduction; and Marika Sherwood, 'Blacks in Elizabethan England,' *History Today*, 53: 10, 2003, pp. 40–42.

[45] Eden, *The Decades of the New World*, pp. 344–350.

[46] *The Oxford English Dictionary*, p. 423; *Oxford Dictionary of English*, p. 595; and Montagu (ed.), *UNESCO Statement on Race*, p. 78.

[47] Author unknown, *The Calendar of the Patent Rolls, Henry III, 1258–1266* (London: HMSO, 1910), p. 28; Michael Ray in Michael Jones (ed.), 'A Black slave on the run in thirteenth-century England,' *Nottingham Medieval Studies*, Volume L 1, University of Nottingham, 2007, pp. 111–119.

[48] Mathew Paris in Henry Richards Luard (ed.), *Flores Historiarum*, Volume III (London: HMSO, 1890), p. 24. The idea that Saracens could be Africans is controversial but is supported by: Maghan Keita, 'Saracens and Black Knights,' *Arthuriana*, 16: 4, 1 December 2006, pp. 65–77; Baron John Emerich Edward David Dalberg Acton Acton, George Walter Prothero, etc. *Cambridge Modern History*, Volume I (Cambridge: University Press, 1912), pp. 9, 10, Volume IX (1906), pp. 9, 349; Debra Higgs Strickland, *Saracens, Demons, and*

Jews: Making Monsters in Medieval Art (New Jersey: Princeton University Press, 2003), p. 169; Geraldus Cambrensis, Joseph Stevenson (tr.), *Concerning the Instruction of Prince ...* (Felinfach, JMF Books, 1991), p. 59; Rebecca Martin, *Wild Men and Moors in the Castle of Love: The Castle-Siege Tapestries, in Nuremberg, Vienna, and Boston (German (Alsace) Weavers)* (Chapel Hill: University of North Carolina, 1983), p. 82; and John Skelton, in MacCullough, *The Negro in English Literature*, p. 42.

[49] Sue Black, 'Human Skeletal Remains from Wolsey Street, Ipswich, (IAS5003),' January 2009, Report unpublished, pp. 6, 25, 49–51 (contains DNA tests proving the Ipswich Man is an African); And featured in: Neil Ferguson (dr.), Tania Lindon (pr.), History Cold Case, Episode 1, BBC2, 6 May 2010; and Adrian Bell, 'History Cold Case' Email, sent 08/05/10, 10/05/10, accessed 10/05/10, 12/05/10, respectively.

[50] Elizabeth Francis Rogers (ed.), Thomas More, *The Correspondence of Sir Thomas More* (Princeton: Princeton University Press, 1947), p. 4; and *Best, A True Discourse*, pp. 28–32.

[51] Wiltshire and Swindon Records Office, Wiltshire Family History Society, *Colne Parish Register* Vol. 1 *1538–1602* (London: A Webb, 1944), n. p.; Wiltshire and Swindon Records Office, *Colne Parish Register*, ref. 2083/1, n.p.

[52] Barnabe Rich, *The Famous Hystory of Herodotus, Conteyning the Discourse of Dyuers Countreys, the Succession of theyr Kyngs, etc. Deuided into Nine Bookes, Entituled with the Names of the Nine Muses* (London: Thomas Marshe, 1584), n. p. passim; Minsheu, *A Dictionarie in Spanish and English*, p. 175; and Pory (tr.), Africanus, *A Geographical Historie of Africa*, p. 6; et. al.

[53] Jonson, *The Character of Two Royall Masques*, pp. 3–5.

[54] Similar arguments are expressed by Onyeka in, 'What's in a Name?,' pp. 34–39.

[55] Hall, *Things of Darkness*, pp. 13, 211.

[56] Harry Lee Faggett, *Black and Other Minorities in Shakespeare's England* (Prairie View: Prairie View Press, 1971), pp. 95–107; Fraser, Vigne, Littleton (eds.), *From Strangers to Citizens* (2001), pp. 254, 255; Smith, *Race and Rhetoric in the Renaissance* (2009), pp. 46–62; Barthelemy, *Black Face, Maligned Race* (1987), pp. x, 1–18, 35–42, 144; James Andrew Scarborough MacPeek, *The Black Book of Knaves and Unthrifts. In Shakespeare and other Renaissance ...* (Storrs: University of Connecticut, 1969), pp. 1–21, 252–262 (on otherness); Bartels, *Speaking of the Moor* (2008), n. p. preface, introduction; Emily C. Bartels, *Spectacles of Strangeness: Imperialism, Alienation, and Marlowe* (Philadelphia: University of Pennsylvania Press, 1993), n. p. introduction; and Hall, *Things of Darkness* (1996), pp. 13, 211.

[57] Casper Van Senden and Thomas Sherley, 'Cecil Papers Petition, no 151, Merchant of Lubeck to the Queen,' *Calendar of the Manuscripts of the Most Honourable the Marquess of Salisbury*, November 1600, Volume 14 (London: Historical Manuscripts Commission, 1883–1976), p. 143.

[58] Ibid.; Casper Van Senden and Thomas Sherley, 'Cecil Papers Petition, Merchant of Lubeck to the Queen,' 29 November 1600, 29 December, 1600: Volume 10, pp. 399, 431; Author unknown, Letter to the Lord Mayors signed 11 July 1596; Author unknown, Letter to the Lord Mayors signed 18 July 1596; Author unknown, Proclamation ca 1601. A contrary view is offered by Fryer, *Staying Power*, pp. 1, 5, 8, 9; Hall, *Things of Darkness*, pp. 13, 211; and Kenneth Little, *Negroes in Britain* (London: Routledge, Kegan Paul, 1947), p. 187.

[59] The quotations in Latin are from Richard Devizes, in Ruth Morse (ed.), *Truth and Convention in the Middle Ages: Rhetoric, Representation, and Reality* (Cambridge: Cambridge University Press, 1991), pp. 109–110. The translations are from the same, but also include those of Stephen Donaldson, Wayne Dynes, *History of Homosexuality in*

Europe and America (London: Taylor and Francis, 1992), p. 162: Donaldson's translation includes 'kinds,' instead of 'sorts' and the words 'black magicians.'

[60] Appleby (ed.), *The Chronicles of Richard of Devizes,* pp. preface, 65; John Appleby, *John King of England* (New York: Knopf, 1959), p. 179; V. J. Scattergood, 'Reading the past: essays on medieval and renaissance literature,' *Medieval Studies* (Dublin: Four Courts Press, 1996), pp. 19–20; some historians regard the idea of 'Garamantes' being Africans as controversial see: Charles Daniels, *The Garamantes of Southern Libya* (Stoughton: Oleander Press, 1970), pp. 32–35; John Allen Giles, *The Chronicles of Richard of Devizes … also Richard of Cirencester's Description of Britain* (Oxford/ London: James Bohn, 1841), p. 60; Ranulphus Higden, in Churchill Babington (ed.), John Trevisa (tr.), *Polychronicon,* pp. 158–161; Wayne Chandler, in Ivan Van Sertima (ed.) *Golden Age of the Moor* (Piscataway; Transaction Publishers, 1992), pp. 25, 111–119, 127–135, 157; and Gustav Jahoda, *Images of Savages: Ancient Roots of Modern Prejudice in Western Culture* (London: Routledge, 1999), pp. 30–33.

[61] Author unknown, Proclamation ca January 1601.

[62] Appleby (ed.) *The Chronicles of Richard of Devizes,* p. 65; Author unknown, Proclamation ca 1601; and Casper Van Senden, Thomas Sherley, 'Cecil Papers Petition, no 151, Merchant of Lubeck to the Queen,' p. 143.

[63] The inscriptive etymology that Devizes uses is also present in some early modern fiction, for example in *Volpone* by Ben Jonson written in 1606, he describes 'bastard servants,' 'begot on beggars/ Gypsies, and Jews, and blackamoors …' whose drunkenness and idle behaviour would no doubt have rivalled their parents, see, *Volpone or the Fox …* (1606, new edition, London: T, Thorpe, 1607), Act I Scene 5 line 43–45, n. p.

[64] Barnabe Rich, *The Famous Hystory of Herodotus* (London: Thomas Marshe, 1584), fol or p. 96; and Pliny the Elder, *Begin. Caius Plynius Marco suo Salutem. [Fol. 3:] Caii Plynii Secundi Naturalis Historiae Liber. I. End. [Colophon:] Caii Plynii Secundi Naturalis Historiae Libri Tricesimiseptimi et Ultimi Finis, etc* (Venetiis: Nicolaum Jenson, 1472), passim.

[65] Philemon Holland, *The History of the World Commonly Called the Natural Historie of C Plinius Secondus, Translated by Philemon Holland* (London: Adam Philip, 1601), pp. 96, 146–147, 157.

[66] Pory (tr.), Africanus, *A Geographical Historie of Africa,* n. p. introduction; and Eden, *The Decades of the New World,* n. p. introduction.

[67] Quotations are from Best, *A True Discourse,* p. 30. Other evidence in Pory (tr.), Africanus, *A Geographical Historie of Africa,* pp. 6, 42; Rich, *The Famous Hystory of Herodotus,* fol. or p. 96; and Pliny the Elder, *Plynii Secundi Naturalis Historiae Liber* (Venetiis: Nicolaum Jenson, 1472), n. p. passim. Different views are offered on these matters in Benjamin Braude, 'The Sons of Noah and the Construction of Ethnic and Geographical Identities in the Medieval and Early Modern Periods,' *William and Mary Quarterly LIV,* January 1997, pp. 103–142; and David M. Whitford, *The Curse of Ham in the Early Modern Era: The Bible and the Justifications for Slavery* (Farnham: Ashgate, 2009), pp. 102, 105,106, 116, 117, 120.

[68] Best, *A True Discourse,* p. 30. I am aware of the inherent contradiction, in the way that Best uses the term original Man to describe a person, family, and group of people.

[69] Ibid., pp. 30, 31; Braude, 'The Sons of Noah and the Construction of Ethnic … Identities,' pp. 103–142; and Folarin Shyllon, *Black People in Britain 1553–1833* (Oxford: Oxford University Press, 1977), p. 3 (on the 'curse').

[70] On Meredith Hanmer's life see Thomas Cromwell, *Walks Through Islington; Comprising an Historical and Descriptive …* (London: Sherwood Gilbert and Piper, 1835), pp. 78–79.

⁷¹ Meredith Hanmer, *The Baptizing of a Turke A Sermon* ... (London: Robert Walde-Grave, 1586), E2 (on Chinano's age and origins).

⁷² Hanmer, *The Baptizing of a Turke*, p. B 4.

⁷³ The question of where this idea first started is convoluted see Thomas Browne, *Pseudodoxia Epidemica: or, Enquiries into Very Many Received Tenents and Commonly Presumed Truths* (London: Edward Dod, 1646), pp. 332–368 (offers other origins for where the idea came from); as does, Sujata Iyengar, *Shades of Difference: Mythologies of Skin Colour in Early Modern England* (Philadelphia: University of Pennsylvania Press, 2008), pp. 7–13, 67, 76–78; But David Goldenberg, *The Curse of Ham: Race and Slavery in Early Judaism, Christianity, and Islam* (Princeton: Princeton University Press, 2003), pp. 4–8, 107, 132, 133, 138 (Ottoman Empire).

⁷⁴ Whitford, *The Curse of Ham*, pp. 102, 105, 106, 116, 117, 120; Best, *A True Discourse*, pp. 28–32; and the legacy of this idea remains with the term 'Hamitic' used by some anthropologists to define Africans in Ashley Montagu (ed.), *UNESCO Statement on Race*, pp. 9, 78.

⁷⁵ Thomas Matthew, John Rogers, William Tyndale, *The Byble, Which is all the Holy Scripture: In whych are Contayned the Olde and Newe Testament Truly and Purely Translated into Englysh by Thomas Mathew [or Rather, the Books from Genesis to Chronicles and the New Testament Translated by W. Tyndale and the Remaining Books by Miles Coverdale ... [With Woodcuts.]* (London/Antwerp: R. Grafton & E. Whitchurch, 1537), pp. 3–7.

⁷⁶ Best, *A True Discourse*, pp. 28–32; Author unknown, *A Forensic Dispute on the Legality of Enslaving Africans held at the Commencement in Cambridge New England, July 21, 1773* (Boston: John Boyle, 1773), pp. 5, 25–27, 39; Douglas Lorimer, *Colour, Class and the Victorians: English Attitudes to the Negro in the Mid-Nineteenth Century* (New York: Leicester University Press, 1978), pp. 131–161; Skinner, *Peoples and Cultures of Africa*, pp. 61–63; and Greenberg, *The Languages of Africa*, pp. 24, 42, 45.

⁷⁷ Guildhall Library, St Olave, P69/OLA1/A/01/GL Ms 28867, p. 50.

⁷⁸ Hanmer, *Baptizing a Turke*, passim.

⁷⁹ Ibid., p. 5 'the Great Turke.' Hanmer's rant againt the papacy can be read in, *The Great Bragge and Challenge of M. Champion a Jesuite, Commonlye Called Edmunde Campion, Latelye Arrived in Englande* ... (London: Thomas Marshe, 158)1, passim. The rebuttal of his views are in Robert Persons, *A Defence of the Censure, Given Upon Two Bookes of William Chake and Meredith Hanmer Mynysters, Whiche They Wrote Against M Edmond Campian and Against his Offer of Disputation, etc.* (Rouen: Robert Persons, 1582), passim.

⁸⁰ Hanmer, *Baptizing a Turke*, p. 2.

⁸¹ Ibid., p. E5

⁸² Ibid., p. F 3.

⁸³ Ibid., p. 5.

⁸⁴ Ibid., p. E 4 (slavery).

⁸⁵ John Weever, *Ancient Funeral Monuments within the United Monarchie of Great Britain ... Intermixed and Illustrated with Variety of Historical Observations* ... (London: Thomas Harper, 1631), p. 427; and Cromwell, *Walks Through Islington*, pp. 78–79.

⁸⁶ John Strype, *Annals of the Reformation and Establishment of Religion ... During the First Twelve Years of Elizabeth I's Happy Reign*, Volume III (London: John Wyatt, 1709), pp. 216–217.

⁸⁷ Cromwell, *Walks Through Islington*, pp. 78–79.

⁸⁸ Ibid.; Henry Ellis, *The History and Antiquities of the Parish of Saint Leonard Shoreditch* ... (London: J. Nicholas, 1798), p. 24.

[89] Best, *A True Discourse*, p. 30. These sorts of ideas are also in Holland, *The Natural Historie of C Plinius Secondus*, pp. 96, 146–147, 157. The later writers are discussed in Lorimer, *Colour Class and the Victorians*, p. 132; and Higginbotham, *In the Matter of Colour*, pp. 10, 19–28.

[90] Minsheu, *A Dictionarie in Spanish and English*, p. 175; *Oxford Dictionary of English*, p. 171; and Moore, *The Name Negro its Origin and Evil Use*, p. 60, preface.

[91] William Shakespeare, *Othello* in Richard Proudfoot, Ann Thompson and David Scott Kastan (eds.), *The Arden Shakespeare* ... (Walton on Thames: Thomas Nelson and Sons, 1998), Act I, Scene I–3, pp. 941–945, *Titus Andronicus*, Act V, Scene I, Line 40–51, pp. 1145–1146; and Christopher Marlowe, *Lust's Dominion or the Lascivious Queen a Tragedie* (London: FK for Robert Parker, 1657), Act I, Scene I, Line 21, p. B3.

[92] William Shakespeare, *Othello* in Richard Proudfoot, Ann Thompson and David Scott Kastan (eds.), *The Arden Shakespeare Complete Works*, Act I, Scene III, Line 95–170, p. 945.

[93] The quotations are from Shakespeare's *Titus Andronicus* in Barthelemy, *Black Face, Maligned Race*, pp. 77, 96, 99. Writers that share this view include: David Dabydeen, *The Black Presence in English Literature* (1983, new edition, Manchester: Manchester University Press, 1985), p. 3; and Annette Drew-Bear, *Painted Faces on the Renaissance Stage: The Moral Significance of Face-Painting Conventions* (Lewisburg/London: Bucknell University Press, 1994), pp. 102–104.

[94] Author unknown, Letter to Lord Mayors, signed 11 July 1596; Author unknown, Letter to the Lord Mayors signed 18 July 1596; Author unknown, Proclamation ca 1601; John Stubbs, *The Discoverie of a Gaping Gulf, The Discoverie of a Gaping Gulf Whereinto England is like to be Swallowed by an other French Marriage, if the Lord Forbid not the Banes, by Letting her Maiestie see the Sin and Punishment Thereof* (London: H Singleton, 1579), pp. 4, 30–33, 35, 42; and Whitford, *The Curse of Ham in the Early Modern Era*, pp. 105–108 (suggests a different view but with no evidence related to Tudor England).

[95] Stubbs, *The Discoverie of a Gaping Gulf*, pp. 4, 30– 33, 35, 42; suggested by Faggett, *Black and Other Minorities in Shakespeare's England*, pp. 9–29, 95–107; and Sokol, *Shakespeare and Tolerance*, pp. 117–121.

[96] Thomas More, William Rastell (ed.), *The Works of Sir Thomas More Knyght ... The First Boke* (London: John Cawod, Richard Tottell, 1557), p. 126.

[97] Francis Bacon in, *Novum Organum* (1620), in, James Spedding (ed.), *The Works of Francis Bacon Collected and Edited by James Spedding* ... (London: Longman and Co, 1857), p. 473; Browne, *Pseudodoxia Epidemica*, pp. 332–368; and Siobhan Collins and Louise Denmead, 'There is All Africa [...] Within Us': Language, Generation and Alchemy in Browne's Explication of Blackness,' in Kathryn Murphy and Richard Todd (eds.), *"A Man Very Well Studyed": New Contexts for Thomas Browne* (Leiden/Boston: Brill, 2008), pp. 127–146. For a more detailed discussion on heliotropism see, Sujata Iyengar, *Shades of Difference*, pp. 6–8, 84–85.

[98] On this legend see Sujata Iyengar, *Shades of Difference*, pp. 26, 110; and Holland, *The Natural Historie of C Plinius Secondus*, p. 146.

[99] Quotations are from More, *The First Boke*, pp. 125–126.

[100] Bacon, *The Works of Francis Bacon*, p. 473; and Browne, *Pseudodoxia Epidemica*, pp. 332–368.

[101] Bacon, *Novum Organum* (1620), Spedding (ed.), *The Works of Francis Bacon*, p. 473.

[102] Browne, *Pseudodoxia Epidemica*, p. 332.

[103] Reid Barbour and Claire Preston (eds.), *Sir Thomas Browne: The World Proposed* (Oxford: Oxford University Press, 2008), n. p. preface, introduction.

[104] More, Rastell (ed.), *The First Boke*, p. 125.

[105] The term 'Inde' is discussed in more detail in the following: Sidney Lee, 'Caliban's visits to England,' *Cornhill Magazine*, 34, 1913, pp. 333-345; James Laurence Bolton (ed.), *Alien Communities of London in the Fifteenth Centuries* (Stamford: Richard III and York History Trust with Paul Watkins, 1998), pp. 29, 42; and *The Oxford English Dictionary*, pp. 815, 880, 1171.

[106] Rogers (ed.), More, *The Correspondence of Sir Thomas More*, p. 4.

[107] Sherwood, 'Blacks in Elizabethan England,' *History Today*, pp. 40-42; and Habib, *Black Lives*, pp. 274-294.

[108] Native-Americans are 'a member of any of the indigenous peoples of North and South America and the Caribbean Islands:' Oxford *Dictionary of English*, p. 1171; and John Stow, *The Annales of England, Faithfully Collected Out of the Most Autenticall Authors, Records ... untill ... 1592* (London: R. Newbery, 1592), p. 485.

[109] *Best, A True Discourse*, pp. 28-32.

[110] Suggested by the more numerous occurrence of Africans in: London, GL Ms 9243-9245, GL Ms 4310, GL Ms 9222; Author unknown, *St Martin in the Fields Parish Register*, Volume I (London: No publisher, 27 September 1571), p. 116; Plymouth and West Devon Record Office, Plymouth, St Andrews/MF1-4; Devon Record Office, East Allington/20/08/1577 PR; Northampton Records Office, Northampton, Microfiche 120, pp. 1-3; other evidence is referenced in the Bibliography.

[111] Plymouth and West Devon Record Office, Registers of St Andrews/October 22/1602/MF1-4 (what seems to be the rare baptism of a Native-American in Tudor England); Ann Fienup-Riordan, *Eskimo Essays, Up'ik Lives and How We See Them* (New Jersey: Rutgers University Press, 1990), pp. 11-12; and William Biddulph, *The Travels of Certain Englishmen into Africa, Asia, Troy, Bythnia, Thracia, and to the Black Sea ... Began in the Year ... 1600 ... Finished this Year 1608 ...* (London: TH. Hoveland for W. Aspley, 1609), pp. 65, 75.

[112] Alden Vaughan, 'Sir Walter Raleigh's Indian Interpreters, 1584-1618,' *The William and Mary Quarterly*, 59.2, 2002, pp. 341, 347; Lee, 'Caliban's visits to England,' pp. 333-345; and James Laurence Bolton (ed.), *Alien Communities of London*, pp. 29, 42.

[113] A definition of who 'Inuit people' are is contained in *The Oxford English Dictionary*, p. 999; *Oxford Dictionary of English*, p. 591; John White, 'An Eskimo man with bow,' Watercolour, Paper, British Museum, Prints and Drawings, London, 1585-1593, 1.29, Size 225 by 163 millimetres, ref. 1906,0509 and an 'Eskimo woman with baby,' Watercolour, Paper, British Museum, London, 1585-1593, Size 223 by 166 millimetres, ref. 1906,0509.1.30; see figures 6 and 7; Fienup-Riordan, *Eskimo Essays, How We See Them*, pp. 11-12.

[114] Paul Slack, *Poverty and Policy in Tudor and Stuart England* (London: Longman, 1988), pp. 91-99; and Judith Okely, *The Traveller-Gypsies* (Cambridge: Cambridge University Press, 1983), pp. 2-7.

[115] David Mayall, *Gypsy Identities, 1500-2000: From Egipcyans and Moon-men to the Ethnic Romany* (London: Routledge, 2004), pp. 5-11, 18-24; MacPeek, *The Black Book of Knaves and Unthrifts*, pp. 1-21, 252-262; and Ian Hancock, 'The Struggle for the Control of Identity,' *Perspectives*, http://www.osi.hu/rpp/perspectives1f.htm, accessed 06/07/07.

[116] Mayall, *Gypsy Identities, 1500-2000*, pp. 5-11, 45; Brian Belton, *Questioning Gypsy Identity: Ethnic Narratives in Britain and America* (Walnut Creek: Alta Mira Press, 2005), pp. 74, 176. Implied by the numerous proclamations against vagrants in Humfrey Dyson (collator), *A Book Containing all such Proclamations as were Published by the Reigine of the Late Queen Elizabeth 1559-1602* (London: Bonham Norton and John Bull, 1618), pp. 1- 6, 300, 324, 356, et. al.

117 *The Oxford English Dictionary*, p. 351; Charles Knight, *The English Encyclopaedia* (London: Bradbury Evans, 1868), pp. 613–616; and suggested by David MacRitchie, *Scottish Gypsies under the Stewarts* (Edinburgh: D. Douglas, 1894), pp. 25–33, 42, 51; Gypsy Lore Society, *Journal of the Gypsy Lore Society*, 2: 2, 1891, pp. 34–37; Faggett, *Black and Other Minorities in Shakespeare's England*, pp. 95–107; and Belton, *Questioning Gypsy Identity*, pp. 74, 176.

118 Mayall, *Gypsy Identities*, pp. 5–11, 45; *The Oxford English Dictionary*, pp. 257, 357–358; Paul Slack, *Poverty and Policy in Tudor and Stuart England* (London: Longman, 1988), pp. 91–99; Okely, *The Traveller-Gypsies*, pp. 2–7; and Hancock, 'The Struggle for the Control of Identity.'

119 This evidence includes that for London, GL Ms 9243–9245, GL Ms 4310, GL Ms 9222; Author unknown, *St Martin in the Fields Parish Register*, Volume I (London: No publisher, 27 September 1571), p. 116; Plymouth and West Devon Record Office, Plymouth, St Andrews/MF1-4; Devon Record Office, East Allington/20/08/1577 PR; and Northampton Records Office, Northampton, Microfiche 120, pp. 1–3.

120 *Token Books of St Saviour Southwark*, 1579, ref book 183, p. 7, line 33, these records are at the London Metropolitan Archives. On the 'liberty of the clink' see Jessica Browner, 'The wrong side of the river: London's disreputable Southbank in the sixteenth and seventeenth century,' *Essays in History*, 36, 1994, http://etext.virginia.edu/journals/EH/EH36/EH36.html accessed 12/06/2007.

121 Boorde, *Introduction to the Book of Knowledge*, pp. 88–89; and Thomas Earle and Kate Lowe (eds.), *Black Africans in Renaissance Europe* (Cambridge: Cambridge University Press, 2005), pp. 37, 38, 147, 176, 182, 183, etc.

122 Cesare Vecellio, *Degli Habiti Antichi et Moderni di Diverse Parti del Mondo* ... (Venice: Italy, 1590), pp. 480, 481, 487, 488, 'Moors,' pp. 470, 471, 473 (see figure 8), 'Ethiopians,' pp. 485, 486, 489.

123 Author unknown, *Domesday Abbreviatio* [Abridgement], Exchequer: Treasury of the Receipt, Miscellaneous Books, p. 196, National Archives, Kew, London, Ref. E36/284 (Why he is looking up at the letter I is still not known), see figure 9.

124 Nikolaus Pevsner, *The Buildings of England, London 1, The Cities of London and Westminster* (Harmondsworth: Penguin Books, 1957), p. 405; and William Lethaby, *Westminster Abbey Re-examined* (London: Duckworth, 1925), p. 192.

125 Laura Kinsey, 'History Cold Case Westminster,' Westminster Abbey Press Office (Email) sent and accessed 22/10/10.

126 This includes the image of 'The King of Garamantes Restored by his Dogs' in Paul Binski, *The Painted Chamber at Westminster* (London: Society of Antiquaries of London, 1986), p. 44; The Royal Archaeological Institute, *The Archaeological Journal of Great Britain*, Volumes 118–119 (London: Royal Archaeological Institute, 1943–1986), p. 179; and George Richard Jesse ... *The History of the British Dog from Ancient Laws* ...Volume I (London: R Hardwicke, 1866), p. 187.

127 Boorde, *Introduction to the Book of Knowledge*, pp. 88–99; Herbert Edmund Poole (ed.), *The Wisdom of Andrew Boorde* (London: E Backus, 1936), pp. 1–10 (suggests Boorde never went to Africa).

128 Eden, *The Decades of the New World*, p. 360.

129 Ranulphus Higden, in Churchill Babington (ed.), John Trevisa (tr.), *Polychronicon: Together with the English Translations of John Trevisa* ... (London: Longman, 1865), pp. 53, 158–161, 169, 189; Ranulphus Higden, in William Caxton (ed.), John Trevisa (tr.), *Polychronicon (the Description of Britain)* ... (London: William Caxton, 1480), n. p. passim; Great Britain Royal Commission on Historical Manuscripts, *Fourth Report of the Royal*

Commissions on Historical Manuscripts (London: Eyre and Spottiswoode, 1874), p. 414; and William Blades, *The Life and Typography of William Caxton* ... (London: Oxford University, 1861), pp. ix, 74, 194-5.

[130] Higden, in Babington (ed.), Trevisa (tr.), Polychronicon, pp. 53, 158-161, 169, 189 (these comments are that the 'humores' of Africans and not the Sun makes their hair 'crispedde [curly],' in other words they would keep their colour if they lived outside of Africa). He also compares Africans to white people and says the latter are 'moore bolde [in nature].'

[131] Quotations from Best, *A True Discourse*, pp. 28-29. Other historians have similar views, Luu, *Immigrants and the Industries of London, 1500-1700*, pp. 142-144; and Faggett, *Black and Other Minorities*, pp. 1-6.

[132] Best, *A True Discourse*, pp. 28-32.

[133] Evidence in Bristol Record Office, Bristol, Ref P/ST PJR/1/1/CMB 1576-1621, n. p.; London: GL Ms 9243-9245, GL Ms 4310, GL Ms 9222; Author unknown, *St Martin in the Fields Parish Register*, Volume I (London: No publisher, 27 September 1571), p. 116; Plymouth and West Devon Record Office, Plymouth, St Andrews/MF1-4; Devon Record Office, East Allington/20/08/1577 PR; and Northampton Records Office, Northampton, Microfiche 120, pp. 1-3.

[134] On Tudor marriages see David Cressy, *Birth, Marriage, and Death: Ritual, Religion, and the Life-Cycle in Tudor and Stuart England* (Oxford: Oxford University Press, 1997), pp. 298-307; and Leonidas Rosser, *Baptism: Its Nature, Obligation, Mode, Subjects and Benefits* (Philadelphia: Leonidas Rosser, 1854), pp. 19-23, 30-33, 379-386.

[135] Plymouth and West Devon Record Office, St Andrews Dec/24/1594/MF1-4; and Best, *A True Discourse*, pp. 28-32.

[136] Plymouth and West Devon Record Office, Registers of St Andrews/November 17/1594/MF1-4.

[137] Jonson, *The Character of Two Royall Masques*, pp. 11-14; and Wilson, *English Ethnicity and Race in Early Modern Drama*, pp. 111-130.

[138] G. L. Registers of St Botolph Bishopsgate, GL Ms 4515/1. Of course the child could have suffered from 'albinism' see the *Oxford Dictionary of English*, p. 37.

[139] Some of these children's complexion is also called 'Tawny,' meaning 'of an orange brown or yellowish-brown colour' see Best, *A True Discourse*, pp. 28-29; *The Oxford English Dictionary*, pp. 1058, 1808 (dictionary quotation); *Chambers Dictionary of Etymology*, p. 676; Johnson, *A Dictionary of the English Language*, p. 510; Shakespeare, *Titus Andronicus* in Proudfoot, Thompson and Kastan (eds.), Act IV, Scene II, Line 68, p. 1141, Act V, Scene I, Line 27, p. 1145; *The Merchant of Venice*, Act II, Scene I, Line 1-46, pp. 835-836, Act II, Scene VII, Line 1-79, p. 840, Act III, Scene IV, Line 35-41, p. 848 (Moroccan Ambassador); Richard Eden, *The History of Travel in the West and East Indies* ... (London: Richard Iugge, 1577), pp. 348-349.

[140] Thomas Underdowne (tr.), *An Æthiopian Historie Written in Greeke by Heliodorus: very Wittie and Pleasaunt, Englished by Thomas Underdoune. With the Argumente of Euery Booke, Sette Before the Whole Woorke* (London: Henry Wykes, 1569), passim; Iyengar, *Shades of Difference*, p. 21.

[141] A view shared by, Geoffrey Paul Edwards, *Early African Presence in the British Isles, an Inaugural Lecture* ... (Edinburgh: Centre of African Studies, Edinburgh University, 1990), n. p. passim; and David Killingray, *Africans in Britain* (London: Taylor and Francis, 1994), pp. 1-5.

[142] Benjamin Z. Kedar, *Crusade and Mission: European Approaches Toward the Muslims* (Princeton: Princeton University Press, 1984), pp. 52-53, 80-84, 146-151; John Morris, *The*

Life and Martyrdom of Thomas Becket ... (London: Percy and Sons, 1845), pp. 375, 401–402; Edward Grim in James Craig Robertson (ed.), etc. al., *Vita Sancti in Thomae Materials for the History of Thomas Becket, Archbishop of Canterbury* ... (1875, new edition, London: Longman, 1965), p. 401; Sue Niebrzydowski, 'The Sultana and her sisters: black women in the British Isles, before 1530,' *Women's History Review*, Volume 10:2, 2001, pp. 187–210; Geoffrey Chaucer, *The Boke of Chaucer Named Canterbury Tales* (London 'Westmestre': William Caxton, 1498), pp. fii–gii; and Martin, *Wild Men and Moors*, pp. 84, 85, 86.

[143] Morris, *The Life and Martyrdom of Thomas Becket*, pp. 375, 401–402; and Grim in Robertson (ed.), etc. al., *Vita Sancti in Thomae Materials*, p. 401.

[144] Chaucer, *The Prologue to the Canterbury Tales*, pp. 1526–1530 (Becket's importance as a saint); Paul Alonzo Brown, *The Development of the Legend of Thomas Becket* (Philadelphia: University of Pennsylvania, 1930), pp. 1–20; William Holden Hutton, *Thomas Becket – Archbishop of Canterbury* (London: Pitman and Sons Ltd, 1910), p. 4; and Niebrzydowski, 'The Sultana and her sisters: black women in the British Isles, before 1530,' pp. 187–210.

[145] Richard Grafton, *A Chronicle at Large, and meere History of the Affayres of England; and Kinges of the Same, Deduced from the Creation of the Worlde, unto the First Habitation of Thys Islande, and is by Contynuance to the First Yeere of ... Queene Elizabeth* ... Volume 2 (London: Henry Denham for R. Tottle and H. Toye, 1569), p. 53, 'Thomas Becket a Londoner borne, the sone of Gilbert Beckett and of a woman of Siria;' William Holden Hutton, *Thomas Becket – Archbishop of Canterbury* (London: Pitman and Sons Ltd, 1910), p. 4; and Bromley, *The Armorial Bearings of the Guilds of London*, pp. 28–30, Hutton and Bromley doubt whether the Becket legend was true but suggest that it was believed in medieval and Tudor times.

[146] Robert James Blackham, *The Soul of the City. London's Livery Companies. Their Stored Past, Their Living Present* (London: Sampson Low and Company, 1931), p. 144; and Anon, *Whitbread's Brewery Incorporating the Brewer's Art* (London: Whitbread's Brewery, 1948, new edition, London: Read Books, 2008), p. 50.

[147] Anthony Gerard Barthelemy, *Black Face, Maligned Race: The Representation of Blacks in English Drama from Shakespeare to Southerne* (London: Louisiana State University Press, 1987), n. p. preface. On Lambert Waterson see Richard Kirk and Ernest Kirk (eds.), *Returns of Aliens Dwelling in the City and Suburbs of London, Volume III* (1907), p. 407; Habib, *Black Lives*, p. 304; and Bolton (ed.), *Alien Communities of London in the Fifteenth Centuries*, pp. 1–15, 42 (the idea of otherness in Tudor England).

[148] *The Oxford English Dictionary*, pp. 945, 946; and Smith, *Race and Rhetoric in the Renaissance: Barbarian Errors*, pp. 46–62.

[149] Shakespeare, *Othello* in Proudfoot, Thompson and Kastan (eds.), *The Arden Shakespeare Complete Works*, Act I, Scene I, Line 110, p. 942.

[150] Kirk and Kirk (eds.), *Returns of Aliens Dwelling in the City and Suburbs of London*, Volume III (1907), p. 407; and Bolton (ed.), *Alien Communities of London in the Fifteenth Centuries*, pp. 1–15, 42.

[151] Philippa Maddern, "In Myn Own House:' The Troubled Connections Between Servant Marriages, Late Medieval English Households Communities and Early Modern Historiography,' in, Susan Broomhall and Stephanie Tarbin, *Women, Identities and Communities in Early Modern Europe* (Aldershot: Ashgate, 2008), p. 62.

[152] The ideas of 'belonging' and 'community' in Tudor England are of course complex subjects and are discussed by Anthony P. Cohen, *The Symbolic Construction of Community* (Chichester: Ellis Horwood, 1985), p. 85; Joshua Phillips, *English Fictions of Communal Identity, 1485–1603* (Farnham, Ashgate, 2003), pp. 11–22, passim (on how medieval and

Tudor fiction saw 'belonging'); and Joyce A. Youings, *Sixteenth-Century England* (London: Allen Lane, 1984), pp. 88–102.

[153] London, Metropolitan Archives, Registers of St Dunstan; and All Saints Church, Stepney, LMA P93/DUN/255.

[154] Registers of All Saints Parish, Centre for Kentish Studies, All Saints Church, Staplehurst Parish, Kent, ms P 347 ref 560, ms P347, ref 800.

[155] Similar perspectives are given by William Brewer Stephens, *Sources for English Local History* (Cambridge: Cambridge University Press, 1981), pp. 52–56; Habib, *Black Lives*, pp. 7, 19–63, 96, 119; Paul Griffiths, 'Secrecy and Authority in sixteenth and seventeenth century London,' *Historical Journal*, 40–4, 1997, pp. 925–51; and David Cressy, *Birth, Marriage, and Death: Ritual, Religion, and the Life-Cycle in Tudor and Stuart England* (Oxford: Oxford University Press, 1997), pp. 99–107.

[156] Worcestershire Archive and Archaeology Service, *Holt Parish Registers*, ref. 985, p. 19.

[157] On the meaning of the word 'Jet' please see *Oxford Dictionary of English* (Oxford: Oxford University Press, 2nd edition 2003), p. 931, the term is also discussed in more detail in the Afterword.

[158] Please see the Afterword for more on 'Henrie Jetto' and his family, and the Bibliography for references to them.

[159] Wiltshire and Swindon Records Office, *Salisbury St Thomas Parish Register*, no ref. 26 January, 1653, n.p.; *Salisbury St Thomas Parish Registers and Bishop's Transcripts 1530–1837, Burials* (Devizes: Wiltshire Family History Society, new edition 2011), p. 67.

[160] London, Metropolitan Archives, London, Registers of Mary Magdalene, Bermondsey, P71/MMG/002, Microfiche X 097 MF 004; and Habib, *Black Lives*, pp. 1–17, 45–49 (marriage records), 140, 307.

[161] Kirk and Kirk (eds.), *Returns of Aliens ... in ... London*, Volume II, pp. 84, 329.

[162] On immigrant silk weavers from Europe present in early modern England see, Luu, *Immigrants and the Industries of London*, pp. 21, 55–76, 176–217; on silk weavers in Oudenaarde in Flanders and Europe see, *The New Encyclopaedia Britannica*, Volume 11 (London: Encyclopaedia Britannica Company, 1983), p. 156; Maarten Roy Prak (ed.), *Craft Guilds in the Early Modern Low Countries: Work, Power and Representation* (Aldershot: Ashgate, 2006), pp. 111–125. Patrick Wallis a historian at the London School of Economics suggests the entry merely records his name (personal communication undated).

[163] Quotation from Kirk and Kirk (eds.), *Returns of Aliens ... in ... London*, Volume II, p. 84; for Moorish silk weavers see: Mary Schoeser, *Silk* (New Haven/London: Yale University Press, 2007), p. 45; and Stanley Lane-Poole, *Story of the Moors of Spain* (London: Fisher Unwin, 1887), pp. 141–147.

[164] Kirk and Kirk (eds.), *Returns of Aliens ... in ... London*, Volume II, pp. 84, 329.

[165] Rogers, *World's Great Men of Colour*, Volume I and II, p. 94; and Rogers, *Sex and Race*, Volume I, p. 86.

[166] Author unknown, National Archives, Kew, London, Court of Chancery: Six Clerks Office: *Early Proceedings, Richard II to Philip and Mary, 1518–1529*, C 1/831/71–72; and *Merriam Webster's Spanish-English Dictionary* (Springfield: Merriam Webster, 1997), p. 186.

[167] Carol R. Ember, Melvin Ember and Ian Skoggard (eds.), *Encyclopedia of Diasporas: Immigrant and Refugee Cultures around the World*, Volume 2 (New York: Springer, 2004), p. 20.

[168] Northampton Records Office, Northampton, Microfiche 120, p. 3.

169 Ibid.; Ronald Leslie Greenall, *A History of Northamptonshire* (London: Phillimore, 1979), pp. 35–42, 48–52; and Julia Bush, et. al., *Sharing the Past, Northamptonshire, Black History* (Northampton: Northamptonshire Black History Association, 2008), pp. 1–7.

170 Moore, *The Name Negro its Origin and Evil Use*, pp. 72–75.

171 Habib, *Black Lives*, n. p. preface; and echoed by Barthelemy, in, *Black Race Maligned Race*, n. p. preface.

172 G. L. Registers of St Olave Hart Street, GL Ms 9223, p. 121.

173 G. L. Registers of St Botolph without Aldgate, GL Ms 9222, GL Ms 9222/1.

174 G. L. Registers of St Olave Hart Street, GL Ms 9223.

175 GL Ms 9234/6.

176 Blount (tr.), Conestaggio, *The Historie of the Uniting of the Kingdom of Portugal to the Crowne of Castill ... The Description of Portugal, their Principal Townes* ... (1600), pp. 5–7.

177 Faggett, *Black and Other Minorities in Shakespeare's England*, p. 46; including evidence of Africans in: GL Ms 9243–9245, GL Ms 4310, GL Ms 9222; Author unknown, *St Martin in the Fields Parish Register*, Volume I (London: No publisher, 27 September 1571), p. 116; City of Westminster Archives Centre, London, 1601/2 January/21/St Clements Dane/ Volume1Burials/MF 1; and Rory Lalwan (ed.), *Sources for Black and Asian History at the City of Westminster Archives* (London: Westminster City Archives, 2005), pp. 9, 10.

178 Rich, *The Famous Hystory of Herodotus*, pp. fol. 89, 94, 96; Aubrey de Selincourt (tr.), Herodotus, *The Histories* (1954, new edition, London: Penguin, 1974), pp. 129, 130, 152–153, 165, 167, 186; and Holland, *The Natural Historie of C Plinius Secondus*, pp. 96, 146–147, 157.

179 Samuel Purchas, *Purchas his Pilgrimage; or Relations of the World and the Religions Observed in all Ages and Places Discovered from the Creation unto the Present ...* (London: William Stansby for Henrie Fetherestone, 1613), pp. 38, 39, 47, 60, 187, 188 (Moses' Wife), 189, 463, 464; Robert Greene, *Perimedes the Blacke-Smith, a Golden Methode How to Use the Minde in Pleasant and Profitable Exercise ...* (London: John Wolfe, Edward White, 1588), p. 7 (Africans and science); Thomas Wilson (tr., ed.), *The Three Orations of Demosthenes, Chiefe Orator, among the Grecians* ... (London: Henrie Denham, 1570), pp. 7, 10 (Africans and science); Christopher Marlowe, *The Tragedy of Dido, Queen of Carthage* (London: Thomas Nashe, 1601), n. p. passim; Eden, *The Decades of the New World*, pp. 344–345 (Solomon and Sheba), 356, 357 (legend of Prester John); and Walter Thomas Rogers (ed.), Scheltco Geveren, *Of the End of this World, and Second Coming of Christ ...* (London: Henrie Middleton, 1583), pp. 11 (Ancient Egyptians and science). On Sheba also see figures 10 and 11.

180 On Balthazar see Vincent Boele, Ernest Schreuder and Elmer Kolfin (eds.), *Black is Beautiful: Rubens to Dumas* (Amsterdam: Die Nieuwe Kerk, 2008), pp. 35, 36, 182; Ann Sutherland Harris, *Seventeenth-Century Art and Architecture* (London: Laurence King, 2008), p. 212; David L. Jeffrey, *A Dictionary of Biblical Tradition in English Literature* (Grand Rapids: W. B. Eerdmans, 1994), p. 472. In some traditions this king is called Melchior and he is King of Nubia see Ebenezer Cobham Brewer, *Character Sketches of Romance, Fiction, and the Drama*, Volume 2 (Jerusalem/New York: The Minerva Group, 2004), p. 376; Hieronymus Bosch, *The Epiphany or the Adoration of the Magi*, 1510, oil on wood panel, Museo del Prado, Madrid, 138 x 72 cm, by 138 x 34 cm, ref 21032 see figures 24 and 25; And Artist unknown, *Adoration of the Magi*, part of a rood Screen panel, oil and gilt on oak, circa 1520, made in England, ref. W.54-1928 @ Victoria and Albert Museum, London, SW7 2RL, figures 12 and 13.

181 Fred Gustafson, *The Black Madonna* (Boston: Sigo Press, 1990), passim; Małgorzata Oleszkiewicz Peralba, *The Black Madonna in Latin America and Europe: Tradition and*

Transformation (Albuquerque: University of New Mexico Press, 2007), passim; Ean Begg, *The Cult of the Black Virgin* (London: Arkana, 1985), passim; Regina Buccola and Lisa Hopkins (eds.), *Marian Moments in Early Modern British Drama* (Aldershot: Ashgate, 2007), pp. 75–86; Ivan Van Sertima (ed.), *Black Women in Antiquity* (New York: Transaction Publishers, 1984), pp. 138–154, 167–182; Lucia Chiavola Birnbaum, *Black Madonnas: Feminism, Religion, and Politics in Italy* (Boston: Northeastern University Press, 1993), pp. 3, 13, 30, 31, 95, 105.

[182] A view shared by, Buccola (ed.), in, *Marian Moments in Early Modern British Drama*, pp. 75–86; Sertima (ed.), *Black Women in Antiquity*, pp. 138–154, 167–182.

[183] Rogers (ed.), Geveren, *Of the End of this World, and Second Coming of Christ*, p. 4; and John Stow, *A Summary of the Chronicles of England, Abridged and Continued unto 1598* ... (1565, new edition, London: R. Bardocke, 1598), p. 748.

[184] Iyengar, *Shades of Difference*, pp. 42–58, 62–65.

[185] Evidence in, Jean Devisse, Michel Mollat, *The Image of the Black in Western Art* (Cambridge: Harvard University Press, 1979), p. 93; and Rebecca Martin, *Wild Men and Moors in the Castle of Love: The Castle-Siege Tapestries, in Nuremberg, Vienna*, pp. 1–10, 83, 97, 100, 102.

[186] Sertima, *Golden Age of the Moor*, Volume 11, pp. 65–66; Joel Augustus Rogers, *Nature Knows no Colour Line* (St Petersburg: Helga Rogers, 1952), pp. 56–57; and Maghan Keita, 'Saracens and Black Knights,' *Arthuriana*, 16: 4, 1 December 2006, pp. 65–77.

[187] Habib, *Black Lives*, pp. 31–37.

[188] On Saint Maurice see, Sertima, *Golden Age of the Moor*, Volume 11, pp. 65–66; St Clair Drake, *Black Folk Here and There: An Essay in History and Anthropology*, Volume II (Berkley: Centre for Afro American Studies University of California, 1991), p. 196; Boele, Schreuder, Kolfin (eds.), *Black is Beautiful*, pp. 23–25.

[189] A view supported by evidence in, Jessica Laidlay Weston, *The Romance of Morien* (London: David Nutt, 1901), pp. 12–13, 29, 31, 32, 35, 38–41, 150; and Keita, 'Saracens and Black Knights,' pp. 65–77, see figure 15. And see images from Europe of Black knights with St Maurice as an archetype, see figures 15, 16 and 17.

[190] Appleby (ed.) *The Chronicles of Richard of Devizes*, p. 65; and Artist unknown, Author unknown, *Westminster Tournament Roll 1511*, The College of Arms, London.

[191] Martin Biddle, Sally Badham, *King Arthur's Round Table: An Archaeological Investigation* (Woodbridge: Boydell and Brewer, 2000), pp. 1–17; Roger Sherman Loomis, *The Grail. From Celtic Myth to Christian Symbol* (Cardiff: University of Wales Press, 1963), pp. 218–221; Thomas Malory, *La Morte D'Arthur. Translated from the French by Sir T. Malory* (London: William Copleand, 1557), n. p. preface, book nine (The African/Saracen character is called Palamides); Irene Groves (tr.), Walter Johannes Stein, *The Ninth Century and the Holy Grail* (London: Temple Lodge, 1988), pp. 71, 83–84, 86, 92, 96, 127, 253, 259, 262 (Another African character is called Feirefis); and John Pitcher, Robert Lindsey, Susan Cerasano, *Medieval and Renaissance Drama in England*, Volume 13 (New York: Fairleigh Dickinson, University Press, 2001), pp. 310–311.

[192] Weston, *The Romance of Morien*, pp. 12–13, 29, 31, 32, 35, 38–41, 150; and Robert List, *Merlin's Secret: The African and Near Eastern Presence in the Ancient British Isles* (New York: University Press of America, 1999), p. 356.

[193] Bart Besamusca, in Norris J. Lacy (ed.), *The New Arthurian Encyclopedia*, (New York: Garland, 1991), pp. 329–330; Jessica Laidlay Weston, *Arthurian Romances Unrepresented in Malory's, 'Morte d'Arthur,'* Volume IV (London: David Nutt, 1901), p. 12; List, *Merlin's Secret: The African and Near Eastern Presence in the Ancient British Isles*, p. 356; and Weston, *The Romance of Morien*, pp. 9, 12, 13, 17, 29, 35, 38–41.

194 Peter Morien's records are at: Author unknown, *Accounts of the Lord High Treasurer of Scotland*, The National Archives of Scotland, H. M. General Record Office, Edinburgh, Ref E21/5-10, Volume II, *1503/4,* pp. 96– 97, 99, 106, 417, 422, etc.

195 A similar view is expressed by Marika Sherwood, 'Blacks in Elizabethan England,' pp. 40–42; Salisbury Cathedral records, Wiltshire and Swindon History Centre, Wiltshire, Register 1, X3/84/1.

196 Sherwood, 'Blacks in Elizabethan England,' pp. 40–42; and Imtiaz Habib, 'Othello, Sir Peter Negro and the Blacks of Early Modern England: Colonial Inscription and Post Colonial Excavation,' *Literature Theory Interpretation Theory* 9/1, 1998, pp. 15–30.

197 Habib, *Black Lives,* pp. 296–302.

198 Habib, 'Was Sir Peter Negro Black,' *Black and Asian Studies Association Newsletter,* xlvi, November 2006, p. 5; Miranda Kaufmann, 'Sir Pedro Negro What Colour was his Skin?' *Oxford Journals, Notes and Queries,* 55(2), 2008, pp. 142–146.

199 Pitcher, Lindsey, Cerasano, *Medieval and Renaissance Drama in England,* pp. 310–311; James Douglas Merriman, *The Flower of Kings; a Study of the Arthurian Legend in England between 1485 and 1835* (Lawrence: University Press of Kansas, 1973), pp. 35–37, 47; and John E. Housman, 'Higden, Trevisa and Caxton and the Beginnings of Arthurian Criticism,' *The Review of English Studies,* 23, No. 91, July 1947, pp. 209–217.

200 These matters are discussed in detail by Jessica Laidlay Weston in, *The Legend of Sir Gawain and the Green Knight: Studies Upon its Original Scope and Significance* (London: David Nutt, 1897), pp. 1–3, 17; Seth Lerer, *Courtly, Letters in the Age of Henry VIII, Literary Culture and the Arts of Deceit* (Cambridge: Cambridge University Press, 1997), p. 106; Ralph Warren Victor Elliot, *The Gawain Country* (Leeds: University of Leeds School of English, 1984), p. 69; Malory, *La Morte D'Arthur,* n. p. book nine.

201 On the influence of Arthurian legends on Tudor culture see, Pitcher, Lindsey, Cerasano, *Medieval and Renaissance Drama in England,* pp. 310–311; Merriman, *The Flower of Kings,* pp. 35–37, 47; Housman, 'Higden, Trevisa and Caxton and the Beginnings of Arthurian Criticism,' pp. 209–217; and Weston, *The Legend of Sir Gawain and the Green Knight: Studies Upon its Original Scope and Significance,* pp. 1–3, 17.

202 Quotations from Rogers (ed.), Geveren, *Of the End of this World, and Second Coming of Christ,* p. 4. A perspective developed by Iyengar, *Shades of Difference,* pp. 47–52, 58–61 (black convert is better than white heathen), 110, 'primary conditions of human beings is black not white,' 139 (whiteness as other and different in early modern England).

203 Iyengar, discusses these matters at length and quotes from ancient and early modern sources many of which support the interpretation I have given, *Shades of Difference,* pp. 44–49, 51, 58, 61, 62–63 'The Anglican Church is both black and comely …', 65–68; this includes the classical writer Origen who says that 'blackness represents the 'Primal Image' of God … rather than tainted white flesh,' 69–72.

204 Buccola, Hopkins (eds.), *Marian Moments in Early Modern British Drama,* pp. 75–86; Małgorzata Oleszkiewicz Peralba, *The Black Madonna in Latin America and Europe: Tradition and Transformation* (Albuquerque: University of New Mexico Press, 2007), passim; Ean Begg, *The Cult of the Black Virgin* (London: Arkana, 1985), passim; Fred Gustafson, *The Black Madonna* (Boston: Sigo Press, 1990), passim.

205 Similar views are expressed in, Ivan Van Sertima (ed.), *Black Women in Antiquity* (New York: Transaction Publishers, 1984), pp. 138–154, 167–182; Birnbaum, *Black Madonnas,* pp. 3, 13, 30, 31, 95, 105.

206 George Bagshawe Harrison, *Shakespeare at Work 1592-1603* (London: Routledge, 1933), pp. 310, 311; Sertima (ed.): *African Presence in Early Europe,* p. 207; *Black Women*

in Antiquity (Piscataway: Transaction Publishers, 1984), p. 140; and *Golden Age of the Moor* (1992), p. 344.

[207] Ibid.; Edward Scobie, *Black Britannia: A History of Blacks in Britain* (Chicago: Johnson Publishing Company, 1972), p. 6; Habib, *Black Lives*, pp. 308, 326, 327 (Other 'Black' female prostitutes?); Sherwood, 'Blacks in Elizabethan England,' pp. 40–42 (Dennis Edward's letter); and Samuel Schoenbaum, *William Shakespeare: A Compact Documentary Life* (Oxford: Clarendon Press, 1977), p. 125. But Gustav Ungerer states that the legends relate to two different people in, 'Recovering a black African's voice in an English Lawsuit,' *Medieval and Renaissance Drama in England* (Madison: Fairleigh Dickinson University Press, 2004), pp. 255–271 (note 4).

[208] Sertima (ed.), *Golden Age of the Moor,* Volume 11, pp. 342–345; Sertima, *African Presence in Early Europe,* pp. 201, 207, 292; Rogers, *Nature Knows no Colour Line*, pp. 76, 77, 81; Simon Schoenbaum, *Shakespeare's Lives* (London: Clarendon, 1991), p. 688; Hugh Calvert, *Shakespeare's Sonnets and Problems of Autobiography* (Braunton: Merlin, 1987), pp. 203–206, 220; Brenda James, *Henry Neville and the Shakespeare Code* (Bognor Regis: Music for Strings, 2008), pp. 150–154; and Robert Nye, *The Late Mister Shakespeare: A Novel* (London: Chatto and Windus, 1998), pp. 281–285, 289–297 (fictional retelling of Lucy legend).

[209] William Shakespeare, *Shakespeare's Sonnets, Never Before Imprinted* (London: G.L. for T.T, 1609), Line 25, p. H3, Line 3, 27, p. H5, Line 9/10, p. H6. There is more discussion on this matter by, MacCullough, *The Negro in English Literature*, pp. 41–47; Annette Drew-Bear, *Painted Faces on the Renaissance Stage, the Significance of Face Painting Conventions* (Lewisburg/London: Bucknell University Press, 1994), pp. 93–107; James Joseph Davey, *The Function of the Dark Lady in Shakespeare's Sonnets* (Trieste: Università Degli Studi di Trieste, 1986), n. p. passim ('though art or I am Black but comely' in the Song of Solomon'); and Katherine Duncan Jones (ed.), *Shakespeare's Sonnets* (London: Arden Shakespeare, 1997), pp. 29, 47–55, 80, 88, 100, 368.

[210] Edward Herbert, John Churton Collins (ed.), *The Poems of Lord Herbert of Cherbury* (1665, 2nd edition, London: Chatto and Windus, 1881), pp. 6, 58, 59. Iyengar, goes further and says in, *Shades of Difference,* p. 75, that Herbert wants the 'the reader, the poet ... to be turned black' to understand blackness.

[211] Author unknown, Proclamation ca January 1601; G. L. Registers of Holy Trinity the Less, GL Ms 9155; *Chambers Dictionary of Etymology,* p. 676; and *The Oxford English Dictionary,* p. 1058.

[212] Boorde, *Introduction to the Book of Knowledge,* pp. 88–89; Best, A True Discourse, pp. 28–32; Minsheu, *A Dictionarie in Spanish and English,* p. 72; Blount (tr.), Conestaggio, *The Historie of ... Portugal,* pp. 10, 39; and Pory (tr.), Africanus, *A Geographical Historie of Africa,* p. 6.

[213] Ungerer, *The Mediterranean Apprenticeship of British Slavery,* pp. 11–12,17, 69; Habib, *Black Lives,* p. 7; and Griffiths, 'Secrecy and Authority,' pp. 925–51.

[214] G. L. London, Census for Coleman Street Ward, London, 15 December, 1567 Returns Coll/SP/E. 1: 460.

[215] Reginald Godfrey Marsden (ed.) Selden Society, *Select Pleas in the Court of Admiralty.* Vol. I. *The Court of the Admiralty of the West (A.D. 1390-1404) and the High Court of Admiralty (A.D. 1527-1545),* Volume II (London: Publications of the Selden Society, 1897), p. xvi.

[216] Best, *A True Discourse,* pp. 28–32; and suggested by Faggett, *Black and Other Minorities,* pp. 9–29, 95–107.

[217] Stubbs, *The Discoverie of a Gaping Gulf*, pp. 10, 19, 32, 35, 41, 67; suggested by Faggett, *Black and Other Minorities*, pp. 9–29, 95–107.

[218] An opposite view to this is offered by Smith on the question of linguistics in *Race and Rhetoric in the Renaissance*, pp. 15, 17, 73, 80, 121, 131, 133–137.

[219] Best, *A True Discourse*, pp. 28–32. Similar views are expressed by James Walvin (ed.), *Black Presence: A Documentary History of the Negro in England, 1555–1860* (London: Orbach and Chambers, 1971), pp. 33–37; Braude, 'The Sons of Noah,' pp. 103–142; and Folarin Shyllon, *Black People in Britain 1553–1833* (Oxford: Oxford University Press, 1977), p. 3.

[220] Author unknown, Proclamation ca January 1601.

[221] Kirk and Kirk (eds.), *Returns of Aliens Dwelling in ... London,* Volume I, pp. preface, xii, 391; GL Ms 9223,9222/1; G. L. Author unknown, *St Botolph without Aldgate Memorandum Day Book,* Volume VI (London: Parish of St Botolph without Aldgate, 1596–7), p. 118, Ref P69/BOT2/ A/ 01/MS 9234/6; Habib, *Black Lives in the English Archives,* p. 320; and G. L. 'Black and Asian people discovered in records held by the Manuscripts Section,' Manuscripts Section, Aldermanbury, London.

[222] Registers of St Botolph Bishopsgate, GL Ms 4515/1; Arthur Meredyth Burke (ed.), *Memorials of St Margaret's Church Westminster. The Parish Registers, 1539–1660* (London: Eyre and Spottiswoode, 1914), p. 58; and Habib, *Black Lives,* p. 320.

[223] Plymouth and West Devon Record Office, St Andrews/ June 23/1603 MF 1–4.

[224] Author unknown, Proclamation ca 1601.

Fig. 1. Abd el-Ouahed Ben Messaoud ... [the] Moorish Ambassador, 1600. Reproduced by kind permission of the University of Birmingham Research and Cultural Collections.

Fig. 2. 'John Blanke' in *Westminster Tournament Roll* … 1511.
Reproduced by permission of the Kings, Heralds and Pursuivants of Arms, London.

Fig. 3. Juriaen Van Streeck. *A Still Life with a Moorish Servant* ...1632–1687.

Fig. 4. Jan Brueghel. *Study of Moorish Heads,* 1568–1625.
Reproduced with kind permission of Bridgeman Art Library, Ltd. London.

ABOVE: Fig. 5. Peter Paul Rubens. *Studies of the Head of a Negro*, circa 1615. Musees Royaux des Beaux-Arts de Belgique, Brussels, Belgium. © 2013. Photo Art Media/Heritage Images/Scala, Florence.

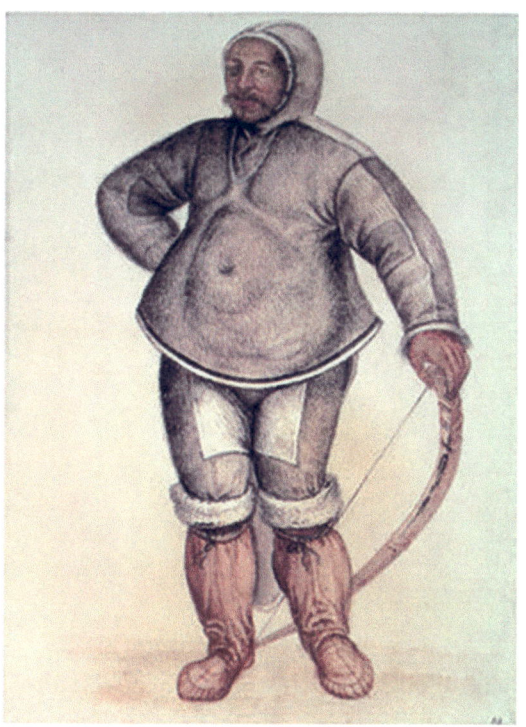

LEFT: Fig. 6. John White. '*An Eskimo Man with Bow*,' 1585–1593.

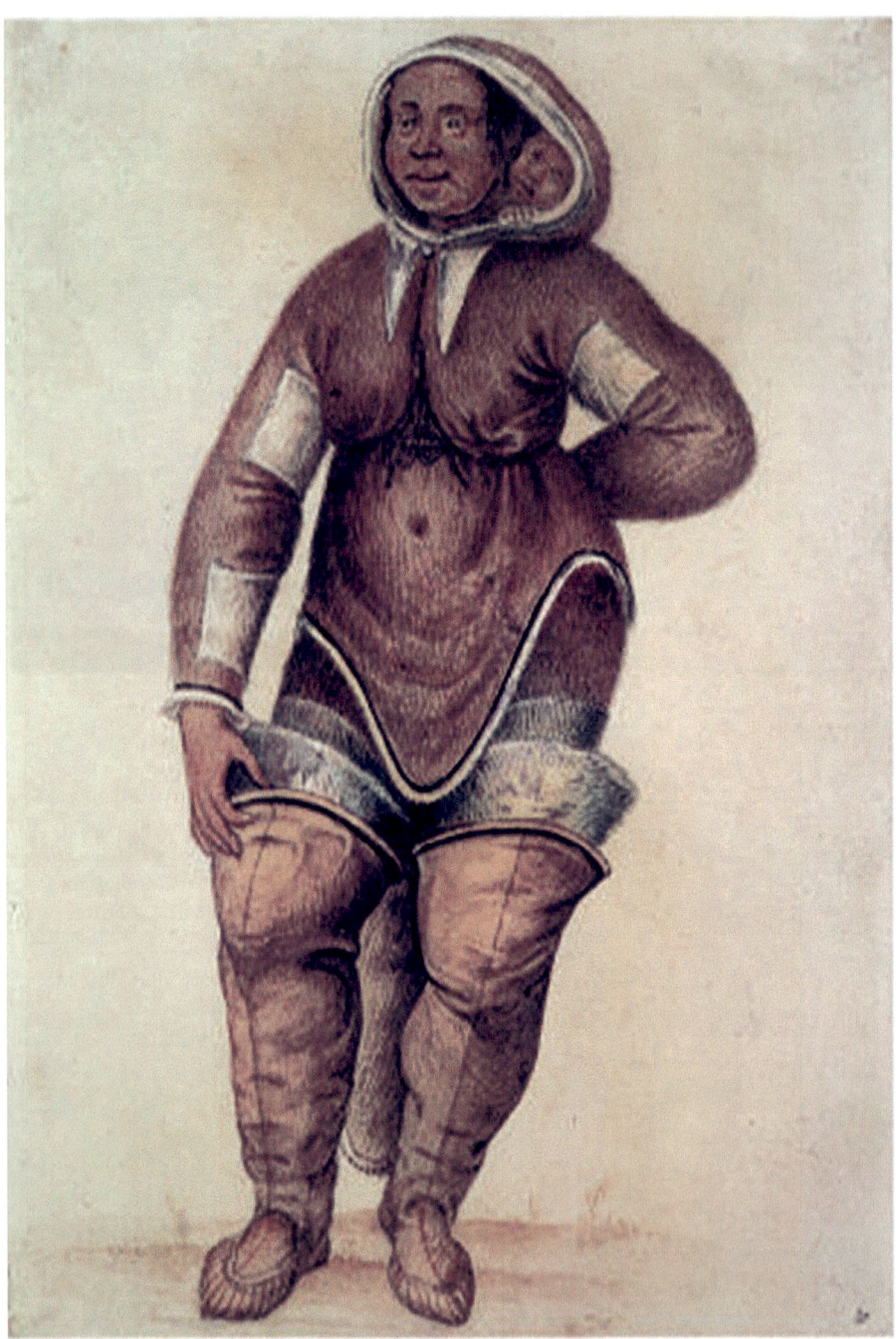

Fig. 7. John White. *'An Eskimo Woman with Baby,'* 1585–1593 (all rights reserved). Both images reproduced by kind permission of the © Trustees of the British Museum.

Fig. 8. Cesare Vecellio. *Degli Habiti Antichi...*, 1590, pp. 470–473.

Fig. 9. *Domesday Abbreviatio*, 1241, England, p. 196.
Reproduced by kind permission of the National Archives Image Library, Kew, London.

Fig. 10. Nicolas Verdun. *Verdun Altar* [King Solomon and the Queen of Sheba], circa 1181, Austria. By kind permission of Erich Lessing. Erich Lessing Culture & Fine Arts Archive, Vienna, Austria.

LEFT: Fig. 11. Conrad Kyeser. *De Bellifortis* [Queen of Sheba], 1405, Germany. By kind permission of Georg-August-Universität Göttingen, Germany.

BELOW: Fig. 12. Artist unknown. *The Adoration of the Magi*, 1520, England. © Victoria and Albert Museum, London

Fig. 13. Artist unknown. *The Adoration of the Magi*, (Detail), England, 1520. © Victoria and Albert Museum, London.

ABOVE: Fig. 14. Hans Baldung Grien. *Adoration of the Magi*, 1507. From the Staatliche Museum, Berlin, Germany. © 2013. Photo Art Media/Heritage Images/Scala, Florence.

LEFT: Fig. 15. Artist unknown. *African Knight*, possibly Saint Maurice, circa 16th century, St Mary's Church, Uffculme, England. Granted with kind permission of Revd Garner, The Vicarage, Uffculme, Cullompton, England.

Relief carving of a black saint (Saint Maurice?) at Uffculme parish church.

BLACKAMOORES: AFRICANS IN TUDOR ENGLAND

Fig. 16. Lucas Cranach the Elder and workshop, 1472–1553. *Saint Maurice*, (Detail), ca.1522–25.
New York, Metropolitan Museum of Art. Oil on wood, 1525. Bequest of Eva F. Kollsman, 2005. Inv.2006.469 © 2013. Image copyright The Metropolitan Museum of Art/Art Resource/Scala, Florence.

Matthias Grunewald. *Erasmus of Formulae and Saint Maurice*, (Detail), 1517–1523.
bpk | Bayerische Staatsgemaldesammlungen (50009493) – Erasmus and St Maurice Ref.

Lucas Cranach the Elder. *Pfirtscher Altar*, (Detail), 1472–1553. Hl. Mauritius, Aschaffenburg, Staatsgalerie im Schloss Johannisburg, Bayerische Staatsgemaeldesammlungen. Buchenholz.
93,2 × 41 cm. Inv. 6263 © 2013. Photo Scala, Florence/BPK, Bildagentur fuer Kunst, Kultur und Geschichte, Berlin.

Hans Baldung Grien. *Adoration of the Magi*, (Detail), 1507.
bpk / Gemaldegalerie, SMB /Jorg P Anders. (00009686)

LEFT: Fig. 17. Matthias Grunewald. *Erasmus of Formulae and Saint Maurice*, 1517–1523, oil on wood, Germany. bpk | Bayerische Staatsgemäldesammlungen (50009493) – Erasmus and St Maurice Ref.

Fig. 18. Artist unknown. *African Head*, Coat of Arms of Sir Thomas Sonds, St Michael and All Angels, Throwley Church, England, circa 16th century. Photography by Julian P Guffogg.

Fig. 19. Albrecht Durer. Portrait of *Caterina, the Mulatta of the Portuguese Bradao*, 1471–1528, no.1060 E. Florence, Gabinetto dei Disegni e delle Stampe degli Uffizi. © 2013. Photo Scala, Florence – courtesy of the Ministero Beni e Att. Culturali.

Fig. 20. 'John Blanke' in *Westminster Tournament Roll* ... 1511.
Reproduced by permission of the Kings, Heralds and Pursuivants of Arms, London.

CHAPTER 3

Africans from continental Europe in Tudor England

There were Africans who came to Tudor England from other European countries. However, it is sometimes difficult to find out which countries these were, as the parish records in which Africans are described often make no reference to where they came from or their origins. Moreover, it can be difficult to prove that simply because someone came from or via a place that they originated from there. Often only an inference can be drawn about a person's origins from the evidence that is available in Tudor records;[1] since for some priests noting the place of birth or origin of an African living in their parish may not have been important. However, by taking a different approach to this issue we can discover more. Where someone is an adult at the time of their baptism it is likely that they may be foreign-born: such as with 'Julyane a blackamore servant, Wyth Mr Alldermanne Bannying' who was '22 yeares' old at her baptism on 29 March 1601 at St Mary Bothaw, London; or with 'Cristofer Adam' described as 'a blackamore' and baptised in Bromley on the '22 daie of April,' 1593 where he is referred to as 'a man growne.'[2] Therefore, although it is difficult to prove that Julyane or Cristofer came from or via Europe it is not unreasonable to assume they are foreign-born. This is because it was a standard practice in Tudor England for children to be baptised at birth and for someone not to have been until their twenty-second year, or until they were 'growne,' implies they have either changed religion, lived outside of any parish, are new to the country, or all of the aforementioned.[3] This is especially as in Cristofer's case because the recorder has chosen to note he is 'a man growne,' but not how old he is, perhaps because neither he, nor Cristofer knows, but the clerk feels that his adult status and adult conversion to Christianity is significant.

In other Tudor parish records where Africans are described their origins may be mentioned in a vague way. But it still may be possible to work out from this information that some of them came from or via continental Europe, and to suggest how their origins may have affected their status in Tudor England. Pursuant to this it appears that some of these Africans had been particularly effective at integrating themselves into Tudor society.

This would be because of their experiences in Europe which gave them the capacity to live amongst European immigrants such as the 3,160 Dutch citizens mentioned in the subsidy rolls who were present in London in 1571.[4]

This integration may also explain why some Tudor records show a connection between an African and a continental European but do not explain the origins of the former. An example of this can be found in the record of an African woman called Mary who gave birth to a daughter called 'Cristen' whose 'supposed' father was 'John Kinge, a Dutchman.' Cristen was baptised on 17 November 1594 at St Andrew's Plymouth.[5]

Cristen's record also illustrates that in parish records, clerks and priests often only wrote a line about the persons they baptised, christened, married or buried, a summary of an entire conversation between themselves and their African subject.[6] This line could indicate to the priest or clerk the origin of that African, but as we read it now it may be difficult for us to understand. So Mary may have been born in England, originated from her employer John White's work and travels as the Governor of the Virginia Company in North America, or come from continental Europe.[7] In this chapter I will discuss the European connections of Africans such as Mary to see how this affected their status in Tudor England.

Africans in Tudor England who came from continental Europe

This chapter will focus on those Africans who came to Tudor England from Spain and Portugal because in English records we have more information about 'those kindes of people.' Nevertheless there were Africans living throughout Europe in the fifteenth and sixteenth centuries. Historians such as J. A. Rogers have listed Africans in the armorial bearings of a number of aristocratic European families, which suggests at this time some of 'those kindes of people' had status and power in Austria, Belgium, Germany, and Eastern European countries such as Poland.[8] However, historians such as Barbara Hanawalt, Habib and Ungerer all propose that Africans were mostly slaves in countries such as France, Holland and Italy[9] and that they brought this status to Tudor England. I challenge this latter view not only because as I suggested in Chapter 1, English law had no power to keep Africans on the basis of their colour or ethnic origins as perpetually-inferior slaves, but also because there are complex issues regarding the status of Africans in continental Europe. For example, the sixteenth-century Italian historian Caelius Augustinus Curio says that in France and Italy Africans came as conquerors; and they had certainly been present in those countries since the Moors invaded Southern Europe in the eighth century;[10] whilst Thomas Bourke the nineteenth-century historian claims that '100,000 [Moors] went to France and Auxere' as exiles from the persecutions which took place in Spain and Portugal and J. A. Rogers confirms this.[11]

The presence of Africans on the coats of arms of a number of European aristocratic families, and some in England, underlines the connections between Africans and Europeans. In other words as J. A. Rogers has suggested this iconography is more than a display of the fantastic or strange.[12] But this iconography is not always easy to explain, such as with the African man depicted on the tomb of the coat of arms of the sixteenth-century English knight Sir Thomas Sonds who fought in Europe, he died on 8 February 1592 and was from Throwley in Kent.[13]

So, some of these connections are difficult to decipher. But we know that Africans were present throughout Europe in the sixteenth and seventeenth centuries and that they were employed by continental Europeans. Some of these Africans came to England with their employers and were recorded in English records as servants. Other African servants such as Frauncis may simply have been employed by a Dutch or Frenchman but had been born in England or elsewhere. But all of these African servants once in England, and if they had skills, are likely to have become part of their employer's exclusive professions and their privileged sodality. For example, Frauncis worked for a Peter Miller a Dutch 'beare brewer' living in St Hallows, Barking, London in 1568. Frauncis is described as 'a negar' and Miller's 'servant' in records contained in the Barking Parish Register and the *Parish Clerk's Memorandum Daybook*. He was buried at the age of thirty-one on 3 March 1596/7 at East Smithfield/Clerkenwell, London. Frauncis was buried with the 'best cloth' and had 'four bearers' at his funeral, which suggests he had been a valued employee in a beer brewing profession which few people in England had access to.[14] This is because the beer brewing profession was organised by a small number of very exclusive guilds and secret societies, mostly run by Dutch immigrants, who employed only a few trusted employees who could keep their 'secrets.'[15]

There are other Africans present in England who came from countries such as Italy, who can help us understand more clearly how and why 'those kindes of people' were present here, and what their status was. One of these Africans is Maria Moriana who came from Venice in Italy with her employer. We do not know the date when she arrived in England, but in the 1470s she was living in Southampton in the household of her employer Filippo Cini. In Southampton, Cini 'hatched a base plot to have her sold' as a slave to one of his Italian colleagues called Dominic who was from

Genoa. Earlier in the fifteenth century Cini had been an important person in Southampton because he helped Italian merchants maintain their control of trade in that city.[16] This control was protected by trade agreements created through Italian merchants' participation in local politics. For example, through these connections Cini and Andrea Morosimi another Italian merchant were able to oust an Englishman called John Payne from the position of Mayor of Southampton. However, towards the second half of the fifteenth century, although the Italian community continued to be influential in that city, Cini suffered economic hardship.[17]

Notwithstanding Cini's difficult economic situation, Moriana his African servant appears to have remained loyal to him. Her testimony on this matter is recorded in the English Chancery records of 1470 where she states she got 'from him only meat and drink' and no payment.[18] Moriana is described in those records as being 'very Innocent' and also unmarried – both of which suggest she was still young despite twenty years of service to him, and that she had entered Cini's employment when she was a small child. It is interesting that despite this loyalty Cini still tried to have her sold, and got other Italian merchants in England involved. Using this fact, Hanawalt suggests that Moriana was 'probably a slave' in Italy before she reached England.[19] But I suggest it is more probable that the reason why Cini felt he could try and sell Moriana in England was because the 'said Oratice ['Orator': Moriana] … cannot speke nor understand Englisshe nor Latyn,' and therefore she did not initially know her rights were being taken away.[20] In other words Cini knew that Moriana was not a slave in Italy or England and that was why he used subterfuge.

An African from Italy present in Tudor England whose status raises similar issues to Moriana's is Jacques Francis. His employer's name was Piero Paule and he brought Jacques to Italy from West Africa. Jacques' status is discussed through his and other witnesses' testimonies given in the High Courts of the Admiralty in 1547–8. The case was about Jacques' employer allegedly stealing tin and lead. In the course of the proceedings Italian witnesses such as Niccolo de Marini and Domencio de Milanes displayed a dismissive contempt for the validity of the testimony of Jacques. As a result, they revealed their attitudes regarding the status of Africans, and perhaps showed that they were used to 'those kindes of people' occupying subservient positions in their Italian and English households.[21]

However, as Steven Epstein and other historians point out the Africans who lived in Italy were not automatically slaves, because there was an absence of national laws which imposed a perpetually-inferior position on them.[22] This is similar to what was happening in Tudor England, where Africans and their children appear to have determined their own status based on the skills they offered.

There is another group of Africans present in Tudor England who can help us see more connections between the presence of 'those kindes of people' in Italy and those here. Some of these Africans present in Southampton are associated in an obvious way with Italian employers as Moriana was, whilst others have links which require more investigation. One of the latter is an African described as 'a blakman' in the *Southampton Book of Fines*. This book describes fines for minor and petty infractions and lists this 'blakman' as being assaulted by a Richard Harterrell sometime in 1491/2. This African was a 'taboryn' or musician working on a ship owned by Peter Trevison. The name Trevison may be an anglicised version of the name Treviso that is a place in Italy near Venice known for 'fine wines,' and may mean that he and the 'blakman' were from there.[23] But this 'blakman' is not the only African in Southampton who has connections to Italy. There are other unnamed Africans who are listed in the *Book of Fines* and because of the presence and influence of Italian merchants in Southampton it may be that some of these Africans also came to England from that country.[24]

Some of the Africans present in Southampton are likely to have come to Tudor England because of international trade with Italy. And indeed, some of the merchants who facilitated this trade may have been Africans from Italy. However, it is difficult to prove this when all we have to rely on is their name being 'Nigro' or 'Negro.'[25] Nevertheless, there is a person called 'Carbew Lazia' who is described as 'a Negro Marche' in the Tudor records where he appears. Carbew was buried on 11 March 1591 at St Andrew's Plymouth.[26] His parish record does not tell us his age which may mean that he was foreign-born, an idea supported by the connection some of his names have to Italy and France, as the word 'Lazia' suggests a relationship to Lazio where Rome is the capital city;[27] whilst the word 'marche' in French means to 'walk,' 'trade' or 'market goods especially wine.' This may make Carbew one of the few African merchants identified as such in English records. But it is also possible that the word 'marche' could be an Italian word meaning to 'brand' or 'mark' and this may indicate that Carbew is a servant or even a slave.[28] However, I think the latter is less likely because his employer's name would probably be included in his record as we have seen with others discussed in this book. These sorts of issues are now discussed in more detail as I examine the Africans present in Tudor England who came from Spain and Portugal.

Africans who came from Spain and Portugal

The evidence in this chapter and throughout this book suggests that an African population in Spain and Portugal (Iberia) had a direct effect on an African presence in Tudor England. This has been acknowledged by writers such as Scobie, Sertima, File and Power but sometimes in a rather cursory or vague way.[29] Furthermore, we saw in Chapter 1 that the 1601 Proclamation makes a connection between an African presence in England and England's war against Spain in 1585, even though we know that Iberian Africans were present in England long before 1585. Moreover in Chapter 2, I stated that many of the names used in Tudor England to describe Africans such as Blackamoore, Moor and Negro owe their origins to how they or other similar terms were used in Spain and Portugal. In other words, English writers were being influenced by some of the ideas about Africans found in these countries. But I suggest it was not just the words used to describe Africans which came to Tudor England from Iberia, but Africans as well.

The case of Pero or Pedro Alvarez illustrates this point. He was present in England in 1490 although we do not know when he arrived. Pero is described in Portuguese archives as a 'negro e forro' which literally means a 'foreign or strange black.'[30] The word 'forro' is also a language spoken in Sao Tome and Principe in West Africa and this may indicate that he originated from there before he came to Portugal or England.[31] Pero was called an 'escravo' in the Portuguese records but evidence suggests that this term did not mean he was a perpetually-inferior slave.[32] This is proved by the fact that once in England Pero obtained his freedom on 13 March 1490 from Henry VII 'Reg de Inglaterra,' and later when Pero voluntarily returned to the Royal Court of Portugal (I have not yet found the date), his manumission was upheld by John II.[33]

The evidence in this chapter shows that there are other Iberian Africans present in Tudor England, but they had a different status to Pero Alvarez. However, discovering their status is difficult as Spain and Portugal from 711 and up to 1492 were not countries as we now know them, but were a series of much smaller nations some of which were controlled by independent African kings. Some of these kingdoms owed their origins to when Tarik Ibn Ziyad landed in Spain in 711 with 7,000–6,000 troops 'most of whom were Moorish Africans':[34] 'Black of complexion.'[35] There were subsequent invasions of various other peoples from North Africa and Arabia and some of these invasions also brought dark-skinned Africans to Iberia. This shows that not only were there dark-skinned Africans in Iberia but that some of this initial population had their own systems of kingship, traditions and culture. Initially the status of these Africans relied on the power of the independent nations they created in Iberia. These kingdoms were later known by different names and included Al Andalus or Andalusia, meaning the 'Land of Light.'[36] Al Andalus at its height included Granada, Castile, Leon, Catalonia, Septimania and Aragon with another place that Jonson refers to in 1605 as 'Swarth [Black] Lusitania' a province of Portugal.[37] A hundred years earlier, the name 'Lusitania' appears in English records when a 'Peter of Lusitania' also known as 'Petrus du Campo Portugaliensis,' studied at Oxford University from 15 June 1506 to 9 June 1509, although there is insufficient evidence to confirm he was an African.[38]

The status of Iberian Africans present in Tudor England was affected by the power of the Moorish kingdoms they were from. This idea can be explored through the Africans who Katherine, later Queen of England brought to Plymouth on 2 October 1501.[39] Katherine was from the Kingdom of Aragon in Spain which emerged through the Reconquista, when 'white Christian Princes' deposed Moorish rulers.[40] By 1492 the last independent Moorish kingdom known as Granada was defeated.[41] However, by the time that Christian rulers had taken over Katherine's province of Aragon in 1035,[42] this kingdom had experienced over three hundred years of Moorish leadership. This historic link with Moorish kingdoms in Europe explains why Katherine brought Iberian Africans to England, and that 'those kindes of people' by their influence on her culture, also affected the way Tudor society developed. An example of this can be seen in the persistence of the image of the pomegranate in English heraldry. The pomegranate was known in the medieval and early modern period as a fruit that the Moors had cultivated and brought to Europe from Africa. It was the emblem for the Moorish city of Granada which was also known as the 'last seed of the pomegranate.' But this symbol became an emblem of Katherine's branch of the English royal family, so much so that when Anne Boleyn replaced her as Henry VIII's wife she chose as one of her emblems an image of a dove or falcon pecking at a pomegranate.[43]

Furthermore, Iberian Africans were not only indirectly influencing English culture with their emblems and motifs, but their presence in England had a direct affect on fashion in Tudor society. An example of this is the Farthingale which is Moorish in origin, and seems to have first been brought to England by Iberian Africans, and white Spanish women who were part of Katherine's entourage. The Farthingale was described by Tudor writers as 'certayn rownde hopys [hoops] berying owte their gownes from their bodies aftir their country['s] maner,' with a 'busteous and marvellous' 'straunge dyverstie of raiment.' The Farthingale later became an integral part of Tudor dress perhaps because of the Iberian African and other Spanish women who brought this style to England. Katherine and her Moorish attendants were certainly dressed in this style when they arrived in London.[44] The Tudor politician Sir Thomas More was living in the area of Charterhouse in 1501 when he saw them, and he made the following comments in a letter dated 12 November of that year:

> [Katherine's] Spanish escort – good heavens, – what a sight! If you had seen it I am afraid you would have burst with laughter, they were ludicrous. Except for three or at most four of them, they were not too much to look at: hunchbacked, undersized, barefoot pygmy Ethiopians. If you had seen them you would have thought they were refugees from hell.[45]

Upon a first reading More's comments seem to be merely a negative rant against Africans resembling others that were discussed in the last chapter. However, his letter provides a key to unlock the ethnicity of Katherine's ladies in waiting. In addition, More's letter added to other evidence (cited below), suggests that these 'barefoot ... Ethiopians' are the same women who Katherine speaks about in 1527 as being her loyal attendants who had been in her service for twenty-six years. More's remarks are also important because they are the Tudor politician's eye-witness observations of Katherine's entourage made to his friend John Holt.[46] More is attempting to convey what he saw without courtly or diplomatic reserve, and perhaps he is writing in confidence as he was probably too wily a politician even at twenty-three to publicly scorn the Queen of England's attendants.[47] As a consequence More uses different words to describe Katherine's entourage from those used in official accounts where the 'lady princes' ethnicity is obscured. This may be because for the official recorders, within the context of the grand spectacle of that day, the 'lady princes' race may not have seemed important enough to emphasise. Furthermore, some of the official accounts compiled by Englishmen such as Sir Richard Guildford, Thomas Grey 2nd Marquis of Dorset and Sir Christopher Wickham were made several months or years after the events they describe. Their accounts were often an amalgamation of earlier reports written by heralds who saw Katherine come to London.[48] However, a close examination of some of these texts, with the information that More has given us, shows us these other writers may also be describing Iberian Africans in Katherine's entourage.[49]

One of these texts is the *Cotton Vitellius Chronicles*. These are a series of manuscripts detailing parts of England's early history although much of the original accounts have been added to by Tudor writers such as Raphael

Holinshed or John Stow. The historian Charles Kingsford has gathered together these manuscripts and in his work there is a recurring statement that Katherine's entourage consisted of women who were 'marvellously dressed but were not the fairest.' In the *Receyt of the Ladie Kateryne*, a compilation of Tudor texts brought together by the historian Gordon Kipling, Katherine's ladies in waiting are described in an almost identical way as having 'apparel [which] was busteous and marvellous but they were not the fairest women of the company.' Stow continuing Holinshed's *Chronicles* in 1615 uses similar phrases.[50]

Unlike the descriptions above, More's statements were probably never intended for publication. His reference to 'barefoot pygmies' is his personal and subjective but honest opinion of the appearance of the people he saw. The phrase 'not the fairest,' repeated in *Vitellius* and the *Receyt* seems to be an 'official' description of the same women who More is talking about and may imply that these women are dark-skinned.[51] It is More's use of the word 'Ethiopian' which reveals that all of these accounts could be talking about people who are of African descent.

However, More's description of Katherine's entourage goes beyond merely calling these people Africans. He seems to be implying that these people are part of some kind of circus or dejected carnival show. For a modern reader it may appear peculiar for the 'First lady of Europe' to have 'barefoot pygmies' of any race in her entourage, as More's phrase 'barefoot' implies they are poor and 'in rags.'[52] This idea is especially at odds with the description that Stow gives over a hundred years later, when he appears to describe the same women as being in 'sumptuous manner apparelled' and says they created a positive 'stir' wherever they went.[53] Stow's account shows us that the women in Katherine's entourage could not have been 'barefoot' or 'in rags,' since the Queen's entrance into London was not just 'public theatre,' but 'a significant object of public attention,' that provided a spiritual, political, and national statement of her intention to be part of the English nation. Indeed this was its purpose,[54] and therefore everyone who was part of this event including these Iberian Africans would have been dressed to fulfil this purpose.

Habib offers an explanation for the way the Tudor politician describes these ladies in waiting. He says that these women only looked as if they were 'barefoot,' but were wearing 'flat-soled shoes' or 'sandals.' In fact these sandals were fashionable amongst Moorish women in Iberia.[55] If this theory is correct More is demonstrating his ignorance, or indifference of a cultural norm that was more sophisticated than the one that existed in early Tudor England.

More continues this indifferent attitude when he describes Katherine's ladies in waiting as 'pygmies,' 'hunchbacked' and 'undersized.' These comments suggest that these Moorish women are deformed in some way. When added to the previous remarks they suggest a very strange spectacle. But the people who More is talking about are probably 'not yet fully grown.'[56] Stow's comments support this idea when he says that Katherine was accompanied by 'many virgins.' In other words, the people being described are actually Moorish children. This may be better understood by exploring the tone of More's letter when he says that 'they were not too much to look at.'[57] Habib translates the phrase 'tollerabiles' that More uses as 'tolerable to look at' but the meaning is the same. More is looking at Katherine's train with the subjective eyes of a young man, so he appears to have found some of Katherine's entourage unappealing because they were 'not yet fully grown.'

In addition, More may have found Katherine's servants unattractive because they had Moorish blood or 'a lick of the tar brush.' Ironically, More's comments in 1501 on Katherine's entourage appear to reveal something about 'black blood'[58] being present not just amongst those classified as 'Moors' in Spain, but also amongst the rest of her attendants. Therefore his remark that only 'three or at most four of them' were attractive may imply more than Habib, Sherwood or others have been willing to state. In other words, that 'black blood' was present in the ethnic make-up of most of Katherine's entourage and many of them looked as 'black' as 'Ethiopians.'[59] This is not as far-fetched a statement as it may initially appear as 'black blood' was strongly present in the blood-line of many people in sixteenth-century Spanish society, and seems to have been difficult to expunge because the Moors were numerous and had been present in Spain for hundreds of years; as the Spanish Converso physician Juan Huarte said in 1588 '... Blacks pass their colour on to their descendants even in Spain away from their homeland.'[60] This matter is one of the major reasons why when Charles V took over control of Spain in 1516 he introduced 'blue blood inheritance,' or 'sangri azul.' The idea of this system was to ensure that only those with proven non-Moorish lineage could inherit land or wealth.[61] More's comments may inadvertently have referred to a 'problem' of racial admixture that Charles V a decade and a half later sought to change.

Nevertheless, Africans such as those in Katherine's entourage were an integral part of Iberian society, and despite 'sangri azul' Moors were maintained in the households of other members of her family. This includes Ferdinand of Aragon, Isabella of Castile and Charles V (despite his policies).[62] Katherine as an urbane trendsetter was continuing this tradition by having 'lady princes' who were Iberian Africans.[63] As J. A. Rogers says Africans were also included in the households of Iberian royalty in Portugal; and Ungerer supports this idea by stating that in the 1530s, King John II of Portugal and his wife Catherine of Austria had 25 'escravos' including 'Africans' and 'Amerindians'.⁶⁴ The Africans who served these powerful European families illustrated to English aristocracy that Africans were useful and important: in other words, what the first families of Europe did would be copied by a number of aristocratic families in Tudor England.

However, Katherine of Aragon did not just have Iberian Africans in her entourage because of fashion. In Tudor England these Moorish 'lady princes' were familiar faces in an initially unfamiliar country, helping the Spanish princess in an alien country. This may be why as Stow tells us in 1501, the 'lady princes' accompanied Katherine wherever she went from Plymouth to 'the archbishop of Canterbury's [premises in London]'.⁶⁵ It seems, the 'lady princes' Stow talks about are the same Moorish children More describes in 1501, so that by the time of Katherine's estrangement from Henry VIII in 1527 they are likely to have become some of her most trusted employees. In the same year Katherine writes to Henry confirming some of this when she says:

> I beseech your highness, to succour my servants and to grant them favours ... From the day that I have arrived in this kingdom they have always served me in the hope that things would be mended ... they serve me still with the same good will as though I granted them every day new favours.

Katherine clearly valued these women's services so they are unlikely to have been maintained in her court merely as decorative accessories. These women probably had skills that white English servants in the court of Henry VII or VIII did not have (something I discuss below). This may be why she left them '£10' each (a large sum) in her will.⁶⁶ But this is not the only information we have on these Iberian-African women. Mariano Roca de Togores a nineteenth-century historian has researched the correspondence between Katherine and Henry and has found information which may help us to name at least one of these Moorish women.⁶⁷

She is called Catalina de Cardones and is referred to in contemporary documents as a 'More' and 'escravo'. Togores' research reveals that Catalina's husband was a Moorish crossbowman 'hace vallestas/ballestas,' who she may have married in Granada, and their record is one of the few of a marriage between two Africans in the Tudor period. Interestingly, the historian Giles Tremlett adds a little more information about this Moorish crossbowman, and names him 'Oviedo,' in his recently published book *Catherine of Aragon: Henry's Spanish Wife*, but it is difficult to trace the author's source for this name.⁶⁸

Catalina's role was as the 'lady of the toilet' or the 'lady of the bedchamber,'[69] which meant that she was responsible for the most intimate of Katherine's 'womanly matters.' Katherine had to have complete confidence in any servant who held this role and it is significant that she chose a Moorish woman. In fact Catalina's Iberian-Moorish heritage may have been a major reason why she held this position. Moorish women from Iberia were well-known for having skills in their 'knowledge of the body' and for producing remedies to enhance the 'arts of love.' These skills were especially associated with Moorish women who came from noble and aristocratic families as Katherine's ladies in waiting are likely to have done. Perhaps Catalina originated from one of the noble Moorish families of Granada that Ferdinand and Isabella, the parents of Katherine conquered in 1492 just nine years before.[70] This is all the more likely since although the last king of Granada Boabdil Abu abd Abdullah Muhammad XII was exiled abroad, many other aristocratic Africans remained in Spain. Some Moorish women who were part of the upper classes in Granada were employed in roles as servants of their new Christian overlords. As the early modern historian Blount says these Iberian Africans 'continued their new navigation [work] with greater service' but 'quiet[ly].'[71] In other words, Iberian-African women such as Catalina of noble Granadian birth, were now occupying positions as servants in English society because of what had happened to their people in Spain.

Katherine's daughter Mary I probably grew up with Catalina and other Iberian Africans as attendants. Therefore it is not surprising that Mary herself had an African in her employment. He is described as 'Fraunces Negro' or 'Fraunces ye negro' and worked in Mary's royal stables. In 1523 Fraunces' presence is noted in the subsidy rolls where it appears he was paid more than his white counterparts.[72] This may have been because he was part of the Iberian-Moorish 'Jinetes,' many of whom originated from the African nation known as Zanata. These 'Jinetes' were internationally known for riding without stirrups and fashionable European stables employed them because this skill was rare in Europe.[73] Fraunces may have been with the Iberian servants who first came with Katherine or he may have arrived in England independently. He is referred to in the subsidy rolls as an Alien and foreign-born, but there is no record of him paying any extra taxes and this may be because as a royal employee he was exempt.[74]

Katherine and Mary were not the only Tudor monarchs to employ Africans amongst their staff. Elizabeth I had at least one African servant who she called her 'littel black a More.' His presence in the Tudor court shows that in the seventy years between Katherine coming to England and Elizabeth being Queen, the idea had remained that African attendants could offer an important and valuable service to members of English royalty. This African boy is mentioned in a warrant dated 14 April 1574, where it is stated that the Queen ordered the clothes maker Henry Henre to make for him a 'garcon coat ... of white taphata cutt and lyned ... striped with gold and silver with buckeram bayes ... knitted stockings [and] white shoes.' This African boy was employed until at least the following year 13 April 1575, when a further warrant granted this 'littel black a More' another set of clothing. This time the clothes were to be made by the designer Thomas Ludwell and they included:

> a Cassocke ... trimmed with silver ... purple lase of grene silke ... silke with buttons of silke and silver fused with taphata lined with bayes and bukeram ... a tuft mockado gown faced with thirty-seven black coney skins.[75]

Another servant of Elizabeth I that Habib claims is of Iberian-Moorish origin was a woman called Thomasina de Pais.[76] However, there is little evidence written or visual which proves conclusively what her ethnic origins were. A painting called *Queen Elizabeth Dancing with the Earl of Leicester* includes an image of a diminutive white woman, that the historian John Southworth claims is Thomasina.[77] But this is unlikely, as the historian Barbara Ravelhofer states, because the painting actually depicts characters from a sixteenth-century French Valois court.[78] Instead we must examine other evidence to discover Thomasina's ethnic origins. She first appears in English records in 1574 where she is described as 'a woman dwarf.' She was present in the court of Elizabeth I and may have had the same position in Elizabeth's court as Catalina did in Katherine's.[79] Thomasina was not a common name in Tudor England and in the Aramaic language that it comes from her name means 'little twin.'[80] Moreover, the language of Aramaic was not written or spoken by many people in sixteenth-century Europe. Most of the people who did both were Moors and Jews from Andalusia:[81] suggesting that she had connections with these peoples and had been given this name long before she came to Tudor England. The first part of this idea is confirmed by the fact that Thomasina had a sister called Prudence de Pais. It is also interesting that the second part of their names de Pais means 'of the country' or from the country and it is Spanish.[82]

The dress of Thomasina may tell us more about the status of this woman but probably not more about her origins. A 1574 warrant orders a dress made for her which is as ostentatious as the clothes made for the 'littel black a More.' This dress also includes taffeta, silk and so on; and this is significant as a royal edict made circa 1577 had stated that taffeta could 'only ... be worn by maidens [bachelors] of honour, knight's daughters [sons], wives of Barons, gentlewomen of the private bed chambers.'[83] This edict and other evidence in Janet Arnold's '*Lost From her Majesties Back*,' suggests that since Thomasina's dress was specifically requested by Elizabeth; and because 'the woman dwarf' often wore other clothes 'made from her [the Queen's] old gowns,' that 'the woman dwarf' was a trusted member of the Queen's 'bed chamber,' and/or 'a gentlewoman' of noble birth.[84]

It is unlikely as Southworth implies, however, that Thomasina or the unnamed 'littel black a More' were merely fools or playthings for Elizabeth. 'Elizabeth kept far fewer personal servants than her forbears' and those she had tended to offer useful skills. For example Monarcho or Monarch the Italian jester was dismissed from the Queen's court because he offered no more service than his 'fooling.' The historian Leslie Hotson supports the idea that Thomasina was more than a mere 'fool,' when he claims to have found Tudor records indicating she had her own servant or servants, and had administrative duties inside the court. The fact she was also issued with a pen from the Queen may support this latter notion.[85]

Thomasina is probably the same 'Mrs Tomasin' referred to as the 'Queen's dwarf' in the private diary of John Dee. Dee was an alchemist, historian and personal advisor to Elizabeth I and in his diaries he refers to 'Mrs Tomasin' visiting him on 7 June 1581. The 'Mrs' indicates that by the time she visited Dee she was married but so far the name or ethnicity of her husband has not been discovered. Dee's entry regarding 'Mrs Tomasin' states that she called on him in a social capacity and reinforces the idea that some Iberians were an integral part of polite society in Tudor England.[86] But after this entry of 1581, I have found no more evidence relating to Thomasina's origins or life although, according to Arnold, Thomasina was employed at Elizabeth's court 'until the end of Elizabeth's reign.'[87]

We now turn our focus away from Thomasina towards someone who we can definitively prove was an African present in Tudor England, and who may also have had an Iberian heritage. This is the 'blacke trumpeter' called John Blanke. He appears in a prominent position on the *Westminster Tournament Roll* of 1511 which was created to celebrate the birth of Katherine's son.[88] Blanke may have come to England as part of Katherine's entourage in 1501, although he is not named in the letters between the officials representing Ferdinand, Isabella or Henry VIII written a year earlier.[89] If Blanke came to England with Katherine then he is likely to have participated in the coronation of Henry VIII in 1509.

In the *Westminster Tournament Roll* of 1511, Blanke is shown twice as the *Roll* shows the procession to and from Westminster – unless there are two 'blacke trumpeter[s]' who look identical, which is possible but unlikely. One is drawn to the images of Blanke on the *Roll* almost as if the creators wanted us to focus on him. This is not just because of Blanke's blackness, but also because he is surrounded by a troop of white musicians. These white musicians look pale and sanguine in comparison to Blanke who is depicted actively blowing his trumpet, his cheeks are rounded and his face is 'bright … and full of life.' Blanke appears in both depictions on the *Tournament Roll* sitting on a black or dark grey horse, whilst his white counterparts sit on white or light grey ones and perhaps this was arranged to also emphasise his blackness.[90]

The images of Blanke on the *Roll* also stand out because in both depictions he is wearing a sort of turban or round hat on his head, while the white musicians are not wearing head attire, and their straight hair is hanging limply by the sides of their faces. Perhaps Blanke's natural 'nine ether' or Afro hair would have marked him as too different from them and that is why Blanke covers his head.[91] But if the object of the turban was to obscure what made Blanke 'different,' the opposite happens. Instead Blanke's turban makes him more noticeable amongst his white counterparts and this is even more evident since Blanke's turban appears to change colour. In the first image on the *Roll* it looks brown whilst the next time Blanke is depicted it is green and is now laced with gold.[92] Turbans are not the ordinary attire for courtly musicians in early Tudor England. However, it did later become a feature for African entertainers and African regiments inside the British Army and perhaps individuals such as Blanke were the forerunners of this kind of tradition.[93] It may be that Blanke's turban was a small token of his cultural antecedents and a reflection of his Spanish-Moorish heritage. Iberian Africans were often known to wear such attire as illustrated by a woman called Katharina. She is wearing a simple turban held in place with a brooch in the line sketch drawing of 1521 by Albrecht Dürer. Katharina was a servant to John or Joao Brandao the King of Portugal's agent. She travelled from Portugal with him to Antwerp in Belgium in the first quarter of the sixteenth century. The sketch of Katharina is drawn with softness and humanity and shows the twenty-year old as a quietly dignified African woman (see Fig. 19).[94]

Whether Katharina was of noble birth we do not know, but we do have information about Blanke which suggests that he was. This is because on the *Westminster Tournament Roll* above Blanke's second depiction are the words: 'Les sons des Trompettes, A l'hostel.' These words literally mean 'The sound of the Trumpets, A l'hostel.' Recent research by Fiona Collins uses evidence from Sydney Anglo's work on pageantry to explain that the exclamation of

'A l'hostel' ended the 'lists' of the pageant. In other words, Blanke was part of a group of musicians who officially brought the pageant to an end. It was a task which was reserved for those who were not just musicians but also knights and gentleman,[95] and suggests that Blanke was recognised as being of noble birth, and that is why he had such a prominent role.

The issue of what status Blanke had in Tudor England raises questions however, about whether his name is a pun related to the French word 'Blanc' meaning white as Habib suggests.[96] I suggest if he was a gentleman or knight from the sophisticated Iberian community and he was well respected in the Tudor court, it is unlikely he would self-select a name that mocked his skin complexion. In Chapter 2, I proposed that if Africans chose names which referred to their skin colour, these names tended to emphasise their blackness – and were not used to mock it. This is especially the case for those Africans involved in pageantry such as Blanke or Peter 'the Moryan' in Scotland. That is why the word Blanke may be related to old English words which describe blackness as the expression Moryan does, and the former could be phonetically associated to a word such as 'Blac' which means 'black, bright and shiny.'[97]

Furthermore, it is not only the fact that Blanke and Peter have monikers that makes them similar, but they also had comparable roles in England and Scotland. In the sixteenth-century Scottish court Peter was responsible for performing as a musician as Blanke did in Tudor England. But Peter also planned and organised events for King James IV of Scotland, and it may be that Blanke had a similar role, and that this was influenced by skills he had acquired from his Iberian background. There are at least 35 entries for Peter in Scottish treasury records.[98] These payments are primarily for his wages and to cover the costs of events he organised between 1500 and 1505. There may indeed be more entries which relate to him, but by 1506 there is at least one other 'More taubronar' in the Scottish court and references thereafter may be for him rather than Peter.[99]

In a similar way to Peter, we have records of payments made to Blanke and these are in the contemporary *Treasurer Chamber Records* starting on 7 December 1507.[100] In another set of Tudor records called the *London Exchequer Accounts*, there are references to Blanke receiving the gift of an expensive 'violet cloth' or gown with a 'bonnet and hat' (this might be another turban) 'against his marriage' on '14 January 1511/1512.'[101] It was unusual for the National Treasury to pay for wedding gifts for their employees and this suggests that Blanke was valued. Moreover, this record shows that Blanke was about to start a family in Tudor England.[102] However, after 1512 we do not have any more records which talk of a 'John Blanke blacke trumpeter.' This may be because Blanke and his descendants were so integrated in Tudor England that ideas about their blackness became less significant for the all reasons discussed in the last chapter.

To illustrate this possibility it is worth examining references to the name 'Blanke' in Tudor records to see if there are references to his family. Having looked at over 250, 000 entries, I have found only four references to a 'Blanke' and they are contained in the subsidy rolls. All these Blankes are found in London parishes so it is possible because the name is so rare that they are connected to John Blanke. But they are unlikely to describe the 'blacke trumpeter,' because even if his race was not mentioned his occupation probably would have been as with 'Guylham the King's mynstrell' who lived in Westminster on 3 November 1540, or 'Anthony ... Hailes ...' 'The Sergeant of the Trumpeters,' who lived at Saint Peter the Poor's Ward, London on 10 January 1564.[103] Nevertheless, it is worth mentioning that the entries with the name Blanke are from the areas of the Liberty of Tower Wharf, London, and date from November 1540, Saint Peter's Parish near the Tower of London on 1 October 1543, and St Katherine's next to the Tower of London on 3 April 1549. The last 'John Blanke' may be the same person who is also referred to as being resident in St Katherine's Parish, Aldgate, London on 14 May 1559. Finally, a 'Johannes Blanke' appears in the subsidy rolls for Middlesex in the Ward of the Lane Beneath on 17 April 1550.[104]

The records above lead us to another issue concerning John Blanke. This is that it is unlikely that Blanke would have been able to move large numbers of his family from sixteenth-century Spain to England. This is because in Spain during the first half of the sixteenth century the political climate restricted the movement of Moors and religious non-conformists. This discrimination was maintained by the Spanish Inquisitions which had been initiated by Ferdinand and Isabella in 1478.[105] Those Iberian Africans who remained in Spain to escape persecution often voluntarily discarded the more 'dangerous' aspects of their culture. Some of these Africans were retained by the Spanish authorities and financially rewarded for their skills such as the 'Moorish preceptor' (teacher/instructor) for Charles V, or the African man pictured in the painting of Jan Mostaert (dated 1520) where the subject is believed to be a servant of the Habsburg King (Fig. 21).[106] In Spain, some of these Iberian Africans chose to be baptised in mass conversions and they took on classical Christian names such as John and Peter. These 'Moriscos' believed that if they 'laboured to be admitted' into the 'New Spain' they could prosper.[107] So if John Blanke was a Morisco, which is likely, he would be aware of persecution in Spain, and as I later discuss, may have developed skills of how to 'negotiate' through a European society that was hostile to him.

The evidence indicates that Blanke's Iberian cultural background was a fundamental reason why he had such a prominent position at the Westminster Tournament celebrations. In Blanke's case, his colour showed he was part of an Iberian culture that was well-known and in many ways well-respected in Tudor England. In other words, I am suggesting his colour may have enhanced his official status, not detracted from it. Blanke is not the same as those Africans who allegedly 'danced naked until they died' for James VI of Scotland at his wedding to Anne of Denmark in 1589.[108] These Africans were an exotic diversion, but this does not seem to be Blanke's role at the Tournament. Despite Blanke's turban, which distinguishes him from his white counterparts, he is not a popinjay or a curiosity but seems to be a central part of the seriousness of the royal celebrations. Blanke's status may well have arisen from him belonging to an Iberian-African community which was part of the 'most powerful nation in the world (Spain).' The people who came from sixteenth-century Spain were perceived as being part of a sophisticated and urbane culture. Iberian Africans such as Blanke and Katherine's ladies in waiting were 'ambassadors,' offering a 'translation' of this 'Modern society's' culture for people living in England.[109] This role seems to have been accepted by the majority of people living in Tudor England, despite More's comments.

The idea that Blanke's presence at the Westminster Tournament was used to advertise England's desire to be part of 'Modern Europe;' needs to be analysed in more detail, as he is absent from the depictions of other Tudor festivals that he logically ought to have been part of. These include the *Great Tournament Roll* of 1545 which commemorated the meeting of Henry VIII and the Emperor Maximilian I of Germany in 1513, but his absence may be because this *Roll* was created over three decades later than the events that it depicts and therefore offers a less accurate version of those proceedings. Blanke also does not appear on the richly illuminated *Field of the Cloth of Gold* created in 1520. But this may be because this painting focuses on King Henry VIII and those around him and does not show the entire pageant.[110] It is unlikely that Blanke would be missing from these events if he was still employed by Henry VIII, because having African trumpeters involved in pageants was a popular tradition in parts of fifteenth- and sixteenth-century Europe. African trumpeters participated in major cultural, political and religious festivals in countries such as Spain, Portugal, Italy, Holland and Germany (especially in Nuremberg).[111] This shows us that Blanke's presence at Westminster may have drawn on Henry's VII and VIII's 'determined effort[s] to catch up' with what was already happening in Europe. Blanke showed that Tudor England could stage festivals which were 'equal in magnificence and status … [to] any … in [Modern] Europe.'[112]

Africans such as Blanke were also employed in pageants in sixteenth-century Europe because their presence advertised an idea about the diversity of the 'family of man.' This idea is further illustrated in some of the visual images of Africans included in Renaissance paintings by artists such as Hieronymus Bosch. Bosch was a Dutch painter who in 1510 created *The Epiphany* or *Adoration of the Magi*. The image is of Balthazar and he is noble and dignified and wearing the most distinguished costume of any of the Kings. He is attended by an African child who is equally dignified and may be his daughter (Figures 24 and 25).[113] Some of these kinds of images of Africans become so animated that they no longer seem to represent actual people, but become caricatures as can be seen with some of the Moorish heads found in sixteenth-century Europe.[114] But this is not so with the Africans in Hieronymus Bosch's painting nor with Blanke on the *Westminster Tournament Roll*.

However in Tudor England, Iberian Africans such as Blanke were employed by English royalty not merely to offer a visual image of success, but because African communities in Spain were known to have a 'higher culture' that 'brought great profit to the [Spanish] crown.'[115] In other words, Iberian Africans had 'gifts' and knowledge which in some ways were more *advanced* than their white counterparts in Spain, and than most Englishmen in Tudor England.

So these Iberian Africans were not bringing Spanish-Moorish culture to Tudor England but Moorish-Spanish culture. This is because Moorish Spain had an 'astonishing population' which had 'opulence, industry ... and immense resources.'[116] Moorish cities such as Valencia and Cordoba in Al Andalus were magnificent with running water, underground heating and street-lighting. These two cities also housed some of the most renowned universities in Europe. Cordoba had over 70 public libraries paid for by its citizens who numbered over 200,000,[117] and Moorish 'schools in philosophy, poetry and medicine' had students 'skilled in medicine pharmacy and surgery.'[118] As the nineteenth-century historian Bourke claims, the Moors of Spain were the highest example of culture and 'carried the art [s,] [science, maths, etc.] so little known to [others in] Europe ...' It was these Moors who are likely to have initiated Spain's renaissance,[119] because these people were some of the first in Europe to begin to systematically translate the Greek and Latin works of Herodotus, Pliny, Virgil and Tacitus. In Tudor England many of the books written in Latin and English were in fact based on work which had previously been written in Arabic.[120] Iberian Africans were known in Europe for their intellectual prowess and are likely to have brought some of this dynamic culture to England. As a result they would have attracted the respect of people living in Tudor society. However, how we prove this is difficult because, if an African such as Fortunatus who was Robert Cecil's servant translated classical works for him this may have been known only to them, and when they both died that information would have died with them.[121]

For other Africans from Iberia as suggested above, we can presume their abilities were recognised because they were paid more than their white counterparts, or were kept in continuous employment. Some of these Africans may also have provided their employers with intellectual 'gifts.' What seems evident is that the skills and usefulness of Iberian Africans seems to have been recognised not only by Englishmen but also by others such as Jewish immigrants from Iberia. This may explain why we find Iberian Africans living in the homes of Jewish people in sixteenth-century England, and how their relationships with each other are linked to complex issues about how both sets of people were seen in Tudor society.

Iberian Africans living in Jewish households

It was mostly white Sephardic Jews who Iberian Africans lived with in Tudor England.[122] The reasons for this are to be found in Iberia and are the result of the Spanish Inquisitions, and other persecutions which forced Moors, Jews, religious non-conformists and Animists to live together in Al Andalus.[123] In Granada in Al Andalus, Jewish culture became an integral element of Moorish-Spanish culture and both sets of people became culturally connected.[124] The Sephardic Jews who employed Africans in Tudor England came from communities where Falasha or 'Black Jews' and West African Jews known as 'Bilad el Sudan' also lived.[125] However, through the rules of 'blue blood inheritance' Africans including 'Black Jews' were forced into servile positions. As the Inquisitions intensified in the second half of the sixteenth century it was mostly 'white' Jews who were converted to Christianity and became known as Conversos.[126] Some of these Conversos became involved in exploiting Africans as servants or even slaves. This is despite these Conversos once being part of communities where 'Black Jews' existed and who had earlier been governed by Moorish rulers.[127]

When some of these Conversos were driven out of Spain and came to England at the end of the sixteenth century, they brought Africans with them because of the connections between both sets of people. This is why we find the records of these Africans being employed in the English households of Conversos.[128] One of these Conversos called Doctor Hector Novimies does not appear to have understood that there were no laws in Tudor England which automatically classified Africans as slaves; because he came from a Spanish society which saw some Africans treated in that way in the last quarter of the sixteenth century. Novimies was living in London when he brought his African servant to the English Court of Chancery in 1587 for 'utterly refusing to work' for him.[129] As stated in Chapter 1, Novimies had no 'remedie' because the 'said Ethiopian' was acting according to English law and he could not be compelled or forced to work as a slave.

Ungerer suggests that this Novimies is the same person as a Doctor Hector Nunez or Nonnez who was a Converso from Portugal/Spain who also had African servants living with him in Tudor England, although Habib suggests that they are two different people.[130] Nunez was an important Converso who worked as a doctor for the politician Robert Cecil. Nunez had an African woman servant called Elizabeth who Ungerer believes had the status of a 'slave' in Tudor England. Ungerer also says that she was named after Nunez's sister-in-law called Elizabeth Freire. The latter is likely, but the first theory is less so for all the reasons outlined so far about the status of Africans in Tudor England. But Elizabeth is not the only African woman in Nunez's household. There was also a servant called Grace 'a nigro oute of Dcor Hector's' who is mentioned in the records from St Olave Hart Street, and she was 'buried on 13 July in 1590.'[131] If this 'Dcor Hector' is Nunez, which is probable, Ungerer may be right to conclude that she too is named after another of his sisters-in-law called 'Gratia' or Grace Freire,[132] whilst a third African woman called 'Mary' or 'Mioury' described as a 'blackamore from Doc-r Hector's Edward Brunyarde' died on '28 January in 1587/8,' and was also buried in St Olave Hart Street, London. We know nothing more about 'Mary,' but we do know that 'Edward Brunyarde' was a business associate of Nunez.[133] The evidence suggests therefore that Nunez's English household had a significant number of Africans within it.

Nunez appears to have constructed his household in London so that it resembled his home in Iberia. In other words, Nunez felt comfortable with Africans in his household in England because of his Iberian background. But it was not just the African servants that Nunez employed who affected his life. Another Converso living in Tudor England called Ferdinando Alvarez had two African servants who testified in Nunez's court case of 1587. Nunez was appearing in court for 'unpaid obligations' and 'outstanding debt.'[134] Alvarez's servants were two unnamed 'blackamore maids' who gave testimony in Nunez's case by proxy through a white servant called Thomas Wilson.[135] These African women's testimonies revealed that Nunez and Alvarez were practising Jewish customs in secret and were suspected of having hidden wealth. It is significant that it was Africans present in Tudor

England who were being used against these wealthy Conversos, and illustrates that either these African women were dumb subalterns being used by anti-Semitic members of the English establishment, or that these African women had grievances against their employers and saw this as an opportunity to get revenge.[136] Whichever theory is true, these two African women's testimonies reinforced the anti-Semitic stereotype of the 'money-lending Jew' who stole from his trading partners.[137]

Even when Nunez became disillusioned with public life and a recluse, he still employed other African servants in his household. This shows that some African women who were living in the English homes of Conversos played important parts in their personal lives, and had the potential to cause them harm or provide them with solace. Africans such as the servants of Nunez may have seen the private sphere of Tudor society as a convenient place to remain, if they had experienced persecution in Iberia. This experience would have invested these Africans with an understanding that obscurity can be an effective method of surviving the politics present in mainland Europe, or sixteenth-century England. In hindsight, the Africans' approach seems to have been strategically more successful than that adopted by their Converso employers.[138]

Nunez died on the 13 September 1591 and he was 'carried to Stepney to be buried.' In his will no Africans are specifically identified such as Elizabeth; and Grace and Mary had already passed away. But what is interesting is that neither in Nunez's will nor in any other documents have I found evidence of Nunez owning African slaves in England.[139]

There is also a further Converso living in Tudor England called Doctor Roderigo Lopez, who Ungerer suggests was involved in the enslavement of Africans and worked with Englishmen to bring them from the Senegambia to England.[140] What is worthy of note is that Lopez in a similar way to the other Conversos mentioned here was convicted on the testimonies of his servants, and was executed in 1594. The roots of the action taken against him appear to have been spurred on by anti-Semitism, although I suggest that Jews in Tudor England were not treated to the systemic abuse those people suffered in Spain and Portugal.[141] This pattern is mirrored by the way that Iberian Africans did not experience the same level of discrimination in Tudor society as they did in Spain and Portugal; and is an idea which is explored in more detail as we look at more of 'those kindes of people' present in England in the later part of the sixteenth century.

Iberian Africans in England in the later part of the sixteenth century

So far in this chapter, except for the presence of Africans in the homes of Conversos, most of 'those kindes of people' who have been discussed were those present in England in the first part of the sixteenth century. However, evidence suggests that there were more Iberian Africans present in late Tudor England. But as I stated in Chapter 1, this is unlikely to be because 'great numbers' of 'those kindes of people' suddenly arrived. Some of the Iberian Africans who did come to Tudor England in the second half of the sixteenth century may have been seeking refuge from the persecutions which took place before and after the Morisco Revolt of Spain in 1568. The Morisco Revolt was led by the Moorish leaders Ferag ben Ferag and Diego Lopez Ben Abu and they were fighting against the persecution of Moors in Spain.[142]

This persecution of Iberian Africans in Spain prior to the Morisco Revolt may explain why we find in Tudor England people such as 'Moore Robert Tego,' described as 'a Morisco, servuant with Thomas Castlyn not denizens.' Tego is recorded as living in the Vintry St Olave and Old Jewry Ward, London on 15 December 1567.[143] He is described as a 'Moor' and a 'Morisco' which emphasises the likelihood that he is an Iberian African as already discussed. Furthermore, the name 'Tego' is not Spanish, English, Latin or Ancient Greek and probably reflects the influence of North-African culture on some Andalusian names.[144] The way Tego's record is written is also interesting as it implies that he is a servant of Thomas Castlyn and that both are 'not denizen.' This may mean that both Tego and Castlyn come from Castile in Spain which may be where Castlyn got his name.[145]

In late Tudor England the status of Iberian Africans such as Tego seems to have been dependent on their skills, whereas in Spain at the same time, 'those kindes' of people's status was determined by their race. In Spain, Philip II and Philip III the descendants of Charles V, began to systematically discriminate against Moors. Moors who became Moriscos were still routinely regarded with suspicion by Spanish rulers because some members of the Spanish establishment believed that these Iberian Africans had retained their own 'infidel religion' in secret.[146] Furthermore, the kings of Spain believed that Granada could be used as a base for 'foreign powers' to invade Spain because it had strong Muslim and non-conformist communities.[147] So Philip II enforced a set of draconian measures which included the forced separation of Moorish children from their parents, a general prohibition against the speaking of Non-European or Christian languages and the banning of Moorish dances and customs,[148] despite the fact as we have already stated, by the sixteenth century many of these customs had already become embedded in Spanish culture. By the last quarter of the sixteenth century more measures were created by the rulers of Spain and they imposed death, slavery or expulsion against Africans who remained in Granada.[149] From the 1570s until 1609, the historian Robert Scott suggests that over 300,000 Moors were expelled from Spain.[150] Some of these Iberian Africans became servants, and Ungerer suggests others became slaves, and that these make up a major part of the African presence in late Tudor Society.

Ungerer suggests English slave traders such as Thomas Malliard and Robert Thorne were the principal means by which Africans were brought to Tudor England. In other words Englishmen such as the Sherleys and Banes were not the first Englishmen to be involved in these types of activities. But this first idea is difficult to prove, even though Malliard had Africans in his household in Spain, because there is little evidence linking his slave trading to 'those kindes of people' in Tudor England.[151] Rather, evidence in this chapter suggests that the majority of Iberian Africans found their way to Tudor England through other routes, and when they arrived they do not seem to have been treated as the Moors in Spain were in the last quarter of the sixteenth century.[152]

One of the Africans who illustrates this idea is Katherin 'the negar' who was buried on 24 August 1594 at St Stephen Coleman Street, London. This Katherin was 'dwelling with the prince of Portingal' in London, and she died just one year before he did in 1595.[153] Ungerer claims that Katherin was a slave who had been obtained from the Prince of Portugal's sponsorship of slave trading in the Senegambia in West Africa, and suggests that Katherin had not been living in Europe long.[154] These ideas can be explored by examining the activities of the Prince of Portugal and looking more carefully at Katherin's record.

The Prince of Portugal was also known as Don or Dom Antonio of Crato/Crreto and he had unsuccessfully fought against the Emperor of Spain Philip II. The nineteenth-century historian John Morris claims that the Portuguese Prince arrived here 'for the first time' in 1581,[155] and this would seem plausible since it coincides with Philip II's attempt to annex Portugal from Spain in 1580. The Prince came to England to gain support from Elizabeth I so he could win the Portuguese throne back. However, according to Ungerer, the Prince was also sponsoring slave trading practices with an Englishman called Anthony Dassell. According to official records written at the time both of them appear to have utilised the services of Lopez who I mentioned earlier.[156]

It is possible that these connections explain Katherin's presence in Tudor England. However, she may also have originated from the Moorish population of Iberia, whose descendants we have been talking about throughout this chapter. What is certain is that Katherin is not referred to or described as a slave in English parish records. She is likely to be the personal servant of Don Antonio although, what 'dwelling with' means in her record is not clear.[157] It may imply that Katherin had a close relationship with the Prince of Portugal perhaps even conjugal, but of a morganatic kind and this is plausible as these types of relationships were not unusual in Tudor England and were relatively common in parts of Iberia.

Another Iberian African who illustrates that these 'kindes of people' did not all suddenly arrive in Tudor England on slave ships is a man who Ungerer calls Pedro Fernandes. Moreover, Fernandes was not fleeing persecution in Portugal, but arrived in England with the Prince of Portugal during the last quarter of the sixteenth century. Ungerer suggests he was known in England as a 'mulato.'[158] The use of the word 'mulato' or 'mulatto' is rare in Tudor records and it comes from the Latin word 'mulus' which describes the offspring between a horse and donkey. In Spain and Portugal the word 'mulato' was a popular term and a euphemism to describe people who are of mixed African and white ancestry.[159] This use of the term Mulatto to describe Fernandes may suggest derogatory ideas about his ethnicity – but it is more likely to be a legacy of his Iberian heritage.

To explain this further it may be useful to briefly mention another person who was also referred to as a 'Mullato' in Tudor records. He is a man known as 'Frances the Mullato' whose burial took place on 19 February 1603 at Gravesend in Kent, England. He too may have been of Iberian extraction because of how the word 'Mullato' was used in his record to describe him. Moreover, in Frances' case the term 'Mullato' does not appear to have been a secret term of mockery, but almost seems to be a title reflecting how he described himself in his life. Frances lived in Gravesend and may have been connected to the profession of the 'Long Ferry,' which was the system of porters who worked along the river Thames. But without more information it would be difficult to say conclusively, although, according to the nineteenth-century historian Robert Peirce Cruden, some people of 'foreign birth' were known to operate the 'Long Ferry' in the sixteenth- and early-seventeenth centuries.[160]

Amongst the Iberian Africans present in Europe there were 'many industrious, skilful Artificers' [161] although, in Tudor England in the case of Katherin, Fernandes, and Frances their skills are not explicitly stated. But the Tudor records for the St Botolph area of London reveal a group of skilled Iberian Africans whose talents seem to have been more openly talked about. Interestingly, St Botolph is the same area where according to my research Africans may have constituted 6% of the total population by the end of the sixteenth century.[162] One African who may have been connected to the group of Iberian artisans present there was Mary Fillis who we mentioned earlier. She was baptised at St Botolph without Aldgate on 3 June 1597. Ungerer calls Mary the 'black slave of Millicent Porter [a seamstress]' but he provides little evidence to support his view.[163] Moreover, in the *Memorandum Daybook* that includes an extraordinarily long (the longest for any commoner in the book) and detailed entry about Mary's life, there is no reference to her being a slave. Mary's record says that she is a 'basket maker' and her father was a 'Basket ... and ... shovel maker' 'of Morisco'. Her entry includes explicit detail about her conversion to Christianity and how she recited 'the Lord's prayer in English' desired to be 'gifted' into the 'holy church' and 'made part of the same'. The focus of Mary's record is on her conversion to Christianity and her father's profession. This emphasis suggests that these two issues were the most important in determining her status, and that Mary was a respected servant whose father was a skilled artisan from Granada and that is why he is described as being 'of Morisco'.[164]

Mary may have been connected to other Iberian Africans who also lived in the St Botolph without Aldgate area of London. These include a Susanna Pearls, Suzanna Peiries (perhaps the same person) and a Symon Valencia. Their parish records reveal that they are living side by side as tenants, servants or both, with a further man John Despinois living amongst them who may also be an Iberian African.[165] It is possible that Symon and perhaps Susanna and Suzanna were from Valencia. In Symon's case this is not just because of his name, but it is also related to his occupation, as his burial record of 20 August 1593 says he is a 'servant to Stephen [illegible] a nedellmaker'.[166] Valencia was a large and important city in Moorish dominated Spain; the artisans of this city were internationally known for being metal workers and needle makers in particular.[167] This may indicate that Symon was part of this industrious Iberian culture before he came to England and was now merely continuing his art 'but more quietly'.

Nevertheless, Symon is not the first Iberian African noted as being part of the needle-making industry of Tudor England. The first is an unnamed African living in England between 1545 and 1553 in Cheapside, London. This African was an independent craftsman making 'fine Spanish needles ... but would never teach his art to any'. In the book *Birmingham and Midland Hardware District* the authors make an important claim. They suggest that this unnamed African was the first person to bring the art of making 'fine' steel needles to England. This idea is reiterated in John Bromley's *The Armorial Bearings of the Guilds,* where the author claims that the original reference to this man comes from the Tudor historian Stow in his *Annales.* However in the 1592 copy of Stow's book there is no mention of this 'negro'. It is only in those accounts of the *Annales* written in and after 1615 by George Buck and Edmund Howes that this African is mentioned. It means that the entry for this man was probably written by them retrospectively and not by Stow.[168] But why Stow did not mention this African is difficult to explain, it seems that Buck and Howes were more effective at gathering information than their predecessor. This idea is substantiated by the fact that it is actually William Harrison in 1577 who first mentions this African. In his *Description of England* he says:

> Spanish needles was first taught in Englande, by Elias Growse a Germaine, about the eight year of Queen Elizabeth, and in Queen Maries time, there was a Negro made fine Spanish needles in Cheapside, but would never teach his art to any.[169]

This shows that by the time that the later writers came to talk about this African his name may have been forgotten – but his skill and art were not. This becomes even more evident when we explore a nineteenth-century reference to this African which adds to our understanding. The account is in *Haydn's Dictionary*

> Needles were first made in England in Cheapside, London, in the time of Mary I, by a Negro from Spain, but was lost at his death, and not recovered till 1566, in the reign of Elizabeth, when Elias Growse … [170]

Haydn seems to have come to similar conclusions as those I have reached here. These are that the African was from Spain, lived in Cheapside, and had skills which no one else had, and that the knowledge he had was temporarily lost. What Haydn adds is a date when this happened 1566. This means that the 'negro' since he was alive in the reign of Mary I from 1553–1558, must have died some time between 1558 and 1566. The evidence gathered so far from the sixteenth century and after, seems to overwhelming show that this 'negro' was a real person living and working in Tudor England.

In trying to discover more about this African I examined the parish records in East Smithfield, London. In those records there is a Martin Blacke who was buried on 17 January 1587. He was 'the son of Richard Blacke a needlemaker'. The word 'Blacke' by itself would not prove that he was connected to the 'needlemaking' 'negro;' but it is because Buck, Howes and the other historians claim that until 1566 this was a skill only known to this African, that the word 'Black' becomes significant, perhaps, it denotes some relationship between this family and the skilled African – but without more evidence it would be difficult to say conclusively.[171]

Moreover, I acknowledge that there are other needle makers in London in the sixteenth-century. I have identified four others on the subsidy rolls. And even though these needle makers are unlikely to be related to the 'Negro' who 'would never teach his art to any,' their presence in Tudor England is worth noting. The first is a Stephen Oluvio from France who lived at Chancery Lane and had been present in England for one year. Then there is John Langent from Flanders who was present in Tower Ward 'with his wife,' three children and one maid. He had been present in London for three years. The third needle maker is called Lewes Franke and he was 'born in Portingale' and had been present in the Aldersgate Ward, London for two years. Whilst the fourth 'Jerry Jane and his wife' were 'born in Valence [Italy]' and had been in the Tower Ward London for three years. Jane appears to have been quite prosperous and had four servants who were also Italians. These needle makers were all present in London on 5 May 1571.[172]

The records of these needle makers are significant because despite most of these artisans appearing to be settled and prosperous in Tudor England, none of them are remembered in the same way as the 'Negro' who 'would never teach his art to any.' This idea is strongly supported by Bromley who suggests the Worshipful Company of Needlemakers were inspired by the African 'needlemaker' when they created their crest which includes an image of him. By 1656, the Worshipful Company of Needlemakers had become a powerful organisation and it is significant that an African living in Tudor England was an inspiration for their heraldic sign.[173] The evidence above now makes it easier to question what Habib proposes about the status of this African 'needlemaker.' Habib suggests that this Iberian African was suffering from discrimination and that is why he would not teach other people his craft.[174] But I suggest that this man had skills his competitors did not have, and that is why he would 'never teach' them. This is all the more likely as he appears to have been an Iberian Moor with special knowledge in making 'fine Spanish needles.' This idea is supported by the seventeenth-century historian Thomas Fuller who says:

> ... the first Spanish needles in England were made, in the Reign of Queen Mary, in Cheapside, by a Negro but such his envy, that he would teach his art to noone, so that it dyed with him. More charitable was Elias Crowse ...[175]

Fuller's account confirms that this African was not suffering discrimination, but was covetous of his art and did not help others so that he could maintain his monopoly.

Almost fifty years later (circa 1593) Symon Valencia does not seem to have had the same restrictive working practices as the 'negro' from Cheapside. Symon had been working with 'Stephen [the] … nedellmaker' and the African was part of a group of artisans connected together in St Botolph.[176] It may have been that by the last quarter of the sixteenth century these Iberian artisans and craftsmen were now established in London in a way that their predecessors had not been fifty years earlier.

It is certain that the skills of some of these Iberian-African craftsmen left an impression on the metal working professions present in Tudor England. An indication of this can be found in the use of the term 'moriscoworke'. This is a term used to describe ornate metal work of an ostentatious and elaborate kind. It is a term used throughout the sixteenth century, for example in an inventory of items owned by Henry VIII, including eyeglasses in 1545; and it is even used to describe the craftsmanship on items given to Thomasina in 1578.[177] The term 'moriscoworke' indicates the enduring legacy of Iberian Africans such as the 'needlemaking' 'negro' and their contribution to the metal working professions.

Englishmen at the end of the sixteenth century appear to have been willing to give respect to some Iberian-Moorish craftsmen, and this may have been because those Englishmen had a greater understanding of the oppression that took place in Spain. This understanding made it easier for people such as Symon to settle and work in Tudor England than in Spain at the same time. If Symon told 'a round unvarnished tale' about his life in Valencia, and perhaps his escape from the Inquisition as the character Othello did about his exploits, this would have made the Africans' persecutions pertinent to Englishmen.[178] This is especially as Iberian Africans' first-hand experience of discrimination would have prepared Englishmen for what they as Protestants would also begin to suffer in mainland Europe during the last decades of the sixteenth century.[179]

Conclusion

Africans came to Tudor England from various parts of Europe but especially from Spain and Portugal. This is despite more white immigrants coming to Tudor England from countries such as Holland, France and Italy. Those Africans present in Tudor England who came from a country such as Italy may have found that in both societies their status was not determined by national laws which categorised them as perpetually inferior because of the colour of their skin or ethnic origins. Moreover some places in Italy where Africans lived such as Venice and Florence, were cosmopolitan and multicultural in a similar way to some parishes in London and Plymouth.[180]

Some Africans from continental Europe settled in English cities such as London, Plymouth, Bristol and Southampton because these were their ports of entry. There is evidence that some of the Africans who were present in London at the end of the sixteenth century were from Iberia and congregated in specific areas of the city operating as a self-sufficient community.[181] Some of these Iberian Africans were skilled artisans, and had professions, trades and knowledge which were acknowledged by the royalty of Europe including members of England's aristocracy. These Africans may have had superior skills to their white counterparts and helped Englishmen translate the more 'advanced' culture found in areas of continental Europe. Ironically, one African in Tudor England who achieved an iconic status for having skills no one else had would not share his 'gifts,' and this was 'the Negro ... that would never teach his art to any.'

The notion that some Iberian Africans brought skills to Tudor England that people in English society needed, may help to explain why this country never implemented the kind of racial policies that were present in Spain and Portugal during the sixteenth and seventeenth centuries. In England the skills of these Iberian Africans were probably more important in determining their status than their race was. Late Tudor England, despite the existence of the Letters and the Proclamation, seems to have been a less racially-conscious society than Spain was at the same time. For example in Tudor England there is a lack of evidence of Africans being forced into becoming Christians, or Moorish children being separated from their parents as happened in Spain.[182] This explains why attempts by Senden, Sherley (elder) and Banes to classify some or groups of Africans as slaves, under the Letters and the Proclamation, were not successful. However at a similar time in Spain, Africans were being discriminated against, enslaved and sold by merchants and traders.[183] Perhaps this was because the conquest and establishment of Moorish kingdoms in Iberia had left a racial awareness in Spain and Portugal that did not exist in Tudor England. Or it could be because Africans in Tudor England did not offer numerically, politically or militarily the same threat to English society that the Moors were presented as offering in Spain. Rather in England other people such as white Frenchmen and Spanish Catholics, appear to have been targeted more often for physical and intellectual attacks.[184]

Therefore in Spain and Portugal, the changing status of Africans is linked to a decline in power of Moorish kingdoms. But in Tudor England this change does not seem to have affected the status of Africans in the same way. Notwithstanding this, some Iberian Africans were being bought and sold in Spain by English merchants and some of these traders may have facilitated 'those kindes' of people's arrival in Tudor England. However, though some of these Iberian Africans upon arrival in Tudor England may have been called 'slaves'; – their status appears to have changed because of the skills they offered, and principles present in English law.

Other Iberian Africans appear to have entered Tudor England as free people who were fleeing persecution. The arrival of 'those kindes of people' corresponds to periods when discrimination in Iberia reached intolerable levels for them. Some of these Africans came to England with their employers but others may have travelled on their own and been artisans and traders. But no matter how these Africans arrived, a significant number of them appear to have been capable of determining their own status in Tudor society. This is an idea which explains the status of Africans who were the servants of Conversos in Tudor England. In late sixteenth-century Spain, some Conversos were used to 'those kindes of people' being slaves. But in their English households these same Conversos appear to have developed familial relationships with the Africans they employed. Significantly, these familial relationships remained whilst the attempt at treating Africans as slaves seems to have failed.

Moreover, the kind of discrimination which was present in Spain and Portugal created opportunities for Englishmen to create connections with Iberian Moors, and for the former to gain access to the knowledge these Africans had. This includes not only the 'gifts' of Iberian, but also of continental Africans. England portrayed itself in the last decade of the sixteenth century as an ally to Spain's enemies, and through this strategy Englishmen such as the unscrupulous pirates Hawkins and Drake, by associating with Iberian and continental Africans gained an opportunity to make 'great profit.'[185] By negotiating with Africans these Englishmen were even able to gain control of some Spanish colonies without bloodshed.[186] In the next chapter, we will see how these connections in West Africa were influential in why some West Africans were present in Tudor England.

Notes

[1] Similar issues are raised by Imtiaz Habib, in *Black Lives in the English Archives ...* (London: Ashgate, 2008), pp. 7, 19–63, 96, 119.

[2] G. L. Registers of St Mary Bothaw, GL Ms 4310; Bromley Records Office, Bromley, *Composite Register Baptisms and Burials 1559–1681*, P92/1/1, p. 1.

³ David Cressy, offers the same views in, *Birth, Marriage, and Death: Ritual, Religion, and the Life-Cycle in Tudor and Stuart England* (Oxford: Oxford University Press, 1997), pp. 97–124.

⁴ Richard Kirk and Ernest Kirk (eds.), *Returns of Aliens Dwelling in the City and Suburbs of London,* Volume I (Aberdeen: Huguenot Society, The Publications of the Society, 1900), p. xii.

⁵ Plymouth and West Devon Record Office, Registers of St Andrews/November 17/1594/MF1-4.

⁶ William Brewer Stephens, *Sources for English Local History* (Cambridge: Cambridge University Press, 1981), pp. 52–56; and Paul Griffiths, 'Secrecy and Authority in sixteenth and seventeenth century London,' *Historical Journal*, 40-4, 1997, pp. 925–951.

⁷ Plymouth and West Devon Record Office, Registers of St Andrews/November 17/1594/MF1-4 (Reference to John White being her employer); Edmund Randolph, Arthur Shaffer (ed.), *The History of Virginia* (Charlottesville: University of Virginia, 1970), pp. 11–14 Randolph queries whether John White who drew the Inuits was the same man who became Governor; John White, Paul Hope Hulton, *America, 1585: The Complete Drawings of John White* (The University of North Carolina: British Museum, 1984), passim.

⁸ Joel Augustus Rogers, *Nature Knows no Colour Line* (St Petersburg: Helga Rogers, 1952), pp. 83, 86, 88–91, 95–98, 100–107; Edward Scobie, in Ivan Van Sertima (ed.), *African Presence in Early Europe* (New Brunswick: Transaction Publishers, 1985), passim; and John Brackett, Thomas Earle, Kate Lowe (eds.), *Black Africans in Renaissance Europe* (Cambridge: Cambridge University Press, 2005), passim, but Lowe suggests Africans did not have power. I also acknowledge that Austria etc. were not countries with the same geographical boundaries that exist today (see note below).

⁹ I refer to Italy as such but throughout the sixteenth and most of the seventeenth centuries it was made up of a number of independent states see Julius Kirshner, *The Origins of the State in Italy, 1300–1600* (Chicago: University of Chicago Press, 1996), passim.

¹⁰ Caelius Augustinus Curio, *A Notable History of the Saracens ...* (London: William How and Abraham Veale, 1575), pp. 31, 46–51 (Africans in France), 67, 68, 79 ('Saracens' from 'Mauritania' in Italy). Regarding Africans in Europe see Jacob van Maerlant, 'Charlemagne killing a Moorish leader,' image on vellum, size 32 by 233 cm, in *Spiegel Historiael* (West Flanders: publisher unknown, 1325–1355), n. p. ; Anne Marsh-Caldwell, *The Song of Roland, as Chanted Before the Battle of Hastings, by the Minstrel Taillefer* (London: Hurst and Blackett, 1854), passim; Ivan Van Sertima (ed.), *Golden Age of the Moor* (Piscataway: Transaction Publishers, 1992), p. 372; and John Bagnall Bury, *The Cambridge Medieval History,* Volume II (London: The University Press, 1964), pp. 374–375.

¹¹ Thomas Bourke, *A Concise History of the Moors in Spain from the Invasion of that Kingdom to their Final Expulsion from it* (London: Rivington Hatchard, 1811), pp. 252–253; Rogers, *Nature Knows no Colour Line*, pp. 143, 145; and Ben Jonson, *The Character of Two Royall Masques, the One of Blacknesse. The Other of Beautie ... 1605 and 1608 at White hall* (London: Thomas Thorp, 1605), pp. 3–5, 9 (suggests Africans were in Aquitania France in the sixteenth and early-seventeenth centuries).

¹² Rogers, *Sex and Race*, Volume I , pp. 86–88; Rogers, *Nature Knows no Colour Line*, pp. 76, 78, 83–110; Other Africans are in Artist unknown, Author unknown. *Schoenbartbuch Nurnberg* [Nuremberg Carnival Book]. (Nuremberg: publisher unknown, 1590–1620); see figures 33, 34, 35, 36 and 37.

¹³ See Fig. 18. For more information on Sir Thomas Sonds' life and tomb, but not on why an African is depicted on the latter, see, Readers Digest Association, *Past All Around Us: An Illustrated Guide to the Ruins, Relics, Monuments, Castles, Cathedrals, Historic*

Buildings, Industrial Landmarks of Britain (London: Readers Digest Association, 1979), p. 297; Nikolaus Pevsner, John Newman, *The Buildings of England: North East and North Kent* (Harmondsworth: Penguin, 1969), p. 459. Other members of the Sonds' family also have images of Africans on their tombs see Zechariah Cozens, *A Tour Through the Island of Thanet: and Some Other Parts of East Kent* (London: J. Nicholas, 1793), pp. 261-266.

[14] Kirk and Kirk (eds.), Returns of Aliens Dwelling in ... London, Volume I (1902), pp. preface, xii, 391; GL Ms 9223, 9222/1; Author unknown, St Botolph without Aldgate Memorandum Daybook, Volume VI (London: Parish of St Botolph without Aldgate, 1596-7), p. 118, Ref P69/BOT2/ A/ 01/MS 9234/6. On the exclusive nature of this profession see Author unknown, *The Booke of Secrets ... Skill to Ordering Wines ... Beer Making ... Translated out of the Dutch ...* (London: Adam Islip, 1596), passim; Lien Luu, 'The Dutch and their Beer Brewing,' in A. Kershen (ed.), *Food in the Migrant's Experience* (Aldershot: Ashgate, 2002), pp. 101-133; and Richard W. Unger, *Beer in the Middle Ages and the Renaissance* (Philadelphia: University of Pennsylvania Press, 2004), pp. 99-104.

[15] In Tudor England the profession was the 'art of brewing,' the trade was 'the selling of.' A beer brewer such as Peter Miller probably did both, see Unger, *Beer in the Middle Ages and the Renaissance*, pp. 296-302 (guilds), 302-361 (beer brewing and Dutch immigrants). For more on how the term 'profession' was applied to doctors, lawyers and clergymen in the middle of the seventeenth century, see Rosemary O. Day, *The Professions in Early Modern England, 1450-1800: Servants of the Commonweal* (Harlow: Longman, 2000), pp. 13-14 (definition of profession), 21-23 (exclusive nature of most guilds and professions in Tudor England).

[16] Alwyn Ruddock, *Italian Merchants and Shipping in Southampton 1270-1600* (Southampton: University College, 1951), pp. 95, 126-7.

[17] Ibid. and Giovanni Manzini, Venice Archivio di Stato, Venezia (Venice) Italy, Ref. Cassia IV, Box 3, Series 18, folios 6v -7, no year.

[18] Moriana's case is discussed in more detail by, Barbara Hanawalt, *Growing up in Medieval London: The Experience of Childhood in History* (Oxford/London: Oxford University Press, 1993), p. 186.

[19] Alwyn Ruddock, *Italian Merchants and Shipping in Southampton*, pp. 95, 126-7; and Barbara Hanawalt, *The Wealth of Wives: Women, Law and Economy in Late Medieval London* (Oxford: Oxford University Press, 2007), p. 195.

[20] Quotations from original records (dated 1470) in the National Archives, Kew, London, *Early Chancery Proceedings* (ECP), C1/148/67, C1/29/150; and Alwyn Ruddock, *Italian Merchants and Shipping in Southampton*, pp. 126-127, 138.

[21] National Archives, Kew, London, *High Courts of Admiralty Reports*, 1547, Ref. 24/39/49-51.

[22] Stephen Milner (ed.), Steven Epstein, *At the Margins: Minority Groups in Premodern Italy* (Minneapolis and Bristol: University of Minnesota Press, 2005), pp. 219-220; Edward Scobie, in Sertima (ed.), *African Presence in Early Europe*, pp. 196, 203, 206; Brackett, Earle and Lowe (eds.), *Black Africans in Renaissance Europe*, pp. 303-326; B. J. Sokol, *Shakespeare and Tolerance* (Cambridge: Cambridge University Press, 2008), pp. 83, 128-133; Gaio Servadio, *Renaissance Women* (London/New York: I.B.Tauris, 2005), p. 20 (African woman Simonetta da Collavechio in Medici family of Italy); and Rogers, *Nature Knows no Colour Line*, p. 165 (image of Simonetta da Collavechio).

[23] Cheryl Butler, Edward Andrew Spicer (eds.), *The Book of Fines: The Annual Accounts of the Mayors of Southampton, 1488-1540*, Volume I (Southampton: Southampton University, 2008), p. 15; and Christopher Kleinhenz, *Medieval Italy an Encyclopedia*, Volume II (New York/London: Routledge, 2004), p. 1096 (trading in Treviso).

[24] Butler, Spicer (eds.), *The Book of Fines ... Southampton*, Volume I, pp. 15, 17, 34, 117, 121.

[25] Including 'Galiace de Nigro' who was present in England between the dates of 1475–1485, in Author unknown, National Archives, Kew, London, *Court of Chancery: Six Clerks Office: Early Proceedings, Richard II to Philip and Mary,* 1475–1485, C1/66/389.

[26] Plymouth and West Devon Record Office, St Andrews/March 11/1591/ MF 1–4.

[27] Roy Domencio, *The Regions of Italy: A Reference Guide to History and Culture* (Westport: Greenwood Publishing Group, 2002), pp. 151–153 (on Lazio).

[28] *Merriam Webster's French-English Dictionary* (Springfield: Merriam Webster, 1999), p. 220; Piero Rébora, Francis Guercio, et. al., *Cassell's Italian Dictionary: Italian-English, English-Italian* (London: Oxford: Macmillan, 1977, 4th Edition), p. 308; and the word 'Marche' is also a region in Italy and this may indicate Carbew is from there in Augusto Morello, *Culture of an Italian Region: The Marche, Guzzini and Design* (Rome and Milan: Electa, 2002), pp. 31–34.

[29] Scobie, in Sertima (ed.), *African Presence in Early Europe,* pp. 190–203; Folarin Shyllon, *Black People in Britain 1553–1833* (Oxford: Oxford University Press, 1977), p. 3; Nigel File, Chris Power, *Black Settlers in Britain 1555–1958* (London: Heinemann Educational Books, 1981), pp. 5, 6, 7; and Stanley Lane-Poole, *Story of the Moors in Spain* (London: Fisher, Unwin, 1887), pp. 13, 36.

[30] Pedro De Azeved (ed.), *Archivo Historico Portuguez* (Madrid: Libano da Silva, 1903), p. 300; and Antonio Vieyra, Jacinto Dias do Canto, *A Dictionary of the Portuguese and English Languages, in Two Parts ...* (1773, 2nd edition, London: J Collingwood, 1827), p. 351.

[31] Albert Gerard (ed.), *European-Language Writing in Sub-Saharan Africa,* Volume I (Budapest: Akademiai Kiado, 1986), p. 432.

[32] Suggested by Peter Fraser, 'Slaves or Free people, the status of Africans in England 1550–1750' ... (Eastbourne: Sussex Academic Press, 2001), pp. 254–261, but especially 257. Africans in some British colonies such as Virginia in the eighteenth century were legally regarded as being 'destitute of every means of improvement,' 'simple plain honest and ignorant' as well as being 'degenerate' and 'bound for service' in Virginia State Legislature, *A Forensic Dispute on the Legality of Enslaving the Africans held at the Public Commencement in Cambridge, New England, July 21 1773* (Boston: John Boyle, 1773), pp. 5, 25–27, 37; and James Stephen, *England Enslaved by her Own Slave Colonies: An Address to the Electors and People of the United Kingdom* (London: R. Taylor, for Hatchard and son, and J. and A. Arch, 1826), passim.

[33] Azeved (ed.), *Archivo, Historico, Portuguez,* p. 300.

[34] Evidence in: Edward Blount (tr.), Ieronimo Conestaggio, *The Historie of the Uniting of the Kingdom of Portugal to the Crowne of Casti ...* (London: A. Hatfield for E. Blount, 1600), pp. 1, 5–7, 39; Tarif Abentarique, *The History of the Conquest of Spain by the Moors. Together with the Life of the Most Illustrious Monarch Menesh Almanzar and of the Several Revolutions of the Mighty Empire of the Caliphs and of the African Kingdoms ... Now made English* (London: Fleach, sold by T Fox, 1687), p. 36; Stanley Lane-Poole, *The Story of the Moors in Spain,* pp. 13, 36, 53.

[35] Supported by evidence in, Samuel Purchas, *Purchas his Pilgrimage; or Relations of the World ...* (London: William Stansby for Henrie Fetherstone, 1613), pp. 193–195(quotation); Sertima (ed.), *African Presence in Early Europe,* pp. 140, 152, 166, 171; Abentarique, *The History of the Conquest of Spain by the Moors,* p. 51; and Rogers, *Nature Knows no Colour Line,* pp. 55–57.

[36] Sertima (ed.), *African Presence in Early Europe,* pp. 134–143; Caelius Augustinus Curio, *A Notable History of the Saracens ...* (London: William How and Abraham Veale, 1575), pp. 18, 26–28, 29, 134; there are other definitions of the words 'Al Andalus' in Jere L Bacharach, Josef W. Meri (eds.), *Medieval Islamic Civilization,* Volume 2, *An Encyclopedia* (New York/London: Routledge, 2006), pp. 43–44.

[37] Jonson, *The Character of Two Royall Masques*, p. 9; Curio, *Notable History of the Saracens* ... pp. 28, 29, 53, 121, 122; and Franz Heinrich Ungewitter, *Europe, Past and Present: A Comprehensive Manual of European Geography* ... (New York: Putnam, 1850), p. 67.

[38] Joseph Foster, *Alumni Oxonienses: The Members of the University of Oxford, 1715–1886* ... *Alumni Oxonienses: The Members of the University of Oxford 1500–1714* (Oxford: Parker and Co., 1888–1892), p. 950; and Ian Smith, *Race and Rhetoric in the Renaissance* ... (Basingstoke: Palgrave Macmillan, 2009), p. 64 (the idea of Africans being present in Lusitania).

[39] Raphael Holinshed, *The Late Volume of Chronicles England, Scotland and Ireland with their Descriptions* (London: J. Harrison, 1587), p. 1465; and John Stow, *The Chronicles* (1615), p. 483.

[40] John Huxtable Elliott, *Imperial Spain 1469–1716* (London: Edward Arnold, 1963), pp. 14–20; and Jean Pierre Claris de Florian, Robert Heron (tr.), *Gonsolvo or Cordova or The Conquest of Granada* (London: Morison and Son, 1792), pp. preface, 91–137.

[41] Bourke, *A Concise History of the Moors in Spain*, p. 252; Jonathan S. C. Riley-Smith, *New Cambridge Medieval History*, Volume VII (Cambridge: Cambridge University Press, 1995), p. 162; Ieronimo Conestaggio, *Dell'unione del Regno di Portogallo. Alla Corona di Castiglia. Istoria* (Genoua: Girolamo Bartoli, 1585), passim; and Derek Lomax, *The Reconquest of Spain* (London: Longman, 1978), p. 78.

[42] Philip Limborch, *The History of the Inquisition* (London: Samuel Handler, 1731), p. 120 (although Zargoza or Saragossa in Aragon was not conquered until 1118).

[43] On the pomegranate and Katherine see, Susan Brigden, *New Worlds, Lost Worlds: The Rule of the Tudors, 1485–1603* (London: Allen Lane, 2000), p. 111; The British Archaeological Society Association and Royal Archaeological Institute of Great Britain and Ireland, *Archaeological Journal*, Volume 69 (London: Royal Archaeological Institute, 1912), p. 485; and Robert Chambers, William Chambers, *Chambers Miscellany of Useful and Entertaining Tracts* (Edinburgh: William and Robert Chambers, 1846), pp. 26, 30 (Mary I of England later readopted the pomegranate as one of the symbols of her branch of the Tudor Royal family).

[44] Stow, *The Chronicles* (1615), p. 314. Quotations from Gordon Kipling (ed.), *The Receyt of the Ladie Kateryne* (Oxford: Oxford University Press, 1990), pp. 31, 33, 43; Barbara Fuchs, *Exotic Nation: Maurophilia and the Construction of Early Modern Spain* (Philadelphia: University of Pennsylvania Press, 2008), pp. 6–8, 22, 60–67, 95, 102, 143 (on the importance of the Farthingale); and Janet Arnold, *Queen Elizabeth's Wardrobe Unlock'd* ... (London: W.S. Maney & Son Ltd, 1988), pp. 146, 214. Other evidence is contained in the rest of this chapter.

[45] Elizabeth Francis Rogers (ed.), Thomas More, *The Correspondence of Sir Thomas More* (Princeton: Princeton University Press, 1947), p. 4, 'At Hispanorum comitatus, proh deorum atque hominum fidem, quails erat! Vereor ne si aspexisses ruptus ridendo fuisses, ita ridicule errant: facies praetor tres aut ad summumquattuor vix tollerabiles; curui errant, laceri, nudipedes pigmei Ethiopes; se affuisses ex inferis euasisse putauisses.' The word 'Ethiopes' appears to mean 'Ethiopians' rather than 'from Ethiopia' a similar suggestion is made by Habib, *Black Lives*, pp. 38, 274–276. Charles Kingsford (ed.), *The Chronicles of London* (London: Clarendon Press, 1905), p. 334 (on More's presence in London).

[46] John Holt and Thomas More were friends for many years and compiled the *Lac Puero M Holti Mylke for Chyldren*, [A Latin Grammar, with two epigrams] (London: Wynkyn de Worde, 1508?).

[47] Robert M. Keane, 'Thomas More as a Young Lawyer,' *Moreana*, Volume 41/160, December 2004, pp. 41–71.

[48] Official accounts were written on the 2 April 1502, August 1502 and 1598 etc. in Kipling (ed.), *The Receyt of the Ladie Kateryne*, pp. xxlv, xxv, xxv, xxviii, xxxiii.

[49] Stow, *The Chronicles* (1615), p. 314; Kipling (ed.) *The Receyt of the Ladie Kateryne*, (1990), p. 33; and Kingsford (ed.) *The Chronicles of London* (1905), p. 334.

[50] Kingsford (ed.) *The Chronicles of London*, p. 334; Kipling (ed.), *The Receyt of the Ladie Kateryne* (1990), p. 33; and Stow, *The Chronicles* (1615), p. 483.

[51] For a longer discussion on the word 'fair' please see Earle and Lowe (eds.), *Black Africans in Renaissance Europe*, p. 102.

[52] Kipling (ed.), *The Receyt of the Ladie Kateryne*, fol. 42, ii. 741–45 p. 33; 'Third Chronicle in BLMS Vitellus A XVI, Book II fol. 193' in Kingsford (ed.) *The Chronicles of London*, p. 334; and the last quotation is from Habib, *Black Lives*, pp. 275–276.

[53] Stow, *The Chronicles* (1615), p. 314.

[54] Judith M. Richards, 'Public Identity and Public Memory: Case Studies of Two Tudor Women,' in, Susan Broomhall and Stephanie Tarbin (eds.), *Women, Identities and Communities in Early Modern Europe* (Aldershot: Ashgate, 2008), p. 202 ('public theatre' quotation); Sybil Jack, 'In Praise of Queens: The Public Presentation of the Virtuous Consort in Seventeenth-Century Britain,' *Women, Identities*, p. 212 ('public attention' quotation); Robert Smuts, 'Public Ceremony and Royal Charisma: The English Royal Entry in London, 1495–1642,' in, A. L. Beier, David Cannadine and James R. Rosenheim (eds.), *The First Modern Society: Essays in English History in Honour of Lawrence Stone* (Cambridge: Cambridge University Press, 1989, pp. 65–94.

[55] Stow, *The Chronicles* (1615), p. 483; Habib, *Black Lives*, p. 25; and Samuel Parsons Scott, *History of the Moorish Empire in Europe*, Volume II (Philadelphia/London: Lippincott, 1994), p. 190.

[56] Habib, *Black Lives*, pp. 24–5.

[57] Stow, *The Chronicles* (1615), p. 483; and Rogers (ed.), More, *The Correspondence of Sir Thomas More*, p. 4.

[58] Habib, *Black Lives*, pp. 24–5; Coleman, *History of Cant and Slang Dictionaries, 1758–1858* (Oxford: Oxford University Press, 2004), p. 320 ('tar brush'); and St Clair Drake, *Black Folk Here and There: An Essay in History and Anthropology*, Volume II (Berkley: Centre for Afro American Studies University of California, 1991), pp. 257, 260 (definition of 'black blood').

[59] Katherine's 'personal wardrobe' also consisted of a 'Maria Mudarra' who may have been an African in Mariano Roca de Togores (ed.), *Cronica del Rey Enrique Octavo de Inglaterra* (Madrid: Libreria de los Bibliofilos, 1874), pp. 325, 329, 344, Appendix E; it is possible that another African may have been 'Donna Elvira de Manuel.' In 1504 she became infected with an eye disease and Katherine sought leave from King Henry VIII for her to go to Flanders for treatment in Mairlee Hanson, 'Katherine of Aragon letter dated 2 December 1505,' Contemporary Descriptions of Anne Boleyn, *EnglishHistory.net. 2004*. http://englishhistory.net/tudor/annedesc.html, accessed 11/8/08; There were also '52 [other] people' including 'foreign musicians, singers, [and] dancers' see Habib, *Black Lives* , pp. 38–9 and 'two slaves' who will 'attend on the maid[s] of honour' during their time in England. Whether these 'two slaves' are African and whether the 'maid[s] of honour' are Katherine's ladies in waiting is uncertain in Gustav Bergenroth, *Calendar of Letters, Dispatches, and State Papers Relating to the Negotiations Between England and Spain …* (London: Longmans Green Reader and Dyer, 1868), p. 246; and Gustav Ungerer, *The Mediterranean Apprenticeship of British Slavery* (Madrid: Verbum Editorial, 2008), p. 97.

[60] Juan Huarte, *Examin de Ingenious Para les Sciencias* (1588), p. 250, quoted in Jonathan Schorsch, *Swimming the Christian Atlantic: Judeoconversos, Afroiberians, and Amerindians in the Seventeenth Century* (Leiden/Boston/Biggleswade: Brill Extenza Turpin), p. 361.

[61] On 'blue blood' inheritance see Robert Lacey, *Aristocrats* (London: Hutchinson, 1983), p. 67; David Brewster, *Brewer's Dictionary of Phrase and Fable …* (London: H Altemus, 1870),

p. 131; Fuchs, *Exotic Nation*, pp. 116, 124–128, 170; Blount (tr.), Conestaggio, *The Historie of the Uniting of the Kingdom of Portugal*, p. 6; and Susan Adams, et. al., 'The Genetic Legacy of Religious Diversity and Intolerance … Christians, Jews, and Muslims in the Iberian Peninsula,' *The American Journal of Human Genetics*, 83: 6, 4 December 2008, pp. 725–736.

[62] Bourke, *A Concise History of the Moors in Spain*, p. 90, 'the Moorish preceptor of Charles V.' Some of Katherine's Moorish servants had originally been employed by Ferdinand and Isabella see Catalina de Cardones (below); and Jacob Michael Levin, *Agents of Empire: Spanish Ambassadors in Sixteenth-Century Italy* (Ithaca: Cornell University Press, 2005), p. 208.

[63] Antonia Fraser, *The Wives of Henry VIII* (New York: Vintage, 1993), pp. 9–26 (Katherine as a fashion trendsetter).

[64] Ungerer, *The Mediterranean Apprenticeship*, pp. 75, 137, 124; Rogers, *Nature Knows no Colour Line*, pp. 63, 66, 76, 77, 82–93, 100–110, 119, 121–123, 143, 144–145; and Anne Marie Jordan, 'Image of Empire, Slaves in the Lisbon household and court of Catherine of Austria,' in Earle and Lowe (eds.), *Black Africans in Renaissance Europe*, pp. 155–181.

[65] Stow, *The Chronicles* (1615), p. 483; Kingsford (ed.), *The Chronicles of London*, p. 332.

[66] Quotations from Gustav Bergenroth (ed.), *Supplement to Volume I and II of Calendar of Letters, Despatches and State Papers* … (London: Longman Green Reader, 1868), p. 102; and Habib, *Black Lives*, p. 24.

[67] Togores (ed.), *Cronica del Rey Enrique Octavo de Inglaterra*, pp. 325, 328, 329.

[68] Ibid., pp. 42, 325, 326, 328, 331(on the marriage, the ethnicity of Catalina's husband and his occupation) ; and Ungerer, *The Mediterranean Apprenticeship*, p. 97; Giles Tremlett, *Catherine of Aragon: Henry's Spanish Wife* (London: Faber and Faber, 2010), p. 337.

[69] Togores (ed.), *Cronica del Rey Enrique Octavo de Inglaterra*, pp. 42, 325, 326, 328.

[70] Ruth Pike, 'Sevillian society in the sixteenth century: Slaves and freedmen,' *The Hispanic American Historical Review*, 47.3, 1967, pp. 345–359; and Abentarique, *The History of the Conquest of Spain by the Moors*, p. 51.

[71] Blount (tr.), Conestaggio, *The Historie of the Uniting of the Kingdom of Portugal* (1600), pp. 5, 6 (quotation), 7. Similar views are stated by Derek Lomax in *The Reconquest of Spain* (London: Longman, 1978), p. 78; John Edwards, *The Spain of the Catholic Monarchs 1474–1520, History of Spain*, Volume V (Oxford/Hoboken: Wiley Blackwell, 2000), p. 173; and Limborch, *The History of the Inquisition*, pp. 128–132.

[72] Kirk and Kirk (eds.), *Returns of Aliens Dwelling in … London, Volume I* (1902), p. 2 and Volume III (1907), p. 301.

[73] Americo Castro, Willard F. King, et. al. *The Spaniards: An Introduction to their History* … (Berkeley/London: University of California Press, 1971), p. 284 (Jinetes); Richard Fletcher, *Moorish Spain* (London: Weidenfeld and Nicholson, 1992), p. 159; and Sertima, *Golden Age of the Moor*, pp. 58–61 (images of Zanata horsemen).

[74] National Archives, Kew, London, *Lay Subsidy Returns Series* (179) 1523–4.3: 301; Habib, *Black Lives*, pp. 45, 294.

[75] Quotations from two warrants issued 14 April 1574 B. L. Egerton 2806 and on 13 April 1575, in, Arnold, *Queen Elizabeth's Wardrobe Unlocked*, p. 106.

[76] Imtiaz Habib, *Shakespeare and Race: Postcolonial Praxis in the Early Modern Period* (Lanham: University Press of America, 1999), p. 28; Habib, *Black Lives*, p. 2, 72. But the following historians suggest she was 'Italian' without mentioning what colour her skin was see, James Walvin, *Black and White: The Negro and English Society* (London: Allen Lane and the Penguin Press, 1973), p. 9; Paul Johnson, *Elizabeth I a Biography* (New York/London: Holt Rinehart and Winston, 1974), p. 202; and Alison Weir, *Life of Elizabeth 1st* (New York: Ballantine, 1998), p. 253.

⁷⁷ Marcus Gheeraerts (?), *Queen Elizabeth Dancing with the Earl of Leicester*, c. 1580, oil on canvas, no reference, Penshurst Place, Tonbridge, Kent; John Southworth, *Fools and Jesters at the English Court* (Stroud: Sutton, 2003), pp. 251–252.

⁷⁸ Barbara Ravelhofer, in, Crista Jansohn (ed.), *Queen Elizabeth I: Past and Present* (Munster/London: Transaction, 2004), p. 110. This view is also supported by Mariusz Misztal in, *The Elizabethan Courtier: Ideal Versus Reality Embodied in Robert Dudley the Earl of Leicester* (Karkow: Wydawnictwo Naukowe Akademii Pedagogicznej, 2002), p. 223; and Peter Holman, *Four and Twenty Fiddlers: The Violin at the English Court, 1540–1690* (Oxford: Oxford University Press, 1993), p. 116.

⁷⁹ Habib has a different view about her status in *Black Lives*, pp. 2, 72; as does Dabydeen and Gilmore (eds.), *The Oxford Companion to Black British History*, p. 145.

⁸⁰ I acknowledge that some scholars suggest that the name 'Thomasina' in the form of 'Tamsin' was already common in Medieval England, see Terry Freedman, Iseabail Mcleod, *The Wordsworth Dictionary of First Names* (Ware: Wordsworth editions, 1995), p. 214.

⁸¹ On Aramaic being used by the Moors and Jews of Spain, see, Mark Abley, *Spoken Here: Travels Among Threatened Languages* (London: Heinemann, 2003), p. 206; and Nathan Ausubel, *The Book of Jewish Knowledge: An Encyclopedia of Judaism and the Jewish People Covering all Elements of Jewish Life from Biblical Times to the Present* (New York: Crown Publishers, 1964), pp. 10, 227. On the few people who studied Aramaic in Tudor England see, Gareth Lloyd Jones, *The Discovery of Hebrew in Tudor England: A Third Language* (Manchester: Manchester University Press, 1983), pp. introduction, 21, 78, 123–125, 137, 240, 263. On Robert Wakefield a Tudor academic's investigations into Aramaic see pp. 107, 183–184, 216n. And John Dee's possession of Aramaic books, pp. 249, 275.

⁸² *Merriam-Webster's Spanish-English Dictionary* (Springfield: Merriam Webster, 1997), p. 201. On Prudence de Pais, see, Southworth, *Fools and Jesters* (1998), p. 141.

⁸³ Humfrey Dyson (collator), *A Book Containing all such Proclamations as were Published by the Reigine of the late Queen Elizabeth 1559–1602* (London: Bonham Norton and John Bull, 1618), p. 157.

⁸⁴ Janet Arnold, *'Lost from her Majesties Back:' Items of Clothing and Jewels Lost or Given Away by Queen Elizabeth I between 1561–1585, Entered in One of the Day Books Kept for the Records of the Wardrobe of the Robes* (Bury: Costume Society, 1980), pp. 58, 64, 78; Southworth, *Fools and Jesters* (2003), p. 141 (first quotation); and Southworth, *Fools and Jesters* (1998), p. 107–108 (other quotations). Similar perspectives on Thomasina's status are offered by Meg Lota Brown, Kari Boyd McBride, *Women's Roles in the Renaissance* (Westport: Harcourt Education, 2005), p. 288; and Suzanne W. Hull, *Women according to Men: The World of Tudor-Stuart Men* (Walnut Creek/London: Alta Mira Press, 1996), p. 178.

⁸⁵ Alison Weir, *Elizabeth the Queen* (London: Jonathan Cape, 1998), p. 253 (quotation); Paul Johnson, *Elizabeth I: A Study in Power and Intellect* (London: Weidenfield and Nicolson, 1974), pp. 201–202 (lists of the Queen's servants their duties and status); Southworth, *Fools and Jesters* (1998), pp. 110 (Thomasina's pen), 112–113 (the Italian jester); and Leslie Hotson, in *Mr W.H.* (London: Hart-Davis, 1964), p. 247. But I acknowledge that 'A Master fool had his or her own servant,' in, Southworth, *Fools and Jesters* (2003), p. 57. On the function and role of fools in the Tudor court see Sandra Billington, *A Social History of the Fool* (Brighton: Harvester, 1984), passim.

⁸⁶ James Orchard Haliwell (ed.), John Dee, *The Private Diary of John Dee and the Catalogue of his Library of Manuscripts* (London: Camden Society, 1842), p. 7; and Christopher Hill, *Intellectual Origins of the English Revolution, Revisited* (Oxford: Clarendon, 1997), p. 142 (on the influence of John Dee).

⁸⁷ Arnold, *Queen Elizabeth's Wardrobe Unlocked*, p. 108.

⁸⁸ Artist unknown, Author unknown, *Westminster Tournament Roll 1511*, The College of Arms, London, E 36/214 f.109, see figure 2; and Dale Hoak (ed.), *Tudor Political Culture* (Cambridge: Cambridge University Press, 2002), pp. 10, 78–86 (the importance of the *Tournament Roll*).

⁸⁹ Bergenroth, *Calendar of Letters, Dispatches, and State Papers, Relating to the Negotiations Between England and Spain*, p. 246.

⁹⁰ Artist unknown, Author unknown, *Westminster Tournament Roll 1511*. The 2ⁿᵈ quotation is from Jonson, *The Character of Two Royall Masques*, p. 4.

⁹¹ Habib, *Black Lives*, pp. 39–40; and Peter Braun, Manfred Weinburg, *Ethno/Graphie ... of Literatur und Anthropologie*, 17 (Turbingen: Narr, Francke, Attempto, Furlang, 2002), p. 374 ('nine ether hair').

⁹² Artist unknown, Author unknown, *Westminster Tournament Roll 1511*, see figures 2 and 20; and Sydney Anglo, *The Great Tournament Roll of Westminster: A Collotype Reproduction of the Manuscript*, Volume II (Oxford: Clarendon Press, 1968), pp. 85, 98.

⁹³ William Duane, *A Military Dictionary, or, Explanation of the Several Systems of Discipline ...* (London: William Duane, 1810), p. 704; Scott Hughes Myerly, *British Military Spectacle: from the Napoleonic Wars through the Crimea* (London/New York: Harvard University Press, 1996), p. 150; Peter Fryer, *Staying Power ...* (1984, reprint, London: Pluto Press, 1989), p. 81.

⁹⁴ Albrecht Durer, *Katharina allt 20 jor. [aged twenty]* Portrait, Graphics, Silverpoint drawing on paper, 20 x 14 cm, Galleria degli Uffizi, Florence, Italy, 1521, see figure 19; Northrup, *Africa's Discovery of Europe*, p. 7 (Katharina's life); Earle, Lowe (eds.), *Black Africans in Renaissance Europe*, pp. 30, 31, 131, 140, 148 (Africans with turbans in sixteenth-century Europe); Jean Vercoutter, J. Devisse, M. Mollat, *The Image of the Black in Western Art*, Volume II (New York and Cambridge: Harvard, Mollat, 1976, 1979), pp. 104, 109, 136; and Joanne Bubolz Eicher, *Dress and Ethnicity: Change across Space and Time* (Oxford: Berg, 1995), pp. 212–215 (the turban does not mean Jacques or Katharina were Muslims).

⁹⁵ Fiona Collins, Gabrielle Hodges and Morag Styles (eds.), 'Storyseeds creating curriculum stories,' *Tales, Tellers and Text* (London: Continuum International Publishing Group, 2000), pp. 50–51; and Anglo, *The Great Tournament Roll of Westminster*, pp. 85, 98.

⁹⁶ Habib, *Black Lives*, pp. 39 (note)–40, 45, 136.

⁹⁷ Northcote T. Toller (ed.), Joseph Bosworth, *An Anglo-Saxon Dictionary ... Supplement ...* (1882, new edition, Oxford: Clarendon Press, 1921), p. 106 (meaning of 'Blac.').

⁹⁸ Author unknown, *Accounts of the Lord High Treasurer of Scotland*, The National Archives of Scotland, Edinburgh, E21/5–10, Volume II, 1503/4, pp. 318, 415, 417, 420, 422, 427 etc., Volume III, 1505–1506, pp. 101, 108, 118, 121, 122, 124, 132, 148, 155, etc., Volume IV, 1506–1513, pp. 51, 59, 61, 62, 64, 82, etc. and Habib, *Black Lives*, pp. 277–284.

⁹⁹ Ibid. and Habib, *Black Lives*, pp. 284–294.

¹⁰⁰ National Archives, Kew, London, Author unknown, *Exchequer Rolls of Henry VII*, Westminster Arch E 36/214, 7 Dec 1507, f. 109; and Rory Lalwan (ed.), *Sources for Black and Asian History at the City of Westminster Archives ...* (London: Westminster City Archives, 2005), pp. 9, 10.

¹⁰¹ National Archives, Kew, London, *Exchequer Accounts*, 417 (6) folio 50 RO in Letters and Papers Henry VIII 1.1.505# 1025.

¹⁰² Habib, *Black Lives*, pp. 39–40 (offers a similar view).

¹⁰³ Kirk and Kirk (eds.), *Returns of Aliens Dwelling in ... London*, Volume I (1902), pp. 24, 296.

¹⁰⁴ Ibid., *Volume I* (1902), pp. 20, 155, 199, 252 and Volume III (1907), p. 314.

[105] Thomas Bourke, *A Concise History of the Moors in Spain*, p. xviii; and Janet Lloyd, *The Spanish Inquisition: A History* (London: New Haven: Yale University Press, 2006), pp. 44–46, 54, 105.

[106] Bourke, *A Concise History of the Moors in Spain*, p. 90; and the painting of the unnamed African man in Jan Mostaert, *Portrait of an African Man*, Rijksmuseum, Amsterdam, circa 1520–1530, ref. Sk-A-4986, Oil on Panel, 30.8 x 21.2 cm, see figure 21. On the African man's employment see *Rijksmuseum*, http://www.rijksmuseum.nl/collectie/aanwinsten2005/portret-van-een-afrikaanse-man?lang=en, accessed 13/02/10.

[107] Quotations from Lane-Poole, *The Story of the Moors in Spain*, p. 270; Limborch, *The History of the Inquisition*, pp. 129–132; Blount (tr.), Conestaggio, *The Historie of the Uniting of the Kingdom of Portugal*, pp. 5–7.

[108] John Allyne Gade, *Christian IV: King of Denmark and Norway: A Picture of the Seventeenth Century* (Boston: Houghton Mifflin, 1928), p. 62.

[109] The first quotation is from Robert O. Bucholz, Newton Key, *Early Modern England, 1485–1714: A Narrative History* (Wiley-Blackwell, 2004), p. 375; and Bourke, *A Concise History of the Moors in Spain*, pp. xxi, xxviii.

[110] Frederick Bouterwerk, 'Meeting at the field of cloth of Gold,' oil on canvas, 1520 Palace of Versailles, France; and Artist unknown, 'The Meeting of Henry VIII and Maximilian, in 1513,' *Great Tournament Roll 1545*, oil on a panel, Queen Elizabeth collection 2008 in Adrian Louis Montrose, *The Subject of Elizabeth: Authority, Gender, and Representation* (Chicago: University of Chicago Press, 2006), pp. 21–22.

[111] Earle and Lowe (eds.), *Black Africans in Renaissance Europe*, pp. 38, 158; and Rebecca Martin, *Wild Men and Moors in the Castle of Love: The Castle-Siege Tapestries, in Nuremberg, Vienna, and Boston (German (Alsace) Weavers)* (Chapel Hill: University of North California, 1983), pp. 1–10, 82, 83, 111; see figures 22, 23.

[112] Kipling (ed.), *The Receyt of the Ladie Kateryne*, pp. xxIv, xxv, xxv, xxviii, xxxiii.

[113] Hieronymus Bosch, *The Epiphany or the Adoration of the Magi*, 1510, oil on wood panel, Museo del Prado, Madrid, 138 x 72 cm, by 138 x 34 cm, ref 21032, see figures 24 and 25; similar images of 'noble' Africans are in Jean Vercoutter, J. Devisse, M. Mollat, *The Image of the Black in Western Art*, Volume II, pp. 101, 113, 136, 140, 141, 164, 179, 183, 214, 248, 249; and Vincent Boele, Ernest Schreuder and Elmer Kolfin (eds.), *Black is Beautiful: Rubens to Dumas* (Amsterdam: Die Nieuwe Kerk, 2008), pp. 15, 20, 24, 37, 39, 59, 61, 69, 74, 93, 96, 157 (Black Angels), 170, 172, 180 ('African' goddess Sibyl), 197, 199 (African King and Queen from the *Aethiopica* or *An Æthiopian Historie*).

[114] Earle and Lowe (eds.), *Black Africans in Renaissance Europe*, pp. 182–183.

[115] The 2nd quotation is from, Blount (tr.), Conestaggio, in, *The Historie of the Uniting of the Kingdom of Portugal*, pp. 6–7, 39. On this 'higher culture' see, Limborch, *The History of the Inquisition*, p. 128; A. C. de C. M. Saunders, *A Social History of Black Slaves and Freedmen in Portugal 1441–1555* (Cambridge: Cambridge University Press, 1982), pp. 29–33, 59–60, 87, 149; and Pike, 'Sevillian society in the sixteenth century, slaves and freedmen,' pp. 345–359.

[116] Quotations from Abentarique, *The History of the Conquest of Spain by the Moors*, preface; Lane-Poole, *The Story of the Moors in Spain*, pp. 54, 217; Florian, Heron (tr.), *Gonsolvo or Cordova or The Conquest of Granada*, p. 97; and Chandler, Sertima (ed.), *African Presence in Early Europe*, pp. 144–176.

[117] Bourke, *A Concise History of the Moors in Spain*, pp. xxi, xxv, xxviii; Pory (tr.), Africanus, *A Geographical Historie of Africa*, p. 359; and Florian, Heron (tr.), *Gonsolvo or Cordova or The Conquest of Granada*, p. 77.

[118] Quotations from Ivan Van Sertima, *African Presence in Early Europe* (New Jersey: Transaction Books, 1985), pp. 159, 168; and Florian, Heron (tr.), *Gonsolvo or Cordova*, p. 77.

[119] Bourke, *A Concise History of the Moors in Spain*, pp. xxi, xxviii, on Spain's renaissance before Italy, p. 188.

[120] A view shared by Daniel Weissbort, Astraour Eystiensson, *Translation – Theory and Practice: A Historical Reader* (Oxford/London: Oxford University Press, 2006), pp. 260–261; and Robert Tittler and Norman Jones (eds.), *Companion to Tudor Britain* (Oxford: Wiley, Blackwell), p. 511. And evidence in: Ptolemy, *Ptolemaei Planisphaerium [translated from Arabic into Latin] Iordani [Nemorarii] Planisphaerium. Federici Commandini Urbinatis in Ptolemaei Planisphaerium Commentarius* (Venice: Aldus, 1558); Aristotle, *Doubtful or Superstitious Work, Mystica Ægyptiorum et Chaldæorum a Platone, Voce Tradita, ab Aristotele, Excepta et Conscripta Philosophia.* [A Latin version by P. N. de Castellaniis of the Arabic translation of Abenama.] (Rome: Apud J Mazochium, 1519); Pory (tr.), Africanus, *A Geographical Historie of Africa, Written in Arabicke and Italian ... by Iohn Leo a More ...* (London: John Pory, 1600); Conrad Gessner, George Baker (tr.), *The, Newe Jewell of Health ...* (London: H. Denham, 1576), pp. preface, Bi , 2.

[121] City of Westminster Archives Centre, London, 1601/2 January/21/St Clements Dane/Volume1Burials/MF 1.

[122] David Katz, *Jews in the History of England, 1485–1850* (1994, new edition, Oxford: Oxford University Press, 1997), pp. 1–107 (a general account of the Jewish Tudor population); and C.J. Sisson, 'A Colony of Jews in Shakespeare's London,' *Essays and Studies*, Volume 23, 1938, pp. 38–51.

[123] Bourke, *A Concise History of the Moors in Spain*, preface, xviii, 'supplication of the old Moor,' p. 199; Janet Lloyd, *The Spanish Inquisition: A History* (London/New Haven: Yale University Press, 2006), pp. 44–46, 54, 105; and John Robert Scott, *A Dissertation on the Expulsion of the Moors from Spain and the Protestants from France and the Low Countries* (Dublin: Joseph Hill University Press, 1779), p. 7.

[124] Suggested by evidence in, Florian, Heron (tr.), *Gonsolvo or Cordova or The Conquest of Granada*, pp. 94–99; Ian Davidson Kalmar, 'Moorish Style: Orientalism, the Jews, and Synagogue Architecture,' *Jewish Social Studies History Culture and Society*, Spring/Summer 2001, Vol. 7, No. 3, pp. 68–100; and Yeshiva, University Museum, *The Sephardic Journey 1492–1992* (New York: Yeshiva University Museum, 1992), p. 291.

[125] On West African Jews see, Pory (tr.), Africanus, *A Geographical Historie of Africa*, p. 379; Purchas, *Pvrchas his Pilgrimages*, pp. 42, 133–138; Rodrigo Diaz de Bivar, Robert Southey (tr.), *Chronicle of the Cid ...* (London: Longman, Hurst, Rees, Orme, 1808), pp. xv.

[126] Susan Adams, et al, 'The Genetic Legacy of Religious Diversity and Intolerance: Paternal Lineages of Christians, Jews, and Muslims in the Iberian Peninsula,' *The American Journal of Human Genetics*, 83: 6, 4 December 2008,' pp. 725–736.

[127] Ibid.

[128] Ungerer, *The Mediterranean Apprenticeship*, pp. 11–12, 99; C.J. Sisson, 'A Colony of Jews in Shakespeare's London,' pp. 38–51; Lucien Wolf, 'Jews in Tudor England,' *Essays in Jewish History*, 1934, pp. 73–90.

[129] Robert Weston Evans, offers different views on the same case in, *Curiosity and Wonder from the Renaissance to the Enlightenment* (London: Ashgate, 2006), pp. 180–181; and Habib, *Black Lives*, pp. 313–314.

[130] Ungerer, *The Mediterranean Apprenticeship*, pp. 11–12; and Habib, *Black Lives*, p. 110.

[131] GL Ms 28867.

[132] Ungerer, *The Mediterranean Apprenticeship*, pp. 92–93.

¹³³ GL Ms 28867; William Bruce Bannerman (ed.), *Registers of St Olave, Hart Street, London, 1563–1700* (London: Harleian Society, 1916), p. 121; and Habib, *Black Lives*, p. 314.

¹³⁴ National Archives, Kew, London, 'Will of Hector Nunez,' Prerogative Court of Canterbury, Register: Sainberbe Quire Numbers, 56–94, 13 September 1591, PROB 11/78; Ungerer, *The Mediterranean Apprenticeship*, p. 92; Habib, *Black Lives*, pp. 110–111, Habib suggests that the court case continued until 1599. But my research suggests that Nunez died in 1591 which means Habib has made an error or the court case proceeded with Nunez in absentia.

¹³⁵ Evidence in, Charles Meyers, Elizabethan 'Marranos' unmasked, *Kulanu all of us*, http://www.kulanu.org/anousim/unmasked.php, accessed 20/07/09

¹³⁶ Ibid.; Charles Meyers, 'Lawsuits in Elizabethan courts of law the Adventurers of Dr Hector Nunez, 1566–1599 a précis,' *Journal of European Economic History*, Volume 25/1, 1996, pp. 157–168; Sisson, 'A Colony of Jews in Shakespeare's London,' pp. 38–51; and Wolf, 'Jews in Tudor England,' pp. 73–90.

¹³⁷ Ibid.; William Shakespeare, *The Merchant of Venice* in Richard Proudfoot, Ann Thompson and David Scott Kastan (eds.), *The Arden Shakespeare Complete Works,*, Act IV, Scene I, Line 173–394, pp. 850–852; and Christopher Marlowe, Prologue to, *The Famous Tragedy of the Rich Jew of Malta as it was Played Before the King and Queene …* (London: Nicholas Vavasour, 1633), pp. A5, A6.

¹³⁸ A different view on this latter issue is offered by Habib, *Black Lives*, pp. 110–111, 314; Ungerer, *The Mediterranean Apprenticeship*, p. 92; and Meyers, 'Elizabethan 'Marranos' unmasked.'

¹³⁹ In Nunez's Will there are references to 'Marit' or 'Manit' and a 'Joanne' named as Nunez's 'maid servantes' who may be Iberian Africans and are given the 'somme of three pounds,' but without more evidence this is difficult to prove in National Archives, Kew, London, 'Will of Hector Nunez,' Prerogative Court of Canterbury, Register: Sainberbe Quire Numbers, 56–94, 13 September 1591, PROB 11/78; GL Ms 28867; and Bannerman (ed.), *Registers of St Olave, Hart Street, London, 1563–1700*, p. 121.

¹⁴⁰ Ungerer, *The Mediterranean Apprenticeship*, pp. 11–12, 99.

¹⁴¹ Dominic Green, *The Double Life of Doctor Lopez: Spies, Shakespeare and the Plot to Poison Elizabeth I* (London: Century, 2003), pp. 6, 308; and Harry Lee Faggett, *Black and Other Minorities in Shakespeare's England* (Prairie View: Prairie View Press, 1971), pp. 52–80.

¹⁴² Bourke, *A Concise History of the Moors in Spain*, pp. 252–253; Joseph Perez, Janet Lloyd (tr.), *The Spanish Inquisition: A History* (2004, new edition, London/ New Haven: Yale University Press, 2006), pp. 44–46; Lane-Poole, *The Story of the Moors in Spain*, p. 270; Benjamin Ehlers, *Between Christians and Moriscos: Juan de Ribera and Religious Reform in Valencia, 1568– 1614* (Baltimore: John Hopkins University Press, 2006), p. 35 (The Moorish Revolt was put down harshly.)

¹⁴³ St Michael Paternoster Church, Vintry Ward, London, ref. Vintry Ward MF 0574365; and Habib, *Black Lives*, p. 303.

¹⁴⁴ Lu Ann Homza, *The Spanish Inquisition, 1478–1614: An Anthology of Sources* (Indianapolis: Hackett Publishing, 2006), pp. xxxv, 45, 52–56; and Limborch, *The History of the Inquisition*, pp. 129–132.

¹⁴⁵ Thomas Henry Dyer, *The History of Modern Europe: From the Fall of Constantinople …* Volume I (London: John Murray, 1861–1864), pp. 56–62 (Moors in Castile).

¹⁴⁶ Homza, *The Spanish Inquisition, 1478–1614*, pp. xxxv, 45, 52–56; and Limborch, *The History of the Inquisition*, pp. 129–132.

¹⁴⁷ Limborch, *The History of the Inquisition*, p. 130; and Helen Rawlings, *The Spanish Inquisition* (London: Wiley Blackwell, 2006), pp. 72–89.

[148] Charles Henry Lea, *The Moriscos of Spain: Their Conversion and Expulsion* (London: Bernard Quaritch, 1901), pp. 232, 311, 321–326; Rawlings, *The Spanish Inquisition*, pp. 72–89; and Limborch, *The History of the Inquisition*, pp. preface, 128, 130.

[149] Rawlings, *The Spanish Inquisition*, pp. 72–89; and Blount (tr.), Conestaggio, *The Historie of the Uniting of ... Portugal*, pp. 6, 39.

[150] Scott, *A Dissertation on the Expulsion of the Moors from Spain*, pp. 17, 27; Bourke, *A Concise History of the Moors in Spain*, p. 252 (quotes similar figures).

[151] Ungerer, *The Mediterranean Apprenticeship*, p. 27; and Florian, Heron (tr.), *Gonsolvo or Cordova*, p. 21.

[152] Alonso Martin Pedraz, *Enciclopedia del Idioma ... Volume II* (Madrid: Aguilar, 1958), p. 281 ('colour difference' in Spain).

[153] GL Ms 4448 (Katherin's record); Richard Wernham (ed.), Public Record Office, *List and Analysis of State Papers, Foreign Series: January to December 1595* (London: Her Majesty's Stationery Office, 1964), p. 208 (the Prince's death).

[154] Ungerer, *The Mediterranean Apprenticeship of British Slavery*, pp. 81–83.

[155] John Morris, *The Troubles of our Catholic Forefathers Related by Themselves* (London: Burns and Oates, 1875), p. 133; Ungerer, *The Mediterranean Apprenticeship*, pp. 81, 84, 90 (suggests the Prince came to England between 1578–80).

[156] Andrew Sharpe Hume (ed.), et al, Public Record Office, *Calendar of Letters and State Papers, 1580–1586* (London: Eyre and Spottiswoode, 1896), p. 403; Arthur John Butler (ed.), et. al., Public Record Office, *Calendar of State Papers, Foreign Series, of the Reign of Elizabeth ... Volume I* (1863, new edition, London: Her Majesty's Stationery, 1914), p. 214; and M. Busk, *The History of Spain and Portugal, 1000BC to AD 1814* (London: Baldwin and Craddock, 1831), pp. 129–132.

[157] GL Ms 4448.

[158] Ungerer, *The Mediterranean Apprenticeship of British Slavery*, p. 81.

[159] Jack Forbes, *Africans and Native Americans: The Language of Race and the Evolution of Red-Black Peoples* (1988, new edition, Urbana: University of Illinois Press, 1993), pp. 140–141.

[160] Medway Archives and Local Studies Centre, Strood, Kent, 19/February/1603/Gravesend/ MF1 and Robert Peirce Cruden, *The History of the Town of Gravesend ...* (London: William Pickering, 1843), pp. 13–14, 59, 120–125, 199, 322.

[161] Quotation from, Scott, *A Dissertation on the Expulsion of the Moors from Spain*, p. 16.

[162] Evidence in St Botolph without Aldgate parish records including: GL Ms 9243–9245, GL Ms 4515/1, St Botolph without Aldgate *Memorandum Daybooks*, Volume I–VI (London: Parish of St Botolph without Aldgate, 1586–1603) etc., references P69/BOT2/A/01/MS 9234/1-6; some of the records containing these Africans are cited in the bibliography.

[163] Ungerer, *The Mediterranean Apprenticeship*, p. 76; and Habib has similar ideas in *Black Lives*, pp. 91–2, 142–3, 241–2.

[164] Author unknown, *St Botolph Without Aldgate Memorandum Daybook*, Volume VI (London: Parish of St Botolph without Aldgate, 1596–7), pp. 257–258, P69/BOT2/ A101/Ms 9234/6 and GL Ms 9234/6.

[165] GL Ms 9222/1, pp. 223, 288, 303.

[166] GL Ms 9222/1, p. 288.

[167] Hugh Chisholm, *The Encyclopaedia Britannica: A Dictionary of Arts, Sciences, Literature and General Information* (London: University Press, 1911), p. 339; and Jose Hinojosa Montalvo, *Jews of the Kingdom of Valencia: From Persecution to Expulsion, 1391–1492* (Jerusalem: Magnes Press, Hebrew University, 1993), p. 205 (Moorish needle makers).

168 R. S. Bartlett, J. M. Woodward, Samuel Timmins (ed.) ... *Birmingham and the Midland Hardware District* (Abingdon: Frank Cass and Company, 1866), p. 197; John Bromley, *The Armorial Bearings of the Guilds of London: A Record of the Heraldry of the Surviving Companies with Historical Notes* (London: F Warne, 1960), p. 181; John Stow, *The Annales of England, Faithfully Collected Out of the Most Authenticall Authors* (London: 1592), pp. 1037–1045; John Stow, Edmund Howes, *The Annales, or Generall Chronicle of England, Begun First by Maister Iohn Stow, and After Him Continued ... Unto the Ende of this Present Yeere 1614, by E. Howes* (London: 1615), p. 948; and Arnold, *Queen Elizabeth's Wardrobe Unlocked*, p. 182.

169 William Harrison, in Frederick James Furnivall, John Norden (eds.), et. al. *Harrison's Description of England in Shakespeare's Youth ... Volume II and III* (1577, 1584, 1877, new edition, London: New Shakespeare Society, 1878), p. 34.

170 *Haydn's Dictionary of Dates Relating to all Ages and Nations for Universal Reference* (1841, new edition, London: Ward and Locke, 1906), p. 509.

171 Author unknown, *St Botolph Without Aldgate Memorandum Daybook*, Volume I (London: Parish of St Botolph without Aldgate, 1586–1588), p. 18; and GL Ref P69/BOT2/A/ 01/MS 9234/1.

172 Kirk and Kirk (eds.), *Returns of Aliens Dwelling in the City and Suburbs of London*, Volume I (1902), pp. 422, 436, 455, 456.

173 Bromley, *The Armorial Bearings of the Guilds of London*, pp. 181–182; and David Henshaw, John de Courcy, *The Worshipful Company of Needlemakers, 1656–2006: A Commemoration of 350 Years* (London: The Worshipful Company of Needlemakers, 2006), introduction.

174 Habib, *Black Lives*, pp. 44–45.

175 Thomas Fuller, *The Histories of the Worthies of England* (1662, new edition, London: F. C. and J. Rivington, 1811), p. 50.

176 GL Ms 9222/1, GL Ms 9221 and GL Ms 9234/6.

177 David Starkey (ed.), *The Inventory of King Henry VIII: The Transcript*, Volume I, Volume 56 (London: Society for Antiquaries of London, 1998), pp. 80, 83, 88; Vincent Ilardi, *Renaissance Vision From Spectacles to Telescopes* (Philadelphia: American Philosophical Society, 2007), p. 130 (Henry VIII's spectacles); Victoria and Albert Museum, *Princely Magnificence: Court Jewels of the Renaissance, 1500–1630 [exposition] 15 October 1980–1 February 1981* (London: Debrett's Peerage in association with the Royal Albert Museum, 1980), p. 33 (sixteenth-century jewelled iron box); Peter Brown, *British Cutlery: An Illustrated History of its Design, Evolution and Use* (London: Philip Wilson, 2001), p. 21 (sixteenth-century cutlery); Southworth, *Fools and Jesters* (2003), p. 223, Thomasina's personal items include 'a handell ... of Moriscoworke with Venice gold and silver.'

178 Shakespeare, *Othello* in Proudfoot, Thompson and Kastan (eds.), *The Arden Shakespeare Complete Works*, Act I, Scene III, Line 91, p. 945.

179 Anthonye de Corro, *A Supplication to the King of Spain ...* (London: Coldocke and Bynneman, London, 1577), pp. 1, 10, 11, 61, 123; Limborch, *The History of the Inquisition*, pp. 120–121, 127; and Robert Greene, *The Estate of the English Fugitives Under the King of Spain and his Ministers* (London: John Drawater, 1595), pp. 1–2, G1–G3.

180 Milner (ed.), Epstein, *At the Margins: Minority Groups in Premodern Italy*, pp. 224–232; Jacques Heers, *Genes Au XVe siecle: Activite Economique et Problemes Sociaux* (Paris: SEVPEN, 1961), pp. 29, 555; and Jacques Heers, *Esclaves et Domestiques au Moyen Age Dans le Monde Mediterranean* (Paris: Fayard, 1981), pp. 135–181.

181 Similar perspectives on this matter are offered in BBC, 'Britain's first Black Community in Elizabethan London,' *BBC News Magazine*, http://www.bbc.co.uk/news/

magazine- 18903391, accessed 20/07/12; Rebecca Dobbs (pr) Michael Wood (presenter), *The Great British Story*, Episode 5, BBC 2, 20/07/12.

[182] Evidence in: G. L. GL Ms 9243–9245, GL Ms 9222; Author unknown, *St Martin in the Fields Parish Register*, Volume I (London: No publisher, 27 September 1571), p. 116; Plymouth and West Devon Record Office, Plymouth, St Andrews/MF1-4; Devon Record Office, East Allington/20/08/1577 PR; Northampton Records Office, Northampton, Microfiche 120, pp. 1–3; and Bristol Record Office, Bristol, Ref P/ST PJR/1/1/CMB 1576–1621, n. p.

[183] Author unknown, Letter to Lord Mayors, signed by Queen Elizabeth, National Archives Kew, London, PC 2/21, p. 304, 11 July 1596; Author unknown, Letter signed by Queen Elizabeth, National Archives, Kew, London, PC 2/21, f.306, 18 July 1596; and Author unknown, Proclamation ca January 1601, National Archives, Kew, London, *Tudor Royal Proclamations*, 1601/ 804.5-805.

[184] Also suggested by Faggett, *Black and Other Minorities in Shakespeare's England*, pp. 2–6.

[185] Blount (tr.), Conestaggio, *The Historie of the Uniting of the Kingdom of Portugal*, pp. 6, 7, 39.

[186] Evidence in, Thomas Greepe, *The True and Perfecte Newes of the Woorthy and Valiaunt Exploytes Performed and Doone by that Valiant Knight Syr F. Drake; Not Onely at Sancto Domingo and Carthagena, etc... Giving an Account of the late Successes Against the Spaniards ...* (London: Publisher unknown, 1587), n. p. passim; and Kent Williams, 'African Heritage in Central America,' http://www.bjmjr.com/afromestizo/imp_dates.htm, accessed 12/03/2006.

CHAPTER 4

West Africans present in Tudor England

In this chapter I will examine why West Africans such as Jacques Francis appear in Tudor records and how their origins affected their status in England. The West Africans who are discussed in this chapter are all men as at present there is insufficient evidence to discuss West-African women in detail. This may reflect that there were only a few West-African women in Tudor England because of the difficulties they faced travelling there in the sixteenth and the beginning of the seventeenth centuries. It is also likely to be because women were so important to the stability of communities in West Africa that they were tied to their land in a way that men were not.[1] This means that a disproportionate number of single West-African men were present in Tudor England, and that they had little opportunities to marry or have sexual relationships with West-African women: this is an idea, the implications of which I return to in the Conclusion.

Some of the West-African men who were present in Tudor England are found in English households and appear to have had skills and abilities which were respected by English aristocrats. In the first part of this chapter I discuss what skills these West Africans had, and how this could have made them valuable servants and friends to some Englishmen of power. I then examine how West Africans were seen in Tudor England, and discuss whether the ideas expressed by Habib, Ungerer and Fryer shows that West Africans were considered as inferior. These ideas primarily relate to whether West Africans were considered as nude-pagan savages in Tudor England.[2] Habib, Ungerer and others use the work of some fifteenth- and sixteenth-century African writers such as the Moorish historian Leo Africanus and the Moroccan Sultan Ahmad Al Mansur to show that some West Africans were perceived as being primitive and savage, 'extremely … lazy,' 'ignorant' and 'ugly,' always naked, and that their Animist beliefs meant they were without a religion.[3] Some of the letters and books of Africanus and others that contain these sorts of views were available to Englishmen, and the ideas that they promote appear to have been echoed in some sixteenth-century English fiction.[4] But I suggest that West Africans were not necessarily perceived in this way in Tudor England, and they were certainly not treated as Habib and Ungerer suggest. Rather, the evidence I have found suggests that Habib and Ungerer's ideas about West Africans originate from the way some of 'those kindes of people' were treated in England in the nineteenth and early-twentieth centuries.[5]

Furthermore, I suggest that in Tudor England some Englishmen acknowledged that parts of West Africa had wealth and contained powerful kingdoms. Some Tudor writers associated wealth with West-African people and this gave Englishmen reasons to invite these Africans to England and trade with them. This explains why West Africans from specific African kingdoms were present in Tudor England, and how these relationships had a significant influence on why West Africans were not automatically exploited in the way that Fryer and other historians have suggested.

Nevertheless analysing the status of West Africans in Tudor England is difficult because we have little evidence written by West Africans themselves. So we rely on the contemporary work of others such as Africanus and the letters of Englishmen as we attempt to find the facts, and some of the latter when they talk about West Africans in Tudor England can provide misleading information about their status. This is because they sometimes describe the Africans they encounter in such a way as it increases the writer's fame, but diminishes the Africans' contribution to the activities they were both engaged in. In this chapter I will analyse some of these issues to discover the status and origins of West Africans in Tudor England.

West Africans present in Tudor England

Most of the West Africans present in Tudor England who are discussed in this chapter, appear to have had skills which were considered important to people living in that society. Nevertheless, in Chapter 1 of this book I suggested that there were Africans present amongst the poor and destitute in Tudor London. Some of these Africans described in parish registers and other records could have come from West Africa, but this may not have always been stated. This is because some Tudor parish clerks and priests might not have had the knowledge to describe West Africans in a different way from other Africans. More specifically, Tudor writers do not appear to have separated West Africans from other Africans using science, religion or linguistics as some contemporary anthropologists do. But a number of West Africans do appear in Tudor records described by terms such as 'Ginnye' or 'Guinea' in conjunction with other words such as 'Blackamoore.' For example as with a man called Domingo described as a 'Ginnye negar,' who was buried on 27 August 1587 at St Botolph, London. In the *Parish Clerk's Memorandum Daybook* written at the same time Domingo is also described as a 'negaro' 'servaunt to the Right worshipfull Sr William Winter knight.'[6] But in the contemporary parish register where Domingo is also recorded he is merely referred to as 'a black neigro servaunt [to] ... Winter,' without any reference to his West-African origins. This may be for a number of reasons. The first is that the writer of the parish register and the daybook are two different people: one with the knowledge of Domingo's origins, the other without.

The second theory is that the writer of the register may not have felt that Domingo's West-African origins were important. But interestingly, both writers did feel that Domingo's race was, and that is why references to this are recorded in both documents. A third theory may explain this, which appears the most likely, and that is more details about his ethnicity have been left off the register for the sake of brevity, with the recorder in the *Daybook* having more time and space to write such information. Linked to this idea is the notion that the *Daybook* may have been written by a more meticulous writer. This is indicated by the fact that the *Daybook* includes details that Domingo lived in 'abbye place' in 'Eastsmithfield,' London, and that he was buried with 'the best clothe [when he died of] Con[sumption?].'[7] All of these details are missing from the parish register. However, in neither the parish register, nor the *Memorandum Daybook* have I found evidence that supports Ungerer's idea that Domingo was a slave 'taken in Guinea from a former Portuguese owner:' Winter's 'business partner,' or that '[Domingo] may have been part of Winter's personal booty.'[8]

Domingo, in a similar way to the Africans discussed in the last chapter, probably had skills that were useful to his English employer. One of these may have been his ability to understand several languages because of his West-African heritage. This is because many sixteenth-century West-African societies were multilingual where the people spoke African Creole or Krio: a mixture of native West-African and European languages such as Portuguese or Spanish. Therefore, Domingo may have had his Spanish name before he came to England.[9] However, there are further issues linked to Domingo's name and this is that he may have come to England via the Caribbean and the island of Hispaniola (Santa Domingo/Haiti), especially because in Santo Domingo English pirates such as Francis Drake, who were sponsored by Winter enslaved Africans for profit.[10] Drake's first foray into Santa Domingo was on 11 January 1586 less than two years before Domingo's death. So it is possible that Domingo came to Tudor England via this route and that he had only been present in England for a short time before he died.

We can thus potentially trace Domingo's origins by examining the activities of Winter his employer. Winter was a naval captain who rose to the rank of Admiral in 1588 during Elizabeth I's reign.[11] Winter and Drake became prominent in the Tudor court by acquiring wealth from raiding Spanish and Portuguese plantations that existed in islands off the coast of West Africa such as Sao Tome and Principe. If Domingo came from these colonies, rather than Santo Domingo or others in the Caribbean, he could have given Winter information about how Africans often unwillingly served their Spanish and Portuguese employers.[12] If Domingo had been useful to Winter in this way it may explain why the West African was buried with the 'best cloth,' a practice in England that appears to have been reserved for the wealthy, or those who had given exemplary service to their employers.[13]

Domingo was not the only West African present in Tudor England, and there are images of what could be another West-African man in Drake's diadem or jewel (see Fig. 26). This diadem was given to Drake by Elizabeth I either in 1586 or 1588, although, it could have been made much earlier as it includes an 'inset miniature' of Elizabeth's portrait which had been created by Nicholas Hilliard in 1575. The diadem is richly ornate and encrusted with gold, silver leaf and pearls. The image of the African man in the diadem looks detailed and intricate and it appears to have been created from a live subject. All of this may suggest that the African person it was based on was present in England when the diadem was created, which could mean that it is one of the few visual representations of an African living in Tudor England. However, the historian Karen Dalton suggests that it portrays a 'Black Emperor' of West-African origin, or perhaps an African ruler from a kingdom in the Caribbean. I have yet to find evidence to confirm these ideas but the African does appear noble and dignified and most importantly he is not depicted as a slave. The image of the African is super-imposed over that of a white face. It is interesting that this last image does not seem to have been based on a real person and is a highly stylised and generic representation of a white youth. Dalton suggests that the images in the diadem portray the unity or victory of the 'peoples' of the world against Catholicism. There is more discussion on this matter in Dalton's work, but the important point is that the diadem's image of the 'noble' African fits with other positive representations of Africans that have been discussed throughout this book.[14]

Another 'noble' West-African present in Tudor England who may have been the subject or inspiration for the image in Drake's diadem is a man called Diego Negro. He came to England with Drake on 9 August 1573. Diego travelled on a 'fantastic' journey from the Caribbean before he reached England and this provides clues about his status in Tudor society.

Diego became acquainted with Drake through the latter's voyage to Panama, Peru, and the Caribbean Islands, and these journeys were described in the Englishman's letters and published in 1628 as *Sir Francis Drake Revived*.[15] Later in 1659, some of Drake's other letters were developed into a play by William Davenant called *The History of Sir Francis Drake*. This play uncovers important information about Diego's exploits which suggest that the African had an important role in Drake's adventures. As the nineteenth-century explorer John Barrow says, Davenant's play reveals the adventures that Diego and Drake were involved in 'pretty correctly,' and more recently the historian Derek Hughes says something similar.[16]

Taking into consideration all the evidence it appears that Diego was a Symeron or Maroon. These were people originally from West Africa who had separated themselves from 'their Spanish masters,' and formed independent kingdoms which participated in trade that stretched from North to South America. By the time that Drake arrived in the Caribbean many of these Symeron kingdoms were almost eighty-years old. The Symerons were a culturally diverse set of people who synthesised elements of West-African cultures and religions with elements of Catholicism inherited from their former owners. These communities in the Americas were often opposed to slavery and freed slaves wherever they found them.[17] Understanding this makes us look with caution at some of Drake's statements that Diego was simply a slave 'who had been used by his [Spanish] masters' to betray the Symerons 'divers times.'[18] It is more likely as Davenant's work states, that Diego had guile and sagacity, and chose to work with Drake because he hated slavery, and had pledged to fight against Spanish slave traders. Diego's cultural heritage and knowledge ended up being invaluable to Drake, and the Englishman acknowledges some of this in his letters when he says that Diego did 'great service' as both he and the other Symerons had 'special skills in the erection of small houses,' were 'well acquainted with the countrey,' and more importantly appear to have shown the English how to wage guerrilla warfare against the Spanish.[19]

The fact that Drake brought Diego to Plymouth with him may be a further indication of how important this African was to Drake's current activities and future plans. Diego was in England for four years from 1573 until 13 December 1577 when Drake was commissioned to circumnavigate the globe. But as of yet I have not discovered where Diego lived, although it is likely that he spent at least some time in Plymouth helping Drake either draw maps or provide information about the Americas. Diego's skills as a navigator are acknowledged in Davenant's work where he claims that Diego was Drake's 'chief conductor,' and that the African showed the Englishmen new routes to 'the North and South Atlantic'.[20] This is all the more likely since Drake's previous navigator the Frenchman Guillaume Le Testu[21] had been killed in 1573 (see below).

It is also probable that Diego had another equally important role in England linked to Drake needing to corroborate his activities to his English sponsors, as the African was in a unique position to support stories that the Englishman told. An indication of why this was important can be seen in evidence which is being revealed here for the first time. This evidence is a letter written in 1586, by the Tudor politician Edward Stafford to the Principal Secretary of State Francis Walsingham, and does not refer to Diego but another African present in sixteenth-century Europe who is connected to the exploits of Drake:

> … There [is in this town] here a [N]egro [with a cut on his face] who [sayeth] he came with Sir Francis Drake, and stole sway when he landed in England. He gives out that [Sir Francis] Drake has brought home little or nothing, and has done less, and that his taking of Cartagena, Nombre de Dios and the rest is false. But the man is never away from the Spanish ambassador, and I think is supposed by him to give out these things. I would be glad to know whether any such [a person] has escaped from Sir Francis Drake [or no,] and also as much as may be known of the particular successes of his journey. I would make them blown abroad to his honour …[22]

This letter states a number of important points. The first is that according to Stafford the African mentioned 'stole away' with Drake to England after the events at Nombe de Dios in Panama. That means he probably came to England in 1573 with Diego, and this could mean that he was a Symeron as well. But we do not know how long he lived in England, although the words 'stole away' suggest the African took an active role in his decision to go with the Englishman and was not merely captured or enslaved.

Furthermore, Stafford's letter states that the African says he was with Drake during the military engagements that took place in Nombre de Dios. Nombre de Dios was one of the most important ports and trading posts used by the Spanish in Central America. Drake claimed in other correspondence that he and the privateer Guillaume robbed a silver mule train.[23] This train operated along an improvised trail which the Spanish used to transport the gold and silver they had 'won' from their colonies in the Americas. Guillaume was captured and killed as a result of these activities, leaving Drake as the principal narrator of the events that took place there.[24] In this regard the testimonial of the African 'with a cut on his face' takes on a greater significance, since Drake claimed to have successfully fought against the Spanish, 'won' renown, and more importantly gold and silver which he buried.[25] What part Africans played in this fighting none of the contemporary evidence has disclosed, and our failure to gain this information underlines issues already stated in this book.

However, fourteen years later from the events in Nombre, the African with 'a cut on his face' appears in France, with the Spanish ambassador, offering his version of the events in Central America – although how the African came to be in France I have not been able to ascertain. But what is certain is that even though Stafford acknowledges that the African may be 'supposed' to say what he is saying. In other words, that the African may have been put up to do it – his safety, (hence his closeness to the Spanish Ambassador) is considered important to his sponsors. Moreover, the African's testimonials appear to have been impressive enough for Stafford to feel compelled to gather more information so that he can compete against him and exhort Drake's honours.

Certainly Stafford feels this matter is significant enough to ask Walsingham if he knows more. Walsingham at this time was responsible for England's internal and external security and the nation's intelligence services.[26] So the fact that Stafford is writing to him is important. Of course the one person who could have offered another version of the events in Nombre was Diego. This is an idea that the historian Alexander McKee takes further, and suggests that Diego was the foremost 'oral historian' of Drake's escapades,[27] and that Diego acted as Drake's principal interpreter since the African 'spoke Spanish and English.' It also probable that Diego through his Symeron heritage, also spoke a number of Native-American languages and therefore, as an interpreter he would have been indispensable to the Englishman.[28]

But Diego died before 1586, so in his absence the African 'with a cut on his face' appears to have gone unchallenged when he spoke in Paris. All of this evidence underlines that the testimonials of Africans such as Diego, and this 'Negro,' could have an impact on international politics, even though their full involvement in the adventures that they were part of is obscured.

Once Diego left Plymouth, English records are silent until they record his death on 28 November 1578, when he was ambushed and killed by 'Natives' on the 'island of La Mocha [near Chile]' with 'poison arrows.' Drake was also severely wounded in this encounter, but he survived. Diego was probably buried at sea since no record of any land burial has been uncovered.[29] Nevertheless, it appears certain that Diego discharged all his roles with aplomb, as Davenant quotes Drake as saying '[Diego has] in several forms ... all/ ... [that] we merit call.'[30]

The evidence that we have about Domingo, Diego and the African 'with a cut on his face' provides proof of their existence, and tells us something about their status and origins – but there is also a great deal that we do not know about them. For example in the case of Domingo although his presence in England is recorded in public documents we have no indication of the effect he had on public events. By contrast with Diego we have evidence of his exploits before he came to England in 1573, and what he did after he left in 1577, but little of his life here. So, despite his very public adventurers with Drake, Diego's private life in Tudor England is hidden. Finally, with the African 'with a cut on his face,' we know from Stafford's letter he came to Tudor England with Drake probably in 1573, and that he was present in Paris in 1586, and that what he said had sufficient probity to cause concern to the Englishman. So the evidence that we have for these Africans does not record their whole lives, instead English writers appear to have noted the parts that they felt were useful to promote their fame, and as a consequence the Africans' true voice is lost.

Ungerer, however, suggests that facts about the origins and exploits of Africans such as Domingo and Diego have been concealed for other reasons. He says this is because these Africans were slaves and evidence of their status would have highlighted their employers' involvement in illegal activities.[31] But, if Englishmen such as Drake intended to hide the presence or existence of an African, they would probably not bring them to England at all. This can be seen in the example of an African 'wench' called Maria who Drake and his men 'had use of.' This African woman was accompanied by two African men, one of whom was named Francisca and they were all deliberately marooned by Drake on an island on 12 December 1580. (The exact location of this island is in doubt.) McKee suggests that Maria was left on this island for her own safety because she was pregnant. But contemporary records suggest that Maria may have been expecting Drake's child, and he was married, and therefore her pregnancy would have brought shame on the Englishman.[32] If she came to Tudor England and had her child they may have been recorded in Tudor parish records as we have seen with other African women and their children. If Maria claimed alimony from Drake she would have needed supporting testimonies, and this may be why Francisca and the other African were marooned on this island because they were the ones most likely to provide that kind of information.[33]

Maria and Francisca are absent from official public records but another African called Bastien who may have had West-African origins is not. Bastien lived in England in the household of William and John Hawkins and he was buried on 10 December 1583 in Plymouth. We have no record of Bastien's baptism; and it is possible he was not born here, and that he came to England via one of the three voyages that William, John or Richard Hawkins undertook to the Caribbean.³⁴ Furthermore, in a similar way to Diego, Bastien's presence reinforces the idea that some West Africans in Tudor England may have come via and had a cultural heritage from the Caribbean.

Three of the expeditions that might have brought Bastien to England include one that took place in 1562 when John Hawkins took 3 ships, 100 men, and captured 300 Africans from Sierra Leone in West Africa 'partly by the sword, and partly by other means.' These Africans were mostly sold in Haiti. Hawkins filled his ships with 'local produce, hides, ginger, sugars and pearles' and '1 year later … [he] returned to England … with prosperous success and much gaine to himself and the aforementioned adventurers.' The second expedition happened in 1564–5 when Hawkins conducted a voyage to the Caribbean, trading with some Africans and fighting and capturing others.³⁵ Hawkins' third voyage in 1567 to 1569 was not so 'successful,' since many of his men 'died of sickness.' In addition he hoped 'to obtain some Negroes where we gatt but fewe and those with great hurte and damage to our men.' The 'Spanish ruthlessly defeat[ed] and killed Englishmen,' and a significant number of West Africans showed armed resistance to Hawkins' attempts to enslave them and he was even wounded by a poisoned arrow.³⁶ Hawkins writes that it would not have been possible to get any Africans at all but for a 'Negroe sente from a[n] [African] kynge oppressed by other kings hys neighbours [who were] desiring [of] our aide.' It was an alliance with this unnamed West-African 'kynge' who was probably a local chief that enabled Hawkins to achieve his mission and 'assault and take towns [probably villages],' and enslave some of the inhabitants.³⁷ It is possible that Bastien could have participated with John Hawkins or other members of Hawkins' family in these sorts of activities in West Africa, as Diego did with Drake in the Caribbean, but without more information it would be difficult to say conclusively.

Bastien was not the only African working for the Hawkins family, another was a 'Negro page' called Samuel. One of the few references to him comes from the writer Ray Unwin who claims that during a naval battle at some point during Hawkins' 1567–9 voyage Samuel gave the Englishman a 'tankard of beer.' Habib discusses this matter in some detail, and points out that in contemporary accounts such as those by Job Hortop a sailor who accompanied Drake, either Samuel is missing or he is not described as a 'Negro.'³⁸ However, Hortop's omission of Samuel does not mean that he did not exist as the sailor was writing his account to glorify their expedition. For example, he states that Hawkins and his men 'fought with 15,000 Negroes' and 'slew many of them' and lost only 'one man,' or when Hortop claims that '300 Spaniards' were blown up and then states in the next paragraph that a further '440' were killed.[39] So writers such as Hortop may have left Samuel out of their accounts because this African's role did not add to the heroic adventure they were touting.

We have no images of Samuel, and the one of an African that is associated with the Hawkins' family is a highly stylised one on the Hawkins' Coat of Arms which does not appear to have been drawn from life. The African on the crest is naked and appears to be androgynous with the breasts of a woman and what seems to be the face of a man: the lower half of the body is not shown. The image of this African may be a generic representation of those Africans with whom the Hawkins' family had been in contact.[40] In that sense the image of this African is very different to the man in Drake's diadem, but both depictions do show that contrary to what Ungerer suggests, the connections existing between Africans and the families of the Drakes and the Hawkins were publicly acknowledged at the time.

Winter, Drake and the Hawkins were not the only people in Tudor England to have West Africans in their employment, there was also the Italian Piero Paul Corso the employer of Jacques Francis. According to Ungerer, Corso also employed a 'George Blak or black' as a diver although what ethnicity he or the rest of Corso's team were is not known.[41] Jacques identified himself as coming from 'Jnsula de Gynney' when he gave testimony to the High Court of Admiralty in London, England in 1547/8. Ungerer suggests that the word 'Jnsula' means peninsula or island and that this may refer to the island of Arguin off the coast of Mauretania in West Africa. According to Jacques' testimony he began to work for Corso at the age of eighteen, and he was probably taken from Arguin as a boy or a very young man by Italian merchants. Jacques had been two years in the employment of Corso before he arrived in England in 1546, and this made him twenty-years old at the beginning of the court case. By the time Jacques came to England he was 'head diver,' and for a young man of twenty to be head diver of such an important international operation suggests that he was very skilled at his work, and possessed abilities that made him invaluable to his employers.[42]

However, Ungerer suggests that Jacques was a slave because Arguin was used as a base to transport Africans to the Caribbean and elsewhere. I question this idea, although I acknowledge that Arguin did attract Europeans from many countries, and that a castle or trading fort was built by the Portuguese in 1461 to facilitate slavery on this island. I also recognise that the castle at Arguin was part of a network of slave forts that extended to

Elmina in modern day Ghana, West Africa. But despite all this, I suggest that Jacques was recognised in Tudor England as a skilled professional who had abilities which his white counterparts in Italy or England did not have. This is because the island of Arguin had also been known for hundreds of years as a place where deep-sea pearl divers lived. These African divers could hold their breath and open their eyes under water for extraordinarily long periods of time. Africans on the island of Arguin were employed by merchants of all nationalities because of this skill. Jacques was probably one of these gifted and skilled Africans and this made him the ideal employee for salvaging goods from the bottom of the sea, and may have been one of the reasons why he was head diver.[43]

These are not the only skills that Jacques possessed because of his West-African origins. Jacques like Domingo was probably multilingual, as in Arguin they spoke the languages of Soninke and Fula used in commerce by local African people, and a patois called 'fala da Guine' or 'fala dos negros' which was used for international trade. The latter language literally means the language of 'Guinea' or the 'language of the blacks,' and it contains the African languages mentioned earlier with Arabic, Portuguese and Spanish.[44] Jacques could also have had a working knowledge of Italian because he had been employed by Corso for two years; and he may have learnt sufficient English to converse with local people since he had been in England since July 1546. But he was apparently not proficient enough in English to give his testimony at the High Court since the records show that an Englishman called John Tyrart translated for him.[45]

Jacques was employed to recover 'cargo' and 'equipment salvage' from England's sunken flagship the *Mary Rose*.[46] Initially, William Paget the Secretary of State, Charles Brandon the brother-in-law of King Henry VIII, and John Dudley the Admiral of England employed men to rescue the entire ship, but this proved unsuccessful.[47] Nevertheless, this did not stop the salvage operations since rescue attempts were about saving English pride as much as the 'valuable ordinances' that the ship contained. As Corso and Jacques proceeded to recover equipment they were granted permission to bring back 'ordinances' from other sunken ships in and around Southampton and the Isle of Wight in an area known as the 'Needles.' As a result of this operation in the 'Needles,' Corso was accused of theft and Jacques gave evidence in support of Corso's innocence during his case at the High Court.[48]

As stated in the last chapter, at the High Court some Italian witnesses protested that Jacques could not give evidence because he was a mere 'escravo,' an 'infidel,' 'a bond man' or owned by another and a 'gynno born.' These statements made to discredit him focussed on his status, religion, race and origins, but not his professionalism or the competency of his work which was never in dispute.⁴⁹

And, so, the English Judges at the High Court allowed Jacques to testify and this may show the African's professionalism was respected. Indeed, for most Englishmen Jacques' profession and experience may have meant he appeared more akin to a traveller from a new advanced world, than a pagan slave.⁵⁰ Moreover, Jacques claimed that his own status was as a 'Famulus' (family servant) and that he had a familial relationship with Corso. This claim is plausible since Jacques had been relatively young when he came into Corso's employment and he may have seen Corso as a mentor and perhaps a guardian. As I stated in the last chapter it was not uncommon for an African to enter a European household and initially be perceived as an outsider, and then end up becoming a socially equal part of the family they were employed to serve. However, despite any respect that the court may have had for Jacques' skills, his statement of Corso's guiltlessness does not appear to have been strong enough to counteract the weight of evidence against him, because Corso was convicted and sentenced to life imprisonment.⁵¹

How West Africans were seen in Tudor England

Some of the Italian witnesses in Corso's case were promoting a negative idea about Jacques' West-African origins to prescribe his status. But although the English courts appear to have rejected this attempt, historians such as Ungerer and Habib strongly suggest West Africans such as Jacques were considered as inferior because they were thought of as naked-pagan savages.⁵² Habib suggests that these ideas are also behind why George Best makes his negative statements about Africans present in Tudor England.⁵³ Habib and Ungerer propose that Tudor Englishmen automatically associated nudity with inferiority, and that both of these notions were applied to West Africans in England as well as those in Africa. But I suggest that this kind of prejudice which expects the West African to be naked on arrival is a feature of a later imagination, prejudice, and fantasy.⁵⁴ It is Africanus despite some of his negative statements about West Africans, who gives us a more pragmatic perspective on this issue, and what he says appears to echo how Tudor Englishmen saw this matter. Africanus says that nudity in West Africa is a consequence of the 'heat of their countrey,' and he underlines this idea by stating that in the fifteenth-century Kingdom of Bornu in modern day Nigeria 'foreign merchants both black and white' go 'naked in the Summer.'⁵⁵ Tudor Englishmen seem to have had a similar perspective, and do not appear to have put on shows depicting West Africans as naked symbols of savagery, ignorance and innocence as Englishmen did in the nineteenth and early-twentieth centuries.[56]

Having said this there is one incident reported by the historian John Allyne Gade that is worthy of discussion, because even though it relates to a dramatic performance, it is used by Habib to explain attitudes towards West Africans not only in Oslo, Norway where it allegedly took place, but also in Tudor England.[57] Gade states that the event happened on 29 November 1589 in Oslo during the marriage celebrations of James VI of Scotland and Anne of Denmark. During these celebrations 'four young Negroes danced naked in the snow' until they died from exposure.[58] However, the historian Claire McManus claims that the incident never happened, since she cannot find any contemporary evidence that substantiates it. Gade's is the earliest reference in 1928, with Ethel Carelton Williams relying on this in her book *Anne of Denmark*, and Habib quoting from her.[59] Even if the incident did occur it would have been a rare event in sixteenth-century Europe, and it is much later in England's history that we find evidence of these types of nude African performances being sponsored and patronised. But of course Anne of Denmark did have 'those kindes of people' amongst her servants in England, as illustrated in the 1617 painting by the English painter Paul Van Somer of her and an African attendant at her English estates (see Fig. 27).[60]

The African in Somer's painting is smartly attired in a red doublet and hose, and this is similar to other representations of Africans in sixteenth-century England. West Africans in the same way as Anne's servant were not expected to be naked to fulfil an English fantasy of what a West African should be. Rather Africans such as Domingo and Jacques even if they had what was perceived to be a naked-pagan past, were expected to conform to what Tudor society regarded as acceptable standards of dress and behaviour.[61] We see a similar pattern with four young West-African men who were also present in Tudor England. They were called Binne, Genie, Anthony and George and they came to England in 1554 from Benin with the Englishman John Lok. Evidence by Lok and others suggests that these Africans were dressed up 'as Englishmen,' despite as Purchas says, the people of Benin being 'naked until they are married' and 'then ... [only] clothed from the[ir] waste to the[ir] knees.'[62]

This idea of 'dressing' the African also seems to have been an important issue in the case of a man called 'Coree the Saldanian' who was a Khoi Khoi or San from Southern Africa. The name Coree appears to be an abbreviation of the 'Kora' or 'Gorachoqua' clan which he was from. The Khoi Khoi are traditionally nude except for a pouch over their genitals. However, when Coree came to England in 1613, he was dressed in the 'finest rich apparel' and even a full suit of armour was made for him. But Coree rejected this attempt at 'civilising' him, and he wanted in his own words to 'goe home go.' When he did, the Englishmen who accompanied him were horrified when he threw off his English clothes and went as 'God had made him,' but for his 'sheep skin,' the 'guts about his neck' and 'a perfumed cap.'[63]

In England, however, Coree conformed to the conservative standards of dress present here, as West Africans in Tudor England did.[64] Moreover, it is interesting that in Tudor times some English writers were questioning the truth of stories told about nude-pagan West Africans such as those mentioned by Williams, or others discussed in Chapter 2. For example, the Tudor writer Richard Madox does this in 1588, when he suggests that many of the 'fantasticall stories' told about Africans are 'illusions' created by the Africans themselves, and then retold to Europeans in 'mockery, sometyme a report of ignorance, sometyme a tale of deceyt.' Madox concludes that these stories were often embellished by rival African merchants and others to 'scare us [Englishmen] away' from 'all the trade' in West Africa.[65] Purchas suggests something similar and adds that some of these stories are merely a product of prurient diversion.[66] Ironically, whilst some negative stories may have been doubted, other positive ones about West Africans seemed to have been believed. This is evident in Madox's diary, which he compiled whilst he was a chaplain sailing on the 1582 voyage to West Africa under the flag of the exiled Portuguese Prince Don Antonio. Madox's voyage was sponsored by Francis Walsingham and Alderman Banning, and it is possible that the Africans who later went to live with Banning originated from these voyages in the Caribbean and West Africa, more information about this idea can be obtained by looking at the work of Habib.[67]

Madox's accounts of Africa are important because he describes West Africans in a positive way and this is linked to similar sorts of ideas about West Africa itself. These ideas are likely to have meant that these West Africans would also be seen as wealthy and prosperous in Tudor England. The areas that Madox visited were the islands of Verde, Tenerife, Lanzarote and a number of coastal towns in West Africa. Madox describes these places as a paradise, 'a type of heaven' with 'marvellous goodly lands and pastures' with people reaching over the age of a hundred and states the 'Aethiopians ... [there are] ... loyal and compassionate' with kings who are 'champion[s] of justice.'[68] The book called the *Description and Historical Account of the Gold Kingdom of Guinea* by the Dutch traveller Pieter de Marees also reflects the idea that West Africans had wealth.[69]

These ideas of West Africans coming from a type of paradise are likely to have influenced Samuel Purchas in his anthology of letters written by Tudor explorers called the *Pilgrimages*. Purchas confirms that in West Africa there are 'vineyards' tended by conscientious and diligent Africans and that the lands are filled with 'great wine,' 'palm trees' which yield a variety of 'velvets,' 'satins,' 'taffetas,' and 'damasks.' Purchas suggests that there was a fertile region that stretched from the Guinea coast to the Congo in Central Africa and in it 'dates,' 'bread fruit,' 'cocoa trees' and 'pineapples' were in abundance.[70] This wealth also included precious metals and is illustrated in the Atles Catala drawn in 1375 by the Majorcan cartographer Abraham Cresques, which shows the Emperor Mansa Musa of Mali holding a huge gold nugget. In Tudor times this promoted the exaggerated notion that in 'nowhere else but' West Africa could such wealth be found (see Fig. 28).[71]

John Hawkins was searching for this gold and 'found' '200,000 pounds' worth after he and the Spanish co-operated in sacking a village in 'Ginnye' during his third voyage to West Africa in 1567 to 1569.[72] However, in the fifteenth and sixteenth centuries, gold and other commodities could not all be obtained by Englishmen using the 'gun and the sword.' As the English explorer Robert Baker discovered in his voyages to Guinea from 1562 to 1563, when he went 'to seek for golde, as Orpheus sought his wife.' But Baker was less 'successful' than Hawkins and he not only fought and lost against West Africans but ended up surrendering to their mercy.[73] The voyages of Hawkins and Baker illustrate that in West Africa during the sixteenth century if Englishmen wanted 'gold,' 'riches,' and 'renown' they could not merely rely on ruthlessness, and they needed to be able to negotiate with West Africans. This gave Englishmen pragmatic reasons to invite some West Africans to Tudor England and treat them with hospitality as the Africans had resources that Englishmen were in dire need of.

Nevertheless, it may be that in Tudor England the hospitality some West Africans received may have been to encourage them not only to give up their wealth, but also their Animist or Pagan beliefs. Moreover, the conversion of West Africans to Christianity in England may have made it easier for Englishmen to gain access to resources found in West Africa. This is because West Africans with Animist beliefs strongly tied to an African culture are likely to have been more difficult to trade with. This might account for some of the views about Animism expressed by Englishmen and other European merchants. For example Thomas Middleton describes these Africans as people who 'give all adoration to the Sunne, The Moone and stars.'[74] But other Englishmen such as Eden suggested that some West Africans have no 'God, lawe, religion or commonwealth;'[75] whilst Iberian Muslims such as Africanus interpreted these beliefs as some West Africans having 'no religion.'[76]

Such ideas may explain why some West Africans such as Dederi and Walter who were living in England, and who sought access to 'God's grace and forgiveness,' had their adult conversion to Christianity celebrated by English recorders. Purchas echoing this idea says that the 'tawny Moore, black Negro, duskie Libyan, Ash coloured Indian, olive coloured American should with the whiter European become one sheep-fold' under a Christian God.[77] But as stated in the last chapter, there is a lack of evidence that any Africans in Tudor England were forced into becoming Christians and therefore it is likely that West Africans were only baptised because they wanted to be. This may be because in late Tudor England, Englishmen had grown to abhor forced conversions, perhaps because this reminded them of their past when these practises were committed against Protestants.[78] It is an idea echoed in records such as those for Mary Fillis of Morisco, who was living in London, where it states that it was thirteen years before she became a Christian and suggests that she was converted in her own time and by her own 'wishe[s]'.[79] The idea that forced conversions were morally wrong is also presented eloquently by the French lawyer and writer Jean Bodin whose work was widely read and translated in England. Bodin's seminal work on religious harmony and tolerance published in 1588 is called the *Colloquium of the Seven about the Secrets of the Sublime*.[80] His work articulates ideas of tolerance also present in Tudor England, which explains why Africans such as Mary were not forced into becoming Christians by English priests.

The baptising of West Africans in Tudor England, however, was not just about Christianising 'those kindes of people' but also anglicising them too. When England became a Protestant country and the stigma of reading English Bibles declined, Ungerer writes that 'no adult ... [was] baptised until [they] know the Lord's Prayer ... the Ten Commandments and the articles of faith [in English].'[81] West Africans present in Tudor England who converted to this Christianity may have done so for genuine reasons of faith which can be difficult for us to prove, or, because they saw the religion as a route to citizenship which they may have felt gave them leverage in diplomacy and trade. The latter reason is one that I shall explore in more detail, especially as records for West Africans such as Dederi reveal that in the late sixteenth and early-seventeenth centuries baptisms showed the subject's allegiance and desire to become a member of an English parish community, nation, and an international 'Protestant family.'[82]

As a result some West Africans such as Dederi who were present in England at the end of the Tudor period and the beginning of the seventeenth century, seem to have converted to Christianity for strategic reasons: and there appears to be agency in 'Caddi-bah ['s]' (Dederi's father's) decision to permit his son to come to England. Moreover, that Dederi's willingness to 'show his opinion concerning Jesus Christ and his faith in him,' and the 'repeat[ing of] the Lords prayer in English at the fonte' were not just innocent statements of religious conviction. [83] Through Dederi's conversion to Christianity in England he may have been seeking the 'magic,' 'spiritual force and soul power' of the Europeans' 'lethal killing machines [guns and cannons].' This is because some West Africans associated these 'powers' with the Christian religion.[84] It was the European efficiency for 'killing' that made European Christianity attractive to some West-African kings, as demonstrated by the respect shown to John Hawkins once he had demonstrated his skill for taking life on his third voyage to 'Ginnye.'[85] These West-African kings such as the Oba Ozolua of the Kingdom of Eweka in modern day Nigeria in 1514, openly expressed a desire to acquire European' weapons 'to make himself more powerful against his neighbours.' It was for this purpose that the Oba sent his servant and ambassadors to Portugal to become Christians.[86] It is likely that these sorts of reasons may have been why other West-African leaders chose to send their sons to Tudor England to be baptised.

In Tudor England the baptism of these West-African dignitaries was sometimes preceded by the Africans' vociferous statement of their conviction to the 'new faith.' West Africans such as Dederi and Walter professed that they had been ignorant of the Christian religion, but when in England, or as they came into contact with Englishmen 'showed [their faith] ... concerning Jesus Christ,' and as the characters in *Triumphs of Truth* proclaim 'only ... [The Christian God] do I adore.'[87] In reality some of this ignorance of Christianity may have been feigned to establish or build good relations with English merchants. A significant proportion of West Africans may have already had a working knowledge of Christianity before they came to Tudor England because of the interchange of religions, cultures and trade in West Africa.[88] For example in the sixteenth century, through trade and immigration cities such as the port town of Kabara near Timbuktu contained Christian missionaries and West-African Jewish and Muslim scholars, with the latter having holy books which contained similar stories and heroes as the Bible.[89]

This means that some West Africans were acquainted with and/or possessed ideas akin to Christianity before they came to Tudor England or had contact with Englishmen. As Madox points out, the Animist beliefs of some West-African people such as 'an eye for an eye, a tooth for a tooth [and] for he that kylleth shall be killed' were perceived by some sixteenth-century Englishmen as being akin to Old Testament Christian ideas.[90] Purchas adds to this idea by suggesting that some African rituals resemble Catholic or 'Popish' 'tricks.' Purchas may be proposing this idea to discredit Catholicism or African Animism, or it may be his genuine opinion on the similarities between some Christian rituals and African-Animist ones.[91] Bodin takes this idea further and says that African Animists have a 'pure' concept of God in a similar way to 'true' Christians, and 'worshipped Gods without images for more than 130 years.'[92]

Therefore, the idea that some Africans' Animist beliefs resembled aspects of Christianity, and the fact that many West Africans in the sixteenth and early-seventeenth centuries were more familiar with the latter religion than they themselves were often willing to publicly state, may mean that 'those kindes of people' in Tudor England were far more aware of European mores than modern historians have thus far acknowledged. This means that some West Africans in Tudor England acted with guile, and that their conversions and baptisms concealed their 'true faith.' In this sense these Africans were shrewder than the English officials who 'converted' them. An example of an African appearing to demonstrate this perspicacity is James Ongunby, described as 'a negro' in his parish records and baptised on 7 June 1593 at the Holy Trinity Minories in London.[93] This is because the last part of James's name 'Ongunby' is almost certainly a reference to the Yoruba words 'Ogun' and 'biyi.' 'Ogun' is a river in Nigeria, but originates from the name of the Yoruba God of Iron and War whilst, the word 'biyi' is an abbreviation of 'biyesi' which means 'to give reverence or respect to': so his name means to honour a Yoruba God devoted to warfare.[94] When translated Ongunby's name seems inappropriate for a Christian to have and it is likely that a Tudor priest if he had understood it would have thought the same.[95]

Furthermore, Ongunby is likely to have known the meaning and significance of his name. To the Yoruba now, and certainly those of the sixteenth century, their names are the most important statements of their identity which help them define their own humanity and divinity. When Yoruba children are born they are given a name after seven days, this is their first or personal one. This is the one that Ongunby has probably dropped in a favour of the English 'James.' In Yoruba culture this personal name is considered the least important one that a person may have. Far more significant is the family name, and another which is given to them if they complete their rites of passage. Both of these names a Yoruba man or woman has to earn.

In the sixteenth century the rites of passage of Yoruba people involved dangerous and life-threatening challenges. When or if they passed these tests they would be invited to a naming ceremony in which the whole community was present. At this naming ceremony all initiates would be expected to quote the meaning of the names that were bestowed upon them. Sixteenth-century Yoruba families would be unwilling to grant their name to any young man or woman who did not have this erudition. Then the family and additional name would be given to the initiate. The latter would reflect how they had performed in their tests during the rites of passage programme. In Ongunby's case this would be the word 'biyi' or 'biyesi'. The new name 'Ogun biyi' or 'Ongunby' would then be reflective of his family and national heritage, personal character and past achievements. When we understand this we can see that Ongunby would not only know the meaning of his name, but it would explain why he chose to retain it.[96]

Of course this discussion of the rich cultural heritage of the Yoruba of the sixteenth century makes us question why Ongunby coming from such a background would wish to be baptised in Tudor England at all. The possible answers are complex, and are linked to what was happening in the West-African kingdoms that he and others came from. This discussion also helps us understand where some of these Africans learnt the skills that they used in Tudor society.

Africans in Tudor England and their relationship to African kingdoms

The developments that took place within West-African civilisations affected the status of West Africans in Tudor England. For example, some of the cultural connections that West-African kingdoms had with Moorish Spain explain why important Englishmen such as Winter and Drake employed West Africans in similar roles as Iberian Moors. This is because some West Africans also had skills which their white counterparts did not have. Cultural connections provided the means by which some of these Africans obtained their skills, as the links between West-African kingdoms and Moorish Spain were strong. For example, West Africans were amongst the soldiers who invaded Iberia in 711, France in 732 and were part of later conquests. West Africans were also present in fifteenth- and sixteenth-century Spain as merchants, traders, intellectuals, diplomats, and so on.[97]

Therefore, some of the Africans who came from West Africa to Tudor England brought a culture that had links to Moorish traditions which stretched into sixteenth-century Europe. An example of this is the flat soled 'classical shoes' I suggested Katherine of Aragon's ladies in waiting wore in London in 1501. These 'classical shoes' were as much a part of the cultural dress amongst Africans in Gobir in Nigeria as they were in Moorish Spain.[98] This African culture travelled on what UNESCO has called the 'African Ink

Road': literally a network of pathways by land and sea across the continent of Africa and beyond, that knowledge and commerce travelled along. Its existence is the reason why in Timbuktu modern scientists have found over 3,000 manuscripts from Moorish-Spain. Ultimately the 'African Ink Road' created the conditions which contributed to West Africans coming to England – but it was initially created by Africans to facilitate trade between Africans as the sixteenth-century West-African scholar Muhammad Baghayogho states.[99] To illustrate this, Africanus the Moorish scholar and poet from Spain visited Timbuktu in 1510, travelling along the 'African Ink Road' when he made his negative and positive references about West-African civilisations.[100] Muhammad Ibn Abd Allah al-Lawati a Moroccan poet and writer also known as Ibn Battuta, journeyed along the same 'African Ink Road' from Al Andalus in Spain to Timbuktu and spent eight months living in Mali in 1341, whilst the Emperor Mansa Kankou Musa travelled along these routes from Mali to North Africa on his Hajji to Mecca in 1324, where he met the Iberian-Moorish poet and architect Es-Saheli.[101]

Our understanding of the 'African Ink Road' provides more information about the culture that West Africans brought to Tudor England, but by following it we cannot ignore the contribution that the Empire of Songhai had on its development. Moreover, Songhai's power and influence in international politics had an indirect effect on why and how some Africans came to Tudor England.[102] For example the fifteenth- and sixteenth-century pearl trade from Jacques Francis' home of Arguin was initiated and organised by African traders from Mali and Songhai until 1443. So the abilities that made Jacques Francis so useful in Tudor England had originally been developed through the influence of these West-African kingdoms.[103]

The Songhai Empire dominated West Africa: at its zenith it was the size of Western Europe, and its power is the reason why we find Africans present in Tudor England who originated from smaller kingdoms adjacent to it. This is because although Europeans were attracted to the wealth of Mali and Songhai, they also feared their power, and attempted to work with smaller African kingdoms because they felt that they would be more accommodating. An example of this strategy can be seen with the Italian merchant Alvise Ca' da Mosto, who in 1455 sought support from local village leaders along the Senegalese coast before attempting negotiations with the powerful kings of Mali.[104] But it was the Spanish and Portuguese who took this method of working with less powerful West-African rulers to a more advanced level. For example King Bunmi Jeleen of the Jolof, in what is now modern day Senegal, established a relationship with King Joao of Portugal that involved the African potentate sending his nephew and '100 slaves' to Portugal in

1487. The Portuguese King later trained an army so Bunmi could retake his kingdom because Joao saw this as a way of gaining access to the 'richest trades and markets of gold in the world.'[105]

The Englishman John Lok was trying to emulate these Italian, Portuguese and Spanish merchants when he brought Binne, Genie, Anthonie and George to Tudor England from Benin in 1554. The events surrounding the presence of these West Africans in Tudor England have been discussed by a number of historians but often with contradictory conclusions. Habib states that Binne, Genie and the others came with an English merchant called William Towerson, and that Lok brought four other Africans.[106] However, Carole Levin suggests that Lok brought five not four Africans to England and it was Towerson who later returned them to Africa. This idea seems the most plausible because of the arguments that Purchas makes (although Levin is one of the few historians to state that five Africans came).[107]

Lok in his letters provides more information about Binne and his companions but that which relates to their status is misleading. This is because Lok says they were kidnapped and brought to England as 'slaves' by Robert Gainsh who was captain of a ship called the *John Evangelist*. In his account Lok also states that one of them was an 'African Chief's son' and 'they' had 'all their gold … about them;' but this seems to contradict the Englishman's previous statement that they were slaves when he came across them. Habib also suggests the West Africans were taken from a village near Lagos in Nigeria, and this theory may be likely, because from this port English merchants had access to trading stations established by the Portuguese;[108] whilst, Ungerer claims that these Africans had 'little chance' of 'asserting their own personalities, but once groomed as commercial and cultural brokers [they] may have been manumitted as was the custom in Portugal.'[109]

However, it is unlikely that these West Africans were slaves in Tudor England because of all the issues stated in this book, and because they had the potential to be utilised as diplomats, ambassadors and navigators. For example we know that Lok's second voyage to Guinea early in 1555 was in emulation of the Portuguese explorer Prince Henry the Navigator, and may well have been aided by the information that these West Africans provided.[110] If this is so, their role may have been similar to Diego's, making them too useful not to be treated with hospitality in Tudor England.

This usefulness is also linked to an idea that Binne and his companions may have been from the Kingdom of Benin.[111] One of the reasons that this is likely is based on these Africans' names. For example the name 'Binne' actually relates to the 'Bini' Edo-speaking people of Benin, whilst the name 'Genie' is probably a play on the word 'Guinea' and relates to this man's

West-African origins.[112] The other two names Anthony and George, because they are English do not help us know more about these Africans' origins, but do probably show that they are Christians, perhaps baptised in England.[113]

There are other factors which indicate that Binne and his group were from Benin. One of these is that there was a cultural exchange between this African kingdom and a number of European countries. Since 1486, the Kingdom of Benin had maintained diplomatic relations with countries such as Portugal. Later the King of Benin sent his ambassador to Portugal and he was well received as 'a man of good speech and natural wisdom.'[114] Thereafter delegations of Africans from Benin were common in Portugal by the fifteenth century, but in this closeness lay the seeds for Benin's dissatisfaction. By 1554, Portugal began to seek control of the gold trade which was organised by Hausa traders from Kano in Nigeria along the 'African Ink Road.'[115] The Portuguese began to meddle in the politics between Kano and Benin by supplying or withholding guns from them.[116] As a result this caused friction between these two African kingdoms, so that by the middle of the sixteenth century, Benin began to acknowledge that European countries outside of Portugal and Spain could be their allies and a source for firearms and cannons. Africans from Benin were present in Tudor England because of these developments as they provided a reason for the African nation to enter diplomatic relations with English officials.

Sometimes these relations were initiated and facilitated through the activities of English pirates present in Benin such as Lok in 1554–5 and Thomas Wyndham in 1553, although, as Eden and Marees state in 1602, Benin was a strong trading nation and had its own merchants and agents working on the 'African Ink Road' and beyond.[117] It appears that Binne and his group were chosen to act as ambassadors, and that is why Lok selected 'taule and stronge men [who] … coulde wel agree with our meates and drynkes. [Even though] The colde and moyst aire doth somewhat offend them.' One of these Africans married a white English woman and Lok may have arranged this to forge an alliance between England and Benin akin to what the Portuguese authorities later did in 1607 in the Kingdom of Warri.[118]

A year after Lok's second voyage three of these Africans went back to Africa. The fourth African who remained in England may have been the one who married the white English woman. Once they went back to West Africa, according to Lok's letters, Binne and the others became 'well known' to the local people and by their 'persuasion' encouraged local Africans to trust Lok's crew men and board their ships.[119] But whether their activities led to other West Africans being brought to Tudor England or elsewhere Lok does not tell us.

How Africans such as Binne and his companions came to be present in Tudor England helps us understand that some Englishmen even in the sixteenth century were seeking relationships with West-African kingdoms. But it also shows that some West-African kingdoms desired greater connections with England and this sentiment appears to have intensified after 1591. This is because of the destabilisation caused by the destruction of Songhai and other semi-independent West-African kingdoms such as Timbuktu.[120] This may explain why we find Africans such as Dederi Jaquoah and Walter Annerby (discussed below) in England. Songhai was defeated at the Battle of Tondibi by a multi-ethnic army of Moroccan, Egyptian and Ottoman troops that used European cannons acquired from Turkey and Spain. This army was led by a Moroccan-Spanish-born leader called Sultan Ahmad I al-Mansur Saadi who was sponsored by the Ottoman Empire. After the battle of Tondibi the Moroccan leader killed some African scholars, and enslaved others such as Abu Abbas and Ahmad Baba who originated from Timbuktu.[121] In 1593, further purges supported by religious jingoism took place in Timbuktu that involved the wanton destruction of libraries and the burning of books.[122]

The evidence suggests that the destruction of Songhai and Timbuktu made smaller neighbouring West-African states more responsive to the outside world.[123] A number of these West-African states such as Benin and Kaabu appear to have sought England as an ally because they were afraid that what had occurred to Songhai may happen to them. As a result, some of the West Africans who we find in Tudor England were trying to facilitate trade with English merchants which would ensure their own nation's survival.

Trade and the presence of West Africans in late Tudor England

Ungerer also claims that West Africans were present in late Tudor England because of trade, but he suggests they were the objects being traded by English merchants. Amongst the Africans who Ungerer and Habib claim were 'brought here' are a few children, some of whom have a West-African origin or heritage. Some of these African children may have been working in the homes of Spanish and Portuguese plantation owners and traders in the Caribbean before being 'liberated' by English pirates. An example of an African who may have been employed in this manner was a boy called 'Charles' who was baptised in 1597 at St Luke's Church, Kensington, London, and who was 'aged about 10 or 11' when he was brought from Guyana in South America by Walter Raleigh. As Marika Sherwood suggests, this 'boy' may have been one of the two who 'entered domestic service in London,' and who served Raleigh 'during the early years of his imprisonment.'[124] A second of these African children is a boy called 'Anthony' 'a blackamore from Guinea' who the historian Alfred Leslie Rowse discusses. He appears in the files of a Tudor family called the Throckmortons and Rowse suggests that Anthony lived in the Raleigh's home in Northampton.[125]

The employment of African children by Tudor merchants was the beginning of a practice that later became fashionable in the seventeenth and eighteenth centuries, where they were portrayed as mute-visual representations of England's power and wealth.[126] But in Tudor England, African children do not often appear as visual adornments of the wealthy and powerful, and those children who were in English households are likely to have performed practical roles in that society similar to adults.

Moreover, the numbers of African children who were employed by Englishmen in Tudor England was small. The reason for this is because Englishmen could not fully exploit trade in West Africa, since in the fifteenth and sixteenth centuries, treaties and international agreements officially kept England out of West-African trade. As stated in Chapters 1 and 3, from 1452 up until as late as 1595, Spain and Portugal had papal authority over 'all trade' in West Africa.[127] Thus, the power and influence of Spain and Portugal in the fifteenth and sixteenth centuries gives us another reason why English monarchs officially abstained from slavery in West Africa. In other words, English monarchs were prevented by international treaties, bilateral agreements and a lack of power from bringing large numbers of Africans as slaves to England. Even in the one example in Bristol, where Africans are purported to have come in great numbers they were sent back to Portugal within a week.[128]

England was in no position until the last quarter of the sixteenth century to openly oppose Spain. Nor were England's governments from Edward IV until the end of Elizabeth's reign convinced that this 'kind of trade' would produce 'live profits.'[129] This may be why in Tudor times men such as Hawkins and Lok despite being emboldened with ideas from books such as *A Packe of Spanish Lies,* and feeling that they had a right to conduct their own activities as other Europeans did,[130] – were sometimes regarded even by other Englishmen as mavericks, interlopers, and pirates and why they were forced to recruit criminals into their ranks to carry out their activities.[131]

So contrary to what Ungerer claims it appears that English merchants did not have the capacity to bring large numbers of Africans to Tudor England. This is underlined by the fact that in the sixteenth century most members of the Merchant Adventurers (an English trading company established in

1546) did not have Africans living with them, and this includes Lord Lisle, even though he supported Sebastian Cabot in his slave trading activities abroad.[132] Furthermore, I have not found evidence of Africans living in Tudor England with Sir George Carew or Martin Frobisher, despite them having links to trade in West Africa.[133] Indeed there are only a few members of the Merchant Adventurers who had Africans in their English residences including Thomas Wyndham in 1551, who had two 'Moors' from North Africa in his home.[134]

One group of English merchants who operated within the Merchant Adventurers and did have Africans in their households were the 'Consortium'. The members of the Consortium include people who have been discussed throughout this book such as William, John and Richard Hawkins and others such as Walter Raleigh, Francis Drake and Paul Banning.[135] But even the connections that members of the Consortium had with Africans do not seem to have been formed because of a stated policy of their organisation, but rather to be a consequence of their individual activities. Moreover, as I proposed in Chapter 1, by the beginning of the seventeenth century some of these Englishmen had died, and others were disillusioned with politics or out of favour at court so as a consequence English trade with West Africa declined. This is despite, as Holinshed claims, the Merchant Adventurers being 'ten thousand merchants by land and sea' who had the power to 'purchase lands' and 'make bye-laws'.[136] In Tudor times they were restricted to acts of sporadic commercial piracy.

Therefore, there is a relationship between England's mercantile activities and the presence of West Africans in Tudor England but this is more complex than Ungerer states. Furthermore, although England's international status did change when it defeated the Spanish Armada in 1588, most English merchants were logistically unable to exploit this. This is despite them creating legal entities such as the Morocco or Barbary Company in 1585, the Company of Senegal Adventurers and the First English Guinea Company in 1588.[137] Even as late as 1592, Englishmen were still regarded and thought of themselves as interlopers in West Africa, and this is illustrated by the activities of Anthony and Thomas Dassell.

The Dassells were Englishmen who brought two West Africans to England from 'beyond Ginnye' between the years of 1587 and 1592. These two unnamed Africans were being brought to England at a time when the total dominance of Spain and Portugal in international relations was coming to an end. Despite this the activities of the Dassells appear to have been criticised even by other English pirates such as Richard Kelly. At the High Court of the Admiralty in 1592, Anthony Dassell claimed that the two young Africans 'made sute to come' to England 'voluntarie,' and 'without any compulsion.' But Kelly claimed that they had been taken 'against their wills' and that the Dassells had 'smuggled the[se] Africans into England illegally against the kinges of that realme [Benin] and his officers comma[u]ndements.' These statements show that the kings of Benin were either opposed to slavery, or that they were against high born sons being taken. Kelly and other English merchants feared that the Dassells' activities would lead to the 'utter overthrow[e] and disturba[u]nce of that trade in those partes,'[138] and may 'awaken the prejudice of merchants [of] that society.'[139] This shows that at the end of the sixteenth century the voice of West-African merchants and kings was important, and that Englishmen still needed Africans' authority and goodwill to trade in West Africa: this authority resting with the kind of African families that these young men were from.

So, the West Africans the Dassells brought to England are unlikely to have been slaves because of what was said by writers at the time. Anthony Dassell admitted that these two West Africans 'were of some accompt' since they were 'sons to the chiefe justice of their country' and therefore, would be treated with 'good entertaynment here,' and to this end they appear to have been kept in Dassell's home. But Anthony Dassell revealed that the real reason for this hospitality was the hope that the Africans 'will be more beneficial and commodious to the Queen [Elizabeth I]' 'in regarde of the trade then all the serva[u]nts of Dom Antonio can do good in going thither.'[140] Therefore, the Dassells were attempting to seduce these Africans into being advocates for English interests and into opposing the influence of the Prince of Portugal in West Africa. But whether this was achieved is unlikely as within the year the Africans were back in West Africa, and the Dassells were later arrested by authorities in North Africa for their involvement in piracy.[141]

The Dassells were not the last Englishmen to attempt schemes of opportunism involving Africans. In Chapter 1 I discussed the ten Africans brought to Tudor England by Thomas Baskerville from Puerto Rico, who Edward Banes, the Sherleys, and Casper Van Senden attempted to exchange or 'sell' for English prisoners from Spain in 1596. However, not all West Africans who arrived in England in the last decade of the sixteenth and the beginning of the seventeenth centuries came through people-smuggling or exchanges – some appear to have come on their own cognisance. This is best illustrated by two West Africans who we mentioned earlier in this chapter called Nosser/Walter Annerby and Dederi/John Joaquah. These two Africans have connections to specific places in West Africa which are named in English records. In that sense the record of their presence in England differs from some of the other Africans we have been discussing whose origins we have had to deduce.

Walter Annerby was 'baptised upon the thirde day of February being Shrove sundaie, in the Eight yeare of King James, anno 1610' at Tottenham, London.[142] Walter was 'borne in the kingdom of Dungala in Africa' which is probably a reference to Dungal in the Kingdom of Kaabu in modern day Oio in Guinea Bissau. The Islamic professor and historian Charles Beckingham suggests that Dungala is in fact Dongola or Dunqula/Dunqulah in Sudan, North Africa.[143] However this is unlikely, since by 1610, English merchants had not established those kinds of diplomatic relations there. It is more probable that Walter's entry in 1610 is akin to Dederi's entry a year later (below). In other words, they both relate to some Englishmen's strategic desire to develop trade with West-African kingdoms.

Walter was from Dungal in Kaabu, a kingdom which was developed by indigenous Mandinka people and emerged from the decline of the Empire of Mali in the fourteenth century. The Kingdom of Kaabu lay on the border of Songhai but retained its independence from its more powerful neighbours. Nosser's name is Arabic and in Kaabu society the Arabic language and Islam played an important part as it did in Songhai.[144] Kaabu was a culturally diverse nation and it is likely that Walter spoke Mandinka, Fula and Bambara since these languages were used in local commerce and trade as well as Portuguese and/or Spanish for all the reasons stated in this chapter.[145]

Dungal in Kaabu was strategically important to Europeans. By 1610 the Cape Verde islands were still held under the authority of the Empire of Kaabu despite Spain and Portugal's long sojourn there. The Portuguese reluctantly paid Kaabu annual taxes so they could trade and run plantations on these islands, but the Europeans were secretly plotting how they could overthrow the leadership within the African kingdom. The leadership of Kaabu understood this and that is why some of these African rulers chose English merchants as allies. Charles Beckingham states that Walter's father's name 'Nosser' means 'help aid' or 'help from God.'[146] This suggests that he was not the King of Kaabu who was known as 'Farim Cabo,' but an official or provincial governor who was attempting to establish an independent relationship with the English, possibly to acquire European guns to take power for himself.[147]

The willingness of West-African kings or leaders such as Nosser to send their sons to England suggests a desire to establish international relations with England. Perhaps these Africans in a similar way to that suggested with James Ongunby were converting to Christianity as a strategy. But then because of what was happening in sixteenth- and early-seventeenth-century

West Africa, they may have also genuinely lost confidence in indigenous African ways.

Another African present in England who illustrates these ideas is Dederi who was baptised as 'John Jaquoah.' He was the son of 'Caddi-biah king of the river of Cetras or Cestus in the cuntrey of Guinny.' Dederi was 'baptised and named' 'by the Parson of' the church of St Mildred's Poultry, London, on 1 January 1611. *The Oxford Companion to Black British History* suggests that Cestus or Cetras is in fact 'Cestos,' or the river Cess in the modern country of Liberia in West Africa,[148] but the actual word 'Cestos' is Portuguese and means 'basket.' The Portuguese traders gave the name 'Cestos' to an area that included a coastal trading port within Liberia which was famous in the sixteenth century for Africans who wove baskets and exported them along the West-African coast and beyond.[149]

Dedrei from 'Cestos,' was probably in England for similar reasons as Walter, because by 1610 West-African leaders such as Caddi-bah and Nosser Annerby had seen in a similar way to the character Othello, two decades of the 'flinty and steele couch of war.'[150] But Dederi's and Walter's presence in England, even though it was diplomatic and strategic, later on may have proved disastrous to the African nations they came from. This can be seen in the example of Don Affonso or Alphonso from the Kingdom of Bakonga or Kongo. As recounted by the English traveller Andrew Battell who was present in the kingdom for sixteen months in 1600.[151] The Portuguese and the Spanish baptised and politically indoctrinated the leadership of the Bakonga Kingdom for over two generations from the 1480s onwards.[152] Affonso was taken to Portugal and Spain and was in awe of European culture and power. Thereafter in his letters written in 1526 he calls the Pope his 'great father' and Affonso genuinely believed the personal relationships he had with Europeans would prevent wholesale slavery taking place in his country – in fact, the Pope was well aware of the slave trade in Bakonga and was secretly profiting from it.[153]

Habib suggests English merchants intend to exploit Dederi in a similar way, partly because he was only '20 years old' when he came to England and therefore may have been impressionable. But also because the Englishmen who sponsored Dederi included a 'John Davies [the] haberdasher' who dabbled in slave trading, and his ship *Abigail of London* which was used to bring Dederi to England, had previously transported enslaved Africans.[154] By 1610, Davies may have learnt that the best way to facilitate trade in West Africa was to work with West-African leaders and charm them. This echoes ideas present in Middleton's *The Triumphs of Truth*. In this masque the 'King of the Moores and his Queene' arrive in England and wonder as

Binne, Dederi and Walter may have done if the image of England portrayed to them by 'English merchants, factors [and] travellers' actually matches the real England that they will find. These concerns though probably spoken in Middleton's masque by white actors in black-face may have mirrored real doubts expressed by African dignitaries who visited Tudor England.[155]

Conclusion

There were West Africans amongst the Africans present in Tudor England, and there were others of 'those kindes of people' who had a West-African heritage in addition to cultural connections to the Caribbean and Europe. The places these West Africans present in Tudor England came from were diverse, ranging from small villages in Arguin to larger kingdoms such as Benin. Some of these places were also culturally diverse as the Moorish kingdoms in Iberia were, and blessed some of these West Africans with multilingual skills and an ability to integrate with other people in their local parishes. These skills also made them useful to Englishmen such as Hawkins and Drake who worked with some West Africans present in England to establish trade and diplomatic links for the purpose of circumventing international treaties.

Consequently, these Africans often had complex relationships with the Englishmen with whom they worked. In some cases these Africans' contributions are hidden in the private sphere of Tudor society despite the very public benefits they seemed to have offered. But most importantly, Africans such as Diego were too useful and important to be treated as slaves in Tudor England, although in some documents they may have been referred to as such.

Other West Africans who were temporary visitors to Tudor England also appear to have been treated with hospitality. The behaviour of West Africans in West Africa was influencing how Englishmen behaved towards Africans in England. Englishmen in West Africa, such as Madox were often fed, clothed and sheltered by the local people because as Africanus says, Africans do not 'make war on anyone' and they 'will not easily doe injurie to any ... [especially a] European.'[156]

However in West Africa this hospitality seems to have relied on Englishmen complying with West-African customs, including sitting on the floor at the feet of West-African kings,[157] or being naked as European and African merchants apparently were in Bornu. In a similar way, West Africans in Tudor England were expected to embrace English customs, dress and religion. But how far Africans were willing to conform to acculturation in

Tudor England appears to have been influenced by the places that they came from. We have seen that 'Coree the Saldanian' from Southern Africa resisted integration. However, those Africans from West Africa such as Domingo and Bastien may have been integrated members of their English parishes. A probable reason for this is that the civilisations these West Africans came from had closer links to England and their own desire or need to work with the English establishment was greater.

Other West Africans such as James Ongunby, however, may have adopted English culture including Protestant Christianity as a veneer, or as part of a strategy, and this was because of what was happening in West Africa. In other words these West Africans arrived in Tudor England with their own agenda. Events such as the destruction of the Empire of Songhai in 1591 had a major impact on West-African interaction with countries such as England. The African kingdoms that felt this impact the most were those nearest to Songhai such as the kingdoms of Kaabu and Benin. This is probably one of the reasons why we find Africans from these nations in sixteenth- and early-seventeenth-century England.

Moreover, the detrimental effects of colonial exploitation by Ottoman, Portuguese and Spanish rulers gave English and Dutch Protestants the opportunity to portray themselves as potential West-African allies.[158] Some West Africans may have initially been reluctant to enter into relationships with another set of foreigners who the Africans considered 'devils,' 'strange' 'demons,' or 'cannibals' who made 'devilish weapons.'[159] However, no matter how 'devilish' guns may have seemed to some Africans, after 1591 many more West-African nations felt they needed them. But English merchants were not always able to fully exploit the opportunities that the destruction of Songhai created and build trade links based on their victory against Spain in 1588. There was still uncertainty as to what role England should play in international relations. As suggested in Chapter 1, the death of John Hawkins and Drake in 1595 may have made some Englishmen fear not only that God's judgement had been called upon those who practised slavery, but also that this kind of trade was not feasible.

So that despite some West Africans being present in Tudor England to facilitate trade, English merchants were still interlopers in that trade. For example in the West-African Kingdom of Kanem Bornu in the sixteenth century, the Spanish maintained and trained a unit of 500 musketeers to preserve their influence in that kingdom,[160] and in Lisbon, Portuguese authorities staged grand festivals to honour West-African chiefs. Englishmen were still trying to 'catch up' with this level of international power and diplomacy.[161] Nevertheless, the presence of Dederi and Walter in England in the early part of the seventeenth century appears to have come about because of what had been learnt by English merchants in the sixteenth century. The difference is that the visit of Africans such as Dederi and Walter appears to have been better organised and co-ordinated than those earlier ones which led to embarrassing court cases or bungled attempts at deportations by Tudor merchants: suggesting that some English merchants in the early-seventeenth century had learnt valuable lessons from what had taken place in Tudor times.

Notes

[1] On women in sixteenth-century West-African societies see: John Donnelly Fage, Roland Anthony Oliver, Richard Gray (eds.), *The Cambridge History of Africa* ... Volume V (Cambridge: Cambridge University Press, 1976), pp. 188, 267, 285; Susan Joekes, *Women in Pastoral Societies in East and West Africa* (London/Edinburgh: International Institute for Environment and Development, 1991), preface, introduction; and Mariane Conchita Ferme, *"Hammocks Belong to Men, Stools to Women;"* Constructing and Contesting Gender Domains in a Mende Village (Sierra Leone, *West Africa*) Volume I (Chicago: University of Chicago, 1992), preface, introduction.

[2] Imtiaz Habib, *Black Lives* ... (London: Ashgate, 2008), pp. 1–18; Gustav Ungerer, *The Mediterranean Apprenticeship of British Slavery* (Madrid: Verbum Editorial, 2008), pp. 11–12, 17, 69; and Peter Fryer, *Staying Power* ... (1984, reprint, London: Pluto Press, 1989), pp. 133–146.

[3] The quotations are from Brion David Davis, *The Problem of Slavery in Western Culture* (1966, new edition, Oxford: Oxford University Press, 1988), p. 340 (Leo Africanus says some West Africans are 'primitive'); and John Hunwick, *Timbuktu and the Songhay Empire: Al Sadis Tarikh Al-Sudan Down to 1613 and Other Contemporary Documents* (Leiden: Brill, 1999), pp. 272, 274, 278, 276, 287–290, 291, 294–296 (Al Mansur).

[4] Gerard Barthelemy, *Black Face, Maligned Race: The Representation of Blacks in English Drama, from Shakespeare to Southerne* (London: Louisiana State University Press, 1987), p. 118; Margo Hendricks, Patricia Parker, *Women, 'Race' and Writing in the Early Modern Period* (New York: Routledge, 1994), p. 164; and Norman Verrle MacCullough, *The Negro in English Literature* (Ilfracombe: A. Stockwell, 1962), pp. 48–49, 143–144.

[5] Fryer, *Staying Power*, pp. 146–190.

[6] Author unknown, *St Botolph without Aldgate Memorandum Daybook*, Volume I (London: Parish of St Botolph without Aldgate, 1586–1588), p. 127; Guildhall Library, London (G. L.), Ref P69/BOT2/ A/ 01/MS 9234/1; GL Ms 9234; and *Oxford Dictionary of English*, p. 772 (the word 'Guinea').

[7] Ibid.

[8] Ungerer, *The Mediterranean Apprenticeship*, p. 81.

[9] Gerda Mansour, *Multilingualism and Nation Building* (Clevedon: Multilingual Matters, 1993), pp. 11–22, 59–66; and Loreto Todd, *Pidgins and Creoles* (1974, new edition, London: Routledge, 1990), pp. 1–22, 31.

[10] Roy Russell, Beatriz Galimberti Jarman, et. al., *The Oxford Spanish Dictionary* ... (London: Oxford University, 3rd edition 2003), p. 298 ('Domingo' means 'Sunday'); and David Hannay, *A Short History of the Royal Navy 1217–1815* (London: Methuen, 1898), p. 82 (piracy).

[11] Raphael Holinshed, *The Chronicles* ... (London: John Harrison, 1577), p. 1833 (On William Winter).

[12] There are examples of other Africans doing this in, William Rogers Louis, Alaine Low and Nicholas Canny (eds.), *The Oxford History of the British Empire: Volume IV: The Twentieth Century* (Oxford/ New York: Oxford University Press, 1998), pp. 61–62; and Hannay, *A Short History of the Royal Navy 1217–1815*, p. 82.

[13] The view that funerals can indicate status is supported by Clare Gittings, in, *Death, Burial and the Individual in Early Modern England* (London: Croom Helm, 1984), p. 172; Christopher Daniell, *Death and Burial in Medieval England, 1066–1550* (London: Routledge, 1998), pp. 43–54, 155, 170; and Ralph Anthonye Houlbrooke, *Death, Religion, and the Family in England, 1480–1750* (Oxford: Clarendon Press, 1998), pp. 268–269, 340, 342.

[14] Hugh Thomas, *The Slave Trade: The Story of the Atlantic Slave Trade, 1440–1870*, p. 155; Artist unknown, *The Drake Jewel [or Diadem]*, gold and enamel, ruby and diamonds, with sardonyx, circa 1575/1586, Nicholas Hilliard, Painting on parchment, Inset miniature in The Drake Jewel [or Diadem], 1585/1588, Victoria and Albert Museum, London, Ref: LOAN: MET.ANON.1–1990, Gallery 57A, Case 12, see figure 26; and Karen Dalton, Peter Erickson (ed.), Clarke Hulse (ed.), *Early Modern Visual Culture: Representation, Race, Empire in Renaissance England* (Philadelphia: University of Pennsylvania Press, 2000), pp. 178–215.

[15] Francis Drake, *Sir Francis Drake Revived Calling Upon the Dull or Effeminate Age to Follow his Noble Steps for Gold and Silver* (London: Nicolas, Bourne, 1628), n. p. preface, introduction.

[16] Francis Drake, William Davenant, *The History of Sir Francis Drake, Expressed by Instrumentall and Vocal Musick* ... (London: Henry Herringman, 1659), pp. 11–12, 14, 15–19, 20–21, 28–29 (Diego is called Pedro); John Barrow, *The Life, Voyages, and Exploits of Admiral Sir Francis Drake ... with Numerous Original Letters* (London: John Murray, 1843), pp. 72–74; and Derek Hughes (ed.), *Versions of Blackness: Key Texts on Slavery from the Seventeenth Century* (Cambridge: Cambridge University Press, 2007), pp. 307–312 (Maroons).

[17] Drake, *Sir Francis Drake Revived* ... pp. 7, 13–14; and Richard Price (ed.), *Maroon Societies: Rebel Slave Communities in the Americas* (New York: Anchor Books, 1973), pp. 11–15.

[18] Drake, *Sir Francis Drake Revived* ... p. 18; and Habib, *Black Lives*, pp. 305–306.

[19] Quotations from Drake, *Sir Francis Drake Revived* ... pp. 25, 29, 30, 66, 70; Pedro Sarmiento de Gamboa, Nuna da Silva, *New Light on Drake: A Collection of Documents Relating to his Voyage of Circumnavigation, 1577–1580* (London: Hakluyt Society, 1968), p. 302; and Philip Nicols, *Sir Francis, Drake Revived* (1882, new edition, Whitefish: Kessinger Publishing, 2004), pp. 14, 26.

[20] Drake, Davenant, *The History of Sir Francis Drake*, pp. 12, 14, 18, 19; and Gamboa, et. al., *New Light on Drake*, pp. introduction, 302 (they attempted to leave England on 13 November 1577 but failed).

[21] On Guillaume le Testu's work see his books including: *Cosmographie Universelle Selon les Navigateurs, Tant Anciens que Modernes*, 1555 (Vincennes: Bibliothèque du Service Historique de l'Armée de Terre, DLZ 14), f. 32, 33, 34, 37, 39. On Guillaume's knowledge see Albert-Marie-Ferdinand Anthiaume, 'Un pilote et cartographe havrais au XVIe siècle: Guillaume Le Testu,' *Bulletin de Géographie Historique et Descriptive*, Paris, Nos 1–2, 1911, pp. 135–202.

22 Sophie Crawford Comes (ed.), Edward Stafford, *Calendar of State Papers, Foreign Series*, Volume 21(London: Her Majesty's Stationery, 1927), p. 73. Added in parenthesis my readings of Edward Stafford, *Letter to Francis Walsingham, Secretaries of State; State Papers Foreign*, France (June–December 1586), 20 August 1586, National Archives, Kew, ref. SP 78/16, f. 90–91.

23 John Sugden, *Sir Francis Drake* (London: Random House, 2006), p. 72.

24 Kenneth Andrews, *Trade, Plunder and Settlement: Maritime Enterprise and the Genesis of British Empire, 1480–1630* (Cambridge: Cambridge University Press, 1984), p. 131; Peter Whitfield, *Sir Francis Drake* (New York: New York University Press, 2004), p. 34.

25 Ibid.

26 Robert Hutchinson, *Elizabeth's Spy Master: Francis Walsingham and the Secret War that Saved England* (London: Weidenfeld and Nicolson, 2006), passim.

27 Alexander McKee, *The Queen's Corsair: Drake's Journey of Circumnavigation, 1577–1580* (London: Souvenir Press, 1978), pp. 43, 124–5, 278.

28 Alexander McKee, *The Queen's Corsair: Drake's Journey of Circumnavigation, 1577–1580* (London: Souvenir Press, 1978), pp. 43, 124–5, 278. Similar views are expressed by Julian Stafford Corbett, in, *Drake and the Tudor Navy: With a History of the Rise of England as a Maritime Power* (London: Longman Green, 1898), p. 262; and Stephen Coote, *Drake: The Life and Legend of an Elizabethan Hero* (London /New York: Simon and Schuster, 2003), pp. 97, 145–146.

29 Quotations from Corbett, *Drake and the Tudor Navy*, p. 262; McKee, *The Queen's Corsair*, pp. 43, 124–5, 278; and Coote, *Drake: The Life and Legend of an Elizabethan Hero*, pp. 97, 145–146.

30 Drake, Davenant, *The History of Sir Francis Drake*, pp. 12, 14, 18, 19.

31 Ungerer, *The Mediterranean Apprenticeship*, pp. 11–12, 17, 69.

32 On Maria's sexual relationship with Drake see Anita Pacheco (ed.), *A Companion to Early Modern Women's Writing* (Oxford: Wiley Blackwell, 2002), p. 369. The quotations are from Zelia Nuttall, *New Light on Drake: A Collection of Documents Relating to his Voyage of Circumnavigation, 1577–1580. Translated and Edited by Zelia Nuttall ...* (London: Hakluyt Society, 1914), pp. 31–32; McKee, *The Queen's Corsair, Drake's Journey of Circumnavigation, 1577–1580*, p. 278; and The British Library, *Sir Francis Drake an Exhibition to Commemorate Francis Drake's Voyage Around the World 1577–1580* (London: British Museum Publications, 1977), p. 90 (although why Drake named the island 'He Francisca' after the African called Francisca whom he marooned there is not known.)

33 On Tudor women in her predicament see, R. B. Outhwaite (ed.), Vivien Brodsky-Elliott, *Single Women in the London Marriage Market: Age, Status and Mobility, 1598–1619* (London: Europe Publications, 1981), pp. 81–100.

34 Plymouth and West Devon Record Office, Plymouth, St Andrews/December 10/1583/ MF1–4 (Bastien's record).

35 Also quoted in, James Walvin, *Black Ivory: A History of British Slavery* (London: Harper Collins, 1992), p. 25.

36 John Hawkins, *A True Declaration of the Troublesome Voyage of Mr John Hawkins to the Parties of Guyana and the West Indies, in the Yeares of Our Lord in 1567 and 1568* (London: Thomas Purfoot, 1569), pp. 2, 19, 20.

37 Ibid. pp. 3, 5.

[38] Rayner Unwin, *The Defeat of John Hawkins* (London: Allen Unwin, 1961), p. 205; Habib, *Black Lives*, pp. 70–71; and Job Hortop, *The Rare Travails of Job Hortop, an Englishman who was not Heard of Three and Twenty Years Passé ... Wherin is Declared he Escaped in his Voiage to Gyinne much Slavery and Bondage in the Spanish Galley* (London: William Wright, 1591), pp. A1–C4.

[39] Hortop, *The Rare Travails*, pp. B2, B3.

[40] On this image see: Faiza Ghazala, Greater London Council Ethnic Minorities Unit, *A History of the Black Presence in London* (London: Greater London Council, 1986), pp. 6–7; and Harry Kelsey, *Sir John Hawkins* (London: Yale University Press, 2003), p. 32.

[41] Gustav Ungerer, 'Recovering a black African's voice in an English Lawsuit,' *Medieval and Renaissance Drama in England* (Madison: Fairleigh Dickinson University Press, 2004), pp. 255–271.

[42] National Archives, Kew, London, *High Courts of Admiralty (HCA) Reports*, 1547, Ref. 24/39/49–51.

[43] Fage, Oliver, Gray (eds.), *The Cambridge History of Africa* ...Volume IV, pp. 221, 222 (the history of Arguin); William Philips, *Slavery from Roman Times to the Transatlantic Trade* (Manchester: Manchester University Press, 1995), p. 139 (slavery in Arguin); Habib, *Black Lives*, pp. 50–53 (Jacques Francis); Nicholas Jay Saunders, *The Peoples of the Caribbean: An Encyclopedia of Archaeology and Traditional Culture* (Santa Barbara: ABC Clio, 2005), p. 219 (pearl divers); Thomas, *The Slave Trade ... 1440–1870*, p. 51 (African pearl divers); and Corbett, *Drake and the Tudor Navy*, pp. 79, 96, 97 (slave forts).

[44] Thomas, *The Slave Trade*, p. 64; and Edward Blount (tr.), Ieronimo Conestaggio, *The Historie of ... Portugal ...* (London: A. Hatfield for E. Blount, 1600), p. 7 (trade in Arguin).

[45] National Archives, Kew, London, *High Courts of Admiralty (HCA) Reports*, 1547, Ref. 24/39/49–51.

[46] Ungerer, 'Recovering a black African's voice in an English Lawsuit,' pp. 255–271. On the importance of the *Mary Rose* see James Gairdner, Robert Henry Brodie, et. al. (eds.), *Letters and Papers, Foreign and Domestic, Henry VIII, Volume 20, Part 2: August-December 1545* (London: Longman Green, 1907), pp. 1–24.

[47] On rescue and salvage attempts see, Peter Marsden, 'Salvage, Saving and Surveying the *Mary Rose*,' in, *Your Noblest Shippe: Anatomy of a Tudor Warship. The Archaeology of the Mary Rose*, Volume 2 (Portsmouth: The Mary Rose Trust, 2009), pp. 12–14; and Peter Marsden, *Sealed by Time: The Loss and Recovery of the Mary Rose. The Archaeology of the Mary Rose*, Volume 1 (Portsmouth: The Mary Rose Trust, 2003), p. 28.

[48] National Archives, Kew, London, *High Courts of Admiralty (HCA) Reports*, 1547, Ref. 24/39/49–51.

[49] Habib, *Black Lives*, pp. 51–53; and Ungerer, 'Recovering a black African's voice in an English Lawsuit,' pp. 255–271.

[50] In this way Jacques resembles the character Othello who also challenges negative ideas about his status and ethnicity in William Shakespeare, *Othello* in Richard Proudfoot, Ann Thompson, David Scott Kastan (eds.), *The Arden Shakespeare Complete Works* (Walton on Thames: Thomas Nelson and Sons, 1998), Act I, Scene III, Lines 140, 168–169, p. 945.

[51] Ungerer, 'Recovering a black African's voice,' pp. 255–271 (Corso's sentence was later reduced and he was released from prison on 26 March 1550.)

[52] Ibid. and Habib, *Black Lives*, pp. 51–53.

⁵³ Habib, *Black Lives*, pp. 101–104; and George *Best, A True Discourse of the Late Voyages of Discovery, for the Finding of a Passage to Cathya, by the Northwest, under the Conduct of Martin Frobisher* ... (London: H Bynyman, 1578), pp. 28–32.

⁵⁴ Fryer, *Staying Power*, pp. 53, 65, 229–230; Bata Kindai Amgoza Ibn LoBagola, *LoBagola: An African Savage's Own Story* (Leipzig: Bernhard Tauchnitz, 1930), p. 69 (Lobagola was an African-American impostor who posed as a continental African but did arrive naked in Scotland in March 1896 fuelling the 'naked savage' myth), passim; and Bata Kindai Amgoza Ibn LoBagola, *Folktales of a Savage* (London: AA Knopf, 1930), passim.

⁵⁵ Hunwick, *Timbuktu and the Songhay Empire*, p. 289.

⁵⁶ Bernth Lindfors (ed.), *Africans on Stage; Studies in Ethnological Show Business* (Bloomington; Indiana University Press, 1998), pp. 85, 228; Philippa Levine, *The British Empire: Sunrise to Sunset* (Harlow: Longman, 2007), p. 152 (Sara Baartman an African woman from South Africa was displayed naked in London in 1810 as a 'freak of nature'); and Marcus Garvey, Robert A. Hill (ed.), *The Marcus Garvey and Universal Negro Improvement Association Papers* (London/Berkeley: University of California Press, 1983), p. 569 (A Pan-African response in 1921 to the idea of the 'naked African savage.')

⁵⁷ John Allyne Gade, *Christian IV: King of Denmark and Norway: A Picture of the Seventeenth Century* (Boston: Houghton Mifflin, 1928), p. 62; and Habib, *Black Lives*, p. 316.

⁵⁸ Ethel Carleton Williams, *Anne of Denmark Wife of James VI of Scotland, James I of England* (New Jersey: Prentice Hall Press, 1970), p. 21.

⁵⁹ Clare McManus, *Women on the Renaissance Stage: Anna of Denmark and Female Masquing in the Stuart Court (1590 –1619)* (Manchester: Manchester University Press, 2002), p. 76; and Gade, *Christian IV: King of Denmark and Norway*, p. 62; and Habib, *Black Lives*, p. 316.

⁶⁰ Paul Van Somer, *Anne of Denmark*, 1617 @ the Royal Collection, London. For more on this image see Bindman, Gates, *The Image of the Black in Western Art*, Volume III, part 1, p. 249, see figure 27.

⁶¹ Brian Cummings, 'Animal Passions and Human Sciences: Shame, Blushing and Nakedness in Early Modern Europe and the New World,' in Erica Fudge (ed.), *At the Borders of the Human: Beasts, Bodies and Natural Philosophy in the Early Modern Period* (Basingstoke: Macmillan, 1999), pp. 26–51(looks at wider issues of nudity and sexuality).

⁶² Samuel Purchas, *Purchas his Pilgrimage; or Relations of the World and the Religions Observed in all Ages and Places* ... (1613), p. 541.

⁶³ The quotations are from Edward Terry, *A Voyage to East India* (London: J. Martin and J. Allestrye, 1655), pp. 20–21; Mohamad Zuhdi Yakan, *Almanac of African Peoples and Nations* (London: Transaction Publishers, 1999), pp. 336, 413–415; and Maghan Keita, *Conceptualizing/Re-Conceptualizing Africa: The Construction of African Historical Identity* (Leiden: Brill, 2002), pp. 90–105 (nudity amongst the Khoi Khoi).

⁶⁴ This matter is examined by Carol Kazmierczak Manzione, in 'Sex in Tudor London, Abusing their bodies with each other,' in Jacqueline Murray, Konrad Eisenbichler (eds.), *Desire and Discipline: Sex and Sexuality in the Premodern West* (Toronto: University of Toronto Press, 1996), pp. 87–100; Jennifer Lyle Morgan, *Laboring Women: Reproduction and Gender in New World Slavery* (Philadelphia: University of Pennsylvania Press, 2004), pp. 14–20. 'Dressing' Native-Americans is discussed by John Stow in *The Annales of England, Faithfully Collected Out of the Most Autenticall Authors, Records ... untill ... 1592* (London: R Newbery, 1592), pp. 484–485; and John Winter Jones (ed.), Richard Hakluyt, *Diverse Voyages, Touching the Discovery of America and the Islands Adjacent* (London: Hakluyt Society, 1850), p. 23.

65 Purchas, *Pvrchas his Pilgrimages* (1613), pp. 5, 15, 21; and Elizabeth Story Donno (ed.), Richard Madox, *An Elizabethan in 1582: The Diary of Richard Madox, Fellow of All Saints* (London: Hakluyt Society, 1976), pp. 18, 49, 173, 193. Donno calls Madox 'the most educated' and 'intelligent person' on the journey and implies his observations are rational and astute.

66 Purchas, *Pvrchas his Pilgrimages,* pp. 538, 541, 582-585; and B. J. Sokol, *Shakespeare and Tolerance* (Cambridge: Cambridge University Press, 2008), pp. 10, 21(offers a similar view).

67 Habib, *Black Lives,* pp. 78-9, 82, 87-88, 194, 317, 331; and GL 4310 (The African women living with Banning).

68 Donno (ed.), Madox, *The Diary of Richard Madox,* pp. 48, 49, 173, 182-3, 319 (African women had 'equal rights' in matriarchal societies). On the idea of a 'type of heaven' see George Bull, Robert Nelson, *Some Important Points of Primitive Christianity,* Volume 2 (London: Richard Smith, 1713), pp. 290-291.

69 Pieter de Marees, *Description et Recit Historial du Riche Royaume d'or de Gunea, Aultrement Nommé, la Coste de l'or de Mina ... P. D. M. [Pieter de Marees]...* (Amsterdam: Claesson, 1605), pp. 1-5, 17, 19-20, 91-92; Pieter de Marees, Albert Dantzig (tr.), Adam Jones (tr.), *Description and Historical Account of the Gold Kingdom of Guinea* (1602) (Oxford: Oxford University Press, 1987), pp. 15, 27, 158-166, 201; and Pieter Marees, *Beschryvinge Ende Historische Verhael ... vant Gout Koninckrijck van Gunea ...* (Amsterdam: Cornelius Claesz, 1602), p. 29.

70 Purchas, *Pvrchas his Pilgrimages* (1613), pp. 538, 541, 582-585; and Marees, *Beschryvinge ende Historische Verhael,* pp. 47-50.

71 Abraham Cresques, *The Catalan Atlas,* oil on canvas, 1375, BNF, ESP, 30, Bibliotheque Nationale, Paris; see figure 28; Real Alcazar, *Ibn Khaldun: The Mediterranean in the Fourteenth Century: Rise and Fall of Empires* (Seville: Foundation Jose Manuel Lara, 2006), pp. 88, 119, 215-216 (describes Abraham Cresques); and Hunwick, *Timbuktu and the Songhay Empire,* pp. preface, lvii and 280. The phrase 'nowhere else' and 'nowhere on earth [but],' in relation to the wealth of African civilisations was coined by James H. Breasted, in, *A History of Egypt from the Earliest Times to the Persian Conquest With Two Hundred Illustrations and Maps* (London: Hodder and Stoughton, 1906), pp. 12-13; and quoted again by Yosef Ben-Jochannan, in *Africa: Mother of Western Civilisation* (Baltimore: Black Classic Press, 1997), pp. 549-550.

72 Hawkins, *Declaration of the Troublesome Voyage* (1569), p. 8.

73 Robert Baker, *Travails in Guinea/ Robert Baker's 'Brefe Discourse.'* 1568, in, Richard Hakluyt (ed.), *The Principal Navigations ...* (London: Hakluyt's Collection, 1598), pp 7-8, 27 (African resistance), 24 (quotation), 37 (surrender to Africans).

74 Purchas, *Pvrchas his Pilgrimages* (1613), pp. 5, 21, 463, 467; John Pory (tr.), Leo Africanus, *A Geographical Historie of Africa, Written in Arabicke and Italian ... by Iohn Leo a More ...* (London: John Pory, 1600), pp. 27-28; Marees in Dantzig and Jones (trs.), *Description and Historical Account of the Gold Kingdom of Guinea,* pp. 19-21, 66-74, 167-172; and the quotation is from Thomas Middleton, *The Triumphs of Truth ...* (London: Nicholas Okes, 1613), p. 22.

75 Richard Eden, *The History of Travel in the West and East Indies ...* (London: Richard Iugge, 1577), pp. 342, 343, 349, 399; and Purchas, *Pvrchas his Pilgrimages* (1613), p. 544 (although they offer contradictory ideas about these beliefs in the same books).

76 Africanus, in Barthelemy, *Black Face, Maligned Race,* p. 118 (of course Africanus did convert to Christianity in 1520).

77 Purchas, *Pvrchas his Pilgrimages* (1613), p. 546; and MacCullough, *The Negro in English Literature*, pp. 48, 49.

78 John Foxe, *Book of Martyrs: Wrytinges Horrible Troubles, That Have Bene Wrought and Practised by the Romishe Prelates, Speciallye in this Realme of England* (1554, revised edition, London: John Day, 1563).

79 'This Marie Fillis being abowt the age of xx yeares and having beene in England for the space of xiii or xiiii yeares, and as yt was not Christned, and now being becom servant with one Millicent Porter a seamster dwelling in the libertie of Eastsmithfield, and now taking some howld of faith in Jesus Chryst, was desyrous to become a Christian.' GL Ms P69/Bot2/A01/Ms 9234/6, pp. 257–258. Her full record contains more evidence which supports my theory and it can be found in the Bibliography.

80 Jean Bodin, Marion Leathers Daniels Kuntz (tr., ed.), *Colloquium of the Seven about Secrets of the Sublime* (Princeton, London: Princeton University Press, 1975), pp. xv–xxviii, xlvii–lxvi (family of man), 144, 145, 146, 147, 153, 162 (harmony of music, food and man is an ideal), 470, 471 (persecution of Moors of Spain morally wrong); by contrast one of Bodin's other major works expresses religious intolerance of witchcraft *De la Demonomanie des Sorciers* ... (Paris: Du Puys, 1580), n. p. passim.

81 Ungerer, *The Mediterranean Apprenticeship of British Slavery*, p. 21.

82 Josias Nicols, *An Order of Household Instruction: by Which Every Master of a Family May Easily and in Short Space Make his Whole Household to Understand, the ...Christian Religion* (London: Thomas Man, 1596), pp. B9, B10, B12, H3, H4; Richard Greaves, *Society and Religion in Elizabethan England* (Minneapolis: University of Minnesota Press, 1981), pp. 287–290; and Leonidas Rosser, *Baptism: Its Nature, Obligation, Mode, Subjects and Benefits* (Philadelphia: Leonidas Rosser, 1854), pp. 19–23, 30–33, 379–386.

83 GL Ms 4429/1 (Dederi's record).

84 David Northrup, *Africa's Discovery of Europe: 1450–1850* (New York/Oxford: Oxford University Press), pp. 12, 18, 19, 26, 27, 31.

85 Hawkins, *Declaration of the Troublesome Voyage*, pp. 2–4.

86 Northrup, *Africa's Discovery of Europe*, pp. 12, 24–31.

87 The first quotation is from the parish record of Dederi or 'John Jaquoah:' G. L. St Mildred Poultry, GL Ms 4429/1, Parish register, baptised 1 January 1610/11. The second quotation is from Middleton, *The Triumphs of Truth*, p. 22.

88 Similar views are stated by Northrup in, *Africa's Discovery of Europe*, pp. 8, 12. But not by Nabil Matar, 'The 1st Turks and Moors in England' in Randolph Vigne (ed.), Charles Littleton (ed.), *From Strangers to Citizens: The Integration of Immigrant Communities in Britain, Ireland, and Colonial America, 1550–1750* (Eastbourne: Sussex Academic Press, 2001), pp. 261, 262.

89 Hunwick, *Timbuktu and the Songhay Empire*, pp. 281, 282; Edith Bruder, *The Black Jews of Africa: History, Religion, Identity* (New York/Oxford: Oxford University Press, 2008), pp. 7, 51–59, 97–132; and Zoltán Szombathy (ed. and tr.), *The History of Bidyini and Kaabu* ... (Piliscsaba: Avicenna Institute of Middle Eastern Studies, 2007), p. 61.

90 Donno (ed.), Madox, *The Diary of Richard Madox*, p. 308.

91 Purchas, *Pvrchas his Pilgrimages* (1613), p. 583.

92 Bodin, Kuntz (tr., ed.), *Colloquium of the Seven*, pp. 157, 163, 193.

93 GL Ms 9239, p. 12.

94 Thomas Jefferson Bowen, *Grammar and Dictionary of the Yoruba Language. With an Introductory Description of the Country and People of Yoruba* (New York: Smithsonian Institute, 1858), pp. ix, 23, 60–61.

⁹⁵ Scott Smith-Bannister, *Names and Naming Patterns in England, 1538-1700* (Oxford: Clarendon, 1997), pp. 28-30, 95-96; William Chambers, *Chambers Miscellany of Instructive and Entertaining Tracts*, Volumes 13-14 (London: Chambers, 1869), pp. 34-36 (meaning of 'Christian' names); and John Bossy, 'Blood and Baptism: Kinship, Community and Christianity in Western Europe from the Fourteenth to the Seventeenth Centuries,' in Derek Baker (ed.) ... *Studies in Church History*, 10 (Oxford: Blackwell, 1973), pp. 129-143.

⁹⁶ Andrew Herman Apter, *Black Critics and Kings: The Hermeneutics of Power in Yoruba Society* (Chicago/London: University of Chicago Press, 1992), pp. 125-131, 151 (the name makes you 'human'), 205 (mixing English and Yoruba names together); Frank Aig-Imoukhuede (ed.), *A Handbook of Nigerian Culture* (1st edition not known, 2nd edition, Lagos: Department of Culture Federal Ministry of Information and Culture, 1992), pp. 30, 52, 132 (on Ogun ceremonies and festivals); William Russell Bascomb, *The Yoruba of Southwestern Nigeria* (London/New York: Holt Rinehart and Winston, 1969), pp. 10, 43, 53-57, 72-79; and Jacob Obafemi, Kehinde Olupona, *Kingship, Religion, and Rituals in a Nigerian Community: A Phenomenological Study of Ondo Yoruba Festivals* (Stockholm: Almqvist and Wiksell International, 1991), pp. 26, 39, 142, 151-152.

⁹⁷ Blount (tr.), Conestaggio, *The Historie of the Uniting of the Kingdom of Portugal*, pp. 1-7, 39 (West Africans part of the initial invasion of Iberia); Ivan Van Sertima, *African Presence in Early Europe* (New Brunswick: Transaction Publishers, 1985), pp. 12, 151, 199, 235 (West Africans as soldiers etc. in Iberia); Lawrence McCrank (ed.), *Discovery in the Archives of Spain and Portugal: Quincentenary Essays, 1492-1992*, Volumes III-IV (New York: Haworth Press, 1992/1993), pp. 382-389; Adu Boahen, Alvin Josephy, *The Horizon History of Africa*, Volume II (New York: American Heritage Publishing, 1971), p. 355.

⁹⁸ Hunwick, *Timbuktu and the Songhay Empire*, pp. 283-285.

⁹⁹ Ibid., pp. preface, xxxiv, xxx; Cape Town University, *The Annual Review of Islam in South Africa*, Issues 3-8 (Cape Town: Centre for Contemporary Islam, 2000), p. 34; Abraham Curtis, 'Stars of the Sahara,' *New Scientist*, Number 2617, 18 August 2007, pp. 37-39; and The UNESCO, 'African Ink Road International Symposium,' http://portal.unesco.org/ci/en/ev.php-URL_ID=26012&URL_DO=DO_TOPIC&URL_SECTION=-473.html accessed 12/09/09 and Nabil Matar (ed. tr.), *In the Lands of the Christians: Arabic Travel Writing in the Seventeenth Century* (New York: Routledge, 2002), pp. introduction, xli (on Muhammad Baghayogho).

¹⁰⁰ Pory (tr.), Africanus, *A Geographical Historie of Africa*, pp. preface, introduction, 6, 39-41.

¹⁰¹ Hunwick, *Timbuktu and the Songhay Empire*, preface; and Edward William Bovill, Robin Hallett, *The Golden Trade of the Moors: West African Kingdoms in the Fourteenth Century* (London: Oxford University Press, 1958), pp. 85-91, 91-97 ('The Emperor' later brought Es Saheli to live in Mali and there he built the Djinguereber Mosque in 1327.)

¹⁰² Franco Alfonso Silva, *La Esclavitud en Sevilla y su Tierra a Fines de la Edad Media* (Seville: Diputacion Provincial de Sevilla, 1979), p. 294 (power of Songhai); Abraham Cresques, *The Catalan Atlas*, (Songhai's influence on the 'African Ink Road'); see figure 28.

¹⁰³ More on the influence of Songhai see: Thomas, *The Slave Trade*, p. 64; and Ira Berlin, *Many Thousands Gone: The First Two Centuries of Slavery in North America* (1998, new edition, New York: Harvard University Press, 2000), pp. 20-21.

¹⁰⁴ Purchas, *Pvrchas his Pilgrimages* (1613), pp. 538-539, 590; and Northrup, *Africa's Discovery of Europe*, p. 9. Al Mansur the Sultan of Morocco did the same in Bornu in John Hunwick, *Timbuktu and the Songhay Empire*, pp. preface, xlii.

¹⁰⁵ Northrup, *Africa's Discovery of Europe*, pp. 26-27.

[106] Habib, *Black Lives*, p. 68; and Marika Sherwood, 'Blacks in Elizabethan England,' *History Today*, 53: 10, 2003, pp. 40–42.

[107] Carole Levin, *The Reign of Elizabeth I* (Basingstoke: Palgrave Macmillan, 2002), pp. 119–120; and Purchas, *Pvrchas his Pilgrimages* (1613), pp. 540–541.

[108] Quotations from, Richard Hakluyt, *The Principal Navigations, Voyages, Traffiques & Discoveries of the English Nation: Made by Sea or Overland to the Remote and Farthest Distant Quarters of the Earth at Any Time Within the Compass of These 1600 years* (1598, new edition, London: JM Dent and Sons, 1927), p. 131. Also quoted in: Walvin, *Black Ivory*, p. 1; and Fryer, *Staying Power*, pp. 5–6.

[109] Ungerer, 'Recovering a black African's voice in an English lawsuit,' p. 261.

[110] Suggested by Eric Ash in *Power, Knowledge, and Expertise in Elizabethan England* (London: Baltimore, John Hopkins University, 2004), p. 99, 103, 126, 235 (Iberian pilots with knowledge of Africa).

[111] Levin, *The Reign of Elizabeth I*, pp. 119–120 (suggests they were from Ghana).

[112] Hans Joachim Melzian, *A Concise Dictionary of the Bini Language of Southern Nigeria* (London: Kegan Paul and Co, 1937), introduction; Robert Oakley Collins ... *Western African History* (Princeton: Markus Wiener, 1990), p. 135; and Edward William Lane, Francis Jenkins Olcott, *More Tales from the Arabian Nights* (London: Holt, 1915), pp. 139–141 (The name Genie may also relate to the mythological 'Genie' found in Islamic and West-African mythology.).

[113] Fryer, *Staying Power*, pp. 5–6.

[114] The quotation is from Northrup, *Africa's Discovery of Europe*, pp. 5, 29, 30.

[115] Walvin, *Black Ivory*, pp. 17, 19; and Hunwick, *Timbuktu and the Songhai Empire*, pp. preface, xxxiv, xxii, 287.

[116] Evidence in: John Thornton, 'Early Kongo Portuguese, Relations 1483–1575, A new interpretation,' *History in Africa*, Volume VIII, 1981, p. 191; Alan Frederick Charles Ryder, 'Missionary Activity, in the Kingdom of Warri to the Early Nineteenth Century,' *Journal of the Historical Society of Nigeria*, 2: 1, December 1960, pp. 5–10; and Pory (tr.), Africanus, *A Geographical Historie of Africa*, p. 42.

[117] Eden (1553) quoted in, Basil Davidson, *African Civilisation Revisited* ... (Trenton: Africa World Press 1991), pp. 229–231; Eden and Wyndham, *The History of Travel in the West and East Indies* ... pp. 342, 343, 349, 399; Wyndham, Hakluyt, *The Principall Navigations*, pp. 86–7; and Marees, in Dantzig, Jones (trs.), *Description and Historical Account of the Gold Kingdom of Guinea*, pp. 15, 31 'they are very clever at trading,' 51–57, 59–61.

[118] The quotation is from John Lok and quoted in Kenneth Little, *Negroes in Britain* ... (London: Routledge, Kegan Paul, 1947), p. 166; and Ash, *Power Knowledge and Expertise in Elizabethan England*, p. 126. The Portuguese arranged a marriage between King Warri of the Niger Delta and a white Portuguese noblewoman in George T. Stride, Caroline Ifeka, *Peoples and Empires of West Africa: West Africa in History, 1000–1800* (New York: Africana Publishing Corporation, 1971), p. 337.

[119] Quotations from Levin, *The Reign of Elizabeth I*, pp. 119–121; Hakluyt, *The Principal Navigations* ... pp. 216–219; Charles Malcolm Macinnes, *England and Slavery* (London: Arrowsmith 1934), p. 18; and Julia Reid, 'The origins of English attitudes towards the Black African 1554–1807,' MA Thesis, University of Hull (unpublished), 1975, passim.

[120] Timbuktu was an intellectual and military centre whose semi-independent ruler according to Africanus had over '3,000 cavalry' and 'a huge number of foot soldiers' in Hunwick, *Timbuktu and the Songhay Empire*, pp. preface, xliii. By 1610, it had been an

intellectual centre for over a thousand years for African civilisations including Ancient Ghana, Mali and Songhai, in Purchas, *Pvrchas his Pilgrimages* (1613), pp. 527, 544; and Northrup, *Africa's Discovery of Europe*, preface.

[121] Al Mulay Ahmed Mansur, letter to Askiya Ishaq of Songhai, December 1589 in Hunwick, *Timbuktu and the Songhay Empire*, pp. 193, 201, 218–232, 281, 283, 294–295, 305, 312–315, 319; and Donno (ed.), Madox, *The Diary of Richard Madox*, p. 315.

[122] Jarita Medupe (ed.), et. al., *African Cultural Astronomy: Current Archaeoastronomy and Ethnoastronomy Research in Africa* (New York/Berlin: Springer, 2008), pp. 179–209; and Hunwick, *Timbuktu and the Songhay Empire*, pp. 294–296, 299, 300–303, 305 (Songhai challenged the Eastern-Islamic orthodoxy that the 'leadership of the Islamic world should rest with the descendants of Quraysh' and that the 'red and the black [African Muslims]' should submit to the Imams of Istanbul.)

[123] Thomas Bourke, *A Concise History of the Moors in Spain from the Invasion of that Kingdom ...* (London: Rivington Hatchard, 1811), p. 252; and Al Mulay Ahmed Mansur in John Hunwick, *Timbuktu and the Songhay Empire*, pp. 193, 201, 218–232, 305, 312–315, 319.

[124] More information about these children can be found in Sidney Lee, 'Caliban's visits to England,' *Cornhill Magazine*, 34, 1913, pp. 333–345; and Sherwood, 'Blacks in Elizabethan England,' pp. 40–42.

[125] Alfred Leslie Rowse, *Raleigh and the Throckmortons* (London: Macmillan Company/ New York, St Martin's Press, 1962), p. 121.

[126] Walvin, *Black Ivory: Slavery in the British Empire*, p. 17; James Walvin, *Slaves and Slavery: The British Colonial Experience* (Manchester: Manchester University Press, 1992), p. 19; GL Ms 7635/2 and GL Ms 4449/2 (records of African children in late-seventeenth-century England).

[127] James Walvin, *Slaves and Slavery: The British Colonial Experience* (Manchester: Manchester University Press 1992), pp. 17–19; and William Philips, *Slavery from Roman Times to the Early Transatlantic Trade* (Manchester: Manchester University Press, 1985), pp. 142–144.

[128] William Hopkins, *Letter to Lord Burghley*, October 1590, in *Lansdowne Manuscripts*, no. 115, item 83, pp. 236–239.

[129] Walvin acknowledges this but later seems to forget it, in Walvin, *Black Ivory*, p. 19.

[130] Author unknown, *A Packe of Spanish Lies Sent Abroad in the World: First Printed in Spain, in the Spanish Tongue, and Translated out of the Original. Now Ripped Up, Unfolded, and by just Examination Condemned as Containing False, Corrupt and Detestable Wares, Worthy to be Damned and Burned.* (London: Christopher Barker, 1588), p. 1; and Charles Howard, *A Declaration of the Causes Moving the Queen Majesty ... to ... Send a Navy to the Seas for the Defence of her Realms ...* (London: Christopher Barker, 1596), pp. 1, 3, 6.

[131] Kelsey, *Sir John Hawkins*, pp. 46–51, 53, 157, 236, 269; Hawkins, *Declaration of a Troublesome Voyage*, p. 18; and Richard Hakluyt, *Divers Voyages, Touching the Discovery of America and the Islands Adjacent* (London: Thomas Woodcoke, 1582), p. 8.

[132] Lawrence Stone, 'Social Mobility in England 1500–1700,' *Past and Present*, No. 33, April 1966, pp. 16–17 (they were also known as the 'Fellowship of Merchant Adventurers of the Town and County of Newcastle upon Tyne' and 'Merchant Venturers in the Ports of Brabant beyond the Seas.'); and Eneas Mackensie, 'Incorporated Companies: Merchant Adventurers,' Historical Account of Newcastle-upon-Tyne: Including the Borough of Gateshead, 1827, *British History Online*, pp. 662–670, http://www.british-history.ac.uk/report.aspx?compid=43401 accessed 18/01/08.

[133] Their links to West Africa can be found in: Robert Kerr (ed.), *A General History Collection of Voyages and Travels, Arranged in Systematic Order: Forming a Complete History of the Origin and Progress of Navigation, Discovery, and Commerce, by Sea and Land, from the Earliest Ages to the Present Time,* Volume VII (Edinburgh: W. Blackwood and Sons, 1824), pp. 331–338; John Maclean (ed.), David Watkin Waters, *The Art of Navigation in England in Elizabethan and Early Stuart Times* (London: Hollis and Carter, 1958), p. 84; and George Carew, *Letters from George Lord Carew to Sir Thomas Roe, Ambassador to the Court of the Great Mogul 1615–1617* (London: Camden Society, 1860), pp. 116, 117. But Martin Frobisher did bring Inuits to England in Sherwood, 'Blacks in Elizabethan England,' pp. 40–42.

[134] Kerr (ed.), *A General History and Collection of Voyages and Travels*, pp. 213–217; and Levin, *The Reign of Elizabeth I*, p. 119.

[135] Levin, *The Reign of Elizabeth I*, pp. 119–121; W.E. Miller, 'Negroes in Elizabethan London,' *Notes and Queries*, No. 8, 4 April, 1961, p. 138; and Emeka Abanime, 'Elizabeth I and Negroes,' *Cahiers Elizabethans*, XIX, 19 April 1981, p. 2.

[136] Holinshed, *The Chronicles*, (1577), pp. 1531, 1550, 1572, 1865; Douglas Bisson, *The Merchant Adventurers of England: The Company and the Crown, 1474–1564* (London: Associated University Press, 1993), introduction; and William Ezra Lingelbach, *The Merchant Adventurers of England: Their Laws and Ordinances with other Documents* (New York: B. Franklin, 1971), pp. 1–12.

[137] George Cawston, Augustus Henry Keane, *Early Chartered Companies, A.D. 1296–1858* (Manchester: Ayer Publishing, 1968), pp. 228–229; and Ungerer, *The Mediterranean Apprenticeship*, p. 12.

[138] Quoted in National Archives, Kew, London, HCA 24/39/49–51; and Ungerer, *The Mediterranean Apprenticeship*, pp. 84–85.

[139] Ibid. and Kerr (ed.), *A General History and Collection of Voyages and Travels,* Volume VII, pp. 342–349.

[140] The quotations are from the National Archives, Kew, London, HCA 24/39/49–51. But Gustav Ungerer says these Africans were slaves in, 'The presence of Africans in Elizabethan England and the performance of *Titus Andronicus* at Burley-on-the-Hill, 1595/96,' *Medieval Renaissance Drama in England*, Volume 21, 2005, January 1 2008, pp. 19–56.

[141] Ibid. and Kenneth Andrews, *Trade, Plunder and Settlement: Maritime Enterprise and the Genesis of the British Empire, 1480–1630* (London: Cambridge University Press, 1984), p. 112.

[142] London Metropolitan Archives, London, LMA DRO/015 /A/01/001.

[143] Quoted in Sylvia Collicott, *Connections: Haringey Local-National-World Links* (London: Haringey Community Information Service and Multi-Cultural Curriculum Support Group, 1986), p. 14.

[144] On the culture of Kaabu and Songhai see, Ayi Kwei Armah (tr.), Barry Boubacar, *Senegambia and the Atlantic Slave Trade* (Cambridge: Cambridge University Press, 1998), pp. 7–8, 17–29; Szombathy (ed. and tr.), *The History of Bidyini and Kaabu*, pp. introduction, 17–38, 62, 85–98, 99–145.

[145] A similar perspective on multilingualism in these kingdoms is given by Armah (tr.), Boubacar, *Senegambia and the Atlantic Slave Trade*, pp. 35–36; and Cornelia Giesing, Valentin Vydrin (eds. trs.), *Ta:rikh Mandinka de Bijini (Guinée-Bissau): la Mémoire des Mandinka et Sòoninkee du Kaabu* / Traduction, Notes et Commentaires par Cornelia Giesing and Valentin Vydrine (Leiden/Boston: Brill, 2007), preface, introduction.

¹⁴⁶ Beckingham in Collicott, *Connections: Haringey Local-National-World Links,* p. 14.

¹⁴⁷ Collicott, *Connections,* pp. preface, 14; and Szombathy, *The History of Bidyini and Kaabu,* pp. 60-62.

¹⁴⁸ The quotations are from GL Ms 4229/1; and Dabydeen and Gilmore (eds.), *Oxford Companion to Black British History,* p. 403.

¹⁴⁹ Hunwick, *Timbuktu and the Songhay Empire,* p. 280.

¹⁵⁰ London Metropolitan Archives, London, LMA DRO/015 /A/01/001; and the quotation is from Shakespeare, *Othello* in Proudfoot, Thompson and Kastan (eds.), *The Arden Shakespeare Complete Works,* Act I, Scene III, Line 231, p. 947.

¹⁵¹ Andrew Battell, *The Strange Adventures of Andrew Battell of Leigh, in Angola and Adjoining Regions* (London: Hakluyt Society, 1901), pp. 110, 136; and Robert Oakley Collins ... *Central and South African History* (Princeton: Markus, Weiner Publishers, 1990), pp. 42-47 (Bakonga included the modern day Republic of the Congo, the Democratic Republic of the Congo and Angola).

¹⁵² Northrup, *Africa's Discovery of Europe,* pp. 5, 6; Collins, *Central and South African History,* pp. 49-57; and Purchas, *Pvrchas his Pilgrimages* (1613), pp. 584-585.

¹⁵³ On this exploitation see: Chancellor Williams, *The Destruction of Black Civilisation* ... (Chicago: Third World Press, 1987), pp. 245-260; Ann Hilton, *The Kingdom of Kongo* (Oxford: Clarendon, 1985), pp. 21-3, 57-85; Helen Weaver (tr.), Georges Balandier, *Daily Life in the Kingdom of the Kongo from the Sixteenth to the Eighteenth Century* (1965, new edition, New York: Allen and Unwin, 1968), pp. 52-55; and Antonio Brasio (ed.), *Monumenta Missionaria Africana* ... (Lisbon: Lisboa, 1ˢᵗ series, 1952-1968), pp. 294-323.

¹⁵⁴ The quotations are from Dederi's parish record GL Ms 4229/1; and are also quoted in Habib, *Black Lives,* pp. 93-94, 141-143, 249; and Marina Warner, *Signs and Wonders: Essays on Literature and Culture* (London: Chatto and Windus, 2003), pp. 257-258.

¹⁵⁵ I also acknowledge that this was not the purpose of Thomas Middleton's masque since it was created to honour the Lord Mayor of London see *The Triumphs of Truth* ... (London: Nicholas Okes, 1613), pp. 1, 21, 22, 23; and an alternative view on the purpose of this Triumph is contained in Jonathan Burton, *Traffic and Turning: Islam and English Drama, 1579-1624* (Newark: University of Delaware Press, 2005), pp. 174-177.

¹⁵⁶ Quotations are in Hunwick, *Timbuktu and the Songhay Empire,* pp. 272-274; and Purchas, *Pvrchas his Pilgrimages* (1613), p. 541.

¹⁵⁷ Marees, *Description du Riche Royaume d'or de Gunea,* p. 95; and Marees, Dantzig (tr.), Jones (tr.), *Description of the Gold Kingdom of Guinea,* pp. 51-57, 59-61, 63, 202-206, 207-212.

¹⁵⁸ Marees, in Dantzig, Jones (trs.), *Description of the Gold Kingdom of Guinea,* pp. 202-206, 207-212.

¹⁵⁹ The quotations are from statements made by Africans, and reported by sixteenth-century European travellers see Northrup, *Africa's Discovery of Europe,* pp. 9, 12, 24-31; and Purchas, *Purchas his Pilgrimages* (1613), pp. 538-539, 590.

¹⁶⁰ Hunwick, *Timbuktu and the Songhay Empire,* p. 327; Robert Sydney Smith, *Warfare and Diplomacy in Pre-Colonial West Africa* (London: Methuen, 1976), pp. 43, 55, 81, 125, 126, 129; and Ahmed Ibn Fartua, Herbet Richmond Palmer (tr.), *History of the First Twelve Years of the Reign of Mai Idris, Alooma of Bornu (1571-1583) / by his Imam, Ahmed Ibn Fartua, Together with the 'Diwan of the Sultans of Bornu' and 'Girgam of the Magumi;' translated from the Arabic* ... (Lagos: Government Printer, 1926), introduction.

[161] Northrup, *Africa's Discovery of Europe*, p. 9; Robert Lacey, *Aristocrats* (London: Hutchinson, 1983), p. 67; and Bailey Diffie, George Winius, Boyd Shafer (ed.), *The Foundations of the Portuguese Empire 1415-1580, of Europe and the World in the Age of Expansion,* Volume I (Minneapolis: University of Minnesota Press, 1977), pp. 166-175.

Fig. 21. Jan Mostaert. *Portrait of an African Man*, circa 1520–1530, Holland. Reproduced by kind permission of the Rijksmuseum, Netherlands.

Fig. 22. Author unknown. *Marriage of St Ursula to Prince Conan*, circa 1520, panel of the Santa Auta Altarpiece, from the Monastery of Madre de Deus in Lisbon, Portugal.
© photographer Jose Pessoa 1993, reproduced by kind permission of Mestre do Retabulo de Santa Auta and Direcao-Geral do Patrimonio Cultural/Arquivo de Documentacao Fotografica (DGPC/ADF).

Fig. 23. Rembrandt. *A Black Drummer and Commander on Mules,* 1638, Hague, Holland. Reproduced by kind permission of the © Trustees of the British Museum.

Fig. 24. Hieronymus Bosch. (copy) *Adoration of the Magi* (after the central panel of the *Epiphany Triptych* in the Museo del Prado), 1450 ca.-1516, Philadelphia, Philadelphia Museum of Art.
Oil on canvas, 37 × 29 5/16' (94 x 74.4 cm). John G. Johnson Collection, 1917.
© 2013. Photo The Philadelphia Museum of Art/Art Resource/Scala, Florence (Code A184683).

Fig. 25. Hieronymus Bosch. (copy) *Adoration of the Magi* (Detail), (after the central panel of the *Epiphany Triptych* in the Museo del Prado), 1450 ca.-1516, Philadelphia, Philadelphia Museum of Art.
Oil on canvas, 37 × 29 5/16' (94 × 74.4 cm). John G. Johnson Collection, 1917.
Madrid, Prado. © 2013. Photo Scala, Florence (code 0109884).

BLACKAMOORES: AFRICANS IN TUDOR ENGLAND

Fig. 26. Artist's impression of, *The Drake Jewel* [or Diadem], 1575/1586, England.
©Victoria and Albert Museum, London.

Fig. 27. Paul Van Somer. *Anne of Denmark*, 1617, England.
Reproduced by kind permission of the Royal Collection Trust/© Her Majesty Queen Elizabeth II 2013.

Fig. 28. Abraham Cresques, *The Catalan Atlas*, 1375, 'The Emperor Mansa Musa'. Bibliothèque nationale de France.

Fig. 29. Govaert Flinck. *Young Archer*, 1639–1640.
Reproduced © by kind permission of the Trustees of the Wallace collection.

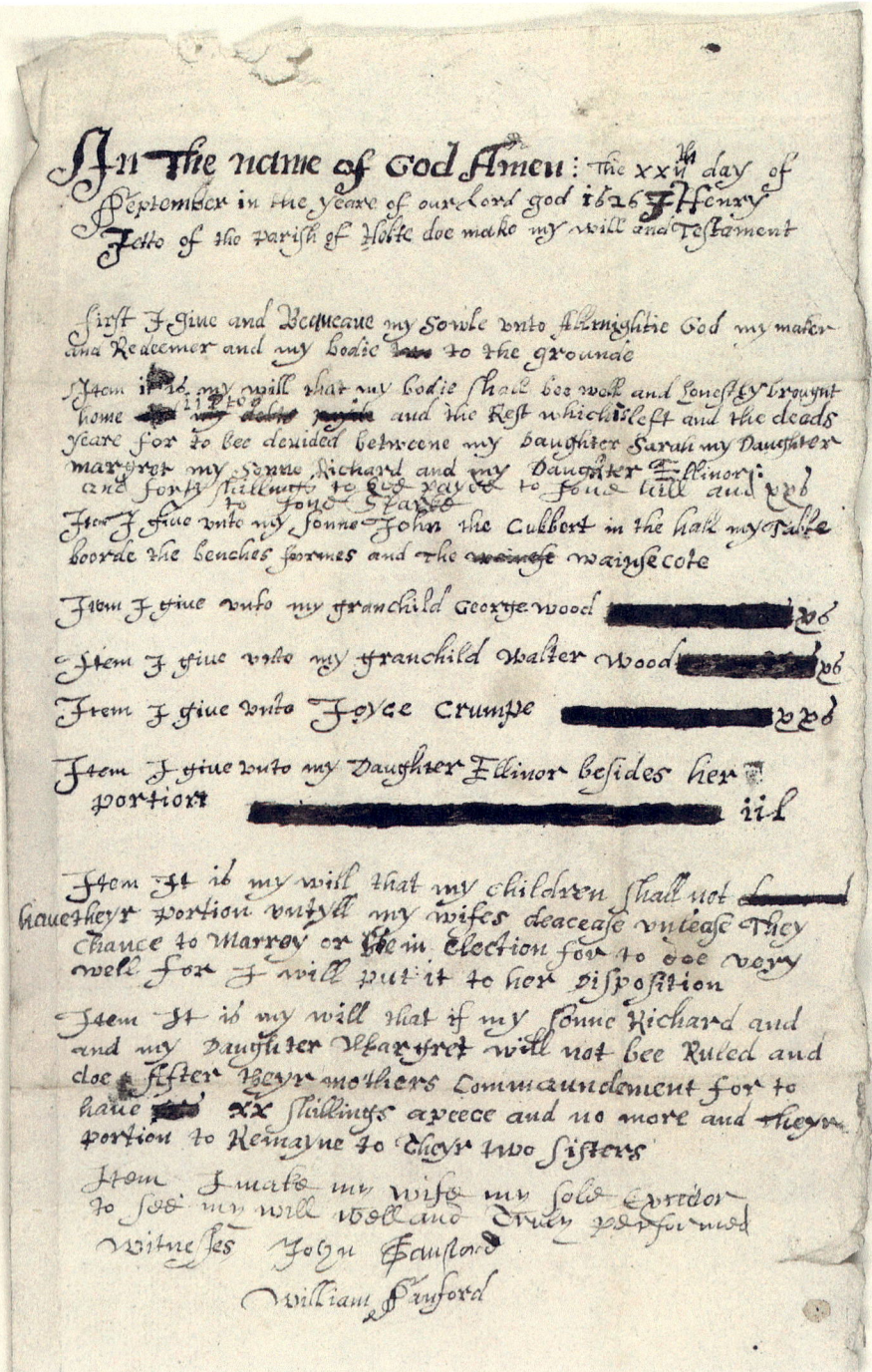

Fig. 30. *Henrie Jetto's Will* 'in his own hand,' 1626, Worcester Archives.

Fig. 31. *Peter Bluck.* Picture reproduced by kind permission of Peter Bluck.

Fig. 32. *Peter Bluck's father.* Picture reproduced by kind permission of Peter Bluck.

Fig. 33. *Schoenbartbuch Nurnberg* [Nuremberg Carnival Book], 1590–1620. With kind permission of Universitats-und Landesbibliothek Dusseldorf, urn.

Fig. 34. *Schoenbartbuch Nurnberg* [Nuremberg Carnival Book], 1590–1620. With kind permission of Universitats-und Landesbibliothek Dusseldorf, urn.

Fig. 35. *Schoenbartbuch Nurnberg* [Nuremberg Carnival Book], 1590–1620. With kind permission of Universitats-und Landesbibliothek Dusseldorf, urn.

Fig. 36. *Schoenbartbuch Nurnberg* [Nuremberg Carnival Book], 1590–1620. With kind permission of Universitats-und Landesbibliothek Dusseldorf, urn.

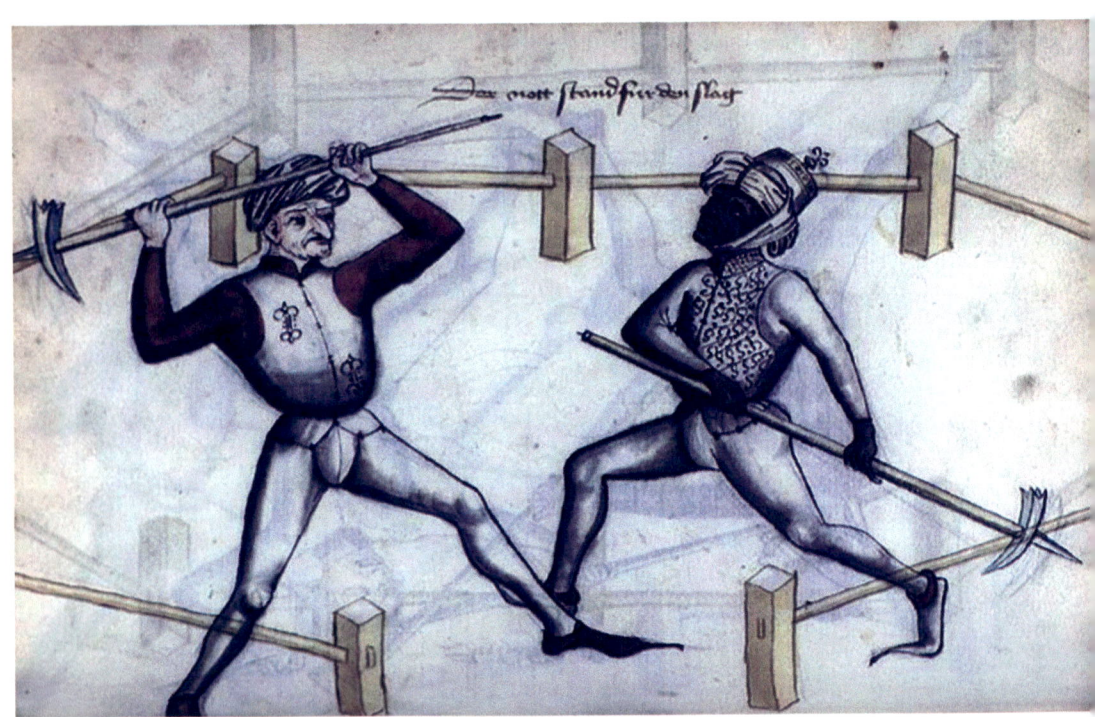

Fig. 37. *Schoenbartbuch Nurnberg* [Nuremberg Carnival Book], 1590–1620. With kind permission of Universitats-und Landesbibliothek Dusseldorf, urn.

Africans in Tudor England: Their Presence, Status and Origins

The Conclusion

This book is the first major research on the status and origins of Africans present in Tudor England. In it I reveal that 'those kindes of people' were living in various cities, towns and villages in sixteenth- and early-seventeenth-century England including: Domingo and Symon Valencia in London, Bastien and Cristian in Plymouth, Thomas Pontying in Bristol, Maria Moriana in Southampton, Anthony in Barnstable, Maria Mundula in Colne and Henrie Jetto of Holt in Worcestershire.[1] In the later half of the sixteenth century, in areas of London such as St Botolph without Aldgate and St Olave Hart Street, this African population constituted more than a 'few strolling players' and represented a significant presence. In St Botolph for example, there are over thirty-two entries in parish registers for African men, women and children, detailing their baptisms and burials, and they may have constituted 6% of that parish's population.[2] However, with the possible exception of the unconfirmed numbers in the Bristol case, a mass influx of 'great numbers' of Africans did not suddenly arrive in Tudor England from Spain, Portugal or elsewhere – despite what the Letters and the Proclamation suggest. Furthermore, it is unlikely that even in cities such as London that Africans constituted the threat that the Letters and the Proclamation imply.

Having said that, I also question the ideas proposed by writers such as Habib and Ungerer which reiterate those by Fryer and Little that Africans in Tudor England were all transient immigrants or slaves, foreign in birth, culture and thought, who occupied the lowest portions of English society. It is also interesting that historians such as Habib and Ungerer, who have found important evidence of an African presence in Tudor England, have interpreted their findings using the ideas of these earlier writers who had less information than they had. But these ideas on Africans all being slaves or that they were considered as inferior in Tudor society, are even older than Fryer and Little's work, and appear to have first been stated by an African-American writer called Luther Porter Jackson in his article 'Elizabethan

Seamen and the African Slave Trade' written in 1924. Jackson suggested that Africans settled in England as a result of slavery conducted by English pirates such as John Hawkins and Drake.[3] So the idea that all Africans in Tudor England are slaves is almost ninety-years old, but it is only now in this book that it is being systematically challenged.

Nevertheless, the evidence that I have discovered about the presence, status and origins of Africans in Tudor England has not been easy to find. This is because documents such as *The Chronicles* written at the time do not always say the people who they are talking about are Africans. It had been thought that this showed there were no Africans in Tudor England, but now with a re-examination of the same documents we are forced to think again. It is more likely that the reticence of most Tudor writers to discuss the race of the people who they talk about, or an African presence in general is because of what I suggest here. This is that many Africans were integrated members of their parishes, or were born in the local area, and for them, race would have become less important. These Africans are likely to have felt a sense of 'belonging' to their parish community, even though as Laura Gowing points out, belonging is a matter of 'negotiation' – if this is so; many of the Africans discussed in this book are avid negotiators.[4] Only a few Africans, such as those mentioned in the Bristol case, or the two apparently poor and destitute 'Blackamoores' mentioned in the last chapter, appear to have been living within the jurisdiction of a parish, without being wholly part of it by being a member of the church or by having familial or employment connections to others in their area.[5]

Since many Africans appear to have been integrated within Tudor society it is doubtful whether they would be specifically targeted during xenophobic 'outrages.' In this regard, Africans in Tudor England appear to have been treated differently from how Iberian Moors in Spain were during the Reconquista, the Inquisitions or through the policy of 'blue-blood inheritance.'[6] In Tudor England, the group of people who did suffer xenophobia, hysterical animosity and routine suspicion akin to that which the Moors and Jews in Iberia suffered at the end of the sixteenth century were 'Egyptians.' This may have been because some Egyptians in a similar way to the Moors in Spain claimed, or did owe their origins to independent nations present in Europe which were consanguineous, and whose history predated the nations they were now part of. I have not found evidence of Africans in Tudor England who publicly declared this kind of heritage, although David MacRitchie appears to offer a contrary view.[7]

Furthermore, other Africans who we know were present in Tudor England are not always easy to find in Tudor documents. In fact in some cases these

Africans seem to be missing or are obscured. This includes the 'needle making' 'Negro who would never teach his art to any' who is not in the Tudor editions of *The Chronicles,* despite being present in later versions and other Tudor texts.[8] Other Africans appear to be absent from parish records and the subsidy rolls. This includes Katherine of Aragon's ladies in waiting, John Blanke, the four Africans who came with John Lok, others who arrived with the Dassells, and Diego Negro. However, the absence of these Africans from some Tudor documents does not appear to be the result of a systematic policy by writers at the time to erase them from history. Instead in each individual case the African's non-appearance can be explained by reasons other than those related to race, such as the fact that some parish records did not cover the areas where they lived, or they were engaged in activities or the kinds of employment which made them exempt from inclusion.

However, even where Africans are described in Tudor documents with reference to the colour of their skin or ethnic origins this may be with a single word or a moniker. In the case of parish records this word or words may reflect a long conversation between an adult African and a clerk or priest. But of course not all Africans were baptised as adults, and as children their ethnicity may have been ignored although, their fathers' and mothers' may not have been (see below). But where Africans are described with words that relate to their ethnicity these terms vary, perhaps reflecting the different ways those 'kindes of people' saw themselves, and even echoing how they wanted to be known or remembered. This is especially as many of the Africans present in Tudor England do not appear to have been dumb subalterns and would have had their own ideas about their identity.

The last idea is reflected in the use of words such as 'Blackamoore,' 'Negro' and 'Ethiopian' that all appear to be describing Africans in Tudor records who we now regard as 'dark skinned' with 'nine ether hair.'[9] But, in Tudor England these terms do not appear to have been used to separate Africans into indivisible groups where some of 'those kindes of people' were systematically defined as having no history or culture, as some modern anthropologists and historians do. In this sense, many of the Tudor writers discussed in this book seem to have an absence of the 'scientific' theories which were later used to define Africans as being 'doomed to slavery.'[10] In other words in Tudor society no such science existed, and even when Tudor writers such as Best do discuss theories which seem to have religious or quasi-scientific ideas behind them such as the 'curse of Ham,' this seems to only be an attempt at 'explaining' the 'blacknesse' of Africans they have seen in sixteenth-century England. Interestingly, in popular Tudor books such as the *Gentlemans Academie* or the *Book of St Albans* published in 1595 by Gervase

Markham, the 'curse of Ham theory' is quoted and discussed but not linked to Africans. Instead Markham claims that Africans are the descendants of Sem or Shem.[11]

Furthermore, Africans in Tudor England were not automatically thought of as slaves, and when the term 'slave' was used to describe a person's status it could relate to a person of any race as demonstrated in the Cartwright case (1569), and by the white English sailor Job Hortop (1550–1591) who claims that the Spanish made him into a 'slave.'[12] And this is further demonstrated by the English traveller Andrew Battell of Leigh (1565–1614?), who appears to have been treated as a slave by the Portuguese in 1600, in Bakongo in Africa itself.[13]

Moreover, even where powerful men and women in England called some Africans 'slaves' or 'escravos' these seem to have been nominal or temporary labels, borrowed from the country they were from as with Pero Alvarez – but this does not mean that he or other Africans had always been regarded as such, or that they would retain that status perpetually. For example, in Spain and Portugal the status of Iberian Moors appears to have been strongly influenced by the power of the Moorish kingdoms in Europe that many of them came from. As these kingdoms declined some Englishmen and other Europeans acknowledging this change in position may have tried to take advantage of 'those kindes of people,' such as the Mayor of Bristol William Hopkins. This also helps to explain the attitude of employers in the cases of Maria Moriana and the Ethiopian 'who utterly refused to serve.' But in Tudor England, English jurists would not legally support the employers of these Africans trying to treat them as slaves. The same seems to apply when the Dutch slave trader Senden and Englishmen such as Banes and the Sherleys attempted to obtain Africans living in Tudor England and sell them elsewhere.[14] All an African had to do was assume or assert they had rights, and sixteenth-century English jurisprudence seems to have been unwilling to take those rights away.

The reasons stated above help to explain why the Letters and the Proclamation are unlikely to have had sufficient validity or cogency to be enforced as law. In the sixteenth century no responsible English lawyer or politician appears to have been willing to create 'special race laws' to impose slavery on Africans living in England.[15] However, these documents also failed because they would be unlikely to appeal to the patriotism that they make reference to. In 1596 or 1601 it is unlikely that it would be seen as patriotic to publicly 'procure' and then trade the servants of Englishmen with an alien-enemy power. England was still at war with Spain and remained so until 1604. Those English merchants such as Thomas Malliard or Robert

Thorne who did trade with Spain during these years did so secretly. This provides another pragmatic reason why Robert Cecil did 'not like a patent of this sort,' in other words he did not want to be seen to be trading with a foreign adversary.[16]

In a similar way Elizabeth's lack of desire or 'pleasure' to be involved in domestic slavery are likely to have been spurred on by pragmatism. Most Englishmen in Tudor times did not have the power or interest in bringing large numbers of African slaves to Tudor England or of making the country a major slave trading nation, even in the Bristol case the Africans seem to have been returned to Portugal with no profit being made.[17] As late as 1621, the English merchant and trader Richard Jobson when he was invited to participate in the slave trade in West Africa said that 'we [the English] were a people who did not deal in any such commodities, neither did we buy or sell one another, or any that had our own shape ...' Jobson goes on to say that those Europeans who had historically been involved in slavery were 'another kind of people different from us.'[18] But we know that some English merchants were involved in slavery in the sixteenth and early-seventeenth centuries, but they were mostly middle-men despite receiving sponsorship or support by individuals inside the English government, exiled members of the Portuguese aristocracy, Iberian Conversos, some African dignitaries, and even a few avaricious merchants from Spain itself.[19] But none of these relationships were durable enough in the sixteenth century to make England a dominant player in that trade.

Furthermore, those Englishmen such as Winter, Drake, Raleigh and the Hawkins family, who were involved in slavery abroad, do not appear to have treated Africans in England as slaves. This can be seen in the examples of Domingo, Diego and others who were living in Tudor England.[20] It is unlikely that a merchant such as Drake automatically categorised every African as a slave simply because of the colour of their skin. It was expediency and probably not modern notions of racism which shaped Drake's and other English pirates' attitudes and behaviours towards Africans.

This expediency may also have shaped official silence on the status of Africans in Tudor England, and it means that without permanent laws to classify Africans as perpetually inferior, the status of 'those kindes of people' was often determined in the private sphere of sixteenth-century English society.[21] In that arena the status of Africans was linked to the skills 'those kindes of people' offered. In this way these Africans' status was being determined by factors that decided the position of other people in Tudor England. But ironically, some of the skills Africans possessed originated from or were developed in parts of continental Europe and West Africa. For example

Frauncis who I suggested may have been born in England, could still have learnt in Holland those skills which made him useful to his employer Peter Miller.

The skills some of these Africans had were useful to people present in Tudor England and gave them an advantage over their white counterparts. This may explain why in sixteenth-century English society Africans were not often displayed as mute-visual representations of their employers' power. Perhaps, some employers wanted to keep the 'gifts' of these Africans to themselves.

Moreover, if an African was from late sixteenth-century Iberia, or somewhere else where they had experienced persecution they may have strategically chosen to remain in the private sphere of Tudor society. Of course, once they were there, they are likely to have 'quietly' influenced the development of that society without being the subject of public attention. In that domain their 'gifts' appear to have been discreetly acknowledged by powerful people in Tudor England such as Henry VIII, Mary I, Elizabeth I, Katherine of Aragon, John Hawkins, Francis Drake, Walter Raleigh, William Winter, Hector Nunez, Hector Noviemies, John White, Paul Banning and Robert Cecil, as they employed Africans either indirectly at the English court, or in their households. It is difficult to imagine Africans being employed by these pre-eminent people if the former were not extremely competent at what they did. Moreover, some of these powerful men and women such as Katherine of Aragon may even have relied on the Africans they employed, and regarded them as familiar companions at times when other people in England were antipathetic to them.

Nevertheless, this does not mean there were not some pejorative notions about Africans present in Tudor society and we see evidence of this expressed in views about beauty.[22] Thomas More does this with Iberian Moors present in Tudor England, and the Scottish poet William Dunbar in 1507–8 mocks the presence of an African woman called 'Blak Margaret' at the 'Black Lady Day' pageants in Scotland.[23] But, Dunbar's comments about 'Blak Margaret' and More's on Katherine's ladies in waiting, do not seem to reflect the prevailing views of Scotsmen and Englishmen living in Scotland and England in the sixteenth century, especially since some Africans continued to be involved in pageantry in both countries.[24]

Pageantry and positive iconography sometimes go together as illustrated by the image of the young African man in Flinck's *Young Archer* (see Fig. 29). In Flinck's painting the African is holding a bow, echoing this weapon's ancient and classical association with Africans. Interestingly, in Flinck's painting the young man is holding the bow in his right hand, either indicating he is left handed, or that this is a symbolic weapon. The bow in West Africa in the fourteenth, fifteenth and sixteenth centuries was a representation of power.[25]

Some of the inclusion of Africans in Tudor pageantry also seems to have been because of positive ideas and images associated with 'those kindes of people' in medieval England. Medieval characters such as Morien and legends about Becket's mother may indicate an 'Old English' idea that Africans and blackness could be an indicator of nobility and dignity. Few historians have discussed this latter idea.[26] Moreover, it is likely that the symbolic representations of Africans in medieval England may have been psychologically important to a Tudor society that looked back. Englishmen in Tudor times, who went into the past to define their identity in their present, would have seen that medieval historians such as Richard Cirencester did not have strident views that linked Englishness to whiteness.[27] This may explain why most Englishmen in the Tudor period did not adopt a systematic racial policy which excluded Africans from being part of English history. Many Tudor writers were not willing to say who the first people in England were, perhaps reflecting what medieval English writers such as Cirencester had said that the 'original inhabitants of Britain whether indigenous or foreign are like most other countries unknown.'[28]

The images of Africans found in medieval and Tudor England may also echo this lack of a coherent negative racial agenda. These images include those in Westminster Abbey, the *Abbreviatio Domesday Book* and in Tudor times of John Blanke on the *Westminster Tournament Roll*. Other medieval images based on medieval English stories about Africans created iconic representations of 'those kindes of people' in Tudor towns and cities. In two cases this means that there were Africans such as Frauncis and Symon Valencia working in Tudor England in the beer making and metal working industries respectively, who were part of professions which had armorial signs depicting other Africans. Conceptually this is a significant finding, and shows how far we can move from an idea that all Africans in Tudor England were slaves.

Some of these African artisans who were present in Tudor England brought their skills from elsewhere, but it is not always easy to prove this as parish records often only provide evidence of a person's first moments and their last. Moreover, some parish clerks and priests may not have fully understood where a foreign-born African had come from, although, it may have been explained to them. This is especially likely as it appears some foreign-born Africans in Tudor England had 'divers' and multiple-ethnic backgrounds and origins, which may have seemed complex, but also interesting to some parish priests and clerks. This helps to explain why some foreign-born Africans such as Mary Fillis are more visible in Tudor documents than English-born 'Blackamoores;' and how their conversion as adults became an indication of the future victory of the newly formed English church over Catholicism. But this does not mean that foreign-born Africans constituted the majority of 'those kindes of people' in Tudor England. These notions explain why we cannot say with certainty whether English-born 'Blackamoores,' Iberian, or West Africans constituted a majority of the African population of Tudor England.

Despite the Africans in Tudor England having multiple-ethnic origins however, many seem to have been influenced by, or possessed cultural mores from Africa, even if these mores came via continental Europe. Indeed this cultural link may have made some of these Africans useful, interesting or appealing to ordinary people in Tudor England. This shows why some cultural styles and idioms were adopted and absorbed in Tudor England such as the Farthingale, fine Spanish needles and Moorish dances. By contrast, shops and businesses promoting aspects of continental-European culture which do not appear to have been influenced by these mores were targeted during the stranger riots.[29]

John Blanke and Katherine's ladies in waiting may have been seen by some in Tudor England not only as ambassadors of a culture which was more sophisticated than its white equivalent, but also of having mores which were more understandable and translatable. There are other examples within a more modern context that may help us to understand how this process worked. These are to be found with the way that aspects of African-American culture such as blues, jazz and soul music since the 1960's have been absorbed internationally – even at a time when other aspects of American culture was and remain highly indigestible.[30]

In sixteenth-century Europe, the skin complexion associated with Africans sometimes appears to have been seen as an indicator that the person was linked to a 'higher' Moorish culture. So this provides another reason why other Africans, in addition to Iberian Moors were retained in some Tudor households and entourages. Some of the Africans employed in this way came to Tudor England with their Italian, Spanish or Portuguese employers, and may have lived in Tudor society amongst these communities.[31] Some of these Africans appear to have been multilingual at a time when many white English people were not, and therefore 'those kindes' of people's skills would have been invaluable to certain sections of Tudor society including translators, historians, politicians, government intelligence officers and so on. But the historian Ian Smith suggests that these Africans would have spoken a broken or 'Black English' and gives a representation of it in *Race and Rhetoric*.³² But it is more likely that some of these Africans would have had a good grasp of other languages including English, since they were often coming from societies which were linguistically and culturally more advanced than Tudor England was.

So in Tudor England whether the Africans came from or via continental Europe, or originated directly from Africa, most do not seem to have been dumb subalterns waiting to be exploited. Pursuant to this some Africans came to Tudor England from Africa because they were active participants in world politics. For example, Africans came to London in 1589, 1595 and 1600 from North Africa with delegations which included Moroccan ambassadors. Thus a lively discourse developed in correspondence between the Moroccan leadership and the Queen of England which even saw the idea promulgated that she should marry one of those North-African princes. These relationships between Muslim leaders and some members of the English aristocracy developed despite warnings from Italian writers such as Caelius Augustinus Curio that such alliances were unholy. But ironically, in Tudor England someone such as Curio may have been considered as stranger than most of the Africans discussed in this book. This is because he was an Italian Catholic, and in many ways they were thought of as dangerous in a way that Iberian Moors, West Africans or English-born Blackamoores present in Tudor England were not.³³ A similar idea applies to the foreign-born Senden and is revealed in the petitions to Robert Cecil written in 1600, and alluded to in the second Letter when the writer admits Senden is a 'stranger,' and asks Englishmen to help him despite this status.³⁴

However, in other contemporary records those described initially appear to represent the epitome of strangeness, but further investigation reveals them not to be. This includes someone such as Lambert Waterson, and another African living in Tudor England called 'George,' his entry raises similar issues to Lambert's although he is not a Christian. George is described as 'a negar,' when he was buried on 11 March 1583 at St Botolph without Aldgate, London. In his record it says that he was called 'George' 'because his other names were not known' and this may have been because they were 'foreign.' Other information in his record also infers this such as the words 'Taethye [?] won [him] from Hambro [?],' and the fact that he was 'no parishioner.' All of this implies that George arrived recently in his parish from abroad, that he was a 'stranger,' and perhaps had the status of a slave when he was 'won.' However, in this entry it also says that George was 'lodged in the house of a John Mythell' 'in the manor of the Eastsmithfield,' and furthermore despite him not being a Christian, when he died his funeral charges were paid from a communal fund. All of this suggests that even though he may not have been in England long enough to be baptised, he was familiar enough to local people to receive their hospitality and compassion.[35] In other words, there is no suggestion that George was barred from becoming a 'parishioner', rather that he had not yet become one.

Moreover, where an African in Tudor England did decide to become a Christian this is likely to have had a positive impact on their status, not only locally, but also internationally as an African by being a member of the English Church would also become part of an international 'Protestant family'.[36] This may explain why people such as Mary Fillis or Lambert Waterson did not need to be forced into becoming Christians as they could see the benefits for themselves. Perhaps Mary Fillis and Waterson's motives resembled those shared by West Africans such as James Ongunby who was also baptised in Tudor England.

The evidence we have about Ongunby's baptism is extremely significant because it suggests his status is different to other West Africans who were taken to the Caribbean and the Americas in the eighteenth and nineteenth centuries. At that time those Africans had their own names taken from them to destroy their sense of identity. This occurred through a systematic policy where they were forced into accepting English names such as Garvey, King, Little and so on because these were the names of their slave owners. These Africans were not allowed to utter their African names and would certainly not be allowed to be baptised with them. Severe punishments including physical torture and mutilations were inflicted on those Africans who persisted in using their own names and this was done because slave owners and traders knew the importance of names to these people.[37] So this is a further indication that someone such as Ongunby is unlikely to be a slave, and as a free man he appears to be deciding for himself which parts of Englishness and Christianity he adopts as his own. In Tudor society baptisms such as that for Ongunby seem to have been used as cultural currency, rather than as a cultural weapon as they were in sixteenth-century Spain. Perhaps some Englishmen were learning how to use Christianity in this way from their interactions with Africans, or from studying the mistakes made by other Europeans.

Thus abuses committed in the Caribbean islands and parts of Africa by the colonial expansion of Spain, Portugal and the Ottoman Empire gave some English and Dutch Protestants opportunities to present themselves as a viable ally.[38] English merchants such as Drake and Hawkins through the Consortium sought relationships with, and had connections to Africans as a practical and logical extension of their desire to interrupt the power of Spain and Portugal in the Iberian Peninsula, Caribbean, West Africa and the Americas. The connections these Englishmen had with Africans from these places were another way for the former to succeed in their missions to acquire money and fame. This seems to have been most evident in the example of Diego Negro, but may also explain the relationships some English merchants had with other Africans from the Caribbean and West Africa. The knowledge some of these Africans had of trade routes to the North and South Atlantic would have made these people indispensable to cartographers and merchants as many white sailors and navigators, their counterparts, would be ignorant of this erudition.[39]

Africans also wanted something from these relationships, however. The international relations between England and some West-African civilisations encouraged a West-African presence in Tudor society. The West Africans such as Dederi from Cestos and Walter from Dungal arrived in England because of some of these diplomatic discourses, and they appear to have exercised a degree of ownership over the relationships they had with the English traders they interacted with. Moreover, these and other West Africans because of their importance in diplomatic relations seem to have been treated with hospitality, and this may have been guided by the way Englishmen were treated in West Africa.

Nevertheless just as Englishmen along with other Europeans were expected to comply with West-African customs in Africa,[40] so West Africans in Tudor England were expected to embrace English manners, customs and dress. But whether all Africans could, or were willing to conform appears to have been influenced by the places they were from. We saw with West Africans such as Domingo, Binne, George (from Benin), Dederi and Walter that they seemed more inclined to acculturate themselves, rather than the southern African 'Coree the Saldanian.' This may be because these West Africans and the societies they were from were advanced and worldly-wise enough to know what benefits such relationships may give. In the sixteenth century some of these West-African societies had in some ways surpassed those present in Tudor England.[41]

Can he speak for himself?!

However, it is unlikely that we are seeing the full extent of these Africans' contributions to Tudor society. This is because we hear about these 'kindes of people' not with their own words, and we see them not through their own eyes. Even in the case of Mary Fillis of Morisco who was baptised in 1597 in St Botolph, although at her baptism the recorder noted that 'shee made sute by hir said m(ist)res to have some conference with the Curat of [the] … parish' and that 'shee answer [ed] … him verie Christian lyke,' and said 'the Lordes Prayer,' and …'articles of hir beliefe …verie decently and well' – we are still deprived of her actual voice, and her true motivations.[42] So without an authentic African voice it is possible we may objectify the Africans present in Tudor England, ending up with research which is merely about 'those kindes of people'. I acknowledge this limitation, unlike most of the other writers who have written on this subject. But because of the need to base conclusions on evidence these issues cannot easily be resolved. But there is some evidence which may help us understand more. Interestingly, this is to be found in the most well-known and frequently read texts written in early modern England. These are the fictional and dramatic works of writers such as Shakespeare and Marlowe in which I suggest there are echoes of the voices of Tudor Africans. This is why the hopes, humour, frustrations and determination found in some of the speeches and asides of these African characters appears to underline that those 'kindes of people' in Tudor England were not naïve-ignorant playthings. Of course, throughout this book I have also acknowledged that some of the plays and masques written by white Englishmen contain negative, pejorative or fantastic ideas about Africans. But notwithstanding this, I am suggesting that African characters such as Othello, Aaron and the Moroccan Ambassador help us to get a glimpse of how some Africans in Tudor England saw the world.[43]

These African characters share a number of characteristics: firstly, all three Africans are formidable individuals who resist being treated or seen as inferior in the place where they are now present. In the case of Othello and Aaron it is suggested that they have no equal and cannot be defeated in the tests of arms. Secondly, they all have their own sense of honour which they fiercely defend, and in the case of Othello and Aaron they are prepared to kill and die for it. Thirdly, none of these Africans are slaves, even though in the case of Othello and Aaron they appear to have been, and they acknowledge that some of 'their people' are elsewhere. Fourthly, all of them are either engaged in relationships with white women or are seeking such a relationship. Fifthly, all three live within integrated communities where they are not segregated from white people because of the colour of their skin. All of these ideas may show that Africans in Tudor England had similar beliefs, background, and patterns of behaviour, and that perhaps as these characters do they demanded respect. These ideas are most evident in a speech Othello makes before the officials of Venice when he is charged with using witchcraft to win Desdemona's love. Because of the evidence in this book we can now look at Othello's words with a new perspective:

Her father loved me; oft invited me;
Still questioned me the story of my life,
From year to year – the battles, sieges, fortunes,
That I have passed.
I ran it through, even from my boyish days,
To th' very moment that he bade me tell it;
Wherein I spake of most disastrous chances,
Of moving accidents by flood and field
Of hair-breadth scapes i' the imminent deadly breach,
Of being taken by the insolent foe
And sold to slavery; of my redemption thence
And portance in my travailous history:
Wherein of antres vast and deserts idle,
Rough quarries, rocks and hills whose heads touch heaven
It was my hint to speak – such was my process –
…

My story being done,
She gave me for my pains a world of sighs,
She swore in faith 'twas strange, 'twas passing strange,
'Twas pitiful, 'twas wondrous pitiful:
…

Yet she wished
That heaven had made her such a man
…

Upon this hint I spake:
She loved me for the dangers I had pass'd,
And I loved her that she did pity them.
This only is the witchcraft I have used:

…
Duke of Venice
I think this tale would win my daughter too.[44]

I am not the first to suggest that such a speech may echo the words of some Africans present in Tudor England, and this is discussed in more detail by writers such as Harry Lee Faggett, B. J. Sokol and Elaine Robinson. However, what I will add is that Othello's speech seems to dramatically present line by line many of the themes discussed in this book. Such as the theory in the last chapter that some Africans in Europe were defining their own identities and were capable of orally articulating this, although, of course in *Othello*, Shakespeare as a white English playwright is doing this for us.

There is another less well-known seventeenth-century African character, also penned by a white writer, who speaks with eloquence and dignity. He is the character called Juan de Meridea and is the hero of the play *El Valiente Negro en Flanders* or *The Gallant Black Man in Flanders*, written by the Spanish author Andres da Claramonte who was born in 1580 and died in 1626. The character Juan Meridea who is identical to Othello rises from obscurity to become loved, feared and respected so much so that he obtains the complete confidence of the Duke of Alba. Once he attains the rank of general he marries the daughter of the man who once held him in bondage. Meridea is robust in the defence of his own humanity and his speeches echo those of his English counterpart. He says:

> Con la infamia del color acabo,
> Y al mundo mi valor significo
> Pues aunque negro soy, no soy escravo.[45]

This translated means:

> With infamy or dishonour my colour is associated,
> [But] To all the world my courage will be more important
> Well then I am Black but, I am no slave.

Similar ideas of self affirmation are echoed in statements recorded by the sixteenth-century Spanish writer Sebastian de Covarrubias Horozco. In his Spanish dictionary called *Tesoro de la Lengua Castellano O Espanola*, first published in 1610 and then revised in 1611, with his description of 'a Negro' he quotes the proverb 'Aunque negros gente somos.'[46] This translates as 'though we are Black we are people.' Covarrubias offers this phrase as one created by Africans, and it suggests a self-effacing, and some may say self-deprecating defence of blackness. But this term originates from a much older and longer phrase that according to the seventeenth-century Spanish writer Gonzalo Correas is 'Aunke somo Negro, onbre somo, alma tenemo.'[47] This means 'Even if Black, we are men, with the souls of human beings': the word 'onbre' being a pronunciation of the Spanish word 'hombre' meaning 'men,' the former being a reflection of the dialect of Africans speaking 'hable de negros,' or 'fala da Guine.'[48] So the latter phrase offers a more spirited defence of humanity, with the eponymous 'Even if,' almost dismissing the idea that Africans are less than human and offering manhood and the human spirit as entirely compatible with the blackness of one's complexion.

Nevertheless, and notwithstanding what I have stated above, we are still left with the fact that we do not have an authentic African voice that represents 'those kindes of people' in Tudor England. Without a voice that helps a modern historian to normalise and contextualise the African presence in Tudor England we may not see them clearly – but with two contradictory perspectives. In other words, Africans in Tudor England are either all dejected slaves or happy-go-lucky kings and queens. But this notion of opposites is more about our recent prejudices concerning race and not necessarily about how Tudor Englishmen saw Africans. Some of these issues are revealed by looking at specific entries in the *Diary of Henry Machyn*.

Machyn's diary was written between the years of 1550 and 1563 and it provides a day-by-day account on the life and times of mid-sixteenth-century London. In his diary there are numerous references to 'Mores danse' and 'mores dance' and 'younge morens.' Historians such as John Forrest and John Cutting suggest that words such as 'Mores' and 'morens' that Machyn uses do not describe Africans.[49] But an earlier historian Jonathan Eastwood identifies the last reference of 'younge morens' as a description of young Africans dancing.[50] It is interesting that in this case it is the more recent historians who believe without obvious, and in some cases negative references to Africans that Tudor writers could not be describing 'those kindes of people.' Other historians such as Anthony Gerard Barthelemy also tend to follow this pattern, and look for derogatory and prejudicial views that fit within their own perspective on how they believe Africans would have been seen.[51] In other words, terms such as 'the people of London,' 'the local population' or 'younge morens' are presumed not to include Africans because they are not pejorative enough. Therefore the way Africans are purported to have been treated in the Bristol case, or comments made by Best, Hanmer or those contained in the Letters and the Proclamation become the only evidence that they will consider actually relates to Africans. Other evidence such as that contained in Machyn's diary is disregarded. Then with this one-sided information about Africans we could conclude that they were thought of as inferior in Tudor England, when in fact our conclusions merely represent our prejudices in collecting, interpreting and understanding the evidence we have.[52]

To explain this further there is another entry in Machyn's diary that this time makes an obvious reference to an African. It is dated 3 November 1554,

> [there] began a grett frey at Charing Cross at viij of the choke [clock?] at night between the Spaniards and Englishmen, the which through wisdom there were

but a fewe hurt and after the next day there were [some or certain] taken that began it; one was a blake-mor, and was brought a-for the … knight–marshall servants.[53]

Machyn's remark that an African was one of those who 'began a grett frey' raises many questions, but also provides clarity to some of the points raised in this book. Perhaps, this African was just singled out because of his colour although, I suggest for all the reasons stated this is unlikely. One issue that does arise here is that in the fight the African must have been on either the English or Spanish side. If we presume the 'blake-mor' is a he, it seems logical from what Machyn tells us that he was not part of a third group of Blackamoore protagonists. In addition, Machyn's comments shows us that this particular Spanish or English 'blake-mor' appears to have been nationalistic enough to be a ringleader and fight on behalf of his nation. Machyn's statements coupled with the evidence in this book suggests that there are other Africans involved in this 'frey,' and bearing in mind all that has been discussed, it is not unreasonable to propose that they could have fought on both sides.[54] Machyn's comments show that this African's existence and ethnicity is significant enough to be noted, but it is not so remarkable that it is worthy of further comment. This 'blake-mor' is unlikely to be the only African that Machyn has heard about, rather his comments seem to reveal that Africans are familiar to him, and he expects them to be familiar to his Tudor audience. So, I am suggesting Machyn is normalising the presence of this African, and offering a context that suggests other Africans are familiar too. This confirms what I have proposed throughout this book, some of which becomes even more evident when we examine the position of African women in Tudor England.

Lucy Negro and her sisters

Throughout this book I have talked about African women being present in Tudor England. However there are some issues about these women which have been raised but not yet fully analysed, and they reveal what happened to the African population as a whole. In examining these issues it is important to state that some African women in the same way as men were servants in Tudor England, and their skills appear to have been useful to their employers. The evidence in parish records suggests that many African women were also integrated members of their Tudor parishes; and were not treated as chattels, 'breeders' and 'mammies' as some of 'those kindes of' women were later to be in the Americas.[55]

Nevertheless, historians such as Barthelemy, Habib, Hall and Ungerer, claim that in Tudor society African women were discriminated against once because of the colour of their skin, secondly because of their sex, and thirdly through their low status. Barthelemy and Hall support their arguments with evidence from the letters of some fifteenth- and sixteenth-century English travellers who had been to West Africa, and reveal an idea of 'white patriarchy,' with the white male explorer dominating the Black female native. But this sort of domination is unlikely to have taken place in Tudor England although it was taking place in some other parts of the world.[56] This is also despite the evidence that historians such as Habib present regarding the disproportionately high numbers of morganatic and interracial unions between African women and white men.[57] I suggest that the relationships described in Tudor parish records are not necessarily an indication of African women being discriminated against because of their colour of their skin. Instead these records may reveal something else more complicated that is happening in Tudor England.

It does appear that in Tudor England many of the African women who are described as being in interracial unions are in domestic service, and they seem to have been made pregnant either by their employers, or others described as important men connected to this employment. The effect of these morganatic unions is likely to have been that the children produced did not inherit any title from the 'supposed father.' In Tudor England, in these situations, the 'supposed fathers' often paid the mother alimony for the child's welfare.[58] But in other cases a single-parent mother may have ended up being unable to work and therefore dependent on charitable relief from within her parish.[59] The question is whether in Tudor England African women found themselves in these circumstances because of their race, and what affect this had on the long-term development of African families in English society.

Let us examine the situation of 'Helene, daughter of Cristian the Negro servant to Richard Sheere, the supposed father binge Cuthbert Holman, illeg.' Helene was baptised on 2 May 1593 at St Andrew's, Plymouth. From this entry we can see there are two people identified here. One is Cristian a 'Negro servant,' the other is her daughter Helene the subject of the baptism. We can infer that Cristian had a relationship with a white person from the lack of racial identification of Cuthbert in comparison with her entry. As with many of the Africans discussed we do not know whether Cristian was born here, and we do not know her age. What we do know is that Cristian was not married to the 'supposed' father of her child Cuthbert Holman.

However, these parish records do not help us answer the question of whether the relationship she had with Cuthbert was consensual and why he did not marry her. But Cristian appears a year later in another record that shows she had a second child who also seems to be illegitimate, because the father is also not named. In this entry as in the first 'Richard Sheer' is described as her employer although, it is possible that this time he may be the father. In this second entry Cristian's child is also named 'Cristian' and she apparently dies within the first year of her life, and is buried on 14 April 1594 at St Andrew's, Plymouth.[60]

This last entry for Cristian's child helps us see the mother's status and position clearer. Cristian is a woman who gives birth to two illegitimate children within a year of each other, and this illustrates what could be an uncertain future for her as a woman servant in Tudor England. We see an almost identical pattern occurring in the same city, and in the same year, with another African woman called 'Mary'. Her child called 'Cristien' was baptised on 17 November 1594 at St Andrew's, Plymouth. This 'Cristien' is described as 'a negro of John Whites' and the 'supposed daughter of John Kinge, a Dutchman illeg.' The Mary under discussion here could be the same one named on 23 June 1603 at St Andrew's, Plymouth, who gives birth to another illegitimate child called Richard. This 'base' child's 'reputed father' is 'Rog Hoggett.' We do not know whether any of the relationships Mary had were consensual.[61]

There is an additional record of a similar kind to the ones mentioned which illustrates that evidence of these types of unions are to be found in other cities, towns and villages in Tudor England. This record is from St George's parish in Bristol and is for 'Richard a Bastard the sonne of Joanne Marya a Blackemore and was not the wife of Thomas Smythe by the latter (?) was baptised the 15 day of August 1600.'[62] The 'Thomas Smythe' mentioned in Richard's record is probably the same famous entrepreneur and merchant who became Governor of the East India Company and a member of the Worshipful Company of Haberdashers and Skinners. Perhaps Marya came to England via Smythe's connections to international trade.[63] In this record the statement 'Joanne Marya [as] ... not the wife of Thomas Smythe' is unusual, but as we read it now it seems to imply that he has a closer connection to her than merely being the sponsor of the child's baptism. If this is so, and he is the father of her child, Smythe was powerful and rich enough to have his name expunged from Richard's parish record, so it is difficult to know why in Marya's case he did not. Perhaps Richard relied on Marya's 'daily work' and 'labour,' and by sponsoring the baptism he sought to comply with one legal enactment the Statute of Artificers 1563, which attempted to force single mothers back into the homes of their masters;[64] whilst avoiding the legal and moral responsibilities of a father.

The final example of an African woman who is a single-parent shows how these unions stretch from the end of the Tudor period into the seventeenth century. This record is for Grace who was living in Hatherleigh in Devon where she was baptised on 13 May 1604. On 10 August 1606 at the same village Grace had a daughter baptised called 'Rebecca,' this child was described as 'a base daughter of Grace, a negyer [negro].' The child did not live long and died on 23 December 1607. Four years later Grace had a second daughter baptised on 8 May 1611 called 'Honour,' who was described as 'a Negro.' This 'illegitimate' child also died young and was buried two years later on 6 June 1613.[65]

The records for Grace reveal her vulnerability as she is unmarried and some of the children she has had with a man or men, have died within a few years of their birth. The fact that she is able to receive baptisms for herself and her daughters suggests that she was an integrated member of her church and parish, despite her bearing two illegitimate children. But what eventually happens to Grace is difficult to discover because after 1613 she drops out of the archives, and this may be because she has moved to another village, or she has passed away. This same pattern appears to have happened with other African women in Tudor England.

There are other explanations however, to the predicament faced by Grace and the other African women mentioned above. One of them, although I doubt its likelihood, is an idea that these records are really describing prostitutes. As stated in Chapter 2, there are legends of a 'Lucy Negro or Banthym' and some evidence of Black female prostitutes or 'black birds' in Tudor London.[66] Nevertheless, I suggest the women above are unlikely to be 'black birds,' because the evidence of African women being involved in morganatic unions in Tudor England is common for women in domestic service. In Tudor England, if a woman became pregnant from one of these unions it would have been her extended family which ensured there was a marriage or provision made for the child.[67] However, if an African woman came to England from another country, or was descended from a person who had come alone, she may not have developed a family network which was strong enough to demand this kind of marriage or provision. This may have made the African women whether foreign or English-born vulnerable. In that situation as the historian Patricia Crawford and others suggest, the church would probably have become that woman's support.[68]

So the records above reveal an underlying inscription of hardship, but do not support the notion that these women's race has marked them as inferior to other people present in their parish. In fact these records in a similar way to others in this book indicate that these African women were integrated enough to receive help from their church. This is supported by the fact that in Tudor parishes the 'notions of charity were giving way to considerations of community, and the idea of belonging ... [was a] crucial' qualification for any charitable provision.[69] So the fact that these women were receiving support from their local churches, and were able to have themselves and their children baptised, indicates they were part of their community.

However, as the historian Philippa Maddern has outlined, there is another factor which may show us what was happening to African women in Tudor England. This is that for a woman in domestic service being pregnant could be perilous no matter what ethnicity they were. It was a danger, it seems, which was unaffected by the woman's martial status, as a pregnant married woman may be unable to join her husband and could have her marriage nullified by the 'master of the house':[70] this power was justified through morality and religion.[71] So it is possible that some of the African women mentioned in this chapter because of their pregnancy were dislodged 'from any networks they had built,' and were reduced to poverty. In other words, as in the case of a woman called Frances Palmer (ethnicity unknown) who gave birth to twins in the Cross Keys area of London in 1603, she 'ended up ... a vagrant, but ... started, like her children's father, as a servant.'[72] Of course in the case of some of the African women discussed in this book, the father of their children or their own status may have started out more elevated than Frances' was. But the important point is that it seems it is not these African women's race per se that has made them poor-single mothers, but it may be the circumstances that they find themselves in through being in domestic service.

These records appear to demonstrate that no matter what skills these African women had, as single mothers they would probably end up in poverty. This is an ignoble end for women who may have had so many 'gifts.' But there is another more intriguing issue; and this pertains to the relationships African women had with African men. From the records discovered so far, it appears that African women and men were so integrated in Tudor society that they may have ended up not having children with each other. Such an idea raises the possibility that they were living parallel lives, highlighted by the fact they were often living side by side in certain areas of London and Plymouth. Ultimately, this parallel existence would have meant very few same-race marriages and this would have had an extremely detrimental effect on the sustainability of an African presence in England.

Those few African men and women who were involved in same-race marriages appear to have been Iberian Moors who brought their spouses with them from abroad, and this includes Catalina de Cardones and her husband who was a man 'from her country' probably Granada in Spain. And another African woman in the early part of the seventeenth century called Anne Vause who was buried on 24 April 1618 at St Botolph without Aldgate, London. Vause is described as 'a Black-more wife to Anthonie Vause, Trompetter of the said Country;' although we do not know whether the 'blacke trumpeter' John Blanke also married a woman of his 'said countrey,' on 14 January 1512.[73]

Interestingly, Miranda Kaufmann has found evidence of four other same-race marriages from the beginning of the seventeenth century. Three of these married couples are located in one parish that is St Dunstans and All Saints in Stepney, London. It is extremely significant to have so many same-race marriages being recorded in one area, bearing in mind that throughout the country during the Tudor period they are hardly recorded at all. This matter is worthy of further investigation and more information can be found on these couples from Kaufmann's research.[74]

As we have discussed Tudor records often leave out a lot of information, and we are left to draw conclusions from what is available.[75] An idea that is connected to this theory is that despite these few same-race marriages, and because of the issues above, Africans in Tudor England would eventually become so integrated they would lose their racial distinctiveness.[76] Therefore, what we are left with in Tudor records are echoes and footprints of this African population, despite their contribution, and the impact they had on various levels of that society. It is ironic that because Tudor England was a less racially-conscious society this may have been the most important factor in the eventual decline of that African population, not through mass expulsions or genocide, but through assimilation. Of course some Africans such as Grace gave birth to children at the end of the Tudor period, and in a different way to her family some of these people survived. However, even those children who survived into the seventeenth century appear to have assimilated to such an extent that their descendants forfeited their racial distinctiveness; although this issue is really the subject of another book.

Notes

[1] Guildhall Library, London, GL Ms 4448 etc.; Plymouth and West Devon Record Office, Plymouth, St Andrews, MF 1–4; Bristol Record Office, Bristol, 15/8/1575/ Ref. Bristol RO P/Dy/R/1a; Bristol Record Office, St Philip and Jacob's Church Bristol, 14/12/1603, etc; National Archives Kew, 'Will of Nicholas Wichehalse,' Barnstable, Devon, 23/9/1570, Ref. Ward 7/13/29; North Devon Record Office, Devon, 6/4/1596, 10/4/1598, 22/5/1596, 22/5/1605 etc. Ref. MFc 46/6–7; Wiltshire and Swindon History Centre, Wiltshire, *Colne Parish Register*, ref. 2083/1, n. p.; Worcestershire Archive, Worcestershire, Holt Parish Register, ref. 985, n. p.

² Guildhall Library, London, GL Ms 9222/3/4, etc; a selection of these entries, and others where the ethnicity is uncertain are included in the Bibliography.

³ Luther Porter Jackson, 'Elizabethan Seamen and the African Slave Trade,' *The Journal of Negro History*, 9: 1, Jan., 1924, pp. 1–17; and Earl Thorpe, *Black Historians: A Critique* (New York: Publisher unknown, 1958, new edition, New York: Morrow, 1971), pp. 111, 177, 234 (on Jackson).

⁴ Laura Gowing, 'Giving Birth at the Magistrates Gate: Single Mothers in the Early Modern City,' in, Susan Broomhall and Stephanie Tarbin (eds.), *Women, Identities and Communities in Early Modern Europe* (Aldershot: Ashgate, 2008), pp. 137–(145 quotations) 150.

⁵ Evidence throughout this book; and in Author unknown, *St Botolph without Aldgate Memorandum Daybook*, Volume I (London: Parish of St Botolph without Aldgate, 1586–1588), pp. 30, 149; St Olave Hart Street, Parish Register, GL Ms 28867; William Bruce Bannerman (ed.), *Registers of St Olave Hart Street, London, 1563–1700* (London: Harleian Society, 1916); Devon Record Office, TD 38 1906 28/08/1570; Richard Kirk (ed.), Ernest Kirk (ed.), *Returns of Aliens Dwelling in ... London*, Volume I–III (Aberdeen: Huguenot Society, The Publications of the Society, 1902–1907), passim.

⁶ Ruth Pike, *Aristocrats and Traders: Sevillian Society in the Sixteenth Century* (Ithaca: Cornell University Press, 1972), p. 188.

⁷ David MacRitchie, *Ancient and Modern Britons ...* (1884, 2ⁿᵈ edition 1985, 3ʳᵈ edition, Los Angeles: Preston, 1986), Volume I, p. 67, Volume II. pp. 125, 186.

⁸ John Stow, Edmund Howes, *The Annales, or Generall Chronicle of England, Begun First by Maister Iohn Stow, and After him Continued ... vnto the Ende of this Present Yeere 1614, by E. Howes* (London: Thomas Dawson for Thomas Adams, 1615), pp. 790, 948.

⁹ Andrew Boorde, *Introduction to the Book of Knowledge ...* (London: William Copeland, 1550), pp. 88–89; George Best, *A True Discourse ...* (London: H. Bynyman, 1578), pp. 28–32; John Minsheu, *A Dictionarie in Spanish and English ...* (London: E. Bollifaunt, 1599), p. 72; Edward Blount (tr.), Ieronimo Conestaggio, *The Historie of ... Portugal ...* (London: A. Hatfield for E. Blount, 1600), 1, 5, 7, 39; and John Pory (tr.), Leo Africanus, *A Geographical Historie of Africa* (London: John Pory, 1600), p. 6.

¹⁰ Last quotation from the *Dred Scott Case, Scott v Sandford*, Chief Justice Roger B. Taney, United States Supreme Court (1857), 60 U.S. 393; Marnie McCuen, *The Genocide Reader: The Politics of Ethnicity and Extermination* (Hudson: Gem Publications, 2000); Leo Kuper Foundation, *The Genocide Reader (Criminology)* (2007, new edition, London: Routledge, 2009), both throughout on science, culture, race and inferiority.

¹¹ Gervase Markham, *The Gentlemans Academie, or the Booke of S. Albans; Containing Three Most Exact and Excellent Bookes: The First of Hawking, the Second of all the Proper Terms of Hunting and the Last of Armorie: All Compiled by Juliana Barnes in the Yere from the Incarnation of Christ 1486: And Now Reduced into a Better Method by G. M. (i.e. Gervase Markham.) ... (by Richard Farmer)* (London: Humfrey Lownes, 1595), pp. 43–44, (Markham links the 'curse of Ham' to the 'curse of Caine' but does not use either idea to stigmatise any race).

¹² Job Hortop, *The Rare Travails of Job Hortop an Englishman Who was Not Heard of ... his ... Slavery and much Bondage with the Spanish Galley* (London: William Wright, 1591), pp. A1–C4; and Case: *In the Matter of Cartwright*, 11 Elizabeth, 2 Rushworth's College (1569), p 468.

¹³ Andrew Battell, *The Strange Adventures of Andrew Battell of Leigh, in Angola and Adjoining Regions* (London: Hakluyt Society, 1901), pp. 110–136.

¹⁴ A different view is expressed by Imtiaz Habib, *Shakespeare and Race ...* (Lanham: University Press of America, 1999), pp. 1–5; and Folarin Shyllon, *Black People in Britain 1553–1833* (Oxford: Oxford University Press, 1977), p. 3.

15 These 'special laws' were created in France in 1685 called 'Code Noir' and they were enforced in their colonies. Similar laws were created in the United States of America during the nineteenth century and were also known as 'Black Codes' or 'Black laws' in Richard Juang, Noelle Morrissette (eds.), *Africa and the Americas: Culture, Politics, and History: A Multidisciplinary Encyclopedia* (Santa Barbara/Oxford: ABC-CLIO, 2008), pp. 277–279; Junius Rodriguez (ed.), *Slavery in the United States: A Social, Political, and Historical Encyclopedia*, Volume 2 (Santa Barbara/Oxford: ABC-CLIO, 2007), pp. 7, 13, 230–231, 541–543; and Molefi Kete Asante, Ama Mazama, *Encyclopedia of Black Studies* (London: Sage Publications, 2005), pp. 188–189.

16 Last quotation from Robert Cecil paraphrased by Casper Van Senden and Thomas Sherley in 'Cecil Papers Petition, Merchant of Lubeck to the Queen,' November day unknown, 29 November, 29 December 1600, *Calendar of the Manuscripts of the Most Honourable the Marquess of Salisbury* (London: Historical Manuscripts Commission, 1883–1976), Volume 10, pp. 399, 431, Volume 14, p. 143; Pauline Croft, 'Trading with the Enemy, 1585–1604,' *Historical Journal*, 32, June 1989, pp. 281–302; Pauline Croft, 'English commerce with Spain and the Armada War, 1558–1603,' in Simon Lester Adams, M. J. Rodriguez-Salgado (eds.), *England, Spain and the Gran Armada, 1585–1604: Essays from the Anglo-Spanish Conferences* (1988, new edition, Edinburgh: Rowman and Littlefield, 1991), pp. 236–263; and Albert Loomie, 'Religion and Elizabethan Commerce with Spain,' *The Catholic Historical Review*, 50, April 1964, pp. 27–51.

17 Hopkins, *Letter to Lord Burghley*, October 1590, in *Lansdowne Manuscripts*, no. 115, item 83, pp. 236–239.

18 Richard Jobson, *The Golden Trade: Or, A Discovery of the River Gambia ... Set Down* [in] ... *the Yeares, 1620 and 1621* (London: Nicholas Oke, 1623), p. 140.

19 A view shared by, Croft, in, 'Trading with the Enemy, 1585–1604,' pp. 281–302; Croft, 'English commerce with Spain and the Armada War, 1558–1603,' pp. 236–263; and Loomie, 'Religion and Elizabethan Commerce with Spain,' pp. 27–51.

20 National Archives, Kew, London, *High Courts of Admiralty (HCA) Reports*, 1547, Ref. 24/39/49–51; and this applies to other Africans in the homes of the Raleighs in Alfred Leslie Rowse, *Raleigh and the Throckmortons* (London/New York: Macmillan Company, St Martin's Press, 1962), p. 121.

21 A different view is presented in Gerard Barthelemy, *Black Face, Maligned Race ...* (London: LSU Press, 1987), pp. introduction, preface, 21, 48, 49; and Thomas Earle, Kate Lowe (eds.), *Black Africans in Renaissance Europe* (Cambridge: Cambridge University Press, 2005), pp. xv, 13, 35, 23, 102–103.

22 Stephen Gundle, 'The Bella Italiana and the English Rose,' in Manfred Pfister, Ralf Hertel (eds.), *Performing National Identity: Anglo-Italian Cultural Transactions* (Amsterdam: Rodopi, 2007), pp. 137–155; and Barthelemy, *Black Face Maligned Race*, p. 55.

23 William Dunbar in Richard Maitland (ed.), *Ancient Scottish Poems Never Before in Print*, Volume I (London and Edinburgh: C. Dilly, 1786), p. 97; (Dunbar calls this African woman 'Anne Blak Moi' and he describes her as having 'mekkle [fulsome] lips,' a 'jaw like an ape,' oily skin like a 'frog' and of being as black as coal 'tar.' 'Blak Margaret' was put forward at the 'Black Lady days' as a symbol of beauty and symbolically betrothed to James IV of Scotland); Patricia Hill Buchanan, *Margaret Tudor Queen of Scots* (Edinburgh/London: Scottish Academic Press, 1985), pp. 52–53(n.), 136 (These African women were brought to England from Portugal by a Scottish merchant Robert Barton. Paul Edwards, James Walvin, *Black Personalities in the Era of the Slave Trade* (London: Palgrave, Macmillan, 1983), p. 33.

24 Thomas More fifty-six years later may have changed his view when he says the 'blackness' of 'black people' is natural in Thomas More, William Rastell (ed.), *The Works of Sir*

Thomas More Knyght ... *The First Boke* (London: John Cawod, Richard Tottell, 1557), pp. 125-127.

[25] Govaert Flinck, *Young Archer*, 1639-1640, oil on oak panel, 66.2 x 50.8 cm, 67.7 x 52 cm, Frame size: 83.5 x 69 cm, Netherlands, ref. P 238, @ Wallace Collection, Hertford House, Manchester, see figure 29. This seventeenth-century 'noble' African reflects ancient and early modern traditions of African archers. Nubia was known as 'the land of the bow,' see Chancellor Williams, *Destruction of Black Civilisation* ... (Chicago: Third World Press, 1987), pp. 57, 144, 198, 209. On African archery in general see Charles E. Grayson, Mary French, *Traditional Archery From Six Continents: The Charles E. Grayson Collection* (Columbia: University of Missouri, 2007), pp. 132-163; Daniel Hays, 'From the Land of the Bow Black Soldiers in the Ancient and Near East,' *Bible Review*, August 1998, pp. 29-33, 50-51. On the bow as a symbol of power see Basil Davidson, *African Civilisation Revisited: From Antiquity to Modern Times* (Trenton: Africa World Press, 1991), p. 98; and David S. Conrad, *Empires of Medieval West Africa Ghana, Mali and Songhay* (New York: Infobase Publishing, 2005), p. 44.

[26] The following writers offer a contrary view Dorothy Auchter, *Dictionary of Literary and Dramatic Censorship in Tudor and Stuart England* (Westport: Greenwood Publishing Group, 2001), pp. 128-129; and Pierre Frederick Inman Portal, W.S. (tr) *An Essay on Symbolic Colours: In Antiquity- The Middle Ages- and Modern Times* (London: J. Weale, 1845), pp. introduction, 9, 7, 10, 12, 20-23, 26, 27, 30.

[27] The concept of English identity being shaped by conflict with the Scots, Welsh, Normans etc. and not necessarily by skin colour is discussed by Benjamin Bradshaw and Peter Roberts (eds.), *British Consciousness and Identity: And the Making of Britain, 1533-1707* (Cambridge: Cambridge University Press, 1998), pp. 2-13, 110-112, 142; and Hans Kohn and Craig J. Calhoun, *The Idea of Nationalism: A Study in its Origins and Background* (New York: Macmillan, 1944), pp. 6-12, 156-162.

[28] Richard Cirencester in John Allen Giles (tr. ed.), *The Chronicle of Richard of Devizes Concerning the Deeds of Richard the First, King of England: Also Richard of Cirencester's Description of Britain* (London: James Bohn, 1841), p. 89; and Geoffrey of Monmouth in his fables and legends includes 'black giants' and Africans amongst some of England's early populations in Aaron Thompson (tr.), *British History, Translated into English from the Latin of Jeffrey of Monmouth* ... (London: J Boyer, 1718), pp. preface, 246, 362, 363, 365.

[29] Stow, *A Summary of the Chronicles of England, Abridged and Continued unto 1598*, pp. 768-769 (stranger riots); and Andrew Spicer, in Nigel Goose, Lieun Luu (eds.) *Immigrants in Tudor and Early Stuart England* (Eastbourne: Sussex Academic Press, 2005), p. 92. Similar views are expressed by Harry Lee Faggett, *Black and Other Minorities* ... (Prairie View: Prairie View Press, 1971), p. 6; and Ian Smith, *Race and Rhetoric in the Renaissance* ... (Basingstoke: Palgrave Macmillan, 2009), pp. 10-12.

[30] Heike Raphael-Hernandez, *Blackening Europe: The African-American Presence* (New York/London: Routledge, 2003), pp. introduction, 142-154; William Dean, *The American Spiritual Culture: And the Invention of Jazz, Football and the Movies* (New York/London: Continuum International Publishing Group, 2006), pp. 52-54, 119-128, 143-144. This idea is illustrated, rather ironically by the revelation that the most strident critic of Americanism Osama Bin Laden had a predilection for soul music, and an obsession for Whitney Houston in Marina Hyde, *Celebrity: How Entertainers Took Over the World and Why we Need an Exit Strategy* (London: Harvill-Secker, 2009), p. 7.

[31] James Laurence Bolton (ed.), *Alien Communities of London in the Fifteenth Centuries* (Stamford: Richard III and York History Trust with Paul Watkins, 1998), pp. 1-15, 23, 35-38.

[32] Ian Smith, *Race and Rhetoric in the Renaissance*, pp. 10, 11, 12, 15, 17, 73.

[33] Richard Hakluyt, *The Principal Navigations* ... Volume VI (London: Hakluyt's Collection, 1598), p. 137 (Moroccan ambassadors); William Percy, Mathew Dimmock, *William Percy's Mahomet and his Heaven: A Critical Edition* (Aldershot: Ashgate Publishing, 2006), pp. 6–11 (Moroccan ambassadors); Nabil Matar, *Islam in Britain, 1558–1685* (New York: Cambridge University Press, 1998), p. 2; Nabil Matar, *Turks Moors and Englishmen in the Age of Discovery* (New York/London: Columbia University Press, 1999), pp. 21, 64; Caelius Augustinus Curio, *A Notable History of the Saracens* ... (London: William How and Abraham Veale, 1575), pp. introduction, preface, 1, 27; and John Stubbs, *The Discoverie of a Gaping Gulf* (1579), pp. 4, 32, 35, 42 (on Moors and a Moorish marriage).

[34] Author unknown, Letter to the Lord Mayors, signed 18 July 1596; Casper Van Senden and Thomas Sherley, 'Petitions to Robert Cecil,' 1600, *Calendar of the Manuscripts of the Most Honourable the Marquess of Salisbury*, Volume 14 (London: Historical Manuscripts Commission, 1883–1976), pp. 143, 144, 154.

[35] Author unknown, *St Botolph without Aldgate Memorandum Daybook*, Volume I (London: Parish of St Botolph without Aldgate, 1586–1588), f. 30 (George was thirty-years old when he died).

[36] Of course this depends on when the African joined the English church. Before 1534 the African would be part of the Roman Catholic Church of England which is also likely to have granted them a certain status. I have not yet found evidence of Africans present in non-conformist churches in Tudor England.

[37] Gwendolyn Midlo Hall, *Slavery and African Ethnicities in the Americas: Restoring the Links* (Chapel Hill: University of North Carolina, 2005), pp. introduction, 22–25, 32–37, 52–54 (anomaly of African names amongst Creoles in Louisiana), 132–134; Yosef Ben-Jochannan, *Cultural Genocide in the Black and African Studies Curriculum* (New York: ECA Associates, 1972), p. 135; Ronald J. Deloach, *Living Without a Name: A View Through Black Eyes* (Pittsburgh: Dorrance Publishing Co. Inc., 2009), pp. 4–10, 22–29; Chantal J. Zabus, *Tempests After Shakespeare* (New York: Basingstoke: Palgrave, 2002), pp. 38, 46–60 (Names, slavery and the renaissance), 144, 149, (African nations also tried to reclaim their former names), 150; and Marcus Garvey, Martin Luther King, Malcolm Little (X) acknowledged the slave roots of their names see Michael Levine, *African American and Civil Rights: From 1619 to the Present* (Phoenix: Oryx, 1996), p. 200.

[38] Gustav Ungerer, *The Mediterranean Apprenticeship* ... (Madrid: Verbum Editorial, 2008), p. 12; and Pieter de Marees, Albert Dantzig (tr.) Adam Jones (tr.), *Description ... of the Gold Kingdom of Guinea* (1602) (Oxford: Oxford University Press, 1987), pp. 202–206, 207–212.

[39] Hugh Thomas, *The History of the Atlantic Slave Trade, 1440–1870* (London: Picador, 1997), p. 100; Linda Maria Heywood, *Central Africans and Cultural Transformations in the America Diaspora* (Cambridge: Cambridge University Press, 2002), pp. 234–236; and Zoltán Szombathy (ed., tr.), *The History of Bidyini and Kaabu: Two Chronicles in Arabic from Guinea-Bissau* ... (Piliscsaba: Avicenna Institute of Middle Eastern Studies, 2007), pp. 60–62.

[40] Pieter de Marees, *Description et Recit Historial du Riche Royaume d'or de Gunea* (Amsterdam: Claesson, 1605), p. 95; and Marees, Dantzig and Jones (trs.), *Description and Historical Account of the Gold Kingdom of Guinea*, pp. 51–57, 59–61, 63, 202–206, 207–212.

[41] Marees, Dantzig and Jones (trs.), *Description and Historical Account of the Gold Kingdom of Guinea*, pp. 15, 24 (West-African children more advanced than white English ones), 31–32 (West-African men 'are all that a fine upright man should be' and public toilets in West-African towns and villages), 75, 187 (houses and towns well constructed); and Sandford Larkey, 'Public Health in Tudor England,' *American Journal of Public Health*, 24, Nov 1934, pp. 1099–1122 (lack of public sanitation in Tudor England.)

⁴² G. L. Registers of St Botolph without Aldgate, GL Ms 9222, GL Ms 9222/1 and GL Ms P69/Bot2/A01/Ms 9234/6, pp. 257–258 (quotations).

⁴³ However, the character of Caliban is more complex in Smith, *Race and Rhetoric in the Renaissance: Barbarian Errors*, pp. 155–162; and Norman Verrle MacCullough, *The Negro in English Literature* (Ilfracombe: A. Stockwell, 1962), pp. 48, 49.

⁴⁴ William Shakespeare, *Othello* in Richard Proudfoot, Ann Thompson, David Scott Kastan (eds.), *The Arden Shakespeare Complete Works* (Walton on Thames: Thomas Nelson and Sons, 1998), Act I, Scene III, Line 129–171, pp. 947–948. In addition, Aaron in *Titus Andronicus* makes statements about his own racial superiority and the power of blackness, and it is possible that this may echo the views or ideas of some Africans in Tudor England in Act IV, Scene II, Line 73–181, pp. 1141–1142. This theory is shared by Jose Piedra, 'In search of the Black stud,' in, Louise Fradenburg and Carla Freccero (eds.), *Premodern Sexualities* (New York: Routlegde, 1996), pp. 22–44; and Faggett, *Black and Other Minorities in Shakespeare's England*, p. 46.

⁴⁵ Andres de Claramonte, *El Valiente Negro en Flanders, Edicion Para Actores y Directores de Nelson Lopez* (Kassel: Reichenberger, 2007), p. 87; Oliver Brachfeld, discusses this character in more detail in *Inferiority Feelings: In the Individual and Group* (London: Routledge, 1999), pp. 244–247.

⁴⁶ Sebastian de Covarrubias Horozco, *Teso de la Lengua Castellano O Espano* (Madrid: Luis Sanchez, 1610, 1611); p. 652.

⁴⁷ Gonzalo Correas, *Vocabulario de Refarnes Y Frases Proverbiales* (Salamanca: Publisher unknown, 1627), p. 33.

⁴⁸ Similar perspectives are offered by Jonathan Schorsch, in *Swimming the Christian Atlantic*, p. 32.

⁴⁹ John Forrest, '*Morris and Matachin*': *A Study in Contemporary Choreography* (London: English Folk Dance and Song Society, 1984), p. 19; and John Cutting, *History and the Morris Dance, a Look at Morris Dancing from the Earliest Days Until 1850* (Alton: Dance Books, 2005), pp. 18, 19, 20, 169.

⁵⁰ Jonathan Eastwood, *The Bible Word-Book: A Glossary of Old English Bible Words* (London/ Cambridge: Macmillan and Co, 1866), pp. 323–324.

⁵¹ Barthelemy, *Black Face, Maligned Race*, pp. 77, 96, 98, 99, 111, 115, 116, 121, 124, 133, 166, 167; Emily Carroll Bartels, *Spectacles of Strangeness: Imperialism, Alienation, and Marlowe* (Philadelphia: University of Pennsylvania Press, 1993), n. p. introduction; Kim Hall, *Things of Darkness …* (New York: Cornell University Press, 1996), pp. 13, 211.

⁵² Quotations from Henry Machyn, in John Gough Nicols (ed.), *The Diary of Henry Machyn Citizen and Merchant Taylor of London* (London: Camden Society, 1848), pp. 20, 33, 89, 191.

⁵³ Ibid., p. 74.

⁵⁴ Ibid., p. 74 (quotations).

⁵⁵ Gwendolyn Midlo Hall, *Social Control in Slave Plantation Societies* (London: John Hopkins Press, 1971), pp. 2, 9–13; Thomas Durant, David Knottnerus, *Plantation Society and Race Relations: The Origins of Inequality* (Westport/London: Greenwood Publishing Group, 1999), pp. 48, 131, 140, 156–157; George Monger, *Marriage Customs of the World: from Henna to Honeymoons* (Santa Barbara: ABC CLIO, 2004), p. 173; George Bourne, *Slavery Illustrated in its Effects on Women and Domestic Society* (Boston: Issac Knapp, 1837), pp. 7, 33–45, 64, 101, 111, 124, 127; and Leon Higginbotham, *In the Matter of Colour …* (1978, new edition, Oxford: Oxford University Press, 1980), passim.

⁵⁶ Rebecca Parker Brienen, *Visions of Savage Paradise …* (Amsterdam: Amsterdam University Press, 2006), pp. 162–171; Smith, *Race and Rhetoric*, pp. 155–162; Richard Eden,

The History of Travel in the West and East Indies and other Countries Lying Either Way Towards the Fruitful and Riche Moluccaes ... (London: Richard Iugge, 1577), pp. 336, 339 (conquering of 'savages'); and Corrine S. Abate, *Privacy, Domesticity, and Women in Early Modern England* (Aldershot: Ashgate Publishing, 2002), pp. 85–87.

[57] Kim Hall, 'Object into Object, Some thoughts on the Presence of Black Women in Early Modern Culture,' pp. 346–380, in, Peter Erickson, Clarke Hulse (eds.), *Early Modern Visual Culture: Representation, Race, Empire in Renaissance England* (Philadelphia: University Press, 2000); Habib, *Black Lives*, pp. 100–112, 205; Ungerer, *The Mediterranean Apprenticeship*, pp. 75–76; Barthelemy, *Black Face*, pp. 22, 27, 40, 131–146, 197–198 (on beauty in interracial unions). Race is not listed as a bar in Tudor marriage ceremonies in Vivien Brodsky-Elliot, 'Single women in the London Marriage market: Age status and mobility, 1598–1619,' *Studies in the Social Mobility of Marriage* (London: RB Outhwaite, 1981), pp. 81–100; and David Cressy, *Birth, Marriage, and Death: Ritual, Religion, and the Life-Cycle in Tudor and Stuart England* (Oxford: Oxford University Press, 1997), pp. 298–307.

[58] This view of morganatic unions is shared by: Leonidas Rosser, *Baptism: Its Nature: Obligation, Mode, Subjects and Benefits* (Philadelphia: Leonidas Rosser, 1854), pp. 19–23, 30–33, 379–386; Laura Gowing, 'Giving Birth at the Magistrates Gate: Single Mothers in the Early Modern City,' in, Susan Broomhall and Stephanie Tarbin (eds.), *Women, Identities and Communities in Early Modern Europe* (Aldershot: Ashgate, 2008), pp. 137–150; and Jeannie Dalporto (ed.), *Women in Service in Early Modern England* (Aldershot: Ashgate, 2008), introduction.

[59] These authors offer a similar view: Laura Gowing, 'Giving Birth at the Magistrates Gate,' pp. 137–141; Jodi Mikalachki, 'Women's Networks and the Female Vagrant: a Hard Case,' in, Susan Frye and Karen Robertson (eds.), *Maids and Mistresses, Cousins and Queens: Women's Alliances in Early Modern England (Seminar) 1993* (New York: Oxford University Press, 1998), pp. 52–69.

[60] Plymouth and West Devon Record Office, St Andrews/May 2/1593/MF1–4, St Andrews/April 14/1594/MF1–4.

[61] Plymouth and West Devon Record Office, St Andrews/November 17/1594/ MF 1–4, St Andrews/ June 23/1603/MF1–4.

[62] Bristol Record Office, Bristol, P/ST PJR/1/1/CMB 1576–1621, n. p.

[63] On the influence and power of Thomas Smythe see, Edward Foss, *Biographia Juridica, A Biographical Dictionary of the Judges of England: from the Conquest to the Present Time* ... (New Jersey: Law Book Exchange, new edition 1999), p. 617; Maine Historical Society, *Collections of the Maine Historical Society*, Volume 18, (Portland: Maine Historical Society, 1831), pp. 34–36; and Robert Brenner, *Merchants and Revolution: Commercial Change, Political Conflict, and London* ... (London: Verso, 2003), pp. 96–100, 109, 154, 216, 223, 433, 434, 526, 529.

[64] Laura Gowing, 'Giving Birth,' p. 139 (quotations).

[65] Quotations are from Grace's records at the Devon Record Office, Devon, Hatherleigh 13/05/1604 PR1, Hatherleigh 10/08/1606 PR1, Hatherleigh 23/12/1607 PR1, Hatherleigh 08/05/1611 PR1, Hatherleigh 06/06/1613 PR1. On this subject, Harry Lee Faggett suggests the same in, *Black and Other Minorities in Shakespeare's England* (Prairie View: Prairie View Press, 1971), pp. 49, 50.

[66] Duncan Salkeld Duncan, 'Black Luce and the 'curtizans' of Shakespeare's London,' *Signature* 2, Winter 2000, pp. 1–10; but Kathy (Kathleen) Chater has a contrary view about 'black birds' in *Untold Histories: Black People in England and Wales During the Period of the British Slave Trade, c. 1660–1807* (Manchester: Manchester University Press, 2008), pp. 41–50. Interestingly Leslie Hotson in *Mr W.H.* (London: Hart-Davis, 1964), pp. 244–255,

claims that 'Lucy Negro' is Lucy Morgan. But that she was 'no more an Ethiop than the Black Prince,' despite being called a 'Negress,' ' Negroe,' 'black,' 'more' etc. But Hotson traces Morgan's presence through several Tudor records and he claims that up until 1581 she was a servant of Elizabeth I along side Thomasina da Pais, before she became the leader of a 'choir of nuns.' These last points raises issues which are worthy of further research.

[67] Similar views are expressed by Michael Braddick, John Walter (eds.), *Negotiating Power in Early Modern Society: Order, Hierarchy* ... (Cambridge: Cambridge University Press, 2001), pp. 65–69, 76–84, 87, 90; Marliss Desenes, *The Bed-Trick in English Renaissance Drama* ... (Newark: University of Delaware Press, 1994), pp. 17, 34, 94; and Laura Gowing, 'Gender and the Language of Insult in Early Modern London,' *History Workshop Journal*, 35, 1993, pp. 1–21.

[68] David Cressy, *Society and Culture in Early Modern England* (Aldershot: Ashgate Variorum, 2003), pp. 50–51, 311; and Patricia Crawford, *Blood, Bodies and Families in Early Modern England* (Harlow: Longman, 2004), pp. 12–13.

[69] Quotation from Laura Gowing, 'Giving Birth at the Magistrates Gate: Single Mothers in the Early Modern City,' in, *Women, Identities and Communities*, pp. 137–138. On the ideas of 'charity,' and 'community' in Tudor England see, Steve Hindle, 'A Sense of Place? Becoming and Belonging in the Rural Parish 1550–1650,' in, Alexandra Shepard and Phil Withington (eds.), *Communities in Early Modern England: Networks, Place, Rhetoric* (Manchester: Manchester University Press, 2000), pp. 96– 114; and Steve Hindle, 'Exclusion Crises: Poverty, Migration and Parochial Responsibility in English Rural Communities, c. 1560–1660,' *Rural History*, 7, 1996, pp. 125–149.

[70] Philippa Maddern, "In Myn Own House:' The Troubled Connections Between Servant Marriages, Late Medieval English Households Communities and Early Modern Historiography,' in, *Women, Identities*, pp. 51–57; and Laura Gowing, *Domestic Dangers: Women, Words and Sex in Early Modern London* (Oxford: Clarendon Press, 1996), pp. 185–188 (on obedience).

[71] Josias Nicols, *An Order of Household Instruction: by Which Every Master of a Family May Easily and in Short Space Make his Whole Household to Understand, the ...Christian Religion* (London: Thomas Man, 1596), pp. B9, B10, B12, H3, H4 (The 'Pater familias': father of the house, was granted authority from God.)

[72] Laura Gowing, 'Giving Birth at the Magistrates Gate: Single Mothers in the Early Modern City,' in, *Women, Identities*, pp. 140 (both sets of quotations).

[73] Mariano Roca de Togores (ed.), *Cronica del Rey Enrique Octavo de Inglaterra* (Madrid: Libreria de los Bibliofilos, 1874), pp. 325, 344, Appendix E (Catalina de Cardones); GL Ms 9222/1, p. 560 (Anne Vause); on her Iberian roots see Habib, *Black Lives*, pp. 135–6; National Archives, Kew, London, Exchequer Accounts, 417 (6) folio 50 RO in Letters and Papers Henry VIII 1.1.505# 1025 (John Blanke's marriage).

[74] Miranda Kaufmann, 'Africans in Early Modern London: Tales from London Metropolitan Archives,' *Miranda Kaufmann History*, http://www.mirandakaufmann.com/lmaafricans.html accessed 09/04/13.

[75] Malcolm Smuts discusses similar matters, in, *Culture and Power in Tudor England, 1585–1685* (Basingstoke: Macmillan, 1999), pp. 50–51, 62 'the fabrication of cultural memory.'

[76] William Wright, *Black History and Black Identity: A Call for a New Historiography* (Westport: Greenwood Publishing Group 2002), pp. 99–101 (on racial distinctiveness).

Afterword

This section includes an important case study on the family of an African man called Henrie Jetto. The information here corroborates many of the conclusions reached in this book and helps us understand more about the presence and status of Africans in Tudor England.

Henrie Jetto

I have suggested that integration, assimilation and the lack of a coherent racial policy that separated Africans on the basis of race from other people in Tudor England would eventually lead to 'those kindes of people' losing their racial distinctiveness.

We have an example of a modern day family descended from just such an African ancestor which demonstrates the veracity of this suggestion. This is the family now known as Bluck, descended on the maternal side from Thomas Bluck from Worcestershire who married Ann Weabley in 1712.[1] Her direct ancestor was Margaret Jetter, whose grandfather four generations back was Henrie Anthonie Jetto. This Henrie Anthonie Jetto was twenty-six when he was baptised on 3 March 1596 in Holt, Worcestershire and was described as 'A Blackamore … belonging to … Sir Henry Bromley.'[2] This entry written by the clerk Henry Bedell as with so many of those already discussed, follows a familiar pattern with the African referred to as a 'Blackamore;' but also his last name 'Jetto' being a moniker: with the word 'jet' emphasising that his skin complexion is '[a] glossy black colour' resembling the 'polished' 'black' 'jet stone.' It may also be a reference to the French word 'Jaiet' meaning the same thing,[3] and we have seen similar epithets adopted by other Africans. Henrie was an adult at the time of his baptism which suggests that he was born abroad and may have come to England through the port of Plymouth (see below), perhaps from France, which would explain why his names have a connection to that country.[4] This may mean he had these names before he came to England.

On 3 March 1596, Henrie is described as 'belonging' to Sir Henry Bromley which suggests that he had a low status, perhaps inherited from abroad. But this is the last time that we see that particular inscription of servileness applied to him. Henrie was employed for his skills as the estates owned by his employer were vast.[5] Two years later, in the parish records for Henrie's children also written by the clerk Bedell, Henrie is referred to as 'a servante of Sir Henry Bromley.' Nine years later in 1607, he is referred to as 'a gardener to Sir Henry Bromley;' and a year after that as 'Henrie Jetto of Holt.' This suggests a movement in his status from one of 'belonging' to Sir Henry Bromley, to one of belonging to the parish he lived in. Moreover, by the time Henrie came to write his own will on 20 September 1626, he describes himself as 'Jetto of the parish of Holte,' and as a man of independent means and resources who is able to bequeath his legacies including land and money as he sees fit. He even includes in that will a chastisement to two of his recalcitrant children, that if they will not be 'ruled and doe after they'r mother's commandment' they will only receive a 'portion' of their legacy.[6] Henrie's will does not contain the words of a slave, but reveal a man who is firmly lodged in Holt society and his concerns are the same as any man with property living in his times.

Henrie's family include his wife called Persida (ethnicity unknown) and five children who were all baptised in Holt. It also includes numerous other descendants some of whom are referred to in his will or described in Holt parish records from the seventeenth to the twentieth century. Henrie's children are: Sarah baptised on 10 December 1598, Margaret on 29 June 1601, John on 17 August 1604, Helena (or Ellinor) on 26 April 1607 and Richard on 5 March 1608. In the first two baptisms he is called 'a Blackemore,' but after 1604 there are no more references to his race or complexion (except through his name 'Jetto').[7] This is probably because by then his ethnicity probably seemed less important and/or because the word 'Jet' was a reference to his skin colour and indicated the family's heritage. This is also supported by the fact that his ethnicity is not mentioned in his burial records of 1627, or that of his wife's in July 1640, they were both buried in Holt. [8]

Henrie's employer Henry Bromley was the son of the Lord Chancellor Thomas Bromley, and the younger man became MP for Plymouth in 1584 and 1586.[9] He was resident in Plymouth during this time and this may have been the city through which Henrie arrived in England. Bromley later inherited land in Worcestershire and Shropshire in 1587 including Holt Castle, where he moved to, perhaps with Henrie coming with him. Bromley purchased the manor of Upton in Worcestershire from Sir Anthony Bourne in 1593, and became an MP for Shropshire in 1597, and justice of the peace in 1598. However, he was later sent to the Tower of London in 1601, but was released and formed part of the delegation that first greeted King James in 1603 and offered him the crown. Bromley died in 1615, which meant that

AFTERWORD

Henrie survived him by twelve years.[10] What part Henrie played in these great events we may never know. He may even have looked after Bromley's estates during the latter's imprisonment, or by accompanying his employer formed part of the prestigious group that met King James. What we do know is that Henrie's descendants are alive today, their pictures are included overleaf. And it was Peter Bluck (see figure 31) who through Marika Sherwood alerted me to his ancestor's ancestry. Peter Bluck resides in Pembrokeshire, but his descendants are still resident in Worcestershire and Yorkshire.

Notes

[1] Worcestershire Archive and Archaeology Service, Worcester, *Holt Parish Registers*, ref. 985, n. p.

[2] Ibid. p. 19.

[3] Quotations from the *Oxford Dictionary of English* (Oxford: Oxford University Press, 2nd edition 2003), p. 931. About Henry Bedell see same parish register, he was baptised in 1573.

[4] Ibid. Interestingly Henrie's first and second names fluctuate between the French/Latin style and the more anglicised 'Henry,' or 'Anthony.'

[5] On the estates of Holt Castle, see, Thomas Moule, *The English Counties Delineated ...* (London: George Virtue, 1830–1835), p. 147.

[6] 'Will of Henrie Jetto' Will number 102, dated and signed on 20 September 1626, but executed 13 September 1638, Worcestershire Archive, Worcester.

[7] Worcestershire Archive and Archaeology Service, Worcester, *Holt Parish Registers*, ref. 985, p. 19 Henrie's baptism, thereafter the same register 1598–1640, with other descendants noted during that period and after. Significantly, a possible modern day descendant of Henrie Jetto: Grata Jeter Clarke suggests a different origin for the family name see *The Jeter Mosaic: Seven Centuries in the History of a Family* (Mount Pleasant: Arcadia-Clarke, 1987), pp. 8–57, 739 (definitions of the word 'Jetto'), 761 (origins of the 'first' Jetto), 772 (Jetto's family).

[8] Ibid. Nor is it mentioned in Presdia's will dated 1640, same record office Will Probate Records 186–223.

[9] Edmund Burke, *A Genealogical History of the Dormant: Abeyant, Forfeited and Extinct Peerages of the British Empire* (London: Harrison, 1866), p. 76.

[10] Ian Bromley, *Bromley: A Midlands Family – And the Search for the Leicestershire Origin* (Leicester: Troubadour Publishing, 2007), pp. 136–138, 175.

Bibliography

Containing selected evidence and sources

Primary sources
Images: including paintings and sculptures
Anglo, Sydney. *The Great Tournament Roll of Westminster: A Collotype Reproduction of the Manuscript* ...Volume II. Oxford: Clarendon Press, 1968.
Artist unknown, Author unknown. *Domesday Abbreviatio [Abridgement]*, Exchequer: Treasury of the Receipt, dated 1241, ref. E36/284, p. 196, Miscellaneous Books @ National Archives, Kew, London, TW9 4DU, reproduced by kind permission of the National Archives Image library, London.
Artist unknown, Author unknown. *Schoenbartbuch Nurnberg* [Nuremberg Carnival Book]. Nuremberg: publisher unknown, 1590–1620. The book was printed to celebrate the festivals that took place in Nuremberg between 1449 and 1539. It includes representations of Africans on the coats of arms of a number of German royal families, and there are watercolour images of Africans involved in equestrian and martial pursuits, some of which show the Africans as more adept than their white counterparts. Some of these images have been copied and are in this book (Figures 33–37), others have been digitalized and can be seen at *UCLA Library Digital Collections website*, htttp://digital2.library.ucla.edu/viewItem.do?ark=21198/zz000sdcsf.and Universitats- und Landesbibliothek Dusseldorf, urn, *website*, http://digital.ub.uni-duesseldorf.de/ihd/content/titleinfo/1411934 all accessed: 30/ 4/11.
Artist unknown, Author unknown. *Westminster Tournament Roll 1511*, ref. E 36/214 f.109. Reproduced by permission of the Kings, Heralds and Pursuivants of Arms.
Artist unknown. *Abd el-Ouahed Ben Messaoud Ben Mohammed Anoun, Moorish Ambassador to Queen Elizabeth I,* about 1600, oil on oak panel, 1145 by 790 mm, ref. A0427 @ Tate Britain, Millbank, London, from the University of Birmingham, The Barber Institute of Fine Arts, Edgbaston, Birmingham, B15 2TT and reproduced by kind permission of the University of Birmingham Research and Cultural Collections.

BIBLIOGRAPHY

Artist unknown, *Adoration of the Magi*, part of a rood Screen panel, oil and gilt on oak, circa 1520, ref. W.54-1928 @ © Victoria and Albert Museum, London, SW7 2RL.

——. *African Head*, included in the Coat of Arms of the tomb of Sir Thomas Sonds died 1592, stone, wood and plaster, circa 16th century, St Michael and All Angels Throwley Church, Kent, ME13 0PJ, photographer Julian P Guffogg.

——. *African Knight*, possibly Saint Maurice, carving in wood, circa 16th century, @ St Mary's Church Vicarage, Bridge Street, Uffculme, Cullompton, EX15 3AX. Reproduced by kind permission of the Reverend Selina Garner @ the Vicarage, etc.

——. *Agate cameo of a Bacchante and an African man with a gold and enamel mount*, Agate: brown and white banded (cut in one piece); white enamelled gold mount with two translucent red and green enamel rosettes of fruit, white and black enamel suspension loops at top and bottom, cameo and mount late-sixteenth and early-seventeenth centuries, 7.3 by 4.5 cm (cameo 4.9 by 3.7) cm, ref. RCIN 65888 @ The Royal Collection, The Surveyor of The Queen's Works of Art, York House, St James's Palace, London, SW1A 1BQ. Referred to in John Boardman and Christina Aschengreen Piacenti, *Ancient and Modern Gems and Jewels: In the Collection of Her Majesty the Queen*. London: Royal Collection, 2008, pp. 60–61 (the image of the African man is of exquisite detail and according to Boardman and Piacenti appears to have been 'made in England' by the 'French engraver Julien de Fontenay.')

——. *Agate cameo of two African men, banded agate*: black, shades of brown and white; open silver-gilt mount with suspension loop, early-seventeenth century (North Italian [?]), 2.3 by 1.6 cm, ref. RCIN 65851 @ The Royal Collection.

——. *Black marble and white feldspar cameo of an African man*, black marble on an integrated white feldspar; open silver-gilt mount with suspension loop, cameo and mount seventeenth century, 2.7 by 2.0 cm, ref. RCIN 65217 @ The Royal Collection.

——. *Cameo of an African King [?] [Queen]*, agate cameo, second half of the 16th century; gold and enamel mount @ Cabinet des medailles, Bibliothèque Nationale de France Quai Francois-Mauriac, 75706 Paris, France.

——. *Cameo of an African man*, onyx: pink, green, black and grey; closed gold mount with convex back, suspension loop and ring, cameo seventeenth century? mount eighteenth century?, ref. RCIN 65852 @ The Royal Collection. John Boardman and Christina Aschengreen Piacenti,

Ancient and Modern Gems and Jewels, p. 112. The African in the cameo has a 'cap and drop pearl earrings.'

——. *Feldspar cameo of an African man,* the feldspar is black and greyish-white; open silver-gilt mount with a suspension loop, cameo and mount seventeenth century, 2.5 by 1.7 cm, ref. RCIN 65215 @ The Royal Collection.

——. *Flint cameo of an African man,* flint, grey-green on variegated brown ground; open silver-gilt mount with suspension loop, cameo and mount seventeenth century, 3.5 by 2.8 cm, ref. RCIN 65802 @ The Royal Collection.

——. *Master of the St Bartholomew Altarpiece,* 'Meeting of the Three Kings,' oil and gold leaf on panel, circa 1480, 24 3/4 x 28 1/16 inches, ref. 96.PB.6 @ John Paul Getty Museum, 1200 Getty Center Drive, Los Angeles, CA 90049-1687.

——. *Onyx cameo of Lucius Verus (?)* and an African man, onyx white and translucent grey; open gilt-brass collet mount with suspension loop and ring cameo, cameo and mount early-seventeenth century, 3.2 by 2.5 cm, ref. RCIN 65180, The Royal Collection.

——. *Sardonyx cameo of an African woman,* sardonyx dark and light brown, white; open silver-gilt mount with suspension loop, cameo early-seventeenth century, mount seventeenth century, 3.4 by 2.7 cm, ref. RCIN 65805 @ The Royal Collection.

——. *Sardonyx cameo of an African woman,* sardonyx brown and grey-freckled white, open silver-gilt mount, with suspension loop, cameo early-seventeenth century, mount seventeenth century (North Italian [?]), 2.6 by 1.8 cm, ref. RCIN 65850 @ The Royal Collection, 'headdress in cameo resembles Queen Artemisia' from John Boardman and Christina Aschengreen Piacenti, *Ancient and Modern Gems and Jewels,* p.112.

——. *Sardonyx cameo of Isis,* dark brown and white, open silver-gilt mount with suspension loop, cameo 2nd and 1st centuries BCE, mount early-seventeenth century, 2.5 by 1.7 by 0.5 cm, ref. RCIN 65613 @ Royal Collection, [Isis is an Egyptian Goddess but is here depicted as a white woman.]

——. *Saint Maurice* or *Mauritius,* statute, circa 1240, stone, approximately six feet, no ref. (next to the grave of Otto I, Holy Roman Emperor) @ The Cathedral of Saint Catherine and Maurice, Am Dom 1, D-39104 Magdeburg, Germany.

——. *The Adoration of the Magi,* panel part of a rood screen, circa 1520, oil and gilt on oak, height: 93 cm, width: 115 cm, depth: 14.6 cm @ © The Victoria and Albert Museum, London, ref. W.54-1928.

BIBLIOGRAPHY

Artist unknown. *Sir Henry Unton*, oil on canvas, 1596, 29 1/8 inches x 64 1/4 inches or 740 mm by 1632 mm, ref. Number 7/10 @ National Portrait Gallery, London, WC2H 0HE.

——. *The Drake Jewel* [or Diadem], gold and enamel, ruby and diamonds, with sardonyx, circa 1575/1586, Nicholas Hilliard painting on parchment, inset miniature in *The Drake Jewel* [or Diadem], 1585/1588, ref. LOAN: MET.ANON.1-1990, Gallery 57A, Case 12 @ **Victoria and Albert Museum**.

——. 'The Meeting of Henry VIII and Maximilian, in 1513,' *Great Tournament Roll 1545*, oil on a panel, Queen Elizabeth collection 2008 in Montrose, Adrian Louis. *The Subject of Elizabeth: Authority, Gender, and Representation*. Chicago: University of Chicago Press, 2006, pp. 21–22.

Berlinghieri, Francesco. *Geographia di Francesco Berlinghieri Fiorentino in Terza Rima et Lingua Toscana Distincta con le sue Tauole in Varii Siti et Prouincie Secondo la Geographia et Distinctione Dele Tauole di Ptolomeo*. Firenze: Nicolo Todescho, 1480.

Boele, Vincent, Ernest Schreuder and Elmer Kolfin (eds.). *Black is Beautiful: Rubens to Dumas*. Amsterdam: Die Nieuwe Kerk, 2008, pp. 15, 20, 24, 37, 39, 59, 61, 69, 74, 93, 96 etc. (fifteenth, sixteenth and early-seventeenth century religious paintings depicting 'noble' Africans).

Bosch, Hieronymus. *The Epiphany or the Adoration of the Magi*, 1510, oil on wood panel, 38 by 72 cm, by 138 x 34 cm, ref. 21032, © Photo SCALA, Florence, 2013, @ Museo Nacional del Prado, Madrid, 28014, Spain. Photo, John G. Johnson Collection, 1917, The Philadelphia Museum of Art/Art Resource/Scala, Florence.

Bosch, Hieronymus. *The Garden of Earthly Delights*, 1490–1510, oil on wood triptych, central panel 220 by 195 cm, wings 220 by 97 cm, ref. P02823 @ Museo Nacional del Prado, Madrid, Spain.

Bouterwerk, Frederick. *Meeting at the Field of Cloth of Gold*, 1520, oil on canvas, no ref. @ Palace of Versailles, 1 Boulevard de la Reine, Versailles, France 78000.

Brueghel, Jan the Elder. *Study of Moorish Heads*, 1568–1625, oil on canvas, 30 by 25 cm, private collection ref. XAM-066147 @ reproduced by kind permission of the Bridgeman Art Library Berlin, Barbarossastr. 39/10779, Berlin, Germany, see figure 4.

Cresques, Abraham. *The Catalan Atlas*, 1375, oil on canvas, ref. BNF, ESP, 30 @ Bibliotheque Nationale France, Quai François-Mauriac, 75706 Paris, Cedex 13.

Durer, Albrecht. *Katharina allt 20 jor*. [aged twenty], 1521, Portrait, Graphics, Silverpoint drawing on paper, 20 by 14 cm, no ref. © Photo

Scala, Florence, 2013, courtesy of the Ministero Beni e Att. Culturali, @ Galleria degli Uffizi, Florence, Italy.

Flinck, Govaert. *Young Archer*, 1639–1640, oil on oak panel, 66.2 x 50.8 cm, 67.7 x 52 cm, Frame size: 83.5 x 69 cm, Netherlands, ref. P 238, reproduced by kind permission of the Trustees of the Wallace Collection, Hertford House, Manchester Square, London, W1U 3BN.

Fries, Lorenz. 'Tabu Nova Partis Aphri,' in Michael Servetus (ed.), Claudii Ptolemæi Alexandrini Geographicæ Enarrationis Libri Octo ... Lugduni: Melchioris and Gasparis Trechsel, 1535.

Geertgen tot Sint Jans. *Adoration of the Magi*, two versions both 1480–1485, oil on panel, 111 by 69 cm, no ref. @ National Gallery Prague, Staroměstské náměstí 12 110 15 Praha 1, Czech republic.

Gheeraerts, Marcus (?). *Queen Elizabeth Dancing with the Earl of Leicester*, c. 1580, oil on canvas, no ref. @ Solar State room, Penshurst Place, Tonbridge, Kent, TN11 8DG, part of the Viscount de L'Isle Collection.

Hans Baldung Grien. *Adoration of the Magi*, 1507, oil on wood @ Staatliche Museum, Berlin, Germany.

Hondius, Jodocus. *Typus Totius Orbis Terrarum in quo & Christiani Militis Certamen Super Terram*, in *Pietatis Studiosi Gratiam, Graphicè Designatur à Iud. Hondio Caelatore*. (Along the bottom of the map are finely engraved figures of a Christian knight assailed by Mundus, Peccatum, Caro, Diabolus and Mors, with appropriate quotations from Scripture. This subject seems to be derived from an engraving by Jerome Wierix after Martin de Vos. The map is on Mercator's projection, and is dedicated to R. Brewer, H. Briggs and Edward Wright). Amsterdam: I Hondius, 1596.

Jones, Inigo. 'Masquer a daughter of Niger,' Watercolour, in Collections of the Duke of Devonshire, Bakewell, Derbyshire, DE45 1PP, Reference Catalogue 1, Stephen Orgel (ed.). *The Theatre of the Stuart Court. Including the Complete Designs for Productions at Court, for the Most Part in the Collection of the Duke of Devonshire, Together with their Texts and Historical Documentation*. London/Berkely: University of California Press, 1973, p. 65.

Jordaens, Jacob. *Moses and his Ethiopian wife*, circa. 1650, oil on canvas, 116.3 by 14 cm, no ref. @ Rubenshuis, Antwerp, Wapper 9, B-2000 Antwerp, Belgium and in Vincent Boele. *Black is Beautiful*, p. 179.

Kyeser, Conrad. *Bellifortis* [Queen of Sheba], f. 140, circa pre 1405, parchment, 320 by 240 mm, Niedersachsische Universitätsbibliothek, Göttingen, Germany.

Maerlant, Jacob van. 'Charlemagne killing a Moorish leader,' image on vellum, 32 by 233 cm, in *Spiegel Historiael* (West Flanders: publisher unknown,

1325–1355), n. p. ref. 133 H 16 fol.131 @ Koninklijke Bibliotheek, Prins Willem-Alexanderhof 52595 BE Den Haag, Holland and in Vincent Boele (ed.). *Black is Beautiful*, pp. 154–155.

Mantegna, Andrea. *The Triumphs of Caesar, I: The Picture Bearers*, circa 1484–1492, tempera on canvas, 266 by 288 cm, ref. RCIN 403958 @ The Royal Collection. (A 'dignified' African is the central character).

Mostaert, Jan. *Portrait of an African Man*, circa 1520–1530, oil on panel, 30.8 by 21.2 cm, ref. Sk-A-4986, reproduced by kind permission @ Rijksmuseum, Jan Luijkenstraat 1, 1071 CJ Amsterdam, Holland and Rijksmuseum, http://www.rijksmuseum.nl/collectie/aanwinsten2005/portret-van-een-afrikaanse-man?lang=en, accessed 13/02/10.

Nassaro, Matteo del, or Dominicus, Romanus? *Onyx of the Adoration of the Magi*, cameo sixteenth century, mount 1700, onyx: olive-green, white and grey on a dark ground (visually black); open silver-gilt collet mount with suspension loop, 3.4 by 6.5 cm. ref. RCIN 65175 @ The Royal Collection.

Rembrandt, Van Rijn. *A Black Drummer and Commander Riding on Mules*, 1638, drawing on paper, pen and brown ink and red chalk with brown wash touched with white and yellow, verso and gilt edged, size 230 by 171 mms. ref. 00 10. 122 @ British Museum, London, see figure 23. Reproduced by kind permission of the © Trustees of the British Museum.

Rubens, Peter Paul. *Studies of the Head of a Negro*, circa 1615, oil on panel, size 25.98 by 20.08 inches, no ref. © *Photo SCALA, Florence*, 2013, @ Musees Royaux Des Beaux-Arts, Place Royale 3, Brussels 1000, Belgium. Photo ArtMedia/Heritage Images/Scala, Florence.

Rubens, Peter Paul. *Head of a Negro* (the same African man is featured), 1618–1620, oil on panel, size 45.7 by 36.8 cm, ref. cat 447, plate 435 @ Hyde collection, Art Museum, Historic House and Gardens, 161 Warren Street, Glens Falls, New York 12801.

Somer, Paul Van, *Anne of Denmark*, 1617, oil on canvas, size 265.4 by 208.3 cm, ref. RCIN 405887@ The Royal Collection, London. Reproduced by kind permission of the Royal Collection Trust/© Her Majesty Queen Elizabeth II 2013.

Streeck, Juriaen Van. *A Still Life with a Moorish Servant Standing Behind a Table*, 1632–1687, oil on canvas, size 90.5 by 80 cm, no ref. @ Salomon Lilian, Spiegelgracht 5, 1017, J P Amsterdam, The Netherlands, see figure 3.

Unknown, *Marriage of St Ursula to Prince Conan*, circa 1522, size 67 by 72 cm, ref. 1462-A Pint, 00900.01 TC, panel of the *Santa Auta Altarpiece*, from the Monastery of Madre de Deus in Lisbon, Portugal @ Museu Nacional de Arte Antiga, Lisbon, Portugal, © photographer Jose Pessoa 1993, reproduced by kind permission of Mestre do Retabulo de Santa Auta and Direcao-Geral do Patrimonio Cultural/Arquivo de Documentacao Fotografica (DGPC?ADF).

Vangrol, Jean. *Banded Agate cameo of an African woman*, cameo early-seventeenth century, mount c.1640, gold and enamel mount, banded agate (from Scotland): various shades of grey and brown; open gold mount with frame of white 'flames' enamelled suspension loop and ring, 4.2 by 2.7 (cameo 3.4 by 2.3) cm ref. RCIN 43780 @ The Royal Collection. Boardman and Piacenti, *Ancient and Modern Gems and Jewels*, p.112 (the cameo is of exquisite detail).

Various, cropped images of Black knights (Maurice heads) they include images from: Matthias Grunewald. *Erasmus of Formulae and Saint Maurice*, 1517–1523, oil on wood, 226 by 176: cmbpk / Gemäldegalerie, SMB / Jörg P. Anders (00018418) bpk | Bayerische Staatsgemäldesammlungen (50009493), b p k, Bildagentur für Kunst, Kultur und Geschichte, Maerkisches Ufer 16-18, 10179 Berlin, Germany; Alte Pinakothek, 80333 Munich, Germany; Hans Baldung Grien. *Adoration of the Magi*, 1507, oil on wood @ Staatliche Museum, Berlin, Germany; and Lucas Cranach (the elder) and Workshop, *Saint Maurice*, 1472–1553, oil on wood, 137.2 by 39.4 cm ref. gallery 628 no. 2006. 469. © Photo Scala, Florence, 2013, Inv.2006.469. Image copyright The Metropolitan Museum of Art/Art Resource/Scala, Florence and @ the Metropolitan Museum of Art, 1000 Fifth Avenue, New York, USA, NY 10028.

Vecellio, Cesare. *Degli Habiti Antichi et Moderni di Diverse Parti del Mondo* ... Venice: Italy, 1590.

Vercoutter, Jean and Jean Devisse and Michel Mollat (eds.). *The Image of the Black in Western Art*. Cambridge: Harvard University Press, 1976–1979, Volume I–III.

Verdun, Nicolas. *Verdun Altar* [King Solomon and the Queen of Sheba], circa 1181, enamel plaque in champlevé technique on gilded copper, @ Sammlungen des Stiftes, Klosterneuburg, Austria.

White, John. *'An Eskimo Man with Bow,'* 1585–1593, Watercolour, Paper, size 225 by 163 millimetres, ref. 1906,0509. 1.29 @ British Museum, Prints and Drawings, London, WC1A 2RJ. Reproduced by kind permission of the © Trustees of the British Museum.

White, John. *'An Eskimo Woman with Baby,'* 1585–1593, Watercolour, Paper, size 223 by 166 millimetres, ref. 1906,0509.1.30 @ British Museum, London. Reproduced by kind permission of the © Trustees of the British Museum.

White, John and Paul Hope Hulton. *America, 1585: The Complete Drawings of John White*. Chapel Hill: The University of North Carolina, British Museum, 1984.

Willis, Deborah. *The Black Female Body: A Photographic History.* Philadelphia: Temple University Press, 2002.

Parish Records, Registers and Lay Subsidy returns

With selected records noted:

Anon. Lay Subsidy Records, Returns for the City of London in 1292-1392 ... National Archives, Kew, PRO E179/144/2, E179/144/3, (179) 1523-4.3.

Bristol Record Office, B Bond Warehouse, Smeaton Road, Bristol, BS1 6XN, Avon, Dyrham, ref. P/ST PJR/1/1/CMB 1576-1621 and 15/8/1575/, Bristol RO P/Dy/R/1a and St Philip and Jacob's Church Bristol, 14/12/1603.

Bromley Records Office, Central Library, High Street, Bromley, BR1 1EX, *Composite Register Baptisms and Burials 1559-1681*, P92/1/1, p. 1, 'Cristofer Adam a blackamore christen[ened] on the 22 daie of April, a man growne,' baptism 22 April 1593.

Burke, Arthur Meredyth (ed.). *Memorials of St Margaret's Church, Westminster. The Parish Registers, 1539-1660.* London: Eyre and Spottiswoode, 1914.

Cornwall Record Office, Old County Hall, Truro, Cornwall, TR1 3AY, Registers of Bodmin, ref Mf 12 FP 13/1/11, Burials 1558-1757:
7 December 1563, 'Thomas Playne a stranger.'
12 December 1563, 'Marrion S Soda of Morrisce.'
28 December 1588, 'Eliz Moro a lascar woman,' p. 436.
30 October 1593, 'Balthazar a portingale,' p. 733.
22 January 1600, 'John my more [his or] stranger,' p. 729
12 April 1606, 'A stranger woman that ... dyed at ...'
Baptisms:
2 November 1578, 'Wlim daughter to Balthazar Portingall,' p. 21.
19 January 1580, 'T[w]o? sons to Bathazar Portingall,' p. 24.
23 October 1582, 'Frances sons to Balthazar Portingale,' p. 27.
3 February 1592, 'Nigro? sonne to Edward Moore,' p. 38.
30 September 1604, 'Negro? Sonne to Robert Gysy [or Cosy],' p. 52.

City of Westminster Archives Centre, 10 St Anns Street, London, SW1P 2DE, St.Clements Danes, January/21/St Clements Dane/ Volume1Burials/MF 1, 'Fortunatus a blackmoor seruant to Sr Robert Cicill,' burial 21 January 1601/2.

Devon Record Office (DRO), Great Moor House, Bittern Road, Sowton, Exeter, Devon, EX2 7NY, including the following:

DRO, East Allington/20/08/1577 PR TD 38 1906 28/08/1570.

DRO, Hatherleigh, 13/05/1604 PR1, 'Grace a Negyer,' baptised 13 May 1604.

——. 10/08/1606 PR1, 'Rebecca, a base daughter of Grace, a negyer [negro]' baptised 10 August 1606.

——. 23/12/1607 PR1, 'Rebecca a blackmore base daughter of Grace,' burial 23 December 1607.

——. 08/05/1611 PR1, 'Honour a Negro' '… a base daughter of Grace,' baptised 8 May 1611.

——. 06/06/13 PR1, 'Honour' was described as an 'illegitimate' child of Grace, burial 6 June 1613.

Duncan, Lewis Leland, Oswald Barron (eds.). *The Registers of all the Marriages, Christenings and Burials in the Church of St Margaret's Lee in the County of Kent, From 1579-1754*. Lee: C. North for Lewisham Antiquarian Society, 1888.

Gibson, Jeremy and Michael Walcot (eds.). *Where to Find the International Genealogical Index*. Plymouth: Federation of Family History Societies, 1984.

Guildhall Library London (GL), 5 Aldermanbury, London, EC2V 7HH including the following:

——. St Andrew Holborn, GL Ms 6673/1, 'Sebrina, a blackmore wench,' burial 30 January 1589/90.

——. St Ann Blackfriars, GL Ms 4510/1, 'Domyngo, a blackmore,' burial 8 January 1587/8.

——. St Botolph without Aldgate parish records including: GL Ms 9243-9245, GL Ms 4515/1, St Botolph without Aldgate *Memorandum Daybooks*, Volume I-VI. London: Parish of St Botolph without Aldgate, 1586-1603 etc., references P69/BOT2/A/01/MS 9234/1-6 and the following:

——. St Botolph without Aldgate (St Botolph), GL Ms 9222/1, Parish register, p. 1, 'Peter Blacke was buried' 25 November 1558.

——. GL Ms 9222/1, Parish register, p. 7, 'Daniel Moore was buried,' 18 October 1559.

——. GL Ms 9222/1, Parish register, p. 8, 'Edwarde Moore,' burial 24 November 1559.

——. GL Ms 9222/1, Parish register, p. 8, 'John Blackmoore' burial 18 December 1559.

——. GL Ms 9222/1, Parish register, p. 17, 'Anthony Blacke,' burial 20 October 1562.

——. GL Ms 9222/1, Parish register, p. 143, 'George a Negar from John Mithol,' burial 11 March 1583.

——. *Parish Clerk Memorandum Daybook*, P69/Bot2/ A01/Ms 9234/1, in the insert pages at the back, f. 30:

George whose name was not know[n] being lodged ina house of John Mythell on dwelling in the manor of Eastsmithfield this 'George was a negar' which same Taethye won from Hambro and now buried 11 Day of March in 1583, years xxx [old], [his funeral charges were paid from a communal fund as he was] no parishioner … he was buried with the second cloth.

——. GL Ms 9222/1, Parish register, p.156, 'Christopher Cappervert a blackemoore,' burial 22 October 1586.

——. GL Ms 9221, Parish burial register, 'Cristopher Cappeverte a blackmoore who dyed in the whitbell of the high street was buryed the 22 of October.' In the margin is written 'Upper [end of the parish]. Christopher caperverto. Yers [of age] 28,' under the date of 'October 1586.'

——. GL Ms 9222/1, Parish register, p.164, 'Domingo, a negroe,' burial 27 August 1587.

——. GL Ms 9221, Parish burial register, 'Domingo, a black neigro servaunt unto Sir William Winter, was buryed the 27 of August [1587]. East [end]. Con[sumption?]. Yeres 40.'

——. P69/Bot 2/ A01/Ms 9234/4, *Parish Clerk Memorandum Daybook*, p. 127, burial 27 August 1587,
Domingo. Beinge a Ginnye negaro and beinge servaunt to the Right Worshipfull S(i)r William Winter knyght, dwellinge in the abbye place, beinge the mannor howse of Eastsmithfield, was buried the xxviith daye of August [1587]. He had the best clothe. Con[sumption?].

——. GL Ms 9222/1, Parish register, p. 330, 'A Youngman vagrant unknown,' burial 6 October 1587.

——. P69/Bot 2/ A01/Ms 9234/1, *Parish Clerk Memorandum Daybook*, p.149, burial 6 October 1587,
A younge man negroe name not known and not a parishioner and dyed in the street before … no man at the time did [know him] at the liberty of Eastsmithfield no parishioner.

——. GL Ms 9222/1, Parish register, p. 168, 'Martin Blacke the son of Richard Blacke a needle maker,' burial 17 January 1587.

——. P69/Bot 2/ A01/Ms 9234/4, f. 18, *Parish Clerk Memorandum Daybook*, 'Martin Blacke the son of Richard Blacke a needle maker dwelling in the … being in the libertie of Eastsmithfield,' burial 17 January 1587.

——. GL Ms 9222/1, Parish register, p. 193, 'Fraucis a Blackamoor servant to Thomas Parker,' burial 8 January 1591.

——. GL Ms 9222/1, Parish register, p. 223, 'Suzanna Peavis [or Pearis] a blackamore servant to John Despinois,' burial 8 August 1593.

——. GL Ms 9222, Parish burial register, 'Suzanna Pearls ... a blackamoore servant to John Despinois, [a hat bandmaker],' burial 8 August 1593.

——. GL Ms 9222/1, Parish register, p. 303, 'Cassangoe A blacke A moore servant to Mrs Barbor,' burial on 8 October 1593.

——. P69/Bot2/A01/ Ms 9234/4, *Parish Clerk Memorandum Daybook*, Cassanggo, a neagar servant to Mr Thomas Barbor a marchaunt, from his howse at the signe of the Redd Crosse in the libertie of Eastsmithfield, was buried the viiith day of October anno 1593. Yeares xx. Plague. For the common grownd because he was coffind xiid. For the best cloth not used having a black cloth ixd. And for i bearer [blank].East.

——. GL Ms 9223, Paper burial register, 'East. Yeres 20. Plagg. Cassango a blackmoore servaunt to Mr Thomas Barber a marchaunt was buryed the 8 daye of October' 1593.

——. GL Ms 9222/1, Parish register, p. 288, 'Symon Valencia, a Blackamoore,' burial 20 August 1593.

——. GL Ms 9221, Parish burial register, Under 'August 1593':] 'Upper [end]. Yeres [of age] 20. Plagg. Symon Valencia, a black moore servaunt to Stephen Drifyeld a nedellmaker was buryed the 20 daye,' August 1593.

——. GL Ms 9222/1, Parish register, p. 307, 'Robert a Negar being servant to William Mathew a Lentleman' burial 29 November 1593.

——. GL Ms 9223, Parish burial register, 'Robart a black a moore servaunt to William Mathew Jent was buryed the 29 daye of November. East. Yeres 26.Plagg.'

——. P69/Bot2/A01/Ms 9234/4, *Parish Clerk Memorandum Daybook*, Robert a negar being servant to William Mathew a Jentelman dwelling in a garden being behynd Mr Quarles his howse and neare unto Hogg Lane in the libertie of Eastsmithfield was buried in the owter church yeard being withowt the crosse walle before Mr Soda his tenementes ... [date follows]. Yeares xxvi ... He had the second cloth and fower bearers. [In the margin the word 'plague' is marked].

——. GL Ms 9223, Paper burial register, 'A Negar whose name was supposed to be ffrauncis he was servant to Mr Peter miller a bearebrewer,' burial 3 March 1596/7.

——. P69/Bot2/A01/Ms 9234/6, *Parish Clerk Memorandum Daybook*, p. 118. East. Of the sckurvie. A Negar whose name was (now?) supposed to be Frauncis. The late servant of Peter Miller a beare brewer dwelling at the signe of the hartes, borne [Habib says 'horne'] in the libertie of EastSmithfield now buried the third day of March anno 1596 year xxxi. Yeares xxxi he had the best cloth [and] iiii bearers.

———. GL Ms 9223, Paper burial register, 'Mary Fillis, a black more, being abowt xx yeares owld and dwelling with Millicent Porter, a seamester, was baptized' 3 June 1597.

———. GL Ms 9220, Parish register, p. 90, 'Mary Phillis a blackmore beinge about twentye yeres of age and dwellinge with Millicen [sic, for Millicent] Porter sempster' baptised 3 June 1597.

———. P69/Bot2/A01/Ms 9234/6, *Parish Clerk Memorandum Daybook*, pp. 257-258.

Mary Fillis of Morisco, being a black more. She was of late servant with one M(ist)res Barker in Marke Lane, a widdowe. She said hir father's name was Fillis of Morisco, a black more, being both a basket maker and also a shovell maker.

This Marie Fillis being abowt the age of xx yeares and having beene in England for the space of xiii or xiiii yeares, and as yt was not Christned, and now being becom servant with one Millicent Porter a seamster dwelling in the libertie of Eastsmithfield, and now taking some howld of faith in Jesus Chryst, was desyrous to becom a Christian.

Wherefore shee made sute by hir said m(ist)res to have some conference with the Curat of this the parish of St Buttolphees without Aldgate London. Which Curat, named Mr Christopher Threlkeld, demaunding of her certen questions concerning hir faith, where unto shee answering him verie Christian lyke, and afterwardes she being by the said Mr Christopher Threlkeld our Curat willed to say the Lordes Prayer, and also to rehearce the articles of hir beliefe, which she did both say and and [sic] rehearce verie decently and well, confessing hir fayth, then the said Curat demaundid of hir if she weare desyrous to be paptized [sic] in the said fayth, whereunt[o] shee said, "I".

Then the said Curat did go with hir unto the founte, and desyring the congregation with him to call upon God the Father thorowgh our Lord Jesus Chryst, that of his bownteous mercie he wold graunt to her that thing which by nature she could not have, that shee myght be baptized with water and the Holy Gost, and receyved into Ch[r]istes Holy Church and be made a lyvely member of the same, Amen, then the said Curat using the rest of the wordes of the Queenes Majesties booke untill he did com unto the qwestions to be demaunded, which qwestions he did demaunde of her, unto which questions she answered as yt is set downe in the Queenes Majesties booke.

And the Minister afterwardes praying according to order, which being done, he said unto the wittnesses whose names weare, William Benton, Margerie Barrick and Mylicent Porter, saying unto them, you shall name this chyld, who named her, Mary Fillis, of Morisco, the dawghter to Fillis of Morisco, a black more being as shee said in that contrie both a basket maker and a shovell maker.

So that I do say that the said Mary Fillis a black more at this tyme dwelling with Millicent Porter a seamester of the libertie of Eastsmithfield was christned on Fryday being the third day of June, in the presents of the undenamed [sic] and dyvers others, viz William Benton, Margerie Barrick, Millicent Porter, M(ist)res Magdalyne Threlkeld, Mathew Pearson, M(ist)res Young, Gertrud Ponder, Thomas Harrydance, being the parish Clarke, Thomas Ponder, being the sexton, and dyvers others. Baptised 3 June 1597.

——. GL Ms 9222/1, Parish register, p. 403, 'Thomas Barbor merchant,' burial 20 August 1603.

——. GL Ms 9222/1, Parish register, p. 560, 'Anne Vause a Black-more wife to Anthonie Vause, Trompetter of the said Country,' burial 24 April 1618.

G. L. St Katherine by the Tower, GL Ms 9659/2, Parish register, p.16 'Phillip, an Indian blackmore, borne in the East Indies at Zarat,' baptised 20 August 1623.

G. L. Holy Trinity the Less, GL Ms 9155, Parish register, 'James Curres, beinge a Moore Christian and Margaret Person, a maid,' marriage 24 December 1617.

G. L. Holy Trinity Minories, GL Ms 9239, Parish register, p.12, 'James Ongunby, a Negro,' baptised 7 June 1593.

G. L. St Martin in the Fields, GL Ms 9226, Parish register, Volume I. London: No publisher, 27 September 1571.

G. L. St Mary Bothaw, GL Ms 4310, Parish register, 'Julyane, a blackamore, servant with Alldermane Banynge, of the age of 22 yeares, was baptized and namyd Marye,' on 29 March 1601.

G. L. St Mary Woolchurch Haw, GL Ms 7644, Parish register,
a blakmore belonging to Mr John Davies, died in White Chappel parishe, was laied in the ground in this church yarde sine frequentia populi et sine ceremoniis quia utrum christianus esset necne nesciebamus [without any company of people and without ceremony, because we did not know whether he was a Christian or not]' undated burial but between entries for 24 April and 20 May 1597.

G. L. St Mary Woolnoth, GL Ms 7635/2, Parish register, p. 347, 'a Blackamore boy of Mr John Temple, Goldsmith, in the Churchyard,' burial 26 June 1675.

G. L. St Mildred Poultry, GL Ms 4429/1, Parish register, 'John Jaquoah, a king's sonne in Guinnye,' baptised 1 January 1610/11,

BIBLIOGRAPHY

Dederi Jaquoah about the age of 20 yeares, the sonne of Caddi-biah king of the rriver of Cetras or Cestus in the cuntrey of Guinny, who was sent out of his cuntrey by his father, in an english shipp called the Abigail of London, belonging to Mr John Davies of this parish, to be baptised. At the request of the said Mr Davies and at the desire of the said Dedery, and by allowance of authority, [he] was by the Parson of this churche the first of Januarie, baptised and named John. His sureties were John Davies haberdasher, Isaac Kilburne mercer, Robert Singleton churchwarden, Edmund Towers, Paul Gurgeny and Rebecca Hutchens. He showed his opinion concerning Jesus Christ and his faith in him; he repeated the Lords prayer in English at the fonte, and so was baptised and signed with the signe of the Crosse.

G. L. Census for Coleman Street Ward, London, 15 December, 1567 Returns Coll/SP/E. 1: 460.

Bannerman, William Bruce (ed.). *Registers of St Olave, Hart Street, London, 1563–1700.* London: Harleian Society, 1916.

St Olave, P69/OLA1/A/01/GL Ms 28867, p. 50, Parish register, 'Isabell, a blackamore,' burial 6 June 1588.

——. GL Ms 28867, Parish register, p. 50, 'burial of 'a man blackamore laye in the streete,' burial 29 June 1588.

——. GL Ms 28867, Parish register, p. 50, 'Grace, a nigro, oute of Dr Hector's,' burial 13 July 1590.

——. GL Ms 28867, Parish register, p. 51, 'Francisco a Nigro,' burial 5 September 1590.

——. GL Ms 28867, Parish register, 'Peter Marley, a blacamore, dira vira house,' burial 9 November 1594.

——. GL Ms 28867, Parish register, p. 54, 'George a blackeamore out of Mr[s?] Barkers,' burial 23 January 1595/6.

——. GL Ms 28867, Parish register, p. 56, 'Madelen, a blackeamore, oute of Bernade's house,' burial 23 November 1598.

——. GL Ms 28867, Parish register, p. 68, 'the blackamore girle from Mr Pintoe's,' burial 14 Mar 1610.

——. GL Ms 28867, Parish register, p. 27, 'Mark Antonio, a Negro baptised,' 26 January 1616.

——. GL Ms 28867, Parish register, p. 72, 'Mark Antonio, a negro Christian,' burial 28 January 1616.

G. L. St Stephen Coleman Street, London, GL Ms 4448, 'Katherin the negar, dwelling with the prince of Portingal,' burial 24 August 1594.

——. GL Ms 4449/2, 'James Dockey, a Guiney negar boy aged 17 years, Mr Lavington's servant,' baptised 24 July 1687.

Guildhall Library London, 'Black and Asian people discovered in records held by the Manuscripts Section,' Manuscripts Section, Aldermanbury, London.

Hidden, Norman and Joyce Hidden. *Hungerford Berkshire and Wiltshire Parish* Register C-M-B 1559-1619. Hungerford: Norman and Joyce Hidden, 1984.

Kent History Services, Kent History and Library Centre, James Whatman Way, Maidstone, ME14 1LQ, Blean, St Damien and St Cosmos parish, CCA-U3/62/1/1, 'Wylmm, the son of Elizabeth, commonly called the Black Moore. base born,' baptised 24 May 1604.

Kirk, Richard and Ernest Kirk (eds.). *Returns of Aliens Dwelling in the City and Suburbs of London from the Reign of Henry VIII. To that of James I,* Volume I-IV, Quarto Series 10. London: Huguenot Society of London, 1900-8.

Lalwan, Rory (ed.). *Sources for Black and Asian History at the City of Westminster Archives Centre.* London: Westminster City Archives, 2005.

Lancashire Record Office, Bow Lane, Preston, Lancashire, PR1 2RE, Blackburn, St Mary's parish, M/F. PR3073/1/1, 'Leticia' whose father is described as a 'Willm Voclentine Egiptian,' baptised 3 December 1602.

Lang, Richard (ed.). *Two Tudor Subsidy Assessment Rolls.* London: The London Record Society Publications, 1993.

London Metropolitan Archives (LMA), 40 Northampton Road, Clerkenwell, London, EC1R 0HB, Registers of St Dunstan and All Saints Church, Stepney, LMA P93/DUN/255.

LMA, London, Registers of Mary Magdalene, Bermondsey, P 71/MMG/002, Microfiche X 097 MF 004.

LMA, London, All Hallows, Tottenham, Haringey, London, LMA DRO/015 /A/01/001,

Walter Anberey the sonne of Nosser Anberey borne in the kingdom of Dungala in Africa, was baptized upon the third day of February being Shrove Sundaie, in the Eight yeare King James, anno, [1610/11].

Northampton Records Office, Wootton Hall Park, Northampton, NN4 8BQ: Northampton, Eydon Parish, Microfiche 120, pp. 1-3, 'Thomas Bull niger was buried the 16 of December' 1545.

North Devon Record Office, Tuly Street, Barnstable, Devon, EX31 1EL, Registers of St Peters/August 23/1588/MSC46/67-3054A/PR1 and 6/4/1596, 10/4/1598, 22/5/1596, 22/5/1605 etc. ref. MFc 46/6-7.

Medway Archives and Local Studies Centre (MALSC), Strood, Rochester, Kent, ME2 4AU:

——. Dartford Kent, 9/January/1596/7/Dartford/ MF1/P110, 'Iferdynando,' 'a blackamore svannte [servant] to Alexander Neuby' burial on 19 January 1596/97.

——. Gravesend Kent, 26/May/1553/Gravesend/ MF1 1553, 'Anthoine an Egyptian' burial on 26 May 1553.

——. 19/February/1603/Gravesend/ MF1 1603, 'Frances the Mullato' burial on 19 February 1603.

Plymouth and West Devon Record Office, Community Services Department, Unit 3 Clare Place, Plymouth, PL4 0LW, Registers of St Andrews (RSA), MF1–4 including:

——. December 10/1583 MF 1–4, 'Bastien, a Blackmoore of Mr Willm Hawkins' burial on 10 December 1583.

——. March 18/1587 MF1–4, 'Anthony, John, a Neyger' burial 18 March 1587.

——. March 11/1591 MF1–4, 'Carbew, Lazia, a Negro marche' burial 11 March 1591.

——. May 2/1593 MF1–4, 'Helene, daughter of Cristian the negro svant to Richard Sheere, the supposed father binge Cuthbert Holman, illeg,' baptised 2 May 1593.

——. April 14/1594 MF1–4, 'Cristian, daughter of Cristian, Richard Sheer's Blackmoore,' burial 14 April 1594.

——. November 17/1594 MF1–4, 'Cristien, daughter of Mary, a negro of John Whites and the supposed daughter of John Kinge, a Dutchman, illeg' baptised 17 November 1594.

——. December 24/1594 MF1–4, 'Fortunatus, son of a negro of Thomas Kegwins the supposed father being a Portugall,' baptised 24 December 1594.

——. July 1/1596 MF1–4, 'Susan, daughter of a Blackmoore' baptised 1 July 1596.

——. October 4/1596 MF1–4, 'Pedro, Katheren, daughter of don Pedro a basterd Neger' baptised 4 October 1596.

——. November 30/1601 MF1–4, 'a Blackmore at Capt. Sparks' burial 30 November 1601.

——. December 6/1601 MF1–4, 'Mary, a Blackmore at Mr Stallenge' burial 6 December 1601.

——. October 22/1602 MF1–4, 'Gifferdandgorge, an Indian,' burial 22 October 1602.

——. June 23/1603 MF1–4, 'Richard, son of Marye a Neger, base, ye reputed father Rog Hoggett,' baptised 23 June 1603.

Centre for Kentish Studies, County Hall, Maidstone, Kent, ME14 1XX, Registers of All Saints Parish, All Saints Church, Staplehurst Parish Kent, ms P 347 ref 560, ms P347, ref 800.

London Local History and Archives Centre, Lewisham Library, 199–201 Lewisham High Street, London, SE13 6LG, Registers of St Margaret's Lee, Deptford, A78/18M/A1/1.

London Family History Centre, Church of Jesus Christ of Latter-day Saints, 64–68 Exhibition Road, London SW7 2PA, St Michael Paternoster Church, returns for Vintry Ward, London, ref. MF 0574365.

Salisbury Cathedral records held at the Wiltshire and Swindon History Centre, Cocklebury Road, Chippenham, Wiltshire, SN15 3QN, Salisbury Cathedral, Register 1, X3/84/1, 'Mathias the Morian' burial 22 February 1601/2.

Sampson, Mike. 'Friends of Devon Archives, the Black connection,' *Friends of Devon Newsletter,* Issue 25, May 2000, pp.12–15.

Society of Genealogists, International Genealogical Index. London: Society of Genealogists, 1994, et. al.

Staffordshire Parish Registers Society. *Parish Registers of Biddulph Staffordshire* Volume I *1558–1642.* Wolverhampton: Birmingham and Midland Society for Genealogy and Heraldry, 1991.

Suffolk Record Office, Gatacre Road, Ipswich, Suffolk, IP1 2LQ, Ipswich St Clement, Ingham register, p. 6, Microfiche FB98, 'Edmund de Guys son of Francis Gyls shoemaker and Katheryn hs wife (who was borne in Norold in Norff), beinge strangers and travellers both theyre son'e Edmunde who baptised ye Vth of December 1591,' baptism.

——. Ingham register, p. 44, Microfiche FB98,' it'm will'm Johnon (as tranger) was buried ye xixth of July A.o. B'ni:1580,' burial 29 July 1580.

——. Bury St Edmunds, St James Parish register, p. 4, microfiche 1, 'Robert an Egyptian,' baptism 18 February 1563.

Westminster City Archives, Westminster City Hall, 64 Victoria Street, London SW1E 6QP, St Martin in the Fields Parish register, Volume 1, 'Margureta a Moor,' burial 27 September 1571.

Wiltshire and Swindon Records Office, Wiltshire Family History Society, *Colne Parish Register* Vol. 1 *1538–1602.* London: A Webb, 1944, n. p. 'Maria Mandula, stranger and Aethiops,' 10 December 1585 Burial.

Wiltshire and Swindon Records Office, *Colne Parish Register,* ref. 2083/1, n.p. 'Maria Mandula. Advena [e] [visitor or foreigner] et Aethiopo,' 10 December 1585 Burial.

BIBLIOGRAPHY

Salisbury St Thomas Parish Registers and Bishop's Transcripts 1530–1837, Burials. (Devizes: Wiltshire Family History Society, 2011), p. 24, 'white child,' burial 6 June 1597.

——. 'Elizabeth' 'blackmore lives at white hart,' burial 26 January 1653, p. 67.

Salisbury St Thomas Parish Register, no ref. 26 January 1653, 'Elizabeth the Blackmore that lives at white Hart,' burial, n.p.

Salisbury St Thomas Parish Registers … Baptisms (2012).

Wiltshire Family History Society, *Chippenham Parish Registers and Bishop's Transcripts 1577–1837 Burials* (2011). pp. 4, 22 October 1584, [no name] 'a stranger died in Mr Robert Franklyn's house.'

——. p. 13, 19 March 1598, [no name] 'a man unknown.'

——. p. 11, 1593 'Alice Micholl' 'daughter of strange woman.'

——. *Baptisms* (2011).

——. *Corsham Parish Registers … 1563–1837 Burials* (2012). *Baptisms* (2012).

——. *Devizes Parish Registers …* (2011). *Baptisms* (2011).

——. *Malmesbury Abbey Parish Registers …1591-1837, Burials* (2011), p. 4, 'an Irish child died at Wm Knaps …' burial 22 April 1591.

——. *Baptisms* (2011).

——. *Marlborough St Mary Parish Registers …1602–1837, Baptisms* (2011). *Burials* (2011), p. 33, 'Blackman,' [no other names] 'widow,' burial 13 March 1671.

——. p. 40, 11 August 1684, 'Blackman' 'w John' [no other names] burial.

——. *Mere Parish Registers …1561–1837 Burials* (2011). *Baptisms* (2011).

——. *Salisbury St Thomas Parish Registers … 1530–1837, Burials*, p. 28, 'child of a stranger at Maundrills House,' burial 19 January 1596.

——. *Baptisms* (2011).

——. *Steeple Ashton Parish Registers and Bishop's Transcripts 1538–1837, Burials* (2011). *Baptisms* (2011)…

——. *Warminster St Denys Parish Registers … 1556–1837 Burials* (2011). *Baptisms* (2011). n. p. 6 October 1615, 'Morryn Ambros' 'parchment maker,' burial.

——. *Westbury Parish Registers … 1556–1837 Burials* (2011). *Baptisms* (2011) p. 20, 30 October 1597, 'Adolefreus' 'a pauper stranger,' burial.

——. p. 21, 3 January 1598, 'more,' 'infant child of William Penlegh,' burial.

Worcestershire Archive and Archaeology Service, The Hive, Sawmill Walk, The Butts, Worcester, WR1 3PB.

——. *Holt Parish Registers*, ref. 985, p. 19. 'Henrie Anthonie Jetto A Blackemore [and] being 26 or year aboute belonging to the worshipful Sir Henry Bromley knight being Instructed in the Christian faith was [new?] baptised the 21 day of Marche ..' baptism 21 March 1596.

The following records are for his family and all are at Holt.

—. 'The same day was Sara the daughter of Henry Jetto A Blackemore servante to Sir Henry Bromley baptised,' baptism 10 December 1598.

—. 'The 29 June was Margaret daughter of Henry Jetto a Blackemore baptised,' baptism 29 June 1601.

—. 'The 26th of April was Ellinor the daughter of Henry Jetto gardener to Sir John Bromley baptised …' baptism 26 April 1607.

—. The 5 day of March was Richard Jetto sonne of Henry Jetto of Holt baptised,' baptism 5 March 1608.

—. 'Henrie jetto was buried,' burial 30 August 1627.

—. 'Apoline Jetto the wife of John Jetto was buried,' burial 16 August 1637.

—. 'John the sonne of John and Isabell Jetto was baptised,' burial March 17 1638.

—. 'Henry the sonne of John and Isabell Jetto was baptised,' baptism 12 July 1640.

—. 'Persida Jetto widow was buried,' burial 7 July 1640.

—. 'Henry the sonne of John and Isabell Jetto was buried,' burial 14 March 1641.

—. 'John the sonne of John and Joanne Jetto was baptised,' baptism 2 May 1667.

—. 'Henry the son of John and Joanne Jetto was baptised,' baptism 17 October 1671. [Great-grandson of Henrie Jetto].

—. 'Margery the daughter of John and Jane Jetto was baptised,' 6 October 1673.

—. 'Thomas Jetter buried,' burial 15 May 1717.

Also from Holt but not related to Henrie Jetto.

Henry Bedell was the church warden 'baptised 1573.'

—. 'The 1st day of May was Sir Henry Bromley the worthy lord of the manor of Holt buried,' burial 1 May 1615.

—. 'Elizabeth the negro of Horatio Morley was buried,' burial 2 December 1627.

—. 'Henry Sambo a Blakmore servant to right worthy Henry Bromley esquire being taught and instructed in the Church catechism was baptised,' baptism 6 October 1667.

—. Henry Bromley 'died,' 6 October 1670.

—. Chaddesley Corbett Parish Register, ref. x 850, 'Margery childe of an egyptian was baptised,' baptism 12 April 1604.

Court Cases and Legal decisions

Anon. *Early Chancery Proceedings* (ECP), National Archives, Kew, C1/148/67 and C1/29/150, C1/247/18.
Anon. *Court of Chancery: Six Clerks Office: Early Proceedings, Richard II to Philip and Mary, 1518-1529*, National Archives, Kew, C1/831/71-72.
Anon. *Court of Chancery: Six Clerks Office: Early Proceedings, Richard II to Philip and Mary, 1475-1485*, National Archives, Kew, C1/66/389; C1/64/330; C1/66/339.
Anon. *A Forensic Dispute on the Legality of Enslaving Africans held at the Commencement in Cambridge New England, July 21, 1773 ...* Boston: John Boyle, 1773.
Anon. *High Courts of Admiralty* (HCA) Reports, National Archives, Kew, 1547, ref. 24/39/49-51.
Anon. *In the Matter of Cartwright*, 11 Elizabeth, 2 Rushworth's College, (1569), p 468.
Anon. *Shanley v Harvey*, 2 Eden, (1763), pp. 126, 127.
Anon. *The Statutes or Ordinaunces Concernynge Artificers, Seruauntes, and Labourers, Journeymen and Prentyses, Drawen out of the Common Lawes of thys Realme, syth the Tyme of Edwarde the Fyrste, Untyll the Thyrde and Fourth Yeare of Oure ... Kynge Edwarde the vi, wyth the Statute and Order of the Measuryng of Landes*. London: Nycholas Hyll, 1550.
Author unknown. *Somersett's Case, R. v. Knowles, ex parte Somersett*, 20 State Tr, (1772), p.1.
Anon. *The Calendar of the Patent Rolls*, Henry III, 1258-1266. London: HMSO, 1910, p. 28.
Anon. *The Court of Chancery Legal Records*, Req2 /164/17, National Archives, Kew.
Baildon, William Paley (ed.). *Les Reportes del Cases in Camera Stellata 1593 to 1609. From the original MS. of John Hawarde ...* London: Baildon?, 1894.
Butler, Cheryl and Edward Andrew Spicer (eds.). *The Book of Fines: The Annual Accounts of the Mayors of Southampton, 1488-1540*, Volume I. Southampton: Southampton University, 2008.
Caesar, Julius [Sir]. *The Ancient State, Authoritie, and Proceedings of the Court of Requests. 2. Octob. 1596.* London: Caesar, 1597.
Coke, Edward. *Les Reports de Edward Coke ... de Diuers Resolutions & Judgemens Donnes ... per les ... Judges, & Sages de la ley ... Durant les Tresheureux Regiment de ... Roigne Elizabeth ...1600*. New edition, London: Tomas Wight, 1607.

Coke, Edward. *The Famous Case of Robert Calvin a Scots-man; as Contain'd in the Reports of Sir E. Coke ... as it was Argued in Westminster-Hall ...* Edinburgh: James Watson, 1705.

Coke, Edward. *The Lord Coke his Speech and Charge. With a Discouerie of the Abuses and Corruption of Officers* ... London: Nathaniell Butter, 1607.

Coke, Edward. *Le Necessarie vse & Fruit de les Pleadings, Conteine en le lieur de le Tresreuerend Edward Coke, Lattorney General la Roigne* ... London: Thomas Wight, 1601.

Dasent, John Roche (ed.). *Acts of the Privy Council of England. New Series ... 1542, [etc.] Edited by J. R. Dasent ... Published ... Under the Direction of the Master of the Rolls.* London: Stationery Office, 1890.

Marsden, Reginald Godfrey (ed.). *Selden Society, Select Pleas in the Court of Admiralty.* Vol. I. *The Court of the Admiralty of the West (A.D. 1390-1404) and the High Court of Admiralty (A.D. 1527-1545),* Volume II. London: Publications of the Selden Society, 1897.

Leadam, I. S. and Issac Saunders (eds.). *Select Cases in the Court of Requests, A.D. 1497- 1569.* London: Bernard Quaritch for the Selden Society, 1895.

National Archives, Kew. 'Will of Nicholas Wichehalse,' Barnstable, Devon, 23/9/ 1570, ref. Ward 7/13/29, C 142/153/20, C142/100/18, 28 August 1570. 'Anthonye my Negarre' is referred to as a trustee in the will and post mortem inquiries of Nicholas Wichehalse of Barnstaple who died 28 August 1570,'

To Anthonye my negarre bequeath all my lands in the Town and pisshes of Lynton and Counseberye, Peracombe, Loxford Berynarber, ffremention and Barnstable to Marye my wyfe for life and for the satisfaction of my debtes and legacyes and pformaunce of this my wyll. I do make said Mary my hole executrixe, and for overseers I ordaine Mr Robert Appelye and my borther John Drate. Proved P.C.C. 23 Sept 1570 by procurator of Mary the relict.

Taney, Roger B. (Chief Justice). *Dred Scott Case, Scott v Sandford*, United States Supreme Court (1857), 60 U.S. 393.

Worcestershire Archive Office, Worcester. 'Will of Henrie Jetto' Will number 102, dated and signed on 20 September 1626, but executed 13 September 1638.

In the name of God Amen; the xx th day of September in the yeare of our Lord god 1626 Fferrey. Jetto of the parish of Holte doe make my will and testament.

First I give and bequeathe my sole unto Almightie God my maker and redeemer and my body bodie to the ground.

Item as is my will that my bodie shall be well and ... [to?] ... [my?] ...

[dear?] ... [these words have been scribbled out] brought home and the rest which is left ... for to be divided between my daughter Sarah my daughter Margaret my sonne Richard and my daughter Ellinor: and forty shillings to God payed to John will? and xxx for the ... unto my sonne John the Cuthbert in the hath my ... boarde the benches formes ...

Item I give unto my grandchild George Wood ... xx

Item I give unto my grandchild Walter Wood ... xy

Item I give unto Joyce Cru?pe ... x?

Item I give unto my daughter Ellinor besides her portion ...

Item It is my will that my children shall not have theyr portion until my wife's decease unless they chance to marry or in the election for to do very well for I put it to her disposition.

Item It is my will that if my sonne Richard and my daughter Margaret will not be ruled and doe after theyr mother's commandment for to have ... xx, shillings a piece and no more and theyre portion to [the estates] ... to their two sisters.

Item I make my wife my sole executor and for my will and truly performed.

Witness John Sandford

  William Sandford.'

——. Will of 'Persida Jetto widow' July 1640, Will Probate Records 186-223. 1 Noverint universis per presentes nos Johnanes Jette de Hoult in Comiitatu Wigorn' yeoman ct Gulielmus Coxe clericum curatum de Hoult in Comitatu Wigorn' predicto5 teneri et firmiter obligari reverendo in Christo patri domino Johannum Wigorn' episcopo in Vigintis libris bone et legalis monete Anglie solventis eidem reverendo patri aut suo Certo Atturnato Executoribus Administratoribus vel Successoribus suis ad quam quidem solutionem bene et fideliter faciendam obligamus 10 nos et utrumque nostrum per se pro toto et in solidum heredes executores et administratores nostros firmiter per presentes sigillis nostris sigillatas Date vicesimo octavo die Julii Anno Regnis domini nostri Caroli dei gratia Anglie Scotie Francie et Hibernie Regis fidei defensor etc decimo sexton.15 The condition of this obligation is such that if the above bounden John Jettoe the sonne and administrator of all and singular the goodes cattells and debtes of Persidie Jetto late of Hoult in the diocese of Worcester deceased doe will and truly administer the said goodes that is to say doe 20 pay all and singuler the debtes and dueties of the said defunct which are all the tyme of her decease for so far forth as the said goods will thereunto extend and as the lawe will charge him And doe render and yield up a true and perfect Accompte of his Administration in ade of and upon the premises unto the ordinary of 25 the diocese of Worcester for the tyme beinge when he shalbe thereunto lawefully requested and called And for such part and portion as shall remayne uppon his said Accompte he shall stand to and abide the order and decree of the said Ordinarie And lastlie doe defend and save harmeles the above named Reverend Father and 30 all others his Officers and Ministers att all tymes hereafter of and from all manner of person and persons haveinge or pretendinge to have any right title or interest unto the said goods or any parte or parcell thereof them this obligation shalbe void or els shall stand in force Sealed and delivered in 35 the presence of…

Inventory of the Goods and Chattels of 'Persida Jetto' (widow of Henry Jetto) July 1640.

A true and just Inventory of all the Goodes Chattles and Cattles of Persida Jetto widdowe lately deceased taken the ?th day of July Anno domini 1640 li s d

Inprimis all her wearing clothes 100

Item 1 bed-steede 1 bed and boulster and other wearinge clothes 0 13 4

Item 1 bed stead ? of lokes one broked chest and 2 pound of hurdes 0 4 0

Item 3 burrells and 2 boxes 0 4 0

Item one kneadinge tubb one seartes 1 some and hoope 0 2 8

Item 1 table board 1 forme 1 cupboard 2 beuther and 1 peire of wainscott 1 1 00

Item 1 fryinge pan 1 paire of Gobirons 1 soitt 1 paire of Lukes 1 grediron and 1 paire of tongues 0 4 0

Item shovell 1 hacker 1 mattacke 1 peale 1 ? forke and 3 hookes 0 1 4

Item 1 iron racke 0 0 6

Item 2 little kettles 2 candlestickes 2 pewter dishes 1 sawcer and 1 salt 050

Item 2 wheeles 2 reeles and a paire ? ? 020

Item certaine small Greene ware 020

Item 1 chaire 2 formes and 2 stooles 016

Item some small earthen ware 010

Item 5 geese 050

Item 2 pigge 068

Item 2 hennes 010

Item the deade yeare 900

Item for house close and fombe 208

Item one Acre of flaxe 428

The whole summe is 17158

Wittnesses hereunto the day and yeare above written

The marke of Edward Prilthell

The marke of John Theapard.

BIBLIOGRAPHY

Books, printed records and letters

Abelard, Peter in C. K. Scott-Moncrieff (translator (tr.). *The Letters of Abelard and Heloise*. New York: Alfred A. Knopf, 1925.

Abentarique, Tarif. *The History of the Conquest of Spain by the Moors. Together with the Life of the Most Illustrious Monarch Menesh Almanzar and of the Several Revolutions of the Mighty Empire of the Caliphs and of the African Kingdoms ... Now made English*. London: Fleach, sold by T Fox, 1687.

Africanus, Leo and John Pory (tr., ed.). *A Geographical Historie of Africa, Written in Arabicke and Italian ... by Iohn Leo a More ...* London: John Pory, 1600.

Allen, William. *A True Sincere and Modest Defence of English Catholiques that Suffer for their Faith at Home and Abrode: Against a False, Seditious and Slaunderous Libel Intituled; The Execution of Justice in England (by William Cecil, Baron Burghley) ...* Rouen: Robert Persons, 1584.

Alvarez, Francisco (ed.) and Henry Edward Stanley (tr.). *Narrative of the Portuguese Embassy to Abyssinia during the Years of 1520–1527*. New York: Burt Franklin, 1966.

A Moor. *Letters from a Moor at London to his Friend at Tunis. Containing an Account of his Journey through England ... Likewise Remarks on the Publick Charities, with Curious Memoirs Relating to the Life of Mr. Sutton, Founder of the Charter-House. A Description of Bedlam, etc*. London: J. Batley, J. Wood, Richard Wellington, 1736.

Anglerius, Petrus Martyr. *De Nouo Orbe, or The Historie of the West Indies ... Comprised in Eight Decades ... Three ... Formerly Translated into English, by R. Eden ... the Other Fiue ... by ... M. Lok*. London: Thomas Adams, 1612.

Anon. *A Packe of Spanish Lies Sent Abroad in the World: First Printed in Spain, in the Spanish Tongue, and Translated out of the Original. Now Ripped Up, Unfolded, and by Just Examination Condemned, as Containing False, Corrupt and Detestable Wares, Worthy to be Damned and Burned*. London: Christopher Barker, 1588.

——. Accounts of the Lord High Treasurer of Scotland, The National Archives of Scotland, H.M. General Record Office, 2 Princess Street, Edinburgh, EH1 3YY, ref. E21/5-10, Volume II, 1503/4, pp. 318, 415, 417, 420, 422, 427 etc., Volume III, 1505–1506, pp. 101, 108, 118, 121, 122, 124, 132, 148, 155, etc., Volume IV, 1506–1513, pp. 51, 59, 61, 62, 64, 82.

——. 'Anglicanus,' *Gentleman's Magazine* XXXIV, October, 1764, Volume 34, pp. 493, 495.

——. *A Declaration of the Demeanour, and Carriage of Walter Raleigh Knight* ... London: Bonham Norton and John Bull, 1618.

——. *A Declaration of Great Troubles Pretended Against the Realme a Number of Seminaries, Priests and Jesuits, Sent and very Secretly Dispersed in the Same, that Work Great Treasons under a False Pretence of Religion* ... London: Christopher Barker, 1600.

——. *A Hundred Merry Tales*. London: Johannes Rastell, 1526.

——. *An Ease for Overseers of the Poore, Abstracted from the Statutes*. Cambridge: Publisher unknown, 1601.

——. *By the King. A Proclamation (Against those that Call Themselves Blacks, and Disguise Themselves Hunting in the Night, Killing Deer, and Committing other Acts of Violence. 2 Feb. 1723)*. London: J. Baskett, 1722.

——. *By the Priuie Counsel. A Commandement that no Suiters Come to the Court for any Priuate Suite Except their Petitions be Indorsed by the Master of Requests. [20 Aug. 1594.]* London: Deputies of C Barker, 1595.

——. Letter to Lord Mayors, signed by Queen Elizabeth, National Archives, Kew, PC 2/21, p. 304, 11 July 1596.

——. Letter signed [by] Queen Elizabeth, National Archives, Kew, PC 2/21, f. 306, 18 July 1596.

——. Proclamation, National Archives, Kew, Tudor Royal Proclamations, 1601/ 804.5-805, ca. January 1601.

——. *The Booke of Secrets ... Skill to Ordering Wines ... Beer Making ... Translated out of the Dutch* ... London: Adam Islip, 1596.

——. *Exchequer Accounts*, National Archives, Kew, London, 417 (6) folio 50 RO in Letters and Papers Henry VIII 1.1.505# 1025.

——. *The Fyrst Boke of Moses Called Genesis. (The Seconde Boke of Moses, Called Exodus.-The Thyrde Boke of Moses Called Leuiticus.-The Fourthe Boke of Moses Called Numeri.-A Prologe in to the Fyfte Boke of Moses, Called Deuteronomye.) (Followed by the Text. Translated with Prologues and Marginal Notes by William Tyndale, Whose Initials Appear at the Head of the Pages of the Prologues.)* Antwerp: Hans Luft, 1531.

——. 'The romaunce of the Sowdone of Babylone, and of Ferumbras his sone who conquerede Rome,' in *Middle English Dictionary*. Ann Arbor: University of Michigan Press, new edition 1976, p. 672.

——. *The Statutes or Ordinaunces Concernynge Artificers, Seruauntes, and Labourers, Iourneymen and Prentyses, Drawn out of the Common Lawes of Thys Realme, Syth the Time of Edward the Fyrste, Vntil the Thyrde and Fourth Yeare of Oure ... Kynge Edwarde the Vi, Wyth the Statute and Order of the Measuryng of Landes*. London: Nicholas Hyll, 1550.

BIBLIOGRAPHY

——. *Token Books of St Saviour Southwark*, 1579, ref book 183, p. 7, line 33, these records are at the London Metropolitan Archives.

——. *A True Relation of the Inhumane ... Actions and Barbarous Murders of Negroes or Moors: Committed on Three Englishmen in Old Calabar in Guinny ... with a Short ... Account of the Customs and Manners and Growth of the Country ...* London: T. Passinger and B. Hurlock, 1672.

Alvares, Francisco. *Ho Preste Joam das Indias Verdadera das Informacam das Terras do Preste Joam Agora Nouamete Impresso, etc.* Lisbon: L. Rodriguez, 1540.

——. *Viaggio Fatto Nella Ethiopia-Obbedienza Data a Papa Clemente Settimo in Nome del Prete Gianni.* Lisbon: L. Rodriguez, 1550.

——. Lord Stanley (tr.). *The Prester John of the Indies: A True Relation of the Lands of the Prester John, being the Narrative of the Portuguese Embassy to Ethiopia in 1520/ the Translation of Lord Stanley of Alderley (1881) Revised and Edited with Additional Material by CF Beckingham and GWB Huntingford.* Cambridge: Cambridge University Press, 1961.

——. *The Laste Booke of Peter Martyr ... of the Landes and Ilandes Lately Founde: And of the Maners of the Inhabitauntes of the Same*, in Richard Eden. *Decades of the New World ...* London: William Powell, 1555.

Antonio, Don and Federike Morell (tr.). *Psalmes of Confession, Found in the Cabinet of the Most Excellent King of Portingal, Don Antonio ... Written with his Owne Hand ...* London: G. Bishop, R. Nuberie, R. Barker, 1596.

Appleby, John (ed.), Richard Devizes. *The Chronicles of Richard of Devizes, of the Time of the King Richard the First, [written between 1192–1198.]* 1886. New edition, London: Thomas Nelson and Sons, 1963.

Aragon, Katherine, et. al. *Four Curious Documents. I. A Letter from Katherine of Aragon, to Mary, her Daughter. II. Anne Boleyn's Last Letter to Henry VIII. III. The Proclamation of Lady Jane Grey's Title to the Crown. IV. A Letter from the Princess ... Mary, to her Father, Henry VIII. 1536.* Edinburgh: privately printed, 1886.

Arbeau, Thoinot [pseudonym], Jehan Tabourot. *Orchesographie, et Traicte en Forme de Dialogue, par Lequel Toutes Personnes Peuvent Facilement Apprendre & Practiquer L'honneste Exercice des Dances.* Lengres: Des preyz, 1588.

Archer, John. 'J. R. Archer's presidential address to the inaugural meeting of the African Progress Union, 1918,' *West Africa*, II, No. 101, 4 January 1919, pp. 840-842 and quoted in Peter Fryer, *Staying Power ...* London: Pluto Press, 1984, pp. 410-416.

Aristotle. *Doubtful or Superstitious Work ... Mystica Ægyptiorum et Chaldæorum a Platone, Voce Tradita, ab Aristotele, Excepta et Conscripta*

Philosophia ... [A Latin version by P. N. de Castellaniis of the Arabic translation of Abenama.] Rome: Apud J Mazochium, 1519.

Arnold, Janet. *Queen Elizabeth's Wardrobe Unlock'd: The Inventories of the Wardrobe of Robes Prepared in July 1600* ... Leeds: Maney, 1988.

——. *Queen Elizabeth's Wardrobe Unlock'd: The Inventories of the Wardrobe of Robes Prepared in July 1600* ... London: Costume and Fashion Press, 2001.

——. *'Lost from her Majesties Back:' Items of Clothing and Jewels Lost or Given Away by Queen Elizabeth I between 1561–1585, Entered in One of the Day Books Kept for the Records of the Wardrobe of the Robes.* Bury: Costume Society, 1980.

Arnold, Richard. *Begin. in this Boke is Conteined ye Names of the Baylyfs, Cutome Manyers and Sherefys of ye Cte of London ... By Richard Arnold Known as Arnold's Chronicle.* London: Peter Treveris, 1521 in Northcote T. Toller (ed.), Joseph Bosworth, *An Anglo-Saxon Dictionary ... Supplement* ... 1882. New edition, Oxford: Oxford University Press, 1921, p. 759.

Awdelay, John. *Here Begynneth the .xxiiii. Orders of Knaves.* London: J. Awdelay, 1561.

Azeved, Pedro de (ed.). *Archivo Historico Portuguez.* Madrid: Libano da Silva, 1903.

Bacon, Francis. 'Experiment solitary touching the coloration of black and tawny Moors,' in, *Novum Organum* (1620), in, James Spedding (ed.). *The Works of Francis Bacon Collected and Edited by James Spedding* ... London: Longman and Co, 1857.

——. *The Two Bookes of Francis Bacon. Of the Proficience and Advancement of Leaning, Divine and Humane.* London: Henrie Tomes, 1605.

Baker, Robert and P. E. H. Hair (ed.). *Travails in Guinea/ Robert Baker's 'Brefe Discourse.'* 1568. New edition, Liverpool: Liverpool University Press, Liverpool University, 1998.

——. *Travails in Guinea/ Robert Baker's 'Brefe Discourse.'* 1568. in, Hakluyt's *Navigations,* 1589 (see below).

Barnfield, Richard. *The Affectionate Shepheard. Containing the Complaint of Daphnis for the Love of Ganymede.* London: John Danter for T. Gubbin and E. Newman, 1594.

Barnum, Priscilla Heath (ed.). Henry Parker. *Dives and Pauper.* Volume 1. Part 2. London/Oxford: Oxford University Press for the Early English Text Society, 1976.

Baskerville, Thomas. *An Approbation of this Discourse, by Sir Thomas Baskeruile.* London: John Windet, 1596.

Battell, Andrew. *The Strange Adventures of Andrew Battell of Leigh, in Angola and Adjoining Regions*. London: Hakluyt Society, 1901. (I have kept his name as 'Battell' not 'Battel' since that is how it appears to have been recorded in the early texts.)

Beale, Robert. 'A Treatise of the office of a Councellor and Principall Secretaire to her Majesty,' in Conyers Read. *Mr. Secretary Walsingham and the Policy of Queen Elizabeth*, Volume I. Oxford: Clarendon Press, 1925, pp. 423–443.

Behn, Aphra. *All the Histories and Novels Written by the Late Ingenious Mrs. Behn, Entire in One Volume. Viz. I. The History of Oroonoko, or the Royal Slave. Written by the Command of King Charles the Second. II ... and ... The Adventure of the Black Lady ...* 1698. New edition, London: Samuel Briscoe, 1700.

Behn, Aphra and Joanna Lipking (ed.). *Oroonoko: An Authoritative Text, Historical Backgrounds, Criticism*. New York/London: W.W. Norton and Company, 1997.

Bergenroth, Gustav. *Calendar of Letters, Dispatches, and State Papers Relating to the Negotiations Between England and Spain Preserved in the Archives of Simancas and Elsewhere ...* London: Longmans Green Reader and Dyer, 1868.

——. *Supplement to Volume I and II of Calendar of Letters, Despatches and State Papers*. London: Longman Green Reader, 1868.

Bernes, Julyans. [The Book of St Albans] *In so moch that Gentill Men and Honest Persones haue Greete Delite in Haukyng and Desire to haue the Maner to take Haukys ... Dam Iulyans Barnes in her Boke of Huntyng ... Here in thys Booke folowyng is determyned the Lynage of Coote Armuris ...* St Albans: publisher unknown, 1486.

Best, George. *A True Discourse of the Late Voyages of Discovery, for the Finding of a Passage to Cathya, by the Northwest, under the Conduct of Martin Frobisher ...* London: H Bynyman, 1578.

Beze, Theodore de, Robert Fyll (tr.). *A Briefe and Piththie [sic] Summe of the Christian Faith, Made in Form of a Confession, with a Confutation of all such Superstitious Errors, as are Contrary Thereunto Translated out of French by RF.* London: William How, 1572.

Beze, Theodore de, Anthony Gilbie (tr.). *The Psalmes of David, Truly Opened and Explained by Paraphrasis, According to the Right Sense of Every Psalme Set Foorth in Latine by Theodore Beza and Faithfully Translated into English, by Anthonie Gilbie, and by Him Newlie Purged from Sundrie Faultes Escaped in the First Print, etc.* London: Henrie Denham, 1581.

Beze, Theodore de, Arthur Golding (tr.). *A Booke of Christian Questions and Answers Wherin are Set Foorth the Chief Points of the Christian Religion Newly Translated into English by Arthur Golding.* London: William How for Abraham Veale, 1572.

Beze, Theodore de, John Stubbs (tr.). *Christian Meditations upon Eight Psalmes of the Prophet David Made and Newly Set Forth by Theodore Beza Translated out of Frenche, for the Common Benefite, into the Vulgar Tongue by J S.* London: Christopher Barker, 1582.

Biddulph, William. *The Travels of Certain Englishmen into Africa, Asia, Troy, Bythnia, Thracia, and to the Black Sea …Began in the Year … 1600 … Finished this Year 1608 …* London: T. H. Hoveland for W. Aspley, 1609.

Binski, Paul. *The Painted Chamber at Westminster.* London: Society of Antiquaries of London, 1986.

Black, Sue. 'Human Skeletal Remains from Wolsey Street, Ipswich, (IAS5003),' January 2009, Report unpublished.

Blackstone, William, John Frederick Archbold and John Taylor Coleridge, et. al. *Commentaries on the Laws of England.* 1765. New edition, London: GW Childs, 1867.

Bland, William. *Letter to Lord Burghley*, October 1590, in *Lansdowne Manuscripts*, no. 115, item 84, p. 241.

Bodin, Jean in Marion Leathers Daniels Kuntz (trs., eds.). *Colloquium of the Seven about Secrets of the Sublime.* Princeton/London: Princeton University Press, 1975.

Bodin, Jean. *De la Demonomanie des Sorciers …* Paris: Du Puys, 1580.

Bolton, James Laurence (ed.). *Alien Communities of London in the Fifteenth Centuries: The Subsidy Rolls of 1440 and 1483–4.* Stamford: Richard III and York History Trust with Paul Watkins, 1998.

Boorde, Andrew. *The Boke for to Lerne a Man to be Wyse in Buyldyng of his Howse for the Helth of his Soule, and Body …* London: Robert Wyer, 1540.

Boorde, Andrew. *The First Boke of the Introduction of Knowledge. The Whych Doth Teach a Man to Speake and Parte of all Maner of Languages and to Know the Vsage and Fashion of all Maner of Countries, etc with woodcuts.* London: William Copeland, 1550.

Bourne, William. *A Booke Called the Treasure for Traveilers, Divided into Five Books or Partes, Contaynyng Very Necessary Matters, For All Sortes of Travailers, Either by Sea or by Lande.* London: T. Woodcoke, 1578.

Bowen, Thomas (ed.). *Bridewell Hospital, Extracts from the Records and Court Books of Bridewell Hospital …* London: Bridewell Hospital? 1798.

Bowen, Thomas Jefferson. *Grammar and Dictionary of the Yoruba Language. With an Introductory Description of the Country and People of Yoruba.* New York: Smithsonian Institute, 1858.

Brown, Peter. *British Cutlery: An Illustrated History of its Design, Evolution and Use.* London: Philip Wilson, 2001.

Browne, John. *The Marchants Auizo Verie Necessarie for their Sonnes and Servants, When They First Send Them Beyond the Seas etc.* London: Thomas Orwin for William Norton, 1590.

Browne, Thomas. *Pseudodoxia Epidemica: or, Enquiries into Very Many Received Tenents and Commonly Presumed Truths.* London: Edward Dod, 1646.

Browne, Thomas. *The Copie of the Sermon Preached Before the University at St Maries in Oxford, on Tuesday the xxiv of December 1633.* Oxford: John Lichfield, 1634.

Buck, George. *An Abstract of the Expedition to Cadiz 1596, Drawne out of Commentaries Written at large thereof, by a Gentleman who was in the Voyage (i.e. Sir George Buck).* London: Thomas Dawson for Thomas Adams, 1615.

Buck, George. *The Third Vniuersitie of England. Or, a Treatise of the Foundations of all the Colledges, Ancient Schools of Priuiledge, and of Houses of Learning, and Liberall Arts, within and about the Most Famous Cittie of London. With a Briefe Report of the Sciences, Arts, and Faculties therein Professed, Studied, and Practised. Together with the Blazon of the Armes, and Ensignes thereunto belonging. Gathered Faithfully out of the Best Histories, Chronicles, Records, and Archiues, by G. B., Knight (George Buck.)* in John Stow. *The Annales.* London: Thomas Dawson for Thomas Adams, 1615.

Bull, George and Robert Nelson. *Some Important Points of Primitive Christianity ... Volume 2.* London: Richard Smith, 1713.

Bulwer, John. *Anthropometamorphosis: Man Transform'd; or, the Artificial Changeling Historically presented, in the Mad and Cruel Gallantry, Foolish Bravery, Ridiculous Beauty, Filthy Finenesse, and Loathsome Lovelinesse of Most Nations, Fashioning & Altering their Bodies from the Mould Intended by Nature With a Vindication of the Regular Beauty and Honesty of Nature And an Appendix of the Pedigree of the English Gallant By J B Sirnamed, The Chirosopher (John Bulwer) [With an engraved frontispiece].* London: William Hunt, 1653.

Butler, Arthur John (ed.), et. al. *Public Record Office, Calendar of State Papers, Foreign Series, of the Reign of Elizabeth ... Volume I. 1863.* New edition, London: Her Majesty's Stationery, 1914.

Cambrensis, Geraldus and Joseph Stevenson (tr.). *Concerning the Instruction of Princes* ... 1858. New edition, Felinfach: JMF Books, 1991.
Camden, William. *Britannia siue Florentissimorum regnorum, Angliae, Scotiae, Hiberniae, et insularum adiacentium ex intima antiquitate chorographica descriptio, authore Guilielmo Camdeno.* London: Radulphum Newbery, 1586.
Carew, George and Christopher Hunt (trs. eds.). *Godfrey of Bulloigne; or, the Recoverie of Hieruslaem: an Heroicall Poeme Written by Seig. Torquato Tasso, and Translated into English by R. C. C[arew]* ... London: J. Windet for G. Hunt, 1594.
——. *Letters from George Lord Carew to Sir Thomas Roe, Ambassador to the Court of the Great Mogul 1615–1617.* London: Camden Society, 1860.
——. and Thomas Stafford (ed.). *Pacata Hibernia. Ireland Appeased and Reduced. Or, an Historie of the Late Warres of Ireland, Especially Within the Province of Mounster vnder the Government of Sir G. Carew ... Illustrated with Seventeene Severall Mappes* ... London: Aug. Mathewes for Robert Milbourne, 1633.
——. *The Survey of Cornwall. And an Epistle concerning the Excellencies of the English Tongue. Now first Published from the Manuscript ... [written in 1602 and 1605 respectively].* London: Samuel Chapman, 1723.
Casas, Bartolome de las. *The Spanish Colonie* ... London: Thomas Dawson for William Brome, 1583.
Casas, Bartolome de las, John Phillips (tr.). *The Tears of the Indians: Being an Historical and True Account of the Cruel Massacres and Slaughters of Above Twenty Millions of Innocent Peoples; Committed by the Spaniards in the Islands of Hispaniola, Cuba, Jamaica, &c ... to the Total Destruction of those Countries* ... London: Printed by J. C. for Nathanial Brook, 1656.
A Catalogue of the Lansdowne Manuscripts in the British Museum with Indexes of Persons, Places and Matters. London: British Museum Dept. of Manuscripts, 1819, p. 221.
Cecil, Robert. *An Answer to Certaine Scandalous Papers* ... London: Thomas Basson, 1606.
Cecil, Robert. *Copie of a Letter to the Right Honourable Earl of Leicester* ... London: Christopher Barker, 1586.
Cecil, Robert and John Mclean (ed.). *Letters from Sir Robert Cecil to Sir George Carew* ... London: Camden Society, 1864.
Chambers Dictionary of Etymology. New York: Harrap Publishers, 1988.
Chamberlain, John and Sarah Williams (ed.). *Letters Written by John Chamberlain during the Reign of Elizabeth I.* London: Camden Society, 1861.

Chamberlain of Bristol. *Accounts of Disbursements*, October 1590, in *Lansdowne Manuscripts*, no. 115, item 82, p. 235.

Chaucer, Geoffrey. *The Prologue to the Canterbury Tales, the Boke of Chaucer Named the Canterbury Tales* ... London 'Westmestre:' William Caxton, 1498.

———. *The Canterbury Tales ... The Man of Law's Tale* (1498), pp. prologue, fii- gii.

Chaucer, Geoffrey and John Lydgate. *The Complaint of the Black Knight* ... London: R Redmayne, 1718.

Cirencester, Richard in John Allen Giles (tr. ed.). *The Chronicle of Richard Devizes Concerning the Deeds of the Richard the First, King of England: Also Richard of Cirencester's Description of Britain*. London: James Bohn, 1841.

Claramonte, Andres de. *El Valiente Negro en Flanders, Edicion Para Actores y Directores de Nelson Lopez*. Kassel: Reichenberger, 2007.

Coleman, Jane. *A History of Cant and Slang Dictionaries, 1758–1858*. Oxford: Oxford University Press, 2004.

Comes, Sophie Crawford (ed.), Edward Stafford. *Calendar of State Papers, Foreign Series*, Volume 21. London: Her Majesty's Stationery, 1927.

Company of Royal Adventurers in England trading in Africa. *The Several Declarations of the Company of Royal Adventurers of England Trading into Africa ... Together with his Royal Highness James Duke of Yorke ... and the Rest of the Said Royal Companie's Letter to ... Francis Lord Willoughby ... Intimating the Said Companie's Resolution to Furnish his Majestie's American Plantations with Negroes ... Also a List of the Royal Adventurers* ... London: Company of Royal Adventurers, 1667.

Conestaggio, Ieronimo. *Dell'unione del Regno di Portogallo. Alla Corona di Castiglia. Istoria*. Genoua: Girolamo Bartoli, 1585.

Conestaggio, Ieronimo and Edward Blount (tr.). *The Historie of the Uniting of the Kingdom of Portugal to the Crowne of Castill ... The Description of Portugal, their Principal Townes, etc.* London: A. Hatfield for E. Blount, 1600.

Correas, Gonzalo. *Vocabulario de Refranes Y Frases Proverbiales*. Salamanca: Publisher unknown, 1627.

Corro, Anthonye de. *A Supplication to the King of Spain* ... London: Coldocke and Bynneman, London, 1577.

Cotti, Giovanni B., William Barley (tr.). *A Booke of Curious and Strange Inventions called the First Part of Needleworkes* ... London: J. Danter for William Barley, 1596.

Covarrubias, Sebastian de (Horozco). *Tesoro de la Lengua Castellano O Espano*. Madrid: Luis Sanchez, 1610, 1611.

Coverdale, Miles (ed.). *Biblia. The Bible, that is, the Holy Scripture of the Olde and New Testament, Faithfully and Truly Translated out of Douche and Latyn in to Englishe. [Translated by Miles Coverdale, Afterwards Bishop of Exeter. With Woodcut Titlepages, Illustrations, and Map.]* Marburg: E. Cervicornus & J. Soter?, 1535.

Cromwell, Thomas. *Walks Through Islington; Comprising an Historical and Descriptive Account of that District, Both in its Ancient and Present State with Numerous Engravings, by J & H. S. Storer L P.* London: Sherwood Gilbert and Piper, 1835.

Cugoano, Ottobah. *Thoughts and Sentiments on the Evil and Wicked Traffic of the Slavery and Commerce of the Human Species, Humbly Submitted to the Inhabitants of Great Britain.* London: T. Beckett, 1787.

Curio, Caelius Augustinus. *A Notable History of the Saracens ...* London: William How and Abraham Veale, 1575.

Curteys, Richard and Thomas Browne (ed.). *A Sermon Preached Before the Queenes Maistie at Grenewiche, the 14 Day of Marche 1573.* London: Henry Bynneman for Francis Coldocke, 1579.

Dabydeen, David and Paul Edwards (eds.). *Black Writers in Britain 1760–1890.* Edinburgh: Edinburgh University, 1991.

Daniel, Samuel. *The True Discription of a Royall Masque. Presented at Hampton Court, Upon Sunday Night, being the Eight of Ianuary. 1604. And Personated by the Queenes Most Excellent Majestie, Attended by Eleuen Ladies of Honour.* London: Edward Allde, 1604.

Dawson, Thomas Cook. *The Good Huswifes Jewell. Wherein is to be Found Most Excellend and Rare Deuises for Conceites in Cookery, Found out by the Practise of Thomas Dawson. Wherevnto is adioyned Sundry Approved Receits for Many Soueraine Oyles, and the Way to Distill Many Precious Waters, with Diuers Appproued Medicines for Many Diseases. Also Certain Approued Points of Husbandry ... Newly Set Foorth with Additions.* 1565. New edition, London: Edward White, 1596.

Dekker, Thomas. *The Seuen Deadly Sinnes of London: Drawne in Seuen Seuerall Coaches, Through the Seuen Seuerall Gates of the Citie, Bringing the Plague with Them.* London: Edward Allde for Nathaniel Butter, 1606.

Delgadillo de Avellaneda, Bernaldino. *A Libell of Spanish Lies: Found at the Sacke of Cales, Discoursing the Fight in the West Indies, Twixt the English Nauie being Fourteene Ships and Pinasses, and a Fleete of Twentie Saile of the King of Spaines, and of the Death of Sir Francis Drake. With an Answere Briefely Confuting the Spanish Lies ...* London: John Windet, 1596.

Devizes, Richard, in Ruth Morse (ed.). *Truth and Convention in the Middle Ages: Rhetoric, Representation, and Reality*. Cambridge: Cambridge University Press, 1991, pp. 109–110.

Diaz de Bivar, Rodrigo and Robert Southey (tr.). *Chronicle of the Cid ... (Translated mainly from the 'Cronica particular del Cid') ...* London: Longman, Hurst, Rees, Orme, 1808.

Downame, John. *A Plea of the Poore, or a Treatise of Beneficence and Almes-Deeds: Teaching How These Christian Duties Are Rightly to be Performed*. London: E. Griffin for R. Tubbe, 1616.

Drake, Francis. *Sir Francis Drake Revived Calling upon the Dull or Effeminate Age to Follow his Noble Steps for Gold and Silver*. 1621. Revised edition, London: Nicolas, Bourne, 1628.

Drake, Francis and William Davenant. *The History of Sir Francis Drake, Expressed by Instrumentall and Vocal Musick ...* London: Henry Herringman, 1659.

Drake, Francis. *The World Encompassed by Sir Francis Drake, being his Next Voyage to that to Nombre de Dios Formerly Imprinted; Carefully Collected out of the Notes of Master Francis Fletcher, Preacher in this Employment, and Divers Others his Followers in the same, etc. (By Sir F. Drake, Bart., Nephew of the Admiral.)* London: Nicholas Bourne, 1628.

Duane, William. *A Military Dictionary, or, Explanation of the Several Systems of Discipline of Different Kinds of Troops ...* London: William Duane, 1810.

Dunbar, William, in Richard Maitland (ed.). *Ancient Scottish Poems Never Before in Print*, Volume I. London/Edinburgh: C. Dilly, 1786.

Dyson, Humfrey (collator). *A Book Containing all such Proclamations as were Published by the Reigine of the Late Queen Elizabeth 1559–1602 ...* London: Bonham Norton and John Bull, 1618.

Eastwood, Jonathan. *The Bible Word-Book: A Glossary of Old English Bible Words*. London/Cambridge: Macmillan and Co, 1866.

Eden, Richard. *The Decades of the Newe World or West India ...* London: William Powell, 1555.

——. *The History of Travel in the West and East Indies and other Countries Lying Either Way Towards the Fruitful and Riche Moluccaes ...* London: Richard Iugge, 1577.

Elaskary, Mohamed Ibrahim Hassan. *The Image of Moors in [the] Writings of Four Elizabethan Dramatists: Peele, Dekker, Heywood and Shakespeare*. Exeter: dissertation unpublished University of Exeter, 2008.

Eldad, Ha-Dani. *Sefer Eldad*. Mantua: Abraham Conath, 1480.

Elizabeth I. *By the Queene. Proclamation Against Idlers and Vagrants in London. 15 Feb 1601*. London: Barker, 1601.

——. *By the Queene. A Proclamation Against Stubs, 'Gaping Gulf' 27 Sept. 1579*. London: Christopher Barker, 1579.

——. *The History of the Life and Reign of ... Queen Elizabeth I ...* London: Publisher unknown, 1739.

Fabyan, Robert. *The Chronicles of Fabyan ...* London: R. Pynson, 1516.

Fartua, Ahmed Ibn and Herbet Richmond Palmer (tr.). *History of the First Twelve Years of the Reign of Mai Idris, Alooma of Bornu (1571-1583) / by his Imam, Ahmed Ibn Fartua, Together with the 'Diwan of the Sultans of Bornu' and 'Girgam of the Magumi;' Translated from the Arabic ...* Lagos: Government Printer, 1926.

Fitz-Geffrey, Charles. *Sir Francis Drake. His Honorable Lifes Commendation, and his Tragicall Deathes Lamentation (in verse.)* Oxford: Lee Priory, 1596.

Fleetwood, William. *The Effect of the Declaratio Made in the Guildhall by M Recorder of London, Concerning the Late Attempts by Her Quenes Maiesties Euill, Seditious, and Disobedient Subiectes*. London: John Daye, 1571.

Fletcher, John. *Monsieur Thomas, a Comedy in Five Acts and in Verse*. London: T. Harper for J Waterson, 1639 in Northcote T. Toller (ed.), Joseph Bosworth. *An Anglo-Saxon Dictionary ... Supplement*, p.123.

Foster, Joseph. *Alumni Oxonienses: The Members of the University of Oxford, 1715–1886 and Alumni Oxonienses: The Members of the University of Oxford 1500–1714*. Oxford: Parker and Co., 1888–1892.

Foxe, John. *Book of Martyrs*:javascript:open_window(%22http://catalogue.bl.uk:80/F/C1K8S2NG1ESIHCXGSB82JQMLK6YLAYJT77VIB7KCUI9J18UTFA-16688?func=service&doc_number=001282112&line_number=0009&service_type=TAG%22); *Wrytinges Horrible Troubles, That Have Bene Wrought and Practised by the Romishe Prelates, Speciallye in this Realme of England and Scotlande, From the Yeare of Our Lorde, a Thousande, unto the Tyme Nowe Present. Gathered and Collected According to the True Copies Actes and Monuments of these Latter and Perillous Dayes, Touching Matters of the Church, Wherein ar Comprehended and Described the Great Persecutions ... 1554*. Revised English edition, London: John Day, 1563.

Freedman, Terry and Iseabail Mcleod. *The Wordsworth Dictionary of First Names*. Ware: Wordsworth Editions, 1995.

Fulke, William. *A Retentive to Stay Good Christians in True Faith and Religion, Against the Motives of R. Bristow. Also, A Discoverie of the Daungerous Rocke of the Popish Church, Commended by N. Sander*. London: T. Vautroullier for G. Bishop, 1580.

Fuller, Thomas. *The Histories of the Worthies of England*. 1662. New edition, London: F. C. and J. Rivington, 1811.

BIBLIOGRAPHY

Gairdner, James and Robert Henry Brodie, et. al. (eds.). *Letters and Papers, Foreign and Domestic, Henry VIII, Volume 20, Part 2, August-December 1545.* London: Longman Green, 1907.

Gama, Vasco de. 'Round Africa to India 1497–1498,' in Oliver J. Thatcher (ed.). *The Library of Original Sources, Vol. V: 9th to 16th Centuries.* Milwaukee: University Research Extension Co., 1907, pp. 26–40.

Gamboa, Pedro Sarmiento de, Nuna da Silva and Zelia Nuttall (eds.). *New Light on Drake: A Collection of Documents Relating to his Voyage of Circumnavigation, 1577–1580.* London: Hakluyt Society, 1968.

Garvey, Marcus and Amy Jacques Garvey (ed.). *Philosophy and Opinions of Marcus Garvey.* 1st edition not known. 2nd edition, New York: Universal Publishing House, 1923.

Garvey, Marcus and Robert A. Hill (ed.). *The Marcus Garvey and Universal Negro Improvement Association Papers.* London/Berkeley: University of California Press, 1983.

Gessner, Conrad and George Baker (tr.). *The Newe Jewell of Health ...* London: H. Denham, 1576.

Gibbon, Charles. *A Watch-Worde for Warre Not so New as Necessary. Published by Reason of the Disperced Rumors Amongst us, and the Suspected Comming of the Spanyard Against us ...* Cambridge: John Legat, 1596.

Giesing, Cornelia and Valentin Vydrine (eds., trs.). *Ta: rikh Mandinka de Bijini (Guinée-Bissau): la Mémoire des Mandinka et Sòoninkee du Kaabu/ Traduction, Notes et Commentaires par Cornelia Giesing and Valentin Vydrine.* Leiden/Boston: Brill, 2007.

Giles, John Allen. *The Chronicles of Richard of Devizes ... also Richard of Cirencester's Description of Britain.* Oxford/London: James Bohn, 1841.

Giraldi, Cinthio Giovanni Battista. *De gli Hecatommithi di G. Gyraldi Cinthio ... Parte Prima (Seconda, Nella Quale si Contengono tre Dialoghi Della Vita Civile).* L. Torrentino: Monte Regale, [Mendovi,] 1565.

Giraldi, Cinthio Giovanni Battista. 'Il Moro di Venezia,' *De Gli Hecatommithi*, Volume I. Vinegia: Girolamo Scotto, 1566, pp. 324–334.

Giraldus, Cambrensis, in Joseph Stevenson (tr.). *Concerning the Instruction of Princes/ Gerald of Wales.* Felinfach: JMF Books, 1991.

Gosson, Stephen. *Quippes for Upstart Newfangled Gentlewomen (A Glasse, to View the Pride of Vainglorious Women Containing a Pleasant Invective Against the Fantastical Forreigne Toyes, Daylie Used in Women's Apparell.* London: Richard Ihones, 1595.

Grafton, Richard. *A Chronicle at Large, and meere History of the Affayres of England; and Kinges of the Same, Deduced from the Creation of the Worlde,* unto the First Habitation of Thys Islande, and is by Contynuance to the First Yeere of ... Queene Elizabeth ... Volume 2. London: Henry Denham for R. Tottle and H. Toye, 1569.

Great Britain Royal Commission on Historical Manuscripts. *Fourth Report of the Royal Commissions on Historical Manuscripts.* London: Eyre and Spottiswoode, 1874, p. 414.

Greene, Robert. *Perimedes the Blacke-Smith, a Golden Methode How to Use the Minde in Pleasant and Profitable Exercise* ... London: John Wolfe, Edward White, 1588. New edition, London: John Drawater, 1595.

Greene, Robert. *The Estate of English Fugitives under the King of Spain and his Ministers* ... London: John Drawater, 1595.

Greepe, Thomas. *The True and Perfecte Newes of the Woorthy and Valiaunt Exploytes Performed and Doone by that Valiant Knight Syr F. Drake; Not Onely at Sancto Domingo and Carthagena, etc ... Giving an Account of the late Successes Against the Spaniards* ... London: publisher unknown, 1587.

Gregoire, Henrie. *On the Slave Trade and on the Slavery of the Blacks and of the Whites, by a Friend of Men of All Colours* ... London: Josiah Conder, 1815.

Grim, Edward in James Craig Robertson (ed.), et. al. *Vita Sancti Thomae in Materials for the History of Thomas Becket, Archbishop of Canterbury* ... 1875. New edition, London: Longman, 1965.

Hakluyt, Richard. *Divers Voyages, Touching the Discovery of America and the Islands Adjacent.* London: Thomas Woodcoke, 1582.

Hakluyt, Richard (ed.). *The Principal Navigations* ... Volume VI. London: Hakluyt's Collection, 1598.

——. *The Principal Navigations, Voyages, Traffiques & Discoveries of the English Nation: Made by Sea or Overland to the Remote and Farthest Distant Quarters of the Earth at Any Time Within the Compass of These 1600 years.* 1598.

New edition, London: J. M. Dent and Sons, 1927.

——. *Tudor Venturers, Selected From the Principal Navigations* ... 1970. New edition, London: Read Books, 2008.

——. *Voyages of Hawkins, Frobisher and Drake: Select Narratives from the 'Principal Navigations' of Hakluyt [edited by Edward John Payne; with additional notes, maps, etc, by C. Raymond Beazley.]* Oxford: Clarendon Press, 1844–1905.

Haliwell, James Orchard (ed.), John Dee. *The Private Diary of John Dee and the Catalogue of his Library of Manuscripts* ... London: Camden Society, 1842.

Hall, Edward. *Hall's Chronicle; Containing the History of England, During the Reign of Henry the Fourth, and the Succeeding Monarchs, to the End of the Reign of Henry the Eighth, in which are particularly Described the Manners and Customs of those Periods. Carefully Collated with the Editions of 1548 and 1550* ... London: Longman, Hurst, Rees and Orme, et. al., 1809.

Hall, George Derek Gordon (ed.), Glanvilla, Ranulphus de. *The Treatise on the Laws and Customs of the Realm of England Commonly Called Glanvill.* London: Nelson, 1965.

Hanmer, Meredith (tr.). *The Auncient Ecclesiastical Histories by Eusebius, Socrates, and Euagrius whereunto is annexed Dorotheus Bishop of Tyrus, of the Lives and Ends of the Prophets, Apostles, and 70 Disciples etc.* London: M. Sparke 1636.

——. *The Baptizing of a Turke A Sermon [on Mathew Verse 16].* London: Robert Walde-Grave, 1586.

——. *The Great Bragge and Challenge of M. Champion a Jesuite, Commonlye Called Edmunde Campion, Latelye Arrived in Englande* ... London: Thomas Marshe, 1581.

Hardyng, John. *The Chronicle of Jhon Hardyng, from the Firste Begynnyng of Englande, vnto the Reigne of Kyng Edward the Fourth Wher he Made an End of his Chronicle. And from that Tyme is Added a Continuacion of the Storie in Prose (by Richard Grafton) to this Our Tyme, Now First Imprinted, etc.* London: Richard Grafton, 1543.

Harrison, William in Frederick James Furnivall, John Norden (eds.), et. al. *Harrison's Description of England in Shakespeare's Youth* ... Volume II and III. 1577, 1584, 1877. New edition, London: New Shakespeare Society, 1878.

Harvey, Gabriel. *The Trimming of T. Nashe Gentleman, by the Hightituled Patron Don Richardo de Medico Campo, Barber Chirurgion to Trinitie College in Cambridge.* London: P. Scarlet, 1597.

Haughton, William. *English-men for My Money; or, a Pleasant Comedy, [in Prose and Verse] Called, A Woman will Have Her Will.* London: printed by A. M. 1616.

Haynes, Samuel. *A Collection of State Papers Relating to Affairs in the Reigns of Henry VIII., Edward VI., Mary, and Elizabeth, from 1542 to 1570. Transcribed from Original Letters and Other Authentick Memorials Left by W. Cecill Lord Burghley, and Now Remaining at Hatfield House.* London: W. Bowyer, 1740.

Hawkins, John. *A True Declaration of the Troublesome Voyage of Mr John Hawkins to the Parties of Guyana and the West Indies, in the Yeares of Our Lord in 1567 and 1568.* London: Thomas Purfoot, 1569.

———. *Letter to Queen Elizabeth*, 16 September 1567, National Archives, Kew, SP 12/44, f. 16 16/9/1567.
———. Will of 6 June 1595, PRO Prob11/94 fols 100-105.
Hawkins, Richard. *The Observations of Sir Richard Hawkins in his Voyage into the South Sea, an. Dom. 1593 ... Illustrated with Notes ... 1622*. New edition, London: publisher unknown, 1847.
Haydn, Joseph. *Haydn's Dictionary of Dates Relating to all Ages and Nations for Universal Reference ...1841*. New edition London: Ward and Locke, 1906.
Henry VIII in Coates, Tim (ed.). *Letters of Henry VIII, 1526–29: Extracts from the Calendar of State Papers of Henry VIII*. London: Stationery Office, 2001.
Herbert, Edward and John Churton Collins (ed.). *The Poems of Lord Herbert of Cherbury*. 1665. New edition, London: publisher not known, Chatto and Windus, 1881.
Higden, Ranulphus, in William Caxton (ed.), John Trevisa (tr.). *Polychronicon (the Description of Britain)* ... London: William Caxton, 1480.
Higden, Ranulphus. *The Descrypcyon of Englonde. Here Foloweth a Lytell Treatyse the Whiche Treateth of the Descrypcyon of This Londe Whiche of Olde Tyme was Named Albyon and After Brytayne and Now is Called Englande. End. Here Endeth the Descrypcyon of Brytaine, the Which Conteyneth Englonde Wales and Scotlonde, and Also ... Irlonde ...* London: Richard Pynson, 1510.
———. in Churchill Babington (ed.), John Trevisa (tr.). *Polychronicon: Together with the English Translations of John Trevisa* ... London: Longman, 1865.
———. *Polychronicon*. Newport: Barrett and Parke, 1992.
Hinks, Patrick, Flavia Hodges and David Gold. *A Dictionary of Surnames*. New York/Oxford: University Press, 1988.
Holinshed, Raphael. *The Late Volume of Chronicles England, Scotland and Ireland with Their Descriptions*. 1577. New edition, London: J. Harrison, 1587.
Holland, Philemon. *The History of the World Commonly Called the Natural Historie of C Plinius Secondus, Translated by Philemon Holland*. London: Adam Philip, 1601.
Homza, Lu Ann. *The Spanish Inquisition, 1478-1614: An Anthology of Sources*. Indianapolis: Hackett Publishing, 2006.
Hortop, Job. *The Rare Travails of Job Hortop, an Englishman who was not Heard of Three and Twenty Years Passé ... Wherin is Declared he Escaped in his Voiage to Gyinne much Slavery and Bondage in the Spanish Galley*. London: William Wright, 1591.

Howard, Charles. *A Declaration of the Causes Moving the Queen Majesty ... to ... Send a Navy to the Seas for the Defence of her Realms ...* London: Christopher Barker, 1596.

Huarte, Juan. *Examin de Ingenious Para les Sciencias.* 1588, p. 250, quoted in Jonathan Schorsch. *Swimming the Christian Atlantic: Judeoconversos, Afroiberians, and Amerindians in the Seventeenth Century.* Leiden/Boston/Biggleswade: Brill Extenza Turpin, p. 361.

Hughes, Derek (ed.). *Versions of Blackness: Key Texts on Slavery from the Seventeenth Century.* Cambridge: Cambridge University Press, 2007.

Hume, Andrew Sharpe (ed.), et. al., Public Record Office. *Calendar of Letters and State Papers, 1580–1586.* London: Eyre and Spottiswoode, 1896.

Hunwick, John O. *Timbuktu and the Songhay Empire: Al Sadis Tarikh Al-Sudan Down to 1613 and Other Contemporary Documents.* Leiden: Brill, 1999.

Jackman, Charles. *The Discoverie Made by M. A. Pet, and M. C. Jackman, of the Northeast Parts Beyond the Island of Vaigatz* [in] Richard Hakluyt. *Collection of the Early Voyages ...* Volume I. London: R. H. Evans, 1809.

Jobson, Richard. *The Golden Trade: Or, A Discovery of the River Gambia, and the Golden Trade of the Aethiopians. Also, the Commerce with a Great Blacke Merchant, Buckor Sano, and his Report of the Houses Covered with Golde, and other Strange Observations for the Good of Our Owne Countrey; Set Down as They were Collected in Travelling, Part of the Yeares, 1620 and 1621.* London: Nicholas Oke, 1623.

Johnson, Richard. *The Famous History of the Seven Champions of Christendom. St George of England, St Denis of France, St James of Spain ...* London: R. Scott, Thomas Bassett, Richard Chiswell, M. Wotton, G. Conyers, 1687.

Johnson, Samuel. *A Dictionary of the English Language.* 1775. New edition, London: Longman Rees, 1827.

Jones, John Winter (ed.), Richard Hakluyt. *Diverse Voyages, Touching the Discovery of America and the Islands Adjacent.* London: Hakluyt Society, 1850.

Jonson, Ben. *The Character of Two Royall Masques, the One of Blacknesse. The Other of Beautie Personated By the Most Magnificent of Queenes Anne Queene of Great Britain, with her Honourable Ladys 1605 and 1608 at Whitehall.* London: Thomas Thorp, 1605.

——. *Hymenæi: or the Solemnities of Masque, and Barriers ... Performed ... at Court ... to the ... Celebrating of the Marriage-Union, betweene Robert,*

Earle of Essex, and the Lady Frances, Second Daughter to ... the ... Earle of Suffolke.* London: V. Sims for T. Thorpe, 1606.

——. *Volpone or the Fox* ... 1606. New edition, London: T, Thorpe, 1607.

——. in William Gifford (ed.). *The Works of Ben Jonson with Notes, Critical and Explanatory and a Biographical Memoir Part Three*. Montana: Kessinger Publishing, 2004.

——. in Stephen Orgel (ed.). 'The Masque of Blackness, 1605,' *Ben Jonson: Complete Masques*. New Haven: Yale University Press, 1969.

Kerr, Robert (ed.). *A General History and Collection of Voyages and Travels, Arranged in Systematic Order: Forming a Complete History of the Origin and Progress of Navigation, Discovery, and Commerce, by Sea and Land, from the Earliest Ages to the Present Time*, Volume VII. Edinburgh: W. Blackwood and Sons, 1811–1824.

Kingsford, Charles (ed.). *The Chronicles of London*. London: Clarendon Press, 1905 including Author unknown. *Third Chronicle in BLMS Vitellus A XVI, Book II fol. 193*, p. 334.

Kinney, Arthur Frederick (ed.). *Rogues, Vagabonds, and Sturdy Beggars: A New Gallery of Tudor and Early Stuart Rogue Literature Exposing the Lives, Times, and Cozening Tricks of the Elizabethan Underworld*. Barre: Imprint Society, 1973.

Kipling, Gordon (ed.). *The Receyt of the Ladie Kateryne*. Oxford: Oxford University Press, 1990.

Knight, Charles. *The English Encyclopaedia*. London: Bradbury Evans, 1868.

Knighton, C.S., David Loades (eds.). *Letters from the Mary Rose*. Stroud: Sutton, 2002.

Knox, William. *Three Tracts Respecting the Conversion and Instruction of the Free Indians, and Negroe Slaves in the Colonies, etc ...* London: Knox, 1789.

Lambarde, William. *A Perambulation of Kent, Containing the Description, Hystorie, and Customes of the Shyre. Collected and Written (for the Most Part) in the Yeare 1570 ...* London: Henrie Middleton for R. Newberie, 1576.

Laughton, John Knox (ed.). *State Papers Relating to the Defeat of the Spanish Armada, Anno 1588*. Aldershot: Publications of the Navy Records Society, 1987.

Lawson, R. P. (tr. ed.). *The Song of Songs Commentary and Homilies Translated and Annotated by R P Lawson*. London: Longmans, Green and Co, 1957.

Lemon, Robert. *Calendar of State Papers, Domestic Series, of the Reigns of ... Elizabeth ...* 12 Volumes. London: Record Office, 1856–72.

Lerer, Seth. *Courtly, Letters in the Age of Henry VIII: Literary Culture and the Arts of Deceit*. Cambridge: Cambridge University Press, 1997.

Lewkenor, Lewis. *A Discourse of the Visage of the English Fugitives, by the Spaniard*. London: Thomas Scarlet for John Drawatar, 1595.

Lingelbach, William Ezra. *The Merchant Adventurers of England: Their Laws and Ordinances with other Documents*. New York: B. Franklin, 1971.

LoBagola, Bata Kindai Amgoza Ibn. *LoBagola: An African Savage's Own Story*. Leipzig: Bernhard Tauchnitz, 1930.

Lodge, Thomas. *Wits Miserie and the Worlds Madnesse: Discovering the Devils Incarnat of this Age*. London: A. Islip, 1596.

Machyn, Henry, in John Gough Nicols (ed.). *The Diary of Henry Machyn Citizen and Merchant Taylor of London from, A. D. 1550 to A.D. 1563*. London: Camden Society, 1848.

Madox, Richard, in Elizabeth Story Donno (ed.). *An Elizabethan in 1582: The Diary of Richard Madox, Fellow of All Saints*. London: Hakluyt Society, 1976.

Magennis, Hugh (ed. tr.). *The Old English Life of St Mary of Egypt: An Edition of the Old English Text with Modern English Parallel-Text Translation ...* Exeter: Exeter University Press, 2002.

Magnus, Olaus, in Peter Foote and John Granlund (eds.). *Olaus Magnus: Volume III, Description of the Northern Peoples, Rome 1555*. 1968. New edition, London: Hakluyt Society, 1998.

Maine Historical Society. *Collections of the Maine Historical Society*, Volume 18. Portland: Maine Historical Society 1831.

Malory, Thomas. *La Morte D'Arthur. Translated from the French by Sir T. Malory ...* 1529. New edition, London: Wynkyne de worde, William Copleand, 1557.

Mansur, Al Mulay Ahmed. 'Letter to Askiya Ishaq of Songhai,' December 1589 and others, in O. Hunwick. *Timbuktu and the Empire of Songhay*, pp. 294–296, 299–301, 305.

Manzini, Giovanni. Venice Archivio di Stato, Campo dei Frari, 3002–30125 Venezia (Venice) Italy, Ref. Cassia IV, Box 3, Series 18, folios 6v–7, no year.

Marees, Pieter de. *Beschryvinge Ende Historische Verhael ... vant Gout Koninckrijck van Gunea ...* Amsterdam: Cornelius Claesz, 1602.

——. *Description et Recit Historial du Riche Royaume d'or de Gunea, Aultrement Nommé, la Coste de l'or de Mina ... P. D. M. [Pieter de Marees] ...* Amsterdam: Claesson, 1605.

——. Albert Dantzig and Adam Jones (trs.). *Description and Historical Account of the Gold Kingdom of Guinea (1602)*. Oxford: Oxford University Press, 1987.

Markham, Gervase. *The Gentlemans Academie, or the Booke of S. Albans; Containing Three Most Exact and Excellent Bookes: The First of Hawking, the Second of all the Proper Terms of Hunting and the Last of Armorie: All Compiled by Juliana Barnes in the Yere from the Incarnation of Christ 1486: And Now Reduced into a Better Method by G. M. (i.e. Gervase Markham.) ... (by Richard Farmer)*. London: Humfrey Lownes, 1595.

Marlowe, Christopher. *Tamburlaine the Great* ... London: Marlow, 1592.

Marlowe, Christopher or Thomas Dekker. *Lust's Dominion or the Lascivious Queen a Tragedie* ... London: FK for Robert Parker, 1657.

——. in George Robinson (ed.). *The Works of Christopher Marlowe: Lust's Dominion; or, The Lascivious Queen* ...Volume II. London: W. Pickering, 1826.

——. *The Famous Tragedy of the Jew of Malta* ... London: Nicholas Vavasour, 1633.

——. *The Tragedy of Dido Queen of Carthage*. London: Thomas Nash, 1594.

Marsh-Caldwell, Anne. *The Song of Roland, as Chanted Before the Battle of Hastings, by the Minstrel Taillefer*. London: Hurst and Blackett, 1854.

Mary I, et. al. and Anne Everett Wood (ed.). *Letters of Royal and Illustrious Ladies. V3, From the Commencement of the Twelfth Century to the Close of the Reign of Queen Mary*. Whitefish: Kessinger, 2007.

Mayor of Bristol, William Hopkins. *Letter to Lord Burghley,* October 1590, in *Lansdowne Manuscripts,* no. 115, item 83, pp. 238–239.

McCrank, Lawrence (ed.). *Discovery in the Archives of Spain and Portugal: Quincentenary Essays, 1492–1992,* Volumes III–IV. New York: Haworth Press, 1992/1993.

Melzian, Hans Joachim. *A Concise Dictionary of the Bini Language of Southern Nigeria*. London: Kegan Paul and Co, 1937.

Merriam-Webster's French-English Dictionary. Springfield: Merriam Webster, 1999.

Merriam-Webster's Spanish-English Dictionary. Springfield: Merriam Webster, 1997.

Middleton, Thomas. *The Triumphs of Truth. A Solemnity ... at the Confirmation ... of ... Sir Thomas Middleton ... in the ... Office of ... Lord Maior of ... London ... October 29, 1613 ... Directed, Written, and Redeem'd into Forme, from the Ignorance of Some Former Times ... by Thomas Middleton*. London: Nicholas Okes, 1613.

——. *The Roaring Girle. Or Moll Cut-Purse. As it hath Lately beene Acted on the Fortune-Stage by the Prince his Players* ... London: Thomas Archer, 1611.

Mills, David Anthony. *Dictionary of British Place-Names*. New York/Oxford: Oxford University Press, 2003.

Milton, John. *Paradise Lost* ... London: Peter Parker, 1667.

Mithobius, Hector [Doctor]. *Almanach: Auff das Jar nach Jhesu Christi Geburt M.D.LXXXIX. [Gere]chnet durch Hectorem Mithobium Doctorem und Physicum zu Hannober*. Erffurdt: Melchior Sachssen, 1588.

Monmouth, Geoffrey and Aaron Thompson (tr.). *The British History, Translated into English from the Latin of Jeffrey of Monmouth* ... London: J. Boyer, 1718.

Montagu, Ashley (ed.). *UNESCO Statement on Race, An Annotated Elaboration and Exposition of the Four Statements on Race Issued by the United Nations Educational, Scientific, and Cultural Organization*. 1st edition not known. 3rd edition, New York: Oxford University Press, 1972.

More, Thomas and Alvaro De Silva (ed.). *The Last Letters of Thomas More*. Grand Rapids/Cambridge: W.B. Eerdmans, 2000.

More, Thomas and John Holt. *Lac Puero M Holti Mylke for Chyldren, (A Latin Grammar, with two epigrams)*. London: Wynkyn de Worde, 1508?

More, Thomas in William Rastell (ed.). *The Works of Sir Thomas More Knyght ... The First Boke*. London: John Cawod, Richard Tottell, 1557.

Mulcaster, Richard. *Positions wherein those Primitive Circumstances be Examined, which are Necessarie for the Training up of Children, either for Skill in their Booke, or Health in their Bodie* ... London: T. Vautrollier, 1581.

Munday, Anthony. (*Le Masque de la Ligue et de l'Hespagnol Decouvert.*) *The Masque of the League and the Spanyard Discouered. Wherein ... The League is Painted Forth in All Her Collours* ... London: I. Charelywoode for Richard Smythe, 1592.

Nennius. *The 'Historia Brittonum' Commonly Attributed to Nennius: From a Manuscript Lately Discovered in the Library of the Vatican Palace at Rome, Edited in the Tenth Century by Mark the Hermit. With an English Version ... by W Gunn*. London: J and A Arch, 1819.

Nennius and David N. Dumville (ed.). *The Historia Brittonum Edited by David N Dumville. 3. The Vatican Recension*. Cambridge: Brewer, 1985.

Nicols, Josias. *An Order of Household Instruction: by Which Every Master of a Family May Easily and in Short Space Make his Whole Household to Understand, the ... Christian Religion*. London: Thomas Man, 1596.

Nicols, Philip. *Sir Francis, Drake Revived*. 1626. 1882. New edition Whitefish: Kessinger Publishing, 2004.

Nunez, Hector. 'Will of Hector Nunez,' *Prerogative Court of Canterbury*, National Archives Kew, Register Sainberbe Quire Numbers, 56–94, 13 September 1591, PROB 11/78.

Nuttall, Zelia (ed.). *New Light on Drake: A Collection of Documents Relating to his Voyage of Circumnavigation, 1577–1580. Translated and Edited by Zelia Nuttall. Illustrated by a Map and Plates.* London: Hakluyt Society, 1914.

Ockham, William of, and George Knysh (ed.). *Fragments of Ockham Hermeneutics.* Winnipeg: WCU Council of Learned Societies, 1997.

Ortelius, Abraham ... *Epitome of the Theatre of the Worlde* ... London: for James Shaw, 1603.

Oxford Dictionary of English. Oxford: Oxford University Press, 2nd edition 2003.

Paris, Mathew, in Henry Richards Luard (ed.). *Flores Historiarum,* Volume III. London: HMSO, 1890.

Parker, Henry (ed.). *D. Pauper. End. Here Endeth a Compendyouse Treatyse Dyalogue of D. and Pauper. That is to Saye, the Riche the Poore* ... London: Wyken de Worde, 1496. New edition, London: Thomas Bertheleti, 1536.

Peele, George. *The Battle of Alcazar,* in John Yoklavich (ed.). *The Dramatic Works of George Peele.* New Haven: Yale University Press, 1961, pp. 293–347.

Percy, William, in Mathew Dimmock. *William Percy's Mahomet and his Heaven: A Critical Edition.* Aldershot: Ashgate Publishing, 2006.

Percyvall, Richard and John Minsheu. *A Dictionarie in Spanish and English, First Published ... by R Percivale ... Now Enlarged ... by J Minsheu ... Hereunto is Annexed in Ample English Dictionarie ... with the Spanish Words ... Adjoined.* London: E. Bollifaunt, 1599.

Persons, Robert. *A Defence of the Censure, Given Upon Two Bookes of William Chake and Meredith Hanmer mynysters, Whiche they wrote against M Edmond Campian and Against his Offer of Disputation, etc.* Rouen: Robert Persons, 1582.

Pevsner, Nikolaus. *The Buildings of England, London I, The Cities of London and Westminster.* Harmondsworth: Penguin Books, 1957.

Pevsner, Nikolaus and John Newman. *The Buildings of England: North East and North Kent.* Harmondsworth: Penguin, 1969.

Pilbeam, Norma and Ian Nelson (eds.). *Poor Law Records of Mid Sussex, 1601–1835.* Lewes: Sussex Record Services, 2001.

Playford, John. *Courtly Masquing Ayres: Containing Almaines, Ayres, Corants, Sarabands, Morisco's, Jiggs, &c. of Two Parts, Treble and Basse, for Viols or Violins. Composed by ... C. Colman ... W. Lawes, J. Jenkins, M. Lock, B. Rogers ... D. Mell, J. Banister, W. Gregorie, &c. Treble. (With a preface signed: J. P. i. e. John Playford) Philo Music.* London: W. Godbid for J. Playford, 1662.

Pliny the Elder. *Begin. Caius Plynius Marco suo Salutem. (Fol. 3:) Caii Plynii Secundi Naturalis Historiae Liber. I. End. [Colophon:] Caii Plynii Secundi Naturalis Historiae Libri Tricesimiseptimi et Ultimi Finis, etc.* Venetiis: Nicolaum Jenson, 1472.

Pory, John (tr.), Leo Africanus. *A Geographical Historie of Africa, Written in Arabicke and Italian by Iohn Leo a More* ... London: John Pory, 1600.

Ptolemy. *Here Begynneth the Compost of Ptholomeus, Prynce of Astronomye. Translated oute of Frenche in to Englysshe, etc.* London: Robert Wyer, 1540.

Ptolemy. *Ptolemaei Planisphaerium (Translated from Arabic into Latin) Iordani (Nemorarii) Planisphaerium. Federici Commandini Urbinatis in Ptolemaei Planisphaerium Commentarius.* Venice: Aldus, 1558.

Purchas, Samuel. *Purchas his Pilgrimage; or Relations of the World and the Religions Observed in all Ages and Places Discovered from the Creation unto the Present* ... London: William Stansby for Henrie Fetherstone, 1613.

Purchas, Samuel. *Haklvytus Posthumus, or Pvrchas his Pilgrimages, Containing a History of the World, in Sea Voyages and Land Truells, by Englishmen and other* ... 1613. 2nd edition, London: William Stansby for Henrie Fetherstone, 1614.

Purchas, Samuel, in David Brion Davis. *The Problem of Slavery in Western Culture.* 1966. New edition, Oxford: Oxford University Press, 1988.

Purfoot, Thomas. *The Historical Discourse of Muley Hamet's Rising to the Three Kingdoms, of Moruecos Fes and Sus ... The Religion and Policies of the More or Barbarian. The Adventures of Sir Anthony Sherley, and Divers other English Gentleman in those Countries* ... London: Clement Knight, 1609.

Purvis, John Stanley (ed.). *Tudor Parish Documents of the Diocese of York. A Selection, with Introduction and Notes by J. S. Purvis.* Cambridge: University Press 1948.

Raleigh, Walter. *A Declaration of the Demeanour and Cariage of Sir Walter Raleigh, as well in his Voyage as in, and Sithence his Returne; and of the True Motives and Inducements which Occasioned his Maiestie to Proceed in Doing Justice Upon Him, as Hath Bene Done.* London: Bonham Norton and John Bull, 1618.

Raleigh, Walter. *The Discoverie of the Large, Rich and Bewtiful Empyre of Guiana, with a Relation of the Great and Golden Citie of Manoa (which the Spanyards cal El Dorado) And of the Provinces of Emeria, Arromaia, Amapaia and other Countries, with their Rivers Adioyning. Performed in the Yeare 1595, by Sir Walter Ralegh, Knight* ... [in] Richard Hakluyt. *Collection of the Early Voyages.* London: Robert Robinson, 1596.

Randolph, Edmund and Arthur Shaffer (ed.). *History of Virginia.* Charlottesville: University of Virginia, 1970.

Rébora, Piero and Francis Guercio, et. al. *Cassell's Italian Dictionary: Italian-English, English-Italian.* London/Oxford: Macmillan, 4th edition 1977.

Record, Robert. *The Castle of Knowledge* ... 1556. New edition, London: V. Sims, 1596.

Ricart, Robert. *Ricart's Kalendar.* 1479–1895 ref. 04720/1/A. Bristol Records Office, Bristol.

Rich, Barnabe. *The Famous Hystory of Herodotus, Conteyning the Discourse of Dyuers Countreys, the Succession of theyr Kyngs, etc. Deuided into Nine Bookes, Entituled with the Names of the Nine Muses.* London: Thomas Marshe, 1584.

Rid, Samuel. *Martin Mark-All, Beadle of Bridewell; His Defence and Answere to the Belman of London. Discouering the Long Concealed Originall and Regiment of Rogues ... by S. R.* London: John Budge and Richard Bonian, 1610.

Roberts, Humfrey. *An Earnest Complaint of Diuers Vain, Wicked and Abused Exercises, Practised on the Saboth Day: which Tende to the Hinderance of the Gospel, and Increase of Many Abhominable Vices. With a Shorte Admonishment to all Popish Priests and Negligent Ministers.* London: Richarde Iohnes, 1572.

Roca de Togores, Mariano (ed.). *Cronica del Rey Enrique Octavo de Inglaterra* ... 1872. New edition, Madrid: Libreria de los Bibliofilos, 1874.

Rogers, Elizabeth Francis (ed.), Thomas More. *The Correspondence of Sir Thomas More.* Princeton: Princeton University Press, 1947.

Rogers, Walter Thomas (ed.), Scheltco Geveren. *Of the End of this World, and Second Coming of Christ* ... London: Henrie Middleton, 1583.

Russell, Roy and Beatriz Galimberti Jarman, et. al. *The Oxford Spanish Dictionary* ... London: Oxford University, 3rd edition 2003.

Rymer, Thomas, in Curt A. Zimansky (ed.). *The Critical Works of Thomas Rymer.* New Haven: Yale University Press, 1956.

Samuel, Marochitanus. *The Blessed Jew of Marocco; or, a Blackmoor Made White. Being a Demonstration of the True Messias Out of the Law and Prophets, by Rabbi Samuel a Jew, Turned Christian; Written First in the Arabick, After Translated into Latin, and Now Englished. To which are Annexed a Diatriba of the Jews' Sins, and Their Miserie all Over the World. Annotations to the Book, with Large Digressions, Discovering Jewish Blindnesse* ... York: T. Broad, 1648.

San Pedro, Diego de and Iohan Bourchier (tr.). *The Castell of Loue, Translated Out of Spanishe (i.e. from D. de San Pedro's "Carcel de Amor") in to Englyshe, by Iohan Bourchier Knyght, Lorde Bernis, at the Instaunce of the Lady Elizabeth Carew, Late Wyfe to Syr Nicholas Carew Knyght.* The

Whiche Boke Treateth of the Loue Betwene Leriano and Laureola Doughter to the Kynge of Masedonia. London: Robert Wyer for Richarde Kele, 1549.

Senden, Casper Van, 'merchant of Lubeck, to the Queen' to Robert Cecil, but Thomas Sherley may be the author. Day unspecified November 1600. 'In reward for his procuring the release in 1596 of 89 of the Queen's subjects who were prisoners in Spain and Portugal, and transporting them to England, the Queen granted him licence to take up such blackamoores as he could find in the realm and transport them into those countries. The masters of the blackamoores, however seeing by his warrant that he could not take them without the master's good will, would not suffer him to have any of them. Since that time he has procured the release of 200 prisoners in Lisbon, and has sent them home to England. In consideration of these services and seeing that all the blackamoores in England are regarded but only for the strangeness of their nation, and not for service to the Queen, and he may be very well spared out of this country, prays again for a licence to take up and carry away into Spain and Portugall all the blackamoors he shall find, without interruption of their masters or others.' *Calendar of the Manuscripts of the Most Honourable the Marquess of Salisbury*. London: Historical Manuscripts Commission, 1883–1976, Volume 14, p. 143.

———. to Robert Cecil, but Thomas Sherley may be the author. November, 1600. 'His services to distressed English in Spain and Portugal. Prays to be called to personal answer touching the calumniations suggested against him; and for aid in his suit concerning the blackmoors.' *Manuscripts*, Volume 14, p. 144

Sherley, Thomas to Robert Cecil. 29 November, 1600. 'Of the suit concerning the blackemoores, wherof he once moved Cecil for Jasper Van Zenden, whose petition he encloses. When he first moved Cecil therin, Cecil seemed not to like that a commission of that nature, to take what pleased him, should be committed to Van Zenden. Prays Cecil, for his (Sherley's good), to assent to the matter, with such limitations to the commission as he best likes.' *Manuscripts*, Volume 10, p. 399.

———. to Robert Cecil. 29 December, 1600. 'I most humbly thank you for your willingness touching the suit of Van Zenden for the transport of the Moores, at my request. And because I did not perceive by my son that you thought it not meet to have these kind taken from their masters compulsorily, I will forbear to urge you therin; but for expedition sake, I beseech that the letter which Van Zenden formerly had may be renewed to some stronger purpose than before, for which purpose I am bold to send you enclosed how far it is desired to stretch. This matter being by your favour committed to Mr Secretary Herbert 10 days past, lies as it did, in respect that Mr Ceaser his servant lost, as is said, the note of her Majesty's pleasure therin.' *Manuscripts*, Volume 10, p. 431.

The next nine entries are petitions to Robert Cecil grouped together because they concern Casper Van Senden and Thomas Sherley.

Andrews, William. c. 1600. 'Having lost £60 by Casper Van Senden, merchant stranger, arrested him in London, but is threatened to be imprisoned for this arrest, Van Senden showing a warrant from Cecil which, he affirms, protects him. Petitioner was ignorant of the warrant, and prays that Cecil will not impute to him the doing of anything in contempt thereof.' *Manuscripts*, Volume 14, p. 154.

Fanshaw, Thomas. 1596–1603. 'Rembearances of the Executor to the Queen ... difficulties arising amongst the parties [Sir Thomas Shirley and others'] ... rent reserved to the Queen has remained unpaid.' *Manuscripts*, Volume 14, p. 272.

Garges, Fernando. 13 April, 1600. '[about Thomas Sherley (elder)] I never saw poor gentleman in a more miserable estate, afflicted with extremity of sickness, destitute of honest and trusty servants, and matched with an unruly rout of mariners ...' *Manuscripts*, Volume 10, p. 108.

Lumley, E. 1596–1603. 'on behalf of the bearer [unnamed]' 'who has a suit to the council for a warrant to Sir Thomas Shirly for the loss of his horses.' *Manuscripts*, Volume 14, p. 277.

Merchants interested in goods taken by Sir Thomas Shirley the younger to Sir Robert Cecil. After May 1, 1600. 'On their petition to the council caused the goods to be brought from Plymouth to London to be sequested to the true proprietors. Notwithstanding this, two-thirds of the very best of the goods are embezzled by Shirley to the value of £3,000 ... They [the merchants] pray Cecil to procure the council's letter to the judge to give sentence without delay ...' *Manuscripts*, Volume 14, pp. 128–129.

Saye, John and Thomas Wood. 1596-1603. 'Pray for letter to Shirly requiring him to deliver them the bill ... [he unlawfully] detains it.' *Manuscripts*, Volume 14, p. 282.

Senden, Casper Van. c. 1600. 'Casper van Senden Merchant of Lubeck 1598 or later prays for protection for his creditors for three months, in consideration of his having released 200 English prisoners in Portugall.' *Manuscripts*, Volume 14, p. 89.

Sherley, Thomas. April 1600. 'It hath please God to send me the prizes, the one a West Indies man, the other a ship of Hamburg laden with Portingales goods ... Since our strangers in London are very apt to give men impediment where they have any hope to benefit themselves, I am bold to beseech you that I may have my right, with as much favour as may be.' *Manuscripts,* Volume 10, pp. 102-103.

Selincourt, Aubrey de (tr.). Herodotus, *The Histories*. 1954. New edition, London: Penguin, 1974.

Shakespeare, William. *Macbeth, Othello, Romeo and Juliet, The Merchant of Venice, Titus Andronicus,* in Richard Proudfoot, Ann Thompson, David Kastan and David Scott (eds.), *The Arden Shakespeare Complete Works*. Walton on Thames: Thomas Nelson and Sons, 1998.

——. *The Excellent History on the Merchant of Venice. With the Extreme Cruelty of Shylocke the Jew Towards the Said Merchant, in Cutting a Just Pound of his Flesh. And the Obtaining of Portia, by the Choyse of Three Caskets. Written by William Shakespeare*. London: J. Roberts, 1600.

——. *The Most Lamentable Tragedy of Titus Andronicus As it has Sundry Times been Played by the Kings Majesty's Servants*. London: Edward White, 1611.

——. *The Tragœdy of Othello, The Moore of Venice. As it Hath Beene Diuerse Times Acted at the Globe, and at the Black-Friers, by his Maiesties Seruants. Written by William Shakespeare*. London: Richard Hawkins, 1630.

——. *The Tragicall Historie of Hamlet, Prince of Denmarke. By William Shake-speare, as it Hath Beene Diuerse Times Acted by his Highnesse Servants in the Cittie of London: As Also in the Two Vniuersities of Cambridge and Oxford, and Else-where*. London: Nicholas Ling, and John Trundell, 1603.

——. *The Tragical Historie of Hamlet, Prince of Denmark, by William Shakespeare, Newley Imprinted and Enlarged to Almost as Much Again as it was According to True and Perfect Coppie*. London: James Roberts, Nicholas, Ling, 1605.

——. *Shakespeare's Sonnets, Never Before Imprinted*. London: G.L. for T.T, 1609.

——. in Katherine Duncan Jones (ed.). *Shakespeare's Sonnets*. London: Arden Shakespeare, 1997.

——. in Norman Henry Hudson (ed.). *Shakespeare's Othello ... with Introduction and Notes ...* Boston: Ginn and Company, 1881.

Sharp, Granville. *A Representation of the Injustice and Dangerous Tendency of Admitting the Least Claim of Private Property in the Persons of Men, in England ...* London: Publisher unknown, 1792.

Silva, Franco Alfonso. *La Esclavitud en Sevilla y su Tierra a Fines de la Edad Media*. Seville: Diputacion Provincial de Sevilla, 1979.

Spade, Paul Vincent (tr. ed.). *Five Texts on the Mediaeval Problem of Universals: Porphyry, Boethius, Abelard, Duns Scotus, Ockham/ Translated and Edited by Paul Vincent Spade*. Indianapolis: Hackett, 1994.

Spenser, Edmund. *A View of the State of Ireland, Written Dialogue-Wise Betweene Eudoxus and Irenaeus, by Edmund Spenser Esq in 1596*. London: H. Hils, 1633.

Stafford, Edward. *Letter to Francis Walsingham*, Secretaries of State; State Papers Foreign, France (June–December 1586), 20 August 1586, National Archives, Kew, ref. SP 78/16, f. 90–91.

Starkey, David (ed.). *The Inventory of King Henry VIII: The Transcript*, Volume I, Volume 56. London: Society for Antiquaries of London, 1998.

Stephen, James. *England Enslaved by her Own Slave Colonies: An Address to the Electors and People of the United Kingdom*. London: R. Taylor, for Hatchard and Son, and J. and A. Arch, 1826.

——. *Reasons for Establishing a Registry of Slaves in the British Colonies*. London: publisher unknown, 1814.

Stow, John. *The Annales of England, Faithfully Collected out of the Most Autenticall Authors, Records ... untill ... 1592*. London: R Newbery, 1592.

Stow, John and Edmund Howes. *The Annales, or Generall Chronicle of England, Begun First by Maister Iohn Stow, and After him Continued ... vnto the Ende of this Present Yeere 1614, by E. Howes*. London: Thomas Dawson for Thomas Adams, 1615.

Stow, John. *The Chronicles of England A Survay of London, Contayning the Originall, Antiquity, Increase, Moderne Estate, and Description of that Citie ... also an Apologie (or Defence) Against the Opinion of Some Men, Concerning the Citie, the Greatnesse there of. With an Appendix, Containing in Latine*. 1580. New edition, London: J Wolfe, 1598.

——. *A Summarie of Englyshe Chronicles, Conteynyng the True Accompt of Yeres, Wherein Euery Kyng of this Realme of England Began theyr Reigne, howe Long they Reigned: And what Notable Thynges hath bene doone durynge theyr Regynes ... Collected ... in the Yere ... 1565, etc*. London: Thomas Marshe, 1565.

——. *A Summary of the Chronicles of England, Abridged and Continued unto 1598 ... 1565*. New edition, London: R. Bardocke, 1598.

Strype, John. *Annals of the Reformation and Establishment of Religion ... During the First Twelve Years of Elizabeth I's Happy Reign*, Volume III. London: John Wyatt, 1709.

Stubbs, John. *The Discoverie of a Gaping Gulf Whereinto England is Like to be Swallowed by an other French Marriage, if the Lord Forbid not the Banes, by Letting her Maiestie see the Sin and Punishment Thereof.* London: H. Singleton, 1579.

Szombathy, Zoltan (ed. and tr.). *The History of Bidyini and Kaabu: Two Chronicles in Arabic from Guinea Bissau* ... Piliscsaba: Avicenna Institute of Middle Eastern Studies, 2007.

Tawny, Richard Henry and Eileen Edna Power (eds.). *Tudor Economic Documents: Being Select Documents Illustrating the Economic and Social History of Tudor England.* Volume 1–3. 1924. 1953. New edition, Harlow: Longman Green and Company, 1963.

Terry, Edward. *A Voyage to East India* ... London: J. Martin and J. Allestrye, 1655.

Testu, Guillaume le. *Cosmographie Universelle Selon les Navigateurs, Tant Anciens que Modernes.* 1555. Vincennes: Bibliothèque du Service Historique de l'Armée de Terre, DLZ 14, f. 32, 33, 34, 37, 39.

The British Library. *Sir Francis Drake an Exhibition to Commemorate Francis Drake's Voyage Around the World 1577–1580.* London: British Museum Publications, 1977.

The Concise Oxford English Dictionary. New York: Oxford University Press, 11th edition 2008.

The Oxford English Dictionary. London: Oxford University Press, 1998.

Toller, Northcote T. (ed.), Joseph Bosworth. *An Anglo-Saxon Dictionary* ... 1882. New edition, Oxford: Clarendon Press, 1921.

Tolstoi, Lev Nikolaevich (Leo Tolstoy) and Ernest Howard Crosby (ed.). 'Tolstoy on Shakespeare,' in *Shakespeare's Attitude to the Working Class.* 1903. New edition, Christchurch: Free Age Press, 1907, p. 68.

Tourneur, Cyril. *The Transformed Metamorphosis.* London: Valentine Sims, 1600.

Trevisa, John. *A Dialogue Betwene a Knyght and a Clerke, Concerning the Power Spiritual and Temporall. [A Translation by John Trevisa of 'Disputatio Inter Clericum et Militem, etc.', Sometimes Attributed to William of Ochkam.]* London: T Berthelet, 1533.

Tuke, Thomas. *The Treatise Against Painting and Tincturing of Men and Women: Against Murther and Poisoning: Pride and Ambition: Adulterie and Witchcraft Whereunto is Added the Picture of a Picture: Or the Character of the Painted Woman.* London: T. Creed and B Allsope, for E Merchant, 1616.

Tyndale, William, Thomas Matthew (pseudonym) and John Rogers. *The Byble, Which is All the Holy Scripture: In Whych are Contayned the Olde and Newe Testament Truly and Purely Translated into Englysh by Thomas Mathew (or Rather, the Books from Genesis to Chronicles and the New*

Testament Translated by W. Tyndale and the Remaining Books by Miles Coverdale. Revised and Edited by John Rogers) ... Set Forth with the Kinges Most Gracyous Lyceče. (With Woodcuts.)* London/Antwerp: R. Grafton and E. Whitchurch of London, 1537.

Underdowne, Thomas (tr.). *An Æthiopian Historie Written in Greeke by Heliodorus: very Wittie and Pleasaunt, Englished by Thomas Underdoune. With the Argumente of Euery Booke, Sette Before the Whole Woorke.* London: Henry Wykes, 1569.

Usk, Adam of, in Edward Maunde Thompson (ed. tr.). *The Chronicle of Adam of Usk A.D. 1377–1421.* 1st edition not known. 2nd edition 1904. 3rd edition, Felinfach: Llanerch, 1990.

——. *Royal Society of Literature of the United Kingdom, Chronicon Adæ de Usk A.D. 1377–1404.* London: Royal Society of Literature, 1876.

Victoria and Albert Museum. *Princely Magnificence: Court Jewels of the Renaissance, 1500–1630 [exposition] 15 October 1980–1 February 1981.* London: Debrett's Peerage in association with the Royal Albert Museum, 1980.

Vieyra, Antonio and Jacinto Dias do Canto. *A Dictionary of the Portuguese and English Languages, in Two Parts ...1773.* 2nd edition, London: J Collingwood, 1827.

Walker, David. *Walker's Appeal, in Four Articles: Together with a Preamble to the Colored Citizens of the World, but in Particular, and Very Expressly to Those of the United States of America. Written in Boston, in the State of Massachusetts, Sept. 28, 1829.* Boston: David Walker, 1830.

Way, Arthur Sanders. *The Song of Roland Translated into English Verse.* Cambridge: University Press, 1913.

Weever, John. *Ancient Funeral Monuments within the United Monarchie of Great Britain ... Intermixed and Ilustrated with a Variety of Historical Observations ...* London: Thomas Harper, 1631.

Welsh, James. *A Voyage to Benin, Beyond the Country of Guinea ... in the Year 1588.– The Second Voyage to Benin ... in the Year 1590,* in Richard Hakluyt. *Hakluyt's Collection of ... Early Voyages* Volume II. London: R. H. Evans, 1809.

Wernham, Richard (ed.), Public Record Office. *List and Analysis of State Papers:* Volume 6 *Foreign Series: January to December 1595.* London: Her Majesty's Stationery Office, 1964.

Weston, Jessica Laidlay. *Arthurian Romances Unrepresented in Malory's, 'Morte d'Arthur,'* Volume IV. London: David Nutt, 1901.

Weston, Jessica Laidlay. *The Romance of Morien.* London: David Nutt, 1901.

Whitford, Richard (tr.). *Here Begynneth the Boke Called the Pype, or Tonne, of the Lyfe of Perfection. The Reason or Cause Wherof Dothe Playnely Appere in the Processe. (A Worke or Boke of ... Saynt Bernarde, Named by ye Title Thus. De Precepto et Dispensatione. That is to saye, of Commaundement and Dispensacion ... Translate and Tourned into Englyshe by ... Rycharde Whytforde).* London: Robert Redman, 1532.

Wilkinson, Thomas. *An Appeal to England on Behalf of the Abused Africans: A Poem.* London: Publisher unknown, 1789.

Wilson, Thomas (tr., ed.). *The Three Orations of Demosthenes, Chiefe Orator, among the Grecians ...* London: Henrie Denham, 1570.

Winkfield, Anthony. *A True Coppie of a Discourse Written by a Gentleman, Employed in the Late Voyage of Spaine and Portingale [Under Sir Francis Drake and Sir John Norris] ... (Sometimes Attributed to Anthony Winkfield.)* London: Thomas Woodstock, 1589.

Worman, Ernest James (ed.). *Alien Members of the Book-Trade during the Tudor Period. Being an Index to those whose Names occur in the Returns of Aliens, Letters of Denization, and other Documents Published by the Huguenot Society ...* London: Huguenot Society, 1906.

Wycliffe, John and John Gough (ed.). *The Dore of Holy Scripture. (Being the Prologue to Wycliffe's Translation of the Bible Revised and Edited with a Preface by John Gough.)* London: John Gowgh, 1540.

Wyndham, Thomas, in John Hamilton Moore (ed.). *A New and Complete Collection of Voyages and Travels ... Including ... Voyages and Travels. ... With the Relations of Maghellan, Drake, Candish, Anson, Dampier, and all the Circumnavigators, Including ... the ... Voyages and Discoveries ...* London: John Hamilton, 1785.

Wyndham, Thomas. *The First Voyage to Guinea and Benin,* in Richard Hakluyt. *Hakluyt's Collection of ... Early Voyages,* Volume II. London: R.H. Evans, 1809.

Yeshiva University Museum. *The Sephardic Journey 1492–1992.* New York: Yeshiva University Museum, 1992.

Primary electronic records

Author unknown. *Genealogy RootsWeb,* http://freepages.genealogy.rootsweb.ancestry.com/-claudia's family, accessed 07/03/ 06.

——. 'Origin of the Surname Moore,' *Genealogy Rootsweb,* http://freepages.genealogy.rootsweb.ancestry.com/-claudia's family, accessed 07/03/ 06.

——. 'Parish Records: 1538, 1563 and 1598,' National Archives, *Parish Records,* http://www.nationalarchives.gov.uk/familyhistory/guide/people/ parish.htm, accessed 12/08/08.

——. 'Black Settlers in Tudor Times,' National Archives, *Pathways,* http://www.nationalarchives.gov.uk/pathways/blackhistory/early_times/settlers.htm accessed 11/03/06.

BBC. *British History,* http://www.bbc.co.uk/history/british/launch_ani_population.shtml, accessed 01/11/08 and Office for National Statistics, Population estimates for the UK, http://www.statistics.gov.uk/cci/nugget.asp?ID=6, accessed 01/11/08 and 02/03/13.

Bell, Adrian. 'History Cold Case' personal email, sent 08/05/10, 10/05/10, accessed 10/05/10, 12/05/10.

Berke, Shari and Rick Gold. 'The Jews of Timbuktu,' *Washington Jewish Week,* December 30, 1999, kulanu.org/timbuktu/JewsofTimbuktu.php, accessed 21/02/07.

Coffin, Cyril. 'Aliens in Dorset 1525,' *The Dorset Page,* http://www.thedorsetpage.com/history/Aliens/Aliens.htm posted 2000, accessed 02/01/07

Davis, Peter (ed.). *William Looney, Victorian Naval Surgeon,* http://www.pdavis.nl/Legislation.htm, accessed 03/03/09.

Hall, Catherine, Nick Draper et.al. 'Legacies of British Slave-ownership' database, http://www.ucl.ac.uk/lbs/ accessed 27/02/13.

Hanson, Mairlee (ed.). 'Katherine of Aragon letter dated 2 December 1505,' Contemporary Descriptions of Anne Boleyn, *EnglishHistory.net. 2004.* http://englishhistory.net/tudor/annedesc.html accessed 11/8/08.

Harrison, William. 'Description of England,' *Modern History Sourcebook,* http://www.fordham.edu/halsall/mod/1577harrison-england.html, accessed 10/09/07.

Jesus Christ Church of Latter day Saints. *International Genealogical Index,* G Batch N. P003891, File 0845460, Call number 6905932, http://www.familysearch.org/eng/default.asp, accessed 15/08/08.

Kinsey, Laura. 'History Cold Case Westminster,' Westminster Abbey Press Office personal email sent and accessed on 22/10/10.

Kitto, John Vivian. 'St Martins in the fields the accounts of the church wardens, 1525–1603,' *British History Online,* 1901, pp. 457–475, http://www.british-history.ac.uk/report.aspx?compid=81909 accessed 25/10/08.

Office for National Statistics, *Ethnicity and National Identity in England and Wales 2011,* http://www.ons.gov.uk/ons/dcp171776_290558.pdf, new census inc. published 11 December 2012 accessed 02/03/13.

Sampson, Mike. *'Black burials and deaths 16th century'* (Email), from Devon Record Office, Great Moor Street, Bittern Road, Sowton, Exeter, Devon, sent and accessed on 16/04/06.

Secondary Sources

Abate, Corrine S. *Privacy, Domesticity, and Women in Early Modern England*. Aldershot: Ashgate Publishing, 2002.
Abley, Mark. *Spoken Here: Travels Among Threatened Languages*. London: Heinemann, 2003.
The Academy. *The Academy*, Volume 7. London: J Murray, 1875.
Acton, Baron John Emerich Edward David Dalberg Acton and George Walter Prothero, etc. *Cambridge Modern History*, Volume I. Cambridge: University Press, 1912, Volume IX, 1906.
Aig-Imoukhuede, Frank (ed.). *A Handbook of Nigerian Culture*. 1st edition not known. 2nd edition, Lagos: Department of Culture Federal Ministry of Information and Culture, 1992.
Akbar, Naim. *Chains and Images of Psychological Slavery*. Jersey City: New Mind Productions, 1984.
Akbar, Naim. *Breaking the Chains of Psychological Slavery*. Jersey City: Mind Productions and Associates, 1996.
Alcazar, Real. *Ibn Khaldun: The Mediterranean in the Fourteenth Century: Rise and Fall of Empires*. Seville: Foundation Jose Manuel Lara, 2006.
Alexander, Catherine and Stanley Wells (eds.). *Shakespeare and Race*. New York: Cambridge University Press, 2000.
Ali, Ahmed and Ali, Ibrahim. *The Black Celts: An Ancient African Civilisation in Ireland and Britain*. Cardiff: Punite Publications, 1992.
Amrouche, Jean and Richard Serrano (ed.). *Against the Postcolonial: 'Francophone' Writers at the Ends of French Empire*. 2005. New edition, Lanham: Lexington Books, 2006.
Anderson, Ruth Matilda. *Hispanic Costume, 1480–1530*. New York: NY: Hispanic Society of America, 1979.
Andrews, Kenneth R. *Elizabethan Privateering: English Privateering during the Spanish War, 1585–1603*. Cambridge: University Press, 1964.
——. *Trade, Plunder and Settlement: Maritime Enterprise and the Genesis of the British Empire, 1480–1630*. London: Cambridge University Press, 1984.
Anon. *Whitbread's Brewery Incorporating the Brewer's Art*. 1948. New edition, London: Whitbread's Brewery, 2008.
Appiah, Kwame Anthony, Henry Louis Gates. Henry Ellis, *The History and Antiquities of the Parish of Saint Leonard Shoreditch* ... London: J. Nicholas, 1798, Oxford: Oxford University Press, 2005.
Appleby, John Tate. *John King of England*. New York: Knopf, 1959.
Apter, Andrew Herman. *Black Critics and Kings: The Hermeneutics of Power in Yoruba Society*. Chicago/London: University of Chicago Press, 1992.

Archer, Ian. *The Pursuit of Stability: Social Relations in Elizabethan London.* Cambridge: Cambridge University Press, 1991.

Archer, Ian (ed.), F. Douglas Price. *English Historical Documents,* Volume V(A) 1558–1603. London: Routledge, 2011.

Armah, Ayi Kwei (tr.), Barry Boubacar. *Senegambia and the Atlantic Slave Trade.* Cambridge: Cambridge University Press, 1998.

Asante, Molefi and Ama Mazama (eds.). *The Encyclopedia of Black Studies.* 2004. New edition, London: SAGE publications, 2005.

Ash, Eric. *Power, Knowledge, and Expertise in Elizabethan England.* Baltimore: John Hopkins University Press, 2004.

Ashley, Maurice. *England in the Seventeenth Century. The Pelican History of England,* Volume 6. 1955. Revised edition, Baltimore: Penguin, 1966.

Auchter, Dorothy. *Dictionary of Literary and Dramatic Censorship in Tudor and Stuart England.* Westport: Greenwood Publishing Group, 2001.

Ausubel, Nathan. *The Book of Jewish Knowledge: An Encyclopedia of Judaism and the Jewish People Covering all Elements of Jewish Life from Biblical Times to the Present.* New York: Crown Publishers, 1964.

Bacharach, Jere L. and Josef W. Meri (eds.). *Medieval Islamic Civilization,* Volume 2, *An Encyclopedia.* New York/London: Routledge, 2006.

Backscheider, Paula (ed.). *The Intersections of the Public and Private Spheres in Early Modern England.* London: Frank Cass, 1996.

Baker, Christopher (ed.). *Absolutism and the Scientific Revolution, 1600–1720: A Biographical Dictionary.* Westport/London: Greenwood Press, 2002.

Barbour, Reid and Claire Preston (eds.). *Sir Thomas Browne: The World Proposed.* Oxford: Oxford University Press, 2008.

Barrow, John. *The Life, Voyages, and Exploits of Admiral Sir Francis Drake ... with Numerous Original Letters.* London: John Murray, 1843.

Bartels, Emily Carroll. *Speaking of the Moor: From Alcazar to Othello.* Philadelphia: University of Pennsylvania Press, 2008.

——. *Spectacles of Strangeness: Imperialism, Alienation, and Marlowe.* Philadelphia: University of Pennsylvania Press, 1993.

Barthelemy, Anthony Gerard. *Black Face, Maligned Race: The Representation of Blacks in English Drama From Shakespeare to Southerne.* Baton Rouge: Louisiana State University Press, 1987.

Bascomb, William Russell. *The Yoruba of Southwestern Nigeria.* London/New York: Holt Rinehart and Winston, 1969.

Begg, Ean. *The Cult of the Black Virgin.* London: Arkana, 1985.

Beier, A. L. *Masterless Men: The Vagrancy Problem in England 1560–1640.* London: Methuen, 1985.

——. *Studies in Poverty and Poor Relief in Warwickshire, 1540–1680.* New York: Princeton University, 1969.

——. *The Vagrant Poor in Tudor and Early Stuart England.* London: Social Science Research Council, 1976.

——. *The Problem of the Poor in Tudor and Early Stuart England.* London: Methuen, 1983.

Belton, Brian. *Questioning Gypsy Identity: Ethnic Narratives in Britain and America.* Walnut Creek: Alta Mira Press, 2005.

Ben-Jochannan, Yosef. *Africa: Mother of Western Civilisation.* Baltimore: Black Classic Press, 1997.

——. *Cultural Genocide in the Black and African Studies Curriculum.* New York: ECA Associates, 1972.

Bennett, Norman R. *Africa and Europe: From Roman Times to the Present.* New York: Africana Publishing Company, 1975.

Bennett, Tony, Lawrence Grossberg and Meaghan Morris (eds.). *New Keywords: A Revised Vocabulary of Culture and Society.* Oxford: Blackwell, 2005.

Berlin, Ira. *Many Thousands Gone: The First Two Centuries of Slavery in North America.* 1998. New edition, New York: Harvard University Press, 2000.

Besamusca, Bart, in Norris J. Lacy (ed.), et. al. *The New Arthurian Encyclopedia.* New York: Garland, 1991.

Bessel, Richard, Nicholas Guyatt and Jane Rendall (eds.). *War, Empire and Slavery 1770-1830.* [Conference May 2008 in York.] Basingstoke: Palgrave Macmillan, 2010.

Betteridge, Thomas and Anna Riehl (eds.). *Tudor Court Culture.* Selinsgrove: Susquehanna University Press, 2010.

Biddle, Martin and Sally Badham. *King Arthur's Round Table: An Archaeological Investigation.* Woodbridge: Boydell and Brewer, 2000.

Billington, Sandra. *A Social History of the Fool.* Brighton: Harvester, 1984.

Birnbaum, Lucia Chiavola. *Black Madonnas: Feminism, Religion, and Politics in Italy.* Boston: Northeastern University Press, 1993.

Bisson, Douglas. *The Merchant Adventurers of England: The Company and the Crown, 1474-1564.* London: Associated University Press, 1993.

Blackham, Robert James. *The Soul of the City. London's Livery Companies. Their Stored Past, Their Living Present.* London: Sampson Low and Company, 1931.

Blades, William. *The Life and Typography of William Caxton ...* London: Oxford University, 1861.

Blake, John William. *European Beginnings in West Africa, 1454–1578: A Survey.* London: Longmans 1937.

Blakeley, Allison. *Russia and the Negro: Blacks in Russian History and Thought.* Washington: University Press, 1986.

Blumenthal, Debra. *Enemies and Familiars: Slavery and Mastery in Fifteenth-Century Valencia.* Ithaca/London: Cornell University Press, 2009.

Boshen, Adu and Alvin Josephy. *The Horizon History of Africa*, Volume II. New York: American Heritage Publishing, 1971.

Bourke, Thomas. *A Concise History of the Moors in Spain from the Invasion of that Kingdom to their Final Expulsion from it …* London: Rivington Hatchard, 1811.

Bourne, George. *Slavery Illustrated in its Effects on Women and Domestic Society.* Boston: Issac Knapp, 1837.

Bourne, Stephen. *Speak of me as I am: The Black Presence in Southwark since 1600.* London: Southwark Local History Library, 2005.

Bovill, Edward William and Robin Hallett. *The Golden Trade of the Moors: West African Kingdoms in the Fourteenth Century.* London: Oxford University Press, 1958.

Bowers, Jennifer and Peggy Keeran. *Literary Research and the British Renaissance and Early Modern Period: Strategies and Sources.* Plymouth: Scarecrow Press, 2010.

Bowser, Benjamin P., Louis Kushnick, Paul Grant (eds.). *Against the Odds: Scholars who Challenged Racism in the Twentieth Century.* Amherst: University of Massachusetts Press, 2002.

Boyer, Allen. *Sir Edward Coke and the Elizabethan Age.* London: Stanford University Press 2003.

Brachfeld, Oliver. *Inferiority Feelings: In the Individual and Group.* London: Routledge, 1999.

Bradford, Ernle Selby Dusgate. *The Wind Commands Me: A Life of Sir Francis Drake.* London: Harcourt Brace & World, 1965.

Braddick, Michael and John Walter (eds.). *Negotiating Power in Early Modern Society: Order, Hierarchy and Subordination in Britain and Ireland.* Cambridge: Cambridge University Press, 2001.

Bradshaw, Benjamin and Peter Roberts (eds.). *British Consciousness and Identity: And the Making of Britain, 1533–1707.* Cambridge: Cambridge University Press, 1998.

Brasio, Antonio (ed.). *Monumenta Missionaria Africana …* Lisbon: Lisboa, 1952–1968.

Braun, Peter and Manfred Weinburg. *Ethno/Graphie: Reiseformen des Wissens of Literatur und Anthropologie*, Volume 17. Turbingen: Narr, Francke, Attempto, Furlang, 2002.

Breasted, James H. *A History of Egypt from the Earliest Times to the Persian Conquest With Two Hundred Illustrations and Maps*. London: Hodder and Stoughton, 1906.

Brenner, Robert. *Merchants and Revolution: Commercial Change, Political Conflict, and London's Overseas Traders, 1550-1653*. 1991. New edition, London: Verso, 2003.

Brett, Michael and Elizabeth Fentress. *The Berbers*. Oxford: Wiley Blackwell, 1996.

Brewer, Ebenezer Cobham. *Character Sketches of Romance, Fiction, and the Drama*, Volume 2. Jerusalem/New York: The Minerva Group, 2004.

Brewster, David. *Brewer's Dictionary of Phrase and Fable, Giving the Derivation, Source, or Origin of Common Phrases, Allusions and Words ...* London: H. Altemus, 1870.

Brienen, Rebecca Parker. *Visions of Savage Paradise: Albert Eckhout, Court Painter in Colonial Dutch Brazil*. Amsterdam: Amsterdam University Press, 2006.

Brigden, Susan. *New Worlds, Lost Worlds: The Rule of the Tudors, 1485-1603*. London: Allen Lane, 2000.

Brimacombe, Peter. *All the Queen's Men: The World of Elizabeth I*. 2000. New edition, Stroud: Sutton, 2003.

Bromley, Ian. *Bromley: A Midlands Family – And the Search for the Leicestershire Origin*. Leicester: Troubador Publishing, 2007.

Bromley, John. *The Armorial Bearings of the Guilds of London: A Record of the Heraldry of the Surviving Companies with Historical Notes*. London: F Warne, 1960.

Broomhall, Susan and Stephanie Tarbin (eds.). *Women, Identities and Communities in Early Modern Europe*. Aldershot: Ashgate, 2008.

Broomhall, Susan and Jacqueline Van Gent (eds.). *Governing Masculinities in the Early Modern Period; Regulating Selves and Others*. Farnham: Ashgate, 2011.

Brown, Meg Lota and Kari Boyd McBride. *Women's Roles in the Renaissance*. Westport: Harcourt Education, 2005.

Brown, Paul Alonzo. *The Development of the Legend of Thomas Becket*. Philadelphia: University of Pennsylvania, 1930.

Bruder, Edith. *The Black Jews of Africa: History, Religion, Identity*. New York: Oxford University Press, 2008.

Buccola, Regina and Lisa Hopkins (eds.). *Marian Moments in Early Modern British Drama*. Aldershot: Ashgate, 2007.

Buchanan, Patricia Hill. *Margaret Tudor Queen of Scots*. Edinburgh/London: Scottish Academic Press, 1985.

Burke, Edmund. *A Genealogical History of the Dormant: Abeyant, Forfeited and Extinct Peerages of the British Empire*. London: Harrison, 1866.

Burton, Jonathan. *Traffic and Turning: Islam and English Drama, 1579–1624*. Newark: University of Delaware Press, 2005.

Bury, John Bagnall. *The Cambridge Medieval History*, Volume II. London: The University Press, 1964.

Buscaglia-Salgado, Jose F. *Undoing Empire: Race and Nation in the Mulatto Caribbean*. Minneapolis/London: University of Minnesota Press, 2003.

Bush, Julia, et. al. *Sharing the Past, Northamptonshire, Black History*. Northampton: Northamptonshire Black History Association, 2008.

Busk M. *The History of Spain and Portugal, 1000 BC to AD 1814*. London: Baldwin and Craddock, 1831.

Calkin, Siobhain Bly. *Saracens and the Making of English Identity: The Auchinleck Manuscript (Studies in Medieval History and Culture)*. Abingdon: Routledge, 2005.

Callaghan, Dympma. *Shakespeare without Women: Representing Gender and Race on the Renaissance Stage*. London: Routledge, 1999.

Calvert, Hugh. *Shakespeare's Sonnets and Problems of Autobiography*. Braunton: Merlin, 1987.

Canning, Robert Cecil Gordon. *'Boabdil;' or, 'The Twilight of Granada,' and Other Poems*. London: C. F. Hodgson and Son, 1930.

Cape Town University. *The Annual Review of Islam in South Africa*, Issues 3–8. Cape Town: Centre for Contemporary Islam, 2000.

Capp, Bernard. *When Gossips Meet: Women, Family, and Neighbourhood in Early Modern England*. Oxford: Oxford University Press, 2003.

Carroll, William C. *Fat King, Lean Beggar: Representations of Poverty in the Age of Shakespeare*. Ithaca/London: Cornell University Press, 1996.

Castro, Americo and Willard F. King, et. al. *The Spaniards: An Introduction to their History* ... Berkeley/London: University of California Press, 1971.

Cawston, George and Augustus Henry Keane. *Early Chartered Companies, AD 1296–1858*. Manchester: Ayer Publishing, 1968.

Cerasano, Susan. *Medieval and Renaissance Drama in England*, Volume 20. New York: Fairleigh Dickinson University Press, 2003.

Chambers, Edmund Kerchever. *The Elizabethan Stage*. Oxford: Clarendon, 1923.

Chambers, Robert and William Chambers. *Chambers Miscellany of Useful and Entertaining Tracts*. 1846. New edition, Edinburgh/London: William and Robert Chambers, 1869.

Chapman, Don. *1788, The People of the First Fleet*. North Ryde: Cassell Australia, 1981.

Chater, Kathleen (Kathy). *Untold Histories: Black People in England and Wales During the Period of the British Slave Trade, c. 1660–1807*. Manchester: Manchester University Press, 2008.

Chater, Kathy. *How to Trace Your Family Tree in England, Ireland, Scotland and Wales*. London: Anness Publishing Incorporated, 2006.

Chisholm, Hugh. *The Encyclopaedia Britannica: A Dictionary of Arts, Sciences, Literature and General Information*. London: University Press, 1911.

Churchward, Albert. *The Signs and Symbols of Primordial Man ...The Evolution of Religious Doctrines from the Eschatology of the Ancient Egyptians ...* London: EP Dutton and Co, 1910.

Clarke, Grata Jeter. *The Jeter Mosaic: Seven Centuries in the History of a Family*. Mount Pleasant: Arcadia Clarke, 1987.

Claris de Florian, Jean Pierre and Robert Heron (tr.). *Gonsolvo or Cordova or The Conquest of Granada*. London: Morison and Son, 1792.

Cohen, Anthony P. *The Symbolic Construction of Community*. Chichester: Ellis Horwood, 1985.

Collicott, Sylvia. *Connections: Haringey Local-National-World Links*. London: Haringey Community Information Service and Multi-Cultural Curriculum Support Group, 1986.

Collins, Fiona in Gabrielle Hodges and Morag Styles (eds.), 'Storyseeds Creating Curriculum Stories,' *Tales, Tellers and Text*. London: Continuum International Publishing Group, 2000, pp. 50–51.

Collins, Robert Oakley. *African History: Western African History*. Princeton: Markus Wiener, 1990.

——. *African History: Central and South African History*. Princeton: Markus, Weiner Publishers, 1990.

Conrad, David S. *Empires of Medieval West Africa Ghana, Mali and Songhay*. New York: Infobase Publishing, 2005.

Coote, Stephen. *Drake: The Life and Legend of an Elizabethan Hero*. London/New York: Simon and Schuster, 2003.

Corbett, Julian Stafford. *Drake and the Tudor Navy: With a History of the Rise of England as a Maritime Power*. London: Longman Green, 1898.

Cozens, Zechariah. *A Tour Through the Island of Thanet: and Some Other Parts of East Kent ...* London: J. Nicholas, 1793.

Crabb, Ann. *The Strozzi of Florence: Widowhood and Family Solidarity in the Renaissance.* Michigan: University of Michigan Press, 2000.

Crawford, Patricia. *Blood, Bodies and Families: in Early Modern England.* Harlow: Longman, 2004.

——. (ed.). *Exploring Women's Past; Essays in Social History.* Carlton: Sisters Publishing, 1983.

——. *Parents of Poor Children in England 1580–1800.* Oxford: Oxford University Press, 2010.

——. *Women and Religion in England 1500–1720.* London: Routledge, 1993.

——. and Sara Heller Mendelson (eds.). *Women in Early Modern England 1550–1720.* Oxford: Oxford University Press, 1998.

——. and Laura Gowing (eds.). *Women's World's in Seventeenth-Century England.* London: Routledge, 2000.

Cressy, David. *Birth, Marriage, and Death: Ritual, Religion, and the Life-Cycle in Tudor and Stuart England.* Oxford: Oxford University Press, 1997.

——. *Education in Tudor and Stuart England.* London: E. Arnold, 1975.

——. *Society and Culture in Early Modern England.* Aldershot: Ashgate Variorum, 2003.

——. *Literacy and the Social Order: Reading and Writing in Tudor and Stuart England.* Cambridge: Cambridge University Press, 2006.

Cruden, Robert Peirce. *The History of the Town of Gravesend …* London: William Pickering, 1843.

Cummins, Joseph. *The War Chronicles, from Chariots to Flintlocks: New Perspectives on the Two Thousand Years of Bloodshed that Shaped the Modern World.* Beverly: Fair Winds Press, 2008.

Cutting, John. *History and the Morris Dance: A Look at Morris Dancing from the Earliest Days Until 1850.* Alton: Dance Books, 2005.

Dabydeen, David. *The Black Presence in English Literature.* 1983. New edition, Manchester: Manchester University Press, 1985.

——. and James Gilmore (eds.). *The Oxford Companion to Black British History.* Oxford: Oxford University Press, 2007.

Dalporto, Jeannie (ed.). *Women in Service in Early Modern England.* Aldershot: Ashgate, 2008.

Dalton, Karen, in Peter Erickson, Clarke Hulse (eds.). *Early Modern Visual Culture: Representation, Race and Empire in Renaissance England.* Philadelphia: University of Pennsylvania Press, 2000.

D'Amico, Jack. *The Moor in English Renaissance Drama.* Tampa: University of South Florida Press, 1991.

Daniell, Christopher. *Death and Burial in Medieval England, 1066–1550.* London: Routledge, 1998.

Daniels, Charles. *The Garamantes of Southern Libya*. Stoughton: Oleander Press, 1970.

Davenport, Francis Gardiner and Charles Oscar Pullin (eds.). *European Treaties Bearing on the History of the United States and its Dependencies*. Washington: Carnegie Institution of Washington, 1917–1937.

Davey, James Joseph. *The Function of the Dark Lady in Shakespeare's Sonnets*. Trieste: Università Degli Studi di Trieste, 1986.

Davidson, Basil. *African Civilization Revisited: From Antiquity to Modern Times*. Trenton: Africa World Press, 1991.

Davidson, Basil. *Black Mother: A Study of the Precolonial Connection Between Africa and Europe*. London: Longman, 1970.

Davidson, Clifford. *Illustrations of the Stage and Acting in England to 1580*. Kalamazoo: Medieval Institute Publications, Western Michigan University, 1991.

Davies, David Williams. *Elizabethans Errant. The Strange Fortunes of Sir Thomas Sherley and his Three Sons*. Ithaca: Cornell University Press, 1967.

Davis, Edwards Brion. *The Problem of Slavery in the Age of Revolution, 1770–1823*. Ithaca/London: Cornell University, 1975. New edition, New York: Oxford University Press, 1999.

Day, Rosemary O. *The Professions in Early Modern England, 1450–1800: Servants of the Commonweal*. Harlow: Longman, 2000.

Dean, William. *The American Spiritual Culture: And the Invention of Jazz, Football and the Movies*. New York, London: Continuum International Publishing Group, 2006.

Deans, Richard Storry. *The Trials of Five Queens. Katherine of Aragon, Anne Boleyn, Mary Queen of Scots, Marie Antoinette and Caroline of Brunswick* …London: Methuen, 1910.

Debrunner, Hans Werner. *Presence and Prestige – Africans in Europe: A History of Africans in Europe before 1918*. Basel: Basler Afrika Bibliographien, 1979.

Deloach, Ronald J. *Living Without a Name: A View Through Black Eyes*. Pittsburgh: Dorrance Publishing Co. Inc., 2009.

Desenes, Marliss. *The Bed-Trick in English Renaissance Drama: Explorations in Gender, Sexuality, and Power*. Newark: University of Delaware Press, 1994.

Diffie, Bailey, George Winius and Boyd Shafer (eds.). *The Foundations of the Portuguese Empire 1415–1580, of Europe and the World in the Age of Expansion*, Volume I. Minneapolis: University of Minnesota Press, 1977.

Doane, Gilbert Harry. *Searching for your Ancestors. The Why and How of Genealogy.* London/ New York: Mc Graw Hill Book Co, 1937.

Domencio, Roy. *The Regions of Italy: A Reference Guide to History and Culture.* Westport: Greenwood Publishing Group, 2002.

Donaldson, Stephen and Wayne Dynes. *History of Homosexuality in Europe and America.* London: Taylor and Francis, 1992.

Doran, Susan (ed.), Michael Dobson and Nicola Watson. *'Elizabeth's Legacy,' Elizabeth: The Exhibition at the National Maritime Museum.* London: Chatto and Windus, 2003.

Dorson, Richard Mercer. *History of British Folklore.* 1968. New edition, London: Taylor and Francis, 1999.

Douce, Francis. *Illustrations of Shakespeare, and of Ancient Manners: with Dissertations on the Clowns and Fools of Shakespeare; on the Collection of Popular Tales entitled Gesta Romanorum; and on the English Morris Dance.* London: Longman, Hurst, Rees and Orme, 1807.

Diop, Cheikh Anta, in Ivan Van Sertima (ed.). *Golden Age of the Moor.* Piscataway: Transaction Publishers, 1992.

Diop, Cheikh Anta. *Antériorité des Civilisations Nègres: Mythe ou Vérité Historique?* Paris: publisher unknown, 1967.

——. and Mercer Cook (tr.). *The African Origin of Civilisation: Myth or Reality.* New York: L. Hill, 1974.

Drake, St Clair. *Black Folk Here and There: An Essay in History and Anthropology,* Volume II. Berkley: Centre for Afro American Studies University of California, 1991.

Dresser, Madge. *Slavery Obscured: The Social History of the Slave Trade in an English Provincial Port.* 2001. New edition, Bristol: Redcliff Press, 2007.

Dresser, Madge and Peter Fleming. http://www.amazon.co.uk/Bristol-Ethnic-Minorities-City-1000-2001/dp/1860774776/ref=sr_1_2?ie=UT-F8&s=books&qid=1227625951&sr=1-2*Bristol: Ethnic Minorities and the City, 1000–2001.* 2007. New edition, Stroud: Gloucestershire, The History Press Ltd, 2008.

Drew-Bear, Annette. *Painted Faces on the Renaissance Stage: The Moral Significance of Face-Painting Conventions.* Lewisburg/London: Bucknell University Press, 1994.

Duffy, Michael. *The Englishman and the Foreigner.* Cambridge: Chadwyck-Healey, 1986.

Dunbavin, Paul. *Picts and Ancient Britons: An Exploration of Pictish Origins.* London: Third Millennium Publishing, 1998.

Durant, Thomas and David Knottnerus. *Plantation Society and Race Relations: The Origins of Inequality.* Westport/London: Greenwood Publishing Group, 1999.

Dyer, Thomas Henry. *The History of Modern Europe: From the Fall of Constantinople* ... Volume I. London: John Murray, 1861–1864.

Dykes, Eva Beatrice. *The Negro in English Romantic Thought: or, A Study of Sympathy for the Oppressed/ Eva Beatrice Dykes.* Washington: The Associated Publisher, 1942.

Earle, Thomas and Kate Lowe (eds.). *Black Africans in Renaissance Europe.* Cambridge: Cambridge University Press, 2005.

Edwards, Geoffrey Paul. *Early African Presence in the British Isles, an Inaugural Lecture* ... Edinburgh: Centre of African Studies, Edinburgh University, 1990.

Ehlers, Benjamin. *Between Christians and Moriscos: Juan de Ribera and Religious Reform in Valencia, 1568–1614.* Baltimore: John Hopkins University Press, 2006.

Eicher, Joanne Bubolz. *Dress and Ethnicity: Change Across Space and Time.* Oxford: Berg, 1995.

Elaskary, Mohamed Ibrahim Hassan. *The Image of Moors in Writings of Four Elizabethan Dramatists: Peele, Dekker, Heywood and Shakespeare/ by Mohamed Ibrahim Hassan Elaskary.* Exeter: University of Exeter, 2008.

Elliott, John Huxtable. *Imperial Spain 1469–1716.* London: Edward Arnold, 1963.

Elliot, Ralph Warren Victor. *The Gawain Country.* Leeds: University of Leeds School of English, 1984.

Ellis, Henry. *The History and Antiquities of the Parish of Saint Leonard Shoreditch* ... London: J. Nicholas, 1798.

Elton, Geoffrey Rudolph. *The English.* Oxford: Blackwell, 1992.

——. *England under The Tudors.* 1955. Revised edition, London: Methuen, 1974.

——. *The Reformation 1520-1559.* Cambridge: Cambridge University Press, 1990.

——. *Studies in Tudor and Stuart Politics and Government: Papers and Reviews.* 1973. New edition, Cambridge: Cambridge University Press, 2003.

Ember, Carol R., Melvin Ember and Ian Skoggard (eds.), *Encyclopedia of Diasporas: Immigrant and Refugee Cultures Around the World*, Volume I and II. New York: Springer, 2004.

Evans, Robert Weston. *Curiosity and Wonder from the Renaissance to the Enlightenment.* London: Ashgate, 2006.

Fage, John Donnelly, Roland Anthony Oliver and Richard Gray (eds.). *The Cambridge History of Africa ... Volume V.* Cambridge: Cambridge University Press, 1976.

Faggett, Harry Lee. *Black and Other Minorities in Shakespeare's England.* Prairie View: Prairie View Press, 1971.

Fahlander, Frederick and Terje Oestigaard. *The Materiality of Death: Bodies, Burials, Beliefs.* Oxford: Archaeopress, 2008.

Fanon, Frantz. *Black Skin, White Masks.* Paris: Editions du Seuil, 1952.

Farrell, Kirby and Arthur F. Kinney and Elizabeth Hageman. *Women in the Renaissance: Selections from English Literary Renaissance.* Amherst: University of Massachusetts Press, 1990.

Ferme, Mariane Conchita. *"Hammocks Belong to Men, Stools to Women." Constructing and Contesting Gender Domains in a Mende Village (Sierra Leone, West Africa),* Volume I. Chicago: University of Chicago, 1992.

Fiedler, Leslie A. *The Stranger in Shakespeare.* New York: Stein and Day, 1972.

Fienup-Riordan, Ann. *Eskimo Essays: Up'ik Lives and How We See Them.* New Jersey: Rutgers University Press, 1990.

File, Nigel and Chris Power. *Black Settlers in Britain 1555-1958.* London: Heinemann Educational Books, 1981.

Fitzgerald, Sybil. *In the Track of the Moors: Sketches in Spain and Northern Africa ...* London: JM Dent and Co, 1905.

Fleissner, Robert F. *Shakespeare and Africa: The Dark Lady of his Sonnets Revamped and Other Africa-Related Associations.* Philadelphia: Xibris, 2005.

Flesler, Daniela. *The Return of the Moor: Spanish Responses to Contemporary Moroccan Immigration.* West Lafayette: Purdue University, 2008.

Fletcher, Richard. *Moorish Spain.* London: Weidenfeld and Nicholson, 1992.

Floyd-Wilson, Mary. *English Ethnicity and Race in Early Modern Drama.* Cambridge: Cambridge University Press, 2003.

Foot, Susan. *The Effect of the Elizabethan Statute of Artificers on Wages in England.* Exeter: Exeter Research Group, 1980.

Forbes, Jack. *Africans and Native Americans: The Language of Race and the Evolution of the Red-Black Peoples.* 1988. 2nd edition, Urbana: University of Illinois Press University of Illinois, 1993.

Forrest, John. *'Morris and Matachin': A Study in Contemporary Choreography.* London: English Folk Dance and Song Society, 1984.

———. *The History of Morris Dancing, 1458-1750.* Toronto: University of Toronto Press, 1999.

Foss, Edward. *Biographia Juridica: A Biographical Dictionary of the Judges of England from the Conquest to the Present Time ...1870*. New edition, New Jersey: Law Book Exchange, 1999.

Fraser, Antonia. *The Six Wives of Henry VIII*. 1977. Revised edition, London/Arizona: Phoenix, 2002.

——. *The Wives of Henry VIII*. New York: Vintage, 1993.

Fraser, Peter. 'Slaves or Free people, the status of Africans in England 1550–1750,' in Randolph Vigne, Charles Littleton (eds.). *From Strangers to Citizens: The Integration of Immigrant Communities in Britain, Ireland, and Colonial America, 1550–1750*. Eastbourne: Sussex Academic Press, 2001.

Frye, Susan and Karen Robertson (eds.). *Maids and Mistresses, Cousins and Queens: Women's Alliances in Early Modern England (Seminar) 1993*. New York: Oxford University Press, 1998.

Fryer, Peter. *Staying Power: The History of Black People in Britain Since 1504*. 1984. Reprint, London: Pluto Press, 1989.

Fuchs, Barbara. *Exotic Nation: Maurophilia and the Construction of Early Modern Spain*. Philadelphia: University of Pennsylvania Press, 2008.

Fuller, Neely. *The United Independent Compensatory Code/System/Concept a Textbook/Workbook for Thought, Speech and /or Action for Victims of Racism (White Supremacy)*. Place of publication unknown: Neely Fuller, 1957–1980.

Gabriel, John. *Whitewash: Racialized Politics and the Media*. London: Routledge, 1998.

Gade, John Allyne. *Christian IV: King of Denmark and Norway: A Picture of the Seventeenth Century*. 1927. New edition, Boston: Houghton Mifflin, 1928.

Gascoigne, Margaret, George Monger (ed.). *Discovering English Customs and Traditions*. 1969. New edition, Tring: Shire Publications, 1998.

Gerard, Albert (ed.). *European-Language Writing in Sub-Saharan Africa*, Volume I. Budapest: Akademiai Kiado, 1986.

Gerzina, Gretchen Holbrook. *Black London: Life Before Emancipation*. 1995. New edition, New Jersey: Rutgers University, 1997.

Ghazala, Faiza, Greater London Council Ethnic Minorities Unit. *A History of the Black Presence in London*. London: Greater London Council Strategic Policy Unit, 1986.

Gill, Anton and Nick Barratt. *Who Do You Think You Are?: Trace Your Family History Back to the Tudors*. London: Harper Collins, 2006.

Gittings, Clare. *Death, Burial and the Individual in Early Modern England*. London: Croom Helm, 1984.

Goldenberg, David. *The Curse of Ham: Race and Slavery in Early Judaism, Christianity, and Islam*. Princeton: Princeton University Press, 2003.

Gowing, Laura. *Common Bodies: Women, Touch, and Power in Seventeenth-Century England*. New Haven/London: Yale University Press, 2003.

——. *Domestic Dangers: Women, Words and Sex in Early Modern London*. Oxford: Clarendon Press, 1996.

——. *Women, Sex and Honour: The London Church Courts, 1572–1640*. London: University of London, 1993.

Gramsci, Antonio, in Q. Hoare and G. N. Smith (trs. eds.). *Selections from the Prison Notebooks of Antonio Gramsci*. New York: International Publishing, 1971.

Gransden, Antonia. *Historical Writing in England, c. 550–1307*. 1970. New edition, London: Routledge, 1996.

Grayson, Charles E. and Mary French, *Traditional Archery From Six Continents: The Charles E. Grayson Collection*. Columbia: University of Missouri, 2007.

Greaves, Richard. *Society and Religion in Elizabethan England*. Minneapolis: University of Minnesota Press, 1981.

Green, Dominic. *The Double Life of Doctor Lopez: Spies, Shakespeare and the Plot to Poison Elizabeth I*. London: Century, 2003.

Green, Toby. *The Rise of the Trans-Atlantic Slave Trade in Western Africa, 1300–1589*. New York: Cambridge University Press, 2012.

Greenall, Ronald Leslie. *A History of Northamptonshire*. London: Phillimore, 1979.

Greenberg, Joseph. *The Languages of Africa*. 1963. 2nd edition 1966. 3rd edition, Bloomington: Hague by Mouton & Co., 1970.

Griffin, Eric J. *English Renaissance Drama and the Specter of Spain: Ethnopoetics and Empire*. Philadelphia: University of Pennsylvania Press, 2009.

Griffiths, Paul. *Lost Londons: Change, Crime and Control in the Capital City 1550–1650*. Cambridge: Cambridge University Press, 2007.

Grosvenor, Ian D. *Hidden Histories: Cultural Diversity and Heritage in the West Midlands*. London: Heritage Lottery Fund, report 2004, 1st edition 2005.

Groves, Irene (tr.) and Walter Johannes Stein. *The Ninth Century and the Holy Grail*. London: Temple Lodge, 1988.

Gundara, Jagdish S. and Ian Duffield (eds.). *Essays on the History of Blacks in Britain: From Roman Times to the Mid-Twentieth Century*. Aldershot: Averbury, 1992.

Gunther, John. *Inside Africa*. London: Hamish Hamilton, 1955.

Gustafson, Fred. *The Black Madonna*. Boston: Sigo Press, 1990.

Habermas, Jurgen and Martin Heidegger, in Thomas Burger, Frederick Lawrence (eds. trs.). *The Structural Transformation of the Public Sphere: An Inquiry into a Category of Bourgeois Society.* Cambridge: MIT Press, 1989.

Habib, Imtiaz. *Black Lives in the English Archives, 1500–1677: Imprints of the Invisible.* Ashgate: London, 2008.

——. *Shakespeare and Race: Postcolonial Praxis in the Early Modern Period.* Lanham: University Press of America, 1999.

Haigh, Christopher. *English Reformations: Religion, Politics, and Society under the Tudors.* Oxford: Oxford University Press, 1993.

G., W, O. *An Historical Account of the Farthingale and Hoop-Petticoat.* London: E. Philpot, 1863.

Hall, Gwendolyn Midlo. *Social Control in Slave Plantation Societies: A Comparison of St. Domingue and Cuba.* London: John Hopkins Press, 1971.

——. *Slavery and African Ethnicities in the Americas: Restoring the Links.* Chapel Hill: University of North Carolina, 2005.

Hall, Kim. *Things of Darkness: Economies of Race and Gender in Early Modern England.* 1995. 2nd edition, New York: Cornell University Press, 1996.

——. 'Object into Object, Some thoughts on the Presence of Black Women in Early Modern Culture,' pp. 346–380 in Peter Erickson and Clarke Hulse (ed.). *Early Modern Visual Culture: Representation, Race, Empire, in Renaissance England.* Philadelphia: University Press, 2000.

Hanawalt, Barbara. *Growing up in Medieval London: The Experience of Childhood in History.* Oxford/London: Oxford University Press, 1993.

——. *The Wealth of Wives: Women, Law and Economy in Late Medieval London.* Oxford: Oxford University Press, 2007.

Handover, Phyllis Margaret. *The Second Cecil: The Rise to Power 1563–1604 of Sir Robert Cecil Later First Earl of Salisbury.* London: Eyre & Spottiswoode, 1959.

Hannay, David. *A Short History of the Royal Navy 1217–1815.* London: Methuen, 1898.

Harris, Ann Sutherland. *Seventeenth-Century Art and Architecture.* London: Laurence King, 2008.

Harrison, George Bagshawe. *Shakespeare at Work 1592–1603.* London: Routledge, 1933.

——. *The Elizabethan Journals: being a record of those things most talked of during the Years 1591-1603. Comprising an Elizabethan Journal, 1591–4,*

A Second Elizabethan Journal, 1595-8, A Last Elizabethan Journal, 1599–1603, Volumes 1–3. London: Constable and Co., 1928.

Hawkins, John. *A General History of the Science and Practice of Music* ... London: T Payne and son, 1776.

Heers, Jacques. *Esclaves et Domestiques auMoyen-Age Dans le Monde Mediterranean*. Paris: Fayard, 1981.

——. *Genes Au XVe siecle: Activite Economique et Problemes Sociaux*. Paris: SEVPEN, 1961.

Heinze, Rudolph W. *The Proclamations of the Tudor Kings*. Cambridge: Cambridge University Press, 1976.

Hendricks, Margo and Patricia Parker. *Women, 'Race' and Writing in the Early Modern Period*. New York: Routledge, 1994.

Henshaw, David and John de Courcy. *The Worshipful Company of Needlemakers, 1656–2006: A Commemoration of 350 Years*. London: The Worshipful Company of Needlemakers, 2006.

Heywood, Linda Marie. *Central Africans and Cultural Transformations in the America Diaspora*. Cambridge: Cambridge University Press, 2002.

Higginbotham, Leon. *In the Matter of Colour: Race and the American Legal Process: The Colonial Period*. 1978. New edition, New York: Oxford University Press, 1980.

Higgins, Godfrey. *Anacalypsis, An Attempt to Draw Aside the Veil of the Saitic Isis: or, an Inquiry into the Origin of Languages, Nations, and Religions*. 1833. 1878. Reprint, London: TGS publishing, 1927.

Hill, Christopher. *Intellectual Origins of the English Revolution, Revisited*. Oxford: Clarendon, 1997.

Hills, Catherine. *Origins of the English*. London: Duckworth, 2003.

Hilton, Ann. *The Kingdom of Kongo*. Oxford: Clarendon, 1985.

Hindle, Steve. *On the Parish?: The Micro-Politics of Poor Relief in Rural England, c. 1550–1750*. Oxford, Clarendon, 2004.

Hoak, Dale (ed.). *Tudor Political Culture*. Cambridge: Cambridge University Press, 2002.

Hoenselaars, A. J. *Images of Englishmen and Foreigners in the Drama of Shakespeare and his Contemporaries: A Study of Stage Characters and National Identity in English Renaissance Drama, 1558–1642*. Rutherford: Fairleigh Dickinson University Press, 1992.

Holbrook, Jarita Medupe, Rodney Thebe Medupe and Johnson O. Urama (eds.). *African Cultural Astronomy: Current Archaeoastronomy and Ethnoastronomy Research in Africa*. New York/Berlin: Springer, 2008.

BIBLIOGRAPHY

Holbrook, Peter. *Literature and Degree in Renaissance England: Nashe, Bourgeois Tragedy, Shakespeare.* Newark: University of Delaware Press, 1994.

Holman, Peter. *Four and Twenty Fiddlers: The Violin at the English Court, 1540-1690.* Oxford: Oxford University Press, 1993.

Holmes, Colin. *John Bull's Island: Immigration and British Society, 1871-1971.* Basingstoke: Macmillan, 1988.

Horrox, Rosemary and W. Mark Ormrod (eds.). *A Social History of England 1200-1500.* Cambridge: Cambridge University Press, 2006.

Hoskins, William George. *Local History in England.* 1959. 3rd edition, Harlow: Longman, 1984.

Hotson, Leslie. *Mr W.H.* London: Hart-Davis, 1964.

Houlbrooke, Ralph Anthonye. *Death, Religion, and the Family in England, 1480-1750.* Oxford: Clarendon Press, 1998.

Howe, Stephen. *Afrocentrism: Mythical Pasts and Imagined Homes.* 1998. New edition, London: Verso, 1999.

Howell, Martha C. and Walter Prevenier. *From Reliable Sources: An Introduction to Historical Method.* Itacha: Cornell University Press, 2001.

Hull, Suzanne W. *Women according to Men: The World of Tudor-Stuart Men.* Walnut Creek/London: Alta Mira Press, 1996.

Hunter, George Kirkpatrick. *Dramatic Identities and Cultural Tradition: Studies in Shakespeare and his Contemporaries ...* Liverpool: Liverpool University Press, 1978.

——. *Othello and Colour Prejudice, Annual Shakespeare Lecture.* London: Oxford University Press, 1967.

Hutchinson, Robert. *Elizabeth's Spy Master: Francis Walsingham and the Secret War that Saved England.* London: Weidenfeld and Nicolson, 2006.

Hutton, William Holden. *Thomas Becket – Archbishop of Canterbury.* London: Pitman and Sons Ltd, 1910.

Hyde, Marina. *Celebrity: How Entertainers Took Over the World and Why we Need an Exit Strategy.* London: Harvill-Secker, 2009.

Ilahiane, Hsain. *Historical Dictionary of the Berbers (Imazighen).* Lanham: Scarecrow Press Inc, 2006.

Ilardi, Vincent. *Renaissance Vision From Spectacles to Telescopes.* Philadelphia: American Philosophical Society, 2007.

Irving, Washington. *A Chronicle of the Conquest of Granada, From the Manuscript of Fray Antonio Agapido ...* London: John Murray, 1829.

Iyengar, Sujata. *Shades of Difference: Mythologies of Skin Colour in Early Modern England.* Philadelphia: University of Pennsylvania Press, 2008.

Jack, Sybil. 'In Praise of Queens: The Public Presentation of the Virtuous Consort in Seventeenth-Century Britain,' *Women, Identities*, pp. 211–225.

Jackson, John G. *Introduction to African Civilisations*. 1970. New edition, New York: Citadel Press, 2001.

Jacobs, Daniel and Peter Morris. *The Rough Guide to Tunisia*. London: Routledge and Kegan Paul, 1985.

Jahoda, Gustav. *Images of Savages: Ancient Roots of Modern Prejudice in Western Culture*. London: Routledge, 1999.

James, Brenda. *Henry Neville and the Shakespeare Code*. Bognor Regis: Music for Strings, 2008.

Jeffrey, David Lyle. *A Dictionary of Biblical Tradition in English Literature*. Grand Rapids: W.B. Eerdmans, 1994.

Jesse, George Richard. *Researches into the History of the British Dog, from Ancient Laws ...Volume I*. London: R Hardwicke, 1866.

Jessop, William. *Privateering in Elizabethan Bristol: A Case Study on John Hopkins*. Unpublished, 2004.

Joekes, Susan. *Women in Pastoral Societies in East and West Africa*. London/Edinburgh: International Institute for Environment and Development, 1991.

Johnson, Malcolm. *Outside the Gate: St Botolph's and Aldgate 950–1994*. London: Stepney Books, 1994.

Johnson, Paul. *Elizabeth I: a Biography*. New York/London: Holt Rinehart and Winston, 1974.

Johnson, Paul. *Elizabeth I: A Study in Power and Intellect*. London: Weidenfield and Nicolson, 1974.

Jones, Eldred. *Othello's Countrymen: The African in English Renaissance Drama*. London: Oxford University Press, 1965.

Jones, Eldred. *The Elizabethan Image of Africa*. Charlottesville: University of Virginia Press, 1971.

Jones, Gareth Lloyd. *The Discovery of Hebrew in Tudor England: A Third Language*. Manchester: Manchester University Press, 1983.

Jordan, Don and Michael Walsh. *White Cargo: The Forgotten History of Britain's White Slaves in America*. Leicester: W.F. Howes Ltd, 2007.

Jordan, Winthorp D. *White over Black: American Attitudes Towards the Negro, 1550–1812*. Chapel Hill: University of North Carolina Press, 1968.

Juang, Richard and Noelle Morrisette (eds.). *Africa and the Americas: Culture, Politics, and History: A Multidisciplinary Encyclopedia*. Santa Barbara/Oxford: ABC-CLIO, 2008.

BIBLIOGRAPHY

Kassell, Lauren. *Medicine and Magic in Elizabethan London: Simon Forman: Astrologer, Alchemist, and Physician.* 2005. New edition, Oxford: Clarendon Press, 2006.

Katz, David. *Jews in the History of England, 1485–1850.* 1994. New edition, Oxford: Oxford University Press, 1997.

Kaul, Mythili. *Othello: New Essays by Black Writers.* Washington: Howard University Press, 1997.

Kedar, Benjamin Z. *Crusade and Mission: European Approaches Toward the Muslims.* Princeton: Princeton University Press, 1984.

Keita, Maghan. *Conceptualizing/Re-Conceptualizing Africa: The Construction of African Historical Identity.* Leiden: Brill, 2002.

Kelsey, Harry. *Sir John Hawkins: Queen Elizabeth's Slave Trader.* London: Yale University Press, 2003.

Killingray, David. *Africans in Britain.* London: Taylor and Francis, 1994.

Kingsley, Mary Henrietta. *West African Studies.* London: Macmillan, 1901.

Kirshner, Julius. *The Origins of the State in Italy, 1300–1600.* Chicago: University of Chicago Press, 1996.

Kleinhenz, Christopher. *Medieval Italy an Encyclopedia*, Volume II. New York/London: Routledge, 2004.

Kohn, Hans and Craig J. Calhoun. *The Idea of Nationalism: A Study in its Origins and Background.* New York: Macmillan, 1944.

Kottman, Karl A. *Millenarianism and Messianism in Early Modern European Culture*, Volume 175, in James E. Force (ed.). *International Archives of the History of Ideas Millenarianism and Messianism in Early Modern European Culture.* London/Dordrecht: Kluwer Academic, 2001.

Kraemer, Joel L. and Y Tzvi Langermann and Josef Stern (eds.). *Adaptations and Innovations: Studies on the Interaction Between Jewish and Islamic Thought and Literature From the Early Modern Ages to the Late Twentieth Century, Dedicated to the Professor Joel L Kraemer.* Leuven: Peeters, 2007.

———. *Humanism in the Renaissance of Islam: The Cultural Revival During the Buyid Age.* 2nd ed. Leiden, Netherlands: Brill, 1992.

Kris, Lane. *Pillaging the Empire: Piracy in the Americas 1500–1750.* New York: ME Sharpe, 1998.

Kumar, Krishan. *The Making of English National Identity.* Cambridge: Cambridge University Press, 2003.

Lacey, Robert. *Aristocrats.* London: Hutchinson, 1983.

Lancashire, Ian. *Dramatic Texts and Records of Britain: A Chronological Topography to 1558.* Cambridge: Cambridge University Press, 1984.

Lane, Kris. *Pillaging the Empire: Piracy in the Americas, 1500–1750.* New York: ME Sharpe, 1998.

Lane, Edward William and Francis Jenkins Olcott. *More Tales from the Arabian Nights*. London: Holt, 1915.

Lane-Poole, Stanley. *Story of the Moors in Spain*. London: Fisher Unwin, 1886/1887.

Lea, Charles Henry. *The Moriscos of Spain: Their Conversion and Expulsion*. London: Bernard Quaritch, 1901.

Lee Faggett, Harry. *Black and Other Minorities in Shakespeare's England*. Prairie View: Prairie View Press, 1971.

Lefkowitz, Mary. *Black Athena Revisited*. Chapel Hill: University of North Carolina Press, 1996.

Lefkowitz, Mary. *Not Out of Africa: How Afrocentrism Became an Excuse to Teach Myth as History*. New York: Basic Books, 1996.

Leo Kuper Foundation. *The Genocide Reader*. 2007. New edition, London: Routledge, 2009.

Leonard, E. M. *The Early History of English Poor Relief*. Cambridge: Cambridge University Press, 1900.

Lethaby, William. *Westminster Abbey Re-examined*. London: Duckworth, 1925.

Levin, Carole. *The Reign of Elizabeth I*. Basingstoke: Palgrave Macmillan, 2002.

Levin, Jacob Michael. *Agents of Empire: Spanish Ambassadors in Sixteenth-Century Italy*. Ithaca: Cornell University Press, 2005.

Levine, Michael. *African Americans and Civil Rights: From 1619 to the Present*. Phoenix: Oryx, 1996.

Levine, Philippa. *The British Empire: Sunrise to Sunset*. Harlow: Longman, 2007.

Limborch, Philip. *The History of the Inquisition*. London: Samuel Handler, 1731.

Lindfors, Bernth (ed.). *Africans on Stage: Studies in Ethnological Show Business*. Bloomington: Indiana University Press, 1998.

Linebaugh, Peter and Marcus Rediker. *The Many Headed Hydra: Sailors, Slaves, Commoners and the Hidden History of the Revolutionary Atlantic*. Boston: Beacon Press, 2000.

List, Robert. *Merlin's Secret: The African and Near Eastern Presence in the Ancient British Isles*. New York: University Press of America, 1999.

——. *Folktales of a Savage*. London: AA Knopf, 1930.

Little, Arthur L. *Shakespeare Jungle Fever: National-Imperial Re-Visions of Race, Rape, and Sacrifice*. Stanford: Stanford University Press, 2000.

Little, Kenneth. *Negroes in Britain*. London: Routledge and Kegan Paul, 1947.

Lloyd, Janet and Joseph Perez. *The Spanish Inquisition: A History*. London/New Haven: Yale University Press, 2006.
Lomax, Derek. *The Reconquest of Spain*. London: Longman, 1978.
Loomba, Ania. *Colourblind Shakespeare*. New York/London: Routledge, 2006.
——. *Gender Race Renaissance Drama*. Manchester: Manchester University Press, 1989.
——. and Martin Orkin. *Post-colonial Shakespeares*. London: Routledge, 1998.
——. and Jonathan Burton. *Race in Early Modern England: A Documentary Companion*. Basingstoke: Palgrave Macmillan, 2007.
——. *Shakespeare, Race, and Colonialism*. Oxford: Oxford University Press, 2002.
Loomis, Roger Sherman. *The Grail. From Celtic Myth to Christian Symbol*. Cardiff: University of Wales Press, 1963.
Lorimer, Douglas. *Colour, Class and the Victorians: English Attitudes to the Negro in the Mid-Nineteenth Century*. New York: Leicester University Press, 1978.
Louis, William Rogers, Alaine Low and Nicholas Canny (eds.). *The Oxford History of the British Empire, The Twentieth Century*, Volume IV. Oxford/New York: Oxford University Press, 1998.
Lowe, Kate and Thomas Earle. *Black Africans in Renaissance Europe*. London: Cambridge University Press, 2005.
Luu, Lien. *Immigrants and the Industries of London, 1500–1700*. Aldershot, Ashgate, 2005.
Lynch, Andrew and Philippa Maddern (eds.). *Venus and Mars: Engendering Love and War in Medieval and Early Modern Europe*. Nedlands: University of Western Australia Press, 1995.
MacCullough, Norman Verrle. *The Negro in English Literature*. Ilfracombe: A. Stockwell, 1962.
Macdonald, Joyce Green (ed.). *Race, Ethnicity, and Power in the Renaissance*. Madison: Fairleigh Dickinson University Press and London: Associated University Presses, 1997.
Macinnes, Charles Malcolm. *England and Slavery*. London: Arrowsmith, 1934.
MacKeith, Lucy. *Local Black History: A Beginning in Devon*. London: Archives and Museum of Black Heritage, 2003.
MacKenzie, Donald A. *Ancient Man in Britain*. London: Blackie, 1922.
Maclean, John (ed.), David Wakin Waters. *The Art of Navigation in England in Elizabethan and Early Stuart Times*. London: Hollis and Carter, 1958.

Macpeek, James Andrew Scarborough. *The Black Book of Knaves and Unthrifts. In Shakespeare and Other Renaissance Authors.* Storrs: University of Connecticut, 1969.

MacRitchie, David. *Ancient and Modern Britons: A Retrospect*, 2 Volumes. London: Kegan Paul and Company, 1884. New edition, Los Angeles: Preston, 1986.

——. *Scottish Gypsies under the Stewarts.* Edinburgh: D. Douglas, 1894.

Maley, Willy (ed.) and Margaret Tudeau-Clayton. *This England, That Shakespeare: New Angles on Englishness and the Bard.* Farnham: Ashgate Publishing, 2010.

Malik, Sarita. *Representing Black Britain: A History of Black and Asian Images on British Television.* London: SAGE, 2001.

Manaton, John. *Hatherleigh History in Brief.* Exeter: Devonshire Association for the Advancement of Science Literature and Art Parochial History Section, 1951.

Mansour, Gerda. *Multilingualism and Nation Building.* Clevedon: Multilingual Matters, 1993.

Mark, Peter. *African in European Eyes: The Portrayal of Black Africa in 14th & 15th Century Europe.* Syracuse: Maxwell School of Citizenship and Public Affairs Syracuse University, 1974.

Marrapodi, Michele. *Italian Culture in the Drama of Shakespeare and his Contemporaries: Rewriting, Remaking, Refashioning.* Aldershot: Ashgate, 2007.

Marsden, Peter. *Sealed by Time: The Loss and Recovery of the Mary Rose. The Archaeology of the Mary Rose*, Volume 1. Portsmouth: The Mary Rose Trust, 2003.

Marsden, Peter. 'Salvage, Saving and Surveying the *Mary Rose*,' in, Marsden (ed.) *Your Noblest Shippe: Anatomy of a Tudor Warship. The Archaeology of the Mary Rose*, Volume 2. Portsmouth: The Mary Rose Trust, 2009.

Martin, Rebecca. *Wild Men and Moors in the Castle of Love: The Castle-Siege Tapestries, in Nuremberg, Vienna, and Boston (German (Alsace) Weavers).* Chapel Hill: University of North California, 1983.

Massey, Gerald. *A Book of the Beginnings: Containing an Attempt to Recover and Reconstitute the Lost Origines of the Myths and Mysteries, Types and Symbols, Religion and Language, with Egypt for the Mouthpiece and Africa as the Birthplace.* Volume I, *Egyptian Origines in the British Isles*. 1881. Republished, London: Secaucus University Books, 1974.

——. *Ancient Egypt the Light of the World, A Work of Reclamation and Restitution in Twelve Volumes.* London: T. Fisher Unwin, 1907. Reprint, London: Adelphi Terrace Kessinger Publishing, 1990.

———. *Ancient Egypt the Light of the World, Containing an Attempt to Recover and Reconstitute the Lost Origines of the Myths and Mysteries ... with Egypt for the Mouthpiece and Africa as the Birthplace. Egyptian Origines in the British Isles*, Volume I. 1881. New edition, London: Secaucus University Books, 1974.

Matar, Nabil (ed. tr.). *In the Lands of the Christians: Arabic Travel Writing in the Seventeenth Century.* New York: Routledge, 2002.

———. *Islam in Britain, 1558-1685.* 1998. New edition, New York/Cambridge: Cambridge University Press, 1998, 1999.

———. *Turks Moors and Englishmen in the Age of Discovery.* 1999. New edition, New York/Chichester: Columbia University Press, 2000.

Mayall, David. *Gypsy Identities, 1500-2000: From Egipcyans and Moon-men to the Ethnic Romany.* London: Routledge 2004.

McCuen, Marnie. *The Genocide Reader: The Politics of Ethnicity and Extermination.* Hudson: Gem Publications, 2000.

McIntosh, Marjorie Keniston. *Poor Relief in England, 1350-1600.* New York: Cambridge University Press, 2011.

McKee, Alexander. *The Queen's Corsair: Drake's Journey of Circumnavigation, 1577-1580.* London: Souvenir Press, 1978.

McKee, Sally (ed.). *Crossing Boundaries: Issues of Cultural and Individual Identity in the Middle Ages and the Renaissance.* Turnout: Brepols, 1999.

McLean, Antonia. *Humanism and the Rise of Science in Tudor England.* London: Heinemann Educational, 1972.

McManus, Clare. *Women on the Renaissance Stage: Anna of Denmark and Female Masquing in the Stuart Court (1590-1619).* Manchester: Manchester University Press, 2002.

Menocal, Maria Rosa. *The Ornament of the World: How Muslims, Jews and Christians Created a Culture of Tolerance in Medieval Spain.* London: Little Brown, 2002.

Merriman, James Douglas. *The Flower of Kings; a Study of the Arthurian Legend in England between 1485 and 1835.* Lawrence: University Press of Kansas, 1973.

Miller, Lee. *Roanoke: Solving the Mystery of England's Lost Colony.* London: Jonathon Cape, 2000.

Miller, Monica L. *Slaves to Fashion: Black Dandyism and the Styling of Black Diasporic Identity.* Durham: Duke University Press, 2009.

Milner, Stephen (ed.). Steven Epstein. *At the Margins: Minority Groups in Premodern Italy.* Minneapolis/Bristol: University of Minnesota Press, 2005.

Misztal, Mariusz. *The Elizabethan Courtier: Ideal Versus Reality Embodied in Robert Dudley the Earl of Leicester.* Karkow: Wydawnictwo Naukowe Akademii Pedagogicznej, 2002.

Monger, George. *Marriage Customs of the World: From Henna to Honeymoons.* Santa Barbara: ABC CLIO, 2004.

Montalvo, Jose Hinojosa. *Jews of the Kingdom of Valencia: From Persecution to Expulsion, 1391-1492.* Jerusalem: Magnes Press, Hebrew University, 1993.

Moore, Richard B. *The Name Negro its Origin and Evil Use.* Baltimore: Black Classic Press, 1960.

Morello, Augusto. *Culture of an Italian Region: The Marche, Guzzini and Design.* Rome/ Milan: Electa, 2002.

Morgan, Jennifer Lyle. *Laboring Women: Reproduction and Gender in New World Slavery.* Philadelphia: University of Pennsylvania Press, 2004.

Morgan, O. Morien. *The Mabin of the Mabinogion.* London: Whittaker, 1900.

Morris, John. *The Life and Martyrdom of Thomas Becket ...* London: Percy and Sons, 1845.

——. *The Troubles of Our Catholic Forefathers Related by Themselves.* London: Burns and Oates, 1875.

Moule, Thomas. *The English Counties Delineated; or Descriptive View of the Present State of England and Wales; Illustrated by a New Map of London ...* London: George Virtue, 1830-1835.

Mugglestone, Lynda (ed.). *The Oxford History of English.* Oxford: Oxford University Press, 2006.

Munck, Bert De and Steven L. Kaplan, Hugo Soly (eds.). *Learning on the Shop Floor: Historical Perspectives on Apprenticeship.* New York: Berghahn Books, 2006.

Myerly, Scott Hughes. *British Military Spectacle: From the Napoleonic Wars through the Crimea.* London/New York: Harvard University Press, 1996.

Myers, Norma. *Reconstructing the Black Past: Blacks in Britain, 1780-1830.* Liverpool: University of Liverpool, 1990.

Nicholson, Edward Williams Byron. *Keltic Researches: Studies in the History and Distribution of the Ancient Goidelic Language and Peoples.* Oxford: Oxford University Press, 1904.

Northrup, David. *Africa's Discovery of Europe: 1450-1850.* New York/ Oxford: Oxford University Press, 2002.

Nye, Robert. *The Late Mister Shakespeare: A Novel.* London: Chatto and Windus, 1998.

Obafemi, Jacob and Kehinde Olupona. *Kingship, Religion, and Rituals in a Nigerian Community: A Phenomenological Study of Ondo Yoruba Festivals.* Stockholm: Almqvist and Wiksell International, 1991.

Ojior, Omoh. *Africa and Africans in the Diaspora: An Evaluation of the Impact they have on each other*. Hampton: UB and US Communications Systems, 1996.

Okely, Judith. *The Traveller-Gypsies*. Cambridge: Cambridge University Press, 1983.

Oleszkiewicz Peralba, Małgorzata. *The Black Madonna in Latin America and Europe: Tradition and Transformation*. Albuquerque: University of New Mexico Press, 2007.

Olsen, Kirstin. *Daily Life in 18th-Century England*. Oxford: Greenwood Publishing Group, 1999.

Onyeka, *The Black Equestrians: The African Gentlemen of Georgian England*. London: Narrative Eye, 2014.

Orlin, Lena Cowen. *Locating Privacy in Tudor London*. Oxford: Oxford University Press, 2007.

Ostovich, Helen, Mary V. Silcox and Graham Roebuck (eds.). *The Mysterious and Foreign in Early Modern England*. Newark: University of Delaware Press, 1998.

Otto, Beatrice K. *Fools are Everywhere: The Court Jester Around the World*. Chicago/London: University of Chicago Press, 2001.

Outhwaite, R. B. (ed.), Vivien Brodsky-Elliott. *Single Women in the London Marriage Market: Age, Status and Mobility, 1598–1619*. 1980. Revised edition, London: Europe Publications, 1981.

Palliser, D. M (ed.). *The Cambridge Urban History of Britain*. Volume I: c. 600–c.1540. Cambridge: Cambridge University Press, 2000.

Pallua, Ulrich. *Eurocentrism, Racism, Colonialism in the Victorian and Edwardian Age: Changing Images of Africa(ns) in Scientific and Literary Texts*. Heidelberg: Winter, 2006.

Pankhania, Josna. *Liberating the National History Curriculum*. London: Falmer Press, 1994.

Paul, Kathleen. *Whitewashing Britain: Race and Citizenship in the Postwar Era*. New York/London: Cornell University Press, 1997.

Pedraz, Alonso Martin. *Enciclopedia del Idioma* ... Volume II. Madrid: Aguilar, 1958.

Perez, Joseph and Janet Lloyd (tr.). *The Spanish Inquisition: A History*. 2004. New edition, London/New Haven: Yale University Press, 2006.

Perry, Peter John Charles. *The Evolution of British Manpower Policy: From the Statute of Artificers 1563 to the Industrial Training Act 1964*. London: Perry, 1976.

Pevsner, Nikolaus. *The Buildings of England, London 1, The Cities of London and Westminster*. Harmondsworth: Penguin Books, 1957.

Philips, William. *Slavery from Roman Times to the Early Transatlantic Trade.* Manchester: Manchester University Press, 1985.

Phillips, Joshua. *English Fictions of Communal Identity, 1485–1603.* Farnham: Ashgate, 2003.

Piesse, A. J. *Sixteenth-Century Identities.* Manchester: Manchester University Press, 2001.

Pike, Ruth. *Aristocrats and Traders: Sevillian Society in the Sixteenth Century.* Ithaca: Cornell University Press, 1972.

Pimienta-Bey, Jose. *Othello's Children in the 'New world': Moorish History and Identity in the African American Experience.* Bloomington: Authorhouse, 2002.

Pollock, Frederick. *The History of English Law Before the Time of Edward I.* Cambridge: Cambridge University Press, 1895.

Poole, Herbert Edmund (ed.). *The Wisdom of Andrew Boorde.* London: E. Backus, 1936.

Portal, Frederick Pierre and W.S. Inman (tr.). *An Essay on Symbolic Colours: In Antiquity- The Middle Ages- and Modern Times.* London: J. Weale, 1845.

Pound, John. *Poverty and Vagrancy in Tudor England.* London: Longman, 1971.

Prak, Maarten Roy (ed.). *Craft Guilds in the Early Modern Low Countries: Work, Power and Representation.* Aldershot: Ashgate, 2006.

Prest, Wilfrid R. *The Professions in Early Modern England.* London: Croom Helm, 1984.

Price, Richard (ed.). *Maroon Societies: Rebel Slave Communities in the Americas.* New York: Anchor Books, 1973.

Quinn, David B. *Explorers and Colonies: America, 1500–1625.* London: Hambledon Press, 1990.

Ramdin, Ron. *The Making of the Black Working Class in Britain.* Aldershot: Gower, 1987.

Randerson, Geoff and Mark Bateson. *The Continuing Search for Black, Asian and non-European People in Kent.* Kent Archives, unpublished, 2008.

Raphael-Hernandez, Heike. *Blackening Europe: The African-American Presence.* New York/London: Routledge, 2003.

Rashidi, Runoko. *The Global African Community: The African Presence in Asia, Australia, and the South Pacific.* Washington: Institute for Independent Education, 1993.

Ravelhofer, Barbara, in, Crista Jansohn (ed.). *Queen Elizabeth I: Past and Present* Munster/London: Transaction, 2004.

Rawlings Helen. *The Spanish Inquisition.* London: Wiley Blackwell, 2006.

Read, Conyers. *Mr. Secretary Walsingham and the Policy of Queen Elizabeth* ... Oxford: Clarendon Press, 1925.
Reade, John Edmund. *Memnon: And other Poems*. London: Publisher unknown, 1868.
Readers Digest Association. *Past All Around Us: An Illustrated Guide to the Ruins, Relics, Monuments, Castles, Cathedrals, Historic Buildings, Industrial Landmarks of Britain*. London: Readers Digest Association, 1979.
Riley-Smith, Jonathan Simon Christopher (ed.), et. al. *The New Cambridge Medieval History*, Volume VII. Cambridge: Cambridge University Press, 1995.
Robinson, Elaine L. *Shakespeare Attacks Bigotry: A Close Reading of Six Plays*. Jefferson: Mcfarland and Company, 2009.
Rodriguez, Junius (ed.). *Slavery in the United States: A Social, Political, and Historical Encyclopedia*, Volume I and II. Santa Barbara/Oxford: ABC-CLIO, 2007.
Rogers, Joel Augustus. *Nature Knows no Colour Line*. St Petersburg: Helga Rogers, 1952.
——. *Sex and Race, Negro Caucasian Mixing in all Ages and all Lands*, Volume I–IV. 1942. 9th edition, New York: Rogers, 1967.
——. *World's Great Men of Colour*, Volume I and II. 1931. New edition, New York: Touchstone Books, 1995.
Rosser, Leonidas. *Baptism: Its Nature, Obligation, Mode, Subjects and Benefits*. Philadelphia: Leonidas Rosser, 1854.
Rowse, Alfred Leslie. *Raleigh and the Throckmortons*. London/New York: Macmillan Company and St Martin's Press, 1962.
Rubinstein, Annette Teta. *The Great Tradition in English Literature from Shakespeare to Shaw*. 1953. New edition, New York/London: Modern View Paperbacks, 1969.
Ruddock, Alwyn. *Italian Merchants and Shipping in Southampton 1270–1600*. Southampton: University College, 1951.
Russell, Joycelyne Gledhill. *Field of Cloth of Gold: Men and Manners in 1520*. London: Routledge and Kegan Paul, 1969.
Sachar, Abram Leon. *A History of the Jews*. 1930. New edition, New York: Knopf, 1967.
Said, Edward W. *Orientalism*. New York: Pantheon Books, 1978.
Sandhu, Sukhdev. *London Calling: How Black and Asian Writers Imagined a City*. London: Harper Collins, 2003.
Saunders, A. C. de C. M. *A Social History of Black Slaves and Freedmen in Portugal 1441–1555*. Cambridge: Cambridge University Press, 1982.

Saunders, Nicholas Jay. *The Peoples of the Caribbean: An Encyclopedia of Archaeology and Traditional Culture*. Santa Barbara: ABC Clio, 2005.

Schiesaari, Juliana. *Beasts and Beauties: Animals, Gender and Domestication in the Italian Renaissance* ...Toronto: University of Toronto Press, 2010.

Schlebecker, John T. *The Many Names of Country People: A Historical Dictionary from the Twelfth Century Onwards*. New York/London: Greenwood Press, 1989.

Schleiner, Louise. *Tudor and Stuart Women Writers*. Bloomington: Indiana University Press, 1994.

Schoenbaum, Samuel. *William Shakespeare: A Compact Documentary Life*. Oxford: Clarendon Press, 1977.

Schoenbaum, Simon. *Shakespeare's Lives*. London: Clarendon, 1991.

Schofield, Roger. *Taxation under the Early Tudors 1485-1547*. London: Blackwell, 2004.

Schorsch, Jonathan. *Jews and Blacks in the Early Modern World*. Cambridge: Cambridge University Press, 2004.

Schorsch, Jonathan. *Swimming the Christian Atlantic: Judeoconversos, Afroiberians, and Amerindians in the Seventeenth Century*. Leiden/Boston/Biggleswade: Brill Extenza Turpin, 2008.

Schwarzenfeld, Gertrude Von. *Charles V Father of Europe*. London: Hollis and Carter, 1957.

Schwyzer, Philip. *Literature, Nationalism, and Memory in Early Modern England and Wales*. Cambridge: Cambridge University Press, 2004.

Scobie, Edward. *Black Britannia: A History of Blacks in Britain*. Chicago: Johnson Publishing Company, 1972.

Scott, John Robert. *A Dissertation on the Expulsion of the Moors from Spain and the Protestants from France and the Low Countries*. Dublin: Joseph Hill University Press, 1779.

Scott, Samuel Parsons. *History of the Moorish Empire in Europe*. 1904. New edition, New York/Philadelphia/London: Lippincott, 1994.

Selwood, Jacob. *Diversity and Difference in Early Modern London*. Farnham: Ashgate, 2010.

Sertima, Ivan Van (ed.). Edward Scobie. *African Presence in Early Europe*. New Jersey: Transaction Publishers, 1985.

Sertima, Ivan Van (ed.). *Black Women in Antiquity*. New York: Transaction Publishers, 1984.

——. Wayne Chandler. *Golden Age of the Moor*. Piscataway: Transaction Publishers, 1992.

——. Larry Obadele Williams (eds.). *Great African Thinkers*. Volume I, *Cheikh Anta Diop*. New Brunswick: Transaction Books, 1986.

Servadio, Gaio. *Renaissance Woman*. London/New York: I. B.Tauris, 2005.

Sharp, Joanne. *Geographies of Post-colonialism: Spaces of Power and Representation*. London/Los Angeles: SAGE Publications, 2008.

Shepard, Alexandra and Phil Withington (eds.). *Communities in Early Modern England: Networks, Place, Rhetoric*. Manchester: Manchester University Press, 2000.

Shirley, Evelyn Philip. *Stemmata Shirleiana; or, the Annals of the Shirley Family, Lords of Nether Etindon, in the County of Warwick, and of Shirley in the County of Derby*. London: J. B. Nichols, 1841.

Shyllon, Folarin. *Black People in Britain 1553–1833*. Oxford: Oxford University Press, 1977.

Sim, Alison. *Masters and Servants in Tudor England*. Stroud: Sutton, 2006.

Simon, Joan. *Education and Society in Tudor England*. Cambridge: Cambridge University Press, 1979.

Singh, Jyotsna. *Shakespeare's Othello: African Identities, and Racial Conflicts*. New York: Routledge, 1994.

Skinner, Elliott Percival. *Peoples and Cultures of Africa: An Anthropological Reader*. Washington: Natural History Press, 1972.

Slack, Paul. *Poverty and Policy in Tudor and Stuart England*. London: Longman, 1988.

———. *The English Poor Law, 1531–1732*. Basingstoke: Macmillan Education, 1990.

———. *Poverty in Early-Stuart Salisbury*. Devizes: Wiltshire Record Society, 1975.

Smith, Ian. *Race and Rhetoric in the Renaissance: Barbarian Errors*. Basingstoke: Palgrave Macmillan, 2009.

Smith, Robert Sydney. *Warfare and Diplomacy in Pre-Colonial West Africa*. London: Methuen, 1976.

Smith-Bannister, Scott. *Names and Naming Patterns in England, 1538–1700*. Oxford: Clarendon, 1997.

Smuts, Robert Malcolm. *Culture and Power in England, 1585–1685*. Basingstoke: Macmillan, 1999.

Snell, K. D. M. *Parish and Belonging: Community, Identity, and Welfare in England and Wales, 1700–1950*. New York/Cambridge: Cambridge University Press, 2006.

Snowden, Frank M. *Blacks in Antiquity: Ethiopians in the Greco-Roman Experience*. Cambridge: Belknap Press Harvard University Press, 1970.

Sokol, B. J. *Shakespeare and Tolerance*. Cambridge: Cambridge University Press, 2008.

Southworth, John. *Fools and Jesters at the English Court.* 1998. New edition, Stroud: Sutton, 2003.

Spicer, Andrew in Nigel Goose and Lieun Luu (eds.). *Immigrants in Tudor and Early Stuart England.* Eastbourne: Sussex Academic Press, 2005.

Spurgeon, Caroline Frances Eleanor. *Shakespeare's Imagery and what it tells us.* Cambridge: University Press, 1935.

Sreedharan, E. *A Textbook of Historiography, 500 B.C. to A.D. 2000.* New Delhi: Orient Longman, 2003.

Staples, John. *Notes on St. Botolph, without Aldersgate.* London: Printed for Private Circulation, 1881.

Stephens, William Brewer. *Sources for English Local History.* Cambridge: Cambridge University Press, 1981.

Stone, Lawrence and A. L. Beier and David Cannadine and James R. Rosenheim (eds.). *The First Modern Society: Essays in English History in Honour of Lawrence Stone.* Cambridge: Cambridge University Press, 1989.

Strickland, Debra Higgs. *Saracens, Demons, and Jews: Making Monsters in Medieval Art.* New Jersey: Princeton University Press, 2003.

Stride, George T. and Caroline Ifeka. *Peoples and Empires of West Africa: West Africa in History, 1000–1800 ...* New York: Africana Publishing Corporation, 1971.

Strutt, Joseph and Charles Cox (ed.). *The Sports and Pastimes of the People of England ...* London: Methuen, 1801.

Styles, Susan J. *The Poor Law.* London: Macmillan Education, 1985.

Sugden, John. *Sir Francis Drake.* London: Random House, 2006.

Tadmor, Naomi. *The Social Universe of the English Bible: Scripture, Society and Culture in Early Modern England.* Cambridge: Cambridge University Press, 2010.

The Royal Archaeological Institute. *The Archaeological Journal of Great Britain*, Volumes 118–119. London: Royal Archaeological Institute, 1943–1986.

Thomas, Hugh. *The Slave Trade: The History of the Atlantic Slave Trade, 1440–1870.* 1997. New edition, London: Phoenix, 2006.

Thompson, Ayanna (ed.). *Colourblind Shakespeare: New Perspectives on Race and Performance.* London: Routledge, 2006.

Thompson, Brenda. *'For the Better Relief of the Poor of this Parish:' Public Poor Relief in Eighteenth Century Charles Town, South Carolina.* Ann Arbor: ProQuest Information and Learning Company, 2006, pp. 27–32 (on Tudor Poor relief).

Thompson, Edward. *The Making of the English Working Class.* 1963. New edition, Hopkington: Vintage Books, 1966.

Thorpe, Earl. *Black Historians: A Critique.* 1958. New Revised edition, New York: Morrow, 1971.

Timmins, Samuel, R. S. Bartlett and J. M. Woodward (eds.). *The Resources, Products, and Industrial History of Birmingham and the Midland Hardware District* ... Abingdon: Frank Cass and Company, 1866.

Tittler, Robert. *Townspeople and Nation: English Urban Experiences, 1540–1640.* Stanford: Stanford University Press, 2001.

Tittler, Robert and Norman Jones (eds.). *A Companion to Tudor Britain, Blackwell Companions to British History.* Oxford: Wiley Blackwell, 2004.

Todd, Loreto. *Pidgins and Creoles.* 1974. New edition, London: Routledge, 1990.

Tokson, Elliot H. *The Popular Image of the Black Man in English Drama, 1550–1688.* Boston: G. K. Hall, 1982.

Tremlett, Giles. *Catherine of Aragon: Henry's Spanish Wife.* London: Faber and Faber, 2010. Also known as *Catherine of Aragon: The Spanish Queen of Henry VIII.* New York: Walker and Company, 2010.

Trevelyan, Raleigh. *Sir Walter Raleigh.* London: Allen Lane, 2002.

Tribe, David Harold. *Free Thought and Humanism in Shakespeare.* London: Pioneer Press, 1964.

Tuner, Marion. *Chaucerian Conflict: Languages of Antagonism in Late Fourteenth-Century London.* Oxford: Clarendon, 2007.

Unger, Richard W. *Beer in the Middle Ages and the Renaissance.* Philadelphia and Bristol: University of Pennsylvania Press and University Presses Marketing, 2004.

Ungerer, Gustav. *The Mediterranean Apprenticeship of British Slavery.* Madrid: Verbum Editorial, 2008.

Ungewitter, Franz Heinrich. *Europe, Past and Present: A Comprehensive Manual of European Geography and History* ... New York: Putnam, 1850.

Unwin, Rayner. *The Defeat of John Hawkins.* 1960. New edition, London: Allen Unwin, 1961.

Vaughan, Virginia Mason. *Performing Blackness on English Stages, 1500–1800.* Cambridge: Cambridge University Press, 2005.

Vitkus, Daniel (ed.). *Three Turk Plays from Early Modern England: Selimus, A Christian turned Turk, and The Renegado.* New York/Chichester: Columbia University Press, 2000.

Vitkus, Daniel. *Turning Turk: English Theater and the Multicultural Mediterranean, 1570–1630.* New York: Palgrave Macmillan, 2003.

Walker, Robin. *When We Ruled.* London: Every Generation Media, 2005.

Walvin, James. *A Short History of Slavery.* London: Penguin, 2001.

———. *Atlas of Slavery.* London: Longman, 2005.

—. *Black and White: The Negro and English Society, 1555–1945.* London: Allen Lane and the Penguin Press, 1973.

—. *Black Ivory: Slavery in the British Empire.* 1992. 2nd edition, London: Wiley/Blackwell, 2001.

—. *Black Ivory: A History of British Slavery.* London: Harper Collins, 1992. New edition, London: Wiley/Blackwell, 2001.

—. *Black Personalities in the Era of the Slave Trade.* London: Palgrave Macmillan, 1983.

—. *Making the Black Atlantic: Britain and the African Diaspora.* London: Cassell, 2000.

—. in Peter Fryer. *Rhythms of Resistance: African Musical Heritage in Brazil.* London: Pluto Press, 2000.

—. *The Black Presence: A Documentary History of the Negro in England, 1555–1860.* London: Orbach and Chambers, 1971.

—. *The Trader, the Owner, the Slave: Parallel Lives in the Age of Slavery.* 2007. New edition, London: Vintage Reprint, 2008.

—. *Slaves and Slavery: The British Colonial Experience.* Manchester: Manchester University Press, 1992.

Warner, Marina. *Signs and Wonders: Essays on Literature and Culture.* London: Chatto and Windus, 2003.

Washington, Joseph R. *Anti-Blackness in English Religion 1500–1800, Texts and Studies in Religion,* Volume 19. New York: Mellen, 1984.

Weaver, Helen (tr.), Georges Balandier. *Daily Life in the Kingdom of the Kongo: From the Sixteenth to the Eighteenth Century.* 1965. New edition, New York: Allen and Unwin, 1968.

Wegemer, Gerard. *Young Thomas More and the Arts of Liberty.* Cambridge: Cambridge University Press, 2001.

Weir, Alison. *Elizabeth the Queen.* London: Jonathan Cape, 1998.

—. *Life of Elizabeth 1st.* New York: Ballantine, 1998.

—. *The Six Wives of Henry VIII.* New York: Grove Press, 1991.

Weissbort, Daniel and Astraour Eystiensson. *Translation - Theory and Practice: A Historical Reader.* Oxford/London: Oxford University Press, 2006.

Weston, Jessica Laidlay. *The Legend of Sir Gawain and the Green Knight: Studies Upon its Original Scope and Significance.* London: David Nutt, 1897.

Whitfield, Peter. *Sir Francis Drake.* New York: New York University Press, 2004.

Whitford, David M. *The Curse of Ham in the Early Modern Era: The Bible and the Justifications for Slavery.* Farnham: Ashgate, 2009.

Williams, Chancellor. *The Destruction of Black Civilisation: Great Issues of a Race From 4500 BC to 2000 AD*. Dubuque: Kendall/Hunt Publishing Company, 1971. 3rd revised edition, Chicago: Third World Press, 1987.

Williams, Ethel Carleton. *Anne of Denmark: Wife of James VI of Scotland, James I of England*. New Jersey: Prentice Hall Press, 1970.

Williams, Michael Warren. *The African American Encyclopedia*, Volume 2. New York/London: Marshall Cavendish Corporation, 1993.

Winthrop, Jordan D. *White over Black: American Attitudes toward the Negro, 1550-1812*. Chapel Hill: University of North Carolina Press, 1968.

Woolley, Benjamin. *The Queen's Conjurer: The Science and Magic of Doctor John Dee, Advisor to Queen Elizabeth I*. New York: Henry Holt, 2001.

Wright, William. *Black History and Black Identity: A Call for a New Historiography*. Westport: Greenwood Publishing Group, 2002.

Yakan, Mohamad Zuhdi. *Almanac of African Peoples and Nations*. London: Transaction Publishers, 1999.

Yates, Frances. *The Occult Philosophy in the Elizabethan Age*. 1979. New edition, London: Routledge, 2001.

Youings, Joyce A. *Sixteenth-Century England*. London: Allen Lane, 1984.

Youngs, Frederick A. *The Proclamations of the Tudor Queens*. Cambridge: Cambridge University Press, 1976.

Yungblut, Lara Hunt. *Strangers Settled Here Amongst Us: Policies, Perceptions, and the Presence of Aliens in Elizabethan England*. 1996. New edition, London: Routledge, 2003.

Zabus, Chantal J. *Tempests After Shakespeare*. New York/Basingstoke: Palgrave, 2002.

Articles

Abanime, Emeka. 'Elizabeth I and Negroes,' *Cahiers Elisabethains*, XIX, 19 April 1981, p. 2.

Abercrombie, Thomas J. 'When the Moors Ruled Spain,' *National Geographic*, 174, No. 1, July 1988, pp. 86–119.

Adams, Simon. 'At Home and Away: The Earl of Leicester,' *History Today*, 46, Issue 5, May 1996, pp. 22–28.

——. 'New light on the 'Reformation' of John Hawkins: the Ellesmere Naval Survey of January 1584,' *English Historical Review*, 190, pp. 97–111.

Adams, Susan, et. al. 'The Genetic Legacy of Religious Diversity and Intolerance: … Christians, Jews, and Muslims in the Iberian Peninsula,' *The American Journal of Human Genetics*, 83, Issue 6, 4 December 2008, pp. 725–736.

Adler, Doris. 'The Rhetoric of Black and White in Othello,' *Shakespeare Quarterly*, 25, No. 2, Spring 1974, pp. 248–257.

Alford, Stephen. 'Politics and Political History in the Tudor Century,' *Historical Journal*, 42, No. 2. Cambridge University Press, 1999, pp. 535–548.

Alford, Stephen. 'Urban Safe Houses for the Unfree in Medieval England: A reconsideration,' *Slavery and Abolition*, 32, Issue 3, September 2011, pp. 363–375.

Anon. '13 Cheikh Anta Diop Conference Selected Proceedings,' *Journal of Black Studies*, 33, No. 2, 2002, n. p.

Anthiaume, Albert-Marie-Ferdinand. 'Un pilote et cartographe havrais au XVIe siècle: Guillaume Le Testu,' *Bulletin de Géographie Historique et Descriptive*, Paris, Nos 1–2, 1911, pp. 135–202.

Aubrey, James R. 'Race and the Spectacle of the Monstrous in 'Othello,"' *CLIO*, 22, No. 3, March 22 1993, pp. 221–238.

Baker, John. '*Personal Liberty under the Common Law of England, 1200-1600*,' *The Origins of Modern Freedom in the West*. Stanford: Stanford University Press, 1995, pp. 178–202.

Bartels, Emily Carroll. 'Making more of the Moor: Aaron, Othello and Renaissance Refashionings of Race,' *Shakespeare Quarterly*, 41, No. 4, Winter 1990, pp. 433–454.

Bartels, Emily Carroll. 'Too many Blackamoors: Deportation, discrimination and Elizabeth 1,' *Studies in English Literature 1500–1900*, 46, No. 2, Spring 2006, pp. 305–322.

Beier, A. L. 'Poverty and Progress in Early Modern England,' in, Cannadine and Rosenhiem (eds.). *The First Modern Society*, pp. 201–241.

Bernadette, Andrea. 'Black Skin, The Queen's Masques: Africanist Ambivalence and Feminine Author(ity) in the *Masques of Blackness* and *Beauty*,' *English Literary Renaissance*, 29, No. 2, 1999, pp. 246–281.

Bossy, John. 'Blood and Baptism: Kinship, Community and Christianity in Western Europe from the Fourteenth to the Seventeenth Centuries,' in Derek Baker (ed.). *Sanctity and Secularity, Studies in Church History*, 10. Oxford: Blackwell, 1973, pp. 129–143.

Braidwood, Stephen J. 'Initiatives and Organisation of the Black Poor 1786-1787,' Paper presented at International Conference on the History of Blacks in Britain, London 28–30 September 1981.

Braude, Benjamin. 'Collective Degradation: Slavery and the Construction of Race, Ham and Noah: Sexuality, Servitudinism, and Ethnicity:' from proceedings of the Fifth Annual Gilder Lehrman Center International Conference. New Haven Connecticut: Yale University, November 8, 2003, n. p.

——. 'The Sons of Noah and the Construction of Ethnic and Geographical Identities in the Medieval and Early Modern Periods,' *William and Mary Quarterly*, 54, No.1, January 1997, pp. 103-142.

Braxton, Phyllis Natalie. 'Othello: the Moor and the Metaphor,' *South Atlantic Review*, 55, No. 4, November 1990, pp. 1-17.

Britnell, Richard. 'The Economy of British Towns 1300-1540,' in, D. M. Palliser (ed.). *The Cambridge Urban History of Britain: c. 600-c.1540.* Volume I. Cambridge: Cambridge University Press, 2000, pp. 313-333.

——. 'Town Life,' in, Rosemary Horrox (ed.). *A Social History of England 1200-1500.* Cambridge: Cambridge University Press, 2006, pp. 134-178.

Brodsky-Elliott, Vivien. 'Single women in the London Marriage market: Age status and mobility, 1598-1619,' *Studies in the Social History of Marriage.* London: RB Outhwaite, 1981, pp. 81-100.

Burnard, Trevor. 'Slave Naming Patterns: Onomastics and the Taxonomy of Race in Eighteenth-Century Jamaica,' *The Journal of Interdisciplinary History*, XXXI, 3, Winter, 2001, pp. 325-46.

Calvo, Ana Manzanas. 'Conversion narratives: Othello and other black characters in Shakespeare's and Lope de Vega's plays,' *Sederi* VII, 1996, pp. 231-236.

Collington, Phlip D. 'Othello the Liar,' in, Helen Ostovich and Mary V. Silcox and Graham Roebuck (eds.). *The Mysterious and Foreign in Early Modern England.* pp. 187-199.

Collins, Siobhan and Louise Denmead. 'There is All Africa [...] Within Us': Language, Generation and Alchemy in Browne's Explication of Blackness,' in, Kathryn Murphy and Richard Todd (eds.). *"A Man Very Well Studyed": New Contexts for Thomas Browne.* Leiden/Boston: Brill, 2008, pp. 127-146.

Condren, Conal. 'Public, Private and the Idea of the 'Public Sphere' in Early-Modern England.' *Intellectual History Review*, 19, 1, 2009, pp. 15-28.

Connors, Richard and Lynn Botelho, Tim Hitchcock, Ian Archer, Patricia Fumerton, 'London Calling! Paul Griffiths - *Lost Londons: Change, Crime and Control in the Capital City, 1550-1660.*' *Histoire Sociale*, 43, No. 85, 2010, pp. 213-240.

Crawford, Patricia. 'Public Duty, Conscience and Women in Early Modern England,' in, John Morrill and Paul Slack (eds.), et. al. *Public Duty, and Private Conscience in Seventeenth-Century England: Essays Presented to G. E. Aylmer.* Oxford: Clarendon Press, 1993, pp. 201-234.

——. 'Women, Religion and Social Action in England, 1500-1800,' *Australian Feminist Studies*, 13, Issue 28, October 1998, pp. 269-280.

Croft, Pauline. 'Trading with the Enemy, 1585–1604,' *Historical Journal*, 32, June 1989, pp. 281–302.

——. 'English commerce with Spain and the Armada War, 1558–1603,' in Simon Lester Adams and M. J. Rodriguez-Salgado (eds.), *England, Spain and the Gran Armada, 1585–1604: Essays from the Anglo-Spanish Conferences, London and Madrid 1988*. 1988. New edition, Edinburgh: Rowman and Littlefield, 1991, pp. 236–263.

Curtis, Abraham. 'Stars of the Sahara,' *New Scientist*, No. 2617, 18 August 2007, pp. 37–39.

Cummings, Brian. 'Animal Passions and Human Sciences: Shame, Blushing and Nakedness in Early Modern Europe and the New World,' in Erica Fudge (ed.), *At the Borders of the Human: Beasts, Bodies and Natural Philosophy in the Early Modern Period*. Basingstoke: Macmillan, 1999, pp. 26–51.

Gilbert, Susan Wiseman (eds.). *At the Borders of the Human: Beasts, Bodies and Natural Philosophy in the Early Modern Period*. Basingstoke: Macmillan, 1999, pp. 26–51.

Douce, Francis. 'Dissertation III: On the Ancient English Morris Dance,' in *Illustrations of Shakespeare*. London: Longman, 1808, pp. 428–482.

Duncan Salkeld, Duncan. 'Black Luce and the 'curtizans' of Shakespeare's London,' *Signature* 2, Winter 2000, pp. 1–10.

Edwards, Paul and James Walvin. 'Africans in Britain, 1500–1800,' in Martin L. Kilson and Robert L. Rotberg (eds.). *The African Diaspora: Interpretive Essays*. Cambridge: Harvard University Press, 1976, pp. 173–204.

Eltis, David. 'Slavery and Freedom in the Early Modern World,' in Stanley L. Engerman, *Terms of Labour: Slavery, Serfdom and Free Labour*. Stanford: Stanford University Press, 1999, pp. 25–50.

Evans, K.W. 'The Racial Factor in *Othello*,' *Shakespeare Studies*, 5, 1969, pp. 124–140.

Gilchrist, Anne G. 'A Carved Morris Dance panel from Lancaster Castle,' *Journal of the English Folk Dance and Song Society*, 1, No. 2, December 1933, pp. 86–88.

Gowing, Laura. 'Gender and the Language of Insult in Early Modern London,' *History Workshop Journal*, 35, 1993, pp. 1–21.

——. 'Giving Birth at the Magistrates Gate: Single Mothers in the Early Modern City,' Broomhall and Tarbin (eds.). *Women, Identities and Communities*, pp. 137–150.

Griffiths, Paul. 'Secrecy and Authority in late sixteenth- and seventeenth-century London,' *Historical Journal*, 40, No. 4, 1997, pp. 925–51.

Gual Camarena, Miguel. 'Una cofradía de negros libertos en el siglo XV,' *Estudios de la Edad Media en la Corona de Aragón*, 5, 1952, pp. 457–466.

Gundle, Stephen. 'The Bella Italiana and the English Rose,' in Manfred Pfister and Ralf Hertel (eds.). *Performing National Identity: Anglo-Italian Cultural Transactions.* Amsterdam: Rodopi, 2007, pp. 137–155.

Gypsy Lore Society. *Journal of the Gyspsy Lore Society*, II, Issue 2, 1891, pp. 34–37.

Habib, Imtiaz. 'Was Sir Peter Negro Black, Othello, Sir Peter Negro and the (lost) blacks of early modern England: colonial inscription and post colonial excavation,' *Literature Interpretation and Theory*, 9, No.1, 1998, pp. 15–30.

——. 'Was Sir Peter Negro Black,' *Black and Asian Studies Association Newsletter*, xlvi, November 2006, p. 5.

Hair, P. E. H. 'Black African Slaves at Valencia, 1482–1516: An Onomastic Inquiry,'

History in Africa: A Journal of Method, 7, No.1, 1980, pp. 19–39.

Hall, Kim F. 'Beauty and the Beast of Whiteness: Teaching Race and Gender,' *Shakespeare Quarterly*, 47, No. 4, Winter 1996, pp. 461–476.

Harris, Stephen. 'Overview of Race and Ethnicity in Pre-Norman England,' *Literature Compass*, 5, No. 4, 2008, pp. 740–754.

Hays, Daniel. 'From the Land of the Bow Black Soldiers in the Ancient and Near East,' *Bible Review*, August 1998, pp. 29–33, 50–51.

Hendricks, Margo. 'Obscured by dreams': Race, Empire and Shakespeare's A Midsummer Night's Dream,' *Shakespeare Quarterly*, 47, No.1, Spring 1996, pp. 37–60.

Hindle, Steve. 'A Sense of Place? Becoming and Belonging in the Rural Parish 1550–1650,' in, Alexandra Shepard and Phil Withington (eds.). *Communities in Early Modern England: Networks, Place, Rhetoric.* Manchester: Manchester University Press, 2000, pp. 96–114.

Hindle, Steve. 'Exclusion Crises: Poverty, Migration and Parochial Responsibility in English Rural Communities, c. 1560–1660,' *Rural History*, 7, 1996, pp. 125–149.

Hoskins, William George. 'English Provincial Towns in the Sixteenth-Century,' *Transactions of the Royal Historical Association*, 5th Series, 6, 1956, pp. 1–19.

Housman, John E. 'Higden, Trevisa and Caxton and the Beginnings of Arthurian Criticism,' *The Review of English Studies*, 23, No. 91, July 1947, pp. 209–217.

Huxley, Thomas. 'On the Geographical Distributions of the Chief Modifications of Mankind,' *Journal of the Ethnological Society of London*, No. 2. London: Ethnological Society of London, 1870, pp. 404–412.

Jackson, Luther Porter. 'Elizabethan Seamen and the African Slave Trade,' *The Journal of Negro History*, 9, No. 1, January 1924, pp. 1–17.

Johnson, Rosalind. 'African Presence in Shakespearean Drama: Parallels Between Othello and the Historical Leo Africanus,' in Ivan Van Sertima (ed.). *African Presence in Early Europe*. (1985), pp. 276–87.

Jordan, Anne Marie. 'Image of Empire, Slaves in the Lisbon household and court of Catherine of Austria,' in Thomas Earle and Kate Lowe (eds.). *Black Africans in Renaissance Europe*, pp. 155–181.

Kalmar, Ian Davidson. 'Moorish Style: Orientalism, the Jews, and Synagogue Architecture,' *Jewish Social Studies History Culture and Society*, 7, No. 3, Spring/Summer 2001, pp. 68–100.

Kaufmann, Miranda. 'Caspar Van Senden, Sir Thomas Sherley and the 'Blackamoor' project,' *Historical Research*, 81, Number 212, May 2008, pp. 366–371.

——. 'Sir Pedro Negro What Colour was his Skin?' *Oxford Journals, Notes and Queries*, 55(2), 2008, pp. 142–146.

Keane, Robert M. 'Thomas More as a Young Lawyer,' *Moreana*, 41/160, December 2004, pp. 41–71.

Keita, Maghan. 'Saracens and Black Knights,' *Arthuriana*, 16, Issue 4, December 1, 2006, pp. 65–77.

Knutson, Roslyn L. 'A Caliban in St.Mildred Poultry,' *Shakespeare and Cultural Traditions*. Newark: Delaware University Press, 1994, pp. 114–116.

Lee, Sidney. 'Caliban's visits to England,' *Cornhill Magazine*, 34, 1913, pp. 333–345.

Leeson, Peter and Alex Nowrasteh. 'Was Privateering Plunder Efficient?' *Journal of Economic Behaviour and Organization*, 79, issue 3, August 2011, pp. 303–317. A more detailed version is available at http://www.peterleeson.com/Efficient_Plunder.pdf.

Lindow, John. 'Supernatural Others and Ethnic Others: A millennium of World View,' *Scandinavian Studies*, 67, No.1, Winter 1995, pp. 8–31.

Loomie, Albert. 'Religion and Elizabethan Commerce with Spain,' *The Catholic Historical Review*, 50, April 1964, pp. 27–51.

Luu, Lien. 'The Dutch and their Beer Brewing,' in A. Kershen (ed.). *Food in the Migrant's Experience*. Aldershot: Ashgate, 2002, pp. 101–133.

Macdonald, Joyce Green. 'Black Ram, White Ewe: Shakespeare, Race and Women,' *A Feminist Companion to Shakespeare*. Oxford: Wiley Blackwell, 2001, pp. 188–207.

Maddern, Philippa. "In Myn Own House:' The Troubled Connections Between Servant Marriages, Late-Medieval English Households

Communities and Early Modern Historiography,' in *Women, Identities*, pp. 45–59.

Manzione, Carol Kazmierczak. 'Sex in Tudor London, Abusing their bodies with each other,' in Jacqueline Murray and Konrad Eisenbichler (eds.). *Desire and Discipline: Sex and Sexuality in the Premodern West*. Toronto: University of Toronto Press, 1996, pp. 87–100.

Matar, Nabil. 'The 1st Turks and Moors in England' in Randolph Vigne, Charles Littleton (eds.). *From Strangers to Citizens*, pp. 261–267.

Matthews, G. M. 'Othello and the Dignity of Man,' in Arnold Kettle. *Shakespeare in a Changing World*. London: Lawrence and Wishart, 1964, pp 123–145.

Meyers, Charles. 'Lawsuits in Elizabethan courts of law the Adventurers of Dr Hector Nunez, 1566-1599 a précis,' *Journal of European Economic History*, 25/1, 1996, pp. 157–168.

Mikalachki, Jodi. 'Women's Networks and the Female Vagrant: a Hard Case,' in, Susan Frye and Karen Robertson (eds.). *Maids and Mistresses, Cousins and Queens: Women's Alliances in Early Modern England (Seminar) 1993*. New York: Oxford University Press, 1998, pp. 52–69.

Miller, W.E. 'Negroes in Elizabethan London,' *Notes and Queries*, 206, No. 8, 4 April 1961, p. 138.

Morton, Stephen. 'The subaltern: Genealogy of a concept,' in Gayatri Spivak. *Ethics, Subalternity and the Critique of Postcolonial Reason*. Malden: Polity, 2007, pp. 96–97.

Neill, Michael. "'Mulattos,' 'Blacks,' and 'Indian Moors': Othello and Early Modern Constructions of Human Difference,' *Shakespeare Quarterly*, 49, No. 4, Winter 1998, pp. 361–374.

Niebrzydowski, Sue. 'The Sultana and her sisters: black women in the British Isles, before 1530,' *Women's History Review*, 10, No. 2, 2001, pp.187–210.

Nunez, Rafael Velez. 'Beyond the emblem: Alchemical Albedo in Ben Jonson's The Masque of Blackness,' *Sederi* VIII 1997, pp. 257–263.

Onyeka, 'The Missing Tudors, Black People in Sixteenth-Century England,' *BBC History Magazine*, 13, No. 7, July 2012, pp. 32–33.

Onyeka, 'What's in a Name?,' *History Today*, 62, Issue 10, October 2012, pp. 34–39.

Orkin, Martin. 'Othello and the 'plain face' of Racism,' *Shakespeare Quarterly*, 38, No. 2, Summer 1987, pp. 166–168.

Pablos, Juan Antonio Prieto. 'Shakespearean Strategies of (Dis) orientation in Othello, Act 1,' *Sederi* VII, 1996, pp. 225–230.

Pacheco, Anita (ed.). *A Companion to Early Modern Women's Writing.* Oxford: Wiley Blackwell, 2002.

Parker, Patricia. 'Black Hamlet, Battening on the Moor,' *Shakespeare Studies*, 31, 1/1/2003, pp. 127–164.

Patterson, Catherine F. 'Town and City Government,' in Robert Tittler and Norman Jones (eds.). *Companion to Tudor Britain.* Oxford: Wiley, Blackwell, pp. 116–133.

Peabody, Sue. 'Race, Slavery and the Law in Early Modern France,' *The Historian*, 56, No. 3, Spring 1994, pp. 501–510.

Piedra, Jose. 'In Search of the Black Stud,' in Louise Fradenburg and Carla Freccero (eds.). *Premodern Sexualities.* New York: Routledge, 1996, pp. 23–44.

Pike, Ruth. 'Sevillian society in the sixteenth century: Slaves and freedmen,' *The Hispanic American Historical Review*, 47, No. 3, 1967, pp. 345–359.

Pitcher, John and Robert Lindsey and Susan Cerasano. *Medieval and Renaissance Drama in England*, 13. New York: Fairleigh Dickinson, University Press, 2001, pp. 310–311.

Prior, Roger. 'Jewish Musicians at the Tudor Court,' *The Musical Quarterly*, 69, No. 2, Spring 1983, pp. 253–265.

Ray, Michael. 'A Black slave on the run in thirteenth-century England,' in Michael Jones (ed.). *Nottingham Medieval Studies*, Volume L 1, University of Nottingham 2007, pp. 111–119.

Reid, Julia. 'The origins of English attitudes towards the Black African 1554–1807,' MA Thesis, University of Hull (unpublished), 1975.

Richards, Judith M. 'Public Identity and Public Memory: Case Studies of Two Tudor Women,' in Broomhall and Tarbin (eds.). *Women, Identities*, pp. 195–209.

Ryder, Alan Frederick Charles. 'Missionary Activity, in the Kingdom of Warri to the Early Nineteenth Century,' *Journal of the Historical Society of Nigeria*, 2, No.1, December 1960, pp. 1–26.

Sampson, Mike. 'Friends of Devon Archives, the Black connection,' *Friends of Devon Newsletter*, Issue 25, May 2000, pp.12–15.

Savine, Alexander. 'Bondsmen under the Tudors,' *Transactions of the Royal Historical Society*, 2nd series, 17, 1903, pp. 235–286.

Scarsi, Selene. *Translating Women in Early Modern England: Gender in the Elizabethan Versions of Boirado, Ariosto and Tasso.* Farnham: Ashgate 2001.

Scattergood, V. J. 'Reading the past: essays on medieval and renaissance literature,' *Medieval Studies.* Dublin: Four Courts Press, 1996, pp. 19–20.

Scobie, Edward. 'The African Presence in Early Europe,' in Ivan Van Sertima (ed.). *Journal of African Civilizations*. New Jersey: Transaction Publishers, 1986, pp. 190–203.

Scobie, Edward. 'The Moors and Portugal's Global Expansion,' *Department of Black Studies Pamphlet*. New York: City College, City University of New York, 1996, n. p.

Schafer, Jurgen. 'John Minsheu Scholar or Charlatan?' *Renaissance Quarterly*, 26, No. 1, 1973, pp. 23–35.

Shultz, James. 'Shakespeare's Colors: Race and Culture in Elizabethan England,' *Old Dominion University's Quest*, 5, Issue 1.8, January 2002, n. p.

Sherwood, Marika. 'Blacks in Elizabethan England,' *History Today*, 53, Issue 10, 2003, pp. 40–42.

Sisson, C.J. 'A Colony of Jews in Shakespeare's London,' *Essays and Studies*, 23, 1938, pp. 38–51.

Slights, Camille Wells. 'Slaves and Subjects in Othello,' *Shakespeare Quarterly*, 48, No. 4, Winter 1997, pp. 377–390.

Smith, Ian. 'Barbarian Errors: Performing Race in Early Modern England,' *Shakespeare Quarterly*, 49, No. 2, Summer 1998, pp. 168–186.

Smith, Robert. 'In search of Carpaccio's African Gondolier,' *Italian Studies*, 34, 1979, pp. 45–59.

Smith, Warren D. 'Shakespeare's Shylock,' *Shakespeare Quarterly*, 15, No. 3, 1964, pp.193–199.

Smuts, Robert Malcolm. 'Public Ceremony and Royal Charisma: The English Royal Entry in London, 1495–1642,' in, Cannadine and Rosenheim (eds.). *The First Modern Society*, pp. 65–94.

Spivak, Gayatri Chakravorty. 'Can the subaltern speak?' in Cary Nelson and Lawrence Grossberg (eds.). *Marxism and the Interpretation of Culture*. Urbana: University of Illinois Press, 1988, pp. 271–313.

Stone, Lawrence. 'Social Mobility in England 1500-1700,' *Past and Present*, No. 33, April 1966, pp. 16–55.

The British Archaeological Society Association and Royal Archaeological Institute of Great Britain and Ireland. *Archaeological Journal*, Volume 69. London: Royal Archaeological Institute, 1912.

Thornton, John. 'Early Kongo Portuguese, Relations 1483–1575, A new interpretation,' *History in Africa*, Volume VIII, 1981, pp. 183–204.

Ungerer, Gustav. 'Recovering a black African's voice in an English lawsuit: Jacques Francis and the salvage operations of the *Mary Rose* and the *Sancta Maria* and *Sanctus Edwardus*, 1545–ca 1550,' *Medieval and Renaissance Drama in England*. Madison: Fairleigh Dickinson University Press, 2004, pp. 255–271.

——. 'The Presence of Africans in Elizabethan England and the performance of Titus Andronicus, at-Burley-on-the-Hill, 1595-96,' *Medieval Renaissance Drama in England,* 21, 2008, pp. 19–56.

Vaughan, Alden. 'Sir Walter Raleigh's Indian Interpreters, 1584–1618,' *The William and Mary Quarterly,* 59, No. 2, 2002, pp. 341–376. ——. 'Before Othello: Elizabethan representations of Sub-Saharan Africans,' *The William and Mary Quarterly,* 54, No. 1, January 1997, pp. 19–44.

Verkerek, Dorothy Hoogland. 'Black Servant, Black Demon: Color Ideology in the Ashburnham Pentateuch,' *Journal of Medieval and Early Modern Studies,* 31, No. 1, Winter 2001, pp. 57–70.

Vicenta, Cortes Alonso. 'La poblacion negra de Palos de la Frontera (1568–1579),' in Alfredo Jimenez Nunez (ed.). *Actas y Memorias, del XXXVI Congreso Internacional de Americanistas,* 3. Seville: ECESA, 1966, pp. 609–618.

Wallis, Patrick and Christopher Wright. 'Evidence, Artisan Experience and Authority in Early Modern England,' *Cultural Histories of the Material World.* Cambridge (USA): Harvard University Press, 2012.

White, Jeanette S. 'Is black so base a hue?': Shakespeare's Aaron and the politics and poetics of race,' *College Language Association Journal,* 40, March 1997, pp. 336–366.

Whitney, Lois. 'Did Shakespeare Know Leo Africanus?' *Publications of the Modern Language Association of America,* 37, 1922, pp. 470–483.

Woodbridge, Linda. 'Vagrancy, Homelessness, and English Renaissance Literature,' in, P. A. Brown, Canadian Society for Renaissance Studies, *Renaissance and Reformation,* 25; Part 3, 2001, pp. 54–56.

——. A. L. Beier, and P. R. Ocobock. 'The Neglected Soldier as Vagrant, Revenger, Tyrant Slayer in Early Modern England.' *Research in International Studies Global and Comparative Studies Series, Cast Out – Vagrancy and Homelessness in Global and Historical Perspective.* Athens/Ohio/London: Ohio University Press, 2008, pp. 64–87.

Secondary electronic sources

Anon. 'The Black Men of Biddle' *St Chads Church Staffordshire,* http://www.stchadsstafford.co.uk/page.asp?pid=27 accessed 14/6/10.

Anon. 'The racial fuss surrounding the Moors in Europe,' *Angelfire,* http://www.angelfire.com/md/8/moors.html accessed 18/11/08.

Anon. 'What was the position of Black people in Shakespeare's England?' *Yahoo Answers,* http://answers.yahoo.com/question/index;_ylt=AksX-poJrC_Y5CnIDzTGuzq0jzKIX;_ylv=3?qid=20080616111915AApm6gn, accessed 30/8/11.

BIBLIOGRAPHY

Alsford, Stephen. 'Were Towns Sanctuaries for Serfs?,' *Florilegium Urbanum,* http://users.trytel.com/~tristan/towns/florilegium/community/cmmemb01.html, accessed 11/11/12.

Baker, John. 'Human Rights and the Rule of Law in Renaissance England,' *Northwestern Journal of International Human Rights,* 2, Spring 2004, www.law.northwestern.edu/journals/jihr/v2/3/ accessed 10/01/13.

British Broadcasting Corporation. 'Britain's first Black Community in Elizabethan London,' *BBC News Magazine,* http://www.bbc.co.uk/news/magazine-18903391, accessed 20/07/12.

Browner, Jessica. 'The wrong side of the river: London's disreputable Southbank in the sixteenth and seventeenth century,' *Essays in History,* 36, 1994, http://etext.virginia.edu/journals/EH/EH36/EH36/browner1.html, accessed 12/06/07.

Coyne, Stacy M. 'Shakespeare's Othello: The Black Other in Elizabethan Drama, Representations of Othello in History and on Stage,' *Associated Content.* http://www.associatedcontent.com/article/31627/shakespeares_othello_the_black_other.html?cat=38, posted May 2006, accessed 08/08/11.

Hancock, Ian. 'The Struggle for the Control of Identity,' *Perspectives,* http://www.osi.hu/rpp/perspectives1f.htm, accessed 06/07/07.

Humphreys, Natalie. 'Saracens of Biddulph Moor - Cold Case History pt2 ??' personal email sent and accessed 14/06/10.

Kaufmann, Miranda. 'Africans in Early Modern London: Tales from London Metropolitan Archives,' *Miranda Kaufmann History,* http://www.mirandakaufmann.com/history.html. and http://www.mirandakaufmann.com/lmaafricans.html accessed 09/04/13

Kent, Williams. 'Afromestizo, Third root, African Heritage of Central America,' *LWF Communications,* http://www.bjmjr.com/afromestizo/imp_dates.htm, accessed 12/03/2006.

Mackensie, Eneas. 'Incorporated Companies: Merchant Adventurers,' Historical Account of Newcastle-upon-Tyne: Including the Borough of Gateshead, 1827, *British History Online,* pp. 662-670, http://www.british-history.ac.uk/report.aspx?compid=43401, accessed 18/01/08.

Meyers, Charles. 'Elizabethan 'Marranos' unmasked,' *Kulanu all of us,* http://www.kulanu.org/anousim/unmasked.php, accessed 20/07/09.

——. 'Turmoil: The Abject Life of a Portuguese Alien in Elizabethan England,' *Society for Crypto Judaic Studies,* http://www.cryptojews.com/Turmoil_Elizabethan_England.htm, accessed 13/05/11.

——. 'Dr. Hector Nunes, Portuguese Physician, Merchant and Crypto-Jew in Elizabethan England 1547-1591,' *Society for Crypto Judaic Studies*, http://www.cryptojews.com/Dr%20Nunez.htm, accessed 13/05/11.

Northamptonshire Black History Association, 'Peter the Saracen,' *Northants Black History*, http://www.northants-black-history.org.uk/activitiesResearchPeter.asp, seen 03/08/12.

Onyeka, 'Diversity in Early Modern Britain Podcasts,' *The Historical Association*, http://www.history.org.uk/resources/secondary_resource_4714.html, accessed 05/06/12.

Qualifications and Curriculum Authority (QCA). 'Innovating with History,' http://www.qca.org.uk/history/innovating/history_matters/worked_for_me/ks3/cameo9.htm, accessed 18/07/08.

Romain, Gemma. 'Black British History,' Birkbeck University, Faculty of Continuing Education, London, 2007-2008, http://www.bbk.ac.uk/ce/history/documents/FFHI232UACB_003.pdf, accessed 05/11/08.

Sherwood, Marika. 'Britain, Slavery and the Trade in Enslaved Africans,' *History in Focus*, Issue 12, http://www.history.ac.uk/ihr/Focus/Slavery/articles/sherwood.html posted spring 2007, accessed 03/12/08.

——. 'In this curriculum, I don't exist,' The Institute of Historical Research, University of London School of Advanced Study, http://www.history.ac.uk/resources/history-in-british-education/first-conference/sherwood-paper, accessed 27/7/11.

Stratford upon Avon Local Authority. 'Village of Octeselve (Oxhill), 12th century grave of a negro slave called Myrtilla,' wn.com/Stratford-on-Avon_(district) accessed 27/8/11.

United Nations Education Scientific and Cultural Organisation. 'African Ink Road International Symposium,' http://portal.unesco.org/ci/en/ev.php-URL_ID=26012&URL_DO=DO_TOPIC&URL_SECTION=-473.html, updated 21. 02. 2008, accessed 12/09/09.

United Nations Educational Scientific and Cultural Organization, 'The Slave Route Project,' *Culture*, http://www.unesco.org/new/en/culture/themes/dialogue/the-slave-route/, accessed on 12/10/11.

Television Programmes and Films

Curtiz, Michael. *The Private Lives of Elizabeth and Essex*, Warner Brothers, 1939.

Dobbs, Rebecca (pr) Michael Wood (presenter). *The Great British Story*, Episode 5, British Broadcasting Corporation (BBC) 2, 20 July 2012.

Ferguson, Neil (dr.), Tania Lindon (pr.). *History Cold Case*, Episode 1, British Broadcasting Corporation (BBC) 2, 6 May 2010.
Graham, Roderick. *Elizabeth R.*, BBC 2, 17 February 1971–24 March 1971. In Episode 3 one African man is present in the sixteenth-century court of France but says nothing and appears out of place and strange.
Hirst, Michael, et. al. *The Tudors*, Showtime/Reveille/Working Title, 1 April 2007–20 June 2010.
Jarrott, Charles, et.al. *Anne of the Thousand Days*, Universal Pictures, 1969.
Jarrott, Charles. *Mary Queen of Scots*, Universal Pictures, 1971.
Kapur, Shekhar, et.al. *Elizabeth*, Polygram, 1998.
Kapur, Shekhar, et.al. *Elizabeth the Golden Age*, Universal Studios, 2007.
Korda, Alexander. *The Private Life of Henry VIII*, United Artists, 1933.
Lowthrope, Philippa. *The Other Boleyn Girl*, BBC, 28 March 2003
Nunn, Trevor. *Lady Jane*, Paramount Pictures, 1986.
Roberts, Gareth (writer), Charles Palmer (director). *The Shakespeare Code*, Dr Who Series, BBC 1, 7 April 2007.
Schama, Simon, et.al. *A History of Britain*, 2 Entertain Video, 2000–2002.
Shivas, Mark and Ronald Travers (producers). *The Six Wives of Henry VIII*, BBC 1, 1 January-5 February 1970.
Zinnemann, Fred, et. al. *The Man for all Seasons*, Highland Film/Columbia Pictures, 1966.

Music

Krieger, Robby and Jim Morrison, 'The Doors.' *People are Strange*. New York: Elektra Records, 1967.

List of Images

(In the order they are referred to in the text).
1. *Abd el-Ouahed Ben Messaoud [the] Moorish Ambassador, 1600.*
2. 'John Blanke' in *Westminster Tournament Roll ... 1511.*
3. Juriaen Van Streeck. *A Still Life with a Moorish Servant ...1632-1687.*
4. Jan Brueghel. *Study of Moorish Heads,* 1568-1625.
5. Peter Paul Rubens. *Studies of the Head of a Negro,* circa 1615.
6. John White. 'An Eskimo Man with Bow,' 1585-1593.
7. John White. 'An Eskimo Woman with Baby,' 1585-1593.
8. Cesare Vecellio. *Degli Habiti Antichi ...* 1590, pp. 470-473.
9. *Domesday Abbreviatio,* 1241, p.196.

10. Nicolas Verdun. *Verdun Altar* [King Solomon and the Queen of Sheba], circa 1181.
11. Conrad Kyeser. *De Bellifortis* [Queen of Sheba], 1405.
12. Artist unknown. *The Adoration of the Magi,* 1520.
13. ——.
14. Hans Baldung Grien. *Adoration of the Magi,* 1507, oil on wood @ Staatliche Museum, Berlin, Germany.
15. Artist unknown. *African Knight,* possibly Saint Maurice, St Mary's Church, Uffculme, circa 16th century.
16. Image details of Black knights (Maurice heads) fifteenth and sixteenth century.
17. Matthias Grunewald. *Erasmus of Formulae and Saint Maurice,* 1517–1523, Germany.
18. Artist unknown. *African Head,* Coat of Arms of Sir Thomas Sonds, St Michael and All Angels, Throwley Church, circa 16th century.
19. Albrecht Durer: *Portrait of Caterina, the Mulatta of the Portoguese Bradao,* 1521.
20. 'John Blanke' in *Westminster Tournament Roll* … 1511.
21. Jan Mostaert. *Portrait of an African Man,* circa 1520-1530.
22. Unknown. *Marriage of St. Ursula to Prince Conan,* panel 1522, Lisbon, Portugal.
23. Van Rijn Rembrandt. *A Black Drummer and Commander Mounted on Mules.* Hague, Holland, 1638.
24. Hieronymus Bosch. *The Epiphany or the Adoration of the Magi,* 1510. 219
25. ——
26. *The Drake Jewel* [or Diadem], 1575/1586.
27. Paul Van Somer. *Anne of Denmark,* 1617.
28. Abraham Cresques. *The Catalan Atlas,* 1375, 'The Emperor Mansa Musa.'
29. Flinck, Govaert. *Young Archer,* 1639-1640.
30. Henrie Jetto's Will, 1626.
31. Peter Bluck.
32. Peter Bluck's father.
33. *Schoenbartbuch Nurnberg* [Nuremberg Carnival Book], 1590-1620, n. p.
34. ——.
35. ——.
36. ——.
37. ——.

Index

*Page numbers in **bold** signify a major discussion of the topic; page numbers followed by (i) refer to illustrations, and those followed by (n) refer to numbered notes.*

People

Aaron (character), xxvi, 17, 52, 222, 236(n44)
Africanus, Leo, xxv, 42–43, 45, 48–49, 152–153, 163, 166–167, 171, 180
Anne of Denmark, 124, 164, 201(i)
Annerby, Walter, 167, 168, 174, **177–180**, 181–182, 221
Antonio, Don/Dom (Prince of Portugal), xxii, 11, 26, 130, 131, 165, 177

Bacon, Francis, 53
Balthazar (character), 66, 100–102(i), 125, 198–199(i)
Banes, Edward, 4–5, 6, 10, 22–24, 27, 130, 136, 177, 214
Banning, Paul, 176, 216
Baskerville, Thomas, **4–7**, 10, 20, 24, 29, 177
Bastien, xii, 28, **159–160**, 181, 211
Becket, Thomas, **60**, 217
Best, George, xxv, 27, 42, 44, 46, 49–50, 52, 54, **57–59**, 72, 163, 213, 225
Binne, 164, 172–174, 180, 221
Blanke, John, xii, xxvi, 27, 57, 67, 92(i), 106(i), **120–125**, 213, 217, 218, 231

Boleyn, Ann, 113
Boorde, Andrew, xxv, 42–45, 56, 57
Bromley, Henry, **239–241**, 260–261
Browne, Thomas, **53–54**

Cardones, Catalina de, xii, **117–118**, 230–231
Cecil, Robert, xii, 10, 13–14, **23–27**, 28, 126–127, 215, 216, 219, 289–291
Cecil, William, 2, 10
Charles V, 116, 123, 129
Coree the Saldanian, 164–165, 181, 221
Corso, Piero Paul, **161–163**
Cristian (servant of Richard Sheere), xii, 211, **227–228**
Cromwell, Thomas, xix
Curres, James, 43, 45

Dassell, Anthony and Thomas, 130, **176–177**, 213
Dederi (John Jaquoah), 167–168, 174, **177–180**, 181–182, 221, **254–255**
Dee, John, 120
Domingo, xxvi–xxvii, **153–155**, 159, 162, 164, 181, 211, 215, 221
Drake, Francis, xxiv, 6–7, 11, 25, 26, 50, 51, 137, **154–159**, 160–161, 170, 176, 180, 181, 212, 215, 216, 220–221
Dunbar, William, 216

Eleazar (character), **52**
Elizabeth I, xix, xxiv, 3, 4, 6, 9–10,
    12-13, 16–17, 26, 27–28, 55,
    118–120, 130, 155, 177, 200(i),
    215, 216, 219

Ferdinand of Aragon, 116, 118, 120,
    123
Fernandes, Pedro, 131
Fillis, Mary, xii, 28, 65–66, **132**, 167,
    188(n79), 218, 220, 221–222,
    253–254
Fortunatus (servant of Robert Cecil),
    xii, 28, 59, 126
Francis, Jacques, 25, 27, 110, 152,
    161-163, 164, 171
Frobisher, Martin, 11, 55, 176

Grace of Hatherleigh, **229**, 231,
    249–250

Hanmer, Meredith, **49–52**, 72, 225
Hawkins, John, xxvi, 6–7, 11, 25–26,
    137, **159–161**, 166, 168, 175, 176,
    180, 181, 212, 215, 216, 220–221
Hawkins, William, xii, xxvi, 28,
    159–160, 176
Henry VIII, vii, xxiii, 55, 67, 68, 113,
    117, 120, 124, 135, 216
Herodotus, 45, 46, 66, 125
Hopkins, William, 2–3, 25, 71, 214

Isabella of Castile, 116, 118, 120, 123

James I, 67, 124, 164, 240–241
James IV of Scotland, 67, 122
James VI of Scotland *see* James I
Jaquoah, John (Dederi), 167–168, 174,
    177–180, 181–182, 221, **254–255**
Jetto, Henrie, 63, 204(i), 211, **239–241**,
    260, **263–264**
Jonson, Ben, xxv–xxvi, 44, 46, 59, 66,
    78(n63), 113

Katharina (servant of Joao Brandao),
    105(i), **121**
Katherine of Aragon, xii, 46, 54,
    113–118, 120, 142(n59), 170,
    213, 216

Lazia, Carbew, 28, 111
Lok, John, 11, 44, 57, 164, **172-173**,
    175, 213
Lopez, Roderigo, **128**, 130

Machyn, Henry, 225–226
Madox, Richard, **165**, 168, 180
Malliard, Thomas, 130, 214–215
Margaret, Blak, 67, 216, 233(n23)
Mary I, 118, 133, 216
Maurice, St, 67, 102–103(i)
More, Elen, 67
More, Thomas, xxv, 46, 53–54,
    114–116, 216, 233(n24)
Moriana, Maria, 20, 25, **109–110**, 211,
    214
Morien (character), **68**, 217
Moryan, Peter, **67–68**, 122
Mullato, Frances, 131

Negro, Diego, xxiv, **155–159**, 172, 180,
    213, 215, 221
Negro, Fraunces (servant of Mary I),
    xxiii, **118**
Negro, Frauncis (servant of Peter
    Miller), 72, 109, 216, 217
Negro, Lucy, 69–70, 226, 229, 237(n66)
Negro, Peter/Pedro (knight), 68
Negro, 'who would never teach his art,'
    133–135, 213
Negro, 'with a cut on his face,' **157–159**
Nosser, 177–180 *see also* Annerby,
    Walter
Noviemies, Hector, 19, 25, 44, 126–
    127, 216
Nunez, Hector, **127–128**, 148(n139),
    216

# INDEX

Ongunby, James, **169–170**, 178, 181, 220
Othello (character), xxi, xxvi, 52, 61, 63, 135, 179, 185(n50), **222–224**

Philip II, 1, **129–130**
Philip III, 129
Phillis, Mary *see* Fillis, Mary
Pliny, 45, **48–49**, 53, 61, 66, 125
Purchas, Samuel, xxv, 51, 66, 164, 165–167, 168–169, 172

Raleigh, Walter, vii, 11, 25, 55, 174–175, 176, 215, 216

Samuel, 160–161
Senden, Casper Van, **9–14**, **22–27**, 47, 136, 177, 214, 219, **289–291**
Shakespeare, William, xxv–xxvi, 66, 69–70, 222–224
Sherley, Thomas (elder and junior), **10–15**, 17, **22–27**, 47–48, 52, 130, 136, 214, 219, **289–291**
Stow, John, xxiv–xxv, 15, 26, 54, 67, **115–116**, 117, 133
Stubbs, John, 16, 53, 71

Thomasina de Pais, **119–120**, 135
Thorne, Robert, 130, 214–215

Valencia, Symon, xii, 64–65, 132, 135, 211, 217

Walsingham, Francis, 157–158, 165
Walter *see* Annerby, Walter
Waterson, Lambert, 45, 61, 219, 220
Winter, William, 11, 154–155, 161, 170, 215, 216

Places
Antwerp (Belgium), 63, 121

Barnstable, xiv, xx, 211
Belgium, 108
    Antwerp, 63, 121
Bristol, xii, xiv, xx, 2–3, 8, 15, 19, 25, 27, 29, 54, 58, 136, 175, 211, 212, 214, 215, 225, 228

Colne (Wiltshire), 46, 211
Cornwall, 249

Derbyshire, 57
Devon *see* Barnstable; Hatherleigh; Plymouth

Florence (Italy), 136

Germany, 11, 108, 124
    Nuremberg, 124, 206–210(i), 242
Granada (Spain), 113, 117, 118, 126, 129–130, 231

Hatherleigh (Devon), xii, xx, 229
Holt (Worcestershire), xii, 63, 211, 239–241

Italy, 108, **109–111**, 124, 134, 135–136, 162
    Florence, 136
    Venice, 109, 111, 136

Kent, xii, xxii, 62, 109
    Throwley, 104(i), 131

London, xii, xiv, xv, xx–xxi, xxiii, xxv–xxvi, 4, 8, 9, 17, 18, 19, 24, 27, 28, 43, 44, 47–48, 51, 54, 61, 63, 69, 109, 114–115, 117, 122, 123, 127, 129, 130, **132–135**, 136, 153, 161, 167, 169, 170, 174–175, 178–179, 211, 219, 225, 229, 230
    Deptford, 42
    East Smithfield, 72, 109, 133, 154, 219

Olave Hart Street, xx–xxi, 8, 44, 51, 65, 127, 211
Southwark, 8, 56, 64
St Botolph, Aldgate, xii, xx, xxvi–xxvii, 8, 15, 59, 65, 131–132, 134, 135, 154, 211, 219, 221, 231
Stepney, 62, 128, 231
Tottenham, 178
Westminster, xii, xxvi, 57, 72, 120–121, 123, 124, 125, 217
Whitechapel, xxi

Northamptonshire, xx, 64, 175
Norway (Oslo), 164
Nottinghamshire, xx
Nuremberg (Germany), 124, 206–210(i), 242

Oslo (Norway), 164

Plymouth, xii, xiv, xx, xxii, xxvi, 8, 15, 17, 18, 27, 28, 42, 59, 72, 108, 111, 113, 117, 136, 156, 158, 159, 211, 227–228, 230, 240
Portugal, xxv, 1–2, 7, 8, 9–11, 13–14, 59, 64, 65, 108, 109, **112–137**, 168, 171–173, 175, 176, 177, 178, 179, 211, 214, 215, 220

Salisbury, xii, xx, 63, 68
Scotland, xviii, 55, 67, 68, 122, 216

Southampton, xxiii, 27, 109–110, 111, 136, 162, 211
Spain, xiv, xxii, 1, 6–7, **9–14**, 17, 26, 42, 63, 64, 65, 108, 109, **112–137**, 170–171, 173, 174, 175, 176, 178, 179, 211, 212, 214–215, 220
Granada, 113, 117, 118, 126, 129–130, 231

Throwley (Kent), 104(i), 131

Venice (Italy), 109, 111, 136

Wiltshire *see* Colne; Salisbury
Worcestershire, xii, 63, 211, 239–241

Events
Defeat of Songhai, 174, 178, 181

Fall of Granada, 113, 118, 129–130

Marriage of Henry VIII, 113–117

Spanish Armada, 176
Spanish Inquisition, 26, 123, 126, **129–130**, 135, 212
Stranger Riots, 4, 26, 212, 218